College Latin

College Latin
An Intermediate Course

Peter L. Corrigan

Yale UNIVERSITY PRESS
New Haven and London

Yale University Press books may be purchased in quantity for educational,
business, or promotional use. For information, please e-mail
sales.press@yale.edu (U.S. office) or sales@yaleup.co.uk (U.K. office).

Designed by Newgen North America
Set in Arno Pro and Meta type by Newgen
Printed in the United States of America

Library of Congress Cataloging-in-Publication Data

Corrigan, Peter L., author.
College Latin : an intermediate course / Peter L. Corrigan.
pages cm
Includes indexes.
ISBN 978-0-300-19092-2 (pbk. : alk. paper)   1. Latin language—Grammar.
2. Latin language—Textbooks.   I. Title.
PA2087.5.C67 2015
478.2421—dc23
2014024317

A catalogue record for this book is available from the British Library.

This paper meets the requirements of ANSI/NISO Z39.48-1992 (Permanence of Paper).

10 9 8 7 6 5 4 3 2 1

This book is dedicated to the memory of Lyman E. Hawbaker Sr.,

teacher, mentor, colleague, and friend

"How can we come to a creative contact with the grounding of our own life? Only through a teacher who can lead us to the source of our existence by showing us who we are, and, thereby, what we are to do."

—Henri Nouwen

Contents

Preface

The present book has been inspired by many of the same pedagogical instincts that informed Harry L. Levy's *A Latin Reader for Colleges* (New York: Prentice Hall, 1939). This admirable volume, now long out of print, was quite innovatory for its time, anticipating many changes that would occur in foreign-language instruction in the postwar era. Some traditionalists at the time must have greeted Levy's introduction of noncanonical authors like Aulus Gellius and Phaedrus as radical. What probably dates Levy's textbook most from today's perspective is the assumption that students' curiosities are primarily antiquarian. As products of a thoroughgoing presentism, our students today typically don't value antiquarianism per se, and they would meet an intermediate reader just like Levy's with considerable diffidence. Our textbooks need to reflect the progress we've made in understanding our students and their widely varying learning styles.

This text contains material I've worked on and with for nearly thirty years. Over time, innumerable little things have been added to and subtracted from the book, mostly due to students' responses, which I have always tried to take into careful account. So many of my Latin students have "test-driven" significant sections of this book that there isn't space here to thank them all by name. But I know that whatever virtues reside in this text are largely due to them. They have made the teaching of intermediate Latin—an assignment that some instructors dread—a true pleasure for me, and I remain mindful of and grateful to them.

I also extend my heartfelt gratitude to two colleagues who have used my materials in their classes and provided me with invaluable feedback. Dr. Emily B. West of St. Catharine University has shown the utmost patience and forbearance with me as I tested ideas for this book (and others) on her and her students. Dr. Robert Mondi of the University of Northern Colorado has been a treasured friend and collaborator; I have spent many hours imposing on his knowledge of the pedagogy of ancient languages. And he has generously devoted to me long stints of reading drafts and arguing fine points. Because of the input of both these scholars, this book has benefited from countless improvements.

Another debt of gratitude I must acknowledge goes to those inmates I've tutored in an English-literacy program at a local jail. Many of the lessons I learned from teaching English speakers to read English have worked their subtle way into this book. Because of this experience, I no longer teach intermediate Latin as a foreign language but as a familiar language, and my outcomes are much improved. I want to thank the gentlemen I've worked with over the years who contributed a richness to my teaching career while their own lives stood in difficult transitions. Their efforts at self-improvement never failed to inspire me.

The anonymous readers for Yale University Press offered some exceptionally good suggestions for making this a better book, and I am most thankful to them. And the admirable editorial staff at Yale was a delight to work with; I single out Ash Lago and, particularly, Tim Shea for special thanks.

The encouragement of friends R. Amy Elman and W. Trent Foley for this project sustained me and was much appreciated. Last, I thank Junjuan, my wife, and Daniela, my daughter, for their boundless understanding during my push to complete this book. Without all their support, my efforts would be for naught.

Introduction

Teaching intermediate Latin to college or university students offers a variety of challenges. The mix of students can often be quite heterogeneous: besides those who have taken the institution's beginning Latin sequence, there are others enrolled who have studied Latin in high school or at a different college or even through self-study. Moreover, they enter the class having been trained with different introductory Latin texts, informed by different pedagogies. The instructor of such a heterogeneous class needs to homogenize it within a week or so. For students to proceed successfully with the language, therefore, intermediate Latin requires a text and an approach that will "level" all earlier texts and approaches. Intermediate Latin is also difficult because it is the hump course for students to develop the reading skills they'll need in upper-division courses on Latin literature. And to mention just one more of the challenges frequently encountered in intermediate Latin: this is the course where a student discovers that the Romans valued poetry far more than our culture does, and if she or he wants to continue studying Latin, a basic comfort with verse expression must be acquired.

This enumeration is hardly exhaustive. I might add one more difficulty I occasionally encounter. In the introductory sequence, there are some students who fall in love with the tidiness of Latin morphology and the exquisite logic of many grammatical constructions, but these same students, when they first confront the nuances and complexities and ambiguities of literary texts in intermediate Latin, become frustrated and disappointed: How can a language that makes so much sense be used to make such little sense?, they sometimes ask.

I sincerely hope that this text will ameliorate these and most other challenges that intermediate Latin poses. It has certainly worked better in my classes than the alternative texts available, precisely because it begins to model the sort of critical thinking that more advanced literary studies require, and it shows off much of the intriguing complexity of Roman society and culture. At the same time, though, it provides a thorough overview of morphology, syntax, and vocabulary building for the students' recovery and review; thus, throughout the book, students are constantly reminded that proficiency and fluency largely depend on their secure command of these features of the language. This text should definitely lower the elevation of that hump between introductory and advanced Latin courses, with the desired outcome that it will also lower the attrition rate typically observed in enrollments at this stress point in the Latin curriculum.

There is a fundamental threefold purpose to any intermediate Latin course: the recovery and review of morphology and syntax, the continuation of vocabulary acquisition, and the introduction to largely unadapted texts from Roman literature. The comprehensive overview of grammar in part I provides students with all the information they need about the language at this stage in their progress; indeed, it can serve as a useful reference for most of their succeeding upper-division Latin literature courses. To be sure, the numeration system used in this section may seem unnecessarily cumbersome at the time of reviewing it. But its value and purpose will become readily apparent to you on encountering the marginal grammar cues in part III. The exercises in part II reinforce most of the more challenging concepts that part I presents and should be used for that purpose. The vocabulary employed for the illustrations in part I and for the sentences in part II is fairly basic and presumably was mastered during the students' prior study of the language. To help distinguish authentic from "made-up" Latin, I have not capitalized the first words of sentences in parts I or II, unless they are proper nouns.

I have drawn the Latin readings in part III from a great variety of sources over a considerable span of literary history. They weren't necessarily chosen for their high Latinity; in fact, in some places the Latin can be downright poor (the students won't really know it, of course, unless it's pointed out to them). The readings were selected to reflect the breadth of Latin literature and to engage the interests and sensibilities of modern college and university students. Battle narratives and forensic oratory won't be found here; they can be studied and appreciated in upper-division courses. In fact, none of the readings found in this textbook is likely to be reencountered later on in the students' undergraduate study, and a word of explanation to justify this is probably warranted. When I teach advanced Latin courses on Catullus or Ovid or Cicero or Livy, it is a personal bête noire when a student declares to me that he or she "knows" a passage or a poem just because the student's intermediate Latin class read it; getting a student to unlearn to relearn takes a lot of energy on both sides. The truth is, whatever literary analysis that's done at the intermediate level is fairly superficial and selective—and that's how it should be. After using this book, a student will greet the great texts of Roman literature, whether poetry or prose, as a tabula rasa, and I believe there is an advantage to this all around.

A further word on the use of noncanonical authors and texts: of course, typical intermediate students don't fully grasp what is or isn't canon or why, and they need to learn considerably more Latin to make any discussion of canon substantive for them. I find it much more useful at this stage of their learning to employ the noncanonical to whet their palates for the canonical. In my intermediate classes, I can commonly be heard uttering something like "If you think *this* is good/interesting/provocative, just wait till you read ____!" The preceding blank can be filled in with Cicero, Ovid, Vergil, Horace, Terence, Caesar, Catullus, Livy, or Tacitus as situationally appropriate. The readings in this volume offer tasty appetizers; we need to build anticipation for the more substantial and piquant entrées to follow. If we're smart, we'll always be talking up the next courses in our curriculum.

An explanation can be offered for this text's heavy use of fables, aphorisms, and anecdotes. There is an inherent pleasure—one might even say comfort—in fables, as Phaedrus first acknowledged. Students are immediately put at ease when told they are going to read a Latin fable; this information even seems to trump most anxieties about reading poetry. Moreover, ancient Roman thought is markedly less dialectical than ancient Greek. Latin literature relies much on the aphoristic and the anecdotal to capture the truth or essence of any given topic, especially in prose, where the *logos* of aphorism or anecdote commonly replaces the *muthos* of poetic fable and myth.

In part III, grammar cues and vocabulary aids are very generous for the first few selections in prose and verse, but then they taper off some. The intent here is that students will realize that overreliance on these types of assistance will begin to hold them back. At some point in their linguistic development it's better and easier for them to puzzle out that a certain accusative, for example, is a subjective accusative and not a direct object than to double-check it against the grammar of part I. Similarly, we don't want reading facility to be frustrated simply because of a student's weak vocabulary, but at the same time we constantly need to motivate students to improve their vocabulary; apart from these considerations, the broad semantic range of many Latin lexemes requires us to accustom students to the use of dictionaries—not a bad thing. Balancing the various desiderata here is not an easy calculus, but if I've erred, it's usually in the direction of trying to improve reading facility.

That near-equal attention is paid to prose and verse readings requires little comment. In our upper-division Latin curriculum we typically pay near-equal attention to poetry and prose. It only makes sense that the bridge course to advanced studies should reflect what the subsequent curriculum strives for: an equal proficiency in Latin prose and verse.

The book provides fairly copious supplemental readings in part III. Their overall content and pedagogy are consistent with the other readings; in this case, more of the same serves to showcase further the breadth and depth of Roman literature and thought. Students and instructors are free to do with them what they will: self-study, testing, practice, further topical reading, diagnostics, extra credit. However they're used, they can be very beneficial for advancing the students' reading skills, and they should be mined for the resources that they contain.

Every reading is accompanied by questions called "Reading for Information" and "Reading for Understanding." While the obvious common denominator is reading and its promotion, the two kinds of questions do different things. "Reading for Information" questions, together with the headings or introductions, are intended to situate the students in the passage even before they begin reading it. On the principle that all proficient reading is basically anticipatory (that is, when we read, we're always engaged in the active process of expecting what will come next), these questions simply prime the pump by helping the students to anticipate, and the questions should therefore be read and answered carefully—the answers will reveal whether or not the students are reading with precision and attention to detail.

The "Reading for Understanding" questions not only reveal students' comprehension but also can generate some very lively class discussions. These questions often exploit cross-cultural and intercultural pressure points, inviting students to examine their own culture carefully before passing judgment on the Romans'. If a question here or there seems tendentious or partisan, this is because it's meant to elicit a vigorous response. When students begin to be able to discuss what they've just read in critical and factually accurate ways, this becomes a reliable indicator of their readiness for advanced studies and theory.

The purpose of part IV, as adumbrated above, is twofold: to provide students with a concrete and specific strategy for building their Latin vocabulary, and to accustom them to a little dictionary work, in which they will discover, if they haven't already, that Latin diction differs greatly from English. Our dictionaries are more word rich and less definition rich, while a Latin glossary is just the opposite. This difference may prompt some practical resistance, but it only rarely causes any conceptual consternation. There's a great teaching moment to be had by bringing into class the *Oxford Latin Dictionary* and letting the students pore over entries like those for *et*, *res*, *habeo*, and *ut*. After that experience, they'll tend to regard the modest general vocabulary in part IV with more respect.

The appendix, on Latin word order and sentence structure, which constitutes part V, attempts to cover only the basics. It should be assigned reading early in the term and repeatedly referred to thereafter. The topic is certainly not the students' favorite, but any worthy étude requires the student to differentiate between theme and variation. At this stage of Latin study, it suffices if our students recognize the norms of word order and the most common anomalies.

Following the appendix, there is a useful list of authors and texts, which provides some chronological and bibliographical detail. Reference to the original texts will reveal the extent to which I have adapted the readings (not much). This list may also prove helpful if a student desires to do further reading in a particular author, work, genre, or period.

Finally, at the book's end, a synopsis of part I will be found. This can be removed and mounted on heavy paper for use both as ready reference and as a bookmark.

Recommendations for Students

Not to oversimplify things, but success in college Latin depends mostly on your command of Latin vocabulary and your ability to distinguish between different uses of common constructions (e.g., the ablative case or the subjunctive mood). For the former, part IV presents a straightforward strategy; follow that and you will cultivate a strong operative vocabulary, serving you well in your next Latin courses too. As for the latter, keep a careful eye out for those uses or constructions that are high-frequency, make sure you really understand the language logic underlying them, and repeatedly test your understanding with those exercises in part II that are keyed to them. To that end, I strongly recommend that you *don't* write your translations of the exercises in the book itself; rather, write out the Latin of the exercises on separate paper and adjoin your translations thereto. That way, you can repeat the exercises as many times as you need to in order to achieve the desired accuracy and precision in your translations.

Armed with a strong vocabulary and a secure command of grammar and syntax, with your instructor's assistance you will begin to gain a facility in reading Latin—not simply translating it. Remember that reading, whether it's in your first language or a studied language, relies heavily on expectation or anticipation: as we're reading, we're almost always guessing what will come next. Therefore, be guided by the headings for each reading and the "Reading for Information" questions, as well as even the "Reading for Understanding" questions; these will help shape your expectations, create greater fluidity within each reading, and pave the way for your reading fluency.

You'll know you're getting better at reading Latin when you find yourself less often looking down for vocabulary aids and over for grammar cues. Keep in mind that even the most expert Latin scholars occasionally need to consult grammar books and dictionaries, so don't get discouraged in any way just because you're using the assistance provided to facilitate your reading.

Finally, the supplemental readings found in part III offer you great opportunities to practice the skills you're trying to develop. It's a pretty simple truism: the more you practice your Latin skills, the better they'll become. The supplemental readings are interesting, and they'll complement and sophisticate your understanding of the major themes that each of the six reading sections present. One more idea: use these readings to keep "road rust" off your Latin during winter, spring, and summer breaks. Reading Latin is like playing a musical instrument: the best way to get better at it is by practicing every day. Muscle memory is as important for languages as for playing music.

What you find in this textbook is but a foretaste of all that you can enjoy in the vast variety of Roman literature. If you like the fables or the love poetry or the natural sciences or the medical writings or the aphorisms or the historical anecdotes, there are plenty more where these were selected from. Your instructor can point you to similar texts for further reading. Probably the most important thing for you to recognize, though, is the spectacular panorama that is Roman literature. Here can be found nearly every subject and every perspective approximating the sum of human thought, observation, and experience. When you consider that this all took place roughly two thousand years ago, it's nothing short of amazing. The basic challenge for you as you proceed in your firsthand understanding of Roman thoughts and values is to remain open to the ideas they got right as you stay alert to and cognizant of the ideas they got wrong. This understanding will help you in your lifelong effort to make sense of your own culture.

Recommendations for Instructors

Most of the grammar and syntax in part I will be familiar to your students, although they may have learned it under different nomenclature. There will be several items, however, that some students may be encountering for the first time. You will probably need to spend a little extra time on those (and the concomitant exercises in part II). Also, part I, especially the latter half, may somewhat initially disorient some students, because the material has been organized very differently than it was in their primers; someone will doubtless ask you to explain this difference. Because students today like things to be quantified, when I introduce them to a construction whose syntax is unfamiliar to them, I often tell them something like "If you read Latin for one hour every day for a week, you'll probably see this construction X or Y times." This kind of information seems to help them process the grammar better, for some reason. And I occasionally get the student who will blurt out, "You said X or Y times, but this is the Zth time!" which indicates to me that she or he is keeping an eye out for the construction precisely because I did try to quantify it.

Generally speaking, I plan out my Latin classes in one-week blocks: I decide by Monday morning what I want to accomplish before the end of class on the upcoming Friday. Because every group of students is different, I have never followed the same formula twice for using the book. Depending on the class itself and its preparedness for intermediate Latin, for the first four weeks of the term I may spend more time on parts I and II than on part III. But by the last four weeks of the term we're spending almost all our time reading and vocabulary building.

I usually let the students decide which order they'd like to follow in part III. That is, if they want to do the readings about love before undertaking the fables, that is perfectly all right. Each of the six reading topics is an independent unit and does not presume the completion of a previous reading topic. Furthermore, this book provides enough readings that it certainly isn't necessary to complete each and every one under each topic: feel free to pick and choose as you see fit or as the predilections of your students dictate. But however much you pick and choose, I strongly recommend that you divide the readings equally, to the extent you can, between prose and verse selections.

I devote a lot of attention in class to the "Reading for Information" and "Reading for Understanding" questions, making something of a game of the former while applying a stricter critical rigor to the latter. Whenever we get into a spirited discussion over an "Understanding" question, I usually stand back and play only a moderating role, but in that role I'm often asking questions such as "Where in the Latin are you finding support for your claim?" or "When John just made this claim about our culture, do the rest of you concur?" I want the students using both the readings and their classmates to measure and test their assertions. The results are hardly the Tusculan Disputations, but students do learn that ancient argumentation was based on facts, the application of logic and rhetoric, and reference to literary authority.

I've suggested above a wide range of possible uses for the supplemental readings. I encourage you to make full use of them. Almost all of us subscribe to the view that the more reading our students do, the better readers they become. You'll notice that I provide grammar cues for only some of the selections; as a useful exercise, I frequently ask my students to supply the cues for a passage that's lacking them. If you try this exercise yourself, it will quickly disclose to you which of your students either don't grasp or don't employ the methods of the book.

As a bit of a vocabulary-acquisition martinet, I encourage you to require your students to follow the strategy for vocabulary building that part IV presents. I typically spread this over the entire term, testing my students once per week on it. Also, when we encounter a word glossed in part III that's related to a word I've required them to learn, as often happens, I ask my students to explain the relationship.

Of course, it's the goal of every intermediate Latin instructor that all grammar cues and vocabulary aids will become superfluous. As the term progresses, I repeatedly encourage students to wean themselves off these forms of assistance. I'm often saying things like "It's better to look within than to look down" or "It's easier just to learn 12.I.c.1 than to keep looking it up." Most students will agree (however reluctantly) and start to use the aids only as a last resort. Another strategy I employ toward this goal is bringing in an edition of the Latin author or work they'll be studying in the next term and showing them that their next textbook won't be as generous to them as their current one is. They get the message.

I intentionally provide a bare minimum of historical and cultural background for the readings so as to set up opportunities for you, the instructor, to expand on your own enthusiasms. I've found that textbooks only rarely kindle genuine student interests; this is the essential role of the classroom instructor. Students will better remember what you present to them about the elder Scipio, ancient medicine, or Roman marriage, for example, than what I might offer here in the context of an intermediate Latin course.

I leave entirely to your discretion whether to teach your students prosody and scansion for the poetic texts provided. I am aware that opinions on this vary, and I designed the book so that both schools of pedagogical thought can exercise their prerogative freely. For my part, in the last week or two of the school term, I introduce my students to only the barest of the basics (long and short syllables, elision, iambs, trochees, dactyls, and spondees), and I carefully select one or two of the poetic texts to illustrate these basics. (Some prose aphorisms have been included among those in verse because they display a poetry-like concision and even prose rhythm. I would advise against using aphorisms for teaching scansion; look rather to fables and elegies for this purpose.) In this way, my students won't be put off at all by some of the intricacies of prosody, and they can enter their first advanced Latin poetry class with an elementary understanding of technical poetics.

On a related matter, my use (or nonuse) of the macron may initially strike you as odd or idiosyncratic. Indeed, a cogent case could be made for an all-or-nothing approach at the intermediate level. Instructors and even primers of beginning Latin are now inconsistent in their use of or emphasis on macra. As an instructor of intermediate Latin, I always praise the students who have learned and apply their macra properly, but at the same time I reassure the students who are mostly unfamiliar with the macron that, apart from proper pronunciation, the mark will become important later in their study of poetics. I have employed macra in this book to distinguish between two (or more) similar forms or lexical items; when the student sees a macron, he or she should be encouraged to draw a semantically significant distinction ("What would this be/what would it mean if there weren't a macron present?"). Helping our students to develop a discerning eye for fine details will serve them tremendously well in all their subsequent studies. Macra are also commonly provided for particles, those lexemes that, in my experience, Latin students find the most slippery. Advanced philological texts omit macra, as well as vocabulary and grammar aids, and so I've opted to use this text to begin detaching students from such cues when and where they're unnecessary for reading proficiency and understanding.

PART I

Morphology and Grammar Review

A. Nouns

1. Regular Declensions

An asterisk (*) signifies that the declension exhibits a potential alternate ending, for which see the notes under each declension.

I. FIRST DECLENSION

Case	Singular	Plural
Nominative	**fama**	**famae**
Genitive	**famae**	**famarum**
Dative	**famae**	**famis**
Accusative	**famam**	**famas**
Ablative	**famā**	**famis**
Vocative	**fama**	**famae**

I.1. 1st declension nouns are typically feminine in gender, except for a few proper names of men (e.g., Agrippa, Scaevola) and a few occupations (e.g., **agricola**, **poeta**, **scriba**, **pirata**), which are masculine.

II. SECOND DECLENSION

II.1. Masculines

Case	Singular	Plural
Nominative	**cibus**	**cibi**
Genitive	**cibi**	**ciborum***
Dative	**cibo**	**cibis**
Accusative	**cibum**	**cibos**
Ablative	**cibo**	**cibis**
Vocative	**cibe***	**cibi**

II.1.a. 2nd declension nouns ending in **-us** or **-r** are typically masculine in gender, except for the names of trees (e.g., **ornus**, **ulmus**, **pinus**), which are feminine.

II.1.b. Vocative singulars for 2nd declension nouns ending in **-ius** are **-i**, ending in **-us** are **-e**, and ending in **-r** are **-r**.

II.1.c. With certain very common nouns, you can sometimes find **-um** instead of **-orum** in the genitive plural.

II.1.d. In older Latin, any 2nd declension noun whose stem ends in **-v-** or **-qu-** can have **-os** (M) or **-om** (N) in the nominative singular and **-om** in the accusative singular; the archaizing **-om** for **-orum** can also be found in the genitive plural.

II.2. Neuters

Case	Singular	Plural
Nominative	**verbum**	**verba**
Genitive	**verbi**	**verborum**
Dative	**verbo**	**verbis**
Accusative	**verbum**	**verba**
Ablative	**verbo**	**verbis**
Vocative	**verbum**	**verba**

II.2.a. 2nd declension nouns that end in **-um** are neuter in gender.

III. THIRD DECLENSION

III.1. Regulars

Case	Singular	Plural	Singular	Plural
Nomin.	**lex**	**leges**	**cor**	**corda**
Genitive	**legis**	**legum**	**cordis**	**cordum**
Dative	**legi**	**legibus**	**cordi**	**cordibus**
Accus.	**legem**	**leges**	**cor**	**corda**
Ablative	**lege**	**legibus**	**corde**	**cordibus**
Vocative	**lex**	**leges**	**cor**	**corda**

III.1.a. Normal 3rd declension nouns can be masculine or feminine in gender, in which case they behave like **lex**, or neuter in gender, in which case they behave like **cor**.

III.2. *I*-stems

Case	Singular	Plural	Singular	Plural
Nomin.	**ignis**	**ignes***	**mare**	**maria**
Genitive	**ignis**	**ignium**	**maris**	**marium**
Dative	**igni**	**ignibus**	**mari**	**maribus**
Accus.	**ignem***	**ignes***	**mare**	**maria**
Ablative	**igne***	**ignibus**	**mare***	**maribus**
Vocative	**ignis**	**ignes***	**mare**	**maria**

III.2.a. Normal 3rd declension *i*-stem nouns can be masculine or feminine in gender, in which case they behave like **ignis**, or neuter in gender, in which case they behave like **mare**.

III.2.b. Especially in poetry, *i*-stems exhibit the following alternate forms: in the ablative singular, **-i** for **-e** (e.g., **igni** or **mari** for **igne** or **mare**); in the accusative singular, **-im** for **-em** (e.g., **ignim** for **ignem**); in the nominative, accusative, and vocative plural, **-īs** for **-es** (e.g., **ignīs** for **ignes**).

III.2.c. The three rules for recognizing *i*-stems are as follows:

—Masculine and feminine nouns that both are monosyllabic in the nominative singular and have stems ending in two consonants are *i*-stem (e.g., **nox**, **noctis**).

—Masculine and feminine nouns that both end in **-is** or **-es** in the nominative singular and have the same number of syllables in the nominative and genitive singular are *i*-stem (e.g., **ignis**, **ignis**).

—Neuter nouns that end in **-e**, **-ar**, or **-al** in the nominative singular are *i*-stem (e.g., **mare**, **maris**).

III.2.d. Like most rules in Latin, the preceding aren't 100 percent rules. The most common exceptions are **canis**, **iuvenis**, **senex**, and **volucris**, none of which has **-ium** in the genitive plural.

IV. FOURTH DECLENSION

IV.1. Masculines and Feminines

Case	Singular	Plural
Nominative	metus	metūs
Genitive	metūs	metuum
Dative	metū*	metibus*
Accusative	metum	metūs
Ablative	metū	metibus*
Vocative	metus	metūs

IV.1.a. 4th declension nouns ending in **-us** are most often masculine but sometimes feminine in gender.

IV.2. Neuters

Case	Singular	Plural
Nominative	genu	genua
Genitive	genūs	genuum
Dative	genū	genibus*
Accusative	genu	genua
Ablative	genū	genibus*
Vocative	genu	genua

IV.2.a. 4th declension nouns ending in **-u** in the nominative are neuter in gender.

IV.3. In poetry and some older Latin literature, the following alternate forms can be found: in the dative singular, **-ui** for **-ū** (e.g., **metui** for **metū**), and in the dative and ablative plural, **-ubus** for **-ibus** (e.g., **metubus** for **metibus**, or **genubus** for **genibus**).

V. FIFTH DECLENSION

Case	Singular	Plural
Nominative	spes	spes
Genitive	spei	sperum
Dative	spei	spebus
Accusative	spem	spes
Ablative	spe	spebus
Vocative	spes	spes

V.1. 5th declension nouns are most often feminine but sometimes masculine in gender.

2. Irregular Declensions

I. *vis*, F   **II. *domus*, F**

Case	Sing.	Plur.	Sing.	Plur.	Case
Nom.	vis	vires	domūs	domūs	Nom.
Gen.	vis	virium	domūs, domi	domuum, domorum	Gen.
Dat.	vi	viribus	domui, domo	domibus	Dat.
Acc.	vim	vires, virīs	domum	domos, domūs	Acc.
Abl.	vi	viribus	domo, domū	domibus	Abl.

III. *deus*, M   **IV. *dea*, F**

Case	Sing.	Plur.	Sing.	Plur.	Case
Nom.	deus	dei, dii, dī	dea	deae	Nom.
Gen.	dei	deorum, deum	deae	dearum	Gen.
Dat.	deo	deis, diis, dis	deae	deabus	Dat.
Acc.	deum	deos	deam	deas	Acc.
Abl.	deo	deis, diis, dis	deā	deabus	Abl.

V. *bos*, M/F   **VI. *locus*, M/N**

Case	Sing.	Plur.	Sing.	Plur.	Case
Nom.	bos	boves	locus	loci, loca	Nom.
Gen.	bovis	boum	loci	locorum	Gen.
Dat.	bovi	bubus	loco	locis	Dat.
Acc.	bovem	boves	locum	locos, loca	Acc.
Abl.	bove	bubus	loco	locis	Abl.

VI.1. Note that the masculine plural **loci, locorum** are usually unrelated places, while the neuter plural **loca, locorum** are places that share something in common.

VII. *Iuppiter*, M   **VIII. *nemo*, M**

Case	Sing.	Plur.	Sing.	Plur.	Case
Nom.	Iuppiter	——	nemo	——	Nom.
Gen.	Iovis	——	nullius	——	Gen.
Dat.	Iovi	——	nemini, nulli	——	Dat.
Acc.	Iovem	——	neminem	——	Acc.
Abl.	Iove	——	nullo	——	Abl.

3. Review of Cases

I. NOMINATIVE

I.1. Subject of finite verb
Marcus **pugnat.**   *Marcus* fights.

I.2. Subject complement (predicate attribute)
Marcus erit *miles.*   Marcus will be a *soldier.*
Marcus *tribunus* **creatus est.**   Marcus was appointed *tribune.*

II. GENITIVE

II.1. Of possession
mercatoris **taberna**   *the merchant's* shop, the shop *of the merchant*
mercatorum **tabernae**   *the merchants'* shops, shops *of the merchants*

II.2. Partitive (of the whole)
pars *urbis*   part *of the city*
fortissimus *virorum*   the bravest *of the men*

II.3. Of description
femina *magnae sapientiae*   a woman *of great wisdom*

II.4. Of material
urna *auri*   a pitcher *of gold*

II.5. Of characteristic (predicate genitive)
aequē regere est *boni regis.*   It is (the mark) *of a good king* to rule fairly.

II.6. Objective

II.6.a. Nominal
dux *proelii*   the leader *of the battle*
spes *pacis*   a hope *of peace*
pecunia est *belli* **causa.**   Money is the cause *of war.*

II.6.b. Verbal
nos te *ignaviae* **damnamus.**   We accuse you of *cowardice.*
                                         (verbs of accusing and condemning)
meminimus *tuorum factorum.*   We remember *your deeds.*
                                         (verbs of remembering and forgetting)

II.6.c. Adjectival

    urna plena *aquae*   a pitcher full *of water*

    vir *scientiae* doctus   the man learned *in science*

II.7. Of indefinite value

    villam *magni* habeo.   I have a house *worth much*.

    haec villa *parvi* est.   This house is *of little worth*.

II.8. Of definite measurement

    flumen *sex pedum*   a river *of six feet*

    iter *decem dierum*   a journey *of ten days*

III. DATIVE

III.1. Indirect object (with verbs: give, offer, show, tell, etc.)

    ***servo* pecuniam dedi.**   I gave money *to the slave*.

                                 I gave *the slave* money.

III.2. With certain adjectives (e.g., **amicus, inimicus, idoneus, par, proximus, similis, dissimilis, carus, iucundus**)

    vir est amicus *nobis*.   The man is friendly *to us*.

    filius erat similis *patri*.   The son was like *his father*.

III.3. Of advantage or disadvantage (referential)

    librum *nautae* ēmimus.   We bought the book *for the sailor*.

    pontem *hostibus* delevit.   He destroyed the bridge *for the enemy*.

III.4. Of the possessor

    est *mihi* nova villa.   *I* have a new house.

                                 (literally, there is *for me* a new house)

III.5. With certain intransitive verbs (e.g., **credo, faveo, ignosco, impero, noceo, parco, pareo, persuadeo, placeo, studeo**)

    ego *tibi* non credo.   I don't trust *you*.

    ignosce *mihi*!   Forgive *me*!

III.6. Of agent (with passive periphrastics; see 17.IV.3)

    hoc agendum *puellis* est.   *The girls* must do this.

                                   It is necessary *for the girls* to do this.

III.7. With certain compound verbs: many verbs compounded with the prefixes **ad-**, **ante-**, **circum-**, **con-**, **in-**, **inter-**, **ob-**, **post-**, **prae-**, **pro-**, **sub-**, and **super-** govern the dative case (with or without an accusative direct object).

bellum *provinciae* **inferimus.**	We inflict war *on the province.*
legatum *navibus* **praefecit.**	He put the legate in charge *of the ships.*
in viā *patri* **occurri.**	I met *my father* in the street.
legatus *navibus* **praeest.**	The legate is in charge *of the ships.*

III.8. Ethical (always a personal pronoun)

illud *mihi* **scelus non est.**	That isn't a crime *in my opinion/to my thinking/as far as I'm concerned/for my part.*

III.9. Of purpose (of service)

librum *dono* **ēmimus.**	We bought the book *for/as a gift.*
milites *auxilio* **missi sunt.**	The soldiers were sent *for/as help.*

III.10. "Double dative": The so-called double dative is a combination of the dative of purpose with either an indirect object or a referential dative.

servo **pecuniam** *dono* **dedi.**	I gave money *to the slave as a gift.*

IV. ACCUSATIVE

IV.1. Direct object

habeo *multos fratres.*	I have *many brothers.*
docet *nos scientiam.*	He teaches *us science.* (double accusative)
vivemus *longam vitam.*	We will live *a long life.* (cognate accusative)

IV.1.a. Active participles and gerunds, like finite verbs, can produce a direct object:

viventes *longam vitam*	living *a long life*
habens *multos fratres*	having *many brothers*

IV.1.b. The complement or attribute of a direct object is also put into the accusative:

habemus eum *regem.*	we have him *as king.*

IV.2. Of time duration (no preposition; see 4.II.3)

multos annos **vixit.**	He lived *for many years.*

IV.3. Of extent of space

puer saxum *quinque pedes* **portavit.**	The boy carried the rock *five feet.*

IV.4. Subject of infinitive (subjective accusative; see 12.I.4)

nos **discedere nolunt.**	They don't want *us* to leave.
dicit *feminas* **vēnisse.**	He says that *the women* have come.

IV.4.a. Predicate attribute of a subjective accusative

dicit feminas esse *viduas*.   He says the women are *widows*.

IV.5. Of exclamation

***me miserum*!**   O *miserable me*!

***infelicem diem*!**   O *unlucky day*!

IV.6. Of the part of the body affected

viri *oculos* vulnerati sunt.   The men were wounded *in the eyes*.

IV.7. Adverbial

***maximam partem* hoc mihi placet.**   *For the most part* this pleases me.

vir me *nihil* vexat.   The man annoys me *not at all*.

IV.8. With certain prepositions (see 8.I)

ad *urbem*   to *the city*

prope *Italiam*   near *Italy*

post *bellum*   after *the war*

IV.9. Place to which (without preposition; see 4.I.2)

***domum* cucurrit.**   He ran *home*.

***Romam* contendo.**   I'm hurrying *to Rome*.

V. ABLATIVE

V.1. Of means or instrument (no preposition)

***saxo* vulneratus est.**   He was wounded *by/with a stone*.

V.2. Of agent (with the preposition **a/ab**)

***a milite* vulneratus est.**   He was wounded *by a soldier*.

V.3. Of manner

V.3.a. With the preposition **cum**

pugnat *cum virtute*.   He fights *with courage*.

V.3.b. With or without **cum** in the presence of an adjective

pugnat *magnā (cum) virtute*.   He fights *with great courage*.

V.4. Of accompaniment (with the preposition **cum**)

***cum matre* vēni.**   I came *with my mother*.

V.5. Of description (always with an adjective)

vīdi virum *uno oculo*.   I saw a man *with one eye/a one-eyed man*.

femina *digitis longis* est pulchra.   A woman *with long fingers* is beautiful.

V.6. Of time when or within which (see 4.II.1 and 4.II.2)

***nocte* advēnimus.**   We arrived *at night*.

***paucis annis* reveniam.**   I'll return *in a few years*.

V.7. Of cause

cucurrit *timore*.   He ran *because of/out of/from fear*.

V.8. Of comparison

Germani fortiores sunt *Romanis*.   Germans are braver *than Romans*.

V.9. Of degree of difference

hoc monile est *multō* pulchrius.   This necklace is *much/by far* prettier.

Marcus est longior *duobus pedibus*.   Marcus is taller *by two feet*.

V.10. Of respect or specification

est pulcher *corpore et animo*.   He is beautiful *in body and mind*.

V.11. Of route

advēnit *Appiā Viā*.   He arrived *on/by the Appian Road*.

V.12. Of price

vendidi servum *magno pretio*.   I sold the slave *at/for a great price*.

V.13. With certain deponent verbs (e.g., **fruor, fungor, potior, utor, vescor**)

usus est *gladio*.   He used *a sword*.

fruor *vino*.   I enjoy *wine*.

V.14. Of attendant circumstances

flumen *magno clamore* ruit.   The river rushes *with a great clamor*.

V.15. Ablative absolute (see section 13)

V.16. With certain adjectives (e.g., **dignus, indignus, fretus, contentus, laetus**)

dignus *laude*   worthy *of praise*

fretus *virtute*   relying *on courage*

contentus *spe*   content *with hope*

V.17. Of material (with or without the prepositions **de** or **e/ex**)

est statua *(de) marmore* **in foro.**   There's a statue *of marble* in the forum.
navis *(ex) robore* **facta est.**   The ship was made *of oak.*

V.18. Of origin (with or without a preposition)

gente clarā **natus est.**   He was descended *from a famous family.*
e matre pulchrā **natus est.**   He was born *of a beautiful mother.*
flumen *a mari* **oritur.**   The river rises *from the sea.*

V.19. Of separation (with or without the prepositions **a/ab**, **de**, or **e/ex**)

solvite nos *ex carcere***!**   Free us *from prison!*
Caesar te *noxā* **servavit.**   Caesar saved you *from harm.*

V.20. With certain prepositions (see 8.II)

de *reginā*   concerning *the queen*
pro *auxilio*   in return for *the help*
prae *templo*   in front of *the temple* (place where)
in *Italiā*   in *Italy* (place where)
ex *Africā*   out of *Africa* (place from which)
de *monte*   down (from) *the mountain* (place from which)

V.21. Place from which (without preposition; see 4.I.1)

domo **cucurrit.**   He ran *from home.*
Romā **contendo.**   I'm hurrying *from/out of Rome.*

VI. VOCATIVE

VI.1. Direct address

pueri, **est necesse discedere.**   *Boys,* it's necessary to leave.
Marce et Mani, **venite!**   *Marcus and Manius,* come!

VII. LOCATIVE

See 4.I.3.

VIII. APPOSITION

A noun (or a pronoun or even an adjective) can be loosely attached to another noun in order to clarify or restrict it, and is called an appositive. The appositive is always placed in the same case as the noun to which it refers.

Agrippa, *meus pater,* **vocat.**	Agrippa, *my father,* summons.
Agrippam, *meum patrem,* **vocat.**	She summons Agrippa, *my father.*

IX. AMBIGUITY

Since Latin noun (and pronoun) declensions exhibit numerous repeated forms (e.g., **-ae** in the 1st declension genitive and dative singular; **-o** in the 2nd declension dative and ablative singular; **-bus** in the 3rd, 4th, and 5th declension dative and ablative plurals), it may not always be evident to a reader which case (or which use of a case) the author intended. Indeed, the author may even have artfully intended this ambiguity and wanted the reader to consider all the semantic possibilities together.

X. ELLIPSIS

As an economical language, Latin often omits a noun (or pronoun) that can be understood from the context. For example:

interfecerunt meum fratrem et tuum.   They killed my brother and yours.

In the preceding, the word **fratrem** (brother) is construed with **meum** but also understood with **tuum**. This type of omission is sometimes referred to as *brachylogy*.

4. Place and Time Constructions

I. With the names of cities, towns, and small islands and with the nouns **domus** (home), **humus** (ground), and **rus** (country), prepositions are not used in place constructions.

This class of words expresses place in or at which by means of the locative case. Its form is like that of the genitive singular for nouns of the 1st and 2nd declensions (e.g., **Romae**, "at Rome"; **Cypri**, "at Cyprus" or "on Cyprus"; **domi**, "at home"), otherwise like that of the ablative (e.g., **Athenis**, "at Athens"; **Neapoli**, "at Naples"; **ruri** (or **rure**), "in the country").

The following chart provides Latin's different place constructions:

Construction	With Ordinary Nouns	With Cities, Towns, Small Islands, **domus, humus, rus**
I.1. PLACE FROM WHICH	**a/ab, de, e/ex** with ablative	ablative (no preposition)
venit . . .	. . . **ab urbe.**	. . . **Romā/domo.**
She comes . . .	. . . from the city.	. . . from Rome/home.
I.2. PLACE TO WHICH	**ad, in** with accusative	accusative (no preposition)
currit . . .	. . . **ad urbem.**	. . . **Romam/domum.**
She runs . . .	. . . to the city.	. . . to Rome/home.
I.3. PLACE IN OR AT WHICH	**in** with ablative	locative
est . . .	. . . **in urbe.**	. . . **Romae/domi.**
She is . . .	. . . in/at the city.	. . . in/at Rome/home.

II. Latin distinguishes between time when or at which, time during or within which, and time duration (how long).

II.1. A simple ablative usually expresses time when or at which; see 3.V.6.

vēnit nocte.   He came at nighttime.

II.1.a. When the time is just an approximation, the prepositions **ad** or **sub** with the accusative case are used:

vēnit ad/sub noctem.   He came around nighttime.

II.2. A simple ablative usually expresses time within or during which; see 3.V.6.

vēnit nocte.   He came during/in the night.

II.2.a. For greater explicitness, the preposition **in** with the ablative can be used for time during or within which:

vēnit in nocte.   He came exactly at night.

II.3. A simple accusative usually expresses the period during which an action occurred (time duration); see 3.IV.2.

manebat decem dies.   He stayed for ten days.

II.3.a. For greater explicitness, the preposition **per** with the accusative can be used for time duration:

manebat per decem dies.   He stayed for exactly ten days.

B. Adjectives and Adverbs

5. Regular and Irregular Declensions

I. Regular Latin adjectives belong to one or another classification: they decline according to either the 1st and 2nd declensions or else the 3rd declension.

I.1. Most 1st and 2nd declension adjectives decline like **magnus, -a, -um**. A small group ends in **-r** in the nominative masculine singular (e.g., **miser, misera, miserum**).

Case	Masculine	Feminine	Neuter	Case
		SINGULARS		
Nom.	magnus	magna	magnum	Nom.
Gen.	magni	magnae	magni	Gen.
Dat.	magno	magnae	magno	Dat.
Acc.	magnum	magnam	magnum	Acc.
Abl.	magno	magnā	magno	Abl.
		PLURALS		
Nom.	magni	magnae	magna	Nom.
Gen.	magnorum	magnarum	magnorum	Gen.
Dat.	magnis	magnis	magnis	Dat.
Acc.	magnos	magnas	magna	Acc.
Abl.	magnis	magnis	magnis	Abl.

I.2. 3rd declension adjectives are classified as 1-termination, 2-termination, or 3-termination; this refers to the number of distinctive endings in the nominative singular.

I.2.a. 1-termination

Case	Masculine/Feminine	Neuter	Case
	SINGULARS		
Nom.	ingens	ingens	Nom.
Gen.	ingentis	ingentis	Gen.
Dat.	ingenti	ingenti	Dat.
Acc.	ingentem	ingens	Acc.
Abl.	ingenti	ingenti	Abl.
	PLURALS		
Nom.	ingentes	ingentia	Nom.
Gen.	ingentium	ingentium	Gen.
Dat.	ingentibus	ingentibus	Dat.
Acc.	ingentes	ingentia	Acc.
Abl.	ingentibus	ingentibus	Abl.

I.2.a.i. 1-termination adjectives include all present active participles.

I.2.b. 2-termination

Case	Masculine/Feminine	Neuter	Case
	SINGULARS		
Nom.	**omnis**	**omne**	Nom.
Gen.	**omnis**	**omnis**	Gen.
Dat.	**omni**	**omni**	Dat.
Acc.	**omnem**	**omne**	Acc.
Abl.	**omni**	**omni**	Abl.
	PLURALS		
Nom.	**omnes**	**omnia**	Nom.
Gen.	**omnium**	**omnium**	Gen.
Dat.	**omnibus**	**omnibus**	Dat.
Acc.	**omnes**	**omnia**	Acc.
Abl.	**omnibus**	**omnibus**	Abl.

I.2.b.i. 2-termination adjectives include all comparative adjectives.

I.2.c. 3-termination

Case	Masculine/Feminine	Neuter	Case
	SINGULARS		
Nom.	**acer/acris**	**acre**	Nom.
Gen.	**acris**	**acris**	Gen.
Dat.	**acri**	**acri**	Dat.
Acc.	**acrem**	**acre**	Acc.
Abl.	**acri**	**acri**	Abl.
	PLURALS		
Nom.	**acres**	**acria**	Nom.
Gen.	**acrium**	**acrium**	Gen.
Dat.	**acribus**	**acribus**	Dat.
Acc.	**acres**	**acria**	Acc.
Abl.	**acribus**	**acribus**	Abl.

I.2.d. All 3rd declension adjectives, except comparatives, are *i*-stem. They allow the following alternate forms: -īs for -es in the masculine/feminine accusative and vocative plurals, and -e for -i in some 1-termination and 2-termination ablative singulars.

II. IRREGULAR/PRONOMINAL ADJECTIVES

There is a group of 1st and 2nd declension adjectives that are identical to other 1st and 2nd declension adjectives except that they end, like many pronouns, in **-ius** in the genitive singular and in **-i** in the dative singular. For example, **totus, -a, -um** (whole, all):

Case	Masculine	Feminine	Neuter	Masculine	Feminine	Neuter
		SINGULARS			PLURALS	
Nom.	totus	tota	totum			
Gen.	totius	totius	totius	(regular endings like		
Dat.	toti	toti	toti	those of **magnus, -a, -um**)		
Acc.	totum	totam	totum			
Abl.	toto	totā	toto			

II.1. Other adjectives of this group are:

alius, alia, aliud — other

alter, altera, alterum — the other (of two)

ullus, -a, -um — any

nullus, -a, -um — no, none, not any

uter, utra, utrum — which (of two)

neuter, neutra, neutrum — neither

solus, -a, -um — only, sole

unus, -a, -um — one, alone

III. All regular adjectives, regardless of declension, agree with the nouns they modify in all three respects of case, number, and gender.

6. Regular and Irregular Comparisons

I. Most adjectives have three degrees of comparison: the positive, the comparative, and the superlative.

Positive:	**fortis, -e** — brave
	miser, misera, miserum — miserable
Comparative:	**fortior, -ius** — braver, more brave, rather brave, too brave
	miserior, -ius — more miserable, rather miserable, too miserable
Superlative:	**fortissimus, -a, -um** — bravest, most brave, very brave
	miserrimus, -a, -um — most miserable, very miserable

I.1. All positives belong either to the 1st and 2nd declensions (e.g., **bonus, -a, -um**) or to the 3rd declension (e.g., **fortis, -e**).

I.2. All comparatives conform to the 3rd declension.

I.2.a. Comparatives constitute the only group of 3rd declension adjectives which are not *i*-stems.

I.2.b. Comparatives are frequently accompanied by an ablative of comparison (see 3.V.8), an ablative of degree of difference (see 3.V.9), or a relative clause of purpose (see 16.III.2.c).

Germani fortiores sunt Romanis.
Germans are braver than Romans.
hoc monile est multō pulchrius.
This necklace is much/by far prettier.
imperator ad Arabiam proficiscitur quō maiores equos inveniat.
The general is setting out for Arabia to find bigger horses.

I.3. All superlatives conform to the 1st and 2nd declensions.

I.3.a. Superlatives are often accompanied by a genitive of the whole (see 3.II.2).

fortissimus virorum   the bravest of the men

I.4. The most common adjectives exhibiting irregular comparison are:

Positives	Comparatives	Superlatives
bonus — good	**melior** — better	**optimus** — best
	deterior — worse	**deterrimus** — worst
exterus — outward	**exterior** — outer	**extremus** — outmost
inferus — below	**inferior** — lower	**infimus** — lowest
	interior — inner	**intimus** — inmost
magnus — big	**maior** — bigger	**maximus** — biggest
malus — bad	**peior** — worse	**pessimus** — worst
multus — much	**plus** — more	**plurimus** — most
parvus — little	**minor** — less	**minimus** — least
posterus — following	**posterior** — latter	**postremus** — last
	prior — former	**primus** — first
	propior — nearer	**proximus** — nearest
superus — above	**superior** — higher	**supremus/summus** — highest
	ulterior — farther	**ultimus** — farthest

II. Most adverbs derived from adjectives have the same three degrees of comparison: positive, comparative, superlative.

II.1. Most positives derived from 1st and 2nd declension adjectives end in -**ē** (or -**ō**), for instance **carē**, dearly; **tutō**, safely. Most positives derived from 3rd declension adjectives end in -**iter** (or -**ter**), for example **celeriter**, quickly; **audacter**, boldly.

II.2. Most comparatives, regardless of derivation, end in -**ius**, for instance **miserius**, more miserably, too miserably, rather miserably.

II.3. Most superlatives, regardless of derivation, end in -**issimē** (or -**rimē**), for example **saepissimē**, most often; **miserrimē**, most miserably.

II.4. The most common adverbs exhibiting irregular comparison are:

Positives	Comparatives	Superlatives
bene — well	**melius** — better	**optimē** — very well
male — poorly	**peius** — worse	**pessimē** — worst
multum/**multō** — much	**magis** — more	**maximē** — most
parum — too little	**minus** — less	**minimē** — least

III. The adverb **quam** is commonly found with adjectives and adverbs and has differing translations depending on the degree of comparison.

III.1. With a positive:

quam **celeriter cucurrit!**	*How* quickly she ran!
quam **elegans est!**	*How* elegant she is!

III.2. With a comparative:

Cicero est senior *quam* **is.**	Cicero is older *than* he.

III.3. With a superlative:

quam **celerrimē cucurrit.**	She ran *as* quickly *as possible*.
quam **nobilissimus est.**	He is *as* noble *as can be*.

C. Pronouns

7. Declensions

I. PERSONAL PRONOUNS

I.1. 1st person		*I.2. 2nd person*	
		SINGULARS	
Nom.	**ego**	**tu**	Nom.
Gen.	**mei**	**tui**	Gen.
Dat.	**mihi, mi**	**tibi**	Dat.
Acc.	**me**	**te**	Acc.
Abl.	**me**	**te**	Abl.
		PLURALS	
Nom.	**nos**	**vos**	Nom.
Gen.	**nostri, nostrum**	**vestri, vestrum**	Gen.
Dat.	**nobis**	**vobis**	Dat.
Acc.	**nos**	**vos**	Acc.
Abl.	**nobis**	**vobis**	Abl.

I.2.a. **Nostrum** and **vestrum** are used for partitive genitives (see 3.II.2), **nostri** and **vestri** for objective genitives (see 3.II.6).

I.3. 3rd person (determinative)

Case	*Masculine*	*Feminine*	*Neuter*	*Case*
		SINGULARS		
Nom.	**is**	**ea**	**id**	Nom.
Gen.	**eius**	**eius**	**eius**	Gen.
Dat.	**ei**	**ei**	**ei**	Dat.
Acc.	**eum**	**eam**	**id**	Acc.
Abl.	**eo**	**eā**	**eo**	Abl.
		PLURALS		
Nom.	**ei, ii, i**	**eae**	**ea**	Nom.
Gen.	**eorum**	**earum**	**eorum**	Gen.
Dat.	**eis, iis, īs**	**eis, iis, īs**	**eis, iis, īs**	Dat.
Acc.	**eos**	**eas**	**ea**	Acc.
Abl.	**eis, iis, īs**	**eis, iis, īs**	**eis, iis, īs**	Abl.

I.3.a. Behaving similarly is the pronoun **idem, eadem, idem**. Since the consonant cluster **-md-** is inadmissible in Latin, **-nd-** is used in the masculine and feminine accusative singular (**eundem, eandem**) and in the plural genitives (**eorundem, earundem**).

II. INTENSIVE PRONOUN

Case	Masculine	Feminine	Neuter	Case
		SINGULARS		
Nom.	**ipse**	**ipsa**	**ipsum**	Nom.
Gen.	**ipsius**	**ipsius**	**ipsius**	Gen.
Dat.	**ipsi**	**ipsi**	**ipsi**	Dat.
Acc.	**ipsum**	**ipsam**	**ipsum**	Acc.
Abl.	**ipso**	**ipsā**	**ipso**	Abl.
		PLURALS		
Nom.	**ipsi**	**ipsae**	**ipsa**	Nom.
Gen.	**ipsorum**	**ipsarum**	**ipsorum**	Gen.
Dat.	**ipsis**	**ipsis**	**ipsis**	Dat.
Acc.	**ipsos**	**ipsas**	**ipsa**	Acc.
Abl.	**ipsis**	**ipsis**	**ipsis**	Abl.

III. REFLEXIVE PRONOUN (3RD PERSON)

Case	Singular/Plural
Nom.	———
Gen.	**sui**
Dat.	**sibi**
Acc.	**se, sese**
Abl.	**se, sese**

IV. DEMONSTRATIVE PRONOUNS

Case	Masc.	Fem.	Neut.	Masc.	Fem.	Neut.	Case
			SINGULARS				
Nom.	**hic**	**haec**	**hoc**	**ille**	**illa**	**illud**	Nom.
Gen.	**huius**	**huius**	**huius**	**illius**	**illius**	**illius**	Gen.
Dat.	**huic**	**huic**	**huic**	**illi**	**illi**	**illi**	Dat.
Acc.	**hunc**	**hanc**	**hoc**	**illum**	**illam**	**illud**	Acc.
Abl.	**hōc**	**hac**	**hōc**	**illo**	**illā**	**illo**	Abl.

			PLURALS				
Nom.	hi	hae	haec	illi	illae	illa	Nom.
Gen.	horum	harum	horum	illorum	illarum	illorum	Gen.
Dat.	his	his	his	illis	illis	illis	Dat.
Acc.	hos	has	haec	illos	illas	illa	Acc.
Abl.	his	his	his	illis	illis	illis	Abl.

IV.1. Behaving similarly to **ille, illa, illud** is the pronoun **iste, ista, istud**.

V. RELATIVE PRONOUN

Case	Masc.	Fem.	Neut.	Case
		SINGULARS		
Nom.	qui	quae	quod	Nom.
Gen.	cuius	cuius	cuius	Gen.
Dat.	cui	cui	cui	Dat.
Acc.	quem	quam	quod	Acc.
Abl.	quo	quā	quo	Abl.
		PLURALS		
Nom.	qui	quae	quae	Nom.
Gen.	quorum	quarum	quorum	Gen.
Dat.	quibus	quibus	quibus*	Dat.
Acc.	quos	quas	quae	Acc.
Abl.	quibus	quibus	quibus*	Abl.

V.1. The form **quīs** is sometimes found instead of **quibus** in the dative and ablative plural.

V.2. Relative pronouns are frequently used at the beginning of a sentence or clause to refer to something mentioned in the previous sentence or clause. We best translate this usage with one of the English demonstratives.

    quibus rebus auditis   when *these* things were heard

V.3. Similar in declension are the pronouns **quicumque, quidam, quilibet,** and **quivis**.

    V.3.a. For **quidam,** since the consonant cluster -**md**- is inadmissible in Latin, -**nd**- is used in the masculine and feminine accusative singulars (**quendam, quandam**) and in the genitive plurals (**quorundam, quarundam**).

VI. INTERROGATIVE PRONOUN

Case	Masc.	Fem.	Neut.	Case
		SINGULARS		
Nom.	quis	quis	quid	Nom.
Gen.	cuius	cuius	cuius	Gen.
Dat.	cui	cui	cui	Dat.
Acc.	quem	quem	quid	Acc.
Abl.	quo	quo	quo	Abl.
		PLURALS		
Nom.	qui	quae	quae	Nom.
Gen.	quorum	quarum	quorum	Gen.
Dat.	quibus	quibus	quibus	Dat.
Acc.	quos	quas	quae	Acc.
Abl.	quibus	quibus	quibus	Abl.

VI.1. Behaving similarly are the pronouns **aliquis, ecquis, nequis, numquis, quisnam, quispiam, quisquam, quisque,** and **quisquis**.

VI.1.a. For the pronoun **aliquis**, don't forget the little ditty "After **si, nisi, num,** and **ne,** all the **ali**'s drop away." To this list of conjunctions, add **neve** and **neu**.

VII. All the pronouns provided above, except those in I.1, I.2, III, and V, can also function as adjectives.

D. Prepositions

8. Prepositions (and Postpositions)

Key:
   (P) = commonly postpositional (i.e., comes after the positive it governs)
   * = also occurs as an adverb

I. WITH THE ACCUSATIVE CASE

I.1. The more common prepositions:

ad — to, toward; near, at; until; according to
***ante** — before; prior to
apud — among; at the house of; with; according to
***circum** — round, about, near
***contrā** — opposite to, facing; against; contrary to
in — into, onto, toward; against; until
inter — between, among; during; in spite of
***iuxtā** — close to, next to; very like; next door to
ob — on account of, because of
per — through; during, throughout; by means of; for the sake of
***post** — behind; after, since
***praeter** — past, across; beyond, surpassing; contrary to; in addition; except for
***prope** — near, close to, by
propter — near, beside; on account of
super — over, above; beyond; besides
trans — across, over, beyond

I.2. The less common prepositions used with the accusative case:

adversus or **adversum** — toward; against
***circā** — round, in the vicinity of; about
***circiter** — about, near (time or number)
cis — on this side of; within (time)
***citrā** — on this side of, short of; apart from; before (time)
***clam** — unknown to, without the knowledge of
erga — toward; against
***extrā** — outside, beyond; free from; except for
***infrā** — below, beneath, under; later than
***intrā** — inside, within; during; less than, within the limits of
penes — in the power of, in the possession of; in the house of, with

*__pone__ — behind

*__propius__ — nearer to, closer to

*__proximē__ — next to, closest to, nearest to

__secundum__ — behind; after; next to; according to

__sub__ — along, under, up to

__subter__ — beneath, up close to

*__suprā__ — over, above; beyond; before (time); more than

*__ultrā__ — beyond, on the far side of; past (time); over and above

(P) *__versus__ — toward

II. WITH THE ABLATIVE CASE

II.1. The more common prepositions:

__a/ab/abs__ — from; by

__cum__ — with

__de__ — down, down from, from; about, concerning

__e/ex__ — out of, from, of

__in__ — in, on, among, at; during

__pro__ — in front of; on behalf of; instead of; in return for; in proportion to

__sine__ — without

__sub__ — under, beneath; during

*__super__ — upon, above, on top of; concerning; besides

II.1.a. When used with the 1st and 2nd person personal pronouns (see 7.I.1 and 7.I.2) and with the reflexive pronoun (see 7.III), __cum__ becomes both postpositive and enclitic.

__nobiscum__ — with us

__tecum__ — with you

__secum__ — with themselves

II.2. The less common prepositions used with the ablative case:

*__coram__ — in the presence of, before, in front of

*__palam__ — in the presence of

*__prae__ — in front of; compared with; because of

*__procul__ — far from, far away from

*__simul__ — together with; at the same time as

(P) *__tenus__ — as far as, up to (sometimes governs the genitive case)

III. FUNCTIONING LIKE PREPOSITIONS, GOVERNING THE GENITIVE CASE

(P) **causā** — for the sake of, because of
(P) **gratiā** — for the sake of, because of
(P) *****tenus** — as far as, up to (sometimes governs the ablative case)

IV. In a literary figure called *anastrophe*, any preposition (especially those of two syllables) can be used postpositively.

E. Verbs

9. Regular Conjugations

I. FIRST CONJUGATION

Principal parts: **nego, negare, negavi, negatus**

I.1 Indicative mood

I.1.a. Active voice

Present active indicative

Person	Singular	Plural
1	**nego**	**negamus**
2	**negas**	**negatis**
3	**negat**	**negant**

Imperfect active indicative

Person	Singular	Plural
1	**negabam**	**negabamus**
2	**negabas**	**negabatis**
3	**negabat**	**negabant**

Future active indicative

Person	Singular	Plural
1	**negabo**	**negabimus**
2	**negabis**	**negabitis**
3	**negabit**	**negabunt**

Perfect active indicative

Person	Singular	Plural
1	**negavi**	**negavimus**
2	**negavisti**	**negavistis**
3	**negavit**	**negaverunt**

Pluperfect active indicative

Person	Singular	Plural
1	negaveram	negaveramus
2	negaveras	negaveratis
3	negaverat	negaverant

Future perfect active indicative

Person	Singular	Plural
1	negavero	negaverimus
2	negaveris	negaveritis
3	negaverit	negaverint

I.1.b. Passive voice

Present passive indicative

Person	Singular	Plural
1	negor	negamur
2	negaris	negamini
3	negatur	negantur

Imperfect passive indicative

Person	Singular	Plural
1	negabar	negabamur
2	negabaris	negabamini
3	negabatur	negabantur

Future passive indicative

Person	Singular	Plural
1	negabor	negabimur
2	negaberis	negabimini
3	negabitur	negabuntur

Perfect passive indicative

Person	Singular	Plural
1	negatus, -a, -um sum	negati, -ae, -a sumus
2	negatus, -a, -um es	negati, -ae, -a estis
3	negatus, -a, -um est	negati, -ae, -a sunt

Pluperfect passive indicative

Person	Singular	Plural
1	negatus, -a, -um eram	negati, -ae, -a eramus
2	negatus, -a, -um eras	negati, -ae, -a eratis
3	negatus, -a, -um erat	negati, -ae, -a erant

Future perfect passive indicative

Person	Singular	Plural
1	negatus, -a, -um ero	negati, -ae, -a erimus
2	negatus, -a, -um eris	negati, -ae, -a eritis
3	negatus, -a, -um erit	negati, -ae, -a erunt

I.2. Subjunctive mood

I.2.a. Active voice

Present active subjunctive

Person	Singular	Plural
1	negem	negemus
2	neges	negetis
3	neget	negent

Imperfect active subjunctive

Person	Singular	Plural
1	negarem	negaremus
2	negares	negaretis
3	negaret	negarent

Perfect active subjunctive

Person	Singular	Plural
1	**negaverim**	**negaverīmus**
2	**negaverīs**	**negaverītis**
3	**negaverit**	**negaverint**

Pluperfect active subjunctive

Person	Singular	Plural
1	**negavissem**	**negavissemus**
2	**negavisses**	**negavissetis**
3	**negavisset**	**negavissent**

I.2.b. Passive voice

Present passive subjunctive

Person	Singular	Plural
1	**neger**	**negemur**
2	**negeris**	**negemini**
3	**negetur**	**negentur**

Imperfect passive subjunctive

Person	Singular	Plural
1	**negarer**	**negaremur**
2	**negareris**	**negaremini**
3	**negaretur**	**negarentur**

Perfect passive subjunctive

Person	Singular	Plural
1	**negatus, -a, -um sim**	**negati, -ae, -a simus**
2	**negatus, -a, -um sis**	**negati, -ae, -a sitis**
3	**negatus, -a, -um sit**	**negati, -ae, -a sint**

Pluperfect passive subjunctive

Person	Singular	Plural
1	negatus, -a, -um essem	negati, -ae, -a essemus
2	negatus, -a, -um esses	negati, -ae, -a essetis
3	negatus, -a, -um esset	negati, -ae, -a essent

I.3. Imperative mood

I.3.a. Active voice

Singular	Plural
nega	negate

I.3.b. Passive voice

Singular	Plural
negare	negamini

I.4. Infinitives

	Present	Perfect	Future
I.4.a. Active	negare	negavisse	negaturus esse
I.4.b. Passive	negari	negatus esse	negatum iri

I.5. Participles

	Present	Perfect	Future
I.5.a. Active	negans	——	negaturus, -a, -um
I.5.b. Passive	——	negatus, -a, -um	negandus, -a, -um

I.6. Gerunds and supines

	Genitive	Dative	Accusative	Ablative
I.6.a. Gerunds	negandi	negando	negandum	negando
I.6.b. Supines	——	——	negatum	negatū

II. SECOND CONJUGATION

Principal Parts: **moneo, monēre, monui, monitus**

II.1. Indicative mood

II.1.a. Active voice

Present active indicative

Person	Singular	Plural
1	moneo	monemus
2	mones	monetis
3	monet	monent

Imperfect active indicative

Person	Singular	Plural
1	monebam	monebamus
2	monebas	monebatis
3	monebat	monebant

Future active indicative

Person	Singular	Plural
1	monebo	monebimus
2	monebis	monebitis
3	monebit	monebunt

Perfect active indicative

Person	Singular	Plural
1	monui	monuimus
2	monuisti	monuistis
3	monuit	monuerunt

Pluperfect active indicative

Person	Singular	Plural
1	monueram	monueramus
2	monueras	monueratis
3	monuerat	monuerant

Future perfect active indicative

Person	Singular	Plural
1	monuero	monuerimus
2	monueris	monueritis
3	monuerit	monuerint

II.1.b. Passive voice

Present passive indicative

Person	Singular	Plural
1	moneor	monemur
2	moneris	monemini
3	monetur	monentur

Imperfect passive indicative

Person	Singular	Plural
1	monebar	monebamur
2	monebaris	monebamini
3	monebatur	monebantur

Future passive indicative

Person	Singular	Plural
1	monebor	monebimur
2	moneberis	monebimini
3	monebitur	monebuntur

Perfect passive indicative

Person	Singular	Plural
1	**monitus, -a, -um sum**	**moniti, -ae, -a sumus**
2	**monitus, -a, -um es**	**moniti, -ae, -a estis**
3	**monitus, -a, -um est**	**moniti, -ae, -a sunt**

Pluperfect passive indicative

Person	Singular	Plural
1	**monitus, -a, -um eram**	**moniti, -ae, -a eramus**
2	**monitus, -a, -um eras**	**moniti, -ae, -a eratis**
3	**monitus, -a, -um erat**	**moniti, -ae, -a erant**

Future perfect passive indicative

Person	Singular	Plural
1	**monitus, -a, -um ero**	**moniti, -ae, -a erimus**
2	**monitus, -a, -um eris**	**moniti, -ae, -a eritis**
3	**monitus, -a, -um erit**	**moniti, -ae, -a erunt**

II.2. Subjunctive mood

II.2.a. Active voice

Present active subjunctive

Person	Singular	Plural
1	**moneam**	**moneamus**
2	**moneas**	**moneatis**
3	**moneat**	**moneant**

Imperfect active subjunctive

Person	Singular	Plural
1	**monērem**	**monēremus**
2	**monēres**	**monēretis**
3	**monēret**	**monērent**

Perfect active subjunctive

Person	Singular	Plural
1	monuerim	monuerīmus
2	monuerīs	monuerītis
3	monuerit	monuerint

Pluperfect active subjunctive

Person	Singular	Plural
1	monuissem	monuissemus
2	monuisses	monuissetis
3	monuisset	monuissent

II.2.b. Passive voice

Present passive subjunctive

Person	Singular	Plural
1	monear	moneamur
2	monearis	moneamini
3	moneatur	moneantur

Imperfect passive subjunctive

Person	Singular	Plural
1	monērer	monēremur
2	monēreris	monēremini
3	monēretur	monērentur

Perfect passive subjunctive

Person	Singular	Plural
1	monitus, -a, -um sim	moniti, -ae, -a simus
2	monitus, -a, -um sis	moniti, -ae, -a sitis
3	monitus, -a, -um sit	moniti, -ae, -a sint

Pluperfect passive subjunctive

Person	Singular	Plural
1	monitus, -a, -um essem	moniti, -ae, -a essemus
2	monitus, -a, -um esses	moniti, -ae, -a essetis
3	monitus, -a, -um esset	moniti, -ae, -a essent

II.3. Imperative mood

II.3.a. Active voice

Singular	Plural
monē	monete

II.3.b. Passive voice

Singular	Plural
monēre	monemini

II.4. Infinitives

	Present	Perfect	Future
I.4.a. Active	monēre	monuisse	moniturus esse
I.4.b. Passive	monēri	monitus esse	monitum iri

II.5. Participles

	Present	Perfect	Future
I.5.a. Active	monens	——	moniturus, -a, -um
I.5.b. Passive	——	monitus, -a, -um	monendus, -a, -um

II.6. Gerunds and supines

	Genitive	Dative	Accusative	Ablative
II.6.a. Gerunds	monendi	monendo	monendum	monendo
II.6.b. Supines	——	——	monitum	monitū

III. THIRD CONJUGATION

Principal parts: **gero, gerere, gessi, gestus**

III.1. Indicative mood

III.1.a. Active voice

Present active indicative

Person	Singular	Plural
1	gero	gerimus
2	geris	geritis
3	gerit	gerunt

Imperfect active indicative

Person	Singular	Plural
1	gerebam	gerebamus
2	gerebas	gerebatis
3	gerebat	gerebant

Future active indicative

Person	Singular	Plural
1	geram	geremus
2	geres	geretis
3	geret	gerent

Perfect active indicative

Person	Singular	Plural
1	gessi	gessimus
2	gessisti	gessistis
3	gessit	gesserunt

Pluperfect active indicative

Person	Singular	Plural
1	**gesseram**	**gesseramus**
2	**gesseras**	**gesseratis**
3	**gesserat**	**gesserant**

Future perfect active indicative

Person	Singular	Plural
1	**gessero**	**gesserimus**
2	**gesseris**	**gesseritis**
3	**gesserit**	**gesserint**

III.1.b. Passive Voice

Present passive indicative

Person	Singular	Plural
1	**geror**	**gerimur**
2	**gereris**	**gerimini**
3	**geritur**	**geruntur**

Imperfect passive indicative

Person	Singular	Plural
1	**gerebar**	**gerebamur**
2	**gerebaris**	**gerebamini**
3	**gerebatur**	**gerebantur**

Future passive indicative

Person	Singular	Plural
1	**gerar**	**geremur**
2	**gerēris**	**geremini**
3	**geretur**	**gerentur**

Perfect passive indicative

Person	Singular	Plural
1	gestus, -a, -um sum	gesti, -ae, -a sumus
2	gestus, -a, -um es	gesti, -ae, -a estis
3	gestus, -a, -um est	gesti, -ae, -a sunt

Pluperfect passive indicative

Person	Singular	Plural
1	gestus, -a, -um eram	gesti, -ae, -a eramus
2	gestus, -a, -um eras	gesti, -ae, -a eratis
3	gestus, -a, -um erat	gesti, -ae, -a erant

Future perfect passive indicative

Person	Singular	Plural
1	gestus, -a, -um ero	gesti, -ae, -a erimus
2	gestus, -a, -um eris	gesti, -ae, -a eritis
3	gestus, -a, -um erit	gesti, -ae, -a erunt

III.2. Subjunctive mood

III.2.a. Active voice

Present active subjunctive

Person	Singular	Plural
1	geram	geramus
2	geras	geratis
3	gerat	gerant

Imperfect active subjunctive

Person	Singular	Plural
1	gererem	gereremus
2	gereres	gereretis
3	gereret	gererent

Perfect active subjunctive

Person	Singular	Plural
1	**gesserim**	**gesserīmus**
2	**gesserīs**	**gesserītis**
3	**gesserit**	**gesserint**

Pluperfect active subjunctive

Person	Singular	Plural
1	**gessissem**	**gessissemus**
2	**gessisses**	**gessissetis**
3	**gessisset**	**gessissent**

III.2.b. Passive voice

Present passive subjunctive

Person	Singular	Plural
1	**gerar**	**geramur**
2	**geraris**	**geramini**
3	**geratur**	**gerantur**

Imperfect passive subjunctive

Person	Singular	Plural
1	**gererer**	**gereremur**
2	**gerereris**	**gereremini**
3	**gereretur**	**gererentur**

Perfect passive subjunctive

Person	Singular	Plural
1	**gestus, -a, -um sim**	**gesti, -ae, -a simus**
2	**gestus, -a, -um sis**	**gesti, -ae, -a sitis**
3	**gestus, -a, -um sit**	**gesti, -ae, -a sint**

Pluperfect passive subjunctive

Person	Singular	Plural
1	gestus, -a, -um essem	gesti, -ae, -a essemus
2	gestus, -a, -um esses	gesti, -ae, -a essetis
3	gestus, -a, -um esset	gesti, -ae, -a essent

III.3. Imperative mood

III.3.a. Active voice

Singular	Plural
gere	gerite

III.3.b. Passive voice

Singular	Plural
gerere	gerimini

III.4. Infinitives

	Present	Perfect	Future
I.4.a. Active	gerere	gessisse	gesturus esse
I.4.b. Passive	geri	gestus esse	gestum iri

III.5. Participles

	Present	Perfect	Future
I.5.a. Active	gerens	——	gesturus, -a, -um
I.5.b. Passive	——	gestus, -a, -um	gerendus, -a, -um

III.6. Gerunds and supines

	Genitive	Dative	Accusative	Ablative
III.6.a. Gerunds	gerendi	gerendo	gerendum	gerendo
III.6.b. Supines	——	——	gestum	gestū

IV. FOURTH CONJUGATION

Principal parts: **scio, scire, scivi, scitus**

IV.1. Indicative mood

IV.1.a. Active voice

Present active indicative

Person	Singular	Plural
1	scio	scimus
2	scis	scitis
3	scit	sciunt

Imperfect active indicative

Person	Singular	Plural
1	sciebam	sciebamus
2	sciebas	sciebatis
3	sciebat	sciebant

Future active indicative

Person	Singular	Plural
1	sciam	sciemus
2	scies	scietis
3	sciet	scient

Perfect active indicative

Person	Singular	Plural
1	scivi	scivimus
2	scivisti	scivistis
3	scivit	sciverunt

Pluperfect active indicative

Person	Singular	Plural
1	**sciveram**	**sciveramus**
2	**sciveras**	**sciveratis**
3	**sciverat**	**sciverant**

Future perfect active indicative

Person	Singular	Plural
1	**scivero**	**sciverimus**
2	**sciveris**	**sciveritis**
3	**sciverit**	**sciverint**

IV.1.b. Passive voice

Present passive indicative

Person	Singular	Plural
1	**scior**	**scimur**
2	**sciris**	**scimini**
3	**scitur**	**sciuntur**

Imperfect passive indicative

Person	Singular	Plural
1	**sciebar**	**sciebamur**
2	**sciebaris**	**sciebamini**
3	**sciebatur**	**sciebantur**

Future passive indicative

Person	Singular	Plural
1	**sciar**	**sciemur**
2	**scieris**	**sciemini**
3	**scietur**	**scientur**

Perfect passive indicative

Person	Singular	Plural
1	**scitus, -a, -um sum**	**sciti, -ae, -a sumus**
2	**scitus, -a, -um es**	**sciti, -ae, -a estis**
3	**scitus, -a, -um est**	**sciti, -ae, -a sunt**

Pluperfect passive indicative

Person	Singular	Plural
1	**scitus, -a, -um eram**	**sciti, -ae, -a eramus**
2	**scitus, -a, -um eras**	**sciti, -ae, -a eratis**
3	**scitus, -a, -um erat**	**sciti, -ae, -a erant**

Future perfect passive indicative

Person	Singular	Plural
1	**scitus, -a, -um ero**	**sciti, -ae, -a erimus**
2	**scitus, -a, -um eris**	**sciti, -ae, -a eritis**
3	**scitus, -a, -um erit**	**sciti, -ae, -a erunt**

IV.2. Subjunctive mood

IV.2.a. Active voice

Present active subjunctive

Person	Singular	Plural
1	**sciam**	**sciamus**
2	**scias**	**sciatis**
3	**sciat**	**sciant**

Imperfect active subjunctive

Person	Singular	Plural
1	**scirem**	**sciremus**
2	**scires**	**sciretis**
3	**sciret**	**scirent**

Perfect active subjunctive

Person	Singular	Plural
1	**sciverim**	**sciverīmus**
2	**sciverīs**	**sciverītis**
3	**sciverit**	**sciverint**

Pluperfect active subjunctive

Person	Singular	Plural
1	**scivissem**	**scivissemus**
2	**scivisses**	**scivissetis**
3	**scivisset**	**scivissent**

IV.2.b. Passive voice

Present passive subjunctive

Person	Singular	Plural
1	**sciar**	**sciamur**
2	**sciaris**	**sciamini**
3	**sciatur**	**sciantur**

Imperfect passive subjunctive

Person	Singular	Plural
1	**scirer**	**sciremur**
2	**scireris**	**sciremini**
3	**sciretur**	**scirentur**

Perfect passive subjunctive

Person	Singular	Plural
1	**scitus, -a, -um sim**	**sciti, -ae, -a simus**
2	**scitus, -a, -um sis**	**sciti, -ae, -a sitis**
3	**scitus, -a, -um sit**	**sciti, -ae, -a sint**

Pluperfect passive subjunctive

Person	Singular	Plural
1	scitus, -a, -um essem	sciti, -ae, -a essemus
2	scitus, -a, -um esses	sciti, -ae, -a essetis
3	scitus, -a, -um esset	sciti, -ae, -a essent

IV.3. Imperative mood

IV.3.a. Active voice

Singular	Plural
sci	scite

IV.3.b. Passive voice

Singular	Plural
scire	scimini

IV.4. Infinitives

	Present	Perfect	Future
IV.4.a. Active	scire	scivisse	sciturus esse
IV.4.b. Passive	sciri	scitus esse	scitum iri

IV.5. Participles

	Present	Perfect	Future
IV.5.a. Active	sciens	——	sciturus, -a, -um
IV.5.b. Passive	——	scitus, -a, -um	sciendus, -a, -um

IV.6. Gerunds and supines

	Genitive	Dative	Accusative	Ablative
IV.6.a. Gerunds	sciendi	sciendo	sciendum	sciendo
IV.6.b. Supines	——	——	scitum	scitū

V. THIRD CONJUGATION -IO

Principal parts: **pario, parere, peperi, partus**

V.1. Indicative mood

V.1.a. Active voice

Present active indicative

Person	Singular	Plural
1	**pario**	**parimus**
2	**paris**	**paritis**
3	**parit**	**pariunt**

Imperfect active indicative

Person	Singular	Plural
1	**pariebam**	**pariebamus**
2	**pariebas**	**pariebatis**
3	**pariebat**	**pariebant**

Future active indicative

Person	Singular	Plural
1	**pariam**	**pariemus**
2	**paries**	**parietis**
3	**pariet**	**parient**

Perfect active indicative

Person	Singular	Plural
1	**peperi**	**peperimus**
2	**peperisti**	**peperistis**
3	**peperit**	**pepererunt**

Pluperfect active indicative

Person	Singular	Plural
1	**pepereram**	**pepereramus**
2	**pepereras**	**pepereratis**
3	**pepererat**	**pepererant**

Future perfect active indicative

Person	Singular	Plural
1	**peperero**	**pepererimus**
2	**pepereris**	**pepereritis**
3	**pepererit**	**pepererint**

V.1.b. Passive voice

Present passive indicative

Person	Singular	Plural
1	**parior**	**parimur**
2	**pareris**	**parimini**
3	**paritur**	**pariuntur**

Imperfect passive indicative

Person	Singular	Plural
1	**pariebar**	**pariebamur**
2	**pariebaris**	**pariebamini**
3	**pariebatur**	**pariebantur**

Future passive indicative

Person	Singular	Plural
1	**pariar**	**pariemur**
2	**parieris**	**pariemini**
3	**parietur**	**parientur**

Perfect passive indicative

Person	Singular	Plural
1	**partus, -a, -um sum**	**parti, -ae, -a sumus**
2	**partus, -a, -um es**	**parti, -ae, -a estis**
3	**partus, -a, -um est**	**parti, -ae, -a sunt**

Pluperfect passive indicative

Person	Singular	Plural
1	**partus, -a, -um eram**	**parti, -ae, -a eramus**
2	**partus, -a, -um eras**	**parti, -ae, -a eratis**
3	**partus, -a, -um erat**	**parti, -ae, -a erant**

Future perfect passive indicative

Person	Singular	Plural
1	**partus, -a, -um ero**	**parti, -ae, -a erimus**
2	**partus, -a, -um eris**	**parti, -ae, -a eritis**
3	**partus, -a, -um erit**	**parti, -ae, -a erunt**

V.2. Subjunctive mood

V.2.a. Active voice

Present active subjunctive

Person	Singular	Plural
1	**pariam**	**pariamus**
2	**parias**	**pariatis**
3	**pariat**	**pariant**

Imperfect active subjunctive

Person	Singular	Plural
1	**parerem**	**pareremus**
2	**pareres**	**pareretis**
3	**pareret**	**parerent**

Perfect active subjunctive

Person	Singular	Plural
1	**pepererim**	**pepererīmus**
2	**pepererīs**	**pepererītis**
3	**pepererit**	**pepererint**

Pluperfect active subjunctive

Person	Singular	Plural
1	**peperissem**	**peperissemus**
2	**peperisses**	**peperissetis**
3	**peperisset**	**peperissent**

V.2.b. Passive voice

Present passive subjunctive

Person	Singular	Plural
1	**pariar**	**pariamur**
2	**pariaris**	**pariamini**
3	**pariatur**	**pariantur**

Imperfect passive subjunctive

Person	Singular	Plural
1	**parerer**	**pareremur**
2	**parereris**	**pareremini**
3	**pareretur**	**parerentur**

Perfect passive subjunctive

Person	Singular	Plural
1	**partus, -a, -um sim**	**parti, -ae, -a simus**
2	**partus, -a, -um sis**	**parti, -ae, -a sitis**
3	**partus, -a, -um sit**	**parti, -ae, -a sint**

Pluperfect passive subjunctive

Person	Singular	Plural
1	**partus, -a, -um essem**	**parti, -ae, -a essemus**
2	**partus, -a, -um esses**	**parti, -ae, -a essetis**
3	**partus, -a, -um esset**	**parti, -ae, -a essent**

V.3. Imperative mood

V.3.a. Active voice

Singular	Plural
pare	**parite**

V.3.b. Passive voice

Singular	Plural
parere	**parimini**

V.4. Infinitives

	Present	Perfect	Future
V.4.a. Active	**parere**	**peperisse**	**parturus esse**
V.4.b. Passive	**pari**	**partus esse**	**partum iri**

V.5. Participles

	Present	Perfect	Future
V.5.a. Active	**pariens**	——	**parturus, -a, -um**
V.5.b. Passive	——	**partus, -a, -um**	**pariendus, -a, -um**

V.6. Gerunds and supines

	Genitive	Dative	Accusative	Ablative
V.6.a. Gerunds	**pariendi**	**pariendo**	**pariendum**	**pariendo**
V.6.b. Supines	——	——	**partum**	**partū**

VI. NOTES

VI.1. Some of the forms noted above are subject to syncopation; see 20.I.

VI.2. Future passive participles are also called gerundives; see 12.II.

VI.3. The present, imperfect, and future tenses are collectively known as the present system. The perfect, pluperfect, and future perfect tenses are collectively known as the perfect system.

VI.4. The **esse** of all perfect passive and future active infinitives is often omitted in indirect statements; see 14.I.

10. Irregular Conjugations

Note: Parentheses indicate syncopated forms (see 20.I) commonly used in place of unsyncopated forms.

I. EO, IRE, IVI (II), ITUS

I.1. Indicative mood active voice

Present active indicative Imperfect active indicative

Person	Singular	Plural	Singular	Plural
1	eo	imus	ibam	ibamus
2	is	itis	ibas	ibatis
3	it	eunt	ibat	ibant

Future active indicative

Person	Singular	Plural
1	ibo	ibimus
2	ibis	ibitis
3	ibit	ibunt

Perfect active indicative

Person	Singular	Plural
1	ivi (ii)	ivimus (iimus)
2	ivisti (iisti, īsti)	ivistis (iistis, īstis)
3	ivit (iit, īt)	iverunt (ierunt)

Pluperfect active indicative

Person	Singular	Plural
1	iveram (ieram)	iveramus (ieramus)
2	iveras (ieras)	iveratis (ieratis)
3	iverat (ierat)	iverant (ierant)

Future perfect active indicative

Person	Singular	Plural
1	ivero (iero)	iverimus (ierimus)
2	iveris (ieris)	iveritis (ieritis)
3	iverit (ierit)	iverint (ierint)

I.2. Subjunctive mood active voice

Present active subjunctive   Imperfect active subjunctive

Person	Singular	Plural		Singular	Plural
1	eam	eamus		irem	iremus
2	eas	eatis		ires	iretis
3	eat	eant		iret	irent

Perfect active subjunctive

Person	Singular	Plural
1	iverim (ierim)	iverīmus (ierīmus)
2	iverīs (ierīs)	iverītis (ierītis)
3	iverit (ierit)	iverint (ierint)

Pluperfect active subjunctive

Person	Singular	Plural
1	ivissem (īssem)	ivissemus (īssemus)
2	ivisses (īsses)	ivissetis (īssetis)
3	ivisset (īsset)	ivissent (īssent)

I.3. Imperative mood active voice

Singular	Plural
i	ite

I.4. Infinitives

Present	Perfect	Future
ire	ivisse (iisse, īsse)	iturus, -a, -um esse

I.5. Participles

	Present	Perfect	Future
I.5.a. Active	**iens, euntis**	——	**iturus, -a, -um**
I.5.b. Passive	——	**itus, -a, -um**	**eundus, -a, -um**

I.6. Gerunds and supines

	Genitive	Dative	Accusative	Ablative
I.6.a. Gerunds	**eundi**	**eundo**	**eundum**	**eundo**
I.6.b. Supines	——	——	**itum**	**itū**

I.7. Common compounds of **eo, ire, ivi (ii), itus** include:

abeo, abire, abii, abitus — go away, depart; retire

adeo, adire, adii, aditus — go to, approach; undertake, enter upon

anteeo, anteire, anteii, anteitus — precede; surpass

circueo (circumeo), circuire, circuivi (-ii), circuitus — go around, surround, encircle; visit; deceive

coeo, coire, coivi (-ii), coitus — meet, assemble; encounter; mate; agree, conspire

exeo, exire, exivi (-ii), exitus — go out, leave; issue; expire (time); spring up, rise

ineo, inire, inivi (-ii), initus — go in, enter; begin, enter upon, undertake

intereo, interire, interii, interitus — perish, die, be lost

obeo, obire, obivi (-ii), obitus — go to meet; visit; survey, go over; die

pereo, perire, perii, peritus — be lost, perish, die, pass away; be undone; be in love

praeeo, praeire, praeivi (-ii), praeitus — lead the away, go first, precede; outstrip

praetereo, praeterire, praeterii, praeteritus — pass, go past, overtake, surpass; escape, elude; omit, leave out, neglect; reject, exclude; transgress

prodeo, prodire, prodii, proditus — go out, go forward, appear; go ahead, advance

redeo, redire, redii, reditus — go back, return; revert

subeo, subire, subii, subitus — go under, go in, enter; advance; follow, succeed; aid; come secretly; come to mind; submit to, suffer, undergo

transeo, transire, transii, transitus — pass over, cross over; pass through; outstrip, surpass, overstep; change into; pass (time), pass away

II. FERO, FERRE, TULI, LATUS

II.1. Indicative mood

II.1.a. Active voice

Present active indicative   Imperfect active indicative

Person	Singular	Plural	Singular	Plural
1	fero	ferimus	ferebam	ferebamus
2	fers	fertis	ferebas	ferebatis
3	fert	ferunt	ferebat	ferebant

Future active indicative

Person	Singular	Plural
1	feram	feremus
2	feres	feretis
3	feret	ferent

Perfect active indicative   Pluperfect active indicative

Person	Singular	Plural	Singular	Plural
1	tuli	tulimus	tuleram	tuleramus
2	tulisti	tulistis	tuleras	tuleratis
3	tulit	tulerunt	tulerat	tulerant

Future perfect active indicative

Person	Singular	Plural
1	tulero	tulerimus
2	tuleris	tuleritis
3	tulerit	tulerint

II.1.b. Passive voice

Present passive indicative   Imperfect passive indicative

Person	Singular	Plural	Singular	Plural
1	feror	ferimur	ferebar	ferebamur
2	ferris	ferimini	ferebaris	ferebamini
3	fertur	feruntur	ferebatur	ferebantur

Future passive indicative

Person	Singular	Plural
1	ferar	feremur
2	fereris	feremini
3	feretur	ferentur

Perfect passive indicative

Person	Singular	Plural
1	latus, -a, -um sum	lati, -ae, -a sumus
2	latus, -a, -um es	lati, -ae, -a estis
3	latus, -a, -um est	lati, -ae, -a sunt

Pluperfect passive indicative

Person	Singular	Plural
1	latus, -a, -um eram	lati, -ae, -a eramus
2	latus, -a, -um eras	lati, -ae, -a eratis
3	latus, -a, -um erat	lati, -ae, -a erant

Future perfect passive indicative

Person	Singular	Plural
1	latus, -a, -um ero	lati, -ae, -a erimus
2	latus, -a, -um eris	lati, -ae, -a eritis
3	latus, -a, -um erit	lati, -ae, -a erunt

II.2. Subjunctive mood

II.2.a. Active voice

Present active subjunctive   Imperfect active subjunctive

Person	Singular	Plural	Singular	Plural
1	feram	feramus	ferrem	ferremus
2	feras	feratis	ferres	ferretis
3	ferat	ferant	ferret	ferrent

Perfect active subjunctive   Pluperfect active subjunctive

Person	Singular	Plural	Singular	Plural
1	tulerim	tulerīmus	tulissem	tulissemus
2	tulerīs	tulerītis	tulisses	tulissetis
3	tulerit	tulerint	tulisset	tulissent

II.2.b. Passive voice

Present passive subjunctive   Imperfect passive subjunctive

Person	Singular	Plural	Singular	Plural
1	ferar	feramur	ferrer	ferremur
2	feraris	feramini	ferreris	ferremini
3	feratur	ferantur	ferretur	ferrentur

Perfect passive subjunctive

Person	Singular	Plural
1	latus, -a, -um sim	lati, -ae, -a simus
2	latus, -a, -um sis	lati, -ae, -a sitis
3	latus, -a, -um sit	lati, -ae, -a sint

Pluperfect passive subjunctive

Person	Singular	Plural
1	latus, -a, -um essem	lati, -ae, -a essemus
2	latus, -a, -um esses	lati, -ae, -a essetis
3	latus, -a, -um esset	lati, -ae, -a essent

II.3. Imperative mood

II.3.a. Active voice

Singular	Plural
fer	ferte

II.3.b. Passive voice

Singular	Plural
ferre	**ferimini**

II.4. Infinitives

	Present	Perfect	Future
	Present	*Perfect*	*Future*
II.4.a. Active	**ferre**	**tulisse**	**laturus, -a, -um esse**
II.4.b. Passive	**ferri**	**latus, -a, -um esse**	**latum iri**

II.5. Participles

	Present	*Perfect*	*Future*
II.5.a. Active	**ferens**	——	**laturus, -a, -um**
II.5.b. Passive	——	**latus, -a, -um**	**ferendus, -a, -um**

II.6. Gerunds and supines

	Genitive	*Dative*	*Accusative*	*Ablative*
II.6.a. Gerunds	**ferendi**	**ferendo**	**ferendum**	**ferendo**
II.6.b. Supines	——	——	**latum**	**latū**

II.7. Common compounds of **fero, ferre, tuli, latus** include:

adfero, adferre, attuli, adlatus — bring to, present

aufero, auferre, abstuli, ablatus — carry away, carry off

confero, conferre, contuli, collatus — bring together, collect; compare

   se conferre — take oneself, go

defero, deferre, detuli, delatus — bring away, bring down; report; offer

differo, differre, distuli, dilatus — differ

effero, efferre, extuli, elatus — carry out; bring forth

infero, inferre, intuli, illatus — carry into; inflict

offero, offerre, obtuli, oblatus — bring before; offer; expose

refero, referre, rettuli, relatus — bring back; report

suffero, sufferre, sustuli, sublatus — undergo, endure

transfero, transferre, transtuli, translatus — bring across, transport, transfer; transform, translate

III. SUM, ESSE, FUI, FUTURUS

III.1. Indicative mood active voice

Present active indicative   Imperfect active indicative

Person	Singular	Plural	Singular	Plural
1	sum	sumus	eram	eramus
2	es	estis	eras	eratis
3	est	sunt	erat	erant

Future active indicative

Person	Singular	Plural
1	ero	erimus
2	eris	eritis
3	erit	erunt

Perfect active indicative   Pluperfect active indicative

Person	Singular	Plural	Singular	Plural
1	fui	fuimus	fueram	fueramus
2	fuisti	fuistis	fueras	fueratis
3	fuit	fuerunt	fuerat	fuerant

Future perfect active indicative

Person	Singular	Plural
1	fuero	fuerimus
2	fueris	fueritis
3	fuerit	fuerint

III.2. Subjunctive mood active voice

Present active subjunctive   Imperfect active subjunctive

Person	Singular	Plural	Singular	Plural
1	sim	simus	essem	essemus
2	sis	sitis	esses	essetis
3	sit	sint	esset	essent

Perfect active subjunctive   Pluperfect active subjunctive

Person	Singular	Plural	Singular	Plural
1	fuerim	fuerīmus	fuissem	fuissemus
2	fuerīs	fuerītis	fuisses	fuissetis
3	fuerit	fuerint	fuisset	fuissent

III.3. Imperative mood active voice

Singular	Plural
es	este

III.4. Infinitives

Present	Perfect	Future
esse	fuisse	futurus, -a, -um esse

III.5. Participles

	Present	Perfect	Future
III.5.a. Active	[ens]	——	futurus, -a, -um
III.5.b. Passive	——	——	——

III.6. Gerunds and supines

	Genitive	Dative	Accusative	Ablative
III.6.a. Gerunds	——	——	——	——
III.6.b. Supines	——	——	——	——

III.7. Alternate forms include:

III.7.a. For the imperfect subjunctive: **forem, fores, foret, forent**.

III.7.b. For the future infinitive: **fore**.

III.7.c. For the present subjunctive: **siem, sies, siet, siemus**, etc.

III.8. In classical Latin, the participle [**ens**] is found only in compounds.

III.9. Common compounds of **sum, esse, fui, futurus** include:

absum, abesse, afui, afuturus — be away, be absent; be different

adsum, adesse, adfui, adfuturus — be present; support, assist

desum, deesse, defui, defuturus — be lacking, fail

insum, inesse, infui, infuturus — be in, be on; belong to

intersum, interesse, interfui, interfuturus — be between, be among, be present at; elapse (time)

    interest (impersonal) — it concerns, it is of importance

obsum, obesse, obfui, obfuturus — be against, harm

possum, posse, potui — be able, can (see 10.IV)

praesum, praeesse, praefui, praefuturus — be in charge of, command; take the lead

prosum, prodesse, profui, profuturus — be useful, benefit

subsum, subesse — be underneath; be close to, be at hand; underlie, be latent in

supersum, superesse, superfui, superfuturus — be left, survive, remain; be sufficient; be in excess

IV. POSSUM, POSSE, POTUI

IV.1. Indicative mood active voice

Present active indicative

Imperfect active indicative

Person	Singular	Plural	Singular	Plural
1	possum	possumus	poteram	poteramus
2	potes	potestis	poteras	poteratis
3	potest	possunt	poterat	poterant

Future active indicative

Person	Singular	Plural
1	potero	poterimus
2	poteris	poteritis
3	poterit	poterunt

Perfect active indicative

Pluperfect active indicative

Person	Singular	Plural	Singular	Plural
1	potui	potuimus	potueram	potueramus
2	potuisti	potuistis	potueras	potueratis
3	potuit	potuerunt	potuerat	potuerant

Future perfect active indicative

Person	Singular	Plural
1	**potuero**	**potuerimus**
2	**potueris**	**potueritis**
3	**potuerit**	**potuerint**

IV.2. Subjunctive mood active voice

Present active subjunctive   Imperfect active subjunctive

Person	Singular	Plural	Singular	Plural
1	**possim**	**possimus**	**possem**	**possemus**
2	**possis**	**possitis**	**posses**	**possetis**
3	**possit**	**possint**	**posset**	**possent**

Perfect active subjunctive   Pluperfect active subjunctive

Person	Singular	Plural	Singular	Plural
1	**potuerim**	**potuerīmus**	**potuissem**	**potuissemus**
2	**potuerīs**	**potuerītis**	**potuisses**	**potuissetis**
3	**potuerit**	**potuerint**	**potuisset**	**potuissent**

IV.3. Imperative mood active voice

Singular	Plural
——	——

IV.4. Infinitives

Present	Perfect	Future
posse	**potuisse**	——

IV.5. Participles

	Present	Perfect	Future
IV.5.a. Active	**potens**	——	——
IV.5.b. Passive	——	——	——

IV.6. Gerunds and supines

	Genitive	Dative	Accusative	Ablative
IV.6.a. Gerunds	——	——	——	——
IV.6.b. Supines	——	——	——	——

V. **volo, velle, volui**   VI. **nolo, nolle, nolui**   VII. **malo, malle, malui**

1. Active Indicatives

Present:	volo	nolo	malo
	vīs	non vīs	mavis
	vult	non vult	mavult
	volumus	nolumus	malumus
	vultis	non vultis	mavultis
	volunt	nolunt	malunt
Imperfect:	volebam	nolebam	malebam
	volebas	nolebas	malebas
	etc.	etc.	etc.
Future:	volam	nolam	malam
	voles	noles	males
	etc.	etc.	etc.
Perfect:	volui	nolui	malui
	voluisti	noluisti	maluisti
	etc.	etc.	etc.
Pluperfect:	volueram	nolueram	malueram
	volueras	nolueras	malueras
	etc.	etc.	etc.
Future perfect:	voluero	noluero	maluero
	volueris	nolueris	malueris
	etc.	etc.	etc.

2. Active Subjunctives

Present:	velim	nolim	malim
	velis	nolis	malis
	velit	nolit	malit
	velimus	nolimus	malimus
	velitis	nolitis	malitis
	velint	nolint	malint
Imperfect:	vellem	nollem	mallem
	velles	nolles	malles
	etc.	etc.	etc.
Perfect:	voluerim	noluerim	maluerim
	voluerīs	noluerīs	maluerīs
	etc.	etc.	etc.
Pluperfect:	voluissem	noluissem	maluissem
	voluisses	noluisses	maluisses
	etc.	etc.	etc.

3. Active Imperatives

——	noli, nolite	——

4. Active Infinitives

Present:	velle	nolle	malle
Perfect:	voluisse	noluisse	maluisse

5. Active Participles

Present:	volens	nolens	——

6. Gerunds and Supines

	Genitive	Dative	Accusative	Ablative
6.a. Gerunds	——	——	——	——
6.b. Supines	——	——	——	——

VIII. FIO, FIERI, FACTUS

VIII.1. Indicative mood active voice

Present active indicative   Imperfect active indicative

Person	Singular	Plural	Singular	Plural
1	fio	fimus	fiebam	fiebamus
2	fis	fitis	fiebas	fiebatis
3	fit	fiunt	fiebat	fiebant

Future active indicative

Person	Singular	Plural
1	fiam	fiemus
2	fies	fietis
3	fiet	fient

Perfect active indicative

Person	Singular	Plural
1	factus, -a, -um sum	facti, -ae, -a sumus
2	factus, -a, -um es	facti, -ae, -a estis
3	factus, -a, -um est	facti, -ae, -a sunt

Pluperfect active indicative

Person	Singular	Plural
1	factus, -a, -um eram	facti, -ae, -a eramus
2	factus, -a, -um eras	facti, -ae, -a eratis
3	factus, -a, -um erat	facti, -ae, -a erant

Future perfect active indicative

Person	Singular	Plural
1	factus, -a, -um ero	facti, -ae, -a erimus
2	factus, -a, -um eris	facti, -ae, -a eritis
3	factus, -a, -um erit	facti, -ae, -a erunt

VIII.2. Subjunctive mood active voice

Present active subjunctive   Imperfect active subjunctive

Person	Singular	Plural	Singular	Plural
1	fiam	fiamus	fierem	fieremus
2	fias	fiatis	fieres	fieretis
3	fiat	fiant	fieret	fierent

Perfect active subjunctive

Person	Singular	Plural
1	factus, -a, -um sim	facti, -ae, -a simus
2	factus, -a, -um sis	facti, -ae, -a sitis
3	factus, -a, -um sit	facti, -ae, -a sint

Pluperfect active subjunctive

Person	Singular	Plural
1	factus, -a, -um essem	facti, -ae, -a essemus
2	factus, -a, -um esses	facti, -ae, -a essetis
3	factus, -a, -um esset	facti, -ae, -a essent

VIII.3. Imperative mood active voice

Singular	Plural
fi	fite

VIII.4. Infinitives

Present	Perfect	Future
fieri	factus, -a, -um esse	factum iri

VIII.5. Participles

Present	Perfect	Future
——	factus, -a, -um	faciendus, -a, -um

VIII.6. Gerunds and supines

	Genitive	Dative	Accusative	Ablative
VIII.6.a. Gerunds	faciendi	faciendo	faciendum	faciendo
VIII.6.b. Supines	——	——	factum	factū

VIII.7. Common compounds of **fio, fieri, factus** include:

    confio, confieri —be done, be completed, be accomplished, happen

    defio, defieri — fail

    interfio, interfieri —pass away

    superfio, superfieri —be left over

11. Deponents, Semideponents, and *Fio*

I. Deponents are a distinctive class of Latin verbs whose forms are almost all passive but whose meanings are always active. The following are the most common deponent verbs; those in capitals are the very most common—learn them!

aemulor, -ari, -atus — rival, copy; be jealous of

altercor, -ari, -atus — dispute, wrangle

AMPLECTOR, -i, amplectus — embrace; encircle; comprehend

    circumplector — embrace, surround

    complector — embrace, clasp; comprehend; be fond of

APISCOR, -i, aptus — catch, gain, attain

    adipiscor, -i, adeptus — gain, acquire, attain

    indipiscor, -i, indeptus — obtain, get, reach

    redipiscor — get back, regain

ARBITROR, -ari, -atus — think, suppose; testify

aspernor, -ari, -atus — reject, disdain

auguror, -ari, -atus — foretell, predict

auxilior, -ari, -atus — aid, support

bacchor, -ari, -atus — revel; rave, rage

    perbacchor — carouse

BLANDIOR, -iri, -itus — caress; coax, flatter; please, entice

    eblandior — coax out, obtain by flattery

    subblandior — (with dative) flirt with

calumnior, -ari, -atus — slander, misrepresent

causor, -ari, -atus — pretend, make an excuse of

cavillor, -ari, -atus — scoff at, jeer at

comissor, -ari, -atus — make merry, carouse

commentor, -ari, -atus — study, think over; compose, write, invent

comminiscor, -i, commentus — devise, contrive

    recomminiscor — recollect

    reminiscor — (usually with genitive) remember, call to mind

CONOR, -ari, -atus — try, attempt

consilior, -ari, -atus — consult; (with dative) advise

conspicor, -ari, -atus — observe, see, catch sight of

    suspicor — suspect, surmise, suppose

convivor, -ari, -atus — feast together, carouse

cunctor, -ari, -atus — delay, linger, hesitate

depeculor, -ari, -atus — embezzle, plunder

dignor, -ari, -atus — deem worthy, deign

    dedignor — scorn, reject, think unworthy

    indignor — be displeased with, be angry at

dominor, -ari, -atus — rule, be master

epulor, -ari, -atus — feast (on)

expergiscor, -i, experrectus — wake up, stir oneself

EXPERIOR, -iri, expertus — test, make trial of, attempt

fabricor, -ari, -atus — make, build, forge

fabulor, -ari, -atus — talk, converse, say

　　confabulor — talk (to), discuss

famulor, -ari, -atus — serve as slave

FATEOR, -ēri, fassus — confess, acknowledge, reveal

　　confiteor, -ēri, confessus — confess, acknowledge, reveal

　　diffiteor — disown

　　profiteor — declare, profess; promise, volunteer

fatiscor, -i, fessus — crack, split; become exhausted

　　defetiscor, -i, defessus — grow weary

FOR, fari, fatus — speak, utter

　　effor — speak, utter

　　interfor — interrupt

　　praefor — preface, say in advance; predict

　　profor — speak out, utter

FRUOR, -i, fructus — (with ablative) enjoy

　　perfruor — (with ablative) enjoy to the full; fulfill

frustror, -ari, -atus — deceive, trick, thwart

FUNGOR, -i, functus — (usually with ablative) perform, discharge, do

　　defungor — (with ablative) discharge, have done with; die

　　perfungor — (with ablative) perform, discharge; undergo

furor, -ari, -atus — steal, pillage; impersonate

　　suffuror — filch

glorior, -ari, -atus — boast, pride oneself in

GRADIOR, -i, gressus — step, walk

　　adgredior, -i, adgressus — approach; attack; undertake

　　antegredior — precede

　　circumgredior — surround

　　congredior — meet, accost, fight

　　degredior — march down, descend, dismount

　　digredior — separate, part; digress, deviate

　　egredior — go out, come out, march out, disembark; overstep

　　ingredior — go in, enter (upon); walk, march; engage in, commence

　　introgredior — step inside

　　praegredior — go before; pass, surpass

　　praetergredior — pass, march past; surpass

　　progredior — go forward, advance, go out

　　regredior — go back, come back, return, retreat

subgredior — approach, come up close; attack
supergredior — surpass
transgredior — step across, cross (over), exceed
grassor, -ari, -atus — walk about, prowl, loiter
grator, -ari, -atus — rejoice, congratulate
gratulor, -ari, -atus — congratulate, give thanks
  congratulor — congratulate
gravor, -ari, -atus — object to, disdain, feel annoyed
HORTOR, -ari, -atus — urge, encourage, exhort
  adhortor — encourage, urge
  cohortor — encourage, urge
  dehortor — dissuade, discourage
  exhortor — encourage
iaculor, -ari, -atus — throw, hurl, shoot, aim at
  eiaculor — shoot out
imaginor, -ari, -atus — imagine, picture to oneself
IMITOR, -ari, -atus — copy, imitate, portray
infitior, -ari, -atus — deny, repudiate
insidior, -ari, -atus — lie in ambush for, plot against
interpretor, -ari, -atus — interpret, explain, translate
iocor, -ari, -atus — joke, jest
ioculor, -ari, -atus — joke
irascor, -i, iratus — become angry, get furious
  subirascor — be rather angry
iuvenor, -ari, -atus — behave immaturely or indiscreetly
LĀBOR, -i, lapsus — slip, slide, glide; sink, fall; fade, decline, die
  adlābor — fall; move toward, come to
  collābor — fall in ruin, collapse
  delābor — fall down, sink, fly down, come down
  dilābor — dissolve, disintegrate, disperse, vanish, decay
  elābor — glide away, slip off, escape
  illābor — fall into, flow into, glide into
  interlābor — slip between, glide between
  perlābor — glide along, glide through, move on
  praelābor — move past, move along, slip past
  praeterlābor — slide, move forward; fail, fall, sink into ruin
  relābor — sink back, fall back, glide back
  sublābor — sink down, glide away
  subterlābor — flow past under; slip away
laetor, -ari, -atus — rejoice, be glad
lamentor, -ari, -atus — lament, weep (for), bewail
  delamentor — mourn bitterly for

largior, -iri, -itus — give freely, lavish, bestow, confer, donate
    dilargior — give away generously
latrocinor, -ari, -atus — be a pirate; serve as a mercenary
liceor, -ēri, licitus — bid at an auction, bid for
LOQUOR, -i, locutus — speak, talk, say, mention
    adloquor — speak to, address
    colloquor — converse (with), talk to
    eloquor — speak out, speak eloquently
    interloquor — interrupt
    obloquor — contradict, interrupt, abuse
    praeloquor — speak first
    proloquor — speak out
lucror, -ari, -atus — gain, win, acquire
LUCTOR, -ari, -atus — wrestle, struggle, fight
    deluctor — wrestle down
    eluctor — struggle out of, surmount
    obluctor — struggle against
    reluctor — struggle against, resist
luxor, -ari, -atus — live luxuriously
luxurior, -ari, -atus — live luxuriously
machinor, -ari, -atus — devise, contrive, plot, scheme
medeor, -ēri, ——— — (with dative) heal, remedy
meditor, -ari, -atus — think over, contemplate, reflect, study
    commeditor — practice
    praemeditor — think over, work out
MENTIOR, -iri, -itus — lie, deceive, feign
    ementior — tell lies, pretend, fabricate
mercor, -ari, -atus — trade in, purchase
    commercor — buy up
    emercor — purchase
METIOR, -iri, mensus — measure (out); estimate, judge; traverse
    admetior — measure out
    commetior — measure
    demetior — measure out
    dimetior — measure out
    emetior — measure out; traverse, pass over; live through
    permetior — measure out; traverse
    remetior — measure again; go back over
MINOR, -ari, -atus — threaten
    comminor — threaten
    eminor — threaten
    interminor — threaten, forbid threateningly

MIROR, -ari, -atus — wonder (at), admire, be surprised (at)

    admiror — admire, wonder at, be surprised at

    demiror — marvel at, wonder

    emiror — marvel at

miseror, -ari, -atus — pity, deplore

    commiseror — bewail

moderor, -ari, -atus — (with dative) restrain, check; (with accusative) guide, manage, govern

    admoderor — restrain

    emoderor — give expression to

modulor, -ari, -atus — sing, play music

MOLIOR, -iri, -itus — work at, build; move, heave; struggle; undertake

    amolior — remove

    commolior — set in motion

    demolior — pull down, destroy

    emolior — accomplish

    obmolior — throw up as a defense

    praemolior — prepare thoroughly

    remolior — heave back

morigeror, -ari, -atus — (with dative) humor, gratify

MORIOR, -i, mortuus — die, decay, fade

    demorior — die, pass away

    emorior — die, pass away

    immorior — die upon; waste away

    inemorior — die in

    intermorior — die suddenly

    praemorior — die too soon

MOROR, -ari, -atus — delay, stay, loiter; detain

    commoror — wait, stay, sojourn; detain

    demoror — wait, delay; detain

    remoror — linger, stay behind, delay, defer

muneror, -ari, -atus — present, reward

    remuneror — repay, reward

mutuor, -ari, -atus — borrow

NANCISCOR, -i, nactus or **nanctus** — obtain, get; find, come upon

NASCOR, -i, natus — be born, be produced, grow, originate

    enascor — sprout, grow

    innascor — be born in, grow up in

    renascor — be born again, grow again, spring up again

negotior, -ari, -atus — do business, trade

NITOR, -i, nisus or **nixus** — rest on, lean on; press forward, strive, labor, exert oneself

adnitor — lean on; exert oneself

conitor — lean on; strive, struggle

enitor — struggle up, climb; strive; give birth to

innitor — rest, lean on, depend

obnitor — push against, struggle, resist, stand firm

renitor — struggle, resist

nugor, -ari, -atus — talk nonsense; cheat

OBLIVISCOR, -i, oblitus — forget

odoror, -ari, -atus — smell (out); search out

ominor, -ari, -atus — forebode, prophesy

abominor — deprecate; detest

operor, -ari, -atus — work, be occupied, take pains

OPINOR, -ari, -atus — think, suppose, imagine

opitulor, -ari, -atus — (with dative) help

opperior, -iri, oppertus — wait (for)

ORDIOR, -iri, orsus — begin, undertake

exordior — begin

ORIOR, -iri, ortus — rise, spring up; descend

adorior — accost, attack; set about

coorior — rise, appear, break out, begin

exorior — spring up, arise, come out, appear, start

oborior — arise, spring up

suborior — spring up in succession

osculor, -ari, -atus — kiss

deosculor — kiss warmly

exosculor — kiss fondly

otior, -ari, -atus — be on vacation, be idle

paciscor, -i, pactus — make a bargain, agree; barter

compeciscor, -i, compectus — come to an agreement

depeciscor — bargain for, agree about

palor, -ari, -atus — wander about, straggle

palpor, -ari, -atus — stroke, coax, flatter

suppalpor — coax gently

PATIOR, -i, passus — suffer, experience, submit to, allow

perpetior, -i, perpessus — endure patiently, allow

patrocinor, -ari, -atus — (with dative) defend, support

percontor, -ari, -atus — question, inquire

peregrinor, -ari, -atus — travel, be abroad; be a stranger

periclitor, -ari, -atus — test, try, attempt, risk; be in danger

perplexor, -ari, -atus — cause confusion

philosophor, -ari, -atus — philosophize

piscor, -ari, -atus — fish

    expiscor, -ari, -atus — try to find out

POLLICEOR, -ēri, pollicitus — promise, offer

populor, -ari, -atus — ravage, plunder, destroy, ruin

    depopulor — ravage, devastate, destroy

    perpopulor — ravage completely

POTIOR, -iri, potitus — (with genitive or ablative) acquire, get possession of

praedor, -ari, -atus — plunder, rob; profit

praestolor, -ari, -atus — wait for, expect

praevaricor, -ari, -atus — (with dative) favor by collusion

PRECOR, -ari, -atus — pray, beg, entreat

    apprecor — pray to

    comprecor — pray to; pray for

    deprecor — deprecate, intercede for

    imprecor — invoke

proelior, -ari, -atus — fight, join battle

    deproelior — fight it out

PROFICISCOR, -i, profectus — set out, start, proceed; originate

QUEROR, -i, questus — complain, lament

    conqueror — complain bitterly of, bewail

ratiocinor, -ari, -atus — calculate, consider; argue; infer

recordor, -ari, -atus — recall, remember; ponder over

refragor, -ari, -atus — (with dative) oppose, thwart

    suffragor — vote for, support, favor

REOR, rēri, ratus — think, suppose

rimor, -ari, -atus — tear open, search for, probe, examine

ringor, -i, rictus — snarl

    subringor — make a wry face, be rather vexed

rixor, -ari, -atus — quarrel, brawl, squabble

rusticor, -ari, -atus — live in the country

savior, -ari, -atus — kiss

    dissavior — kiss passionately

sciscitor, -ari, -atus — inquire, question

scitor, -ari, -atus — inquire, consult

scrutor, -ari, -atus — search, probe into, examine, find out

    perscrutor — search, examine thoroughly

scurror, -ari, -atus — play the fool

sector, -ari, -atus — follow, attend; chase, hunt

    consector — follow, go after, pursue, chase; emulate

    insector — pursue; attack; criticize

    persector — investigate

SEQUOR, -i, secutus — follow, accompany; ensue; pursue; aim at

    adsequor — overtake, attain; understand

consequor — follow, pursue; result

exsequor — follow, pursue; accomplish; undergo

insequor — follow, pursue, come after; attack; persecute

obsequor — comply with, yield to, indulge

persequor — follow all the way, chase, pursue; copy; perform

prosequor — attend, escort; pursue, attack

resequor — answer

subsequor — follow closely; support; imitate

sermocinor, -ari, -atus — converse

solor, -ari, -atus — comfort, console, relieve, ease

consolor — console, comfort, reassure, relieve

sortior, -iri, -itus — draw or case lots (for); allot, distribute, share

subsortior — choose as a substitute by lot

spatior, -ari, -atus — walk; spread

exspatior — go off course

speculor, -ari, -atus — spy out, watch for, observe

perspeculor — reconnoiter

prospeculor — look out, reconnoiter, watch for

stipulor, -ari, -atus — bargain, stipulate

instipulor — bargain for

restipulor — stipulate in return

stomachor, -ari, -atus — be vexed, be annoyed

suppetior, -ari, -atus — come to the aid of

testificor, -ari, -atus — give evidence, vouch for, make public

TESTOR, -ari, -atus — testify, prove, vouch for; appeal to; make a will

antestor — call a witness

attestor — confirm

contestor — call to witness

detestor — invoke (against), curse, deprecate

obtestor — call to witness, entreat

tortor, -ari, -atus — writhe

tricor, -ari, -atus — make mischief, play tricks

TUEOR, -ēri, tuitus or tutus — see, watch, look; guard, protect, keep

contueor — look at, observe, consider

intueor — look at, watch, contemplate, consider

obtueor — gaze at, see clearly

tutor, -ari, -atus — watch, guard, protect

ULCISCOR, -i, ultus — take vengeance on, punish; avenge

UTOR, -i, usus — (with ablative) use, employ, possess; experience

abutor — (with ablative) use up; misuse

deutor — (with ablative) maltreat

vador, -ari, -atus — to bind over by bail

vagor, -ari, -atus — wander, rove, go far afield; spread

evagor — wander off; spread out

pervagor — range, rove about; extend, spread; pervade

vaticinor, -ari, -atus — prophesy; rant, rave

velitor, -ari, -atus — skirmish

VENEROR, -ari, -atus — worship, revere, pray to, honor, respect

deveneror — worship, avert by prayers

venor, -ari, -atus — hunt, chase

pervenor — chase through, hunt through

verecundor, -ari, -atus — be bashful, feel shy

VEREOR, -ēri, -itus — be afraid (of), fear; revere, respect

revereor — stand in awe of, respect, revere

subvereor — be a little afraid

versor, -ari, -atus — live, be, be situated; be engaged (in), be busy at

adversor — oppose, resist

aversor — turn away, repulse, decline

deversor — lodge, stay as a guest

obversor — move about before, hover

tergiversor — hedge, be evasive

vescor, -i, ———— (usually with ablative) feed (on), eat, enjoy

vociferor, -ari, -atus — cry out loud, shout

II. Semideponents are typically regular verbs in the present system (present, imperfect, and future tenses) but deponent in the perfect system (perfect, pluperfect, and future perfect tenses). The following are common semideponents:

audeo, -ēre, ausus — dare, venture, be brave

esurio, -ire, esuritus — be hungry

fido, -ere, fisus — (with dative or ablative) trust, rely on

confido — (with dative) trust, rely (on), be sure (of)

diffido — (with dative) distrust; despair

subdiffido — be a little doubtful

gaudeo, -ēre, gavisus — rejoice, be pleased (at), delight (in)

soleo, -ēre, solitus — be accustomed, be in the habit (of)

III. The verb **fio**, the irregular passive of **facio**, is, as it were, a reverse semideponent: in the present system, its forms are active but its meanings are passive; in the perfect system, both its forms and its meanings are all passive. See 10.VIII.

fio, fieri, factus: become, arise, be made, be done, happen

12. Infinitives and Participles

I. A normal Latin verb has six infinitives: two in the present tense, active and passive; two in the perfect tense, active and passive; and two in the future tense, active and passive.

	Active	*Passive*
Present:	**audire**	**audiri**
	to hear	to be heard
Perfect:	**audivisse**	**auditus, -a, -um esse**
	to have heard	to have been heard
Future:	**auditurus, -a, -um esse**	**auditum iri**
	to be about to hear	to be about to be heard

Of the six, the future passive infinitive is by far the least common. Indirect statements often omit the **esse** of all perfect passive and future active infinitives; see 14.I.

I.1. Deponent verbs, having only three infinitives, use the future active infinitive instead of the future passive:

Present:	**sequi**
	to follow
Perfect:	**secutus, -a, -um esse**
	to have followed
Future:	**secuturus, -a, -um esse**
	to be about to follow

I.2. An alternate form of the present passive infinitive ending in -**er** can be found in very old or archaizing Latin:

audirier (= **audiri**) — to be heard
amarier (= **amari**) — to be loved
dicier (= **dici**) — to be said

I.3. The chief uses of the infinitive include:

I.3.a. Subjective infinitives

errare est humanum.   To err is human.

I.3.b. Complementary infinitives

desiderabamus discedere.   We wanted to depart.

I.3.c. With certain impersonal constructions (see 20.III)

licet loqui.   It is permitted to speak.
erat necesse loqui.   It was necessary to speak.

I.3.d. In indirect statements (see 14.I)

I.3.e. Prohibitions (see 19.III)

I.3.f. Historical infinitives (see 20.II)

I.3.g. Exclamatory infinitives
   vidēre patriam meam rursus!   O, to see my homeland again!

I.4. Subjects of infinitives are always put in the accusative (the subjective accusative), except in the case of historical infinitives (see 20.II).

II. A normal Latin verb has four participles: the present active participle, the perfect passive participle, the future active participle, and the future passive participle (also known as the gerundive).

	Active	*Passive*
Present:	**audiens**	——
	hearing	——
Perfect:	——	**auditus, -a, -um**
	——	having been heard
Future:	**auditurus, -a, -um**	**audiendus, -a, -um**
	about to hear	(about) to be heard

All of these are declined as 1st and 2nd declension adjectives (i.e., like **magnus, -a, -um**; see 5.I.1) except the present active participle, which is declined as a 1-termination 3rd declension *i*-stem adjective (i.e., like **ingens**; see 5.I.2.a).

II.1. Deponent verbs have four participles as well, but the perfect participle is usually translated as active:

Present:	**sequens**
	following
Perfect:	**secutus, -a, -um**
	having followed
Future:	**secuturus, -a, -um**
	about to follow
	sequendus, -a, -um
	(about) to be followed

II.2. The semantic range of participles, depending on the context, can be considerably broader than the translations above suggest. Temporal, causal, concessive, and conditional senses can be found:

Caesar spectans . . .   Caesar, while watching, . . .

Caesar, since watching, . . .

Caesar, though watching, . . .

Caesar, if watching, . . .

II.3. The most important uses of participles include:

II.3.a. As true adjectives

milites interfecti   the killed soldiers

II.3.a.i. When functioning as a true adjective, the ablative singular present active participle ends in **-i**:

cum milite interficienti   with the killing soldier

II.3.b. As verbal phrases

milites ab hostibus interfecti   the soldiers killed by the enemy

II.3.b.i. When functioning as a verbal phrase, the ablative singular present active participle ends in **-e**:

cum milite hostes interficiente
with the soldier killing the enemy

II.3.c. As nouns

mea amata   my beloved

agenda   things to be done

II.3.d. In ablative absolutes (see section 13)

II.4. Alternate forms in **-undus, -a, -um** and **-iundus, -a, -um** can be found for future passive participles (gerundives) of the 3rd and 4th conjugations; for example:

audiundus, -a, -um for **audiendus, -a, -um**

dicundus, -a, -um for **dicendus, -a, -um**

pariundus, -a, -um for **pariendus, -a, -um**

13. Ablative Absolutes

I. CARDINAL RULE

The noun in the ablative absolute never denotes the same person or thing as the subject or object of the main verb. This explains why it is an absolute (**absolutus, -a, -um** means "grammatically free or unbound").

II. MINIMUM CONSTRUCTIONS

All in the ablative case:

II.1. Noun (or pronoun) and participle

I.1.a. Perfect participle: most common

I.1.b. Present participle: common

I.1.c. Future participle: least common

II.2. Noun (or pronoun) and noun

II.3. Noun (or pronoun) and adjective

Rule: Participles and adjectives must agree with their nouns (or pronouns) in case, number, and gender.

III. TRANSLATIONS

III.1. Temporal: "when," "after," "while," "as"

III.2. Causal: "since," "because"

III.3. Concessive: "although," "despite"

III.4. Conditional: "if"

IV. POSSIBLE EXPANSIONS IN CONSTRUCTION

IV.1. A noun may have a qualifying genitive.

IV.2. A participle may take an object, an adverb, or a prepositional phrase.

EXAMPLES (keyed to information above):

Section	Ablative absolute	Main clause
II.1.a	**rege vulnerato**	**regina in suo cubiculo dormiebat.**
III.1	When the king was wounded, the queen was sleeping in her bedroom.	
II.1.a	**rege vulnerato**	**regina sola regnavit.**
III.2	Because the king was wounded, the queen ruled alone.	
II.1.a	**rege vulnerato**	**nemo regnum occupare conatus est.**
III.3	Though the king was wounded, nobody tried to seize the kingdom.	
II.1.b	**rege veniente**	**principes manebunt.**
III.1	When the king comes, the princes will stay.	
III.2	Since the king is coming, the princes will stay.	
III.4	If the king comes, the princes will stay.	
II.1.c	**rege venturo**	**hostes relinquere nolunt.**
III.3	Although the king is about to come, the enemy refuse to leave.	
II.2	**Caesare duce**	**nos vincemus.**
III.4	If Caesar is leader, we will win.	
II.2	**Arminio rege**	**Germania erat barbarissima.**
III.1	When Arminius was king, Germany was very barbaric.	
II.3	**imperatore fesso**	**exercitus profectus est.**
III.3	Although the general was tired, the army set out.	
II.3	**mercatore improbo**	**nos merces non emimus.**
III.2	Since the merchant is dishonest, we are not buying the goods.	

IV.1	**rege Germaniae vulnerato** Because the king of Germany was wounded, the queen ruled alone.	**regina sola regnavit.**
IV.1	**partibus villae collapsis** When parts of the house collapsed, we left as fast as possible.	**nos quam celerrimē reliquimus.**
IV.2	**imperatore signum dante** When the general gives the signal, the soldiers march into battle.	**milites in proelium incedunt.**
IV.2	**signo militibus dato** When the signal was given to the soldiers, the general mounted his horse.	**imperator equum suum conscendit.**
IV.2	**principibus ad urbem venientibus** If the princes come to the city, the citizens will rejoice.	**cives gaudebunt.**

V. NOTE ON THE POSITION OF ABLATIVE ABSOLUTES

The absolute phrase is usually found before the main clause (e.g., **rege vulnerato regina in suo cubiculo dormiebat**) or after the subject of the main clause (e.g., **regina, rege vulnerato, in suo cubiculo dormiebat**); more rarely, it occurs after the main clause or its verb (e.g., **regina in suo cubiculo dormiebat, rege vulnerato**).

VI. A COMMON IDIOM USING THE ABLATIVE ABSOLUTE

Romans often identified years by naming the two consuls elected or appointed for that particular year. The formula for this kind of dating involves putting the consuls' names in the ablative without a conjunction between.

> **Gn. Pompeio M. Crasso consulibus** [or abbreviated, **coss.**] . . .
> In the year when Pompey and Crassus were consuls . . .

14. Indirect Discourse

I. INDIRECT STATEMENT

The minimum structure of an indirect statement is a "mind" verb (that is, a main verb of perception or cognition; see below) + a subjective accusative (see 3.IV.4) + an infinitive.

putamus Caesarem venire.   We think that Caesar is coming.

Any one of the six forms of infinitive may be used; the future passive infinitive, though, is quite rare. Indirect statements regularly omit the **esse** of all perfect passive and future active infinitives.

I.1. When the action that the infinitive expresses is roughly contemporaneous with the action of the mind verb, either of the present infinitives is used:

putamus Caesarem venire.
We think [today] that Caesar is coming [today].

When the action that the infinitive expresses is prior to the action of the mind verb, either of the perfect infinitives is used:

putamus Caesarem vēnisse.
We think [today] that Caesar came [yesterday].

When the action that the infinitive expresses is subsequent to the action of the mind verb, either of the future infinitives is used:

putamus Caesarem venturum [esse].
We think [today] that Caesar will come [tomorrow].

I.2. The Latin grammar that the previous paragraph describes persists when the mind verb is in a secondary tense; the English translation, however, requires some changes.

putabamus Caesarem venire. (contemporaneous)
We were thinking [yesterday] that Caesar was coming [yesterday].

putabamus Caesarem vēnisse. (prior)
We were thinking [yesterday] that Caesar had come [the day before].

putabamus Caesarem venturum [esse]. (subsequent)
We were thinking [yesterday] that Caesar would come [today].

I.3. When the perfect passive infinitive or the future active infinitive is used, the form must agree with the subjective accusative:

putabamus Caesarem venturum [esse].
We were thinking that Caesar would come.

putabamus milites venturos [esse].
We were thinking that the soldiers would come.

putabamus novercam venturam [esse].
We were thinking that the stepmother would come.

putabamus auxilia ventura [esse].
We were thinking that the auxiliaries would come.

I.4. The mind verbs that most commonly introduce an indirect statement are:

I.4.a. To know or remember: **cognoscere, ignorare, meminisse, nescire, recordari, scire**, etc.

I.4.b. To think or decide: **arbitrari, censēre, constituere, ducere, existimare, iudicare, opinari, putare, statuere, suspicari**, etc.

I.4.c. To say, tell, promise, threaten, swear, pretend, etc.: **adfirmare, concedere, confirmare, confitēri, declarare, defendere, demonstrare, dicere, fatēri, fingere, iurare, minari, narrare, negare, nuntiare, persuadēre, pollicēri, probare, promittere, referre, respondēre, simulare, suadēre**, etc.

I.4.d. To perceive, learn, or discover: **audire, cernere, comperire, discere, invenire, reperire, sentire, vidēre**, etc.

I.4.e. To hope, expect, believe, trust, etc.: **credere, confidere, exspectare, fidere, sperare**, etc.

II. For indirect commands, see 16.IV.

III. For indirect questions, see 16.V.

IV. For subordinate clauses in indirect statement, see 16.XI.

15. Independent Uses of the Subjunctive

I. JUSSIVE (3RD PERSON) AND HORTATORY (1ST PERSON) SUBJUNCTIVES

I.1. The present subjunctive is used to express a wish or command:

discedat!	Let him leave! (jussive)
discedamus!	Let us leave! (hortatory)

I.2. The word **ne** introduces the negative:

ne hoc dicat!	Let him not say this!
ne dormiamus!	Let us not sleep!

II. POTENTIAL SUBJUNCTIVE

II.1. The present subjunctive is used to express present or future potentialities:

tu hoc putes.
You would (might, could) think this. One might think this.
credas eum esse hominem magnum.
You might (etc.) believe that he is a great man. One could believe . . .
ego eis non fidam.
I would not trust them. I might not . . .

II.2. The imperfect subjunctive indicates past potentialities:

tu hoc putares.
You would (etc.) have thought this. One would have . . .
crederes eum esse hominem magnum.
You might (etc.) have believed he was a great man. One could have . . .
ego eis non fiderem.
I would (etc.) not have trusted them.

II.3. The word **non** expresses the negative.

II.4. A potential subjunctive may be introduced by the impersonal **licet** (it is permitted), which in this context may be translated as "although."

licet hoc putes, . . .   Although you might think this, . . .

III. DELIBERATIVE SUBJUNCTIVE

III.1. A speaker or writer might employ a present or imperfect subjunctive to express deliberation or perplexity about a course of action. A deliberative question anticipates either an imperative or no response at all (i.e., it asks a rhetorical question, employed only for rhetorical effect).

quid dicam?	What am I to say? What should I say?
quid dicerem?	What was I to say? What should I have said?

III.1.a. Though this usage is rare, the perfect subjunctive can express rhetorical emphasis, sometimes without any force of tense.

quid dixerim?	What *was* I to have said?
	What *am* I to say?

III.2. **Non** expresses the negative:

non respondeamus?	Are we not to reply? Should we not reply?
non respondēremus?	Were we not to reply? Should we not have replied?

IV. OPTATIVE SUBJUNCTIVE

IV.1. The present subjunctive, alone or introduced with **utinam** or **ut**, communicates an attainable wish for the future.

utinam discedat!	If only he would leave! I wish he would leave!

IV.1.a. The perfect subjunctive expresses the wish for an action that has already been completed or a strongly emphasized wish.

utinam discesserit!
If only he has left! I pray he has left! If *only* he leaves! I *wish* he would leave!

IV.2. The imperfect subjunctive communicates a wish for the present that is unattainable (see present contrary-to-fact conditions, 18.I.3.a). The pluperfect subjunctive communicates an unattainable wish for the past (see past contrary-to-fact conditions, 18.I.3.b).

utinam discederet!	If only he were leaving! I wish he were leaving!
utinam discessisset!	If only he had left! I wish he had left!

IV.3. **Ne** or **utinam ne** introduces the negative:

(utinam) ne discedat!	If only he would not leave! I wish he would not leave!

IV.4. Note that many older textbooks use the archaic English "would that . . ." to express optative subjunctives.

16. Dependent Uses of the Subjunctive

Despite the title of this section, we will discuss some dependent clauses using the indicative mood too. As you will soon see, the subjunctive clauses and the indicative clauses can look very similar, with only subtle differences in meaning.

I. CUM CLAUSES

Besides resembling a preposition meaning "with" (see 8.II.1), **cum** also occurs as a subordinating conjunction meaning "since" or "because" (causal), "although" (concessive), "when" (circumstantial or temporal), or "whenever" (generalizing). In poetry or archaic Latin, the conjunction can sometimes be spelled **quom**. For negation, **cum** clauses use **non**.

    I.1. Causal: takes subjunctive; follows sequence of tenses.
        cum fortiter pugnemus, hostes nostros vincimus.
        Since we are fighting bravely, we are defeating our enemy.
        cum dormirent, impetum fecimus.
        Because they were sleeping, we made an attack.

    I.2. Concessive: takes subjunctive; follows sequence of tenses.
        cum villam incenderemus, non effūgerunt.
        Although we were setting fire to the house, they did not flee.
        cum sint fessi, fortiter pugnant.
        Although they are tired, they fight bravely.

    I.3. Circumstantial: stating the circumstances in which the action of the main verb takes place.

        I.3.a. Past circumstantial: takes subjunctive. If the action of the circumstantial clause is in the past, the imperfect or pluperfect subjunctive is used:
            cum villam incendissemus, discessimus.
            When/after we had set fire to the house, we departed.
            cum milites dormirent, imperator epistulas scribebat.
            When/while the soldiers were sleeping, the general wrote letters.

        I.3.b. Present or future circumstantial: takes indicative. If the action of the circumstantial clause is in the present or future, the present or future indicative is used:
            cum nos fiemus senes, erimus divites.
            When we (will) become old men, we will be rich.
            cum ego te video, laetus sum.
            When I see you, I am happy.

I.4. Temporal: takes indicative.

If the **cum** clause merely fixes the time of the action of the main verb and the two clauses are strictly coordinate, the verb in the **cum** clause is indicative:

cum venies, erit meus dies natalis.

(At the very time) when you (will) come, it will be my birthday.

(Note: there is no connection between the coming and the birthday except for the coincidence of time.)

cum Caesar discessit, rex moriebatur.

(At the very time) when Caesar departed, the king was dying.

(Note: there is no connection between the departing and the dying except for the coincidence of time.)

I.4.a. To distinguish between circumstantial and temporal clauses, ask yourself this: Would the statement of the main clause have been true regardless of the **cum** clause? If so, it is a temporal clause. If not necessarily so, then it is a circumstantial clause.

I.5. Generalizing: takes indicative. When the **cum** clause expresses a generalization, the conjunction is translated as "whenever."

I.5.a. The perfect indicative is used to make a present generalization:
cum ego te vīdi, laetus sum.
Whenever I see [literally, have seen] you, I am happy.

I.5.b. The pluperfect indicative is used to make a past generalization:
cum ego te vīderam, laetus eram.
Whenever I saw [literally, had seen] you, I was happy.

I.5.c. The tense of the **cum** clause (perfect or pluperfect) indicates that the action of the generalization was prior to the action of the main verb.

I.6. If futurity in a subjunctive **cum** clause is being emphasized, the subjunctive future periphrastic (see 17.VI) is employed:

cum cras discessuri simus, nunc obdormimus.

Since we will depart tomorrow, we are going to bed now.

II. RESULT CLAUSES

II.1. Result clauses (also known as consecutive clauses) are subordinate clauses that answer the question "To what extent or to what degree was the action or condition of the main clause carried to an outcome or effect?" They are introduced by **ut** (or **ut non** in negation), and their verbs are in the subjunctive.

II.2. The use of one of several adjectives and adverbs of degree in the main clause often heralds a result clause.

II.2.a. Adjectives: **talis, -e** — such, of such a kind
                         tantus, -a, -um — so great
                         tot (indeclinable) — so many

II.2.b. Adverbs: **adeō** — so (usually with adverbs and adjectives)
                         ita — so (usually with verbs)
                         sīc — in this way (usually with verbs)
                         tam — so (usually with adverbs and adjectives)
                         tantum — so much (usually with verbs)
                         totiens — so often (usually with verbs)

II.3. If the verb in the main clause is in the present or future tense, the result clause uses the present subjunctive:
tanta est tempestas ut reveniamus.
The storm is so great that we are coming back.
obliviscitur totiens ut ei non fidamus.
He forgets so often that we don't trust him.

II.4. If the verb in the main clause is imperfect, perfect, or pluperfect, the result clause uses the imperfect subjunctive:
tanta erat tempestas ut reveniremus.
The storm was so great that we came back.
obliviscebatur totiens ut ei non fideremus.
He used to forget so often that we didn't trust him.

II.4.a. Rarely, a perfect subjunctive is used in this setting to emphasize that the action of the result is complete:
tanta erat tempestas ut revēnerimus.
The storm was so great that we came back.

II.5. If the result clause is emphasizing futurity, it employs the subjunctive future periphrastic:
tanta erit tempestas ut cras reventuri simus.
The storm will be so great that we will return tomorrow.

III. PURPOSE CLAUSES

Purpose clauses answer the question "To what end or with what intention was the action of the main clause done?" A variety of conjunctions (or adverbs functioning as conjunctions) introduce them, and their verbs are in the subjunctive mood. Always be careful to distinguish purpose clauses from complementary infinitives (which express need, desire, or effort rather than purpose).

III.1. Clauses using **ut** and **ne**: if the purpose is affirmed, **ut** introduces the subjunctive verb of the purpose clause; if the purpose is negated, **ne** (or **neve** or **neu**) is used.

III.1.a. If the verb in the main clause is in the present or future tense, the purpose clause uses the present subjunctive:

pugnamus ut vincamus.   We fight to conquer.
                                We fight that we may conquer.
                                We fight in order to conquer.
                                We fight in order that we may conquer.

III.1.b. If the verb in the main clause is imperfect, perfect, or pluperfect, the purpose clause uses the imperfect subjunctive:

pugnabamus ne vinceremur.
We were fighting (in order) that we might not be conquered.

III.2. Relative and adverbial clauses of purpose are introduced by words with antecedents in the main clause. **Ne** typically negates them too.

III.2.a. Relative pronouns:
ego legatum mitto qui regem interroget.
I am sending an envoy (in order) to question the king.
vilicus ancillam invēnit quae dominam curaret.
The bailiff found a slave girl to care for the mistress.

III.2.b. Adverbs of place or location:
quō — (to) where
ubi — where
unde — from where
ego ad culinam contendo ubi cenam inveniam.
I am hurrying to the kitchen, where I might find dinner.
I am hurrying to the kitchen to find dinner there.
captivi carcerem incenderunt unde effugerent.
The captives set fire to the prison to escape from there.

III.2.c. If the purpose clause contains a comparative adjective or adverb, **quō** (ablative, "by which [act]") usually replaces **ut**:
nos pro turbā adgrediebamur quō melius pompam aspectaremus.
We were advancing in front of the crowd to watch the parade better.

imperator ad Arabiam proficiscitur quō maiores equos inveniat.
The general is setting out for Arabia to find bigger horses.

III.3. If a purpose clause is emphasizing futurity, it employs the subjunctive future periphrastic:

nunc discedimus ut cras reventuri simus.
We depart now in order that we will return tomorrow.

IV. INDIRECT COMMANDS

In the sentence "They urge us to conquer," "to conquer" is the indirect command corresponding to a direct command—"They urge us: conquer!" Indirect commands are closely related to purpose clauses: "They urge us (in order) that we conquer."

IV.1. Either **ut** or **ne** introduces the verb of the indirect command, which is subjunctive.

IV.2. Most verbs of begging, warning, ordering, advising, urging, persuading, requesting, etc. (e.g., **cavēre, censēre, hortari, imperare, instare, monēre, orare, persuadēre, petere, postulare, praecipere, precari, quaerere, rogare**), require this construction.

hortantur nos ut vincamus.   They urge us to conquer.

imperabat ne nos relinqueremus.   He was ordering us not to leave.

IV.2.a. Often, especially in poetry, an infinitive clause replaces this construction of **ut** or **ne** with the subjunctive, softening the meaning somewhat. For example:

Livia postulat ut ancillae sint diligentiores.
Livia demands that the slaves be more careful.

Livia postulat ancillas esse diligentiores.
Livia asks/wants the slaves to be more careful.

IV.3. If an indirect command is emphasizing futurity, it employs the subjunctive future periphrastic:

imperat nobis ut cras reventuri simus.
He commands us to return tomorrow.

V. INDIRECT QUESTIONS

An indirect question is a subordinate clause following a verb of knowing, learning, asking, etc. The indirect question is introduced by an interrogative word or phrase, expressed by the subjunctive, and typically negated by **non**.

Direct question	*Indirect question*
ubi erant?	**audivit ubi essent.**
Where were they?	He heard where they were.
quis es?	**scimus quis sis.**
Who are you?	We know who you are.

V.1. Indirect questions follow the complete rule for the sequence of tenses; see 21.III.4.

V.2. If an indirect question is emphasizing futurity, it employs the subjunctive future periphrastic:

rogat quomodo cras reventuri simus.

He asks how we will return tomorrow.

V.3. The most common interrogative adverbs and pronouns are:

cur, why; **num**, whether; **quā**, by what way; **quārē**, why; **quandō**, when; **quid**, what; **quis**, who; **quō**, to where; **quomodo**, how; **quorsum**, to what end; **ubi**, where, when; **unde**, from where; **utrum**, whether; **utrumne**, whether.

VI. CLAUSES OF FEARING

Verbs or phrases expressing fear introduce subjunctive clauses heralded by the conjunction **ut,** to negate the fear, or **ne**, to affirm it. However counterintuitive the deployment of these conjunctions may seem, it is in fact the outcome of a fairly straightforward linguistic evolution: when the Latin language was in its infancy, fear was expressed paratactically (parataxis is the absence of grammatical subordination); sentences were simple and consecutive. Thus, fear was communicated by means of a declarative sentence followed by an optative subjunctive (see 15.IV):

timeo. ut discedat!	I am afraid. If only he would leave!
timeo. ne discedat!	I am afraid. If only he would not leave!

Then, as the language evolved, hypotaxis (the use of grammatical subordination, whereby sentences became complex and comprised one or more dependent clauses) replaced parataxis. From our perspective, this process meant simply the omission of punctuation:

timeo ut discedat.	I am afraid that he is not leaving.
timeo ne discedat.	I am afraid that he is leaving.

Compare the previous examples; it is logical that the objects of one's fear and one's wish would be opposites.

VI.1. Fear clauses adhere to the complete rule for the sequence of tenses: see 21.III.4.

timeo ut discedat.	I am afraid that he is not leaving.
timeo ut discesserit.	I am afraid that he has not left.
timui ut discederet.	I was afraid that he was not leaving.
timui ut discessisset.	I was afraid that he had not left.

VI.2. To emphasize futurity, the future periphrastic is used:

timeo ut discessurus sit.	I am afraid that he will not leave.
timui ut discessurus esset.	I was afraid that he would not leave.

VI.3. Sometimes a negative clause of fearing uses **ne . . . non** (a double negative) instead of **ut**, especially when the fearing verb is negated:

non timeo ne non discedat.	I'm not afraid that he isn't leaving.

VII. CLAUSES OF DOUBTING

VII.1. Affirmed doubt: the subordinate clause is introduced by **num**, **utrum**, or **an** and operates as a simple indirect question.

dubitat an discedam.	He doubts whether/that I am departing.
dubitavit num discederem.	He doubted whether/that I was departing.

VII.1.a. Again, a future periphrastic may occur to emphasize futurity:

dubitat num discessurus sim.
He doubts whether/that I will depart.

VII.2. Negated doubt: **quin** (but that) introduces the subjunctive clause:

non dubitat quin discedam.
He doesn't doubt (but) that I am departing.
non dubium erat quin discessissem.
There was no doubt (but) that I had departed.

VII.2.a. Included in expressions of negated doubt are rhetorical questions such as:

quis dubitat quin discedam?
Who doubts that I am departing?

Since the clear implication is that no one doubts that the speaker is departing, this is called a virtual or implied negative doubt.

VII.3. Note: when an infinitive follows it, the verb **dubito** means not "doubt" but "hesitate":

dubitat discedere.	He hesitates to depart.

VIII. CLAUSES OF PROVISO

The conjunctions **dum**, **modo**, and **dummodo** all mean "provided that," "so long as," or "if only" and are used with present and imperfect subjunctives to express conditional wishes. The negative used is **ne**.

> **veniant dum/modo/dummodo ne sint inimici.**
> Let them come, so long as they are not unfriendly.
> **veniet dum/modo/dummodo laborem confecerit.**
> He will come, provided that he has finished his task.

VIII.1. **Tantum ut** (negative: **tantum ne**) is also used in proviso clauses:

> **veniant tantum ne sint inimici.**
> Let them come, so long as they are not unfriendly.

VIII.2. If a proviso clause is emphasizing futurity, it employs the subjunctive future periphrastic:

> **nunc discedamus dum cras reventuri simus.**
> Let's depart now, so long as we will return tomorrow.

IX. CLAUSES OF PREVENTION

IX.1. The verbs **prohibeo, -ēre, prohibui, prohibitus** (prohibit); **tardo, -are, tardavi, tardatus** (detain); and **veto, -are, vetui, vetitus** (forbid) usually set up complementary infinitives:

> **te veto discedere.** I forbid you to depart.
> **te prohibeo discedere.** I prohibit you from departing.

IX.2. In a type of purpose clause, the following verbs set up a subjunctive construction:

> **deterreo, -ēre, deterrui, deterritus** — deter, prevent
> **impedio, -ire, impedivi (impedii), impeditus** — hinder
> **interdico, -ere, interdixi, interdictus** — ban
> **moror, -ari, moratus sum** — deter, hinder
> **obsisto, -ere, obstiti, obstitus** — resist, stand in the way of
> **obsto, -are, obstiti** — hinder, stand in the way of
> **officio, -ere, offeci, offectus** — hinder, obstruct

IX.2.a. Affirmed prevention: **quominus** or **ne** introduces the subjunctive.

> **(te) deterreo quominus discedas.**
> I prevent you from departing.
> **(te) impedio ne discedas.**
> I hinder you from departing.

IX.2.b. Negated prevention: **quominus** or **quin** introduces the subjunctive.

non deterreo quin discedas.

I don't prevent you from departing.

non impedivi quominus discederes.

I didn't hinder your departing.

IX.2.c. If a prevention clause is emphasizing futurity, it employs the subjunctive future periphrastic:

deterret ne cras reventuri simus.

He deters us from returning tomorrow.

non deterret quin cras reventuri simus.

He isn't deterring us from returning tomorrow.

X. GENERIC RELATIVE CLAUSES (RELATIVE CLAUSES OF CHARACTERISTIC)

A form (usually in the nominative) of the relative pronoun (see 7.V) introduces certain dependent subjunctive clauses. These clauses describe their antecedent in some indefinite property or characteristic relative to a larger, specified group or class to which the antecedent belongs.

est homo qui cito discedat.	He is the sort (of man) who departs quickly.
	He is a person who departs quickly.
	He is the (sort of) person to depart quickly.

Notice that the person is described in terms of his relation to a broader group, of which he is a member. Contrast:

est homo qui cito discedit.	He is *the* (actual) person who is departing quickly.

In this sentence the relative clause defines something specific, not generic.

X.1. The most common introductory phrases for this construction are:

sunt/erant qui	there are/were those who/to
est/erat qui	he is/was one/the sort who/to
quis est/erit qui?	who is there/will there be who/to?
quid est/erat quod?	what is/was there that/to?
solus est/erat qui	he is/was the only one who/to
nemo est/erit qui	there is/will be no one who/to
nihil est/erat quod	there is/was nothing that/to

X.2. **Quin** (= **qui ne**) commonly introduces negative generic relative clauses:

nemo est quin hoc audiverit.	There is no one who did not hear this.

X.3. If a generic clause is emphasizing futurity, it employs the subjunctive future periphrastic:

nos soli sumus qui cras reventuri simus.
We are the only ones of the sort to return tomorrow.

XI. SUBORDINATE CLAUSES IN INDIRECT STATEMENTS

When a subordinate clause is found in an indirect statement, its verb is typically in the subjunctive mood. The tense of the subjunctive is determined by the tense of the verb of the main clause and follows the complete rule for the sequence of tenses (see section 21). Negation is with **non** unless the grammar requires a different negative.

DIRECT STATEMENT

Main clause	Principal clause	Subordinate clause
dicit,	**"viri pugnant**	**quod sunt irati."**
He says,	"The men are fighting	because they are angry."

INDIRECT STATEMENT

Main clause	Principal clause	Subordinate clause
dicit	**viros pugnare**	**quod sint irati.**
He says	that the men are fighting	because they are angry.
dixit	**viros pugnare**	**quod essent irati.**
He said	that the men were fighting	because they were angry.

This use of the subjunctive follows good language logic, inasmuch as the claim of the subordinate clause (about the men's anger) is only assumed or alleged—not affirmed as fact.

XII. SUBJUNCTIVE BY ATTRACTION

Sometimes when a verb occurs in close context with a subjunctive verb, it is attracted into the subjunctive, even though its grammar ordinarily calls for an indicative. For example:

vēnimus ut captivos, qui effūgissent, puniremus.
We came in order to punish the prisoners who had fled.

In this sentence, **effūgissent**, used in a simple relative clause that expects an indicative, has been attracted into the subjunctive because of the proximity of the subjunctive **puniremus**. If the sentence had read **effūgerant** (indicative) instead of **effūgissent** (subjunctive), it would have been both grammatically correct and translated in the same way.

XIII. WITH VARIOUS CONJUNCTIONS

XIII.1. Conjunctions used only with the subjunctive in conformity with the rules for the sequence of subjunctive tenses (see section 21)

XIII.1.a. Concessive:
quamvis — although

XIII.1.b. Comparative:
quasi — as if
tamquam — as if
velut or **veluti** — as if

XIII.2. Conjunctions usually used with the indicative

XIII.2.a. Temporal:
cum primum — as soon as
postquam — after
quandō — when
simul ac or **simulac** — as soon as
simul atque or **simulatque** — as soon as
ubi — when, after, while
ut — when, as, while

XIII.2.b. Causal:
quandō — since
quoniam — since, because

XIII.2.c. Concessive:
etiamsi — even if
etsi — even if, although
quamquam — although
tametsi — even if, even though

XIII.2.d. Comparative:
ceu — like as, just as
praeut — as compared with
prout — according as, just as
sīcut or **sīcuti** — just as
ut or **uti** — as, just as
velut or **veluti** — as, so as, even as, just as

XIII.3. Certain conjunctions take either the indicative or the subjunctive depending largely on the implication of the sentence. Remember: indicative is the mood of fact, while subjunctive is the mood of probability, intention, or assumption. If a subjunctive clause is emphasizing futurity, it employs the subjunctive future periphrastic.

XIII.3.a. Temporal

XIII.3.a.i.   **donec** — until, as long as, while
dum — until, as long as, while
quamdiu — as long as
quoad — until, as long as, while

XIII.3.a.i.A. When the subordinate clause refers simply to a particular time, it uses the indicative:
manet dum/donec/quoad discedimus.
He remains until we (actually) leave.
manebat dum/donec/quoad cupiebat.
He was staying as long as he wanted.
exspectavi dum/donec/quoad locutus es.
I waited while/until you spoke.

XIII.3.a.i.A.1. The so-called historical present, in the indicative, is typically employed with **dum** even when a continued past action is being indicated:
dum tabernam habeo, uxor mortua est.
While I had my shop, my wife died.

XIII.3.a.i.B. The subjunctive mood is used with these conjunctions to express the notion of intent, purpose, or assumption:
exspectavi dum/donec/quoad veniret.
I waited until he should come.
I waited for him to come.
Note: The sentence does not indicate whether he did in fact come.
exspectavi dum/donec/quoad locutus esses.
I waited until you should speak.
I waited for you to speak.

XIII.3.a.ii.   **antequam** — before
priusquam — before

XIII.3.a.ii.A. The indicative mood is used with these whenever they refer to specific times:

discessi priusquam/antequam vēnit.
I left before he came.

XIII.3.a.ii.B. In secondary sequence (see section 21), if the conjunction involves or implies some intent, assumption, or purpose, the subjunctive mood is employed:
discessi priusquam/antequam veniret.
I left before he might/could come.

XIII.3.a.ii.C. Primary sequence (see section 21) typically employs the present or future perfect indicative (less often, the present subjunctive):
discedam priusquam/antequam vēnerit.
I will leave before he will have come.
discedam priusquam venit/veniat.
I will leave before he comes.

XIII.3.a.ii.D. In a rhetorical figure called *tmesis*, the conjunctions **antequam** and **priusquam** are often split:
ante/prius discessi quam veniret.
I left before [literally, sooner than] he could come.

XIII.3.b. Causal:
quia — because, since
quippe (qui) — because
quod — because, since, that

XIII.3.b.i. When the causal clause is factual, it uses the indicative; when assumed, alleged, or intended, it uses the subjunctive:
exspecto quia/quippe qui/ quod venit.
I'm waiting because he is (actually) coming.
exspecto quia/quippe qui/ quod veniat.
I'm waiting because he is (allegedly) coming/because he might/could come.

XIV. SUBJUNCTIVE IN CONDITIONAL SENTENCES

Certain types of conditional sentences use the subjunctive mood.

XIV.1. Future-less-vivid conditions: see 18.I.2.b.

XIV.2. Contrary-to-fact conditions: see 18.I.3.

XIV.3. Conditions in subordinate clauses: see 18.III.

17. Supines, Gerunds, Gerundives, and Periphrastics

I. SUPINE

The supine is a verbal noun of the 4th declension; it occurs only in the accusative and ablative singular and is formed from the 4th principal part. For example, the supines of **portare** are:

portatum (accusative)   **portatū** (ablative)

I.1. The accusative supine is employed without a preposition after verbs of motion to express the purpose or end of that motion:

vēnit pugnatum.   He came to fight.
milites salutatum appropinquavit.   He approached to greet the soldiers.

I.2. The ablative supine is used with certain adjectives (e.g., **difficilis, facilis, dignus, indignus, mirabilis, gravis, incredibilis, honestus, turpis, utilis, iucundus, optimus**) as an ablative of respect (see 3.V.10).

haec amphora est facilis portatū.   This wine jar is easy to carry.

II. GERUND

The gerund is a neuter singular verbal noun of the 2nd declension. In form, it is identical to the neuter singular of the gerundive, and it occurs only in the accusative, genitive, dative, and ablative cases. In translation, it corresponds to the English gerund ending in -ing. The gerunds of **portare** are:

portandi (genitive) — of carrying
portando (dative) — to/for carrying
portandum (accusative) — carrying
portando (ablative) — by/with/in carrying

inter dormiendum somniabat.   He dreamed during sleeping.
labor est pars discendi.   Work is part of learning.
praesum pugnando.   I'm in charge of fighting.
hic est liber de loquendo.   This is a book about speaking.

II.1. The gerund may exhibit its verbal quality by taking an object or by being modified by an adverb.

hic liber est de bene loquendo.   This book is about speaking well.
labor est pars discendi linguam.   Work is part of learning a language.

III. GERUNDIVE

The gerundive is a verbal adjective (namely, the future passive participle). A gerundive phrase is often preferred to having the gerund take a direct object.

Gerund:	**labor est pars discendi linguam.**
Gerundive:	**labor est pars linguae discendae.**
	(literally, work is part of a language to be learned)
Gerund:	**vicit populum vastando agros.**
Gerundive:	**vicit populum agris vastandis.**
	(literally, he conquered the people by means of the fields to be devastated)

IV. PASSIVE PERIPHRASTIC

In Latin grammar, periphrasis is the use of the verb *to be* as an auxiliary. The passive periphrastic consists of a gerundive (the future passive participle) and a form of *to be*. To translate a passive periphrastic, use the auxiliaries *must, should, ought,* or anything expressing duty, obligation, or necessity.

IV.1. With a transitive verb: the gerundive agrees with the subject in case, number, and gender.

milites mittendi sunt.	The soldiers must be sent.
rex capiendus est.	The king should be captured.
villa videnda est.	The house ought to be seen.
amphora portanda erat.	The wine jar had to be carried.
fures puniendi erant.	The thieves had to be punished.
urbes occupandae erunt.	The cities will have to be seized.
servus interficiendus erit.	The slave will need to be killed.

IV.2. With an intransitive verb: the gerundive is in the neuter nominative singular.

effugiendum est.	It is necessary to flee.
pugnandum est.	It is necessary to fight.
vivendum erat.	It was necessary to live.
currendum erat.	It was necessary to run.
dormiendum erit.	It will be necessary to sleep.
veniendum erit.	It will be necessary to come.

IV.3. The dative of agent is used only with passive periphrastics (see 3.III.6).

milites legato mittendi sunt.	The soldiers must be sent by the legate.
villa vobis videnda est.	You ought to see the house.
effugiendum nobis erat.	It was necessary for us to flee.
pugnandum gladiatori erit.	The gladiator will have to fight.
vivendum tibi est.	You should live.
amphorae servis portandae sunt.	Wine jars should be carried by slaves.

V. GERUNDS AND GERUNDIVES USED TO EXPRESS PURPOSE

V.1. In **ad** + accusative:

vēnit ad pugnandum.	He came to fight.

ad salutandum [gerund] **milites appropinquavit.**	
or **ad milites salutandos** [gerundive] **appropinquavit.**	
He approached to greet the soldiers.	

V.2. In the genitive followed by **causā** or **gratiā** (for the sake of):

dormiendi causā/gratiā discessit.	He departed to sleep.

salutandi [gerund] **milites causā/gratiā appropinquavit.**	
or **militum salutandorum** [gerundive] **causā/gratiā appropinquavit.**	
He approached to greet the soldiers.	

VI. FUTURE PERIPHRASTIC

To express a verbal idea intermediate between the present and the future, Latin employs a future periphrastic, which consists of the future active participle and a form of the verb *to be* (the present and imperfect tenses are the most common). Translate future periphrastics with auxiliaries such as "going to," "about to," or "on the point of."

effugituri sunt.	They are going to flee.
pugnaturus est.	He is about to fight.
dormitura erat.	She was on the point of sleeping.
visurae eramus.	We were about to see.
urbem occupaturi fuerant.	They had been about to seize the city.

VI.1. Since there is no future tense in the subjunctive mood, future periphrastics using subjunctives of the verb *to be* are common for expressing futurity.

18. Conditional Sentences

The sentence "If he works, he is happy" is conditional. It consists of two clauses: the *if* clause (called the *protasis*) and the concluding clause (called the *apodosis*). In Latin, **si** (if) or **nisi/ si non** (if not, unless) introduces the protasis.

I. There are three basic categories of conditional sentences in Latin, and each is constructed according to a specific formula.

I.1. Simple (or general) conditions

Present: If (i.e., whenever) he works, he is happy.

Past: If (i.e., whenever) he worked, he was happy.

Latin formula: indicative in both clauses.
  si laborat, felix est.
  si laborabat, felix erat.

I.2. Future conditions are defined in terms of vividness, that is, the likelihood of whether they will be fulfilled.

  I.2.a. More vivid:
    If he works, he will be happy.

English formula: the protasis is usually present tense; the apodosis is future tense.

Latin formula: future indicative in both clauses.
  si laborabit, felix erit.

  I.2.a.i. If the nature of the condition is exceptionally emphatic, the protasis may use a future perfect indicative:
    si laboraverit, felix erit.
    If, and only if, he works (will have worked) will he be happy.

  I.2.b. Less vivid:
    If he should work, he would be happy.

Note that the condition, while in the future, is conceived of as distinctly less vivid, or less certain of being fulfilled.

English formula: If . . . should . . . , then . . . would . . . . *Or:* If . . . were to . . . , then . . . would . . . .
Latin formula: present subjunctive in both clauses.

si laboret, felix sit.
If he should/were to work, he would be happy.

I.2.b.i. Note: For future-less-vivid conditions, the protasis sometimes uses the perfect instead of the present subjunctive, but this is rare. It occurs when the act of the condition (i.e., of the protasis) is regarded as completed before that of the apodosis begins:

si laboraverit, felix sit.
If he should have worked (yesterday), he would be happy (today).

I.3. Contrary-to-fact (contrafactual) conditions state something that is untrue and only supposed.

I.3.a. Present contrary to fact:
If he were (now) working (but he is not), he would be happy.

English formula: If . . . were ____ing, then . . . would . . . .

Latin formula: imperfect subjunctive in both clauses.
si laboraret, felix esset.

I.3.b. Past contrary to fact:
If he had (in the past) worked (but he did not), he would have been happy.

English formula: If . . . had ____ed, then . . . would have ____ed . . . .

Latin formula: pluperfect subjunctive in both clauses.
si laboravisset, felix fuisset.

I.4. Mixed conditions
In addition to the strict formulae given above, one frequently finds mixed conditions, with the protasis and the apodosis in different categories. Such conditions are constructed as logical thought and grammatical rules require. For example: If he had (in the past) worked (but he did not), he would (now) be happy. The protasis is past contrafactual, but the apodosis refers to the present time. Consequently, in Latin the protasis must have its verb in the pluperfect subjunctive, while the verb of the apodosis will be imperfect subjunctive:
si laboravisset, felix esset.

II. TABLE OF CONDITIONALS

TYPE	TIME	PROTASIS		APODOSIS	
		Tense	*Mood*	*Tense*	*Mood*
II.1. Simple/ General	Present	Present	Indicative	Present	Indicative
	Past	Imperf., Perf., Plupf.	Indicative	Imperf., Perf., Plupf.	Indicative
II.2.a. Future more vivid	Future	Future/Fut. Perf.	Indicative	Future	Indicative
II.2.b. Future less vivid	Future	Present (Perfect)	Subjunctive	Present	Subjunctive
II.3. Contrary-to-fact	Present	Imperfect	Subjunctive	Imperfect	Subjunctive
	Past	Pluperfect	Subjunctive	Pluperfect	Subjunctive

III. CONDITIONS IN SUBORDINATE CLAUSES

We've learned that subordinate clauses in indirect statements typically have subjunctive verbs (see 16.XI); we've also seen that in complex sentences using a subjunctive verb, another verb may be "attracted" into the subjunctive (see 16.XII). It should come as no surprise, then, that conditions expressed within subordination rely on the subjunctive mood. Moreover, the three basic categories of conditionals are only partially preserved when used in subordination: The distinction between future less vivid and future more vivid is lost. Contrary-to-fact conditions in indirect statement are distinguishable from other types of conditions by the use of the future active participle plus the word **fuisse** in the apodosis, but in other forms of subordination they are not always distinguishable by form, since all four tenses of the subjunctive are also employed for simple or general conditions.

For the protasis, either the imperfect or the perfect tense is the norm, but the present (or perfect) subjunctive may be used for future conditions. As expected, present contrary-to-fact uses imperfect subjunctive, while past contrary-to-fact uses pluperfect subjunctive. The tense of the subjunctive may appear to violate the rule for the sequence of tenses (see section 21).

The apodosis of the condition follows the grammar established by the type of subordination; for instance, in an indirect statement, the apodosis will be cast as an infinitive, and in a fearing or a doubting construction, the apodosis will be cast as subjunctive.

19. Commands

I. Most commands in Latin are expressed with the imperative mood. The present imperative occurs in the 2nd person, singular and plural.

		Active	*Passive*
I.1. 1st conjugation			
	singular	**nega**	**negare**
	plural	**negate**	**negamini**
I.2. 2nd conjugation			
	singular	**monē**	**monēre**
	plural	**monete**	**monemini**
I.3. 3rd conjugation			
	singular	**gere**	**gerere**
	plural	**gerite**	**gerimini**
I.4. 4th conjugation			
	singular	**sci**	**scire**
	plural	**scite**	**scimini**
I.5. 3rd conjugation **-io**			
	singular	**pare**	**parere**
	plural	**parite**	**parimini**

II. Older Latin literature and legal writers occasionally employ a future imperative. It occurs in the 2nd and 3rd persons, singular and plural, except in the latter's 2nd person passive.

		Active	*Passive*
II.1. 1st conjugation			
	2nd singular	**negato**	**negator**
	2nd plural	**negatote**	——
	3rd singular	**negato**	**negator**
	3rd plural	**neganto**	**negantor**
II.2. 2nd conjugation			
	2nd singular	**moneto**	**monetor**
	2nd plural	**monetote**	——
	3rd singular	**moneto**	**monetor**
	3rd plural	**monento**	**monentor**
II.3. 3rd conjugation			
	2nd singular	**gerito**	**geritor**
	2nd plural	**geritote**	——

	3rd singular	**gerito**	**geritor**
	3rd plural	**gerunto**	**geruntor**
II.4. 4th conjugation			
	2nd singular	**scito**	**scitor**
	2nd plural	**scitote**	——
	3rd singular	**scito**	**scitor**
	3rd plural	**sciunto**	**sciuntor**
II.5. 3rd conjugation **-io**			
	2nd singular	**parito**	**paritor**
	2nd plural	**paritote**	——
	3rd singular	**parito**	**paritor**
	3rd plural	**pariunto**	**pariuntor**
II.6. Irregulars			
II.6.a. **sum, esse**			
	2nd singular	**esto**	——
	2nd plural	**estote**	——
	3rd singular	**esto**	——
	3rd plural	**sunto**	——
II.6.b. **nolo, nolle**			
	2nd singular	**nolito**	——
	2nd plural	**nolitote**	——
	3rd singular	**nolito**	
	3rd plural	**nolunto**	
II.6.c. **eo, ire**			
	2nd singular	**ito**	——
	2nd plural	**itote**	——
	3rd singular	**ito**	——
	3rd plural	**eunto**	——
II.6.d. **fero, ferre**			
	2nd singular	**ferto**	**fertor**
	2nd plural	**fertote**	——
	3rd singular	**ferto**	**fertor**
	3rd plural	**ferunto**	**feruntor**

II.7. Typically, a future imperative can be adequately translated as if it were a present imperative; if, however, the futurity of the command is being emphasized, you can add the phrase "in the future" or "for the future."

II.8. Since English is largely unfamiliar with 3rd person imperatives, the easiest translation employs the 3rd person jussive, "Let/Have him/her/it/them . . . !"
    copias dimittito!   Let/Have him dismiss the troops [for the future]!

III. Negative commands (or prohibitions) are most commonly expressed with **noli** (singular) or **nolite** (plural) plus an infinitive.
    nolite me sequi!   Don't (you [plural]) follow me!
    noli nos odisse!   Don't (you [singular]) hate us!

III.1. **Ne** usually negates future imperatives.
    copias ne dimittito!   Let him not dismiss the troops!

IV. Jussive or hortatory subjunctives (see 15.I), potential subjunctives (see 15.II), or optative subjunctives (see 15.IV) express polite commands.
    hoc temptes!   You might try this!
    ne illud faciatis!   If only you wouldn't do that!

V. Just as in English, a simple future can sometimes have the force of a command.
    hoc temptabis!   You will try this!

V.1. A future perfect can be used in this context for emphasis.
    hoc temptaveris!   You *will* try this!

20. Miscellaneous Verb Information

I. SYNCOPATED (SHORTENED) VERB FORMS

I.1. Passive 2nd person singular in the present system (see 9.VI.3)

The usual personal ending is **-ris**, but **-re** frequently occurs instead:

portare	for	**portaris**
portabare	for	**portabaris**
capere	for	**caperis**
capiere	for	**capieris**
ducēre	for	**ducēris**
ducare	for	**ducaris**
	etc.	

I.2. 3rd person plural, perfect active indicative

The usual form is **-erunt**, but in poetry and high prose style, **-ēre** often occurs instead:

portavēre	for	**portaverunt**
dixēre	for	**dixerunt**
	etc.	

I.3. Perfect active system (see 9.VI.3)

Forms of the perfect active system with **-vi-** or **-ve-** are often shortened by dropping these elements:

portasti	for	**portavisti**
portarunt	for	**portaverunt**
portarim	for	**portaverim**
audisse	for	**audivisse**
audissem	for	**audivissem**
flerunt	for	**fleverunt**
flessem	for	**flevissem**
laudarat	for	**laudaverat**
	etc.	

II. THE HISTORICAL INFINITIVE

Finite verbs in the perfect or imperfect tense are sometimes replaced in passages of historical narrative by present infinitives, which tend to highlight the specific action of the verb rather than its agent(s):

in regionibus provinciae tumultuari, spoliari, comminus pugnare.
In the regions of the province, there was rioting, there was looting, and there was hand-to-hand fighting.

II.1. The subject of a historical infinitive, as different from all other infinitives, is in the nominative case.

viri comminus pugnare.   Men fought hand to hand.

III. IMPERSONAL CONSTRUCTIONS

Such constructions are numerous and varied. Their grammar is, for the most part, simple and familiar.

III.1. Operations of nature and time of day:
  fulgurat, -are — there is lightning
  grandinat, -are — it hails
  lucescit or **luciscit, -ere** — it gets light
  ningit, -ere, ninguit — it snows
  pluit, -ere, pluit — it rains
  rorat, -are — it dews
  tonat, -are, tonuit — it thunders
  vesperascit, -ere — it grows late

III.2. The passive periphrastic of intransitive verbs (see 17.IV.2):
  currendum est.   It is necessary to run.
  effugiendum erat.   It was necessary to flee.
  veniendum nobis erit.   It will be necessary for us to come.

III.3. Neuter adjectives with the verb *to be* and infinitives:
  facile est dormire.   It is easy to sleep.
  difficile erat dormire.   It was difficult to sleep.
  commodum erit dormire.   It will be convenient to sleep.
  certum est . . .   It is resolved/decided . . .
  necesse est . . .   It is necessary . . .
  decorum est . . .   It is proper . . .

III.4. The passive of intransitive verbs (3rd person singular, no subject):
  pugnatur — there is fighting, it is fought
  pugnatum est — there was fighting, it was fought
  curritur — there is (a) running
  ventum est — there was a coming

III.5. Verbs of feeling:

miseret, -ēre, miseruit — pity, sympathize with

paenitet, -ēre, paenituit — repent, regret

piget, -ēre, piguit — disgust, annoy

pudet, -ēre, puduit or **puditum est** — shame

taedet, -ēre, taeduit or **taesum est** — weary, bore

III.5.a. The person or thing prompting the feeling of these impersonal verbs is placed in the genitive case, while the person affected goes into the accusative case.

miseret nos huius casūs.	We pity this misfortune.
taedetne te laboris?	Are you bored of work?
pudebat virum sceleris.	The man was ashamed of his crime.

III.5.b. In lieu of a genitive, the cause or origin of the feeling is sometimes expressed by a neuter pronoun, by a **quod** causal clause (see 16.XIII.3.b), or by an infinitive serving as the grammatical subject of the verb:

hoc nos piguit.	This disgusted us.
me paenitet quod eum necavi.	I repent for killing him.
cenare me taedet.	Dining bores me.

III.6. **Interest** and **rēfert**

The impersonals **interest** and **rēfert** both mean "it concerns," "it is of interest to," "it is in the interest of." They are both construed with the genitive of the person concerned and an infinitive, an **ut** clause, or a demonstrative pronoun in the neuter singular to indicate the thing that is of interest or concern.

regis interest/rēfert pugnare.	It is in the interest of the king to fight.
regis interest/rēfert ut pugnas.	It is in the interest of the king that you fight.
hoc regis interest/rēfert.	This is in the interest of the king.

III.6.a. However, in place of personal pronouns, the following adjectival forms in the ablative case are used: **meā, tuā, nostrā, vestrā, suā**. The adjectives are in fact agreeing with the noun **rē**, the first element in the word **rēfert**. The use of the ablative adjectives with **interest** is due to analogy with **rēfert**.

nostrā interest/rēfert pugnare.	It is in our interest to fight.
tuā interest/rēfert ut pugnas.	It is in your interest that you fight.
hoc meā interest/rēfert.	This is in my interest.

III.7. Other impersonals

III.7.a. With accusative and infinitive

constat, -are, constitit — it is decided, it is known, it is agreed

decet, -ēre, decuit — it is becoming; it is proper, it is fitting

iuvat, -are, iuvit — it benefits; it delights
licet, -ēre, licuit or **licitum est** — it is permitted
oportet, -ēre, oportuit — it is necessary; it is proper
placet, -ēre, placuit or **placitum est** — it pleases, it is pleasing
praestat, -are, praestitit — it is preferable, it is better

oportet eum venire.	It is necessary for him to come.
licebat eum venire.	It was permitted for him to come.
praestat eum venire.	It is better for him to come.

II.7.b. With dative and infinitive
accidit, -ere, accidit — it happens that, it is the case that
constat
contingit, -ere, contigit — it happens that, it turns out that
libet (or **lubet**), **-ēre, libuit** or **libitum est** — it pleases, it is desirable
licet
placet
superest, -esse, superfuit — it remains
vacat, -are, vacavit — there is time, there is the opportunity

superest mihi Italiam vincere.	It remains for me to conquer Italy.
licebat ei venire.	It was permitted for him to come.
accidit nobis discedere.	It happens that we are leaving.

III.7.c. With subjunctive clause introduced by **ut** (or **ne** for negation)
accidit
contingit
evenit, -ire, evēnit — it happens, it comes about, it turns out
licet
restat, -are, restitit — it remains, it is left
superest

evenit ne (nos) discedamus.
It turns out that we are not leaving.
licebat ut (is) veniret.
It was permitted for him to come.
superest ut (ego) Italiam vincam.
It remains for me to conquer Italy.

IV. Ellipsis can occur with verbs as well as with nouns (see 3.X). The verbs whose forms are most often omitted are **agere, dare, dicere, esse, facere,** and **loqui.**

21. Complete Rule for the Sequence of Tenses

I. For all participial phrases, including ablative absolutes (see section 13), the tense of the participle relates to the tense of the main verb. A present participle signifies an action roughly contemporaneous with that of the main verb, a future participle describes an action subsequent to that of the main verb, and a perfect participle defines action prior to that of the main verb.

II. For simple nonindicative sentences that are not questions or statements of fact, Latin uses the four tenses of the subjunctive plus the subjunctive of future periphrastics (see 17.VI.1) to establish distinctions of time and vividness (see 18.I.2).

II.1. The following table illustrates the sequence of tenses in independent uses of the subjunctive:

Subjunctive	*Present or Future Time*	*Past Time*
Jussive or hortatory	*Present tense*	
	amet! Let him love!	
	ametur! Let him be loved!	
Deliberative	*Present tense*	*Imperfect tense*
	quem amet?	**quem amaret?**
	Whom is he to love?	Whom was he to love?
	Whom should he love?	Whom should he have loved?
	quis ametur?	**quis ameretur?**
	Who is to be loved?	Who was to be loved?
	Who should be loved?	Who should have been loved?
Optative		
—Factual	*Present tense*	
	utinam amet.	
	If only he would love.	
	utinam ametur.	
	If only he'd be loved.	
—Contrafactual	*Imperfect tense*	*Pluperfect tense*
	utinam amaret.	**utinam amavisset.**
	If only he were loving	If only he had loved
	(but he isn't).	(but he didn't).

	utinam amaretur. If only he were being loved (but he isn't).	**utinam amatus esset.** If only he had been loved (but he wasn't).
Potential	*Present tense* **eam amet.** He would (could, might) love her.	*Imperfect tense* **eam amaret.** He would (could, might) have loved her.
	ametur. He would (could, might) be loved.	**amaretur.** He would (could, might) have been loved.

II.1.a. Note that the perfect subjunctive may be used instead of a present subjunctive to express an emphatic idea of potential:

eam non amaverit.	He would *never* love her.
non amatus sit.	He would *never* be loved.

III. In complex sentences, it is necessary both logically and semantically to establish the relative times of the main verb and the subordinate verb(s). The actions of subordinate verbs can occur roughly contemporaneously with, prior to, or subsequent to the main verb; syntax and morphology will reflect these three distinctions. The verb of the main clause is said to be in either a primary tense or a secondary tense. The primary tenses are present, future, future perfect, and, sometimes, perfect. The secondary tenses are imperfect, pluperfect, and, sometimes, perfect.

III.1. The perfective perfect, "have/has ____ed," is a primary tense; the aoristic perfect, "____ed" or "did ____," is a secondary tense.

III.2. Latin has three main types of complex sentences: conditional sentences, indirect statements, and sentences requiring the dependent uses of the subjunctive. In the first case, conditional sentences, the protasis is always prior in time to the apodosis, making the syntax quite straightforward (see section 18).

III.3. In the second case, indirect statements, three tenses of the infinitive are available to address the three different time distinctions (see section 14). The following table illustrates the use of tenses in indirect statements:

Main verb	Contemporary action Present infinitive and subjective accusative	Subsequent action Future infinitive and subjective accusative	Prior action Perfect infinitive and subjective accusative
Primary *tenses*			
scio . . . I know . . .	**eum amare.** that he loves.	**eum amaturum esse.** that he will love.	**eum amavisse.** that he loved.
	eum amari. that he is loved.	(**eum amatum iri.** that he will be loved.)	**eum amatum esse.** that he was loved.
Secondary *tenses*			
scivi . . . I knew . . .	**eum amare.** that he loved.	**eum amaturum esse.** that he would love.	**eum amavisse.** that he had loved.
	eum amari. that he was loved.	(**eum amatum iri.** that he would be loved.)	**eum amatum esse.** that he had been loved.

III.3.a. Note that the use of the future passive infinitive is quite rare.

III.3.b. Note also that the ellipsis of **esse** in the perfect passive and future active participles is very common.

III.4. In the case of dependent uses of the subjunctive, the four tenses of the subjunctive plus the subjunctive of future periphrastics (see section 16) can accommodate distinctions of time (and vividness). The basic scheme is as follows:

Tense of main verb	Tense of subjunctive
Primary: present, future, future perfect, or perfective perfect	Present: if the action is contemporary with or later than the action of the main verb
	Perfect: if the action is prior to the action of the main verb
Secondary: imperfect, aoristic perfect, or pluperfect	Imperfect: if the action is contemporary with or later than the action of the main verb
	Pluperfect: if the action is prior to the action of the main verb

If the subsequence of the subordinate verb is to be emphasized, a future periphrastic with **sim, sis, sit**, etc. (for primary sequence), or **essem, esses, esset**, etc. (secondary), is used.

III.4.a. For causal and concessive **cum** clauses (16.I), indirect questions (16.V), doubting clauses (16.VII), clauses of proviso (16.VIII), and characteristic clauses (16.X), see the following table:

Primary Tenses	Present Subjunctive	Present Periphrastic	Perfect Subjunctive
sum laetus cum . . .	amet.	amaturus sit.	amaverit.
I am happy since /			
I am happy although . . .	he loves.	he will love.	he has loved.
rogo num . . .	amet.	amaturus sit.	amaverit.
I ask whether . . .	he loves.	he will love.	he loved.
dubito an . . .	amet.	amaturus sit.	amaverit.
I doubt that . . .	he loves.	he will love.	he has loved.
sum laetus dum . . .	amet.	amaturus sit.	amaverit.
I'm happy so long as . . .	he loves.	he will love.	he has loved.
is est qui . . .	amet.	amaturus sit.	amaverit.
He's the sort who . . .	loves.	will love.	has loved.

Secondary Tenses	Imperf. Subjunctive	Imperf. Periphrastic	Plupf. Subjunctive
eram laetus cum . . .	amaret.	amaturus esset.	amavisset.
I was happy since . . . /			
I was happy although . . .	he was loving.	he would love.	he had loved.
rogavi num . . .	amaret.	amaturus esset.	amavisset.
I asked whether . . .	he was loving.	he would love.	he had loved.
dubitavi an . . .	amaret.	amaturus esset.	amavisset.
I doubted that . . .	he was loving.	he would love.	he had loved.
eram laetus dum . . .	amaret.	amaturus esset.	amavisset.
I was happy so long as . . .	he loved.	he would love.	he had loved.
is erat qui . . .	amaret.	amaturus esset.	amavisset.
He was the sort who . . .	loved.	would love.	had loved.

III.4.b. For result clauses (16.II), purpose clauses (16.III), indirect commands (16.IV), clauses of fearing (16.VI), and clauses of prevention (16.IX), see the following table:

Primary Tenses	Present Subjunctive	Present Periphrastic
est tam bonus ut . . .	amet.	amaturus sit.
He is so good . . .	that he loves.	that he will love.
venio ad eum ut . . .	amet.	amaturus sit.
I come to him . . .	in order that he (may) love.	in order that he will love.
rogo eum ut . . .	amet.	amaturus sit.
I ask him . . .	to love.	to love in the future.

timeo ut . . .	amet.	amaturus sit.
I'm afraid that . . .	he doesn't love.	he won't love.
obsto ne . . .	**amet.**	**amaturus sit.**
I hinder him from . . .	loving.	loving in the future.

Secondary Tenses	*Imperfect Subjunctive*	*Imperfect Periphrastic*
erat tam bonus ut . . .	**amaret.***	**amaturus esset.**
He was so good . . .	that he loved.	that he would love.
vēni ad eum ut . . .	**amaret.**	**amaturus esset.**
I came to him . . .	in order that he (might) love.	in order that he would love.
rogavi eum ut . . .	**amaret.**	**amaturus esset.**
I asked him . . .	to love.	to love in the future.
timebam ut . . .	**amaret.**	**amaturus esset.**
I was afraid that . . .	he didn't love.	he wouldn't love.
obstiti ne . . .	**amet.**	**amaturus esset.**
I hindered him from . . .	loving.	loving in the future.

III.4.b.i. *Note that after secondary tense verbs, result clauses may have a perfect subjunctive emphasizing the perfectiveness of the action.

> **erat tam bonus ut *amaverit*.**
>
> He was so good that he *has loved*.

III.4.c. For subordinate clauses in indirect statement (16.XI), see the following table:

Primary Tenses	*Present Subj.*	*Present Periphr.*	*Perfect Subj.*
ego eum			
amare quod . . .	**sit malus.**	**futurus sit malus.**	**fuerit malus.**
I deny that			
he loves because . . .	he is evil.	he will be evil.	he was evil.
Secondary Tenses	*Imperf. Subj.*	*Imperf. Periphr.*	*Plupf. Subj.*
negavi eum			
amare quod . . .	**esset malus.**	**futurus esset malus.**	**fuisset malus.**
I denied that			
he loved because . . .	he was evil.	he would be evil.	he had been evil.

III.4.d. For subjunctives used with other causal, comparative, concessive, and temporal conjunctions (16.XIII.1 and 16.XIII.3), see the following table:

Primary Tenses	Present Subj.	Present Periphrastic	Perfect Subjunctive
sum laetus quamvis ...	**amet.**	**amaturus sit.**	**amaverit.**
I am happy although ...	he loves.	he will love.	he has loved.
sum laetus quasi ...	**amet.**	**amaturus sit.**	**amaverit.**
I am happy as if ...	he loves.	he will love.	he has loved.
sum laetus donec ...	**amet.**	**amaturus sit.**	**amaverit.**
I am happy while ...	he may love.	he may love in the future.	he may have loved.
sum laetus quia ...	**amet.**	**amaturus sit.**	**amaverit.**
I am happy because ...	he may love.	he may love in the future.	he may have loved.
sum laetus antequam ...	**amet.**	**amaturus sit.**	**amaverit.**
I am happy before ...	he loves.	he will love.	he has loved.
Secondary Tenses	Imperf. Subj.	Imperf. Periphrastic	Plupf. Subj.
eram laetus quamvis ...	**amaret.**	**amaturus esset.**	**amavisset.**
I was happy although ...	he loved.	he would love.	he had loved.
eram laetus quasi ...	**amaret.**	**amaturus esset.**	**amavisset.**
I was happy as if ...	he loved.	he would love.	he had loved.
eram laetus donec ...	**amaret.**	**amaturus esset.**	**amavisset.**
I was happy while ...	he might love.	he might love in the future.	he might have loved.
eram laetus quia ...	**amaret.**	**amaturus esset.**	**amavisset.**
I was happy because ...	he might love.	he might love in the future.	he might have loved.
eram laetus antequam ...	**amaret.**	**amaturus esset.**	**amavisset.**
I was happy before ...	he loved.	he would love.	he had loved.

22. Overview of Dependent Clauses

Type of dependent clause (keyed to section)	Conjunction or equivalent	Negation	Mood or equivalent
14.I. Indirect statement	——	non	infinitive
16.I.1. **Cum** causal	cum	non	subjunctive
16.I.2. **Cum** concessive	cum	non	subjunctive
16.I.3. **Cum** circumstantial	cum	non	
a. past			subjunctive
b. present or future			indicative
16.I.4. **Cum** temporal	cum	non	indicative
16.I.5. **Cum** generalizing	cum	non	indicative
16.II. Result	ut	non	subjunctive
16.III.1. Purpose	ut	ne	subjunctive
16.III.2.a. Relative	relatives	ne	subjunctive
16.III.2.b. Adverbial	quō, ubi, unde	ne	subjunctive
16.III.2.c. Comparative	quō	ne	subjunctive
16.IV. Indirect command	ut	ne	subjunctive
16.V. Indirect question	interrogatives	non	subjunctive
16.VI. Fearing	ne	ut, ne non	subjunctive
16.VII. Doubting			
16.VII.1. Affirmed	num, utrum, an	——	subjunctive
16.VII.2. Negated	——	quin	subjunctive
16.VIII. Proviso	dum, modo, dummodo	ne	subjunctive
16.IX. Prevention			
16.IX.1. **Interdico, prohibeo, tardo, veto**	——	non	infinitive
16.IX.2.a. With **deterreo, impedio, moror, obsisto, obsto, officio** affirmed	quominus, ne	non	subjunctive
16.IX.2.b. With the same verbs negated	quominus, quin	non	subjunctive
16.X. Generic relative	relatives	quin, ne	subjunctive
16.XI. Subordinate clause in indirect statement	variety	non, ne, quin	subjunctive
16.XII. Attraction	variety	non, ne, quin	subjunctive
16.XIII. With conjunctions			
16.XIII.1.	quamvis, tamquam,	ne, non	subjunctive

Type of dependent clause (keyed to section)	Conjunction or equivalent	Negation	Mood or equivalent
	quasi,		
	velut or **veluti**		
16.XIII.2.	**ubi, ut** or **uti** (as, when), **postquam, quandō, cum primum, simul ac** or **simulac, simul atque** or **simulatque, quoniam, quamquam, etsi, etiamsi, tametsi, sīcut** or **sīcuti, velut** or **veluti, prout, praeut, ceu**	**non**	indicative
16.XIII.3.	**dum, donec, quamdiu, quoad, antequam, priusquam, quod, quia, quippe (qui)**	**ne, non**	subjunctive or indicative
18.I. Conditions			
18.I.1. Simple/general	**si**	**nisi, si non**	indicative
18.I.2.a. Future more vivid	**si**	**nisi, si non**	indicative
18.I.2.b. Future less vivid	**si**	**nisi, si non**	subjunctive
18.I.3. Contrafactual	**si**	**nisi, si non**	subjunctive
18.III. In subordinate clauses	**si**	**nisi, si non**	subjunctive
20.III.5–7. With impersonals			
	——	**non**	infinitive
	quod	**non**	indicative
	ut	**ne**	subjunctive

PART II

Exercises

A. Passive Voice

1. sacerdos victimam sacrificat.

2. victima sacrificatur.

3. milites turbam e viā emovent.

4. turba e viā emovetur.

5. nos multa de illā tragoediā dicimus.

6. multa de illā tragoediā dicuntur.

7. tune cupis vitam longam aut pecuniam magnam?

8. vita longa ab hominum pluribus cupitur.

9. ego vos punio quod me verberabatis.

10. vos punimini a me quod a vobis verberabar.

11. parate hoc cubiculum nunc!

12. hoc cubiculum heri parabatur.

13. diu hostis nos tenebat captivos.

14. diu nos tenebamur captivi.

15. milites te audiebant quod putant te esse callidum.

16. tu a militibus audiebaris quod tu putaris esse callidus.

17. ego hos gladios retinebo.

18. hi gladii retinebuntur.

19. cras exploratores nos invenient.

20. cras nos ab exploratoribus inveniemur.

21. noli effugere! hic canis te capiet.

22. noli effugere! tu capieris.

23. heri nos vos vicimus. hodie nos vincemur.

24. heri nos a vobis victi sumus. hodie vos vincemus.

25. olim ego hanc puellam amavi.

26. olim haec puella a me amata est.

27. Romani templum suum sine auxilio refecerunt.

28. templum Romanorum sine auxilio refectum est.

29. iuvenis nos vituperavit quod patrem necaveramus.

30. nos ab iuvene vituperati sumus quod pater eius necatus erat.

31. milites te non exspectaverunt quod imperator te ad urbem iam miserat.

32. tu non exspectatus es quod ab imperatore ad urbem iam missus eras.

33. omnis cibus consumptus erat. itaque nos discessimus.

34. exercitus non profectus est, quamquam nulla aqua inventa erat et nulli hostes visi erant.

35. ego volo amare.

36. ego volo amari.

37. nolite decipere matrem vestram!

38. mater, noli decipi!

39. non poteramus tenēre eum captivum.

40. ille captivus tenēri non poterat.

41. parentes mei dicunt uxorem me relinquere.

42. parentes mei dicunt me ab uxore relinqui.

43. parentes mei dicunt uxorem me reliquisse.

44. parentes mei dicunt me ab uxore relictum esse.

45. parentes mei dicunt uxorem me relicturam esse.

46. parentes mei dicunt me ab uxore relictum iri.

47. rex, regna! cives, regnamini! imperatores, ducite! exercitus, ducere!

48. milites, interficite aut interficimini!

49. sacerdotes mihi dixerunt, "Arruns, adora deos! custodire ab eis!"

50. nos exclamabamus, "fures, exite ex hac officinā aut verberamini his fustibus!"

B. Ablative Absolutes

1. omnibus perditis, cives tamen spem habebant.

2. infans per noctem dormire poterat, nutrice praesente.

3. senatores, Octaviano adveniente, Perusiam occupaverunt.

4. manibus extentis, hostes pacem petebant.

5. bello finituro, milites domum redire sperabant.

6. Liviā puellā, seditio orta erat in castris.

7. Roma erit fortunata, principe Traiano.

8. non difficile nautis erit, tranquillo mare, navigare.

9. invidiā crescente, sapientia dormit.

10. deo volente, nos vitam longam beatamque agemus.

11. fures, parentibus absentibus, domum nostram diripuerunt.

12. Cicerone exsule, omnes Romam amantes lacrimant.

13. vivo Scipione, viri scelesti non prosperabantur.

14. ancillā accusatā, pater erat iratissimus.

15. signo dato, auxilia oppidum cito oppugnaverunt.

16. periculis gravibus, dux tamen signum non dedit.

17. cives, urbe capturā, effugere coeperunt.

18. Nero, nullo senatore adversante, leges scelestas proponit.

19. Gn. Pompeio M. Crasso consulibus, ara nova Fortunae Athenis aedificata est.

20. exercitus victoriā potietur, Caesare imperatore.

21. quis fiet princeps, Tiberio mortuo?

22. Caesare ipso ducente, legiones fortissimē pugnabant.

23. navibus deligatis, omnes nautae domum revēnerunt.

24. omnibus paratis, mea familia ad urbem profecta est.

25. urbe a barbaris oppugnatā, bellum geremus.

26. cena parabitur, cibo empto.

27. militibus tela tradituris, nos tamen adgressi sumus.

28. Aeneas, Turno interfecto, Laviniam in matrimonium duxit.

29. iuvenes Athenaei, Theseo duce, labyrinthum intraverunt et Minotaurum vicerunt.

30. bello contrā Parthicos confecto, copiae Romanorum ad flumen contendebant.

C. Indirect Statement

I.

Give precise translations of the following sentences.

1. **Marcus dicit Arruntem tabernam renovare.**

2. **ego putavi Arruntem tabernam renovaturum esse.**

3. **Sarmillus exclamat Arruntem mox rem prosperē acturum esse.**

4. **nos credimus Arruntem esse probum et honestum.**

5. **meus pater scripsit matrem advēnisse salvam.**

6. **servi respondebant regem non posse nos nunc vidēre.**

7. **uxor Calvii postulat ancillas esse diligentiores.**

8. **vosne speratis tempestatem naves obruisse?**

9. **placet mihi scire meos inimicos esse mortuos.**

10. **nos diximus facile esse dormire.**

11. **nos diximus facile fuisse dormire.**

12. **nos diximus facile futurum esse dormire.**

13. **noli tuae matri narrare nos fregisse hanc sellam!**

14. **vilicus expostulavit servos non laboraturos esse post cenam.**

15. **Ballio dixit Tranionem bibisse vinum, sed Tranio id negavit.**

16. **Ballio dixit Tranionem bibisse vinum, sed eum id negaturum esse.**

17. **iratus pauper clamavit esse diviti Sarmillo multas villas et pecuniam.**

18. **Quinctius commemoravit illam cladem interfecisse suum patrem matremque.**

19. **di immortales signum mittunt montem mox erupturum esse.**

20. **cras militibus nuntiabo eos accepturos esse nullos aureos.**

II.

Supply the correct Latin form(s) of the word(s) in parentheses and translate each sentence.

1. **Domitilla non putat** (that the slave girl) **confecturam esse rem.**

2. **ego scio Marcum** (is better) **quam Lucium.**

3. **Marcus ad nos scripsit Arruntem officinam** (had repaired).

4. **necesse est tibi intellegere** (that a brave man) **esse rarum.**

5. **exploratores nuntiaverunt regem regionem mox** (would leave).

D. Uses of the Subjunctive

I. 15.I–IV and 16.I–II

1. **pueri tam celeriter cucurrerunt—crederes eos esse equos—ut a militibus capi non possent.** (15.II, 16.II)

2. **amor vincit omnia: et igitur nos cedamus amori!** (15.I)

3. **conarer fieri poeta, sed scribere et legere nescio.** (15.II)

4. **gaudeamus quod hodiē est dies natalis imperatoris nostri!** (15.I)

5. **hic servus est tam ebrius ut stultissimē loquatur.** (16.II)

6. **illa puella me amet! ego eam tantum amo ut insanus fiam.** (15.I, 16.II)

7. **legatus periculum tam diu timebat ut tandem exercitum relinqueret.** (16.II)

8. **tali voce locutus sum ut non audirer.** (16.II)

9. **milites adeō fortiter pugnabant ut facile vincerent.** (16.II)

10. **turba est tanta ut meam sororem invenire non possimus.** (16.II)

11. **deus virtutem mihi det! ego hac virtute optimē utar.** (15.I)

12. **urbs nostra est tam pulchra ut multi homines ad eam visitent.** (16.II)

13. **tanta erat difficultas ut villas nostras relinquere nollemus.** (16.II)

14. **cives regi tot dona tulerant ut totum palatium complērent.** (16.II)

15. **ne mentiamur! ne patrem decipiamus! conemur esse probi!** (15.I)

16. **sacra serpens erat tam mansueta ut Tullia eam tangere posset.** (16.II)

17. **cum periculum timuerim, ex urbe proficiscor.** (16.I)

18. **cum periculum timeam, ex urbe proficiscor.** (16.I)

19. **cum periculum timuissem, ex urbe profectus sum.** (16.I)

20. **cum periculum timērem, ex urbe proficiscebar.** (16.I)

21. **meus dominus appellavit me ignavum et furem. quid ei dicerem? quomodo me gererem?** (15.III)

22. **mater non vult nos Romam venire. cur patrem nostrum non visitemus? utinam mater ne sit tam crudelis!** (15.III, 15.IV)

23. **utinam Caesar hac nocte adveniat! magnum exercitum ducat! quid aliud dicam? utinam Caesar nos timore solvat!** (15.IV, 15.I, 15.III)

24. **Caesar non advēnit. o miseros nos! utinam nostri ne oblitus esset! urbem nostram hostibus tradidimus. quid aliud ageremus?** (15.IV, 15.III)

25. **contendo semper ad forum, cum Romam vēni.** (16.I)

26. **cum mater mortua est, in Syriā militabam.** (16.I)

27. **nautae, cum Cyclops apparuisset, magnopere terrebantur.** (16.I)

28. **Scipio, cum Hannibal se traderet, maximam clementiam demonstrabat.** (16.I)

29. **cum Minotaurus sit terribilis, Theseus tamen labyrinthum intrare vult.** (16.I)

30. For all the **cum** clauses above (17–20, 25–29), identify the type (causal, concessive, circumstantial, temporal, or generalizing).

II. 16.III–IX

1. **operae Titio appropinquabant qui necarent.** (16.III)

2. **Statius, monte Vesuvio erupto, e Campaniā effūgit ne interficeretur.** (16.III)

3. **manēre constituimus dummodo tempestas esset tam saeva.** (16.VIII)

4. **dum Cicero Romae sit, populus non timebit.** (16.VIII)

5. **ne Ciceronem populus laudet, modo consilia eius capiat.** (15.I, 16.VIII)

6. **Caesar ad Italiam hieme semper revēnit tantum ne esset aut aeger aut occupatus.** (16.VIII)

7. **Antonius erit fidelis Caesari tantum ut Caesar sit liberalior hostibus suis.** (16.VIII)

8. **timebamus ut iuvenes legibus novis parērent.** (16.VI)

9. **verebamur ut milites urbem nostram cum celeritate defenderent.** (16.VI)

10. **metuo ne mea uxor ante me moritura sit.** (16.VI)

11. **metuo ne mea uxor ante me non moritura sit.** (16.VI)

12. **formidasne ne finis omnium rerum sit proximus?** (16.VI)

13. **dubium non erat quin Antonius esset carus Caesari.** (16.VII)

14. **dubitare voluit num hostes nostrum oppidum vicissent.** (16.VII)

15. **dubitare voluit cum hostes nostrum oppidum vicissent.** (16.I)

16. **dubito tibi dicere tuum fratrem ab hostibus interfectum esse.** (16.VII)

17. **estne dubium ullum quin Caesar fuerit magnus imperator?** (16.VII)

18. **non dubitandum est quin Homerus ante Sophoclem vixerit.** (16.VII)

19. **dubitavi an Cicero fuisset optimus orator illo tempore.** (16.VII)

20. **domina nos prohibuit vinum bibere et cibum consumere.** (16.IX)

21. **pudor me deterret ne facta impia Neronis enumerem.** (16.IX)

22. **Cicero Catilinae obstitit quominus rem publicam delēret.** (16.IX)

23. **vos vetare non possum amicas vestras visere, quod estis non diutius pueri.** (16.IX)

24. **Caesar Ciceronem non impedivit quin multos et magnos honores sibi caperet.** (16.IX)

25. **Livia nobis narrabat quomodo Romani Gallicas gentes superavissent.** (16.V)

26. **magister discipulis imperabit ut saepius studeant.** (16.IV)

27. **Medea Iasonem hortata est ut Argonautae Colchidem quam celerrimē relinquerent.** (16.IV)

28. **si vultis, nunc date mihi illam pecuniam ne amittatis.** (16.III)

29. **non diutius praevaricari potes. mater tua quem ames scit.** (16.V)

30. **pete ne invenias quendam candidatum meliorem Caesare.** (16.IV)

31. **avus noster non certē scit quo anno natus sit.** (16.V)

32. **Orpheus ad infernos iit quō plus dierum cum uxore precaretur.** (16.III)

33. **mercatores multa loca visitant unde metalla importent.** (16.III)

III. 16.X–XIII

1. **Cicero erat solus quin rem publicam hostibus traderet.** (16.X)

2. **estne nemo qui amicitiam et fidem miretur?** (16.X)

3. **in Germaniā nihil est quod dices esse elegans.** (16.X)

4. **illi sunt qui Homerum fuisse meliorem poetam Vergilio arbitrentur.** (16.X)

5. **quis est quin Caesarem et exercitum eius timeat?** (16.X)

6. **hae feminae sunt quae poeticis et musicis artibus faveant.** (16.X)

7. **dum amicam meam amabam, amica alium amabat.** (16.XIII)

8. **quamvis amica alium amaret, ego tamen eam amavi.** (16.XIII)

9. prius ab amicā discessi quam me odisse inciperet. (16.XIII)

10. ut discedebam, amica lacrimavit quia me amaret. (16.XIII)

11. amicam aliam numquam habebo donec aliquam fidelem inveniam. (16.XIII)

12. inquisiverunt quibus occurrissem postquam in Hispaniam pervēnissem. (16.V, 16.XII)

13. credimus nos salvos fore simulatque portum conspiciamus. (16.XI)

14. urbs tot hominibus complebatur ut ad forum ire non possem ubi pater laboraret. (16.II, 16.XII)

15. Medusa sentit Perseum appropinquare qui velit eam necare. (16.XI)

16. turba Ciceronem laudavit, non quod hostem superavisset, sed quia rem publicam servavit. (16.XIII)

17. senatores laudaverunt Ciceronem quoniam optimus consul erat. (16.XIII)

18. etsi populus senatusque Ciceronem laudaverunt, magnā cum ignominiā mortuus est. (16.XIII)

19. Antonius crudelia facta erga Ciceronem vivum et, postquam hic mortuus erat, etiam crudeliora erga corpus eius ille fecit. (16.XIII)

20. Antonius corpus Ciceronis tractavit sīcut lanius bovem trucidat. (16.XIII)

21. corpus caput et manūs amputatum est, quippe quae essent partes corporis quibus Cicero iniuriam Antonio intulisset. (16.XIII, 16.XII)

22. Cicero, postquam orationes contra Antonium capite suo composuerat atque manibus suis exscripserat, suā linguā elocutus est. (16.XIII)

23. Cicero maximus omnium Romanorum vixit, sed mortuus est veluti fuisset pessimus hostis Romae. (16.XIII)

24. dum manetis quattuor dies Athenis, iter periculosum Epidaurum fecimus. (16.XIII)

25. simulac Epidaurum advēnimus, ad templum Aesculapii contendimus. (16.XIII)

26. audivimus sacram serpentem esse in hōc templo, quamquam nemo eam diū vīdisset. (16.XI)

27. cum primum ad templum vēnimus, spectavimus quoad sacerdotes sacrificia faciebant. (16.I, 16.XIII)

28. subitō illa serpens apparuit. o felicem diem! stetimus taciti tamquam miraculum vīdissemus. (16.XIII)

29. praeter nos serpens placidē lapsa est prout multi angues solent. (16.XIII)

30. ceu apparuerat, serpens subitō vanuit antequam sacerdotes eam tenēre conarentur. (16.XIII)

31. tametsi serpentem diū non spectavimus, eramus fortunati quandō rarissimam omnium bestiarum conspexeramus. (16.XIII)

32. ubi Athenas revēnimus, nemo credebat nos serpentem vīdisse. (16.XIII)

33. sed dum vivam, serpentis sacrae numquam obliviscar quamvis totae Athenae me mendacem appellent. (16.VIII, 16.XIII)

IV. 15–16

1. mater videt amphoram vini e cellā deficere ubi omnis cibus vinumque serventur, et quaerit quis eam abstulerit. (16.XI, 16.V)

2. cum meus paedagogus senex Parmenio sit praecipuē bibulosus, mater eum vini ablati accusat. (16.I)

3. Parmenio negat se amphoram cepisse, sed mater nescit ab quo nisi a Parmenione vinum ablatum sit. (16.V)

4. cum ego cogitam Parmenionem amphoram probabiliter cēpisse quod bibendum amet, matri tamen dico eum esse innocentem qui semper fuerit fidelis familiae nostrae. (16.I, 16.XI)

5. inquam, "mater cara, scis quotiens Parmenio me fideliter custodiverit ubi essem parvus." (16.V, 16.XII)

6. mater autem rogat utrum certa indicia innocentiae eius habeam. (16.V)

7. cum negem me habēre, mater constituit se graviter punituram Parmenionem esse quod sit nocens. (16.I, 16.XI)

8. interea aperitur ancillam, quae sit ornatrix, amphoram vini abstulisse. (16.XI)

---

9. historicus Philo quietam vitam vivere vult ut annales scribat. (16.III)

10. Potidea, uxor Philonis, tot amicas ad villam semper invitat ut Philo vexetur et scribere non possit. (16.II)

11. Charita, filia Philonis, amicos quoque invitat qui ad villam veniant. (16.III)

12. amici Charitae sunt causidici et orationes semper habent, sed hi iuvenes sunt adeō mali causidici ut Philo saepe fiat iratus aut quasi aeger. (16.II)

13. dicas illos amicos Charitae esse caudices, non causidici. (15.II)

14. iuvenibus orationes habentibus, Philo conatur esse politus ne filia sua offendatur. (16.III)

15. Philone etiam polito, causidici inter se totiens iurgant ut expellendi sint e villā. (16.II)

16. Philo orat ut causidici pessimi ei quietem dent: "liceat mihi vivere in pace! scribam meas annales ut ego proelia iuvenum in libris meis solum cogitem!" (16.IV, 15.I, 16.III)

17. uxor Potidea verba ultima offert: "senex care, quam stultus es! scis certissimē hoc: si uxorem et liberos pulchros habes, in pace vivere numquam potes."

18. post diem illum, Philo annales scribere non rursus temptavit. quietem tamen in silentio suo inveniebat.

———

19. iuvenis quidam, quia novam domum emere volebat, veterem villam inspexit quae multos annos deserta erat. (16.XIII)

20. etiamsi villa erat paene ruinosa, sine bonā causā iuveni placuit. (16.XIII)

21. itaque iuvenis eam emit et gaudebat quasi palatium opulentum adeptus esset. (16.XIII)

22. primā nocte in hac villā, postquam omnes res suas in eam moverat, cubitum iit contentus. (16.XIII)

23. sed mediā nocte, ubi obdormiverat, iuvenis clamore insolito excitatus est. (16.XIII)

24. iuvenis veritus est ne fur esset in villā, dum tunicam induit. (16.VI, 16.XIII)

25. e cubiculo exiit et tablinum intravit quod putavit clamorem inde exortum esse. (16.XIII)

26. in angulo tablini iuvenis larvam vīdit. iuvenis non erat perterritus tametsi credidit larvas non esse nihil. (16.XIII)

27. larva erat senex qui vestimenta pannosa et cruenta gestabat et lacrimabat.

28. iuvenis, simulatque virtutem receperat, senem rogavit cur lacrimaret. (16.XIII, 16.V)

29. tamquam esset vivus, larva respondit, "olim eram clarus philosophus." (16.XIII)

30. "quamvis multos et bonos discipulos habērem, erat unus discipulus pessimus mihi qui meam vitam semper perdebat." (16.XIII)

31. "quodam die iste discipulus dixit mihi se me necaturum esse, quippe ego meos optimos libros sibi non dedissem." (16.XI)

32. "posteā ego meos optimos libros sub pavimento in cubiculo meo celavi."

33. "postquam discipulus hanc villam diripuerat et quia nihil invēnisset, me necavit." (16.XIII)

34. "sepelivit meum corpus post villam et ex hac urbe effūgit, quamquam nemo scivit eum me interfecisse." (16.XIII)

35. larva dixit se non laetum multos annos fuisse quia libri sui secum non sepulti essent. (16.XI)

36. itaque iuvenis, cum primum libros in cubiculo invēnerat, eos post villam sepelivit. (16.XIII)

37. post illud tempus iuvenis larvam numquam iterum aut vīdit aut audivit, dum in illā villā habitat. (16.XIII)

———

38. Marco apud meos parentes manente, coniuratio talis inter servos fiebat ut periculum esset magnum. (16.II)

39. Marcus meum patrem matremque hortatus est ut essent benigniores in servos. (16.IV)

40. Marco hortato, pater erat benevolens in servos quo diligentius laborarent. (16.III)

41. Rutulius loquebatur, "laboremus! omnis servus opere suo fungatur! omnis ancilla sit occupata!" (15.I)

42. Rutulius tamen servis non persuasit ut laborarent. (16.IV)

———

43. Antonius quosdam viros miserat qui Ciceronem verberarent et necarent. (16.III)

44. Antonius his viris dixerat Ciceronem verberandum eis esse ut Cicero pecuniam suam traderet. (16.III)

45. Cicero oravit ne viri se verberarent. (16.IV)

46. negavit se verberandum viris esse quod esset bonus homo. (16.XI)

47. Cicero mirabatur cur hi viri essent adeō inimici. (16.V)

48. viri Ciceronem tantum verberaverunt ut ambulare vix posset. (16.II)

49. crederes illos viros esse bestias. (15.II)

50. cum viri Ciceronem verberarent, servus eius auxilium petebat. (16.I)

51. Cicero viris dixit, "cum Octavianus apparebit, vos me non verberabitis." (16.I)

52. Cicero negavit viros se verberaturos esse cum Octavianus appareret. (16.XI)

53. cum Octavianus apparuit, viri Ciceronem verberabant. (16.I)

54. Octaviano adveniente, viri Ciceronem verberabant.

55. cum Octavianus advenisset, viri non diutius Ciceronem verberaverunt. (16.I)

56. Cicero iterum miratus est cur viri fuissent adeō inimici. (16.V)

––––––––––

For the following sentences, identify the various uses of the subjunctive and translate accordingly:

57. Gorgona Praxinoaque, duae Alexandrinae feminae, festinant ut pompam spectent.

58. cum Praxinoae infans curandus sit, ancilla Eunoa ad pompam adire non potest.

59. Gorgona rogat cur Eunoa ad pompam adire non possit.

60. Praxinoa respondet manendum Eunoae esse quod infans fuerit aeger.

61. cum feminae discedere incipiunt, de suis maritis loquuntur.

62. Praxinoa dicit maritum suum esse tam stultum ut ēmerit tunicas sordidas.

63. Gorgona admonet ne Praxinoa marito maledicat.

64. Gorgona dicit, "te maledicente, infans omnia verba intellegit. putes infantem esse callidiorem quam nos. coram eo ne diutius loquamur!"

65. cum constituant non diutius loqui, discedunt e villā unde ad pompam festinent.

E. Gerunds, Supines, Gerundives, and Periphrastics

1. est nobis spes habendi pecuniam.

2. discipuli dona tulerunt blandiendi magistro causā.

3. nos pompam visum festinabamus.

4. festinantes pompam visuri eramus.

5. nos ad pompam videndam festinabamus.

6. hoc opus erat difficile factū.

7. Herodas est rex potens et optimus rectū.

8. omnes mariti uxoresque artem amandi scire debent.

9. fortasse maritus uxorque artem amandi cognituri sunt.

10. iuvenes ad bestias interficiendas profecti erant.

11. iuvenes ad bestias interficiendas profecturi erant.

12. ancilla erat anxia de cantando.

13. imperator Germaniam in pace mittendo plures militum retinuit.

14. viri scelesti ad pecuniam postulandam vēnerunt.

15. viri scelesti ad pecuniam postulandam venturi sunt.

16. haec fabula est nimis incredibilis dictū.

17. ille imperator de bello gerendo bene scivit.

18. hic imperator de bello gerendo bene sciturus est.

19. Hercules ad palatium visitandi regem Admetum causā adgrediebatur.

20. erit vobis discendum de Caesare et exercitū eius.

21. Antonius iam discesserat, et Octavianus erat discessurus.

22. remanendum Tiberio est in quo loco exploratores aquam reppererunt.

23. servi relinquendi erant quod satis cibi reperiri non poterat.

F. Conditional Sentences I

1. nisi pluit, est difficile agricolis bene vivere.

2. pater meam sororem parvam portabat, si currendum nobis erat.

3. si tuā rēfert Romam venire, mitte ad me brevem epistulam!

4. cotidiē ad amphitheatrum cum Gaio veniebam nisi eum taedebat spectacula spectare.

5. si oportebat medicum dormire, descendebat de equo et iacebat sub arbore.

6. licuit ut Caesar iter faceret si praestabat se non esse solum.

7. si accidit ut pecuniae meae domi obliviscar, remitte servum qui eam afferat.

8. superfuit tamen Ciceroni populo persuadēre, si senatui iam persuaserat.

9. si certum est cras nos discessuros esse, necesse est mihi nunc valedicere meis parentibus.

10. Paulus erat fortis et fidelis miles nisi tonabat atque fulgurabat.

11. si placebit tibi Romam cras advenire, nunc discedendum nobis erit.

12. eveniet ut Tiberius fiat imperator, si Augustus mox morietur.

13. si pudebit te quod pater fuerit fur, numquam eris laetus.

14. id Caesari intererit, si Antonius filiam eius in matrimonium ducere cupiet.

15. nisi mox lucescet, libebit civibus effugere et tradere urbem.

16. si ningat, omne frumentum agricolarum deleatur.

17. indecorum matronis non sit maritos relinquere, si hi iniurias illis inferant.

18. nisi Caesar sit liberalis et iustus, in viis Romae pugnetur.

19. si eveniat ut Antonius Ciceronem necet, ego mortem illius statim postulem.

20. restat ut Aemilia et Ioanna Graecam linguam discant, si cupiant esse callidissimae omnium discipulorum in ludo suo.

21. Caesar multos annos vixisset nisi tam neglegens fuisset.

22. si Caesar esset vivus hodiē, putaret ducem nostrum esse caudicem.

23. si nostrā rēferret vendere tabernam, id statim agerem.

24. meus pater esset pauper, si Alexandriae mansisset et fuisset sacerdos in templo Isidis.

25. si nautae essent probi, tantum pecuniae non poscerent.

26. vobis numquam credidissem, nisi ego ipse serpentem sacram conspexissem.

27. si sit Quartae aufugiendum, sola domi maneat.

28. senatores fuissent iratissimi, si evenisset ut Antonius veniret.

29. si tu esses callidus, regem interficeres atque reginam in matrimonium duceres.

30. nisi ningeret et si viae essent meliores, iter Romam faceremus.

G. Conditional Sentences II

1. Cicero sibi putat, "nisi Caesar sit Romae, populus gaudeat."

2. Cicero putat si Caesar non sit Romae, populum gavisurum esse.

3. Cicero sibi putavit, "si Caesar non esset Romae, populus gaudēret."

4. Cicero putavit si Caesar non esset Romae, populum gavisurus fuisse.

5. si rex dormiebat, regina saltavit.

6. nos scivimus si rex dormiret, reginam saltare.

7. si Antonius discedat, urbs pacem habeat.

8. senatores senserunt si Antonius discesserit, urbem pacem habituram esse.

9. si Antonius discessit, urbs pacem habebat.

10. senatores senserunt si Antonius discessisset, urbem pacem habuisse.

11. ego iubeo, "si tuus pater loquitur, audi!"

12. ego iubeo si tuus pater loqueretur, te audire.

13. ego iubeo, "si tuus pater loquatur, audiendus tibi sit."

14. ego iubeo si tuus pater loquatur, eum a te auditum iri.

15. ego iubeo, "si tuus pater locutus est, parendum est."

16. ego iubeo si tuus pater locutus esset, parendum esse.

17. Augustus promittit, "ego rem republicam restituam, si cives consentient."

18. Augustus promittit se rem publicam restituturum esse, si cives consentiant.

19. Augustus promiserat, "ego rem republicam restituam, si cives consentient."

20. Augustus promiserat se rem publicam restituturum esse, si cives consenserint.

21. Tiberius dicit, "si sim benignior, provinciae non rebellent."

22. Tiberius dicit si sit benignior, provincias non rebellaturas esse.

23. Tiberius dicit, "si fuissem benignior, provinciae non rebellavissent."

24. Tiberius dicit si fuisset benignior, provincias non rebellaturas fuisse.

25. Caesar auxilium ferret, si bellum conficeretur.

26. cognovimus Caesarem auxilium laturum fuisse, si bellum conficeretur.

27. Caesar auxilium tulisset, si bellum confectum esset.

28. cognovimus Caesarem auxilium laturum fuisse, si bellum confectum esset.

29. si nautae maiorem partem praedae postulabunt, regina alios conducet.

30. legatus nuntiat si nautae maiorem partem praedae postulent, reginam alios conducturam esse.

31. si nautae maiorem partem praedae postulant, regina alios conducit.

32. legatus nuntiat si nautae maiorem praedae postularent, reginam alios conducere.

33. si nautae maiorem partem praedae postularent, regina alios conduceret.

34. legatus nuntiat si nautae maiorem partem praedae postularent, reginam alios conducturam fuisse.

35. Vergilius carmina peiora composuisset, nisi in Graeciā doctus esset.

36. respondendum est Vergilium carmina peiora compositurum fuisse nisi in Graeciā doctus esset.

37. datisne cibum bonum si Cicero est in carcere?

38. rogamus utrum detis cibum bonum si Cicero esset in carcere.

39. detisne cibum bonum si Cicero sit in carcere?

40. rogamus utrum detis cibum bonum si Cicero sit in carcere.

41. daretisne cibum bonum si Cicero esset in carcere?

42. rogamus utrum daretis cibum bonum si Cicero esset in carcere.

43. si nos Romam veniamus, fabulas in theatro videamus.

44. non dubitavimus quin si Romam vēnerīmus, fabulas in theatro vidēremus.

45. si Caesar Germaniam invadet, Germani vincent.

46. evenit ut, si Caesar Germaniam invadat, Germani vincant.

PART III

Annotated Readings

A. Animals and Nature

Prose Readings

1.

This story is told about the extraordinary horse of Alexander the Great, Bucephalas, whose name means "bull head."

READING FOR INFORMATION
1. *After he was decked out for battle, what did Bucephalas refuse to allow?*
2. *After Bucephalas had suffered many wounds, what did he do for Alexander?*
3. *How did Alexander memorialize Bucephalas for his faithful service?*

capite: 3.V.7
**emptum esse,
donatum esse:**
14.II

equo: 3.V.20
memoriā: 3.V.16
ubi: 16.XIII.2.a
passus sit:
16.XIII.3.b.i
cum: 16.I.2

coniectis . . . telis:
13.III.3
vulneribus: 3.V.14

ubi: 16.XIII.2.a

solacio: 3.V.3

partā . . . victoriā:
13.III.1

Equus Alexandri regis capite "Bucephalas" fuit appellatus. Emptum esse quidam scriptor scripsit talentis tredecim et regi Philippo donatum esse; hoc autem aeris nostri summa est sestertia trecenta duodecim. Super hōc equo dignum memoriā est visum, quod, ubi ornatus erat armatusque ad proelium, haud umquam inscendi sese ab alio nisi ab rege passus sit. Id etiam de isto equo memoratum est, quod, cum insidens in eo Alexander bello Indico et facinora faciens fortia, in hostium cuneum non satis sibi providens immisisset, coniectisque undique in Alexandrum telis, vulneribus altis in cervice atque in latere equus perfossus esset, moribundus tamen ac prope iam exsanguis e mediis hostibus regem vivacissimo cursū retulit atque, ubi eum extra tela extulerat, ilicō concidit et, domini iam superstitis securus, quasi cum sensūs humani solacio, animam exspiravit. Tum rex Alexander, partā eius belli victoriā, oppidum in isdem locis condidit idque ob equi honores "Bucephalon" appellavit.

talentum, -i — Greek talent	**facinus, -oris** — deed	**exsanguis, -e** — weak from
sestertium, -i — one thou-	**cuneus, -i** — battle wedge	blood loss
sand sesterces	**provideo, -ēre** — look out for	**vivax, -acis** — lively
trecenti, -ae, -a — three	**immitto, -ere** — drive into	**ilicō** — on the spot
hundred	**conicio, -ere** — hurl	**concido, -ere** — collapse
orno, -are — decorate	**cervix, -icis** — neck	**superstes, -stitis** — surviving
inscendo, -ere — mount	**latus, -eris** — flank	**solacium, -i** — relief
passus sit < **patior**	**perfodio, -ere** — pierce	**exspiro, -are** — perish
memoro, -are — recall	**moribundus, -a, -um** —	**parta** < **pario**
insideo, -ēre — sit on	about to die	**ob** — for the sake of

READING FOR UNDERSTANDING

1. *Stories of animal loyalty, especially those that end in death, are always very touching. Why, when a story also involves someone famous, is it even more popular? Why do the animal rights and animal welfare organizations in our culture rely so heavily on celebrities?*

2. *Alexander the Great's courage in the face of battle was legendary. Bucephalas's protectiveness of one who verged on the reckless also seems legendary. Do you suppose these traits became exaggerated? Why?*

3. *The amount paid for Bucephalas (13 talents, or 312,000 sesterces) was astoundingly high. From the standpoint of storytelling, is it a better tale that the horse was very expensive, or should he have been cheap and of no evident value?*

2.

This story narrates an incident early in the reign (14–37 CE) of the emperor Tiberius. It involves a raven that became something of a neighborhood celebrity, until it met a heinous death.

READING FOR INFORMATION

1. *According to the story, which three Romans did the raven greet by name?*
2. *Who killed the raven? Why did he do it?*
3. *What happened to the killer in the aftermath? What happened to the raven?*

Tiberio principe: 13.III.1 **ex fetū:** 3.V.18 **religione:** 3.V.7 **officinae:** 3.II.6 **domino:** 3.III.3 **sermoni:** 3.III.7 **matutinis:** 3.V.6 **versus:** 3.I.2 **plurium:** genitive plural **officio:** 5.V.7 **aemulatione, iracundiā:** 5.V.7 **excrementis:** 3.V.17 **calceis:** 3.III.7 **impositā...maculā:** 13.III.2 **consternatione:** 3.V.7 **ut:** 16.II **praecedente...coronis:** 3.V.14	Tiberio principe, ex fetū cornicum supra Castorum aedem genito pullus in appositam sutrinam devolavit, etiam religione commendatus officinae domino. Is corvus maturē sermoni adsuefactus, omnibus matutinis evolans, in rostra in forum versus, Tiberium, dein Germanicum et Drusum Caesares nominatim, mox transeuntem populum Romanum salutabat, posteā ad tabernam remeans, plurium annorum adsiduo officio mirus. Hunc sive aemulatione vicinitatis manceps proximae sutrinae sive iracundiā subitā, ut voluit vidēri, excrementis eius impositā calceis maculā, exanimavit, tantā plebei consternatione, ut primo pulsus ex eā regione, mox interemptus sit; funusque aliti innumeris celebratum sit exsequiis, constratus sit lectus super Aethiopum duorum umeros, praecedente tibicine et coronis omnium generum ad rogum usque. Ingenium avis adeō satis iusta causa populo Romano visum est exsequiarum aut supplicii de cive Romano.

fetus, -ūs — brood	**appono, -ere** — place nearby	**adsuefacio, -ere** — train
supra — above	**sutrina, -ae** — shoe store	**matutinum, -i** — morning
Castores, -um — the gods Castor and Pollux	**devolo, -are** — fly down from	**evolo, -are** — fly out
	commendo, -are — entrust	**rostra, -orum** = the forum
genitus < **gigno**	**officina, -ae** — shop	**Germanicus Caesar** — the emperor's nephew
pullus, -i — young bird	**maturē** — from an early age	

Drusus Caesar — the emperor's son

nominatim — by name

remeo, -are — return

adsiduus, -a, -um — unwavering

aemulatio, -onis — jealousy

vicinitas, -tatis — neighborhood

manceps, -ipitis — owner

excrementum, -i — droppings

calceus, -i — shoe

macula, -ae — stain

exanimo, -are — kill

consternatio, -onis — dismay

pulsus < **pello**

interimo, -ere — kill

innumerus, -a, -um — countless

exsequiae, -arum — funeral rites

consterno, -ere — lay, spread

praecedo, -ere — precede

tibicens, -inis — flute player

supplicium, -i — execution

READING FOR UNDERSTANDING

1. *The means of death were related for neither the bird nor the rival cobbler. Why not?*
2. *Would the story seem less remarkable if it didn't involve members of the imperial family?*
3. *The Romans commonly practiced augury and auspicy (divination from the flight and behavior of birds). How does this fact help explain the attention paid to this story's raven, both in life and in death?*

3.

The renegade Sertorius (1st century BCE) fomented a dangerous uprising against the Romans on the Iberian Peninsula. As a former Roman officer, he knew the weaknesses of Roman legions.

READING FOR INFORMATION

1. *How did the Lusitanians want to fight the Romans? Did Sertorius agree with this strategy?*
2. *To illustrate his point, Sertorius used which four figures?*
3. *According to the author, why was this illustration effective after argument had failed?*

robore, consilio: 3.V.10
proscriptione: 3.V.7
cum: 16.I.1
oratione: 3.V.1
ne: 16.III.1
acie: 3.V.1
consilio: 3.V.1
ab, a: 3.V.2
carpi, convelli: 14.II
imperio: 3.III.5
obtemperatum est: 20.III.4
labore: 3.V.7
fatigat: 16.XIII.3.a.i.A.1
senio: 3.III.3
contioni: 3.III.7
tenderet: 16.V
cognoscere: 12.I.3.b
caudae: 3.III.2
possit: 16.XI
celerius: 6.II.2
tradiderit, occupaverit: 16.XI
regi: 12.I
auribus, oculis: 3.V.1

Sertorius verō, corporis robore atque animi consilio parem naturae indulgentiam expertus, proscriptione Sullanā dux Lusitanorum fieri coactus, cum eos oratione flectere non posset ne cum Romanis universā acie confligere vellent, vafro consilio ad suam sententiam perduxit: duos enim in conspectū eorum constituit equos, validissimum alterum, alterum infirmissimum, ac deinde equi validi caudam ab imbecillo sene paulatim carpi; caudam infirmi a iuvene eximiarum virium universam convelli iussit. Obtemperatum imperio est. Sed dum adulescentis dextera se irrito labore fatigat, senio confecta manus ministerium exsecuta est. Tunc barbarae contioni, quorsum ea res tenderet cognoscere cupienti, subicit equi caudae consimilem esse Romanum exercitum, cuius partes aliquis adgrediens opprimere possit, universum conatus prosternere celerius tradiderit victoriam quam occupaverit. Ita gens barbara, aspera et regi difficilis, in exitium suum ruens, quam utilitatem auribus respuerat, oculis pervīdit.

robur, -oris — strength

indulgentia, -ae — endowment

expertus, -a, -um — having experienced

proscriptio, -onis — proscription

Sullanus, -a, -um — Sullan, by L. Sulla

Lusitani, -orum — the Portuguese

cogo, -ere — force

flecto, -ere — sway

confligo, -ere — attack

vafer, -fra, -frum — clever

infirmus, -a, -um — weak

cauda, -ae — tail

imbecillus, -a, -um — feeble

paulatim — gradually

carpo, -ere — pluck

eximius, -a, -um — exceptional

convello, -ere — yank off

obtempero, -are — obey

irritus, -a, -um — useless

conficio, -ere — wear out

ministerium, -i — task

exsequor, -i — complete

barbarus, -a, -um — barbarian

contio, -onis — assembly

quorsum — to what end

tendo, -ere — aim, tend

subicio, -ere — answer

consimilis, -e — like

opprimo, -ere — attack

prosterno, -ere — lay low

occupo, -are — seize, attain

asper, -era, -erum — savage

exitium, -i — ruin

utilitas, -tatis — usefulness

respuo, -ere — reject

pervideo, -ēre — perceive

READING FOR UNDERSTANDING

1. *The value of* **utilitas** (*last sentence*) *seems to characterize this entire passage. What regard was given to the pain inflicted on the horses?*

2. *What practical uses were horses put to in ancient warfare? Were they counted among war's casualties?*

3. *Do you suppose Sertorius would have given up his own horse for this illustration? Why or why not?*

4.

The story of the musician Arion, made famous by the Greek historian Herodotus, is recounted here. As his story begins, Arion travels the ancient Mediterranean, seeking—and making—his fortune. But then his life takes a dangerous turn.

READING FOR INFORMATION

1. *Arion was from what Greek island?*

2. *He became famous in what Greek city? Who was his royal patron there?*

3. *What two lands did Arion then visit, to make a greater name and more money for himself?*

4. *What did the Corinthian sailors plan for him?*

elocutione: 3.V.3.b

fidibus: 3.V.10

loco, oppido: 3.V.10
terrā, insulā: 3.V.10

gratiā: 8.III

Elocutione tereti et candidā fabulam scripsit Herodotus super fidicine illo Arione. "Vetus," inquit, "et nobilis Arion cantator fidibus fuit. Is loco et oppido Methymnaeus, terrā atque insulā omni Lesbius fuit. Eum Arionem rex Corinthi Periander amicum amatumque habuit artis gratiā. Is inde a rege proficiscitur, cupiens terras inclutas Siciliam atque Italiam visere. Ubi eō vēnit auresque omnium mentesque in

pecuniā, re: 3.V.10
Corinthum: 4.I.2
notiores, amiciores:
   6.I.2
Corinthios: 3.IV.4
navi: 1.III.2.b
homine ... provectā:
   13.III.1
praedae, pecuniae:
   3.II.6.c
necando: 17.III
illum: 3.IV.4
pernicie intellectā:
   13.III.2
ut: 16.III.1.b
sibi: 3.III.3
ut: 16.IV.1
commiseritum esse:
   14.II; 20.III.5
ut: 16.II
manibus: 3.V.1
ut: 16.IV.1

utriusque terrae urbibus demulsit, in quaestibus istic et voluptatibus amoribusque hominum fuit. Is tum posteā grandi pecuniā et re bonā multā copiosus Corinthum instituit redire; navem igitur et navitas, ut notiores amicioresque sibi, Corinthios delegit." Sed Herodotus narrat eos Corinthios, homine accepto navique in altum provectā, praedae pecuniaeque cupidos cepisse consilium de necando Arione. Tum illum ibi, pernicie intellectā, pecuniam ceteraque sua, ut haberent, dedisse; vitam modo sibi ut parcerent, oravisse. Navitas precum eius harum commiseritum esse illactenus, ut ei necem adferre per vim suis manibus temperarent, sed imperavisse, ut iam statim coram desiliret praeceps in mare.

elocutio, -onis — style
teres, -etis — polished
fidicens, -inis — lyre player
cantator, -ris — singer
fides, -is — lyre
Methymnaeus, -a, -um — of Methymne
Lesbius, -a, -um — from Lesbos

inclutus, -a, -um — famous
demulceo, -ēre — delight
quaestus, -ūs — profit
grandis, -e — vast
copiosus, -a, -um — wealthy in
delego, -ere — pick, choose
altum, -i — the deep (sea)
proveho, -ere — transport

pernicies, -ei — ruin, death
prex, precis — prayer
commiseret, -ēre — it pities
illactenus — so far as
tempero, -are — refrain from
coram — before their eyes
desilio, -ire — jump, leap

The sailors spare Arion's life and grant him one final request: to wear his robes and perform one last concert. Arion then plunges overboard into the sea, robes and all, and is miraculously rescued.

READING FOR INFORMATION

1. *Arion's last shipboard song was on what subject?*
2. *Why did the sailors permit him to sing and play?*
3. *After Arion jumped overboard, did the sailors wait around to observe his fate?*
4. *How was Arion rescued?*

vitae: 3.II.8
spe perditā: 13.III.2
ut: 16.V
priusquam:
   16.XIII.3.a.ii
casūs: 3.II.3
sui: 7.III
audiendi: 17.II;
   3.II.6

voce: 3.V.1
sublatissimā: 6.I.3

quin: 16.VII
delphinum: 3.IV.4
adnavisse,
   subdidisse: 14.II
homini: 3.III.7
dorso: 3.V.1

"Homo," inquit Herodotus, "ibi territus, spe omni vitae perditā, id unum posteā oravit, ut, priusquam mortem oppeteret, induere permitterent sibi sua omnia indumenta et fides capere et canere carmen casūs illius sui consolabile. Feros et immanes navitas prolubium tamen audiendi subit; quod oraverat, impetrat. Atque ibi mox de more cinctus, amictus, ornatus stansque in summae puppis foro, carmen voce sublatissimā cantavit. Ad postrema cantūs cum fidibus ornatūque omni, sīcut stabat canebatque, iecit sese procul in profundum. Navitae, haudquaquam dubitantes quin perisset, cursum, quem facere coeperant, tenuerunt. Sed novum et mirum et pium facinus contigit." Delphinum repente inter undas adnavisse fluitantique sese homini subdidisse et dorso super

vectavisse: 12.I
corpore, ornatū:
    3.V.14
Taenarum: 4.I.2
devexisse: 12.I

fluctūs edito vectavisse, incolumique eum corpore et ornatū Taenarum in terram Laconicam devexisse.

oppeto, -ere — meet

induo, -ere — put on

indumentum, -i — robe

consolabilis, -e — consoling

immanis, -e — savage

prolubium, -i — desire

cingo, -ere — gird

amicio, -ire — clothe

puppis, -is — stern

postremus, -a, -um — last

profundum, -i — the deep
    (sea)

haudquaquam — not at all

pius, -a, -um — pious

delphinus, -i — dolphin

adno, -are — swim up to

fluito, -are — float about

subdo, -ere — place under

dorsum, -i — back

fluctus, -ūs — wave

edo, -ere — present

vecto, -are — convey

incolumis, -e — safe

Taenarum, -i — promontory
    in southern Greece

Laconicus, -a, -um — Spartan

deveho, -ere — transport

Arion returns to Corinth and King Periander, who sets a trap for the sailors.

READING FOR INFORMATION

1. What did Periander do to Arion in response to his story?
2. How did Periander prove the sailors' guilt?
3. How was Arion's rescue memorialized at Taenarum?

Arionem: 3.IV.4
petivisse: 14.II; 12.I
delphino: 3.V.1
optulisse,
    narravisse: 14.II;
    12.I
sīcuti: 16.XIII.2.d
quasi: 16.XIII.1.b
ablegato Arione:
    13.III.1
interrogasse: 20.I.3
audissent: 20.I.3;
    16.V
vēnissent: 16.XII
eos: 3.IV.4
cum: 16.I.4
irent: 16.XI

Lesbios, Corinthios:
    3.IV.4
viserentur: 16.XI

Tum Arionem prorsus ex eo loco Corinthum petivisse talemque Periandro regi, qualis fuerat delphino vectus, inopinanti sese optulisse eique rem, sīcuti acciderat, narravisse. Regem istaec parum credidisse; Arionem, quasi falleret, custodiri iussisse; navitas requisitos, ablegato Arione, dissimulanter interrogasse, ecquid audissent in his locis, unde vēnissent, super Arione; eos dixisse hominem, cum inde irent, in terrā Italiā fuisse eumque illīc bene agitare et studiis delectationibusque urbium florēre atque in gratiā pecuniāque magnā opulentum fortunatumque esse. Tum inter haec eorum verba Arionem cum fidibus et indumentis, cum quibus se in salum eiaculaverat, exstitisse, navitas stupefactos convictosque ire infitias non quisse. Eam fabulam dicere Lesbios et Corinthios, atque esse fabulae argumentum, quod simulacra duo aenea ad Taenarum viserentur, delphinus vehens et homo insidens.

1–3. **talemque . . . narravisse**: and that he presented himself to a surprised King Periander just as he had been carried by the dolphin, and he told him the story exactly as it happened.

prorsus — in a hurry

inopinans, -tis — caught by
    surprise

optulisse < offero

parum — not fully

fallo, -ere — deceive

requiro, -ere — seek out

ablego, -are — dismiss, send off

dissimulanter — hiding one's
    true intent

ecqui — what if anything

agito, -are — do, fare

delectatio, -nis — pleasure

opulentus, -a, -um — rich

salum, -i — the sea

eiaculo, -are — jump

stupefactus, -a, -um — amazed

convictus, -a, -um — detected

ire infitias — to deny

queo, -ēre — be able

argumentum, -i — evidence

simulacrum, -i — likeness

aeneus, -a, -um — bronze

insideo, -ēre — sit on

READING FOR UNDERSTANDING

1. *Why, presumably, did the dolphin rescue the musician?*
2. *Does the dolphin's behavior seem believable?*
3. *Why do crimes against artists seem particularly heinous?*
4. *Periander and Arion were said to have been friends, but after the latter returned to Corinth, the former called him a fraud. What might have been the reasons behind Periander's distrust of Arion?*

5.

The author here describes a gladiatorial display, involving elephants, that went horribly wrong (55 BCE). The sponsor of the display, Pompey the Great, experienced a significant drop in public opinion as a result of these events.

READING FOR INFORMATION

1. *How many elephants were involved in the incident?*
2. *What did one elephant do after being wounded in the feet?*
3. *What "kill shot" was demonstrated with another elephant?*
4. *How did the elephants finally gain the sympathy of the crowd?*

consulatū: 3.V.6
pugnavēre: 20.I.2
ut: 16.XIII.2.d
Gaetulis . . .
  iaculantibus: 13.III.2
unius: 5.II.1
pedibus confossis:
  13.III.2
voluptati: 3.III.9
spectantibus: 3.III.3
velut: 16.XIII.1.b
uno ictū: 3.V.1
temptavēre: 20.I.2
circumdatis claustris:
  13.III.3
fugae: 3.II.6
amissa . . . spe: 13.III.2
habitū: 3.V.7
supplicavēre: 20.I.2
spectantium: 12.II.3.d
dolore: 3.V.14
ut: 16.II
imperatoris: 3.II.6
munificentiae: 3.II.6
honori: 3.III.9
Pompeio: 3.III.3

Pompei quoque altero consulatū, viginti elephanti pugnavēre in circo aut, ut quidam tradunt, septendecim, Gaetulis ex adverso iaculantibus; mirabili unius dimicatione, qui pedibus confossis repsit genibus in catervas, abrepta scuta iaciens in sublime, quae decidentia voluptati spectantibus erant in orbem circumacta, velut arte, non furore beluae, iacerentur. Magnum et in altero occiso miraculum fuit uno ictū; pilum autem sub oculo adactum in vitalia capitis vēnerat. Universi eruptionem temptavēre, non sine vexatione populi, circumdatis claustris ferreis. Sed elephanti Pompeiani, amissā fugae spe, misericordiam vulgi inenarrabili habitū quaerentes supplicavēre quādam sese lamentatione complorantes, tanto spectantium dolore, ut oblitus imperatoris ac munificentiae honori suo exquisitae, flens populus universus consurgeret, dirasque Pompeio, quas ille mox luit, imprecaretur.

consulatus, -ūs — consulship

circus, -i — circus

Gaetulus, -i — North African

iaculor, -ari — throw javelins

dimicatio, -nis — conflict

confodio, -ere — pierce
through

repo, -ere — crawl

genu, -ūs — knee

caterva, -ae — herd, crowd

abripio, -ere — snatch away

scutum — shield

sublimis, -e — aloft, airborne

decido, -ere — fall down

circumago, -ere — arrange
about

belua, -ae — beast

adigo, -ere — drive in

vitalia, -ium — vitals

eruptio, -nis — breakout

vexatio, -nis — alarm,
disturbance

claustrum, -i — barrier

misercordia, -ae —
compassion

supplico, -are — beg, pray

lamentatio, -nis —
lamentation

comploro, -are — implore
together

munificentia, -ae —
lavishness

exquiro, -ere — pay out

fleo, -ēre — weep

consurgo, -ere — rise up
together

dirae, -arum — curses

luo, -ere — atone for

imprecor, -ari — invoke

READING FOR UNDERSTANDING

1. *Were the Roman spectators right to blame Pompey over a display that he sponsored for their entertainment?*
2. *If the spectators hadn't been shocked into fear by the elephants' attempted escape, would the subsequent sympathy for them have been possible?*
3. *In a society that routinely observed animals being slaughtered in the arena, on altars, and throughout marketplaces, what did it take to trigger compassion for such victims?*

6.

The well-known story of Androclus and the lion is recounted here. The author gives scrupulous attention to citing his authority, Apion, before starting the narrative.

READING FOR INFORMATION

1. *Was Apion considered a good authority? On what subjects was he knowledgeable? On what subject did he publish?*
2. *Where did the incident that Apion (and our author) related take place? Why should Apion's account be trusted?*
3. *What setting is introduced for the story?*

litteris: 3.V.10

scientiā: 3.V.5

audisse: 20.I.3

vitio, studio: 3.V.7
sit: 15.II
praedicandis: 17.III

sese: 3.IV.4
Romā: 3.VIII
oculis: 3.V.1

Apion litteris homo multis praeditus rerumque Graecarum plurimā atque variā scientiā fuit. Eius libri non incelebres feruntur, quibus omnium fermē, quae mirifica in Aegypto visuntur audiunturque, historia comprehenditur. Sed in his, quae vel audisse vel legisse sese dicit, fortassean vitio studioque ostentationis sit loquacior—est enim sanē quam in praedicandis doctrinis sui venditator—hoc autem neque audisse neque legisse, sed ipsum sese in urbe Romā vīdisse oculis suis confirmat. "In Circo Maximo," inquit, "venationis amplissimae pugna populo

Romae: 4.I.3
cum: 16.I.3.a

dabatur. Eius rei, Romae cum forte essem, spectator fui. Multae ibi saevientes ferae, magnitudines bestiarum excellentes, omniumque invisitata aut forma erat aut ferocia."

5. **fortassean . . . loquacior**: perhaps he may be too verbose, either as a defect or out of a desire for self-display.

praedo, -ere — endow

scientia, -ae — learning

inceleber, -bris, -bre — unrenowned

fermē — almost

mirificus, -a, -um — marvelous

comprehendo, -ere — encompass

fortassean — probably

ostentatio, -nis — display

loquax, -acis — verbose

sanē — obviously

praedico, -are — relate, commend

venditator — salesperson

confirmo, -are — affirm

venatio, -nis — staged hunt

saevio, -ire — rage

magnitudo, -inis — number

excellens, -tis — surpassing

invisitatus, -a, -um — unfamiliar

ferocia, -ae — ferocity

The reunion of Androclus and the lion, in the context of a public execution, is described.

READING FOR INFORMATION

1. Which animals at the display commanded the most attention?
2. The largest lion received comment because of what four characteristics?
3. After the lion recognized Androclus, his behavior was like that of what animal?
4. Why was Androclus slower to recognize the lion?

admirationi: 3.III.9

omnīs: 1.III.2.b
impetū, vastitudine, fremitū, toris, comis: 3.V.5

servo: 3.III.4
ubi: 16.XIII.2.a

crura, manūs: 3.IV.6

metū: 3.V.7

contuendum: 17.V.1
quasi: 16.XIII.1.b
mutuā . . . factā: 13.III.2

"Sed praeter alia omnia leonum immanitas admirationi fuit praeterque omnīs ceteros unus. Is unus leo corporis impetū et vastitudine terrificoque fremitū et sonoro, toris comisque cervicum fluctuantibus, animos oculosque omnium in sese converterat. Introductus erat inter complures ceteros ad pugnam bestiarum datos servus viri consularis; ei servo Androclus nomen fuit. Hunc ille leo ubi vīdit procul, repente quasi admirans stetit ac deinde sensim atque placidē, tamquam noscitabundus, ad hominem accedit. Tum caudam more atque ritū adulantium canum clementer et blandē movet hominisque se corpori adiungit cruraque eius et manūs, prope iam exanimati metū, linguā leniter demulcet. Homo Androclus inter illa tam atrocis ferae blandimenta amissum animum recuperat, paulatim oculos ad contuendum leonem refert. Tum quasi, mutuā recognitione factā, laetos et gratulabundos vidēres hominem et leonem."

immanitas, -tatis — enormity

vastitudo, -inis — vastness

terrificus, -a, -um — terrifying

fremitus, -ūs — roar

sonorus, -a, -um — deep

torus, -i — muscle

fluctuo, -are — ripple

introduco, -ere — lead in

complures, -ium — several

consularis, -e — having previously served as consul

admiror, -ari — be surprised

sensim — gradually

noscitabundus, -a, -um — almost recognizing

cauda, -ae — tail

ritus, -ūs — custom

adulo, -are — fawn

clementer — gently

adiungo, -ere — rub up against

crus, cruris — leg

exanimatus, -a, -um — faint

leniter — softly

demulceo, -ēre — stroke

atrox, -trocis — savage

blandimentum, -i — kind attention

recupero, -are — recover

contueor, -ēri — study

recognitio, -nis — recognition

gratulabundus, -a, -um — almost congratulating each other

The proceedings are stopped. The emperor (probably Gaius Caligula) inquires why the lion didn't attack Androclus. Androclus begins to narrate their past encounter.

READING FOR INFORMATION

1. *Why did Androclus run away from his master?*
2. *How did he imagine he would hide in Africa?*
3. *Why did he enter the cave?*

Androclum: 3.IV.4
illi . . . uni: 3.III.5
parsisset: 16.V

admirandam: 17.III
cum: 16.I.3.a

verberibus: 3.V.1
ut: 16.III
mihi: 3.III.3
forent: 10.III.7.a
si: 18.I.4
sole . . . flagranti: 3.V.14

multō: 3.V.9

debili . . . pede: 3.V.5

Eā re prorsus tam admirabili maximos populi clamores excitatos esse Apion dicit, accersitumque a Caesare Androclum esse quaesitamque causam, cur illi atrocissimus leo uni parsisset. Ibi Androclus rem mirificam narrat atque admirandam. "Cum provinciam," inquit, "Africam proconsulari imperio meus dominus obtinēret, ego ibi iniquis eius et cotidianis verberibus ad fugam sum coactus et, ut mihi a domino tutiores latebrae forent, in camporum et arenarum solitudines concessi ac, si defuisset cibus, consilium fuit mortem aliquo pacto quaerere. Tum sole medio rabido et flagranti specum quandam nanctus remotam latebrosamque, in eam penetro et me recondo. Neque multō post ad eandem specum venit hic leo, debili uno et cruento pede, gemitūs edens et murmura dolorem cruciatumque vulneris commiserantia."

prorsus — utterly

excitatus, -a, -um — raise, incite

accerso, -ere — summon

quaero, -ere — inquire

mirificus, -a, -um — remarkable

proconsularis, -e — proconsular

obtineo, -ēre — receive

iniquus, -a, -um — unjust

latebra, -ae — hiding place

arena, -ae — desert

solitudo, -dinis — isolation

desum, -esse — lack, fail

pactum, -i — manner

rabidus, -a, -um — maddening

flagro, -are — blazing

nanciscor, -i — take

latebrosus, -a, -um — shady

penetro, -are — enter

recondo, -ere — hide

debilis, -e — wounded

cruentus, -a, -um — bloodied

edo, -ere — issue, let out

murmur, -is — murmur

cruciatus, -ūs — torment

commiseror, -ari — bewail

Androclus tells how he helped the lion, how they lived together for a time, and on what food he survived.

READING FOR INFORMATION

1. *Why did the lion enter the cave?*
2. *What two things were wrong with the lion's paw?*
3. *How long did Androclus and the lion live together?*
4. *By what means did the man make his food edible?*

sibi: 3.III.3

uti: 16.XIII.2.d

petendae: 17.III
gratiā: 8.III
vulnere: 3.V.18

accuratius: 6.II

operā, medelā:
3.V.1
pede . . . posito:
13.III.2
vīctū: 3.V.1

Atque illīc primo quidem conspectū advenientis leonis territum sibi et pavefactum animum esse dixit. "Sed postquam introgressus," inquit, "leo, uti re ipsā apparuit, in habitaculum suum, videt me procul delitescentem, mitis et mansues accessit et sublatum pedem ostendere mihi et porrigere quasi opis petendae gratiā visus est. Ibi ego stirpem ingentem, vestigio pedis eius haerentem, revelli conceptamque saniem vulnere intimo expressi accuratiusque sine magnā iam formidine siccavi penitus atque detersi cruorem. Illā tunc meā operā et medelā levatus, pede in manibus meis posito, recubuit et quievit, atque ex eo die triennium totum ego et leo in eādem specū eodemque et vīctū viximus. Nam, quas venabatur feras, membra opimiora ad specum mihi subgerebat, quae ego, ignis copiam non habens, meridiano sole torrens edebam.

pavefactus, -a, -um — panic stricken

introgredior, -i — enter

habitaculum, -i — lair

delitesco, -ere — try to hide

mitis, -e — mild

mansues, -suetis — gentle

accedo, -ere — approach

porrigo, -ere — reach out

stirps, -rpis — splinter

revello, -ere — pull out

sanies, -is — infection

intimus, -a, -um — deep

exprimo, -ere — squeeze out

accuratē — carefully

formido, -dinis — fear

sicco, -are — dry

penitus — completely

detergeo, -ēre — wash out

medela, -ae — treatment

levo, -are — relieve

recumbo, -ere — lie down

quiesco, -ere — rest

triennium, -i — three-year period

vīctus, -ūs — food

venor, -ari — hunt

opimus, -a, -um — choice, best

subgero, -ere — bring

meridianus, -a, -um — noonday

torreo, -ēre — bake

edo, edere or **esse** — eat

Finally, we learn how Androclus left the lion and was captured, convicted, and condemned to the arena. The epilogue to the story, the ultimate fate of Androclus and the lion, is then related.

READING FOR INFORMATION

1. *How did Androclus get away from the lion?*
2. *What three things happened because of the vote of the people?*
3. *What became of Androclus and his lion?*

me vitae: 20.III.5.a
pertaesum est:
    20.III.5
leone . . . profecto:
    13.III.1
tridui: 3.II.8
Romam: 4.I.2
rei capitalis: 3.II.6.b
esse damnandum
    dandumque:
    17.III
beneficii,
    medicinae: 3.II.6
populo: 3.III.1
poenā: 3.V.19

suffragiis: 3.V.7

loro: 3.V.1

"Sed ubi me vitae illius ferinae iam pertaesum est, leone in venatum profecto, reliqui specum et viam fermē tridui permensus a militibus visus sum apprehensusque sum, et ad dominum ex Africā Romam deductus sum. Is me statim rei capitalis esse damnandum dandumque ad bestias curavit. Intellego autem hunc quoque leonem me tunc separato captum gratiam mihi nunc beneficii et medicinae referre." Haec Apion dixisse Androclum tradit, eaque omnia populo declarata esse, atque ideō cunctis petentibus dimissum esse Androclum, et poenā solutum esse, leonemque ei suffragiis populi donatum esse. "Posteā," inquit, "videbamus Androclum et leonem, loro tenui revinctum, urbe totā circum tabernas ire, donari aere Androclum, floribus spargi leonem, omnes ubique obvios dicere: 'Hic est leo hospes hominis, hic est homo medicus leonis.'"

ferinus, -a, -um — uncivilized

pertaedet, -ere — it tires, it wearies

venatus, -ūs — a hunt

fermē — almost

triduum, -i — three-day period

permetior, -iri — travel, traverse

apprehendo, -ere — seize

deduco, -ere — lead back

res capitalis — death penalty

declaro, -are — declare

ideō — for this reason

suffragium, -i — vote

lorum, -i — leash

revincio, -ire — restrain

ubique — everywhere

obvius, -a, -um — encountering

hospes, -pitis — host

READING FOR UNDERSTANDING

1. At the two major encounters of Androclus and the lion, in the circus and in the cave, how were the circumstances of the pair similar?
2. Which elements of the story strike you as credible? Which seem incredible?
3. If it has one, what is the moral of this tale?
4. How do you imagine the later fate of Androclus and the lion: making a little money off store grand openings, rich children's birthday parties, the Roman equivalent of late-night community-access TV?

Verse Readings

1.

This pretty little poem on autumn captures that perfect moment when the season is at its height and the harvest has just been completed.

Iam nunc algentes autumnus fecerat umbras,
atque hiemem tepidis spectabat Phoebus habenis,
iam platanus iactare comas, iam coeperat uvas
defecto palmite: adnumerare suas, defecto palmite, vitis:
    13.III.1
ante oculos stabat, quidquid promiserat annus.   5

algeo, -ēre — chill

tepidus, -a, -um —
lukewarm

Phoebus, -i — Sol (the sun
god)

habena, -ae — rein

platanus, -i — sycamore

adnumero, -are — count

palmes, -itis — foliage

READING FOR UNDERSTANDING
1. *How does this poem remind the reader of summer and foreshadow winter?*
2. *Which of the images presented here best epitomizes for you the season of fall?*

2.

The poet here lauds the joys of spring, no less welcome in Mediterranean climes than farther north.

Sentio, fugit hiems, Zephyrisque animantibus orbem
iam tepet Eurus aquis; sentio, fugit hiems.

Parturit omnis ager, persentit terra calores,
germinibusque novis parturit omnis ager.

Laeta virecta tument, folios sese induit arbor,   5
vallibus: 3.V.7 or 3.V.10   vallibus apricis laeta virecta tument.

Ityn: Greek accusative
mensis: 3.III.9   Iam Philomela gemit modulis, Ityn impia mater
oblatum mensis iam Philomela gemit.

monte: 3.V.18   Monte tumultus aquae properat per levia saxa,
et latē resonat monte tumultus aquae.   10

Eoi: Greek genitive   Floribus innumeris pingit sola flatus Eoi,
Tempea: 3.I.1   Tempeaque exhalant floribus innumeris.

Per cava saxa sonat pecudum mugitibus Echo,
iugis: 3.V.19   voxque repulsa iugis per cava saxa sonat.

Vitea musta tument vicinas iuncta per ulmos;   15
fronde maritatā vitea musta tument.

Nōta tigilla linit iam garrula luce chelidon:
dum recolit nidos, nōta tigilla linit.

Sub platano viridi iucundat somnus in umbrā,
sertaque texuntur sub platano viridi.   20

dulce (est): 20.III.3; 20.IV
fila: 3.VI
fusis: 3.V.19

Tunc quoque dulce mori, tunc fila recurrite fusis—
inter et amplexūs tunc quoque dulce mori.

Zephyrus, -i — west wind
animo, -are — bring to life
tepeo, -ēre — grow warm
Eurus, -i — southeast wind
persentio, -ire — feel
calor, -ris — warmth
germen, -inis — seed
folius, -i — greenery
induo, -ere — don, put on
apricus, -a, -um — sunny
Philomela, -ae = the nightingale
modulus, -i — measure, tune
Itys, -yos — son of Philomela; killed and served as a meal to his father

oblatum < **offero**
tumultus, -ūs — rush, swell
resono, -are — resound
flatus, -ūs — breeze
Eos, Eoi — Dawn
Tempea, -orum — valley in Greece
mugitus, -ūs — lowing
repello, -ere — reverberate
viteus, -a, -um — of the vine
mustum, -i — grape skin
iungo, -ere — entwine
ulmus, -i — elm

frons, frondis — foliage
maritatus, -a, -um — wedded
tigillum, -i — branch, twig
garrulus, -a, -um — chatty
chelidon, -onis — swallow, swift
platanus, -i — sycamore
viridis, -e — green
iucundo, -are — delight
sertum, -i — garland
filum, -i — thread (of life)
recurro, -ere — unravel
fusus, -i — shuttle, spool

READING FOR UNDERSTANDING

1. In form, this is an echoic poem: that is, the first two, three, or four words of each couplet also serve as its last two, three, or four words. Does this contribute to the attractiveness of the poem or is it merely a technical virtuosity?

2. The subject of this poem is poetically pretty familiar, the descriptions are also fairly standard, and the diction and grammar are rather straightforward and unremarkable. To your thinking, what makes this poem succeed, if in fact it does?

3. The human presence in this idyllic scene is not very prominent (notice the 1st person singulars in lines 1 and 2 and the references to sleep, embraces, and death in lines 19–22). Is this a virtue of the poem?

4. Poetic connections between lovemaking, sleep, and dying in the springtime of one's life belong more properly to Romantic than to Greco-Roman literature. Does the sensibility of this poem strike you as typically Roman? Can you think of anything to compare this poem to in the Latin you've read so far?

3.

This poem describes the natural effects that time has on all things, even those we consider strong and stable.

videas: 15.II
tempore, usū: 3.V.7

Omne quod Natura parens creavit,
quamlibet firmum videas, labascit:
tempore ac longo fragile et caducum
solvitur usū.

valle: 3.V.11

Amnis insuetā solet ire valle,   5
mutat et rectos via certa cursūs,

cum: 16.I.3.a

rupta cum cedit male pertinaci
  ripa fluento.

Decidens scabrum cavat unda tofum,
ferreus vomis tenuatur agris,   10

digitos: 3.IV.1.a

splendet attrito digitos honorans

auro: 3.V.1

  anulus auro.

quamlibet — however much	**pertinax, -acis** — unyielding	**vomis, -eris** — plow blade
labasco, -ere — decline	**fluentum, -i** — river, flood	**tenuo, -are** — thin, wear down
caducus, -a, -um — short lived	**scaber, -bra, -brum** — rough	**attero, -ere** — grind down
insuetus, -a, -um — unaccustomed	**tofus, -i** — tufa (soft volcanic stone)	**anulus, -i** — ring
	ferreus, -a, -um — of iron	

READING FOR UNDERSTANDING

1. *What is the structure of this poem and its three quatrains?*
2. *How do the exempla of the third stanza differ from those in the second?*
3. *What artful play with juxtaposition and word order do you see in lines 5 and 6?*
4. *Why does the poet describe only the destructive effects of time? Can you write a poem of comparable length describing time's positive and constructive effects?*

4.

This section presents four engaging little poems on the subject of roses.

I.

Vēnerunt aliquandō rosae. Per veris amoeni
ingenium una dies ostendit spicula florum,

pyramidas: Greek accusative plural
nodo: 3.V.18

altera pyramidas nodo maiore tumentes,
tertia iam calathos, totum lux quarta peregit
floris opus. Pereunt hodiē nisi māne leguntur.   5

aliquandō — now, for once	**spiculum, -i** — thorn	**calathus, -i** — calix, flower cup
amoenus, -a, -um — pleasant	**pyramis, -idis** — cone	**perago, -ere** — complete
	nodus, -i — bud	

II.

A, quales ego māne rosas procedere vīdi!

omnibus: 3.III.2   Nascebantur adhūc neque erat par omnibus aetas.

Prima papillatos ducebat tecta corymbos,

umbone: 3.V.18   altera puniceos apices umbone levabat,

tertia iam totum calathi patefecerat orbem,   5

quarta simul nituit nudati germine floris.

dum: 16.XIII.3.a.i   Dum levat una caput dumque explicat altera nodum,

amictū: 3.V.19   sīc, dum virgineus pudor exsinuatur amictū,

pereant: 16.III.1   ne pereant, lege māne rosas: cito virgo senescit.

a — ah	**umbo, -onis** — swelling	**nodus, -i** — bud
procedo, -ere — progress	**calathus, -i** — flower cup,	**virgineus, -a, -um** — virginal
adhūc — already	calyx	**exsinuo, -are** — thrust out
papillatus, -a, -um — nippled	**patefacio, -ere** — open	**amictus, -ūs** — covering
corymbus, -i — rose hip	**niteo, -ēre** — gleam	**senesco, -ere** — grow old
puniceus, -a, -um — red	**nudatus, -a, -um** — exposed	
apex, -icis — tip	**germen, -inis** — seed pod	

III.

Aut hoc risit Amor, aut hoc de pectine traxit

sentibus: 3.III.5   purpureis Aurora comis, aut sentibus haesit

spinis: 3.III.7   Cypris et hic spinis insedit sanguis acutis.

pecten, -inis — comb	**Cypris, -idis** — Venus	**insido, -ere** — settle on
sentes, -ium — spines, thorns	**spina, -ae** — thorn	

IV.

Hortus erat Veneris, roseis circumdatus herbis,

dominae: 3.III.2   gratus ager dominae, quem qui vīdisset amaret.
vīdisset: 16.XII
amaret: 15.II.2   Dum puer hic passim properat decerpere flores
dum: 16.XIII.3.a.i
spinā: 3.V.1   et velare comas, spinā libavit acutā

marmoreos digitos. Mox ut dolor attigit artūs   5

sanguineamque manum, tinxit sua lumina gutta.

Pervēnit ad matrem frendens, defertque querellas:

"Unde rosae, mater, coeperunt esse nocentes?

latentibus armis: Unde tui flores pugnare latentibus armis?
    3.V.1
Bella gerunt mecum. Floris color et cruor unum est!"   10

libo, -are — graze	**artus, -ūs** — limb	**frendo, -ere** — gnash one's
marmoreus, -a, -um — of	**sanguineus, -a, -um** —	teeth
marble	bloodied	**defero, -rre** — relate
attingo, -ere — touch, affect	**tingo, -ere** — tinge	**querella, -ae** — complaint

READING FOR UNDERSTANDING

1. *What evidence can you find that in these poems roses have an erotic significance? Do they seem more of a female symbol or a male symbol?*

2. *Besides the red cultivars, Romans also had yellow and flame-colored roses. Why do we, like the Romans, imagine red whenever we think of roses?*

3. *The effects rather than the functions of rose thorns are sometimes emphasized here. What symbolic significance do you observe for thorns in some of these poems? Why don't all of these poems mention thorns?*

5.

This poem describes in great natural detail a riverside scene of charm and beauty.

READING FOR INFORMATION

1. *How many different kinds of flower does this poem name?*

2. *How many different kinds of wild animal does this poem name?*

3. *At what point are human beings introduced into this natural setting? Are they accorded any description?*

valle: 3.V.14	Amnis ibat inter arva valle fusus frigidā,	
luce: 3.V.7	luce ridens calculorum, flore pictus herbido.	
	Caerulas supernē laurūs et virecta myrtea	
sibilo: 3.V.14	leniter motabat aura blandiente sibilo;	
	subter autem molle gramen flore adulto creverat:	5
	et croco solum rubebat et lucebat liliis,	
	et nemus fragrabat omne violarum sub spiritū.	
	Inter ista dona veris gemmeasque gratias	
	omnium regina odorum vel colorum Lucifer	
flamma: 3.VIII **Diones:** Greek genitive	auriflora praeminebat, flamma Diones, rosa.	10
	Roscidum nemus rigebat inter uda gramina;	
	fonte crebro murmurabant hinc et inde rivuli,	
	antra muscus et virentes intus hederae vinxerant,	
	quā fluenta labibunda guttis ibant lucidis.	
putes: 15.II	Has per umbras omnis ales plus canora quam putes	15
	cantibus vernis strepebat et susurris dulcibus;	
amnis: 3.II.1	hīc loquentis murmur amnis concinebat frondibus,	
quīs: 7.V.1 **melos:** Greek accusative	quīs melos vocalis aurae musa Zephyri moverat.	
	Sīc euntem per virecta pulchra, odora et musica	
	ales, amnis, aura, lucus, flos, et umbra iuverat.	20

18. **quīs . . . moverat**: by which the voiced muse of the west wind's breeze had produced songs

calculus, -i — river stone
herbidus, -a, -um — leafy
caerulus, -a, -um — azure
supernē — above
laurus, -i — laurel tree
myrteus, -a, -um — myrtled
leniter — gently
moto, -are — wave, move
blandior, -iri — coax
sibilus, -i — whisper
gramen, -inis — grass
adultus, -a, -um — grown
crocus, -i — crocus
lilium, -i — lily
fragro, -are — be fragrant

viola, -ae — violet
gemmeus, -a, -um — jeweled
odor, -ris — scent
Lucifer, -i — morning star
auriflorus, -a, -um — golden flowered
praemineo, -ēre — loom over
Dione, -es — mother of Venus
roscidus, -a, -um — dewy
rigeo, -ēre — stand erect
murmuro, -are — murmur
rivulus, -i — rivulet
antrum, -i — cave
muscus, -i — moss
intus — within

hedera, -ae — ivy
fluentum, -i — river
labibundus, -a, -um — gliding
lucidus, -a, -um — shiny
strepo, -ere — sound
susurrus, -i — whisper
concino, -ere — resound
frons, -ndis — leafage
melos, -i — song
vocalis, -e — voiced
Zephyrus, -i — west wind
lucus, -i — grove

READING FOR UNDERSTANDING

1. The **locus amoenus** (attractive place) is a common topos in ancient literature. Sometimes it is a realistic place and sometimes rather utopian. Does the riverside described in this poem seem like it could be real?
2. Why does the poem end as abruptly as it does?
3. In the appreciation of this place, four of the five senses are called on. Does the poet give equal and/or appropriate attention to all four?
4. Of all the images that the poet has created in this poem, which is your favorite?

6.

This charming little poem is about the happiness that comes from living out a simple life amid the fruits of nature.

securo: 3.IX
mero: 3.V.10

Parvula securo tegitur mihi culmine sedes,
uvaque plena mero fecundā pendet ab ulmo.
Dant rami cerasos, dant mala rubentia silvae,
Palladiumque nemus pingui se vertice frangit.
Iam quā diductos potat levis area fontes,   5

mihi: 3.III.3
missura: 12.II
somnos: 3.IV.1.a
alitibus: 3.III.3
libuit: 20.III.5
lino: 3.V.1
novēre: 20.I.2

Corycium mihi surgit olus malvaeque supinae,
et non sollicitos missura papavera somnos.
Praetereā sive alitibus contexere fraudem,
seu magis imbelles libuit circumdare cervos,
aut tereti lino pavidum subducere piscem,   10
hos tantum novēre dolos mea sordida rura.
I nunc, et vitae fugientis tempora vende

divitibus cenis! Me si manet exitus īdem,

hīc, precor, inveniat consumptaque tempora poscat.

divitibus cenis:
   3.V.12
si: 18.I.1
inveniat: 15.I

culmen, -inis — roof	**pinguis, -e** — rich	**imbellis, -e** — peaceful
sedes, -is — house	**frango, -ere** — break	**cervus, -i** — deer
merum, -i — wine	**diduco, -ere** — draw	**teres, -etis** — smooth
fecundus, -a, -um — fertile	**area, -ae** — courtyard	**linum, -i** — fish line
ulmus, -i — elm	**Corycium olus** = kale	**subduco, -ere** — catch
ramus, -i — branch	**malva, -ae** — mallow	**piscis, -is** — fish
cerasus, -i — cherry	**supinus, -a, -um** — drooping	**exitus, -ūs** — end
malum, -i — apple	**papaverum, -i** — poppy	
Palladius, -a, -um — Minerva's	**fraus, -dis** — trap	

READING FOR UNDERSTANDING

1. Why does the poet call hunting, fishing, and birding **doli**?
2. How is the space that the poet here creates bounded? What things manage to cross those boundaries?
3. The only aspect of life outside its cozy, bounded world that the poem mentions is the **divites cenae** of others. Is that a fair and complete picture?

7.

This fascinating poem offers an almost psychological study of dreams. It observes how our dreams are, in a sense, a continuation of our waking lives. Then, sleeplike, the poem breaks off abruptly.

umbris: 3.V.1	Somnia, quae mentes ludunt volitantibus umbris,	
deum: 1.II.1.c	non delubra deum nec ab aethere numina mittunt,	
sibi: 3.III.3 cum: 16.I.3.b sopore: 3.V.1	sed sibi quisque facit. Nam cum prostrata sopore urget membra quies, et mens sine pondere ludit,	
tenebris: 3.V.1	quidquid luce fuit, tenebris agit. Oppida bello	5
	qui quatit et flammis miserandas eruit urbes,	
	tela videt versasque acies et funera regum	
sanguine: 3.V.7	atque exundantes profuso sanguine campos.	
	Qui causas orare solent, legesque forumque	
chorte: 3.V.10	et pavidi cernunt inclusum chorte tribunal.	10
	Condit avarus opes, defossumque invenit aurum.	
undis: 3.V.18	Venator saltūs canibus quatit. Eripit undis	
periturus: 12.II	aut premit eversam periturus navita puppem.	
	Scribit amatori meretrix, dat adultera munus,	
	et canis in somnis leporis vestigia lustrat:	15
	in noctis spatium miserorum vulnera durant.	

somnium, -i — dream
volito, -are — flit
delubrum, -i — sanctuary
aether, -is — heaven
prosterno, -ere — lay out
sopor, -ris — deep sleep
urgeo, -ēre — press
pondus, -eris — weight
quatio, -ere — smash
miseror, -ari — pity
eruo, -ere — destroy

verto, -ere — turn aside
acies, -ei — battle line
exundo, -are — be awash
profusus, -a, -um — profuse
cerno, -ere — perceive
includo, -ere — surround
chorte = cohorte
tribunal, -is — jury panel
avarus, -i — miser
defodio, -ere — dig up
venator, -is — hunter

everto, -ere — wreck
puppis, -is — stern (of a ship)
amator, -ris — lover
meretrix, -icis — prostitute
adultera, -ae — adulteress
lepus, -oris — hare
lustro, -are — track
spatium, -i — span, interval
duro, -are — persevere

READING FOR UNDERSTANDING

1. In what respect do dreams "play with the mind" (**mentes ludunt**)?
2. The conventional wisdom in Greco-Roman times was that dreams were divinely inspired, a position this poem contradicts. Do you believe that sometimes a dream can be externally inspired?
3. Does the poem provide a realistic balance between phobic dreams and wish-fulfillment dreams? Why does it make no mention of surreal or fantastical dreams?
4. The poem ends on a rather pessimistic note. Given this, wouldn't it be more comforting to imagine that dreams are god sent?

8.

This poem, intriguing in a variety of ways, could be categorized as a love poem or as a poem on religion. As it progresses, a kind of poetic biology emerges. It opens, simply enough, in praise of spring and then introduces the goddess Venus—who will hold a festival—with a tactful allusion to the myth of her birth.

READING FOR INFORMATION

1. Whom will Venus lead in the forests tomorrow?
2. What will Venus do from her throne?
3. What does Favonius, the west wind, do?

amet: 15.1   Cras amet qui numquam amavit quique amavit cras amet.
orbis: 3.1.2   Ver novum, ver iam canorum, ver renatus orbis est,
         vere concordant amores, vere nubunt alites,
         et nemus comam resolvit de maritis imbribus.

         Cras amet qui numquam amavit quique amavit cras amet.   5

*   *   *

         Cras amorum copulatrix inter umbras arborum

implicat casas virentes de flagello myrteo:
cras canoris feriatos ducit in silvis choros;
throno: 3.V.1   cras Dione iura dicit fulta sublimi throno.

Cras amet qui numquam amavit quique amavit cras amet.   10

* * *

cum: 16.I.4   Cras erit cum primum Aether copulavit nuptias;
tunc cruore de superno spumeo et ponti globo,
caerulas inter catervas, inter et bipedes equos,
fecit undantem Dionem de maritis imbribus.

Cras amet qui numquam amavit quique amavit cras amet.   15

* * *

Ipsa gemmis purpurantem pingit annum floridis;
ipsa turgentes papillas de Favoni spiritū
urget in nodos tepentes; ipsa roris lucidi,
noctis aura quem relinquit, spargit umentes aquas.

Cras amet qui numquam amavit quique amavit cras amet.   20

* * *

canorus, -a, -um — tuneful
renascor, -i — be reborn
concordo, -are — come together in harmony
resolvo, -ere — let down
maritus, -a, -um — husbandlike
imber, -bri — rain
copulatrix, -tricis — coupler
implico, -are — weave
casa, -ae — arbor, pergola
flagellum, -i — sprig
chorus, -i — choir, chorus

Dione, -es = Venus
fultus, -a, -um — propped up on
thronus, -i — throne
supernum, -i — heaven
spumeus, -a, -um — frothy
pontus, -i — sea
globus, -i — a round mass
caerulus, -a, -um — azure
caterva, -ae — throng
bipes equus = seahorse
undo, -are — surge
gemma, -ae — gem

purpuro, -are — grow red or purple
floridus, -a, -um — flowery
turgeo, -ēre — swell
papilla, -ae — bud, nipple
Favonius, -i — west wind
urgeo, -ēre — press
nodus, -i — bud, belt knot
tepeo, -ēre — grow warm
lucidus, -a, -um — shiny
umeo, -ēre — dampen

The poet describes how the dew helps the rosebuds to open, exposing their brilliant color. Next Venus orders nymphs to commence the festival.

READING FOR INFORMATION
1. *What has Venus ordered the roses to do?*
2. *Who will accompany the nymphs in the myrtle grove?*
3. *How is it known whether or not Cupid is on vacation from his duties?*

Emicant lacrimae trementes de caduco pondere:

orbe: 3.V.18

gutta praeceps orbe parvo sustinet casūs suos.

noctibus: 3.V.6

Umor ille, quem serenis astra rorant noctibus,

peplo: 3.V.19

māne virgineas papillas solvit umenti peplo.

Cras amet qui numquam amavit quique amavit cras amet.   25

*   *   *

En pudorem florulentae prodiderunt purpurae,

nodis: 3.V.18

et rosarum flamma nodis emicat tepentibus.

Ipsa iussit diva vestem de papillis solvere,

ut: 16.III.1
virgines: 3.VIII

ut recenti māne nudae virgines nubant rosae.

Cras amet qui numquam amavit quique amavit cras amet.   30

*   *   *

Facta Cypridis de cruore deque Amoris osculo,

deque gemmis deque flammis deque Solis purpuris,

cras ruborem, qui latebat veste tectus igneā,

nodo: 3.V.19

uvido marita nodo non pudebit solvere.

Cras amet qui numquam amavit quique amavit cras amet.   35

*   *   *

Ipsa Nymphas diva luco iussit ire myrteo:

puellis: 3.III.3
credi: 12.I

it puer comes puellis: nec tamen credi potest

esse Amorem feriatum, si sagittas vexerit.

Ite, Nymphae; posuit arma, feriatus est Amor.

Cras amet qui numquam amavit quique amavit cras amet.   40

*   *   *

tremo, -ere — shimmer	**florulentus, -a, -um** — blooming	**igneus, -a, -um** — fiery
caducus, -a, -um — falling		**uvidus, -a, -um** — moist
umor, -ris — dampness	**prodo, -ere** — produce	**marita, -ae** — bride
serenus, -a, -um — calm	**emico, -are** — flash	**comes, -mitis** — companion
roro, -are — bedew	**tepeo, -ēre** — grow warm	**sagitta, -ae** — arrow
umeo, -ēre — moisten	**recens, -ntis** — fresh	
peplum, -i — gown	**rubor, -ris** — pinkness	

Next we learn about other gods and whether or not they will attend Venus's festival.

READING FOR INFORMATION

1. *Why does Venus order Cupid to come naked to the festival?*
2. *What does Venus want from the goddess Diana? For how long will she want it?*
3. *What other gods will be present at the festival?*

Iussus est inermis ire, nudus ire iussus est,

neu: 16.III.1
quid: 7.VI.1.a

neu quid arcū, neu sagittā, neu quid igne laederet.

Sed tamen, Nymphae, cavete, quod Cupido pulcher est:

totus est in armis īdem, quandō nudus est Amor.

Cras amet qui numquam amavit quique amavit cras amet.   45

*   *   *

pudore: 5.V.5

Compari Venus pudore mittit ad te virgines.

Una res est quam rogamus: cede, virgo Delia,

ut: 16.III or 16.IV

ut nemus sit incruentum de ferinis stragibus

floribus: 3.III.3

et recentibus virentes ducat umbras floribus.

Cras amet qui numquam amavit quique amavit cras amet.   50

*   *   *

si: 18.I.3

Ipsa vellet te rogare, si pudicam flecteret,

decēret: 20.III.7.a

ipsa vellet ut venires, si decēret virginem.

vidēres: 15.II.2
noctibus: 4.II.1

Iam tribus choros vidēres feriatos noctibus

congreges inter catervas ire per saltūs tuos.

Cras amet qui numquam amavit quique amavit cras amet.   55

*   *   *

Floreas inter coronas, myrteas inter casas,

nec Ceres, nec Bacchus absunt, nec poetarum deus.

perviglanda: 17.IV
canticis: 3.V.1
regnet: 15.I

Detenenda tota nox est, perviglanda canticis:

regnet in silvis Dione: tu recede, Delia!

Cras amet qui numquam amavit quique amavit cras amet.   60

*   *   *

inermis, -e — unarmed	**ferinus, -a, -um** — wild	**casa, -ae** — arbor, pergola
arcus, -ūs — bow	**strages, -is** — slaughter	**pervig(i)lo, -are** — stay
compar, -is — similar	**chorus, -i** — choir, chorus	awake
Delius, -a, -um — of Delos	**congrex, -gregis** — assembled	**canticum, -i** — song
(a Greek island)	**caterva, -ae** — throng	**regno, -are** — reign
incruentus, -a, -um —	**saltus, -ūs** — grove	
unbloodied	**floreus, -a, -um** — flowery	

The poem now shifts from Venus's festival to her function as the procreative force in all living things. Venus becomes a divine abstraction as well as a force of nature and an agent in history.

READING FOR INFORMATION

1. Which gods will flank Venus as she presides over the festival?
2. What does Venus tell the nymphs about trusting Cupid?
3. Who "grafted" Trojans onto Latins and mated Sabines with Romans?

floribus: 3.V.17

Iussit Hyblaeis tribunal stare diva floribus;
praeses ipsa iura dicet, adsidebunt Gratiae.
Hybla, totos funde flores, quidquid annus attulit;
Hybla, florum sume vestem, quantus Ennae campus est.

Cras amet qui numquam amavit quique amavit cras amet.   65

*   *   *

Ruris hīc erunt puellae vel puellae montium,
quaeque silvas, quaeque lucos, quaeque fontes incolunt.
Iussit omnes adsidere pueri mater alitis,

Amori: 3.III.5

iussit et nudo puellas nil Amori credere.

Cras amet qui numquam amavit quique amavit cras amet.   70

*   *   *

ut: 16.III
nubibus: 3.V.18

Ut pater totum crearet vernis annum nubibus,
in sinum maritus imber fluxit almae coniugis,

pergeret: 16.III.2.b

unde fetūs perque pontum perque caelum pergeret

corpore: 3.V.1

perque terras mixtus omnes alere magno corpore.

Cras amet qui numquam amavit quique amavit cras amet.   75

*   *   *

Ipsa venas atque mentem permeanti spiritū
intus occultis gubernat procreatrix viribus.
Ipsa Troianos nepotes in Latinos transtulit,
Romuleas ipsa fecit cum Sabinis nuptias.

Cras amet qui numquam amavit quique amavit cras amet.   80

*   *   *

sui: 7.III
tramite: 3.V.1

Pervium sui tenorem seminali tramite
perque caelum perque terras perque pontum subditum

venis: 3.III.7

ipsa duxit, ipsa venis procreantem spiritum

nosse: 20.I.3
nascendi: 17.II

imbuit, iussitque mundum nosse nascendi vias.

Cras amet qui numquam amavit quique amavit cras amet.   85

*   *   *

Hyblaeus, -a, -um — of Hybla
praeses, -sedis — chief
adsideo, -ēre — sit in
    attendance
Hybla, -ae — mountain in
    Greece

adfero, -rre — bring
Enna, -ae — field in Sicily
incolo, -ere — inhabit
fluo, -ere — flow
almus, -a, -um — nurturing
pontus, -i — sea

pergo, -ere — proceed
alo, -ere — feed, nourish
vena, -ae — vein
permeo, -are — permeate
guberno, -are — guide,
    govern

procreatrix, -ricis —
   procreatrix
pervius, -a, -um — accessible

tenor, -ris — course,
   movement
seminalis, -e — seed strewn

trames, -mitis — path
subdo, -ere — set beneath
procreo, -are — procreate

As the poem wraps up, it briefly touches on Venus's role in history, nature, and mythology again, and then in the final stanza the poet speaks up in the first person.

READING FOR INFORMATION

1. *What other Roman matings and offspring was Venus responsible for?*
2. *What creatures of nature does the poet now mention?*
3. *In the last quatrain, after more than a hundred lines of poetry, what does the poet claim that she or he is experiencing?*

unde: 16.III.2.b
posterum: 1.II.1.c

Ipsa Laurentem puellam coniugem nato dedit,
moxque Marti de sacello dat pudicam virginem:
unde Ramnes et Quirites proque prole posterum
Romuli, patrem crearet et nepotem Caesarem.

Cras amet qui numquam amavit quique amavit cras amet.   90

*   *   *

rure: 4.I
natus (esse): 12.I;
   20.IV
cum: 16.I.3.a
osculis: 3.V.14

Rura fecundat voluptas, rura Venerem sentiunt;
ipse Amor, puer Dionae, rure natus dicitur.
Hunc, ager cum parturiret, ipsa suscepit sinū,
ipsa florum delicatis educavit osculis.

Cras amet qui numquam amavit quique amavit cras amet.   95

*   *   *

Ecce, iam super genestas explicant tauri latus,
quisque tutus, quo tenetur, coniugali foedere.
Subter umbras cum maritis, ecce, balantum gregem,
et canoras non tacēre diva iussit alites.

Cras amet qui numquam amavit quique amavit cras amet.   100

*   *   *

ore: 3.V.1

Iam loquaces ore rauco stagna cygni perstrepunt:
adsonat Terei puella subter umbram pōpuli,

ut: 16.II
dici, queri: 12.I.3.d

ut putes motūs amoris ore dici musico,
et neges queri sororem de marito barbaro.

Cras amet qui numquam amavit quique amavit cras amet.   105

*   *   *

Illa cantat, nos tacemus. Quandō ver venit meum?

ut: 16.III

Quandō fiam uti chelidon, ut tacēre desinam?

tacendo: 17.II; 3.V.7   Perdidi Musam tacendo, nec me Phoebus respicit.

cum: 16.I.1   Sīc Amyclas, cum tacērent, perdidit silentium.

Cras amet qui numquam amavit quique amavit cras amet.   110

Laurens puella = Lavinia	**delicatus, -a, -um** — delicate	**perstrepo, -ere** — sound over
natus = Aeneas	**educo, -are** — raise	**adsono, -are** — call out
sacellum, -i — shrine	**genesta, -ae** — broom grass	**Terei puella** = nightingale
virgo = Rhea Silvia	**latus, -eris** — flank	**pōpulus, -i** — poplar tree
Ramnes — an early Roman tribe	**coniugalis, -e** — conjugal	**motus, -ūs** — motion
Quirites — early Romans	**foedus, -eris** — bond, alliance	**queror, -i** — complain
proles, -is — offspring	**subter** — beneath	**chelidon, -nis** — swallow, swift
posterus, -a, -um — later	**balo, -are** — bleat	**respicio, -ere** — regard
patrem = Julius Caesar	**grex, -egis** — herd, flock	**Amyclae, -arum** — town in Greece
nepotem = Augustus	**loquax, -acis** — noisy	
fecundo, -are — make fertile	**raucus, -a, -um** — raucous	
suscipio, -ere — take	**stagnum, -i** — lake	
	cygnus, -i — swan	

READING FOR UNDERSTANDING

1. *What different forms does the concept of love take on in this poem? Are there some forms of love conspicuously absent here?*
2. *In our culture, we tend to view nature rather impersonally. How does this poem show us nature in a very personal light?*
3. *The Romans were not especially good natural scientists. They were, however, quite good religionists and poets. How effectively does this poem work as a creative fusion of biological imperatives, religious awe, and primal love as figured in the goddess Venus?*
4. *What role does the sense of hearing have in this poem?*

Supplemental Readings

1.

The delight of landfall at one's home after a long voyage is the subject of this poem.

READING FOR INFORMATION

1. *What past pleasure had the narrator experienced on these shores?*

O litus vitā mihi dulcius! O mare felix
　　cui licet ad terras ire subinde meas!
O formosa dies! Hōc quondam rure solebam
　　Naiadas alternā sollicitare manū!
Hīc fontis lacus est, illīc sinus egerit algas:　　5

haec statio est tacitis fida cupidinibus.
Pervixi; neque enim Fortuna malignior umquam
eripiet nobis quod prior hora dedit.

subinde — presently   **statio, -nis** — harbor   **malignus, -a, -um** — unkind
Nais, Naiadis — water nymph   **pervivo, -ere** — survive

READING FOR UNDERSTANDING

1. *Is the poet's description of swimming (**Naiadas alternā sollicitare manū**) effective or a little too precious?*
2. *When the poet writes **pervixi** (line 7), does he mean that now, on making landfall, he has survived his ordeal, or that after all his experiences, both bad and good, he has lived a full life?*

2.

This poem offers a distinctively Roman appreciation of beachcombing.

Qui non vult properare mori, nec cogere fata
  mollia praecipiti rumpere fila manū,
hactenus iratum mare nōverit. Ecce refuso
  gurgite, securos abluit unda pedes.
Ecce inter virides iactatur mytilus algas,   5
  et rauco trahitur lubrica concha sono.
Ecce recurrentes quā versat fluctus arenas,
  discolor attritā calculus exit humo.
Haec quisquis calcare potest, in litore tuto
  ludat et hoc solum iudicet esse mare.   10

hactenus — up to this point   **abluo, -ere** — wash, lave   **concha, -ae** — sea snail
refundo, -ere — flow back   **mytilus, -i** — mussel   **attrita** < **attero**

READING FOR UNDERSTANDING

1. *The contrast here between seafaring and being a beach bum is very attractive, but is it realistic?*
2. *Compared with your impressions of the seashore or the lakeshore, does this depiction capture all the appropriate sensations, or would you add others?*

3.

The following aphorisms reveal that the Romans had some notions about nature very different from ours. Ecological and environmental studies have informed us much. And when it comes to human nature, we have benefited from the disciplines of psychology and psychiatry.

dii deos: ellipsis of what verb?	Natura vincit naturam et dii deos.
laedas: use of subjunctive? **cum**: type?	Ingenuitatem laedas, cum indignum roges.
ducas: use of subjunctive?	Nihil proprium ducas quicquid mutari potest.
	Nil non aut lenit aut domat diuturnitas.
	Spina etiam grata est, ex qua spectatur rosa.
	Ingenuitas non recipit contumeliam.
	Virum bonum natura, non ordo, facit.
cum: type? **timore**: use of ablative? **scito**: what form? **tibi**: use of dative? **esse**: use of infinitive? **timendum**: gerund or gerundive?	Cum tibi proponas animalia bruta timore, unum hominem scito tibi praecipuē esse timendum.
	Dat legem natura tibi, non accipit ipsa.
	Terra omnis patria est, quā nascimur et tumulamur.
manū: use of ablative?	Omne manū factum consumit longa vetustas.
	Imago animi sermo est: qualis est vir, talis oratio.
arte: use of ablative? **nulli, homini**: use of dative?	Nullum morosius est animal maioreque arte tractandum quam homo: et nulli magis parcendum quam homini.
defloruerit: tense? **quaeratur**: use of subjunctive?	Quae defloruerit, ne iterum quaeratur rosa.
si: type of condition?	Si fatum est, quid times quod certum est?
homini: use of dative?	Quid est homini inimicissimum? Alter homo.
	Omnes infantes terra nudos excipit:
pudet: type of verb? **sordidius**: adjective or adverb?	non te pudet sordidius vivere quam nasci?
possis: use of subjunctive?	Morieris: stultum est timēre, quod vitare non possis.
	Nihil magnum est in rebus humanis, nisi animus magna despiciens.
	Mira ratio est, quae non vult praedicari, quod gaudet intellegi.

generositas: subject or complement?

Nobilitas animi generositas sensus.

somno: use of ablative?
cum: type?

Stultum est somno delectari et mortem horrēre, cum somnus adsiduus sit mortis imitatio.

ratione: use of ablative?
tempore: use of ablative?

Saepe ea, quae sanari ratione non poterant, sanata sunt tempore.

ingenuitas, -tatis — nobility

diuturnitas, -tatis — length of time

brutus, -a, -um — brute

tumulo, -are — bury

vetustas, -tatis — posterity

defloreo, -ēre — deflower

praedico, -are — praise

generositas, -tatis — generosity

delecto, -are — delight

imitatio, -nis — likeness

READING FOR UNDERSTANDING

1. *In our culture, we have the ideology that nature and humanity are interdependent and function in partnership. What evidence do you see for that ideology in these maxims?*
2. *What views about human nature do you find expressed here? Do you share these views?*
3. *From what you see here, where do the gods seem to belong in the "ecosystem" that the Romans understood? Are the intersections between theology and ecology like those identified in our culture?*

4.

A description of zoological diversity, this poem offers a glimpse of the Romans' general knowledge of natural science.

READING FOR INFORMATION

1. *Unlike other birds, when do crows supposedly lay their eggs?*
2. *How do bear cubs take their form?*
3. *How do tortoises keep their eggs warm?*

> Sīc contrā rerum naturae munera nōta,
>   corvus maturis frugibus ōva refert.
> Sīc format linguā fetum, cum protulit, ursa;
>   et piscis, nullo iunctus amore, parit.
> Sīc Phoebea chelys, nixū resolutā favente   5
>   Lucinā, tepidis naribus ōva fovet.
> Sīc sine concubitū textis apis excita ceris
>   fervet, et audaci milite castra replet.
> Non uno contenta valet natura tenore,
>   sed permutatas gaudet habēre vices.   10

formo, -are — give shape to

protulit < **profero**

Phoebeus, -a, -um — Apollonian

chelys, -lis — turtle

Lucina, -ae — goddess of childbirth

apis, -is — bee

repleo, -ēre — fill

1. *The first line and the last couplet of the poem offer the most interesting propositions. Does the depiction of nature being flexible and dynamic strike you as accurate (despite the dubious illustrative examples)?*

5.

This poem, about the Phoenix, a mythical animal, opens with a description of the bird's "natural" habitat. From the very start of this account, we see just how unique the Phoenix is.

READING FOR INFORMATION
1. *The grove of Sol is found in which direction?*
2. *At what altitude is the grove? Is it mountainous or flat?*
3. *What two mythological events did the grove remain untouched by?*

> Est locus in primo felix oriente remotus,
>> quā patet aeterni maxima porta poli,
> nec tantum aestivos hiemisve propinquus ad ortūs,
>> sed quā Sol verno fundit ab axe diem.
> Illīc planities tractūs diffundit apertos,   5
>> nec tumulus crescit nec cava vallis hiat,
> sed nostros montes, quorum iuga celsa putantur,
>> per bis sex ulnas imminet ille locus.
> Hīc Solis nemus est: et consitus arbore multā
>> lucus perpetuae frondis honore virens.   10
> Cum Phaetontaeis flagrasset ab ignibus axis,
>> ille locus flammis inviolatus erat;
> et cum diluvium mersisset fluctibus orbem
>> Deucalionaeas exsuperavit aquas.

oriens, -tis — east
planities, -ei — plain
tractus, -ūs — region
consero, -ere — scatter
Phaetontaeus, -a,
-um — of Phaeton (would-be charioteer of the sun)
inviolatus, -a, -um — untouched
diluvium, -i — deluge
Deucalionaeus, -a, -um — of Deucalion (the Greco-Roman Noah)
exsupero, -are — rise above

Next, we learn of some of the utopian features of the Phoenix's habitat.

READING FOR INFORMATION
1. *Which calamities, both human and natural, are absent from the grove?*
2. *Without rain, how is the plain watered?*
3. *What is unique about the tree found in this grove?*

Non hunc exsangues Morbi, non aegra Senectus   15
    nec Mors crudelis nec Metus asper adest
nec Scelus infandum nec opum vesana Cupido
    aut Pavor aut ardens caedis amore Furor.
Luctus acerbus abest et Egestas obsita pannis
    et Curae insomnes et violenta Fames.   20
Non ibi tempestas nec vis furit horrida venti
    nec gelido terram rore pruina tegit.
Nulla super campos tendit sua vellera nubes
    nec cadit ex alto turbidus umor aquae.
sed fons in medio est, quem vivum nomine dicunt,   25
    perspicuus, lenis, dulcibus uber aquis.
Qui semel erumpens per singula tempora mensum
    duodeciens undis irrigat omne nemus.
Hīc genus arboreum procero stipite surgens
    non lapsura solo mitia poma gerit.   30

infandus, -a, -um — unspeakable

vesanus, -a, -um — mad

egestas, -tatis — need

obsero, -ere — cover in

pannus, -i — rag

insomnis, -e — sleepless

turbidus, -a, -um — swollen

perspicuus, -a, -um — clear

duodeciens — twelve times

irrigo, -are — water

arboreus, -a, -um — arboreal

procerus, -a, -um — tall

stipes, -itis — trunk

The Phoenix spends each morning in a variety of activities.

READING FOR INFORMATION
1. *To which god is the Phoenix sacred?*
2. *What does the Phoenix do each day at the start of dawn?*
3. *To whom does the Phoenix sing? How is her song distinctive?*

Hoc nemus, hos lucos avis incolit unica Phoenix,
    unica, si vivit morte refecta suā.
Paret et obsequitur Phoebo memoranda satelles:
    hoc Natura parens munus habēre dedit.
Lutea cum primum surgens Aurora rubescit,   35
    cum primum roseā sidera luce fugat.
Ter, quater illa pias immergit corpus in undas;
    ter, quater e vivo gurgite libat aquam.
Tollitur ac summo considit in arboris altae
    vertice, quae totum despicit una nemus,   40
et conversa novos Phoebi nascentis ad ortūs
    exspectat radios et iubar exoriens.
Ast ubi Sol pepulit fulgentis limina portae
    et primi emicuit luminis aura levis,

incipit illa sacri modulamina fundere cantūs   45
    et mirā lucem voce ciēre novam.
Quam nec aedoniae voces nec tibia possit
    musica Cirrheis adsimilare modis;
sed neque olor moriens imitari posse putetur
    nec Cylleneae fila canorae lyrae.   50

obsequor, -i — yield   **modulamen, -minis** — melody   **adsimulo, -are** — imitate

satelles, -itis — attendant   **aedonius, -a, -um** —   **olor, -ris** — swan

rubesco, -ere — grow red   nightingale's   **Cylleneus, -a, -um** —

fugo, -are — banish   **Cirrheus, -a, -um** — Delphic,   Mercury's

quater — four times   Apollonian

The evening of the Phoenix's day is now described, as is the evening of her life, when she starts her final migration.

READING FOR INFORMATION
1. *What does the Phoenix do at day's end?*
2. *What is the Phoenix's natural life span?*
3. *At the end of her life, when she leaves the grove of Sol, where does she fly to? On what kind of tree does she settle?*

Postquam Phoebus equos in aperta effudit Olympi
    atque orbem totum protulit usque
illa ter alarum repetito verbere plaudit
    igniferumque caput ter venerata silet.
Atque eadem celeres etiam discriminat horas   55
    innarrabilibus nocte dieque sonis,
antistes luci nemorumque verenda sacerdos
    et sola arcanis conscia, Phoebe, tuis.
Quae postquam vitae iam mille peregerit annos
    at sibi reddiderint tempora longa gravem,   60
ut reparet lapsum spatiis vergentibus aevum,
    adsueti nemoris dulce cubile fugit.
Cumque renascendi studio loca sancta reliquit,
    tunc petit hunc orbem, Mors ubi regna tenet.
Derigit in Syriam celeres longaeva volatūs,   65
    Phoenicen nomen cui dedit ipsa vetus.
Securosque petit deserta per avia lucos,
    hīc ubi per saltūs silva remota latet.
Tum legit aerio sublimem vertice palmam,
    quae Graium Phoenix ex ave nomen habet,   70
in quam nulla nocens animans prorepere possit,
    lubricus aut serpens aut avis ulla rapax.

ignifer, -a, -um — fiery

discrimino, -are — mark off

innarrabilis, -e — indescribable

antistes, -stitis — master-

arcanus, -a, -um — secret

vergo, -ere — bend, turn

adsuetus, -a, -um — familiar

derigo, -ere — direct

volatus, -ūs — flight

aerius, -a, -um — lofty

Graius, -a, -um — Greek

prorepo, -ere — stalk

rapax, -acis — predatory

Building her last nest and filling it with special substances, the Phoenix finally gives herself up to death.

READING FOR INFORMATION

1. *In what sense is the Phoenix's last nest both a casket and a cradle?*
2. *What are some of the things she brings to her nest? What do they all have in common?*
3. *After she settles back in her nest, what does she do with the things she has accumulated?*

Tum ventos claudit pendentibus Aeolus antris,
　　ne violent flabris āera purpurum,
neu concreta Noto nubes per inania caeli   75
　　submoveat radios solis et obsit avi.
Construit inde sibi seu nidum sive sepulcrum:
　　nam perit ut vivat, se tamen ipsa creat.
Colligit huic sucos et odores divite silvā,
　　quos legit Assyrius, quos opulentus Arabs,   80
quos aut Pygmeae gentes aut India carpit
　　aut molli generat terra Sabaea sinū.
Cinnamon hic auramque procul spirantis amomi
　　congerit et mixto balsama cum folio.
Non casiae mitis, non olentis vimen acanthi   85
　　nec turis lacrimae guttaque pinguis abest.
His addit teneras nardi pubentis aristas
　　et sociat myrrae vim, Panachaea, tuae.
Protinus instructo corpus mutabile nido
　　vitalique toro membra vieta locat.   90
Ore dehinc sucos membris circumque suprāque
　　inicit exsequiis immoritura suis,
tunc inter varios animam commendat odores,
　　depositi tanti nec timet illa finem.

75. **concreta . . . nubes**: a cloud mass condensed by the south wind
86. **nec . . . pinguis**: nor tears of incense but [there was] a fat drop [of it]

Aeolus, -i — god of winds

flabra, -orum — gusts, blasts

concretus, -a, -um — thick, condensed

Notus, -i — south wind

submoveo, -ēre — drive off

obsum, -esse — harm, hinder

Assyrius, -a, -um — Assyrian

Arabs, -bis — Arabian

Pygmeus, -a, -um — of Pygmies

India, -ae — India
Sabaeus, -a, -um — Arabian
cinnamon, -is — cinnamon
amomum, -i — balsam shrub
balsamum, -i — balsam
casia, -ae — wild cinnamon

acanthus, -i — bear's-foot
   (plant)
nardum, -i — nard balsam
pubens, -ntis — flourishing
arista, -ae — crest, beard

Panachaea, -ae — mythical
   island in the Arabian Sea
vietus, -a, -um — withered
dehinc — from here
immorior, -i — die

Miraculous transformations now touch her remains, and the Phoenix is reborn.

READING FOR INFORMATION

1. *What change does her body now undergo?*
2. *What first grows from the ash? What does it metamorphose into?*
3. *After her rebirth, what is her first food?*
4. *As she matures, where does she long to fly?*

morte: use of ablative?	Intereā corpus genitali morte peremptum
	aestuat et flammam parturit ipse calor,
	aetherioque procul de lumine concipit ignem:
	flagrat et ambustum solvitur in cineres.
umore: use of ablative?	Quos velut in massam cineres umore coactos
	conflat; et effectum seminis instar habet.
	Hinc animal primum sine membris fertur oriri,
vermi: use of dative?	sed fertur vermi lacteus esse color:
	creverit immensum subitō cum tempore certo
	seque ovi teretis colligit in speciem.
figurā: use of ablative?	Inde reformatur quali fuit ante figurā
exuviis: use of ablative?	et Phoenix ruptis pullulat exuviis;
cum: type?	ac velut agrestes, cum filo ad saxa tenentur,
filo: use of ablative? **papilione:** use of ablative?	mutari tineae papilione solent.
cuiquam: use of dative?	Non illi cibus est nostro consuetus in orbe
nectare: use of ablative?	nec cuiquam implumem pascere cura subest.
cecidēre: syncopation of what?	Ambrosios libat caelesti nectare rores,
polo: use of ablative?	stellifero tenues qui cecidēre polo.
proferat: use of subjunctive?	Hos legit, his mediis alitur in odoribus ales,
	donec maturam proferat effigiem.
iuventā: use of ablative?	Ast ubi primaevā coepit florēre iuventā,
reditura: what form?	evolat ad patrias iam reditura domos.

Line numbers: 95, 100, 105, 110, 115

genitalis, -e — reproductive
perimo, -ere — extinguish
aetherius, -a, -um — ethereal
ambustus, -a, -um — burned
massa, -ae — heap
conflo, -are — breathe on

effectus, -ūs — effect
instar — like
vermis, -is — worm
lactaeus, -a, -um — milky
reformo, -are — reform
pullulo, -are — hatch

tinea, -ae — caterpillar
papilio, -nis — butterfly
implumis, -e — without
   feathers
ambrosius, -a, -um — ambrosial
stellifer, -a, -um — starry

Before making a pilgrimage to Egyptian Heliopolis, the Phoenix cleans up her nest. The poet now begins a physical description of the bird.

READING FOR INFORMATION

1. *What does the Phoenix do with the "afterbirth" of her regeneration?*
2. *How is the color of the Phoenix described?*
3. *What does her tail look like?*

> Ante tamen, proprio quicquid de corpore restat,
> > ossaque vel cineres exuviasque suas,
> unguine balsameo myrrāque et ture soluto
> > condit et in formam conglobat ore pio.   120
> Quam pedibus gestans contendit Solis ad urbem
> > inque arā residens ponit in aede sacrā.
> Mirandam sese praestat praebetque videnti:
> > tantus avi decor est, tantus abundat honor.
> Principio color est qualis sub sidere caeli   125
> > mitia quem corio punica grana tegunt.
> Qualis inest foliis, quae fert agreste papaver,
> > cum pandit vestes Flora rubente polo.
> Hoc umeri pectusque decens velamine fulget,
> > hoc caput, hoc cervix summaque terga nitent;   130
> caudaque porrigitur fulvo distincta metallo,
> > in cuius maculis purpura mixta rubet.

126. **mitia . . . tegunt**: which tender pomegranates protect with their rind

unguen, -inis — ointment

balsameus, -a, -um — balsamic

conglobo, -are — roll into a ball

corium, -i — skin

punicus, -a, -um — magenta

pando, -ere — open

velamen, -minis — veil

The poet's description of the Phoenix's marvelous appearance continues.

READING FOR INFORMATION

1. *What does her beak look like?*
2. *How are her legs described?*
3. *To what other birds is she compared?*

> Alarum pennas lux pingit discolor, Iris
> > pingere ceu nubes desuper acta solet.
> Albicat insignis mixto viridante smaragdo   135
> > et puro cornū gemmea cuspis hiat.

Ingentes oculos credas geminosque hyacinthos,
      quorum de medio lucida flamma micat.
Aptata est toto capiti radiata corona
      Phoebei referens verticis alta decus.   140
Crura tegunt squamae fulvo distincta metallo,
      ast ungues roseo tingit honore color.
Effigies inter pavonis mixta figuram
      cernitur et pictam Phasidis inter avem.
Magna itidem terris Arabum quae gignitur ales   145
      vix aequare potest, seu fera seu fit avis.
Non tamen est tarda, ut volucres quae corpore magno
      incessūs pigros per grave pondus habent.
Sed levis ac velox, regali plena decore:
      talis in aspectū se tenet usque hominum.   150

Iris — goddess of rainbows	**hyacinthus, -i** — hyacinth	**Phasidis avis** = pheasant
desuper — from above	**radiatus, -a, -um** — glittering	**magna ales** = ostrich
albico, -are — whiten	**Phoebeus, -a, -um** —	**Arabs, -bis** — Arabian
viridor, -ari — shine green	Apollonian	**incessus, -ūs** — gait
cuspis, -pidis — peak, head	**squama, -ae** — scale	

Heliopolis receives the Phoenix with pomp and pageantry. As the poet brings the poem to a close, it presents the bird's biology.

READING FOR INFORMATION

1. *In what ways does Egypt greet her arrival?*
2. *What kind of escort is she given?*
3. *What do we learn about her gender and sexuality at the poem's end? Are these things considered good?*
4. *What is the paradox of the Phoenix's immortality?*

Hūc venit Aegyptus tanti ad miracula visūs
      et raram volucrem turba salutat ovans.
Protinus exsculpunt sacrato in marmore formam
      et signant titulo remque diemque novo.
Contrahit in coetum sese genus omne volantum: 155
      nec praedae memor est ulla nec ulla metūs.
Alituum stipata choro volat illa per altum
      turbaque prosequitur munere laeta pio.
Sed postquam puri pervenit ad aetheris auras,
      mox redit; ista suis conditur inde locis.   160
A fortunatae sortis finisque volucrem,
      cui de se nasci praestitit ipse deus!

> Femina vel mas haec, seu neutrum, seu sit utrumque,
>   felix quae Veneris foedera nulla colit;
> mors illi venus est, sola est in morte voluptas: 165
>   ut possit nasci, appetit ante mori.
> Ipsa sibi proles, suus est pater et suus heres,
>   nutrix ipsa sui, semper alumna sibi:
> ipsa quidem, sed non eadem quia et ipsa nec ipsa est,
>   aeternam vitam mortis adepta bono.   170

Aegyptus, -i — Egypt   **exsculpo, -ere** — sculpt   **stipo, -are** — crowd together

READING FOR UNDERSTANDING

1. *Explain the logic of the biology of the Phoenix. Why does it make sense that she is without gender and asexual?*

2. *There are many versions of the Phoenix story in Greco-Roman literature and many other versions throughout world mythologies. How would you explain the popularity of this myth?*

3. *The myth was also very popular in the early Christian era. Which of its details would have appealed to the early church?*

B. Religion

Prose Readings

1.

Here we have a story about King Tarquin the Proud (traditionally second half of the 6th century BCE), a mysterious old woman, and the collected prophecies about Rome that came to be called the Sibylline Books.

READING FOR INFORMATION

1. *How many volumes did the old woman have to sell?*
2. *From the start, what was Tarquin's attitude toward her? Why?*
3. *How many volumes did Tarquin end up buying?*
4. *What became of the old woman?*

esse: 14.II
velle: 14.II

aetate: 3.V.7
desiperet:
  16.XIII.1.b
cum: 16.I.3.b
vellet: 16.V
multō: 3.V.9
delirare: 14.II

emat: 16.V
ore, animo: 3.V.5
habendam esse:
  17.IV; 14.I
nihilo: 3.V.9
pretio: 3.V.12

loci: 3.II.2

cum: 16.I.3.b
consulendi: 17.IV

In antiquis annalibus memoria super libris Sibyllinis haec prodita est: anus hospita atque incognita ad Tarquinium Superbum regem adiit, novem libros ferens, quos esse dicebat divina oracula; eos velle vendere. Tarquinius pretium percontatus est. Mulier nimium atque immensum poposcit; rex, quasi anus aetate desiperet, derisit. Tum illa foculum coram cum igni apponit, tres libros ex novem deurit et, ecquid reliquos sex eodem pretio emere vellet, regem interrogavit. Sed enim Tarquinius id multō risit magis, dixitque anum iam procul dubio delirare. Mulier ibidem statim tres alios libros exussit atque id ipsum denuō placidē rogat, ut tres reliquos eodem illo pretio emat. Tarquinius ore iam serio atque attentiore animo fit, eam constantiam confidentiamque non insuper habendam esse intellegit, libros tres reliquos mercatur nihilo minore pretio, quam quod erat petitum pro omnibus. Sed eam mulierem tunc a Tarquinio digressam posteā nusquam loci visam esse constitit. Libri tres, in sacrarium conditi, "Sibyllini" sunt appellati; ad eos quasi ad oraculum quindecimviri adeunt, cum di immortales publicē consulendi sunt.

---

annales, -ium — annals
prodo, -ere — publish
hospitus, -a, -um — strange
incognitus, -a, -um — unknown
percontor, -ari — inquire
immensus, -a, -um — absurd

desipio, -ere — be silly
derideo, -ēre — ridicule
foculus, -i — fireplace
coram — right in front of him
deuro, -ere — burn
ecquid — whether
deliro, -are — be insane

ibidem — at the very moment
exuro, -ere — burn
denuō — once again
serius, -a, -um — serious
attentus, -a, -um — attentive
insuper — besides, moreover
mercor, -ari — purchase

digredior, -i — depart
constitit < **constat**

nusquam — nowhere
sacrarium, -i — shrine, chapel

quindecimviri — panel of
minor priests

READING FOR UNDERSTANDING

1. *The Romans revered their Sibylline Books, but at the time when Tarquin bought them, how would they have known the books' worth?*
2. *The Sibyl of Cumae, a famous prophetess of extraordinary old age, isn't named here as the seller of the books, but she is the first to come to mind as the mysterious old woman. Why doesn't the author do more than hint at the identity of the old woman?*
3. *Imagine how the Roman government was benefited by the ability to consult books of "divine prophecy" each time a serious crisis befell it.*

2.

The Romans had a profound ambivalence about all things Greek. This incident, dated to 181 BCE, reflects a strong impulse to preserve Roman cultural purity at the expense of superior Greek learning.

READING FOR INFORMATION

1. *How were the two stone chests discovered?*
2. *What did each of them contain?*
3. *How were the Greek contents treated differently from the Roman?*

conservandae:
17.III; 3.II.6
P. Cornelio . . .
consulibus: 13.VI
cultoribus . . .
versantibus:
13.III.2
altius: 6.II
duabus . . . repertis:
13.III.1
diligentiā: 3.V.3

adservandos: 17.III
solvendam: 17.III

Magna conservandae religionis etiam apud maiores nostros, P. Cornelio Baebio Tamphilo consulibus, cura acta est. Siquidem cultoribus in agro L. Petili scribae sub Ianiculo terram altius versantibus, duabus arcis lapideis repertis, quarum in alterā scriptura indicabat corpus Numae Pompilii fuisse, in alterā libri reconditi erant Latini septem de iure pontificum totidemque Graeci de disciplinā sapientiae, Latinos magnā diligentiā adservandos curaverunt, Grecos, quia aliquā ex parte ad solvendam religionem pertinēre existimabantur, praetor urbanus ex auctoritate senatūs per victimarios, facto igni in conspectū populi, cremavit: noluerunt enim prisci viri quicquam in hac adservari civitate, quo animi hominum a deorum cultū avocarentur.

conservo, -are — preserve
etiam — especially
maiores — ancestors
siquidem — since, when
cultor, -is — plowman
scriba, -ae — scribe

Ianiculum, -i — Roman hill
arca, -ae — strongbox
lapideus, -a, -um — of stone
recondo, -ere — bury
totidem — same number of
adservo, -are — preserve

pertineo, -ēre — pertain
praetor urbanus — police commissioner
victimarius, -i — subordinate
cremo, -are — burn
avoco, -are — divert

READING FOR UNDERSTANDING

READING FOR UNDERSTANDING

1. *What is the significance in the difference between Roman **ius pontificum** and Greek **disciplina sapientiae**?*
2. *Does the introduction of something innovatory in religion necessarily contribute to religion's undoing?*
3. *Why would some people, including Romans, argue this point?*

3.

Set in 390 BCE, this story stresses the importance of the piety of ordinary Roman citizens. It recounts how sacred objects were transferred to a nearby town when Rome was in peril.

READING FOR INFORMATION

1. *Whom did Albanius discover fleeing Rome? Why were they doing so?*
2. *With whom was Albanius traveling?*
3. *What (false) etymology does the author provide for the Latin word **caerimonia**?*

urbe ... captā: 13.III.1 cum: 16.I.3.a onere partito: 13.III.1	Urbe enim a Gallis captā, cum flamen Quirinalis virginesque Vestales sacra, onere partito, ferrent, easque Pontem Sublicium transgressas et clivum, qui ducit ad Ianiculum, ascendere incipientes L. Albanius plaustro
religioni, caritati: 3.III.2 descenderent: 16.IV.2 omisso ... itinere: 13.III.2 Caere oppidum: 4.I ubi: 16.XIII.2.a veneratione: 3.V.3	coniugem et liberos vehens aspexisset, propior publicae religioni quam privatae caritati suis ut plaustro descenderent imperavit, atque in id virgines et sacra imposita, omisso coepto itinere, Caere oppidum pervexit, ubi cum summā veneratione recepta sunt. Grata memoria ad hoc usque tempus hospitalem humanitatem testatur: inde enim institutum est sacra
infracto ... statū: 13.III.1 sordidius: 6.I	caerimonias vocari, quia Caeretani ea, infracto rei publicae statū perinde ac florente, sanctē coluerunt. Illud agreste et sordidius plaustrum tempestivē
aequaverit, antecesserit: future perfects	capax cuiuslibet fulgentissimi triumphalis currūs vel aequaverit gloriam vel antecesserit.

flamen Quirinalis — high priest of the deified Romulus	**plaustrum, -i** — wagon, cart	**infringo, -ere** — weaken
sacra, -orum — sacred objects	**privatus, -a, -um** — private	**perinde** — exactly as
partio, -ire — distribute	**omitto, -ere** — discontinue	**tempestivē** — appropriately
Pons Sublicius — bridge across the Tiber	**perveho, -ere** — transport	**capax, -acis** — suitable
Ianiculum, -i — Roman hill	**veneratio, -nis** — reverence	**fulgens, -ntis** — shiny
ascendo, -ere — climb	**hospitalis, -e** — hospitable	**currus, -ūs** — chariot
	humanitas, -tatis — kindness	**aequo, -are** — equal
	testor, -ari — attest to	**antecedo, -ere** — surpass

READING FOR UNDERSTANDING

1. *According to this story, is piety toward religion or loyalty to family more praiseworthy?*
2. *Do you think our value system would regard Albanius's choice as equally praiseworthy?*
3. *Why is a display of private piety significant in a time of—and in the face of—public crisis?*

4.

Rome suffered one of its worst military losses in 53 BCE, when the Parthians destroyed the tri-umvir M. Licinius Crassus and seven legions at Carrhae, in eastern Syria. This story relates how signs indicated that the campaign was thoroughly doomed. These signs, according to the author, expressed great divine displeasure.

READING FOR INFORMATION
1. Generals' cloaks can be found in what colors? What colors are typically worn on entering into battle?
2. How do soldiers usually greet their general before battle?
3. What is the author's attitude toward Crassus's loss of seven Roman legions?

Non sinit nos M. Crassus, inter gravissimas Romani imperii iacturas numerandus, hōc loco de se silentium agere, plurimis et evidentissimis ante tantam ruinam monstrorum pulsatus ictibus. Ducturus erat a Carrhis adversus Parthos exercitum. Pullum ei traditum est paludamentum, cum in proelium exeuntibus album aut purpureum dari soleat. Maesti et taciti milites ad principia convēnerunt, qui vetere instituto cum clamore alacri accurrere debebant. Aquilarum altera vix convelli a primo pilo potuit, altera aegerrimē extracta in contrariam ac ferebatur partem se ipsa convertit. Magna haec prodigia, sed illae clades aliquantō maiores, tot pulcherrimarum legionum interitus, tam multa signa hostilibus manibus intercepta, tantum Romanae militiae decus barbarorum obtritum equitatū, optimae indolis filii cruore paterni respersi oculi, corpus imperatoris inter promiscuas cadaverum strues avium ferarumque laniatibus obiectum. Vellem quidem placidius, sed quod relatum verum est. Sīc deorum spreti monitūs excandescunt, sīc humana consilia castigantur, ubi se caelestibus praeferunt.

numerandus: 17.III

ictibus: 3.V.1
ducturus erat: 17.VI

cum: 16.I.2
exeuntibus: 3.III.1
vetere instituto: 3.V.7

indolis: 3.II.3
cruore: 3.V.1
laniatibus: 3.III.9

vellem: 15.II.2

ubi: 16.XIII.2.a
caelestibus: 3.III.7

---

iactura, -ae — loss

numero, -are — count

evidens, -ntis — obvious

ruina, -ae — ruin

monstrum, -i — omen, sign

pulso, -are — beat

pullus, -a, -um — gray

paludamentum, -i — cloak

principia, -orum — headquarters

convenio, -ire — meet

institutum, -i — practice, custom

alacer, -cris, -cre — swift

accurro, -ere — run up to

aquila, -ae — battle standard

primus pilus — chief centurion

extraho, -ere — extract

prodigium, -i — prodigy

clades, -is — disaster

aliquantō — rather

interitus, -ūs — destruction

intercipio, -ere — intercept

militia, -ae — military

obtero, -ere — trample

equitatus, -ūs — cavalry

indoles, -is — talent

paternus, -a, -um — fatherly

respergo, -ere — splatter

promiscuus, -a, -um — mixed

cadaverum, -i — corpse

strues, -is — heap

laniatus, -ūs — tearing

obicio, -ere — toss about

sperno, -ere — scorn

monitus, -ūs — warning

excandesco, -ere — grow hot

castigo, -are — belittle

READING FOR UNDERSTANDING

1. *What seems to be the difference between an omen and a prodigy?*
2. *At what point did the gods begin to disfavor Crassus's campaign against the Parthians—before or after it started?*
3. *According to this account, could Crassus's campaign ever have succeeded? If it had succeeded, would the occurrences described in this story as prodigies have been so described? What would the role of the gods have been in Crassus's putative success?*

5.

The origins of Rome's Secular Games, a festival of great antiquity, are given here. The story, more fancy than actual history, narrates a father's desperate efforts to see his sick children cured. Guided by a divine voice, they undertake a journey to find restorative water from a particular place.

READING FOR INFORMATION

1. *What was Valesius doing when he began to pray to his household gods?*
2. *What does he ask the gods to do? Do they do it?*
3. *Why is Valesius so eager to find or make fire?*

Cum ingenti pestilentiā urbs agrique vastarentur, Valesius, vir locuples rusticae vitae, duobus filiis et filiā ad desperationem usque medicorum laborantibus, aquam calidam eis a foco petens, genibus nixus lares familiares ut puerorum periculum in ipsius caput transferrent oravit. Orta deinde vox est, habiturum esse eos salvos, si continuō flumine Tiberi devectos Tarentum portasset, ibique ex Ditis patris et Proserpinae arā petita aqua recreasset. Eo praedicto magnopere confusus, quod et longa et periculosa navigatio imperabatur, spe tamen dubiā praesentem metum vincente, pueros ad ripam Tiberis protinus detulit ac, lintre Ostiam petens, nocte concubia ad Martium campum appulit; sitientibusque aegris succurrere cupiens, igne in navigio non suppetente, ex gubernatore cognōvit haud procul apparēre fumum; et ab eo iussus egredi Tarentum—id nomen ei loco est—cupidē adrepto calice, aquam flumine haustam eo, unde fumus erat obortus, iam laetior pertulit, divinitus dati remedii quasi vestigia quaedam in propinquo nanctum esse se existimans; inque solo magis fumante quam ullas ignis habente reliquias, dum tenacius omen apprehendit, contractis levibus et quae fors obtulerat nutrimentis pertinaci spiritū flammam evocavit, calefactamque aquam pueris bibendam dedit.

Margin annotations:
cum: 16.I.1
vitae: 3.II.3
filiis . . . laborantibus: 13.III.1
eis: 3.III.3
genibus: 3.V.1
ut: 16.IV
habiturum esse: 12.I.3.d
flumine: 3.V.2
Tarentum: 4.I.2
portasset, recreasset: 16.XI; 20.I.3
praedicto: 3.V.7
quod: 16.XIII.3.b
spe . . . vincente: 13.III.1
lintre: 3.V.1
sitientibusque aegris: 3.III.7
igne . . . suppetente: 13.III.2
Tarentum: 4.I.2
adrepto calice: 13.III.1
dum: 16.XIII.3.a.i.A.1
tenacius: 6.II
nutrimentis: 3.V.1
spiritū: 3.V.7
bibendam: 17.III

pestilentia, -ae — plague
vasto, -are — lay waste to
locuples, -letis — wealthy
desperatio, -nis — desperation

calidus, -a, -um — warm
focus, -i — hearth
genu, -ūs — knee
nitor, -i — poise

lar, -is — tutelary household god
familiaris, -e — of the family
flumen, -inis — river

recreo, -are — recover	**navigium, -i** — ship	**remedium, -i** — remedy
praedictum, -i — omen	**suppeto, -ere** — be available	**nanciscor, -i** — get hold of
magnopere — greatly	**gubernator, -ris** —	**fumo, -are** — smoke
confusus, -a, -um — confused	steersman	**tenax, -acis** — persistent
navigatio, -nis — voyage	**fumus, -i** — smoke	**apprehendo, -ere** — grasp
ripa, -ae — riverbank	**egredior, -i** — disembark	**contraho, -ere** — pull
defero, -rre — carry	**adripio, -ere** — grab up	together
linter, -tri — small boat	**calix, -licis** — drinking cup	**levis, -e** — light, flammable
concubium, -i — night's sleep	**haurio, -ire** — drink	**nutrimentum, -i** — tinder
sitio, -ire — be thirsty	**oborior, -iri** — arise	**evoco, -are** — evoke
succurro, -ere — relieve	**divinitus** — divinely	**calefacio, -ere** — heat

As the story continues, the children have a marvelous dream, telling them how to properly offer thanks to the gods. After some difficulty, the rite is performed and the gods are satisfied. Many years later, the consul Publicola repeats the rite in the hopes that Rome might benefit from its healing effect.

READING FOR INFORMATION

1. *According to the cured children, to which gods should sacrifices be made? What other thanksgivings should be offered?*
2. *After Valesius left to purchase an altar, what did his slaves discover while they were digging?*
3. *What did the consul Publicola do to the altar after he repeated the rites of Valesius?*

quā pōtatā: 13.III.2
quiete: 3.V.3
sopiti: 12.II
vi: 3.V.19
vīdisse: 12.I.3.d
a: 3.V.6
ut: 16.IV
hostiae: 3.I
loci: 3.II.2

ut: 16.III.1
empturus: 12.II
relictis viris: 13.III.1
qui: 16.III.2.a
constituendorum: 17.V.2
cum: 16.I.3.a
pedum: 3.II.8
hoc: 3.IV.1
nuntiante servo: 13.III.1
emendae: 17.III
omisso . . . proposito: 13.III.2
Tarenti: 4.I.3
noctibus: 4.II.2
periculo: 3.V.19
studio: 3.V.7
succurrendi: 17.II
civibus: 3.III.7
nuncupatis votis, caesis . . . bubus: 13.III.1; bubus: 2.V
Diti, Proserpinae: 3.III.3
maribus, feminis: 3.VIII
trinoctio: 4.II.2
lectisternio . . . factis: 13.III.1

Quā pōtatā salutari quiete sopiti diutinā vi morbi repente sunt liberati, patrique indicaverunt vīdisse se in somnis a nescio quo deorum spongeā corpora sua pertergēri et praecipi ut ad Ditis patris et Proserpinae aram, a qua potio ipsis fuerat adlata, furvae hostiae immolarentur lectisterniaque ac ludi nocturni fierent. Is, quod eo loci nullam aram vīderat, desiderari credens ut a se constitueretur, aram empturus in urbem perrexit, relictis viris qui fundamentorum constituendorum gratiā terram ad solidum foderent. Hi viri domini imperium exsequentes, cum ad viginti pedum altitudinem humo egestā pervēnissent, animadverterunt aram Diti patri Proserpinaeque inscriptam. Hoc postquam Valesius nuntiante servo accepit, omisso emendae arae proposito, hostias nigras, quae antiquitus furvae dicebantur, Tarenti immolavit, ludosque et lectisternia continuis tribus noctibus, quia totidem filii periculo liberati erant, fecit. Cuius exemplum Valerius Publicola, qui primus consul fuit, studio succurrendi civibus secutus, apud eandem aram publicē, nuncupatis votis caesisque atris bubus, Diti maribus, feminis Proserpinae lectisternioque ac ludis trinoctio factis, aram terrā, ut ante fuerat, obruit.

salutaris, -e — restorative

sopio, -ire — doze, sleep

diutinus, -a, -um — long

nescioquis — some(one) unknown

spongea, -ae — sponge

pertergeo, -ēre — cleanse

praecipio, -ere — instruct

adlata < adfero

furvus, -a, -um — dark, black

hostia, -ae — sacrificial animal

immolo, -are — immolate

lectisternium, -i — religious feast

nocturnus, -a, -um — by night

perrego, -ere — set out

fundamentum, -i — foundation

solidus, -a, -um — solid

fodio, -ere — dig

exsequor, -i — carry out

altitudo, -dinis — depth

egero, -ere — remove

inscribo, -ere — inscribe

omitto, -ere — drop, leave off

propositum, -i — plan

antiquitus — in antiquity

succurro, -ere — relieve

nuncupo, -are — utter

ater, -tra, -trum — dark, black

trinoctium, -i — a three-night period

obruo, -ere — bury

READING FOR UNDERSTANDING

1. Why were the gods Dis Pater and Proserpina honored after the children were healed? What was the significance of the black sacrificial victims?

2. What do the symbols of water, fire, and earth mean in this story? The number 3? The male/female distinction?

3. To achieve his desired end, Valesius must undergo a considerable ordeal and then undertake an elaborate thanksgiving. What seems to be the theological message behind this story?

6.

This anecdote is offered in support of the notion that the Roman gods looked out for the Roman state even in emergencies. A conspicuous omen provides "evidence" that the gods favor Rome as Rome. The scene is set in 390 BCE.

READING FOR INFORMATION

1. If omens aren't accidents of nature, what are they?

2. Where and under what circumstances did the omen in this story occur?

3. From a Roman viewpoint, what was the major difference between the city of Rome and the city of Veii?

motū, providentiā: 3.V.7
quae: 7.V.2
ut: 16.II
deliberantibus . . .
  conscriptis: 13.III.2
migrarent, restituerent:
  16.V
cohortibus redeuntibus:
  13.III.1

vestigio: 3.V.19

Veios: 4.I.2
transeundi: 17.II

diis existimantibus:
  13.III.1
auspiciis: 3.V.14

Ominum etiam observatio aliquo contactū religioni innexa est, quoniam non fortuito motū, sed divinā providentiā constare creduntur. Quae effecit ut, urbe a Gallis disiectā, deliberantibus patribus conscriptis utrum Veios migrarent an sua moenia restituerent, forte eo tempore e praesidio cohortibus redeuntibus, centurio in comitio exclamaret, "Signifer, statue signum, hīc optimē manebimus": eā enim voce auditā, senatus accipere se omen respondit, e vestigioque Veios transeundi consilium omisit. Quam paucis verbis de domicilio futuri summi imperii confirmata est condicio! Credo indignum esse, diis existimantibus Romanum nomen prosperrimis auspiciis ortum,

<table>
<tr><td>appellatione: 3.V.1
mutari, infundi:
12.I.3.c
ruinis: 3.III.3</td><td>Veientanae urbis appellatione mutari, inclitaeque victoriae decus modo abiectae urbis ruinis infundi.</td></tr>
</table>

observatio, -nis — observation	**moenia, -ium** — city walls	**domicilium, -i** — home
contactus, -ūs — connection	**restituo, -ere** — rebuild	**confirmo, -are** — confirm
innecto, -ere — involve	**praesidium, -i** — garrison	**prosperus, -a, -um** — favorable
fortuitus, -a, -um — random	**cohors, -rtis** — cohort, unit	**auspicium, -i** — auspice
providentia, -ae — providence	**centurio, -onis** — centurion	**appellatio, -nis** — name
consto, -are — exist	**comitium, -i** — senate house	**inclitus, -a, -um** — glorious
disicio, -ere — ransack	**exclamo, -are** — shout out	**abicio, -ere** — raze
patres conscripti — senators	**signifer, -i** — standard bearer	**ruina, -ae** — ruin
migro, -are — emigrate	**statuo, -ere** — set, fix	**infundo, -ere** — mingle
	transeo, -ire — transfer, move	
	omitto, -ere — drop, abandon	

READING FOR UNDERSTANDING

1. *Why do omens seem more significant in a time of crisis, especially if they occur in important places or contexts?*
2. *What makes an accident or a random occurrence meaningful?*
3. *What are the implications if a culture can see the potential for omens in virtually anything?*

7.

Here a summary description of the organization and the scrupulousness of Roman religion is provided. The author also articulates a commonly held view, that the greatness of Rome's empire was directly related to Rome's religious piety.

READING FOR INFORMATION

1. *What were the respective duties of pontiffs, augurs, prophets, and haruspices?*
2. *What is the function of prayer? Of vow? Of thanksgiving? Of sacrifice?*
3. *Why has Rome grown and prospered?*

<table>
<tr><td>caerimonias: 3.IV.4
scientiā: 3.V.1
gerendarum: 17.III
auctoritates: 3.IV.4
observatione: 3.V.1
praedictiones: 3.IV.4
libris: 3.V.1
depulsiones: 3.IV.4
disciplinā: 3.V.1
instituto: 3.V.7
rebus: 3.III.1
cum:16.I.3.b
commendandum est: 17.IV
precatione: 3.V.1
exposcendum est: 17.IV
voto: 3.V.1
solvendum est: 17.IV
gratulatione: 3.V.1
inquirendum est: 17.IV
extis, sortibus: 3.V.1
impetrito: 19.I.1
antiquis: 3.III.4
servandae, amplificandae:
17.III</td><td>Maiores nostri statas sollemnesque caerimonias pontificum scientiā, bene gerendarum rerum auctoritates augurum observatione, Apollinis praedictiones vatum libris, portentorum depulsiones Etruscā disciplinā explicari voluerunt. Prisco etiam instituto rebus divinis opera datur: cum aliquid commendandum est, precatione; cum exposcendum est, voto; cum solvendum est, gratulatione; cum inquirendum est vel extis vel sortibus, impetrito; cum sollemni ritū peragendum est, sacrificio, quo etiam ostentorum ac fulgurum denuntiationes procurantur. Tantum autem studium antiquis non solum servandae sed etiam amplificandae religionis fuit. Non mirum</td></tr>
</table>

augendo,
    custodiendo: 17.III

igitur est, si pro eo imperio augendo custodiendoque pertinax deorum indulgentia semper excubuit, quō tam scrupulosā curā parvula quōque momenta religionis examinari videntur, quia numquam remotos ab exactissimo cultū caerimoniarum oculos habuisse nostra civitas existimanda est. Omnia namque post religionem ponenda esse semper nostra civitas duxit, etiam in quibus summae maiestatis conspici decus voluit. Quapropter non dubitaverunt sacris imperia servire, ita se humanarum rerum futura esse regimen existimantia, si divinae potentiae bene atque constanter fuissent famulata.

dubitaverunt:
    16.VII.3
sacris: 3.III.5
imperia: 3.IV.4
se: 3.IV.4
regimen: 3.IV.4.a
potentiae: 3.III.5
fuissent: 16.XI

18–19. **se . . . existimantia**: thinking that they will be the controller of human affairs

status, -a, -um — established
scientia, -ae — knowledge
augur, -is — augur
praedictio, -nis — prediction
vates, -is — prophet
portentum, -i — portent
depulsio, -nis — averting
priscus, -a, -um — ancient
institutum, -i — custom, practice
precatio, -nis — prayer
exposco, -ere — request

gratulatio, -nis — thanksgiving
inquiro, -ere — inquire
exta, -orum — entrails
impetritum, -i — good omen
ostentum, -i — prodigy
fulgur, -is — lightning
denuntiatio, -nis — indication
procuro, -are — procure
amplifico, -are — expand
augeo, -ēre — increase
pertinax, -acis — persistent

excubo, -ere — keep watch
scrupulosus, -a, -um — scrupulous
parvulus, -a, -um — tiny
momentum, -i — influence
examino, -are — examine
exactus, -a, -um — precise
quapropter — for this reason
imperia — "powers that be"
regimen, -inis — control
potentia, -ae — power
famulor, -ari — serve

READING FOR UNDERSTANDING

1. *For a Roman priest or magistrate, what are the benefits of promoting religion?*
2. *What is the significance for the Romans of a religious system that their ancestors handed down to them?*
3. *How is the orderly division and classification of religious duties and observances characteristically Roman?*

8.

This passage describes the odd taboos and conventions surrounding the high priest of Jupiter (flamen Dialis) and even his wife (flaminica Dialis).

READING FOR INFORMATION

1. *What authority does the author cite for the information he relates here?*

2. *Why has a* flamen Dialis *only seldom served as consul?*

3. *What happens if someone condemned to corporal punishment appeals to the* flamen Dialis?

flamini: 3.III.3

Caerimoniae impositae flamini Diali sunt multae, item castūs multiplices, quos in libris, qui de sacerdotibus publicis compositi sunt, lēgimus. Unde

equo: 3.V.1

haec fermē sunt, quae commeminimus: equo Dialem flaminem vehi religio est; item religio est extrā pomerium exercitum armatum vidēre;

cum: 16.I.4

idcircō rarenter flamen Dialis creatus consul est, cum bella consulibus

anulo: 3.V.13

mandabantur; item iurare Dialem fas numquam est; item anulo uti nisi pervio cassoque fas non est. Ignem e flaminis Dialis domo, nisi sacrum

vinctum, vincula: 3.IV.4
si: 18.I.4
introierit: future perfect

efferri ius non est. Vinctum, si aedes eius introierit, solvi necessum est, et vincula per impluvium in tegulas subduci atque inde foras in viam demitti. Nodum in apice neque in cinctū neque aliā in parte ullum habet.

si: 18.I.4
quis: 7.VI.1.a
verberandum: 17.V.1

Si quis ad verberandum ducatur, si ad pedes eius supplex procubuerit, eo die verberari piaculum est. Capillum Dialis, nisi qui liber homo est, non detondet.

castus, -ūs — taboo	**mando, -are** — entrust	**subduco, -ere** — lead over
multiplex, -plicis — manifold	**pervius, -a, -um** — having	**demitto, -ere** — lower
fermē — mostly	perforations	**apex, apicis** — priestly hat
commemini, -isse — recount	**cassus, -a, -um** — not solid	**cinctus, -ūs** — belt
extrā — (with accusative)	**vinctum** < **vincio**	**procubo, -ere** — fall
outside	**introeo, -ire** — enter	before
pomerium, -i — city limits	**impluvium, -i** — opening in	**piaculum, -i** — sacrilege
armatus, -a, -um — armed	the roof above a Roman	**detondeo, -ēre** — trim
idcircō — for this reason	atrium	
rarenter — rarely	**tegula, -ae** — roof tile	

The account continues with more taboos and superstitions, some quite bizarre.

READING FOR INFORMATION

1. *The* flamen *must not sleep away from his own bed for how many nights in a row?*

2. *What modification did the pontiffs recently make concerning the* flamen's *hat-wearing requirements?*

3. *What explanation is given for the taboo against the* flamen *taking off his tunic outdoors?*

Diali: 3.III.3

Capram et carnem incoctam et hederam et fabam neque tangere Diali mos est neque nominare. Propagines e vitibus altius praetentas non succedit. Pedes lecti, in quo cubat, luto tenui circumlitos esse oportet et

trinoctium: 4.II.3

de eo lecto trinoctium continuum non decubat neque in eo lecto cubare

alium: 3.IV.4

alium fas est. Apud eius lecti fulcrum capsulam esse cum strue atque ferto oportet. Unguium Dialis et capilli segmina subter arborem felicem

terrā: 3.V.1

uti: 16.II

remissa esse: 12.I.3.d
facta esse: 12.I.3.d
tunicā: 3.V.19
ne: 16.III.1

terrā operiuntur. Dialis cotidiē feriatus est. Sine apice sub divo esse licitum non est; sub tecto uti liceret, non pridem a pontificibus constitutum est; et alia quaedam remissa esse, gratiaque aliquot caerimoniarum facta esse dicitur. Farinam fermento imbutam attingere ei fas non est. Tunicā intimā, nisi in locis tectis, non exuit se, ne sub caelo, tamquam sub oculis Iovis, nudus sit. Super flaminem Dialem in convivio, nisi rex sacrificulus, haut quisquam alius accumbit.

capra, -ae — she-goat	**trinoctium, -i** — period of	**apex, apicis** — priestly hat
caro, carnis — meat	three nights	**divum, -i** — open air
incoctus, -a, -um — uncooked	**decubo, -are** — sleep	**pridem** — long ago
hedera, -ae — ivy	**fulcrum, -i** — bedpost	**aliquot** — some
faba, -ae — bean	**capsula, -ae** — box	**farina, -ae** — grain
propago, -ginis — shoot	**strues, -is** — sacrificial cake	**fermentum, -i** — yeast
praetentus, -a, -um —	**fertum, -i** — sacred cake	**imbuo, -ere** — soak
extended	**unguis, -is** — fingernail	**intimus, -a, -um** — under-
succedo, -ere — pass under	**segmen, -inis** — clipping	**exuo, -ere** — take off
lutum, -i — mud	**subter** — (with accusative)	**rex sacrificulus** — high priest
circumlino, -ere — smear	beneath	of sacrifices
around	**operior, -iri** — be covered	

Information concerning the flamen's marriage, his wife's duties and taboos, and some final random details close the account.

READING FOR INFORMATION

1. *Is a flamen allowed to divorce or to attend funerals?*
2. *What does a flaminica have in her headwear?*
3. *According to M. Varro, why does the flamen wear a white cap?*

flamonio: 3.V.19
morte: 3.V.7

venenato: 3.V.1

gradibus: 3.V.8

cum: 16.I.3.b

sit: 16.XIII.3.b
Iovi: 3.III.3
hostiā: 3.V.7
id: 3.IV.4
oporteat: 20.III.7.a

Uxorem si amisit, flamonio decedit. Matrimonium flaminis nisi morte dirimi ius non est. Locum, in quo bustum est, numquam ingreditur, mortuum numquam attingit; funus tamen exsequi non est religio. Eaedem fermē caerimoniae sunt flaminicae Dialis; alias seorsum aiunt observitare, veluti est, quod venenato operitur, et quod in ricā surculum de arbore felici habet, et quod scalas escendere ei plus tribus gradibus religiosum est atque etiam, cum it ad Argeos, quod neque comit caput neque capillum depectit. Verba praetoris ex edicto perpetuo de flamine Diali (et de sacerdote Vestae) adscripsi: "Sacerdotem Vestalem et flaminem Dialem in omni meā iurisdictione iurare non cogam." Verba M. Varronis super flamine Diali haec sunt: "Is solum album habet galerum, vel quod maximus sacerdos sit, vel quod Iovi immolatā hostiā albā id fieri oporteat."

flamonium, -i — office of
flamen

decedo, -ere — retire

dirimo, -ere — dissolve

bustum, -i — tomb

funus, -eris — funeral
procession

exsequor, -i — follow

fermē — approximately

seorsum — separately

observito, -are — observe

venenatum, -i — dyed clothing

operior, -iri — be covered

rica, -ae — priestly hat

surculum, -i — a cutting

scala, -ae — ladder

Argei, -orum — a district in
Rome

como, -ere — dress, adorn

depecto, -ere — comb out

edictum, -i — edict

iurisdictio, -nis —
jurisdiction

galerus, -i — cap

immolo, -are — sacrifice

hostia, -ae — victim

READING FOR UNDERSTANDING

1. *The* flamen Dialis *usually came from one of the most prominent families of Rome, and when he was seen in public, it was generally quite a spectacle and he was paid much respect. What parts of the* flamen's *life seem enjoyable to you?*
2. *Nonetheless, throughout the history of this priesthood, it was sometimes difficult to find Romans willing to hold it. How do you account for this?*
3. *Compare some of the more bizarre taboos or superstitions in this account with taboos and superstitions in our culture.*

10.

This account describes many of the conventions and taboos associated with the Vestal Virgins, the prestigious priestesses of the goddess Vesta. The passage opens with some of the priesthood's exemptions and exclusions.

READING FOR INFORMATION

1. *Within what age range are Vestals first chosen?*
2. *What physical conditions exclude a girl from selection?*
3. *When might a father's situation automatically exempt a girl from selection?*

capiendā: 17.III	Qui de virgine Vestali capiendā scripserunt, minorem quam annos sex, maiorem quam annos decem natam, negaverunt capi fas esse; item quae
sit: 16.XI	non sit patrima et matrima; item quae linguā debili sensūve aurium
insignita sit: 16.XI	deminuta aliāve qua corporis labe insignita sit; item quae ipsa aut cuius pater
vivo patre: 13.III.3	emancipatus sit, etiamsi vivo patre in avi potestate sit; item cuius parentes
servierunt: 20.I.3	alter ambove servitutem servierunt aut in negotiis sordidis versantur. Sed
eam: 3.IV.4	et eam, cuius soror ad id sacerdotium lecta est, excusationem merēri aiunt; item cuius pater flamen aut augur aut quindecimvirum sacris faciundis
sponsae: 3.III.1	aut septemvirum epulonum aut Salius est. Sponsae quoque pontificis et
filiae: 3.III.1	tubicinis sacrorum filiae vacatio a sacerdotio isto tribui solet. Praeterea
legendam esse: 17.IV	scriptor quidam reliquit neque eius legendam esse filiam, qui domicilium in
habēret: 16.XI excusandam esse: 17.IV	Italiā non habēret, et excusandam esse eius, qui liberos tres habēret.

patrimus, -a, -um — with a living father

matrimus, -a, -um — with a living mother

debilis, -e — impaired

deminutus, -a, -um — diminished

labes, -is — weakness

insignitus, -a, -um — distinguished

emancipo, -are — emancipate

etiamsi — even if

servitus, -tutis — slavery

verso, -are — engage

excusatio, -nis — exemption

quindecimviri sacris faciundis — midlevel priests responsible for sacrifices

septemviri epulonum — midlevel priests responsible for public feasts

Salii — midlevel priests of Mars and Hercules

tubicen, -inis — trumpeter

vacatio, -nis — exemption

domicilium, -i — domicile

excuso, -are — excuse

We next learn about the legal status of Vestals and the ancient law that prescribes the formal method of their selection. The author describes an alternate procedure more often followed in his time.

READING FOR INFORMATION

1. How is the legal status of Vestals different from that of other young women?
2. According to the law, the pontifex chooses a Vestal from a pool of how many eligible girls?
3. How does the senate get involved if the legal procedure isn't followed?

tempore: 4.II.1	Virgo autem Vestalis, simul est capta atque in atrium Vestae est deducta et pontificibus tradita est, eo statim tempore sine emancipatione ac
faciundi: 12.II.4	sine capitis minutione e patris potestate exit et ius testamenti faciundi
capiundae: 12.II.4	adipiscitur. De more autem rītūque capiundae virginis litterae quidem
antiquiores: 6.I.2	antiquiores non exstant, nisi, quae capta prima est, a Numā rege esse
ut: 16.IV	captam. Sed quandem legem invēnimus, quā cavetur, ut pontificis maximi arbitratū virgines e populo viginti legantur sortitioque in contione ex eo
ut: 16.III.1	numero fiat et, cuius sors virginis ducta erit, ut eam pontifex maximus
Vestae: 3.II.1	capiat eaque Vestae fiat. Sed ea sortitio ex lege illā non necessaria nunc
si: 18.I.4 quis: 7.VI.1.a	vidēri solet. Nam si quis honesto loco natus adeat pontificem maximum atque offerat ad sacerdotium filiam suam, cuius dumtaxat salvis
possit:16.VIII	religionum observationibus ratio habēri possit, gratia Papiae legis per
fit: 10.VIII	senatum fit.

deduco, -ere — escort

emancipatio, -nis — emancipation

caput, -pitis — status

minutio, -nis — decrease

exsto, -are — survive

Numa — Rome's second king

arbitratus, -ūs — decision

sortitio, -nis — selection by lot

contio, -nis — assembly

dumtaxat — so long as

The author discusses how a peculiar verb is used in reference to the selection of Vestals. He adds some details about them and about bequests and ends with an explanation of why Vestals are called Beloved.

READING FOR INFORMATION

1. *Why is a Vestal said to be captured and not selected?*
2. *What other priests, besides Vestals, are said to be captured?*
3. *What becomes of a Vestal's estate if she dies without a will?*
4. *According to this account, why is a captured Vestal called Beloved?*

quia: 16.XIII.3.b
manū: 3.V.1
bello: 3.V.7

oporteat: 16.XI
cum: 16.I.3.b
capiat: 16.XII

faciat: 16.III.2.a
siet: 10.III.7.c; 16.XII
Quiritibus: 5.VIII
lege: 3.V.10

cuiquam: 3.III.3
ei: 3.III.3
fiat: 16.V

capiendum: 17.II

"Capi" autem virgo propterea dici videtur, quia pontificis maximi manū prensa ab eo parente, in cuius potestate est, veluti bello capta, abducitur. In annalibus, quae verba pontificem maximum dicere oporteat, cum virginem capiat, scriptum est. Ea verba haec sunt: "Sacerdotem Vestalem, quae sacra faciat, quae ius siet sacerdotem Vestalem facere pro populo Romano, Quiritibus, uti virgo quae optima lege fuit, ita te, Amata, capio." Plerique autem "capi" virginem Vestalem solam debēre dici putant. Sed flamines quoque Diales, item pontifices et augures "capi" dicebantur. Praeterea in commentariis ad Duodecim Tabulas compositis, ita scriptum est: "Virgo Vestalis neque heres est cuiquam intestato, neque ei intestatae quisquam heres est, sed bona eius in publicum redigi aiunt. Id quo iure fiat, quaeritur." "Amata" inter capiendum a pontifice maximo appellatur, quoniam illius virginis, quae prima capta est, hoc fuisse nomen traditum est.

propterea — moreover
prehendo, -ere — grasp
abduco, -ere — lead away
annales, -ium — annals
Quirites, -ium — Roman civilians

plerique — some
commentarium, -i — commentrary
Duodecim Tabulae — Rome's basic laws

intestatus, -a, -um — intestate
redigo, -ere — redirect
quaeritur = is unknown

READING FOR UNDERSTANDING

1. *From what you've read, does it seem that finding candidates for the Vestal Virgins would have been easy?*
2. *Why is the willingness or unwillingness of candidates to serve not discussed here?*
3. *Does the* Pontifex Maximus *sound to you like the Vestal Virgins' boss, surrogate father, or surrogate husband?*

Verse Readings

1.

"God Helps Those Who ...": The Farmer and His Oxen

READING FOR INFORMATION

1. *In what condition did the farmer abandon his oxen and cart?*
2. *Instead of trying a more hands-on approach, what did the farmer do?*
3. *Hercules informed the farmer that prayers of what type fail to move the gods?*

	Haerentem luteo sub gurgite rusticus axem	
	liquerat et nexos ad iuga tarda boves,	
depositis ... votis: 13.III.2	frustrā depositis confidens numina votis	
ferre: 12.I.3.d **rebus:** 3.III.3	ferre suis rebus, cum residēret, opem.	
cum: 16.I.2	Cui rector summis Tirynthius infit ab astris,	5
	nam vocat hunc supplex in sua vota deum:	
stimulis: 3.V.1	"Perge laborantes stimulis agitare iuvencos,	
manibus: 3.V.1	et manibus pigras disce iuvare rotas.	
viribus: 3.V.1	Tunc quoque congressum maioraque viribus ausum	
fas (est): 20.IV **animis:** 3.III.3	fas superos animis conciliare tuis.	10
numina: 3.IV.4 **votis:** 3.V.1	Disce tamen pigris non flecti numina votis;	
cum: 16.I.3.b	praesentesque adhibē, cum facis ipse, deos."	

luteus, -a, -um — muddy	**resideo, -ēre** — sit back and rest	**iuvencus, -i** — young bull
gurges, -itis — pool		**rota, -ae** — wheel
axis, -is — axle, cart	**rector Tirynthius** = Hercules	**congredior, -i** — face, encounter
linquo, -ere — abandon	**infit** — (defective) starts out	
necto, -ere — join	**pergo, -ere** — continue	**superi, -orum** — the gods
tardus, -a, -um — sluggish	**stimulus, -i** — whiplash	**concilio, -are** — win over
confido, -ere — trust	**agito, -are** — drive	**adhibeo, -ēre** — render

READING FOR UNDERSTANDING

1. *Imagine yourself getting a flat tire at night on an infrequently traveled road. Can you picture yourself, after having sized up the situation, sitting along the side of the road and saying, "Heaven help me!"? What would you do next?*
2. *Why, do you suppose, do gods help those who help themselves? What's the underlying theology?*
3. *Why do you think it was the god Hercules who responded to the farmer?*

2.

"One Sorry Ass": The Priests and the Donkey

READING FOR INFORMATION

1. *What did the priests use the donkey for when it was alive?*
2. *What did they use it for after it died?*
3. *How was the donkey's condition unchanged by death?*

	Qui natus est infelix, non vitam modo	
	tristem decurrit, verum post obitum quoque	
	persequitur illum dura fati miseria.	
Cybeles: Greek genitive	Galli Cybeles circum in quaestūs ducere	
	asinum solebant, baiulantem sarcinas.	5
cum:16.I.3.a **labore, plagis:** 3.V.7 **pelle:** 3.V.18	Is cum labore et plagis esset mortuus, detractā pelle sibi fecerunt tympana.	
delicio: 3.V.10	Rogati mox a quodam, delicio suo	
fecissent: 16.V	quidnam fecissent, hoc locuti sunt modo:	
fore: 10.III.7.b	"Putabat se post mortem securum fore:	10
mortuo: 3.III.3	ecce aliae plagae congeruntur mortuo!"	

decurro, -ere — go through
obitus, -ūs — death
persequor, -i — pursue
miseria, -ae — misery
Galli — priests of Magna Mater

Cybele, -es — Magna Mater
quaestus, -ūs — panhandling
baiulo, -are — tote, lug
sarcina, -ae — pack, bag
plaga, -ae — blow

detraho, -ere — remove
pellis, -is — hide, skin
tympanum, -i — tambourine
delicium, -i — pet

READING FOR UNDERSTANDING

1. *Do you feel any sympathy for the donkey?*
2. *What evidence do you find that the poet intends for you to feel sympathy?*
3. *When you consider that priests in antiquity routinely participated in animal sacrifices, does that excuse these priests' callousness to any degree?*

3.

"Guilt by Association . . . and Illumination": The Thief in the Temple
This tale, simple in the telling, is quite sophisticated in its explication.

READING FOR INFORMATION

1. *How did the thief light his lamp?*
2. *Who addressed him?*
3. *When will the thief supposedly pay the price for his crime?*
4. *What taboos are placed on the use of sacred fires?*

Lucernam fur accendit ex arā Iovis,
ipsumque compilavit ad lumen suum.

cum: 16.I.3.a	Onustus qui sacrilegio cum discederet,
	repente vocem sancta misit Religio:
quamvis: 16.XIII.1.a	"Malorum quamvis ista fuerint munera 5
ut non: 16.II	mihique invisa, ut non offendar subripi,
	tamen, sceleste, spiritū culpam lues,
cum: 16.I.3.b	olim cum adscriptus vēnerit poenae dies.
ne: 16.III.1	Sed ne ignis noster facinori praeluceat,
facinori: 3.III.7	
verendos: 17.III	per quem verendos excolit pietas deos, 10
	veto esse tale luminis commercium."
deum: 1.II.1.c	Itaque hodiē nec lucernam de flammā deum
	nec de lucernā fas est accendi sacrum.
contineat: 16.V	Quot res contineat hoc argumentum utiles
	non explicabit alius quam qui repperit. 15
alueris: 16.XI	Significat primum saepe quos ipse alueris
	tibi inveniri maximē contrarios;
scelera: 3.IV.4	secundum ostendit scelera non irā deum,
irā: 3.V.1	
deum: 1.II.1.c	Fatorum dicto sed puniri tempore;
tempore: 3.V.1	
ne: 16.IV	novissimē interdicit ne cum malefico 20
malefico: 3.V.4	usum bonus consociet ullius rei.

lucerna, -ae — lamp

compilo, -are — rob, plunder

onustus, -a, -um — loaded down

sacrilegium, -i — theft of sacred things

invisus, -a, -um — hated

subripio, -ere — steal

culpa, -ae — sin, fault

luo, -ere — atone for

facinus, -noris — crime

praeluceo, -ēre — illuminate

excolo, -ere — give worship to

commercium, -i — trade, exchange

argumentum, -i — theme

significo, -are — mean

alo, -ere — nurture

secundum — secondly

interdico, -ere — forbid

maleficus, -a, -um — wicked

consocio, -are — associate, link

READING FOR UNDERSTANDING

1. The poet states that three lessons are to be derived from this story. Explain how the story illustrates each.
2. Religio acknowledges that most of the temple plunder that the thief stole had been given by people no better than him. Explain this claim and its significance.
3. Does this story seem to you to be written out of deep and reverent religious sentiment?

4.

"Quick to Judge, Slow to Repent": The Faults of Humankind

READING FOR INFORMATION

1. Where is each knapsack carried?

2. What does each knapsack contain?

3. What human trait does this arrangement explain?

nobis: 3.III.3	Peras imposuit Iuppiter nobis duas:
vitiis: 3.V.10	propriis repletam vitiis post tergum dedit,
alienis (vitiis): 3.V.10	alienis ante pectus suspendit gravem.
	Hac re vidēre nostra mala non possumus;
	alii simul delinquunt, censores sumus.　　　　　5

pera, -ae — knapsack   **delinquo, -ere** — make
repletus, -a, -um — filled   mistakes

READING FOR UNDERSTANDING

1. What significance is there to the fact that the poet calls one knapsack **repleta** and the other **gravis**?

2. What is the best solution to the human fault that this fable describes, particularly if wearing the knapsacks is a divine requirement?

5.

"The Thirteen Commandments": Apollo Speaks
In this poem, the oracle at Delphi issues its instructions for right, proper, and ethical behavior.

sit: 16.V	Utilius nobis quid sit dic, Phoebe, obsecro,
	qui Delphos et formosum Parnasum incolis.
sacratae: 3.IX	Subitō sacratae vatis horrescunt comae,
adytis: 3.V.18	tripodes moventur, mugit adytis Religio,
	tremuntque lauri et ipse pallescit dies.　　　5
numine: 3.V.7	Voces resolvit icta Pytho numine:
	"Audite, gentes, Delii monitūs dei:
superis: 3.III.1	pietatem colite, vota superis reddite;
	patriam, parentes, natos, castas coniuges
armis: 3.V.1	defendite armis, hostem ferro pellite;　　　10
ferro: 3.V.I	
miseris: 3.III.5	amicos sublevate, miseris parcite;
bonis: 3.III.5	bonis favete, subdolis ite obviam;
subdolis: 3.III.3	
(homines) qui: 3.VIII	delicta vindicate, corripite impios,
thalamos . . .	punite turpi thalamos qui violant stupro;
violant: 3.IV.1	malos cavete, nulli nimium credite."　　　15
stupro: 3.V.1	
nulli: 3.III.5; 5.II.1	Haec elocuta concidit virgo furens;
	furens profectō, nam quae dixit perdidit.

17. **quae . . . perdidit**: what she said she completely squandered

obsecro, -are — beg

Delphi, -orum — famous oracle of Apollo in Greece

Parnassus, -i — mountain haunt of Apollo in Greece

incolo, -ere — inhabit

sacro, -are — consecrate

vates, -is — prophetess

horresco, -ere — bristle

tripus, -podis — tripod

mugio, -ire — bellow

adytum, -i — sanctuary

tremo, -ere — quiver

laurus, -i — laurel tree

pallesco, -ere — grow pale

resolvo, -ere — release

Pytho, -nis — priestess of Apollo

Delius, -a, -um — of the island of Delos

monitus, -ūs — warning

superi, -orum — the gods

sublevo, -are — come to the aid of

subdolus, -i — deceit

obvius, -a, -um — head-on

delictum, -i — mistake, crime

impius, -a, -um — impious

thalamus, -i — bedchamber

stuprum, -i — sexual deviance

eloquor, -i — utter

concido, -ere — collapse

furens, -ntis — raving

profectō — indeed

READING FOR UNDERSTANDING

1. *This poem is rather ambiguous as to who issues these commands: is it Phoebus, the priestess, the oracle, Religio? What is the effect of the ambiguity?*
2. *How do these commands compare with the Judeo-Christian Ten Commandments? With the Catonian "Fifty-Eight Commandments" (see section D, verse reading 3)?*
3. *This poem ends on a somewhat pessimistic note. How do you explain it?*

6.

Roman religion is decidedly not characterized by theological depth or great speculation. The following sententiae *reveal fairly conventional reflections on the Romans' pantheon and worship.*

Stultitia est insectari, quem di diligunt.

Unus deus poenam adfert, multi cogitant.

sint, regant: 16.IV   An di sint caelumque regant, ne quaere docēri;
cum: 16.I.1   cum sis mortalis, quae sunt mortalia cura.
cura: 19.I

paucorum: 3.II.5   Paucorum est intellegere, quid donet deus.
donet: 16.V   Improbē Neptunum accusat, qui iterum naufragium facit.

Contrā hominem iustum pravē contendere noli;
semper enim deus iniustas ulciscitur iras.

Contrā felicem vix deus vires habet.

cum: 16.I.3.b

Deos ridēre credo, cum felix vocat.

ut: 16.XIII.2.a

Si deus est animus, nobis ut carmina dicunt,

tibi: 3.III.6
colendus: 17.IV

hic tibi praecipuē sit purā mente colendus.

benefactis: 3.V.1

Benefactis proximē ad deos accedimus.

deo favente: 13.III.4
naviges: 15.II
vimine: 3.V.1

Deo favente naviges vel vimine.

virtutem: 3.IV.4
esse: 12.I.3.d
linguam: 3.IV.1
deo: 3.III.2
ratione: 3.V.7

Virtutem primam esse puto compescere linguam:
proximus ille deo est, qui scit ratione tacēre.

domi: 4.I.3
virum: 3.IV.4
decet: 20.III.7

Domi manēre virum fortunatum decet.

similem: 3.IV.1

Plerumque similem ducit ad similem deus.

intendat: 16.V
sorte: 3.V.1
statuat: 16.V

Quid deus intendat, noli perquirere sorte;
quid statuat de te, sine te deliberat ille.

laudaveris,
  accusaveris:
  19.V.1
te: 3.IV.4
coram: 8.II.2
dicere: 12.I.3.d
videto: 19.II

Neminem cito laudaveris, neminem cito accusaveris:
semper puta te coram diis testimonium dicere.

imitare: 19.I

Quod sequitur specta, quodque imminet ante videto;
illum imitare deum, partem qui spectat utramque.

Tutissima res est timēre nil praeter deum.

Optimus animus pulcherrimus dei cultus est.

cum: 16.I.2

Cum sis ipse nocens, moritur cur victima pro te?

morte: 3.V.1

Stultitia est morte alterius sperare salutem.

Puras deus, non plenas aspicit manūs.

Quid est beneficium dare? Imitari deum.

stultitia, -ae — stupidity	**benefactum, -i** — good deed	**perquiro, -ere** — inquire
insector, -ari — persecute	**navigo, -are** — sail	**coram** — (with ablative) in
dono, -are — bestow (favor)	**vimen, -inis** — twig	front of
naufragium, -i — shipwreck	**compesco, -ere** — control	**testimonium, -i** — testimony
pravē — perversely	**plerumque** — commonly	**imitor, -ari** — imitate
iniustus, -a, -um — unjust	**intendo, -ere** — intend	**ille deus** = Janus

READING FOR UNDERSTANDING

1. *According to these aphorisms, how do humans best approximate the gods, and how are the gods most easily alienated?*
2. *Which of these aphorisms strike you as the most anti-intellectual?*
3. *What evidence do you find in these adages that worship of the gods for the Romans is—or should be—a personal experience?*

7.

"Lady Luck, a Force to Be Reckoned With": The Farmer and the Treasure

READING FOR INFORMATION

1. *What did the farmer do for his oxen after his discovery?*
2. *What god did he make thanksgiving to?*
3. *Fortuna predicts that what will happen to his new-found wealth?*

vomere: 3.V.1	Rusticus impresso molitus vomere terram	
thesaurum: 3.IV.4 **sulcis:** 3.V.19 **animo:** 3.V.14	thesaurum sulcis prosiluisse videt. Mox indigna animo properante reliquit aratra, gramina compellens ad meliora boves.	
Telluri: 3.III.3	Continuō supplex Telluri construit aras, quae sibi depositas sponte dedisset opes.	5
rebus: 3.V.7	Hunc Fortuna novis gaudentem provida rebus	
(esse) se: 3.IV.4 **ture:** 3.V.16	admonet, indignam se quoque ture dolens: "Nunc inventa meis non prodis munera templis	
deos: 3.IV.4	atque alios mavis participare deos;	10
cum: 16.I.3.b **surrepto . . . auro:** 13.III.2 **lacrimis:** 3.V.14	sed cum surrepto fueris tristissimus auro, me primam lacrimis sollicitabis inops."	

imprimo, -ere — push against	**aratrum, -i** — plow	**malo, malle** — prefer
molior, -iri — work	**gramen, -inis** — grass	**participo, -are** — take part in
vomis, -eris — plow blade	**compello, -ere** — drive	**surripio, -ere** — take away
thesaurus, -i — treasure chest	**construo, -ere** — build	**sollicito, -are** — annoy
sulcus, -i — furrow	**sponte** — willingly	**inops** — impoverished
prosilio, -ire — jump out from	**providus, -a, -um** — observing	

READING FOR UNDERSTANDING

1. *Does the farmer strike you as having been conscientious after his discovery of the treasure?*
2. *Do you suppose that a worshiper in a polytheistic religion is frequently uncertain which god to pray or make thanksgiving to? How is this uncertainty best handled?*
3. *What do you think of Fortuna's point that we often underestimate the role of luck (consider the phrase* dumb luck*) when good things befall us but overestimate its role when bad things happen?*

8.

Fortuna, a divinized abstraction as much as a goddess, became an increasingly important figure in Roman cult, consciousness, and concern. Conceptions of the deity, as the following aphorisms illustrate, reveal more subtlety and complexity than observed for most of the traditional pantheon.

Plures tegit Fortuna quam tutos facit.

cum: 16.I.3.b
captatum: 17.I

Fortuna cum blanditur, captatum venit.

Saepe Fortuna innocentem, numquam spes bona deserit.

reperias: 15.II
retineas: 15.II

Fortunam citius reperias quam retineas.

Ex hominum quaestū facta Fortuna est dea.

Fortuna nimium quem fovet, stultum facit.

Fortunam: 3.IV.1
innocens: 3.I.1

Legem nocens veretur, Fortunam innocens.

Homo saepe aliud, Fortuna aliud cogitat.

Levis est Fortuna: cito reposcit, quod dedit.

cum: 16.I.5

Minimum eripit Fortuna, cum minimum dedit.

Nil eripit Fortuna, nisi quod et dedit.

Stultum facit Fortuna, quem vult perdere.

successū: 3.V.16

Successū indignos noli tu ferre molestē;

malis: 3.III.5
ut: 16.III.1

indulget Fortuna malis, ut laedere possit.

Fortuna quō se, eōdem et inclinat favor.

usū, mancipio:
   3.V.10

Fortuna usū dat multa, mancipio nihil.

cum: 16.I.1
ratione: 3.V.1

Cum sis incautus nec rem ratione gubernes,
noli Fortunam, quae non est, dicere caecam.

multis, nulli: 3.III.1

Fortuna multis dat nimis, nulli satis.

Non est tuum, Fortuna quod fecit tuum.

cum: 16.I.5   Disce aliquid; nam cum subitō Fortuna recessit
ars remanet vitamque hominis non deserit umquam.

Fortunae: 3.III.4
quis: 7.VI.1.a   Fortunae invidia est, si quis immeritō miser.

Virtuti melius quam Fortunae creditur.

ius, mores: 3.IV.1   Fortuna ius in homines, mores non habet.

a: 3.V.19   Aberrare a Fortunā tuā non potes; obsidet te.

Magnam Fortunam magnus animus decet.

capto, -are — hunt down   **inclino, -are** — incline   **immeritō** — undeservedly
quaestus, -ūs — profit   **mancipium, -i** — ownership   **aberro, -are** — wander away
foveo, -ēre — coddle   **incautus, -a, -um** — reckless   from
reposco, -ere — demand back   **guberno, -are** — control   **obsideo, -ēre** — besiege
successus, -ūs — success   **caecus, -a, -um** — blind
molestē — with annoyance   **remaneo, -ēre** — remain

READING FOR UNDERSTANDING

1. *What evidence do you find that Fortuna was more "personal" than other Roman gods? Is this evidence also contradicted?*
2. *What is the semantic range of the Latin word **fortuna**? Do you observe the same range illustrated in the depictions of Fortuna?*
3. *What are the differences between treating luck superstitiously (knocking on wood, throwing salt over the shoulder, avoiding sidewalk cracks, etc.) and cultically? What do you think of the baseball player who makes the sign of the cross as he steps into the batter's box?*

9.

This poem adopts the form of a prayer to Mother Earth, and the speaker is portrayed as a doctor or some other practitioner of herbal healing. The first half of the poem describes Earth in terms of her natural attributes and functions.

READING FOR INFORMATION

1. *What is Earth's function vis-à-vis the Underworld?*
2. *What does Earth do with respect to winds, rains, and storms?*
3. *What does Earth do when life ceases?*

Dea sancta Tellus, rerum naturae parens,
quae cuncta generas et regeneras in dies,

gentibus: 3.III.3	quod sola praestas gentibus vitalia,
	caeli ac maris diva arbitra rerumque omnium,
	per quam silet natura et somnos concipit, 5
	itemque lucem reparas et noctem fugas:
	tu Ditis umbras tegis et immensum chaos
	ventosque et imbres tempestatesque attines
cum: 16.I.3.b	et, cum libet, dimittis et misces freta
	fugasque soles et procellas concitas, 10
cum: 16.I.3.b	itemque, cum vis, hilarem promittis diem.
	Tu alimenta vitae tribuis perpetuā fide,
cum: 16.I.3.a	et, cum recesserit anima, in tete refugimus:
	ita, quicquid tribuis, in te cuncta recidunt.

regenero, -are — regenerate	**fugo, -are** — banish	**hilaris, -e** — bright
vitalia, -ium — essentials	**chaos, -i** — chaos, abyss	**alimentum, -i** — nourishment
arbitra, -ae — judge	**attineo, -ēre** — hold back	**-te** — suffix signifying emphasis
sileo, -ēre — be silent	**fretum, -i** — strait	**refugio, -ere** — flee back
reparo, -are — restore	**procella, -ae** — gale storm	**recido, -ere** — retire

The second half of the poem contains the prayer and represents the concerns of the speaker.

READING FOR INFORMATION

1. *Why is Earth rightly called Magna Mater?*
2. *What specific request does the prayer contain?*
3. *If Earth grants the prayer, what will the speaker do?*

deum: 1.II.1.c	Meritō vocaris Magna tu Mater deum, 15
pietate: 3.V.10 **divom:** 1.II.1.d	pietate quia vicisti divom numina;
	tuque illa vera es gentium et divom parens,
	sine qua nil maturatur nec nasci potest;
	tu es magna tuque divom regina es, dea.
	Te, diva, adoro tuumque ego numen invoco, 20
praestes: 19.IV	facilisque praestes hoc mihi quod te rogo;
fide: 3.V.7	referamque grates, diva, tibi meritā fide.
exaudi: 19.I.4 **coeptis:** 3.III.5 **praesta:** 19.I.1	Exaudi me, quaeso, et fave coeptis meis;
	hoc quod peto a te, diva, mihi praesta volens.
	Herbas, quascumque generat maiestas tua, 25
causā: 8.III **gentibus:** 3.III.1 **permittas:** 19.IV	salutis causā tribuis cunctis gentibus:
	hanc nunc mihi permittas medicinam tuam.
veniat: 15.I	Veniat medicina cum tuis virtutibus:
habeat: 15.I	quidque ex his fecero, habeat eventum bonum,
	cuique easdem dedero quique easdem a me acceperint, 30
sanos (esse): 20.IV **eos:** 3.IV.4 **praestes:** 19.IV **mihi:** 3.III.1	sanos eos praestes. Denique nunc, diva, hoc mihi
	maiestas praestet tua, quod te supplex rogo.

maturo, -are — ripen
adoro, -are — adore
invoco, -are — invoke

grates, -ium — thanks
exaudio, -ire — listen to
coeptum, -i — undertaking

eventus, -ūs — outcome
sanus, -a, -um — healthy

READING FOR UNDERSTANDING
1. *What is the purpose of the praise and the description in the poem's first half?*
2. *How is Earth's godhead increased by reference to her as a force and power of nature?*
3. *If you were an ancient Roman, would you believe more in the efficacy of medicinal herbs after reading this poem?*

10.

This poem takes a distinctly irreligious view of the origins and worship of the gods.

READING FOR INFORMATION
1. *What emotion first prompted belief in gods? What triggered that emotion?*
2. *After humans observed some order and routine in nature, what happened next?*
3. *How did humans respond after benefiting from some modest windfall of nature?*
4. *Finally, if a person experienced a great or repeated windfall, what did he or she imagine?*

caelo: 3.V.18

cum: 16.I.3.a
discussa (essent): 20.IV
flammis: 3.V.1
devectus (est), reparatus (est), effusa (sunt), distinctus (est): 20.IV
mensibus: 3.V.1

agricolas: 3.IV.4
Cereri: 3.III.1
messis: 3.II.1
palmitibus: 3.V.1
manū: 3.V.7

aquā: 3.V.1

voti: 3.II.6

certamine: 3.V.3

Primus in orbe deos fecit timor, ardua caelo
fulmina cum caderent, discussaque moenia flammis,
atque ictus flagraret Athos; mox Phoebus ad ortūs,
lustratā devectus humo, Lunaeque senectus
et reparatus honos; hinc signa effusa per orbem,   5
et permutatis distinctus mensibus annus.
Profecit vitium, iamque error iussit inanis
agricolas primos Cereri dare messis honores,
palmitibus plenis Bacchum vincire, Palemque
pastorum gaudēre manū. Natat obrutus, omni   10
Neptuni demersus aquā; Pallasque tabernas
vindicat. Et voti reus, et qui vendidit urbem,
iam sibi quisque deos avido certamine fingit.

arduus, -a, -um — high
fulmen, -inis — thunderbolt
discutio, -ere — shake
Athos — mountain in Greece
lustro, -are — traverse
reparo, -are — restore
permuto, -are — change completely

distinguo, -ere — differentiate
proficio, -ere — succeed
palmes, -mitis — leafage
Pales — god of flocks
pastor, -ris — shepherd
nato, -are — swim
obruo, -ere — shipwreck

demergo, -ere — immerse
reus voti — one indebted by a vow
certamen, -inis — competition
fingo, -ere — make up

READING FOR UNDERSTANDING
1. *Explain how this poem is sort of a reverse creation myth.*
2. *Explain how this creation is completely anthropocentric.*
3. *The human affects at the heart of this poem (fear, desire for order, gratitude, greed) are not by any means exhaustive. If the logic of this poem holds, could there be a deific response to every human emotion, impulse, and sentiment?*

11.

The following poem offers, in the form of a prayer, an intriguing fusion of religious and philosophic thought, highlighted most of all by a pronounced monotheistic perspective.

READING FOR INFORMATION
1. *What difficulty does the speaker have in addressing the god who is the subject of this poem?*
2. *What are some of the divine paradoxes that the poem's first fourteen lines present?*
3. *What does this poem say about cyclical rebirth?*

numero, aevo:
   3.V.10
esto: 19.II.6.a
quo: 7.VI.1.a
nomine: 3.V.1
dignum est (adfari):
   20.III.3; 20.IV
quo . . . ignoto
   (nomine): 3.V.7;
   3.X
quom: 16.I.4
tui: 7.I.2
turbine: 3.V.1
fata: 3.IV.4
rapi: 12.I
vitas: 3.IV.4
involvier: 12.I.2
aevo: 3.V.1
ut:16.III.1
mundo: 3.III.3
quod: 7.V
partubus: 1.IV.3;
   3.V.7
haustus (mundus):
   3.X

> Omnipotens, annosa poli quem suspicit aetas,
> quem sub millenis semper virtutibus unum
> nec numero quisquam poterit pensare nec aevo,
> nunc esto adfatus, si quo te nomine dignum est,
> quo, sacer, ignoto gaudes, quom maxima tellus   5
> intremit et sistunt rapidos vaga sidera cursūs.
> Tu solus, tu multus item; tu primus et īdem
> postremus mediusque simul, mundique superstes.
> Nam sine fine tui lābentia tempora finis,
> altus ab aeterno spectas fera turbine certo   10
> rerum fata rapi vitasque involvier aevo
> atque iterum reduces supera in convexa referri,
> scilicet ut mundo redeat, quod partubus haustus
> perdiderit, refluumque iterum per tempora fiat.

omnipotens — omnipotent	**adfor, -ari** — invoke	**turbo, -binis** — swirl
annosus, -a, -um — long lived	**quom = cum**	**involvo, -ere** — wrap up in
polus, -i — axis of heaven	**intremo, -ere** — quake	**redux, -cis** — brought back
suspicio, -ere — honor	**sisto, -ere** — stop	**convexum, -i** — vault
milleni, -ae — a thousand each	**rapidus, -a, -um** — swift	**scilicet** — obviously
penso, -are — compare	**vagus, -a, -um** — wandering	**haurio, -ire** — wear out
	lābor, -i — slip, pass	**refluus, -a, -um** — refluent
	aeternum, -i — eternity	

The poem now presents the speaker's prayer request of the god, which is, like the god, rather abstract.

READING FOR INFORMATION

1. *What physical features does the speaker ascribe to the god?*
2. *What is the gender of the god? How are the god and the world distinct?*
3. *What does the speaker request of the god?*

	Tu (si quidem fas est in temet tendere sensum	15
quā: 3.V.1	et speciem temptare sacram, quā sidera cingis	
	immensus longamque simul complecteris aethram	
	fulmineis forsan rapidā sub imagine membris)	
quo: 3.V.1 **cuncta**: 3.IV.1	flammifluum quoddam iubar es, quo cuncta coruscans	
	ipse vides nostrumque premis solemque diemque.	20
deum: 1.II.1.c	Tu genus omne deum, tu rerum causa vigorque,	
	tu natura omnis, deus innumerabilis unus,	
sexū: 3.V.16 **tibi**: 3.III.3 **deum**: 1.II.1.c	tu sexū plenus toto, tibi nascitur olim	
flore: 3.V.10	hīc deus, hīc mundus, domus hīc hominumque deumque,	
	lucens, augusto stellatus flore iuventae.	25
quem (mundum): 3.X **aspires**: 19.IV **sit . . . creatus**: 16.V **(sit) genitus factusve**: 16.V **nosse**: 20.I.3 **(mihi) volenti**: 3.X; 3.III.1 **ut**: 16.III.1 **moles**: 3.IV.1 **foedere**: 3.V.7 **sustulerīs**: 16.V **texuerīs**: 16.V **numero**: 3.V.10 **sit**: 16.V	Quem (precor, aspires), qua sit ratione creatus, quo genitus factusve modo, da nosse volenti. Da, Pater, augustas ut possim noscere causas, mundanas olim moles quo foedere rerum sustulerīs, animamque levi quo maximus olim texuerīs numero, quo congrege dissimilique, quidque id sit vegetum, quod per cita corpora vivit.	30

30–32. **animamque . . . vivit**: in what light relation, in what dissimilar and akin relation you, most mighty that you are, once wove life and whatever that animated something is that thrives throughout active bodies

-met — suffix expressing emphasis	**flammifluus, -a, -um** — flame flowing	**aspiro, -are** — help
species, -ei — appearance	**iubar, -ris** — brilliance	**mundanus, -a, -um** — earthly
cingo, -ere — surround	**corusco, -are** — glitter	**moles, -is** — mass, matter
complector, -i — embrace	**innumerabilis, -e** — countless	**sustulerīs** < **tollo**
aethra, -ae — atmosphere	**sexus, -ūs** — gender	**congrex, -gregis** — akin
fulmineus, -a, -um — thundering	**luceo, -ēre** — shine	**dissimilis, -e** — dissimilar
forsan — perhaps	**stellatus, -a, -um** — starry	**vegetus, -a, -um** — animated

READING FOR UNDERSTANDING

1. *In Greco-Roman prayer formulae, it was especially important to address the god by the proper and correct epithet. How does the speaker satisfy the requirement technically and religiously?*

2. *Point out places where monotheistic thinking is most prominent.*

3. *The poem's end seems more scientific than religious. Explain the kind of physics, biology, and archaeology that the speaker seeks through study and prayer.*

12.

Many people have supposed that Apollo and Bacchus were contrary and oppositional forces in Greco-Roman antiquity, but this poet views the gods in a different light.

Sīc Apollo, deinde Liber sīc videtur ignifer:

flammis: 3.V.1, 3.V.7, 3.V.17, or 3.V.18 — ambo sunt flammis creati prosatique ex ignibus;

vite, radio: 3.VIII — ambo de donis calorem, vite et radio, conferunt;

noctis hic rumpit tenebras, hic tenebras pectoris.

ignifer, -i — fire bringer   **radius, -i** — sun ray

prosero, -ere — beget

READING FOR UNDERSTANDING

1. *This poem moves comfortably between the literal and the metaphorical. Is it too facile in that respect?*

13.

The scene of this engaging poem is the god Pan entertaining three shepherd boys with a song in praise of the god Bacchus. The scene is introduced with the boys trying to make music with Pan's pipes.

READING FOR INFORMATION

1. *What was Pan doing when the boys came upon him and his pipes?*
2. *What sort of music did the pipes produce when the boys tried to play them?*
3. *What was Pan's reaction on discovering the boys with his pipes?*

Nyctilus atque Micon nec non et pulcher Amyntas

ilice: 3.V.1 — torrentem patulā vitabant ilice solem,

cum: 16.I.4
venatū: 3.V.7 — cum Pan venatū fessus recubare sub ulmo

somno: 3.V.7 — coeperat et somno laxatus sumere vires;

quem super ex tereti pendebat fistula ramo.   5

tamquam: 16.XIII.1.b — Hanc pueri, tamquam praedam pro carmine possent

sumere fasque esset calamos tractare deorum,

invadunt furtō. Sed nec resonare canorem,

fistula quem suerat, nec vult contexere carmen,

sed pro carminibus male dissona sibila reddit,   10

cum: 16.I.3.b
sonitū: 3.V.7 — cum Pan excussus sonitū stridentis avenae

si: 18.I.4

nulli: 5.II.1

cerā: 3.V.1

ordine: 3.V.10
Baccho: 3.III.3

iamque videns: "Pueri, si carmina poscitis," inquit,
"ipse canam. Nulli fas est inflare cicutas,
quas ego Maenaliis cerā coniungo sub antris.
Iamque ortūs, Lenaee, tuos et semina vitis   15
ordine detexam: debemus carmina Baccho."

torreo, -ēre — torrid	**calamus, -i** — reed, pipes	**sonitus, -ūs** — noise
patulus, -a, -um — wide branching	**tracto, -are** — handle	**stridens, -tis** — high pitched
vito, -are — avoid	**invado, -ere** — rush upon	**avena, -ae** — reed
ilex, -icis — holm oak	**furtō** — furtively	**inflo, -are** — blow into
venatus, -ūs — hunting	**resono, -are** — sound	**cicuta, -ae** — shepherd's pipe
recubo, -are — recline	**canor, -ris** — tune	**Maenalius, -a, -um** — pertaining to a mountain range in southern Greece
ulmus, -i — elm	**suo, -ere** — weave together	**cera, -ae** — wax
laxo, -are — relax	**contexo, -ere** — create	**Lenaeus** = Bacchus
teres, -retis — smooth	**dissonus, -a, -um** — dissonant	**semen, -inis** — seed, origin
fistula, -ae — pipes	**sibila, -orum** — hissing	**detexo, -ere** — compose on
ramus, -i — branch	**excutio, -ere** — shake from	

Pan narrates the birth, infancy, childhood, and adolescence of the god Bacchus in this section of the poem.

READING FOR INFORMATION

1. *What details are given about the conception and birth of Bacchus?*
2. *Who takes care of and raises the baby Bacchus?*
3. *What details are provided about the interactions between the satyr Silenus and the infant Bacchus?*

palmite: 3.V.1

colla: 3.IV.6
capillis: 3.V.5
cum: 16.I.4

ora: 3.IV.1.b

aevi: 3.II.6

Nysae: 4.I.3

gremio: 3.V.18
ulnis: 3.V.1

palmis: 3.V.1

Haec fatus coepit calamis sīc montivagus Pan:
"Te cano, qui gravidis hederatā fronte corymbis
vitea serta plicas quique udo palmite tigres
ducis odoratis perfusus colla capillis,   20
vera Iovis proles. Nam cum post sidera caeli
sola Iovem Semele vīdit Iovis ora professum,
hunc pater omnipotens, venturi providus aevi,
pertulit et iusto produxit tempore partūs.
Hunc Nymphae Faunique senes Satyrique procaces,   25
nosque etiam Nysae viridi nutrimus in antro.
Quin et Silenus parvum veteranus alumnum
aut gremio fovet aut resupinis sustinet ulnis,
evocat aut risum digito motūve quietem
adlicit aut tremulis quassat crepitacula palmis.   30

pectore: 3.V.1	Cui deus adridens horrentes pectore saetas
digitis: 3.V.1	vellicat aut digitis aures adstringit acutas
	applauditve manū mutilum caput aut breve mentum,
pollice: 3.V.1	et simas tenero collidit pollice nares.
pube: 3.V.10	Intereā pueri florescit pube iuventus 35
cornū: 3.V.10	flavaque maturo tumuerunt tempora cornū.
	Tum primum laetas extendit pampinus uvas:
	mirantur Satyri frondes et poma Lyaei.
	Tum deus: 'O Satyri, maturos carpite fetūs,'
	dixit, 'et ignotos primi calcate racemos.'" 40

calamus, -i — reed

montivagus, -a, -um —
  mountain-wandering

gravidus, -a, -um — pregnant

hederatus, -a, -um — ivied

corymbus, -i — ivy berry

viteus, -a, -um — of the vine

sertum, -i — garland

plico, -are — weave

udus, -a, -um — wet

palmes, -mitis — vine branch

perfundo, -ere — perfume

profiteor, -ēri — openly
  display

providus, -a, -um —
  provident

perfero, -rre — gestate

partus, -ūs — delivery

procax, -cacis — rowdy

Nysa, -ae — city in India,
  birthplace of Bacchus

nutrio, -ire — nurture, raise

veteranus, -a, -um — old

alumnus, -i — foster child

gremium, -i — lap

foveo, -ēre — coddle

resupinus, -a, -um —
  reclining

ulna, -ae — elbow

adlicio, -ere — coax

tremulus, -a, -um —
  trembling

quasso, -are — shake

crepitaculum, -i — baby
  rattle

horreo, -ēre — bristle

saeta, -ae — stiff hair

vellico, -are — pluck out

adstringo, -ere — tug at

mutilus, -a, -um — ugly

mentum, -i — chin

simus, -a, -um — pug nosed

collido, -ere — squash
  together

naris, -is — nostril

floresco, -ere — blossom

pubes, -is — manhood

flavus, -a, -um — blond

tumeo, -ēre — swell

pampinus, -i — vine tendril

uva, -ae — grape cluster

frons, -ndis — foliage

pomum, -i — fruit

Lyaeus = Bacchus

fetus, -ūs — fruit

calco, -are — trample

racemus, -i — bunch

After Bacchus bids the satyrs to help him, they make the wine, try the product, and even become drunk.

READING FOR INFORMATION

1. *Which steps does the poet describe in the making of the wine?*
2. *What are the various vessels or means that the satyrs use to sample the wine?*
3. *What attention does this section of the poem pay to Bacchus?*

vitibus: 3.V.19	"Vix haec ediderat, decerpunt vitibus uvas
calathis: 3.V.1 plantā: 3.V.I super: 8.IV	et portant calathis celerique elidere plantā concava saxa super properant: vindemia fervet
pede: 3.V.1	collibus in summis, crebro pede rumpitur uva

musto: 3.V.1   nudaque purpureo sparguntur pectora musto.   45

cohors: 3.VIII
sibi: 3.III.2   Tum Satyri, lasciva cohors, sibi pocula quisque

obvia corripiunt: quae fors dedit, adripit usus.

cornū: 3.V.18   Cantharon hic retinet, cornū bibit alter adunco,

concavat ille manūs palmasque in pocula vertit,

lacū: 3.V.19   pronus at ille lacū bibit et crepitantibus haurit   50

labris: 3.V.1   musta labris; alius vocalia cymbala mergit

atque alius latices pressis resupinus ab uvis

ore: 3.V.19   excipit; at pōtus (saliens liquor ore resultat)

evomit, inque umeros et pectora defluit umor."

---

edo, -ere — order

decerpo, -ere — pluck

uva, -ae — grape cluster

calathus, -i — wicker basket

elido, -ere — crush

planta, -ae — sole of the foot

concavus, -a, -um — concave

vindemia, -ae — grape harvest

ferveo, -ēre — be busy

mustum, -i — grape skin

lascivus, -a, -um — lusty

obvius, -a, -um — ready to hand

cantharon, -i — pot

aduncus, -a, -um — curved

concavo, -are — cup

pronus, -a, -um — on the ground

crepito, -are — smack

vocalis, -e — noisy

cymbalum, -i — cymbal

latex, -icis — liquid

resupinus, -a, -um — lying on the back

pōtus, -a, -um — drunk

salio, -ire — dance, slosh

resulto, -are — jump back out

evomo, -ere — vomit

defluo, -ere — flow down

umor, -ris — liquid

Now drunk, the satyrs engage in riotous behaviors. Silenus adopts the role of the habitual old souse. And Bacchus even offers wine to wild creatures. Once Pan's song is finished, the shepherd boys resume their pressing duties.

READING FOR INFORMATION

1. *After wine, song, and dance, the satyrs' minds turn to what?*
2. *Silenus's blood contains what? His belly contains what?*
3. *What three chores did the shepherd boys perform after Pan completed his song?*

"Omnia ludus habet cantusque chorique licentes;   55

et venerem iam vina movent: raptantur amantes

concubitū: 3.V.10   concubitū Satyri fugientes iungere Nymphas;

crine, veste: 3.V.1   iam iamque elapsas, hic crine, hic veste retentat.

musto: 3.V.16   Tum primum roseo Silenus cymbia musto

plena senex avidē non aequis viribus hausit.   60

venas: 3.IV.6
nectare: 3.V.7
Iaccho: 3.V.7   Ex illo venas inflatus nectare dulci

hesternoque gravis semper ridetur Iaccho.

Iove: 3.V.18   Quin etiam deus ille, deus Iove prosatus ipso,

plantis: 3.V.1   et plantis uvas premit et de vitibus hastas

integit et lynci praebet cratera bibenti."   65

Haec Pan Maenaliā pueros in valle docebat,

donec: 16.XIII.3.a.i
campo: 3.V.19
uberibus: 3.V.19

sparsas donec oves campo conducere in unum
nox iubet, uberibus suadens siccare fluorem
lactis et in niveas adstrictum cogere glaebas.

licens, -ntis — unrestrained

concubitus, -ūs — sex

elābor, -i — slip away, elude

retento, -are — try to hold back

roseus, -a, -um — rosy

cymbium, -i — cup

vena, -ae — vein

inflo, -are — inspire

nectar, -ris — nectar

hesternus, -a, -um — yesterday's

Iacchus = Bacchus

prosero, -ere — beget

hasta, -ae — thyrsus (ritual Bacchic wand)

intego, -ere — cover

lynx, -ncis — lynx

craterum, -i — wine bowl

conduco, -ere — lead together

suadeo, -ēre — urge

sicco, -are — drain

fluor, -ris — flow

niveus, -a, -um — snow white

adstringo, -ere — squeeze

glaeba, -ae — cheese curd

READING FOR UNDERSTANDING

1. *Pan and the satyrs are gods of what sort of territory? Is Bacchus a god of the same territory over which these other gods range?*
2. *Why do "wild" gods so much love a "cultivated" god?*
3. *Besides becoming rather ridiculous, "wild" gods are also rendered somewhat harmless and impotent when drunk. (Note how drunk satyrs always pursue but never catch nymphs.) What is the significance of this?*

Supplemental Readings

1.

The following story, set during the reign of King Servius Tullius (traditionally 578–535 BCE), is an excellent illustration that Roman religious piety didn't necessarily require a degree of ethical behavior.

READING FOR INFORMATION

1. *The cow belonged to a man of what locality?*
2. *The priest at the temple was of what locality?*
3. *How was the cow's owner put off?*
4. *Why did it matter who sacrificed the cow?*

Servio . . . regnante: use of ablative?
patri: use of dative?
magnitudinis, formae: use of genitive?
quam: use of relative?
ut: introducing what subjunctive?
immolasset: syncopation of what?

Servio Tullio regnante, cuidam patri familiae in agro Sabino praecipuae magnitudinis et eximiae formae vacca nata est. Quam oraculorum certissimi auctores in hōc a dis immortalibus editam esse responderunt, ut quisquis eam Aventinensi Dianae immolasset, eius patria totius terrarum orbis imperium obtinēret. Laetus eō dominus bovem summā cum festinatione Romam actam in Aventino ante aram Dianae constituit, sacrificio Sabinis regimen humani generis daturus. De qua re antistes templi certior factus religionem hospiti intulit, ne prius victimam caederet quam proximi amnis se aquā abluisset, eoque alveum Tiberis petente vaccam ipse immolavit, et urbem nostram tot civitatium, tot gentium dominam pio sacrificii furto reddidit.

vacca, -ae — cow

Aventinensis, -e — on the
  Aventine hill

festinatio, -nis — haste

antistes, -titis — chief
  priest

abluo, -ere — cleanse

alveus, -i — riverbank

READING FOR UNDERSTANDING

1. *Why does the author believe the validity of the oracles in this story?*
2. *Is there any suggestion here that the goddess Diana was offended that her temple and priest participated in a gross deception?*
3. *The implication of this story seems to be that world dominion takes precedence over ethics, which can be a dangerous way of thinking. Do you suppose that this mind-set was more dangerous or less because the Romans also believed that gods favored them for world dominion?*

2.

This tale tells how Rome finally captured the town of Veii after a long siege (396 BCE). The victory was based on a prodigy that could have benefited either side.

READING FOR INFORMATION

1. *What prodigy occurred in the Alban Lake?*
2. *Whom did the Romans consult about the prodigy? Whom did the Veientians consult?*
3. *Who ultimately ordered the Romans to act according to divine command?*

Cum bello acri et diutino Veientes a Romanis intrā moenia compulsi capi non possent, eaque mora non minus obsidentibus quam obsessis intolerabilis vidēretur, exoptatae victoriae iter miro prodigio di immortales patefecerunt: subitō enim Albanus lacus, neque caelestibus auctus imbribus neque inundatione ullius amnis adiutus, solitum stagni modum excessit. Cuius rei explorandae gratiā legati ad Delphicum oraculum missi rettulerunt praecipi sortibus ut aquam eius lacūs emissam per agros diffunderent: sīc enim Veios venturos esse in potestatem populi Romani. Quod priusquam legati renuntiarent, haruspex Veientium a milite nostro, quia domestici interpretes deerant, raptus et in castra perlatus futurum esse dixerat. Ergo senatus, duplici praedictione monitus, eodem paene tempore et religioni paruit et hostium urbe potitus est.

diutinus, -a, -um — long
intolerabilis, -e — unbearable
exopto, -are — desire
inundatio, -nis — flood

adiutus < adiuvo
stagnum, -i — pool
excedo, -ere — exceed
exploro, -are — examine

renuntio, -are — report back
interpres, -pretis — soothsayer
perlatus < perfero

READING FOR UNDERSTANDING

1. *What role does luck play in this tale?*
2. *What role does deliberation play in this tale?*
3. *What role does action play in this tale?*
4. *By implication, what distinguished Rome from Veii for victory?*

3.

Most Roman field commanders kept a stock of sacred chickens with them, for the purposes of taking auspices and sacrificing. This incident from 293 BCE involved a general who took issue with his chicken tender and the consequence for a particular battle.

READING FOR INFORMATION

1. *Did the chicken tender report favorable or unfavorable auspices? Was he telling the truth?*
2. *Where did the consul marshal his chicken tender on the battlefield?*
3. *What became of the chicken tender?*

Papirius Cursor consul, cum Aquiloniam oppugnans proelium vellet committere, pullariusque non prosperantibus avibus optimum ei auspicium renuntiasset, de fallaciā illius factus certior, sibi quidem et exercitui bonum omen datum credidit ac pugnam iniit; ceterum mendacem ante ipsam aciem constituit, ut habērent di eum cuius capite, si quid irae conceperant, expiarent. Sive autem casū sive etiam caelestis numinis providentiā directum est, quod primum e contrariā parte missum erat telum in ipsum pullarii pectus, eumque exanimem prostravit. Id ut cognōvit consul, fidente animo et invasit Aquiloniam et cepit. Tam cito animadvertit quo pacto iniuria imperatoris vindicari debēret, quemadmodum violata religio expianda foret, qua ratione victoria apprehendi posset. Egit virum severum, consulem religiosum, imperatorem strenuum, timoris modum, poenae genus, spei viam uno mentis impetū rapiendo.

Aquilonia, -ae — Samnite town southeast of Rome
pullarius, -i — tender of sacred chickens
prosperans, -ntis — favorable
renuntio, -are — report

fallacia, -ae — deception
ineo, -ire — enter
expio, -are — make good
dirego, -ere — guide
exanimis, -e — dead
fido, -ere — be confident

pactum, -i — manner
quemadmodum — how
severus, -a, -um — stern
strenuus, -a, -um — vigorous

READING FOR UNDERSTANDING

1. *Although the author states that the outcome was the result of either chance or divine providence, which option does he seem to prefer?*
2. *The author here credits the consul with many virtues; if the outcome of the incident had been different, what would be the judgment(s) against the consul?*
3. *How would this story be different if the chicken tender had been not a humble figure but a high priest instead?*

4.

This narrative tells the famous story of how, after a long plague, Rome introduced the Greek god Asclepius (Aesculapius) into its pantheon (292 BCE). The embassy that the Romans sent to the Greek cult center of Epidaurus received a favorable welcome.

READING FOR INFORMATION

1. *How long did the plague last before the Romans acted?*
2. *What national resource did they consult in this crisis?*
3. *What animal exhibited the power and will of the god Aesculapius?*

urbi: use of dative?
exsequamur: use of subjunctive?
triennio: use of ablative?
pestilentiā: use of ablative?
cum: type?
misericordiā: use of ablative?
auxilio: use of ablative?
inspectis . . . libris: use of ablative?
salubritatem: use of accusative?
esset accersitus: use of subjunctive?
legatis missis: use of ablative?
impetraturam esse: use of infinitive?
se: use of accusative?
studio: use of ablative?
existimassent: use of subjunctive? syncopation of?
sumerent: use of subjunctive?
obsequio: use of ablative?
Epidauri: case?
oculis: use of ablative?
tractū: use of ablative?

Ut ceterorum quoque deorum propensum huic urbi numen exsequamur, triennio continuo vexata est pestilentiā civitas nostra; cum finem tanti et tam diutini mali neque divinā misericordiā neque humano auxilio imponi vidēret, cura sacerdotum inspectis Sibyllinis libris animadvertit non aliter pristinam recuperari salubritatem posse quam si ab Epidauro Aesculapius esset accersitus. Itaque eō legatis missis, unicam fatalis remedii opem auctoritate suā, quae iam in terris erat amplissima, impetraturam esse se credidit. Neque eam opinio decepit: pari namque studio petitum ac promissum est praesidium, e vestigioque Epidaurii Romanorum legatos in templum Aesculapii, quod ab eorum urbe quinque milia passuum distat, perductos ut quidquid inde salubre patriae laturos se existimassent pro suo iure sumerent benignissimē invitaverunt. Quorum tam promptam indulgentiam numen ipsius dei subsecutum verba mortalium caelesti obsequio comprobavit: si quidem is anguis, quem Epidauri rarō sed numquam sine magno ipsorum bono visum, in modum Aesculapii venerati erant, per urbis celeberrimas partes mitibus oculis et leni tractū lābi coepit.

11–12. **ut . . . sumerent:** to take whatever they thought that, should they bring it, would be helpful to their state

propensus, -a, -um — inclined

pristinus, -a, -um — former

salubritas, -tatis — public health

fatalis, -e — predetermined

disto, -are — be distant

salubris, -e — healthy

laturos < **fero**

promptus, -a, -um — ready

comprobo, -are — approve

anguis, -is — snake

tractus, -ūs — course

As the story resumes, the Romans experience religious celebrations and wonders in Epidaurus before setting off to return to Italy. After a brief stay in Antium, they made their way to Rome and Aesculapius's new temple.

READING FOR INFORMATION

1. When the Romans reembarked on their ship, what joined them? What was the reaction of the ship's crew?
2. What happened with the ship's passenger when landfall was made at Antium?
3. What effect did the passenger have on its eventual arrival in Rome?

Triduoque inter religiosam omnium admirationem conspectus haud dubiam prae se appetitae clarioris sedis alacritatem ferens ad triremem Romanam perrexit, paventibusque inusitato spectaculo nautis eo conscendit, ubi Q. Ogulni legati tabernaculum erat, inque multiplicem orbem per summam quietem est convolutus. Tum legati, perinde atque exoptatae rei compotes expletā gratiarum actione, cultūque anguis a peritis excepto, laeti inde solverunt, ac prosperam emensi navigationem postquam Antium appulerunt, anguis, qui ubique in navigio remanserat, prolapsus in vestibulo aedis Aesculapii myrto frequentibus ramis diffusae superimminentem excelsae altitudinis palmam circumdedit, perque tres dies, positis quibus vesci solebat, non sine magno metū legatorum ne inde in triremem reverti nollet, Antiensis templi hospitio usus, urbi se nostrae advehendum esse restituit, atque in ripam Tiberis egressis legatis in insulam, ubi templum dicatum est, tranavit adventūque suo tempestatem, cui remedio quaesitus erat, dispulit.

9–10. **myrto . . . palmam:** a palm tree of lofty height that overhung a myrtle tree spread out with dense branches

triduum, -i — three days' time

sedes, -is — locale

triremis, -is — trireme

pergo, -ere — make straight for

inusitatus, -a, -um — unaccustomed

conscendo, -ere — board

tabernaculum, -i — tent

convolvo, -ere — coil together

exopto, -are — desire

compos, -otis — in possession of

anguis, -is — snake

peritus, -a, -um — knowledgeable

emetior, -iri — pass, traverse

navigatio, -nis — voyage

vestibulum, -i — atrium

myrtus, -i — myrtle

superimminens, -ntis — overhanging

altitudo, -dinis — height

vescor, -i — eat, feed on

hospitium, -i — hospitality   **dico, -are** — dedicate   **adventus, -ūs** — arrival

adveho, -ere — convey   **trano, -are** — swim across   **dispello, -ere** — dispel

READING FOR UNDERSTANDING

1. *Throughout this story, what seems to be the divine disposition toward Rome?*
2. *Is the plague that prompted this incident represented as god sent or totally unrelated to the gods?*
3. *The Greeks and Romans believed that one or more animal species (theriomorphs) represented each god. What is the logic behind a snake serving as Aesculapius's sacred animal?*

5.

Rome necessarily experienced a significant change of mind-set as it transitioned from an Italian to a Mediterranean power. The following anecdote describes how the younger Scipio Africanus altered religious ritual to reflect a new global reality (circa 141 BCE).

READING FOR INFORMATION

1. *What office did Scipio occupy when he changed the prayer formula?*
2. *Who read the prayer formula that Scipio changed?*
3. *What kind of greediness was Scipio trying to avoid?*

> Ne Africanus quidem posterior nos de se tacēre patitur. Qui censor, cum lustrum conderet inque solitaurilium sacrificio scriba ex publicis tabulis sollemne ei precationis carmen praeiret, quo di immortales ut populi Romani res meliores amplioresque facerent rogabantur, "Satis," inquit, "bonae et magnae sunt: itaque precor ut eas perpetuō incolumes servent," ac protinus in publicis tabulis ad hunc modum carmen emendari iussit. Qua votorum verecundiā deinceps censores in condendis lustris usi sunt: prudenter enim sensit tunc incrementum Romano imperio petendum fuisse, cum intrā septimum lapidem triumphi quaerebantur, maiorem autem totius terrarum orbis partem possidenti ut avidum esse quicquam ultrā appetere, ita abundē felix, si nihil ex eo, quod obtinebat, amitteret.

posterior, -ius — later   **scriba, -ae** — scribe   **incrementum, -i** — increase

lustrum, -i — five-year period of census taking   **praeeo, -ire** — preview   **septimus, -a, -um** — seventh

solitaurilia, -ium — sacrifice of a pig, a sheep, and a bull   **emendo, -are** — emend   **lapis, -idis** — milestone

deinceps — successively   **abundē** — sufficiently

prudenter — prudently

READING FOR UNDERSTANDING

1. *Explain the religious significance of the change from "bigger and greater" to "securer and more lasting."*

2. *Does the author seem to commend Scipio's modification out of religious principle or out of political pragmatism?*

3. *States often undergo lengthy transitions from survival to growth to maintenance to survival again. Was Scipio wise for recognizing that Rome was at a critical time in one of those transitions?*

6.

This charming anecdote recounts the prediction of one famous Roman about a soon to be famous Roman. The story is set in Africa around 134 BCE.

READING FOR INFORMATION

1. *Who made this prediction about Gaius Marius? Did Marius like it?*
2. *Where was the prediction made? Was Marius present?*
3. *The night after Marius's victory over the Cimbrians was announced at Rome, what did the people do?*

> Inhaerent uni voci posterioris Africani septem C. Marii consulatūs ac duo amplissimi triumphi: ad rogum enim usque gaudio exsultavit, quod, cum apud Numantiam sub eo duce equestria stipendia merēret, et forte inter cenam quidam Scipionem interrogasset, si quid illi accidisset, quemnam res publica aequē magnum habitura esset imperatorem, respiciens se suprā ipsum cubantem, "Vel hunc," dixerit. Quo augurio perfectissima virtus maximam orientem virtutem vīderitne certius an efficacius accenderit perpendi vix potest. Illa nimirum cena militaris speciosissimas totā in urbe Mario futuras cenas ominata est: postquam enim Cimbros ab eo deletos esse initio noctis nuntius pervēnit, nemo fuit qui non illi tamquam dis immortalibus apud sacra mensae suae libaverit.

inhaereo, -ēre — pertain
posterior, -ius — later
exsulto, -are — boast
Numantia, -ae — town in
  Spain
equestris, -e — equestrian

stipendium, -i — term of
  service
perfectus, -a, -um — excellent
efficaciter — productively
perpendo, -ere — adjudge
nimirum — doubtless

ominor, -ari — presage
Cimbri, -orum — Germanic
  tribe
nuntius, -i — announcement

READING FOR UNDERSTANDING

1. *Some people seem destined for greatness from an early age. The talents and promise of others aren't readily evident except to a few and only later. Would you rather be a wunderkind or a late bloomer? Why?*

2. *Marius, as we'll see elsewhere (section D, prose reading 3), overcame many obstacles to achieve greatness. Did Scipio's pronouncement predict Marius's future or alter it?*

3. *Although the author doesn't necessarily say so, he hints that Marius's existential status was something greater than human. Is there something sacrilegious in that suggestion?*

7.

This anecdote involves a famous soothsayer, who predicted that Julius Caesar's life was in peril. Despite Caesar's dismissals, the prophet was, in fact, right (44 BCE).

READING FOR INFORMATION

1. *For how long a period did Spurinna predict that Caesar's life was in danger?*
2. *At whose home did Spurinna and Caesar both come to call on the Ides of March?*
3. *What was Spurinna's response when Caesar said his "deadline" was already up?*

Spurinnae in coniectandis deorum monitis efficacior scientia apparuit quam urbs Romana voluit. Praedixerat C. Caesari ut proximos triginta dies quasi fatales cavēret, quorum ultimus erat Idūs Martiae. Eō cum forte māne uterque in domum Calvini Domitii ad officium convēnisset, Caesar Spurinnae dixit, "Ecquid scis Idūs iam Martias vēnisse?" At is, "Ecquid scis illas nondum praeterisse?" Abiecerat alter timorem, tamquam exacto tempore suspecto; alter ne extremam quidem eius partem periculo vacuam esse arbitratus est. Utinam haruspicem potius augurium quam patriae parentem securitas fefellisset!

coniecto, -are — surmise	**fatalis, -e** — fatal	**exigo, -ere** — complete, pass
monitum, -i — warning	**Idūs, -uum** — the thirteenth	**securitas, -tatis** —
efficax, -acis — effective	or fifteenth day of a month	carelessness
praedico, -ere — predict	**ecquid** — at all, of course	

READING FOR UNDERSTANDING

1. *Does the author have a favorable view of Caesar? On what is his view based?*
2. *The worldview expressed here is very deterministic; that is, what is previously destined will necessarily occur. Do you agree with this?*
3. *What is the role of free will in a deterministic universe? Can a decision of an individual alter the dictates of destiny?*

C. Fables

Verse Readings
"Do unto Others"

As these fables show, the early Christians had no copyright on the so-called Golden Rule ("Do unto others as you would have others do unto you"). The precept embraces a powerful truth, regardless of culture, period, or faith.

1.

"What Goes Around . . .": The Panther and the Shepherds

READING FOR INFORMATION

1. What three things did the countrypeople bring for or against the panther?
2. What did most of the people assume would happen when they went home at nightfall?
3. What or whom did the panther kill? What or whom did the panther spare?

referri: 12.I	Solet a despectis par referri gratia.	
	Panthera imprudens olim in foveam decidit.	
vīdēre: 20.I.2	Vīdēre agrestes; alii fustes congerunt,	
saxis: 3.V.1	alii onerant saxis; quidam contra miseriti	
periturae: 12.II, 3.II.6	periturae quippe, quamvis nemo laederet,	5
quamvis: 16.XIII.1.a **misēre:** 20.I.2 **ut:** 16.III.1	misēre panem ut sustinēret spiritum.	
domum: 4.I.2 **inventuri:** 12.II	Nox insecuta est; abeunt securi domum,	
	quasi inventuri mortuam postridiē.	
ut: 16.XIII.2.a	At illa, vires ut refecit languidas,	
saltū: 3.V.1 **foveā:** 3.V.19	veloci saltū foveā sese liberat,	10
	et in cubile concito properat gradū.	
diebus interpositis: 13.III.1	Paucis diebus interpositis provolat,	
	pecus trucidat, ipsos pastores necat,	
	et cuncta vastans saevit irato impetū.	
sibi: 3.III.3 **ferae:** 3.III.5	Tum sibi timentes qui ferae pepercerant,	15
	damnum haut recusant: tantum pro vitā rogant.	
petierit: 20.I.3	At illa: "Memini quis me saxo petierit,	
dederit: 16.V	quis panem dederit; vos timēre absistite;	
illis: 3.III.3 **hostis:** 3.I.2	illis revertor hostis qui me laeserunt."	

imprudens, -ntis — careless	**panis, -is** — bread	**velox, -ocis** — quick
fovea, -ae — pit	**insequor, -i** — come on, follow	**saltus, -ūs** — leap, jump
fustis, -is — club		**libero, -are** — free
onero, -are — weigh down	**postridiē** — on the next day	**concitus, -a, -um** — disturbed
misereor, -ēri — take pity	**languidus, -a, -um** — weak	**interpono, -ere** — intervene

provolo, -are — dash out

trucido, -are — slaughter

pastor, -ris — shepherd

vasto, -are — lay waste to

saevio, -ire — rage

damnum, -i — loss, damage

recuso, -are — denounce

absisto, -ere — cease

READING FOR UNDERSTANDING

1. In all of Roman literature, there are remarkably few anecdotes, such as this one, praising compassion for vulnerable animals. Considering Roman culture, how would you explain this paucity?

2. The people who were merciful toward the panther didn't begrudge their loss of livestock (see line 16). Why not?

3. Though the idea that compassion toward wild animals will be rewarded is attractive, the truth is more often otherwise. What commends compassion for animals, if direct or immediate rewards do not?

2.

"Rewards for the Inconsiderate": The Owl and the Cicada

READING FOR INFORMATION

1. How was the cicada annoying the owl?
2. What liquid did the owl invite the cicada to drink with it?
3. What happened to the cicada?

humanitati: 3.III.7	Humanitati qui se non accommodat	
	plerumque poenas oppetit superbiae.	
noctuae: 3.III.3	Cicada acerbum noctuae convicium	
	faciebat, solitae vīctum in tenebris quaerere	
	cavoque ramo capere somnum interdiū.	5
tacēret: 16.IV multō: 3.V.9 admotā prece: 13.III.2 ut: 16.XIII.2.a	Rogata est ut tacēret. Multō validius clamare occepit. Rursus admotā prece accensa magis est. Noctua, ut vīdit sibi	
esse, contemni: 12.I.3.d	nullum esse auxilium et verba contemni sua,	
	hac est adgressa garrulam fallaciā:	10
	"Dormire quia me non sinunt cantūs tui,	
sonare: 12.I.3.d citharam: 3.IV.4 putes: 15.II pōtare: 12.I.3.b si: 18.I.1 veni: 19.I bibamus: 5.I	sonare citharam quos putes Apollinis, pōtare est animus nectar, quod Pallas mihi nuper donavit; si non fastidis, veni; unā bibamus." Illa, quae arebat siti,	15
vocem: 3.IV.4	simul gaudebat vocem laudari suam,	
obsepto cavo: 13.III.1	cupidē advolavit. Noctua, obsepto cavo, trepidantem consectata est et leto dedit.	
negarat: 20.I.3	Sīc, viva quod negarat, tribuit mortua.	

humanitas, -tatis — thoughtfulness	**ramus, -i** — branch	**unā** — together
accommodo, -are — accommodate	**interdiū** — during the daytime	**areo, -ēre** — be parched
plerumque — often	**occipio, -ere** — begin	**sitis, -is** — thirst
oppeto, -ere — meet with	**garrulus, -a, -um** — talkative	**advolo, -are** — fly to
superbia, -ae — arrogance	**fallacia, -ae** — deceitfulness	**obsepio, -ere** — seal, block
cicada, -ae — cicada	**sono, -are** — sound	**cavum, -i** — hollow
noctua, -ae — owl	**cithara, -ae** — lute	**trepido, -are** — be afraid
convicium, -i — spat	**nectar, -aris** — nectar	**consector, -ari** — chase
vīctus, -ūs — food	**nuper** — recently	**letum, -i** — death
	fastidio, -ire — disdain	

READING FOR UNDERSTANDING

1. *In your view, did the owl give the cicada due warnings?*
2. *In your view, was the deception that the owl employed suitably justified?*
3. *Does the deceptive use of gods' names (Apollo and Minerva) in the owl's ruse strike you as blasphemous in any way?*

3.

"You Get What You Give": The Fox and the Stork

READING FOR INFORMATION

1. *What did the fox serve the stork? How did he serve it?*
2. *What did the stork serve the fox? How did she serve it?*

nulli: 3.III.6
nocendum (est): 17.IV
si: 18.I.4
quis: 7.VI.1.a
multandum (esse): 17.IV
iure: 3.V.3
invitasse: 20.I.3
posuisse: 12.I.3.d
gustare: 12.I.3.b
potuerit: 16.XI
cum: 16.I.1
cibo: 3.V.16
huic: 3.III.7

fame: 3.V.10

cum: 16.I.1

locutam (esse): 20.IV
animo: 3.V.3
pati: 12.I.3.b

Nulli nocendum; si quis vērō laeserit,
multandum simili iure fabella admonet.
Ad cenam vulpes dicitur ciconiam
prior invitasse, et liquidam in patulo marmore
posuisse sorbitionem, quam nullo modo   5
gustare esuriens potuerit ciconia.
Quae, vulpem cum revocasset, intrito cibo
plenam lagonam posuit; huic rostrum inserens
satiatur ipsa et torquet convivam fame.
Quae cum lagonae collum frustrā lamberet,   10
peregrinam sīc locutam volucrem accepimus:
"Sua quisque exempla debet aequo animo pati."

multo, -are — punish	**ciconia, -ae** — stork	**patulus, -a, -um** — flat, open
fabella, -ae — fable	**liquidus, -a, -um** — liquid	**marmor, -ris** — slab of marble

sorbitio, -onis — soup

gusto, -are — taste

esurio, -ire — be hungry

revoco, -are — invite in turn

intero, -ere — grind

lagona, -ae — bottle

rostrum, -i — beak

insero, -ere — insert

satior, -ari — eat one's fill

torqueo, -ēre — torment

conviva, -ae — dinner guest

lambo, -ere — lick

peregrinus, -a, -um — guest-

READING FOR UNDERSTANDING

1. *How would you characterize the hospitality the fox and the stork show each other?*

2. *The fable suggests that eye-for-an eye justice is acceptable. Can this concept be reconciled with the principle underlying the Golden Rule?*

3. *Short of the bedroom, table fellowship is about as intimate as humans routinely get with one another. In what ways can we offend others at table and foreclose that intimacy?*

4.

"Practice What You Preach!": A Young Crab and His Mother

READING FOR INFORMATION

1. *What happened to the young crab that prompted his mother to try to give him advice?*

2. *What does the young crab propose to his mother?*

dum: 16.XIII.3.a.i.A.1	Curva retrō cedens dum fert vestigia cancer,
	hispida saxosis terga relisit aquis.
procedere: 12.I.3.b **gressū:** 3.V.3 **adloquiis:** 3.V.1 **emonuisse:** 12.I.3.d **tibi:** 3.III.5 **placeant:** 15.I **velis:** 19.IV	Hunc genetrix facili cupiens procedere gressū
	talibus adloquiis emonuisse datur:
	"Ne tibi transverso placeant haec devia, nate, 5
	rursus in obliquos neu velis ire pedes,
nisū: 3.V.10	sed nisū contenta ferens vestigia recto
tramite: 3.V.2 **siste:** 19.I **si:** 18.I.2.a.i	innocuos prono tramite siste gradūs."
	Cui natus: "Faciam, si me praecesseris," inquit,
recta: 3.IV.1.a	"rectaque monstrantem certior ipse sequar. 10
cum: 16.I.1 **pravissima:** 3.IV.1 **si:** 18.I.1 **vitiosa:** 3.IV.1	Nam stultum nimis est, cum tu pravissima temptes,
	alterius censor si vitiosa notas."

curvus, -a, -um — winding

retrō — backward

cancer, -eris — crab

hispidus, -a, -um — prickly

saxosus, -a, -um — rocky

relido, -ere — scrape

procedo, -ere — move, proceed

gressus, -ūs — course, way

adloquium, -i — word, discussion

emoneo, -ēre — advise

transversus, -a, -um — transverse, sideways

devius, -a, -um — deviant, wandering

obliquus, -a, -um — oblique, indirect

innocuus, -a, -um — faultless, harmless

pronus, -a, -um — pointing forward

trames, -itis — path, way

sisto, -ere — plant, set

praecedo, -ere — go ahead of   **pravus, -a, -um** — crooked
monstro, -are — show   **vitiosus, -a, -um** — flawed

READING FOR UNDERSTANDING

1. *In what ways does the response of the son seem more strident and disrespectful than the advice of the mother?*
2. *It is easier, to be sure, to observe a fault in another than to notice the same fault in one-self. What happens emotionally, though, when we see a shared fault in a parent or an offspring?*
3. *How is the maxim "Practice what you preach" just a variation on the Golden Rule?*

———

"Be Careful Whom You Trust"
The following fables remind us that our superiors in power and intelligence are not always to be trusted. Being weaker but wary is a perfectly fine condition.

5.

"The Lion's Share": A Four-Way Partnership

READING FOR INFORMATION

1. *Of the four members of the **societas**, which one is described as **patiens iniuriae**?*
2. *What booty have the four captured?*
3. *Divided into quarters, was the booty shared equally by all four members?*

	Numquam est fidelis cum potente societas.
	Testatur haec fabella propositum meum.
iniuriae: 3.II.6	Vacca et capella et patiens ovis iniuriae
fuēre: 20.I.2	socii fuēre cum leone in saltibus.
cum: 16.I.3.a	
corporis: 3.II.3	Hi cum cepissent cervum vasti corporis, 5
partibus factis: 13.III.1	sīc est locutus, partibus factis, leo:
nomine: 3.V.10	"Ego primam tollo nomine hōc quia rex cluo;
	secundam, quia sum consors, tribuetis mihi;
	tum, quia plus valeo, me sequetur tertia;
malo: 3.V.1	malo adficietur si quis quartam tetigerit." 10
si: 18.I.2.a	
quis: 7.VI.1.a	Sīc totam praedam sola improbitas abstulit.

societas, -tatis — affiliation   **capella, -ae** — goat   **consors, -rtis** — partner
testor, -ari — attest to   **saltus, -ūs** — glade, glen **malum, -i** — a bad thing
fabella, -ae — fable   **cervus, -i** — buck, stag   **adficio, -ere** — do, face with
propositum, -i — premise   **vastus, -a, -um** — huge   **improbitas, -tatis** — wickedness
vacca, -ae — cow   **cluo, -ere** — be called   **abstulit < aufero**

1. *Why does the poet say that **improbitas** carried off the booty?*
2. *Does this partnership between three herbivores and a carnivore—and the fact that their bone of contention is over meat—distract you from the fable's message in any way?*

6.

"Taking the High Road (to Avoid the Lowlifes)": The Kid and the Wolf

READING FOR INFORMATION

1. *Where does the kid seek refuge from the wolf?*
2. *Where does the wolf claim that the kid will die if it doesn't leave the city?*
3. *Why, according to the kid, would that be a preferable death?*

cursū: 3.V.10	Forte lupum melior cursū deluserat haedus,	
dum: 16.XIII.3.a.i.A.1	proxima vicinis dum petit arva casis;	
casis: 3.III.2	inde fugam recto tendens in moenia cursū	
cursū: 3.V.1	inter lanigeros adstitit ille greges.	
	Impiger hunc raptor mediamque secutus in urbem,	5
dolis: 3.V.1	temptat compositis sollicitare dolis:	
ut: 16.IV	"Nonne vides," inquit, "cunctis ut victima templis	
morte: 3.V.1	immitem regemens morte cruentet humum?	
nisi: 18.I.4	Quod nisi securo valeas te reddere campo,	
campo: 3.III.1		
mihi: 3.III.8	heu mihi!, vittatā tu quoque fronte cades."	10
vittatā . . . fronte: 3.V.14		
exime: 19.I	Ille refert: "Modo quam metuis, precor, exime curam,	
tecum: 8.II.1.a	et tecum viles, improbe, tolle minas;	
tolle: 19.I		
divis: 3.III.3	nam sat erit sacrum divis fudisse cruorem,	
fudisse: 12.I.3.b		
lupo: 3.III.3	quam rabido fauces exsaturare lupo."	
casū: 3.V.5	Sīc quotiens duplici subeuntur tristia casū,	15
promeruisse: 12.I.3.c	expedit insignem promeruisse necem.	

15. **Sīc . . . casū:** so whenever certain sorrows present themselves with two possible outcomes

lupus, -i — wolf	**raptor, -ris** — predator	**minae, -arum** — threats
deludo, -ere — trick, elude	**sollicito, -are** — harry	**faux, faucis** — throat
haedus, -i — young goat, kid	**nonne** — surely?	**exsaturo, -are** — fill, glut
casa, -ae — house, cottage	**immitis, -e** — cruel	**duplex, -plicis** — twofold, ambiguous
moenia, -ium — town walls	**regemo, -ere** — bellow	
laniger, -era, -erum — wool bearing	**cruento, -are** — make bloody	**expedit, -ire** — it is useful
	heu — alas!	**promereo, -ēre** — be worthy of
adsto, -are — stand amid	**vittatus, -a, -um** — garlanded	
impiger, -gra, -grum — persistent	**eximo, -ere** — remove	
	vilis, -e — worthless	

READING FOR UNDERSTANDING

1. The ancients believed that to be acceptable to the gods, all sacrificial victims should go willingly to sacrifice. How does this fable support that belief?
2. Which death do you think would be preferable, one in support of a noble cause or one in pursuit of a personal goal?

7.

"Divide and Conquer": The Oxen and the Lion

READING FOR INFORMATION

1. What was the nature of the original relationship among these four oxen?
2. How did the lion change this relationship?

iuvencis: 3.III.4 **amicitiae:** 3.II.6 **fuisse:** 12.I.3.d	Quattuor immensis quondam per prata iuvencis fertur amicitiae tanta fuisse fides,
ut: 16.II	ut simul emissos nullus divelleret error, rursus et e pastū turba rediret amans.

collatis . . .
  cornibus: 13.III.2
	Hos quoque collatis inter se cornibus ingens 5
	    dicitur in silvis pertimuisse leo,

dum:
  16.XIII.3.a.i.A.1
	dum metus oblatam prohibet temptare rapinam,
	    et coniuratos horret adire boves.

quamvis: 16.XIII.1.a **factis:** 3.V.10 **viribus:** 3.III.2	Et quamvis audax factisque immanior esset, tantorum solus viribus impar erat. 10
verbis: 3.V.1	Protinus adgreditur pravis insistere verbis,
dissociare: 12.I.3.b	collisum cupiens dissociare pecus.
	Sīc postquam dictis animos disiunxit acerbis, invasit miserum diripuitque gregem.
servare: 12.I.3.b	Tunc quidam ex illis, "Vitam servare quietam 15
discere: 12.I.3.b	qui cupit, ex nostrā discere morte potest.
impleat: 15.I **deserat:** 15.I	Neve cito admotas verbis fallacibus aures impleat, aut veterem deserat ante fidem."

iuvencus, -i — young bull

divello, -ere — separate

error, -ris — wandering

pastus, -ūs — pasture

collatis < confero

pertimeo, -ēre — fear much

coniuro, -are — unite, join together

immanis, -e — mighty

impar — unequal

pravus, -a, -um — sinister

insisto, -ere — press

collido, -ere — dash upon

dissocio, -are — scatter, divide

disiungo, -ere — disunite

invado, -ere — attack

diripio, -ere — ravage

fallax, -acis — deceitful

impleo, -ēre — fill

READING FOR UNDERSTANDING

1. *Why did the oxen's original relationship intimidate the lion?*
2. *One (the last?) of the oxen provides the moral of the fable. How is this more effective than if the poet had simply declared the moral in his own voice?*

8.

"Always Workin' an Angle": The Lion and the She-Goat

READING FOR INFORMATION

1. *The lion advises the she-goat not to graze where? Why?*
2. *Does the she-goat consider the advice sound in any way?*

	Vīderat excelsā pascentem rupe capellam,	
cum: 16.III.1.a	comminus esuriens cum leo ferret iter.	
	Et prior: "Heus," inquit, "praeruptis ardua saxis	
iugis: 3.V.19	linque, nec hirsutis pascua quaere iugis;	
	sed cythisi croceum per prata virentia florem	5
	et glaucas salices et thyma grata pete."	
	Illa gemens: "Desiste, precor, fallaciter," inquit,	
securam (me): 3.X	"securam placidis instimulare dolis.	
instimulare: 12.I.3.b		
dolis: 3.V.1	Vera licet moneas, maiora pericula tollas,	
moneas: 15.II		
tollas: 15.II	tu tamen his dictis non facis esse fidem.	10
dictis: 3.V.10		
quamvis: 16.XIII.1.a	Nam quamvis rectis constet sententia verbis,	
verbis: 3.III.7	suspectam hanc rabidus consiliator habet."	

excelsus, -a, -um — lofty	**linquo, -ere** — abandon	**desisto, -ere** — cease
pasco, -ere — feed, browse	**hirsutus, -a, -um** — thicketed	**fallaciter** — deceitfully
rupes, -is — crag	**pascua, -orum** — food	**instimulo, -are** — goad
capella, -ae — she-goat	**cythisus, -i** — clover	**licet** — although
comminus — close, closer	**croceus, -a, -um** — yellow	**consto, -are** — correspond
esurio, -ire — be hungry	**glaucus, -a, -um** — gray	**suspicio, -ere** — suspect
heus — hey!	**salix, -icis** — willow	**conciliator, -ris** —
praeruptus, -a, -um — sheer	**thymum, -i** — thyme	counselor
ardua, -orum — heights	**gemo, -ere** — bleat	

READING FOR UNDERSTANDING

1. *Which dilemma have you found more difficult to deal with, good advice from a person you didn't trust or respect, or bad advice from a person you did?*
2. *The predator/prey aspect of this fable is pretty obvious. Would the fable be more interesting or more effective if, say, a fox or a large snake replaced the lion?*

"Just Tell Yourself, Ducky, You're Really Quite Lucky!"
It isn't always easy to be content with who one is or what one has. So many pressures—cultural, economic, social, and personal—vex simple contentment. The message of these fables is that true happiness and well-being rest with a basic decision.

9.

"The Grass Is Always Greener": Juno and the Peacock

READING FOR INFORMATION

1. The peacock emulates the voice of what other bird?
2. According to Juno, the fates allotted what attributes to what other birds?
3. Juno affirms that to wish for the impossible produces what effect?

	Pavo ad Iunonem vēnit, indignē ferens	
quod: 16.III.3.b.i	cantūs luscinii quod sibi non tribuerit;	
esse, deridēri: 12.I.3.d	illum esse cunctis auribus mirabilem,	
auribus: 3.III.3 **miserit:** 16.XI	se deridēri simul ac vocem miserit.	
consolandi: 17.V.2 **gratiā:** 8.III	Tunc consolandi gratiā dixit dea:	5
formā, magnitudine: 3.V.10	"Sed formā vincis, vincis magnitudine;	
collo: 3.V.18	nitor smaragdi collo praefulget tuo,	
plumis: 3.V.10 **mi:** 7.I.1	pictisque plumis gemmeam caudam explicas."	
(dedisti): 20.IV **si:** 18.I.1	"Quo mi," inquit, "mutam speciem, si vincor sono?"	
sono: 3.V.10 **arbitrio:** 3.V.7	"Fatorum arbitrio partes sunt vobis datae;	10
tibi, aquilae, luscinio, corvo, cornici: 3.III.1	tibi forma, vires aquilae, luscinio melos, augurium corvo, laeva cornici omina;	
dotibus: 3.V.10	omnesque propriis sunt contentae dotibus."	
noli: 19.III	Noli adfectare quod tibi non est datum,	
ne: 16.III.1	delusa ne spes ad querelam decidat.	15

pavo, -onis — peacock	**praefulgeo, -ēre** — shine forth	**arbitrium, -i** — judgment
luscinius, -i — nightingale		**aquila, -ae** — eagle
mirabilis, -e — marvelous	**pictis** < **pingo**	**melos, -i** — song
derideo, -ēre — mock	**pluma, -ae** — feather	**augurium, -i** — augury
consolor, -ari — console	**gemmeus, -a, -um** — begemmed	**laevus, -a, -um** — unfavorable
magnitudo, -dinis — size		**cornix, -icis** — crow
nitor, -ris — glitter, sheen	**mutus, -a, -um** — mute	**deludo, -ere** — deceive
smaragdus, -i — emerald	**species, -ei** — appearance	**querela, -ae** — complaint

READING FOR UNDERSTANDING

1. *A survey once conducted by one of the American fashion magazines (our great cultural authorities!) revealed that only a very small percentage of the population like their hair, teeth, and hands, all three. What factors lead to this widespread sort of self-dissatisfaction?*

2. *Being beautiful is a great gift; being able to do something beautiful is also a great gift. We usually prize the latter more than the former. So how would you argue for the preservation of, say, a beautiful pristine mountain that could produce many beautiful things through strip mining?*

3. *The fact that the fates allotted each species of bird a particular attribute or function suggests that the poet believed in an ancient equivalent of "intelligent design," that is, a providential architect for all creation. But the peacock's complaint to Juno suggests that the "architecture" can be altered (through adaptation? evolution?). How can you explain or reconcile the coexistence of these seemingly contradictory views?*

10.

"Some Things Never Change": The Donkey and the Old Man

READING FOR INFORMATION

1. *What is the donkey doing as this fable opens?*
2. *Why does the old man suddenly become afraid?*
3. *What is the donkey's basic point to the old man?*

commutando: 17.III	In principatū commutando civium
	nil praeter dominum, non rem mutant pauperes.
esse: 12.I.3.d	Id esse verum, parva haec fabella indicat.
	Asellum in prato timidus pascebat senex.
clamore: 3.V.7 **asino:** 3.III.5 **ne:** 16.III.1 **mihi:** 3.III.3 **impositurum** **(esse):** 12.I.3.d **victorem:** 3.IV.4 **rēfert meā:** 20.III.6 **cui:** 3.III.5 **serviam:** 16.V **dum:** 16.VIII	Is hostium clamore subito territus 5
	suadebat asino fugere, ne possent capi.
	At ille lentus: "Quaeso, num binas mihi
	clitellas impositurum victorem putas?"
	Senex negavit. "Ergo, quid rēfert meā
	cui serviam, clitellas dum portem unicas?" 10

principatus, -ūs — leadership	**suadeo, -ēre** — persuade	**bini, -ae, -a** — doubled
commuto, -are — change	**lentus, -a, -um** — slow	**clitella, -ae** — pack saddle
fabella, -ae — fable	**quaeso, -ere** — beg, pray	**victor, -ris** — winner
pasco, -ere — put to pasture	**num** — whether	**unicus, -a, -um** — single

READING FOR UNDERSTANDING

1. The significance of this fable is circumscribed to **pauperes** and their circumstances (**res**, line 2). While it might matter to a donkey who its master is (because of the different treatment it might receive), is it true that the poorest of the poor don't care about changes of government and political regimes?
2. The socioeconomic status of the old man in this fable isn't given; we are told, however, that he is **timidus**. Do you suppose that a person can sink to a point of poverty where even fear is lost and abandoned?
3. What concerns should the powers that be and society as a whole have if a significant number of citizens fall into apathy, despair, and recklessness as a result of their poverty?

11.

"One in the Hand Is Worth . . .": The Dog in the River

READING FOR INFORMATION

1. What did the dog have in its mouth?
2. What did the dog see in the river?

	Amittit meritō proprium qui alienum appetit.	
cum: 16.I.3.a	Canis, per fluvium carnem cum ferret, natans	
	lympharum in speculo vīdit simulacrum suum,	
ferri: 12.I.3.d	aliamque praedam ab altero ferri putans	
	eripere voluit; verum decepta aviditas	5
ore: 3.V.I	et quem tenebat ore dimisit cibum,	
	nec quem petebat adeō potuit tangere.	

appeto, -ere — desire	**nato, -are** — swim	**simulacrum, -i** — likeness
fluvium, -i — river	**lympha, -ae** — water	**aviditas, -tatis** — greediness
caro, carnis — meat	**speculum, -i** — reflection	

READING FOR UNDERSTANDING

1. Did the dog get what it deserved?
2. If the fable had gone on to relate that the dog next drowned in the river, then would the dog have gotten what it deserved?

12.

"Pretty Is as Pretty Does": The Peacock and the Crane

READING FOR INFORMATION

1. When did the crane and the peacock come into conflict?
2. According to the fable, apart from the peacock's tail, what is the most salient difference between cranes and peacocks?

Thraciam volucrem fertur Iunonius ales

conteruisse:
  12.I.3.d
cibo: 3.V.1

communi sociam conteruisse cibo;

namque inter varias fuerat discordia formas,

magnaque de facili iurgia lite trahunt,

quod: 16.XIII.3.b.i

quod sibi multimodo fulgērent membra decore,   5

caeruleam facerent livida terga gruem;

caudae: 3.II.6

et simul erectae circumdans tegmina caudae,

sparserat arcatum sursus in astra iubar.

certet: 15.II
honore: 3.V.10
vocibus: 3.V.13
usa (esse): 12.I.3.d
quamvis: 16.XIII.1.a

Illa licet nullo pennarum certet honore,

his tamen insultans vocibus usa datur: 10

"Quamvis innumerus plumas variaverit ordo,

humi: 4.I.3

mersus humi semper florida terga geris:

pennā: 3.V.1
sideribus
  numinibusque:
  3.III.2

ast ego deformi sublimis in āera pennā,

proxima sideribus numinibusque feror."

Thracia volucris — Thracian bird = crane	**caeruleus, -a, -um** — light blue	**licet** — although
communis — joint	**lividus, -a, -um** — gray	**penna, -ae** — feather
socia, -ae — partner	**grus, gruis** — crane	**certo, -are** — compete
contero, -ere — belittle	**erigo, -ere** — raise up	**insulto, -are** — insult
discordia, -ae — discord	**tegmen, -minis** — cover	**vario, -are** — vary
multimodus, -a, -um — variegated	**arcatus, -a, -um** — arched	**mergo, -ere** — sink, bury
	sursus — upward	**floridus, -a, -um** — flowery
	iubar, -aris — splendor	**deformis, -e** — ugly

READING FOR UNDERSTANDING

1. *The poet tells us that this competition is a **facilis lis**. What does he mean?*
2. *The aphorism "Pretty is as pretty does" has long been current in North America. What is its significance for this fable?*
3. *Empowerment (i.e., doing something great) and endowment (i.e., being something great) are both wonderful assets. If you're a teacher, like this author, which one do you foster and promote more?*

13.

"Beauty's in the Eye of the Beholder": Jupiter and the Monkey

READING FOR INFORMATION

1. *Besides the monkey, what two species are specifically said to have participated in this competition?*
2. *What was Jupiter's reaction when the monkey presented her baby?*

natorum: 3.II.2
quīs: 7.V.1
daret: 16.V

Iuppiter in toto quondam quaesiverat orbe,

munera natorum quīs meliora daret.

Certatim ad regem currit genus omne ferarum,

homini: 3.III.7   permixtumque homini cogitur ire pecus.

Sed nec squamigeri desunt ad iurgia pisces,   5

volucrum: 3.II.2   vel quicquid volucrum purior aura vehit.

Inter quos trepidae ducebant pignora matres,

iudicio: 3.V.1
discutienda: 17.III   iudicio tanti discutienda dei.

cum: 16.I.3.a   Tunc brevis informem traheret cum simia natum,

ipsum etiam in risum compulit ire Iovem.   10

Hanc tamen ante alios rupit turpissima vocem,

dum generis crimen sīc abolēre cupit:

nōrit: 20.I.3
si: 18.I.4
quem: 7.VI.1.a "Iuppiter hoc nōrit, maneat victoria si quem;

iudicio: 3.V.10
omnibus: 3.III.7   iudicio superest omnibus iste meo."

certatim — competitively	**piscis, -is** — fish	**compello, -ere** — compel
permisceo, -ēre — mix	**trepidus, -a, -um** — trembling	**crimen, -inis** — stigma
squamiger, -era, -erum — scale bearing	**discutio, -ere** — scrutinize	**aboleo, -ēre** — abolish
desum, -esse — be missing	**informis, -e** — ugly	**supersum, -esse** — surpass
	simia, -ae — monkey	

READING FOR UNDERSTANDING

1. *Why don't we have beauty pageants for adult males in our culture?*
2. *Was the mother monkey wrong for promoting her offspring as the most beautiful?*
3. *What's the significance, do you think, of a supreme god who wants to know which species in all of creation has the best offspring?*

14.

"Living the Charmed Life?": The Ox and the Calf

READING FOR INFORMATION

1. *How does the calf reproach the ox?*
2. *How does the ox react? Why does he react that way?*
3. *What is the ultimate fate of the calf?*

cervice: 3.V.5   Pulcher et intactā vitulus cervice resultans

scindentem adsiduē vīderat arva bovem.

pudet: 20.III.5
collo: 3.V.1   "Non pudet, heus," inquit, "longaevo vincula collo

nosse: 20.I.3
positis . . . iugis:
13.III.1   ferre nec haec positis otia nosse iugis,

cum: 16.I.2   cum mihi subiectas pateat discursus in herbas   5

et nemorum liceat rursus opaca sequi?"

verbis: 3.V.7   At senior, nullam verbis compulsus in iram,

vomere: 3.V.1   vertebat solitam vomere fessus humum,

donec:
   19.XIII.3.a.i.B
deposito . . . aratro:
   13.III.1
toro: 3.III.7
aris: 3.III.7
cultro: 3.V.10

(te) expertem: 3.X
iugi: 3.II.6
quamvis: 16.XIII.1.a
(te) tenerum: 3.X
peritura: 12.II
felicibus: 3.III.3
ut: 16.II
cum: 16.I.4
miseris: 3.III.3
(mortem): 3.X

donec deposito per prata licēret aratro

    molliter herboso procubuisse toro.   10

Mox vitulum sacris innexum respicit aris

    admotum cultro comminus ire popae.

"Hanc tibi tristis," ait, "dedit indulgentia mortem,

    expertem nostri quae facit esse iugi.

Proderit ergo graves quamvis perferre labores,   15

    otia quam tenerum mox peritura pati."

Est hominum sors ista, magis felicibus ut mors

    sit cita, cum miseris vita diurna negat.

intactus, -a, -um — untouched	**opacus, -a, -um** — shady	**respicio, -ere** — regard
vitulus, -i — young bull	**compello, -ere** — compel	**cultrum, -i** — knife
resulto, -are — scamper	**vomer, -eris** — plow blade	**comminus** — close
scindo, -ere — split	**aratrum, -i** — plow	**popa, -ae** — religious
heus — hey!	**herbosus, -a, -um** — grassy	attendant
longaevus, -a, -um — aged	**procumbo, -ere** — lie out	**expers, -rtis** — free from
pateo, -ēre — be available	**innecto, -ere** — weave,	**diurnus, -a, -um** — day-to-day
discursus, -ūs — free-run	garland	

READING FOR UNDERSTANDING

1. *This fable suggests that work has value beyond its immediate product or result. What is that value?*
2. *Do you think the moral of the fable (lines 17–18) accurately reflects the fable's meaning?*
3. *Which option sounds preferable to you: a short life of little effort or accomplishment, or a long life of considerable effort but only modest satisfaction?*

15.

"Mom Always Liked You Best": The Monkey Twins

READING FOR INFORMATION

1. *How did the mother feel about her two offspring?*
2. *What happened to the favored twin?*
3. *What became of the less favored one?*

quod: 16.XIII.3.b.i
partum: 3.IV.1.a

amore: 3.V.3

alterius: 3.II.6
odiis: 3.V.7
ut: 16.XIII.2.a

condicione: 3.V.3

manibus, pectore:
   3.V.1

Fama est quod geminum profundens simia partum,

    dividat in varias pignora nata vices;

namque unum caro genetrix educit amore,

    alterius odiis exsaturata tumet.

Coeperit ut fetam gravior terrēre tumultus,   5

    dissimili natos condicione rapit:

dilectum manibus vel pectore gestat amico,

dorso: 3.V.1	contemptum dorso suscipiente levat.
cum: 16.I.1 **plantis:** 3.V.1	Sed cum lassatis nequeat consistere plantis,
	oppositum fugiens sponte remittit onus. 10
collo: 3.III.7	Alter at hirsuto circumdans bracchia collo
	haeret, et invitā cum genetrice fugit.
	Mox quoque dilecti succedit in oscula fratris,
heres: 3.I.2 **avis:** 3.III.3 **ordine verso:** 13.III.1 **humiles:** 3.IV.1	servatus vetulis unicus heres avis.
	Sīc multos neglecta iuvant, atque, ordine verso, 15
	spes humiles rursus in meliora refert.

profundo, -ere — issue

simia, -ae — monkey

divido, -ere — distinguish

——, vicis — position, status

educo, -ere — raise

exsaturo, -are — fill

feta, -ae — mother

tumultus, -ūs — disturbance

dissimilis, -e — differing

dorsum, -i — back

suscipio, -ere — support

lassatus, -a, -um — wearied

nequeo, -ēre — be unable

consisto, -ere — persist

planta, -ae — foot

oppono, -ere — place opposite

sponte — of one's own accord

onus, -eris — load, burden

hirsutus, -a, -um — shaggy

invitus, -a, -um — reluctant

succedo, -ere — become heir

vetulus, -a, -um — ancient

unicus, -a, -um — sole

humilis, -e — lowly

READING FOR UNDERSTANDING

1. This fable suggests that luck plays a greater role than parental love and provision in survival and success. Do you agree?
2. Define the condition known as survivor's guilt. Does the surviving monkey twin exhibit any signs of that condition? Why does he react to the loss of his twin as he does?

"Vanity of Vanities! All Is Vanity"
The age-old fault of vanity makes us overvalue things that aren't important and undervalue things that are—specifically when these things are our own! Can you see any of your behaviors in the following fables?

16.

"A Fool and His Cheese Are Soon Parted": The Fox and the Crow

READING FOR INFORMATION

1. Where did the crow get the cheese?
2. What parts of the crow's body did the fox praise?
3. The crow, in his vanity, wanted the fox to praise what?

verbis: 3.V.1	Qui se laudari gaudent verbis subdolis,
paenitentiā: 3.V.3	seri dant poenas turpi paenitentiā.
cum: 16.I.3.a	Cum de fenestrā corvus raptum caseum

comesse vellet, celsā residens arbore,

vulpes invīdit, deinde sīc coepit loquī: 5

"O quī tuārum, corve, pinnārum est nitor!

decoris: 3.II.2
corpore, vultū: 3.V.10
Quantum decoris corpore et vultū geris!

Sī vōcem habērēs, nulla prior āles foret."

si: 18.I.3
foret: 10.III.7.a
dum: 16.XIII.3.a.i.A.1
ore: 3.V.19
At ille stultus, dum vult vōcem ostendere,

lātō ōre ēmīsit cāseum; quem celeriter   10

dentibus: 3.V.1
dolōsa vulpēs avidīs rapuit dentibus.

Tum dēmum ingemuit corvī dēceptus stupor.

subdolus, -a, -um — deceptive	**comedo, comesse** — eat	**dolosus, -a, -um** — tricky
paenitentia, -ae — regret	**celsus, -a, -um** — high	**avidus, -a, -um** — greedy
fenestra, -ae — window	**pinna, -ae** — feather	**ingemo, -ere** — groan, sigh
caseus, -i — cheese	**nitor, -ris** — luster, sheen	**stupor, -ris** — stupidity

READING FOR UNDERSTANDING

1. *Having read this fable, do you praise the fox for being clever or condemn him for being manipulative?*

2. *Does the fact that the cheese was already stolen figure in your answer to the previous question? Should it?*

3. *For the crow, what was the takeaway message here: don't take pleasure in being praised (which is vanity), or don't be gulled by **verba subdola**?*

17.

"A Lesson Learned Too Late": The Buck at the Pool

READING FOR INFORMATION

1. *What was the buck doing before he gazed at his reflection?*
2. *What was his assessment of his legs?*
3. *Where did he meet his end?*

laudatis: 3.V.8
utiliora: 3.IV.4
contempseris: 16.XI
testis: 3.I.2
cum: 16.I.3.a
Laudātis ūtiliōra quae contempserīs,

saepe invenīrī testis haec nārrātiō est.

Ad fontem cervus, cum bibisset, restitit,

et in liquōre vīdit effigiem suam.

dum: 16.XIII.3.a.i.A.1
Ibi dum rāmōsa mīrāns laudat cornua   5

crūrumque nimiam tenuitātem vituperat,

vēnantum subitō vōcibus conterritus,

per campum fugere coepit, et cursū levī

canēs ēlūsit. Silva tum excēpit ferum,

cornibus: 3.V.7
in quā retentīs impedītus cornibus   10

morsibus: 3.V.7 | lacerari coepit morsibus saevis canum.

Tum moriens edidisse vocem hanc dicitur:

me: 3.IV.5
mihi: 3.III.2
fuerint: 16.V
laudaram: 20.I.3
luctūs: 3.II.2
habuerint: 16.V

"O me infelicem, qui nunc demum intellego,

utilia mihi quam fuerint quae despexeram,

et, quae laudaram, quantum luctūs habuerint."   15

testis, -is — witness	**crus, cruris** — leg	**impedio, -ire** — hinder
narratio, -onis — story	**tenuitas, -tatis** — thinness	**lacero, -are** — tear apart
cervus, -i — buck, stag	**vitupero, -are** — curse	**morsus, -ūs** — bite, biting
liquor, -ris — water, liquid	**venor, -ari** — hunt	**saevus, -a, -um** — savage
effigies, -ei — image	**conterreo, -ēre** — frighten	**edo, -ere** — issue
ramosus, -a, -um — branching	**eludo, -ere** — escape	**luctus, -ūs** — grief

READING FOR UNDERSTANDING
1. Could the buck have avoided the outcome of this fable if he had never admired his reflection? That is, if pride comes before a fall, will there be no fall if there is no pride?
2. Is vanity learned or a natural attribute, like the buck's fleetness of foot?
3. The buck's final words, uttered while dogs were ripping him apart, seem pretty unrealistic (whatever that means for a fable!). Does that lack of realism diminish the credibility of the fable's message?

18.

"All Bite, No Bark": The Dog and His Bell

READING FOR INFORMATION
1. What is unusual about the dog in this fable?
2. What does the dog's owner do in response?
3. How does the dog misinterpret the owner's response?

latratibus: 3.V.3 | Forte canis quondam, nullis latratibus horrens,

rictibus: 3.V.5 | nec patulis primum rictibus ora trahens,

caudae: 3.II.1 | mollia sed pavidae submittens verbera caudae,

dente: 3.V.1 | concitus audaci vulnera dente dabat.

ne: 16.III.1
quem: 7.VI.1.a
| Hunc dominus, ne quem probitas simulata latēret,   5

    iusserat in rabido gutture ferre nolam.

faucibus: 3.III.7 | Faucibus innexis crepitantia subligat aera,

quae: 16.III.2.a
cavenda: 17.III
ferri: 12.I.3.d
| quae facili motū signa cavenda darent.

Haec tamen ille sibi credebat praemia ferri,

    et similem turbam despiciebat ovans.   10

Tunc insultantem senior de plebe superbum

    adgreditur tali singula voce monens:

"Infelix, quae tanta rapit dementia sensum,
        munera pro meritis si capis ista dari?
Non hoc virtutis decus ostentatur in aere,   15
nequitiae: 3.II.6   nequitiae testem sed geris inde sonum."

latratus, -ūs — barking   **guttur, -ris** — throat, neck   **singuli, -ae, -a** — several,
patulus, -a, -um — open   **nola, -ae** — bell   individual
rictus, -ūs — jaw   **faux, faucis** — throat   **dementia, -ae** — madness
submitto, -ere — lower   **innecto, -ere** — join, attach   **ostento, -are** — show off,
concitus, -a, -um — excited **crepito, -are** — ring, tinkle   display
dens, -ntis — tooth   **subligo, -are** — tie under   **nequitia, -ae** — wickedness
probitas, -tatis — forthrightness **praemium, -i** — prize, badge **testis, -is** — testimony,
simulatus, -a, -um —   **insulto, -are** — be abusive   witness
    pretended

READING FOR UNDERSTANDING

1. *Did the dog's owner in this fable act responsibly? Why do you think that?*
2. *If you saw a dog with a bell around its neck, would you expect it to be ornery and snappish?*
3. *Have you ever known people who wear their faults, shortcomings, or scars proudly? Are these people oblivious to their disgrace, as the second dog of the fable suggests, or merely trying to cope with their vulnerabilities?*

19.

"Once an Ass, Always an Ass": The Donkey and the Farmer

READING FOR INFORMATION

1. *What effect did the lion skin have on the donkey?*
2. *How did the livestock react to the donkey?*
3. *How did the farmer react to the donkey?*

Exuvias asinus Gaetuli iam forte leonis
spoliis: 3.V.1   repperit et spoliis induit ora novis.
ora: 3.IV.1
membris: 3.III.3   Aptavitque suis incongrua tegmina membris,
honore: 3.V.1   et miserum tanto pressit honore caput.
ubi: 16.XIII.2.a   Ast ubi terribilis mimo circumstetit horror,   5
mimo: 3.III.7   pigraque praesumptus vēnit in ossa vigor,
feris: 3.III.2   mitibus ille feris communia pabula calcans
                        turbabat pavidas per sua rura boves.
postquam: Rusticus hunc magnā postquam deprendit ab aure,
  16.XIII.2.a
vinclis   correptum vinclis verberibusque domat;   10
  verberibusque:
  3.V.1
tergo: 3.V.19   et simul abstracto denudans corpora tergo,

vocibus: 3.V.1	increpat his miserum vocibus ille pecus:
murmure: 3.V.1 **fallas:** 15.II **mihi:** 3.III.8	"Forsitan ignotos imitato murmure fallas, at mihi, qui quondam, semper asellus eris."

exuviae, -arum — pelt, hide

Gaetulus, -a, -um — North African

spolium, -i — booty, plunder

induo, -ere — don, put on

apto, -are — make fit

incongruus, -a, -um — ill suited

tegmen, -inis — cover, covering

terribilis, -e — frightful

mimus, -i — farce, mimicry

circumsto, -are — surround

horror, -ris — horror

praesumo, -ere — assume

vigor, -ris — vigor

mitis, -e — mild

communis, -e — common

pabulum, -i — pasture

calco, -are — trample

turbo, -are — throw into panic

rusticus, -i — farmer

deprendo, -ere — seize

domo, -are — beat

abstraho, -ere — drag off

increpo, -are — rebuke

forsitan — perhaps

mumur, -ris — roar

fallo, -ere — trick, dupe

READING FOR UNDERSTANDING

1. *Vanity is bad enough; false vanity is even worse! But was the farmer justified in beating the donkey?*

2. *When we wear a costume for a Halloween party and get into character, is that a form of vanity?*

3. *Imagine trading places with a president or a prime minister but without getting their knowledge, experience, or sensibility. How long would the fantasy be fun or good for: Ten minutes? An hour? A day? A week?*

Supplemental Readings

1.

"What Have You Done for Me Lately?": The Weasel and the Man

READING FOR INFORMATION

1. *According to the weasel, why should the man spare his life?*

2. *According to the man, the weasel was in competition with what animal for food?*

3. *In the end, what does the man do to the weasel?*

cum: type? **mihi:** use of dative? **tibi:** use of dative? **muribus:** use of ablative?	Mustela ab homine prensa, cum instantem necem effugere vellet, "Parce, quaeso," inquit, "mihi, quae tibi molestis muribus purgo domum."
si: type of condition? **fruaris:** use of subjunctive? **reliquiis:** use of ablative?	Respondit ille, "Faceres si causā meā, gratum esset et dedissem veniam supplici. Nunc quia laboras ut fruaris reliquiis,

5

rosuri: what form?
devores: use of subjunctive?
imputare: use of infinitive?

quas sunt rosuri, simul et ipsos devores,
noli imputare vanum beneficium mihi."
Atque ita locutus improbam leto dedit.
Hoc in se dictum debent illi agnoscere,   10

sibi: use of dative?

quorum privata servit utilitas sibi,

imprudentibus: use of dative?

et meritum inane iactant imprudentibus.

7. **simul . . . devores**: and at the same time you eat [the mice] them[selves]

mustela, -ae — weasel   **insto, -are** — press   **devoro, -are** — gobble up

prehendo, -ere — capture   **rodo, -ere** — gnaw on   **agnosco, -ere** — recognize

READING FOR UNDERSTANDING

1. *Probably the hardest part of translating this fable is picking just the right English word(s) for* **imprudentibus** *in the last line. What can you come up with?*

2. *Is it true, do you think, that we owe no gratitude to a person who benefits us out of self-interest? Could you argue that everyone operates out of self-interest and therefore we owe nobody any gratitude?*

3. *Even if the man's assertions about the weasel were all true, was he justified in treating the creature as he did?*

2.

"Wealth Wasted in Worry": The Dog and the Vulture

READING FOR INFORMATION

1. *According to the author, who should take to heart the message of this fable?*

2. *Whom did the dog offend by digging up the treasure?*

3. *How did the dog perish?*

Haec res avaris esse conveniens potest,
et qui, humiles nati, dici locupletes student.
Humana effodiens ossa thesaurum canis
invēnit, et, violarat quia Manes deos,
iniecta est illi divitiarum cupiditas,   5
poenas ut sanctae religioni pendēret.
Itaque, aurum dum custodit oblitus cibi,
fame est consumptus. Quem stans vulturius super
fertur locutus, "O canis, meritō iaces,
qui concupisti subitō regales opes,   10
trivio conceptus, educatus stercore."

effodio, -ere — dig up   **trivium, -i** — crossroad   **stercus, -coris** — dung
vulturius, -i — vulture

READING FOR UNDERSTANDING
1. *Why is it appropriate that a vulture utter the final verdict over the dog?*
2. *Should the dog have followed a different course of action regarding the treasure? Would his fate have been any different?*
3. *What are your thoughts on the nouveaux riches? Are they entitled to their wealth? Should they behave differently with it from those who were born to wealth?*

3.

"Sour Grapes": The Vixen in the Vineyard

READING FOR INFORMATION
1. *Why does the fox want to eat the grapes?*
2. *What is supposedly wrong with the grapes?*

> Fame coacta vulpes altā in vineā
> uvam appetebat, summis saliens viribus.
> Quam tangere ut non potuit, discedens ait:
> "Nondum matura es; nolo acerbam sumere."
> Qui, facere quae non possunt, verbis elevant,   5
> adscribere hoc debebunt exemplum sibi.

vinea, -ae — vineyard   **acerbus, -a, -um** — sour   **elevo, -are** — minimize

READING FOR UNDERSTANDING
1. *What is the effect of having the vixen address the grapes in the 2nd person?*
2. *Did she give up the effort to reach the grapes too soon?*
3. *Would this fable have a different impact if a different animal—say, a possum—had been cast in the vixen's role?*

4.

"Brain Power Does It!": The Crow

READING FOR INFORMATION
1. *Why couldn't the crow get to the water?*
2. *What was its first strategy to reach the water?*
3. *What strategy finally worked?*

Ingentem sitiens cornix aspexerat urnam,
    quae minimam fundo continuisset aquam.
Hanc enisa diū planis effundere campis,
    scilicet ut nimiam pelleret inde sitim,
postquam nulla viam virtus dedit, admovet omnes   5
    indignata novā calliditate dolos.
Nam brevis immersis accrescens sponte lapillis
    pōtandi facilem praebuit unda viam.
Viribus haec docuit quam sit prudentia maior,
    qua coeptum cornix explicuisset opus.   10

adspicio, -ere — catch sight of	**enitor, -i** — struggle	**accresco, -ere** — increase
urna, -ae — pitcher	**scilicet** — obviously	**lapillus, -i** — pebble
fundus, -i — bottom	**indignatus, -a, -um** — indignant	

READING FOR UNDERSTANDING

1. *This fable celebrates the principle that sometimes the best solution is the simplest solution. Can you name other elegant solutions that illustrate this principle?*
2. *The Romans tended to be far more impressed than we are with the intelligence of crows and ravens (see section A, prose reading 2). Can you suggest a different animal, one we admire more, for this fable?*
3. *Can you provide a two-line moral for this fable? Can you put it in Latin?*

5.

"Dancing Your Life Away": The Ant and the Grasshopper

READING FOR INFORMATION

1. *In what different ways did the ant and the grasshopper spend their summers?*
2. *How did the ant spend the winter?*
3. *What attitude did the grasshopper assume when it approached the ant?*

solibus: use of ablative?
hiemi: use of dative?
cavis: use of ablative?

Solibus ereptos hiemi formica labores
    distulit, et brevibus condidit ante cavis.
Verum ubi candentes suscepit terra pruinas
    arvaque sub rigido delituēre gelū,

corpore: use of ablative?

pigra nimis tantos non aequans corpore nimbos,   5
    in laribus propriis humida grana lēgit.

precibus: use of ablative?
sono: use of ablative?
cum: type?

Discolor hanc precibus supplex alimenta rogabat,
    quae quondam querulo ruperat arva sono:
se quoque, maturas cum tunderet area messes,

cantibus aestivos explicuisse dies.   10

Parvula tunc ridens sīc est adfata cicadam;

    nam vitam pariter continuare solent:

"Mi quoniam summo substantia parta labore est,

    frigoribus mediis otia longa traho.

At tibi saltandi nunc ultima tempora restant,   15

    cantibus est quoniam vita peracta prior."

cantibus: use of
  ablative?
mi: alternate form
  of?
labore: use of
  ablative?
frigoribus: use of
  ablative?
tibi: use of dative?
saltandi: gerund or
  gerundive?
cantibus: use of
  ablative?

formica, -ae — ant

cavum, -i — hole, nest

candens, -ntis — glistening

pruina, -ae — frost

rigidus, -a, -um — stiff

gelu, -ūs — chill

humidus, -a, -um — damp

querulus, -a, -um —
    complaining

tundo, -ere — beat

cicada, -ae — grasshopper

continuo, -are — finish

substantia, -ae — livelihood

parta . . . est < **pario**

salto, -are — dance

READING FOR UNDERSTANDING

1. *Which do you defend, the grasshopper's request or the ant's response?*

2. *Explain the ant's logic that rest was its reward for labor but dancing was the grasshopper's reward for singing.*

3. *Line 12 points out that ants and grasshoppers are usually equally short lived. How does that detail affect your understanding of this fable?*

D. Preeminence

Prose Readings

1.

These two incidents from the career of Julius Caesar, the first dated to 57 BCE and the second to 47 or 46 BCE, illustrate the commander's great bravery and leadership on the battlefield.

READING FOR INFORMATION

1. *What was Caesar's intention in seizing a shield from one soldier and fighting amid others?*
2. *How did he react to the fleeing standard bearer?*
3. *Where do we get evidence from this passage that Caesar was not just a rearguard general?*

cum: 16.I.3.a
multitudine, impetū: 3.V.7
aciem: 3.IV.4
timidius: 6.II
pugnanti militi: 3.III.3
eo: 3.V.1
quo: 7.V.2
facto: 3.V.7
ardore: 3.V.7
ineundae: 17.III
gratiā: 8.I
faucibus: 3.V.1
manibus, adhortatione: 3.V.1
vinci: 12.I.3.b

Divus Iulius, cum innumerabili multitudine et feroci impetū Nerviorum inclinari aciem suam vidēret, timidius pugnanti militi scutum detraxit, eoque tectus acerrimē proeliari coepit. Quo facto fortitudinem per totum exercitum diffudit, lābentemque belli fortunam divino animi ardore restituit. Īdem alio proelio legionis Martiae aquiliferum, ineundae fugae gratiā iam conversum faucibus comprehensum, in contrariam partem retraxit, dexteramque ad hostem tendens, "Quorsum tu," inquit, "abis? Illīc sunt cum quibus dimicamus." Et manibus quidem unum militem, adhortatione verō tam acri omnium legionum trepidationem correxit, vincique paratas vincere docuit.

innumerabilis, -e — countless
multitudo, -dinis — multitude
ferox, -ocis — fierce
Nervi, -orum — Belgic Gauls
inclino, -are — repulse
acies, -ei — battle line
scutum, -i — shield
detraho, -ere — pull from
tectus < tego

proelior, -ari — do battle
fortitudo, -dinis — bravery
diffundo, -ere — inspire
restituo, -ere — restore
Martius, -a, -um — Martial, of Mars
aquilifer, -i — standard bearer
ineo, inire — pursue
fauces, -ium — throat

comprehendo, -ere — seize
retraho, -ere — drag back
quorsum — where to
dimico, -are — fight
adhortatio, -nis — encouragement
trepidatio, -nis — fear
corrigo, -ere — reverse

READING FOR UNDERSTANDING

1. *What are the greatest challenges for field generals of armies who enter every battle expecting to win?*
2. *Caesar seems to exhibit more anger with the standard bearer than with the soldier in the first incident. Is this greater anger justified?*
3. *Teaching troops prepared to be prevailed over to prevail (**vinci paratas vincere docēre**) seems like a line from a job description in a Monster.com listing for a general. What other desirable traits would that job listing advertise, were it written by ancient Romans?*

2.

The Romans devoted remarkably little attention to the notion of creative greatness. Vergil, Rome's greatest poet and the author of the Aeneid, *is the subject of this passage, which provides some information about the production and performance of the epic.*

READING FOR INFORMATION

1. *What two rhetorical means did Augustus Caesar employ to get a preview of the* Aeneid?
2. *What books did Augustus hear recited?*
3. *How did Augustus's sister, Octavia, react when she heard her son eulogized?*

Augustus verō—nam forte expeditione Cantabricā aberat—supplicibus atque etiam minacibus per iocum litteris efflagitarat, ut "sibi de *Aeneide*," ut ipsius verba sunt, "vel primum carminis exemplum vel quodlibet excerptum mitteretur." Cui tamen multō post perfectāque demum materiā tres omnīnō libros recitavit, secundum, quartum, et sextum; sed hunc notabili Octaviae adfectione, quae cum recitationi interesset, ad illos de filio suo versūs, "tu Marcellus eris," defecisse fertur atque aegrē focilata est. Recitavit et pluribus, sed neque frequenter et ea ferē de quibus ambigebat, quo magis iudicium hominum experiretur.

efflagitarat: 20.I.3
ut: 16.III.1
ut: 16.XIII.2.d
cui: 7.V.2
multō: 3.V.9
perfectā . . .
   materiā: 13.III.1
cum: 16.I.1

quo magis:
   16.III.2.c

expeditio, -nis — expedition
Cantabricus, -a, -um — of Cantabria (a region in Spain)
minax, -acis — menacing
efflagito, -are — insist

excerptum, -i — excerpt
materia, -ae — material
omnīnō — entirely
recito, -are — recite
notabilis, -e — well known
adfectio, -nis — emotion

recitatio, -nis — recitation
focilo, -are — revive
frequenter — frequently
ferē — usually
ambigo, -ere — hesitate
experior, -iri — test

READING FOR UNDERSTANDING

1. *What was Vergil's motive in giving recitations? What was he actually testing?*
2. *If you could have a private audience with your favorite musician, which would you prefer to hear, a polished composition or a work in progress?*
3. *Augustus and Octavia had a lot riding on the publication of the* Aeneid, *both personally and politically. Vergil was a notoriously slow and fastidious composer. What tension do you imagine existed between this reclusive writer and his rulers?*

3.

The struggles of Gaius Marius, a famous **novus homo** *(political newcomer) of the late 2nd century and early 1st century BCE, to achieve political prominence are described here.*

READING FOR INFORMATION

1. *What place did Marius come in when he ran for the praetorship?*

2. Was he well regarded in his hometown of Arpinum?

3. Against whom were his three most famous military victories?

Fortunae: 3.III.3	Iam est C. Marius, maxima Fortunae luctatio: omnes enim eius impetūs
honoribus: 3.III.2	quā corporis quā animi robore fortissimē sustinuit. Arpinatibus honoribus
Romae: 4.I.3	iudicatus inferior, quaesturam Romae petere ausus est. Patientiā deinde

repulsarum irrupit magis in curiam quam vēnit. In tribunatūs quoque et aedilitatis petitione consimilem campi notam expertus, praeturae candidatus supremo in loco adhaesit, quem tamen non sine periculo

ambitūs: 3.II.6	obtinuit: ambitūs enim accusatus, vix atque aegrē absolutionem ab
Arpini: 4.I.3	iudicibus impetravit. Ex illo Mario, tam humili Arpini, tam ignobili
Romae: 4.I.3 **fastidiendo:** 17.III	Romae, tam fastidiendo candidato, ille Marius evasit, qui Africam subegit;

qui Iugurtham regem ante currum egit; qui Teutonorum Cimbrorumque exercitūs delevit; cuius bina tropaea in urbe spectantur; cuius septem in

cui, proscripto: 20.III.7.b **contigit:** 20.III.7 **condicione:** 3.V.8 **inconstantius,** **mutabilius:** 6.II **quem:** 7.V.2 **si:** 18.I.2.a.i	fastis consulatūs leguntur; cui post exsilium consulem creari proscriptoque facere proscriptionem contigit. Quid huius condicione inconstantius aut mutabilius? Quem si inter miseros posueris, miserrimus, si inter felices, felicissimus reperietur.

5. **consimilem . . . expertus**: having experienced a similar disgrace of the poll booth

luctatio, -nis — contest, wrestling

robur, -oris — strength

Arpinas, -tis — of Arpinum

iudico, -are — judge

quaestura, -ae — quaestorship

repulsa, -ae — rejection, loss

irrumpo, -ere — burst onto

curia, -ae — senate house

tribunatus, -ūs — tribunate

aedilitas, -tatis — aedileship

petitio, -nis — pursuit

consimilis, -e — similar

experior, -iri — experience

praetura, -ae — praetorship

supremus, -a, -um — last

adhaereo, -ēre — cling to

obtineo, -ēre — achieve

ambitus, -ūs — vote buying

absolutio, -nis — acquittal

humilis, -e — lowly

ignobilis, -e — undistinguished

fastidio, -ire — scorn, disdain

evado, -ere — emerge

subigo, -ere — subjugate

Iugurtha, -ae — rebel king of North Africa

Teutoni, -orum — Germanic tribe

Cimbri, -orum — Germanic tribe

deleo, -ēre — destroy

bini, -ae, -a — both

tropaeum, -i — victory commemorative

fasti, -orum — state records

consulatus, -ūs — consulship

exsilium, -i — exile

inconstans, -ntis — unstable

mutabilis, -e — changeable

READING FOR UNDERSTANDING

*1. What does the author mean by saying that Marius was Fortuna's greatest wrestling match (**maxima Fortunae luctatio**)?*

2. On the whole, does the author seem to approve of the career of Marius?

3. What qualities of Marius does the narrative commend? What allowed or caused him to achieve preeminence?

4.

This fascinating little tale tells how the great Scipio Africanus entertained some rather disreputable (and starstruck) visitors at his country villa after he had retired from public life (early 2nd century BCE).

READING FOR INFORMATION

1. Scipio thought that the pirates appeared in order to do what?
2. What did the pirates do after they were granted an audience with Scipio?
3. In what ways did the pirates regard Scipio Africanus as a living god?

videndum: 17.V.1
quos: 7.V.2
cum: 16.I.1
faciendam: 17.V.1
existimasset: 20.I.3
repellendis: 17.III
animo et apparatū: 3.III.10
quod: 7.V.2
ut: 16.XIII.2.a
dimissis . . . armis: 13.III.1
ianuae: 3.III.7
voce: 3.V.1
novis: 3.III.1
ne: 16.III.1
fores: 3.IV.4
eos: 3.IV.4
qui: 7.V.2

positis . . . donis: 13.III.1
quod: 16.XIII.3.b.i
contigisset: 20.III.7.b
fructū: 3.V.8
hostis: 3.II.1

admiratione: 3.V.1
sui: 7.III
spectaculo: 3.V.1
si: 18.I.2.b
venerationis: 3.II.2

Ad Africanum in Literninā villā se continentem complures praedonum duces videndum eodem tempore forte confluxerunt. Quos cum ad vim faciendam venire existimasset, praesidium domesticorum in tecto collocavit, eratque in his repellendis et animo et apparatū occupatus. Quod ut praedones animadverterunt, dimissis militibus abiectisque armis, ianuae appropinquant, et clarā voce nuntiant Scipioni non vitae eius hostes, sed virtutis admiratores vēnisse, conspectum et congressum tanti viri quasi caeleste aliquod beneficium expetentes: proinde securum se novis spectandum praebere ne gravetur. Haec postquam domestici Scipioni retulerunt, fores reserari eosque intromitti iussit. Qui, postes ianuae tamquam aliquam religiosissimam aram sanctumque templum venerati, cupidē Scipionis dexteram apprehenderunt ac diu osculati, positis ante vestibulum donis, quae deorum immortalium numini consecrari solent, laeti, quod Scipionem vīdisse contigisset, ad naves reverterunt. Quid hōc fructū maiestatis excelsius, quid etiam iucundius? Hostis iram admiratione sui placavit, spectaculo praesentiae suae latronum gestientes oculos vīdit. Delapsa caelo sidera, hominibus si se offerant, venerationis amplius non recipiant.

Literninus, -a, -um — of Campanian Liternum
complures, -ium — several
praedo, -nis — pirate
confluo, -ere — come together
praesidium, -i — guard
domesticus, -i — household slave
colloco, -are — station
repello, -ere — drive off
apparatus, -ūs — preparation
abicio, -ere — drop

appropinquo, -are — approach
admirator, -ris — admirer
congressus, -ūs — meeting
caelestis, -e — divine
expeto, -ere — seek out
proinde — then
gravo, -are — trouble
foris, -is — door
resero, -are — unbolt
intromitto, -ere — let in
religiosus, -a, -um — hallowed
apprehendo, -ere — seize

osculor, -ari — kiss
vestibulum, -i — vestibule
consecro, -are — consecrate
fructus, -ūs — enjoyment
excelsus, -a, -um — lofty
iucundus, -a, -um — delightful
admiratio, -nis — admiration
placo, -are — soothe
spectaculum, -i — sight
praesentia, -ae — presence
gestio, -ire — be eager
delābor, -i — fall from
veneratio, -nis — veneration

READING FOR UNDERSTANDING

1. *After Julius Caesar and Augustus Caesar, the concept of a living god was considerably less alien to Romans. Do you see any resistance to the concept in this passage?*
2. *Is the adulation that the pirates show Scipio a mark of ignorance or lack of education? Can intelligent and sophisticated people be starstruck as these pirates were?*
3. *How would you describe Scipio's response to his fans? Did he react responsibly and admirably?*

5.

Q. Caecilius Metellus Macedonicus (2nd century BCE) is represented here as having received the constant and complete support of Fortuna throughout his long life.

READING FOR INFORMATION

1. *What are some of the advantages that Fortuna conferred on Metellus?*
2. *What were some of the accomplishments of his children?*
3. *What kind of death did Metellus meet?*

videamus: 15.I
gradibus: 3.V.3
indulgentiā: 3.V.14

perduxerit: 16.V
eum: 3.IV.4

ut: 16.III.1
pudicitiā et fecunditate: 3.V.10
ut: 16.III.1

nuptum: 17.I

sinū: 3.V.1

cum: 16.I.2

contemplare: 19.I

spatio: 3.V.13
genere: 3.V.3
rogo: 3.III.7

Videamus quot gradibus beneficiorum Fortuna Q. Metellum a primo originis die ad ultimum usque fati tempus numquam cessante indulgentiā ad summum beatae vitae cumulum perduxerit. Nasci eum in urbe terrarum principe voluit; parentes ei nobilissimos dedit; adiecit animi rarissimas dotes et corporis vires, ut sufficere laboribus posset; uxorem pudicitiā et fecunditate conspicuam conciliavit; consulatūs decus, imperatoriam potestatem, speciosissimi triumphi praetextum largita est; fecit ut eodem tempore tres filios consulares, unum etiam censorium et triumphalem, quartum praetorium vidēret, utque tres filias nuptum daret earumque subolem sinū suo exciperet. Tot partūs, tot incunabula, tot viriles togae, tam multae nuptiales faces, honorum, imperiorum, omnis denique gratulationis summa abundantia, cum interim esset nullum funus, nullus gemitus, nulla causa tristitiae. Caelum contemplare, vix tamen ibi talem statum reperies, quoniam quidem luctūs et dolores deorum quoque pectoribus a maximis vatibus adsignari videmus. Hunc actum consentaneus vitae eius finis excepit: namque Metellum, ultimae senectutis spatio defunctum lenique genere mortis inter oscula complexūsque carissimorum pignorum exstinctum, filii et generi umeris suis per urbem latum rogo imposuerunt.

origo, -inis — birth
cesso, -are — cease
cumulus, -i — addition
perduco, -ere — attend
sufficio, -ere — be sufficient

fecunditas, -tatis — fertility
conspicuus, -a, -um — conspicuous
concilio, -are — win over

imperatorius, -a, -um — of a commander
speciosus, -a, -um — spectacular
praetextus, -ūs — robe

largior, -iri — bestow

consularis, -is — ex-consul

censorius, -i — ex-censor

triumphalis, -is —
  ex-triumphator

praetorius, -i — ex-praetor

suboles, -is — offspring

incunabulum, -i — cradle

nuptialis, -e — wedding-

gratulatio, -nis — rejoicing

abundantia, -ae — abundance

interim — all the while

gemitus, -ūs — groaning,
  hardship

contemplor, -ari — ponder

status, -ūs — status

luctus, -ūs — grief

vates, -is — poet

adsigno, -are — attribute

consentaneus, -a, -um —
  fitting

spatium, -i — span

defungor, -i — complete

lenis, -e — gentle

complexus, -ūs — embrace

latum < fero

READING FOR UNDERSTANDING

1. According to the values of this author, what things contribute to a happy, fortunate life?

2. In your opinion, are there any constituent parts of a happy, fortunate life that the author has omitted?

3. By Roman standards, does Metellus seem to rise to the status of true greatness?

6.

This anecdote relates the misfortunes that befell the famous L. Aemilius Paullus (consul in 168 BCE) and how he regarded his loss as, in some sense, Rome's gain.

READING FOR INFORMATION

1. What happened to the first two of Paullus's four sons?

2. Within the span of a week, what three events occurred in the life of Paullus?

3. What prayer to the gods had Paullus made on behalf of the Roman people?

formae, indolis:
  3.II.3
sibi: 3.III.1

ei: 3.III.3

donandos: 17.III
quem: 7.V.2
sustinuerit: 16.V
adiciendo: 17.II
ambiguum: 3.IV.1
nulli: 3.III.2
cum: 16.I.1
ne: 16.VI
quid: 7.VI.1.a
mali: 3.II.2
ut: 16.IV
quid: 7.VI.1.a
adversi: 3.II.2
immineret: 18.III
adnuendo: 17.II
ut: 16.III.1
casū: 3.V.7

Aemilius Paulus, nunc felicissimi, nunc miserrimi patris clarissima repraesentatio, ex quattuor filiis formae insignis, egregiae indolis duos iure adoptionis in Corneliam Fabiamque gentem translatos sibi ipse denegavit; duos alteros ei Fortuna abstulit. Quorum alter triumphum patris funere suo quartum ante diem praecessit, alter in triumphali currū conspectus post diem tertium exspiravit. Itaque qui ad donandos usque liberos abundaverat, in orbitate subitō destitutus est. Quem casum quo robore animi sustinuerit, orationi adiciendo hanc clausulam ambiguum nulli reliquit: "Cum in maximo proventū felicitatis nostrae, Quirites, timērem ne quid mali Fortuna moliretur, Iovem Optimum Maximum Iunonemque Reginam et Minervam precatus sum ut, si quid adversi populo Romano imminēret, totum in meam domum converteretur. Quapropter bene habet: adnuendo enim votis meis id egerunt, ut vos potius meo casū doleatis quam ego vestro ingemiscerem."

8–9. **ambiguum . . . reliquit**: he left ambiguous to no one

repraesentatio, -nis —
    exemplar

indoles, -is — talent

adoptio, -nis — adoption

denego, -are — deny

praecedo, -ere — precede

exspiro, -are — die

orbitas, -tatis — childlessness

destituo, -ere — abandon

robur, -oris — strength

clausula, -ae — conclusion

ambiguus, -a, -um —
    ambiguous

proventus, -ūs — success

Quirites, -ium — Roman
    citizens

molior, -iri — contrive

quapropter — for this reason

adnuo, -ere — agree to

ingemisco, -ere — bewail

READING FOR UNDERSTANDING

1. *In a culture that prized sons highly, why did Paullus give up two of his sons for adoption?*

2. *In the Roman worldview, preeminence usually exacts a steep price in personal sacrifice. In our worldview, do we commonly think the same thing?*

3. *The notion that Fortuna contrives something evil whenever a state or a person has experienced considerable success posits a pessimistic, even hostile universe. Do we regard Lady Luck in a similar light?*

7.

In 390 BCE, Gauls unexpectedly stormed and ravaged Rome. This story narrates the behavior of those Romans too old to contribute to the military defense of the city.

READING FOR INFORMATION

1. *Why were older Roman men excluded from the Capitoline and the Arx?*

2. *After their exclusion, how did the older men behave? What did they do?*

3. *What did Marcus Atilius do when a Gaul stroked his beard?*

exercitū: 3.V.7
cum: 16.I.3.a

relinquendorum:
    17.III
quō: 15.III.2.c

virtutis: 3.II.6

honoribus: 3.V.13
ianuis: 3.V.14

ut: 16.III.1

sustinendos: 17.V.1

novitate: 3.V.7
magnificentiā: 3.V.7
genere: 3.V.7
hostibus . . .
    commotis: 3.III.2
dubitaret: 15.II.2
quin: 16.VII
conversuri essent:
    17.VI
Gallo: 3.III.3
ictū: 3.V.1
capiti: 3.III.7

Magnum fortitudinis exemplum antiquitas offert. Romani Gallorum exercitū pulsi, cum se in Capitolium et in arcem conferrent, inque his collibus morari omnes non possent, necessarium consilium in planā parte urbis relinquendorum seniorum ceperunt, quō facilius iuventus reliquias imperii tuēretur. Ceterum ne illo quidem tam misero tamque luctuoso tempore civitas nostra virtutis suae oblita est: defuncti enim honoribus apertis ianuis in curulibus sellis cum insignibus magistratuum, quos gesserant, sacerdotiorumque, quae adepti erant, consederunt, ut et ipsi in occasū suo splendorem et ornamenta praeteritae vitae retinērent et plebi ad fortius sustinendos casūs suos exemplum praebērent. Venerabilis eorum aspectus primō hostibus fuit et novitate rei et magnificentiā cultūs et ipso audaciae genere commotis. Sed quis dubitaret quin et Galli et victores illam admirationem mox in risum et in omne contumeliae genus conversuri essent? Non exspectavit igitur hanc iniuriae maturitatem M. Atilius: verum barbam suam permulcenti Gallo scipionem vehementi ictū capiti inflixit, eique propter dolorem ad se

occidendum: 17.V.1
capi: 12.I
dedecus: 3.IV.1
fortunae: 3.III.7
fato: 3.V.8

occidendum ruenti cupidius corpus obtulit. Capi ergō virtus nescit, patientiae dedecus ignorat, fortunae succumbere omni fato tristius ducit, nova et speciosa genera interitūs excogitat—si quisquam interit, qui sīc exstinguitur!

18. **fortunae ... ducit**: it considers succumbing to a fortune sadder than any fate

fortitudo, -dinis — courage
antiquitas, -tatis — antiquity
arx, arcis — citadel
moror, -ari — stay
planus, -a, -um — level
tueor, -ēri — keep watch over
luctuosus, -a, -um — mournful
oblita est < **obliviscor**
defungor, -i — perform
apertus, -a, -um — open
curulis sella — chair of civic
office
insignia, -ium — insignia

magistratus, -ūs — magistracy
adepti sunt < **adipiscor**
consedeo, -ēre — be seated
occasus, -ūs — decline, death
splendor, -ris — splendor
praetereo, -ire — pass
venerabilis, -e — venerable
aspectus, -ūs — appearance
novitas, -tatis — novelty
magnificentia, -ae — grandeur
commotus, -a, -um — struck
admiratio, -nis — admiration
contumelia, -ae — insult

maturitas, -tatis — moment
permulceo, -ēre — stroke
scipio, -nis — dagger
vehemens — violent
infligo, -ere — strike
dedecus, -oris — disgrace
ignoro, -are — disregard
succumbo, -ere — succumb
speciosus, -a, -um —
spectacular
interitus, -ūs — death
excogito, -are — ponder
intereo, -ire — die

READING FOR UNDERSTANDING

1. *Why did the elder men don their former insignia and symbols of authority?*
2. *In many cultures (e.g., ancient Greece), stroking an old man's beard is a gesture of respect and self-subordination. Why does the author regard this gesture as one of mockery and contempt?*
3. *What was the usual fate of elderly prisoners of war in the ancient world?*

8.

In this story, which almost has a fairy-tale feel, a master proscribed by the Second Triumvirate is rescued by his slave, who sacrifices his own life.

READING FOR INFORMATION

1. *In what ways did the slave impersonate his master?*
2. *What events does the author imagine without narrating?*
3. *How did the master memorialize his loyal slave?*

fidei: 3.II.3
cum: 16.I.1
cognosset: 20.I.3
indicio: 3.V.7
occidendum: 17.V.1
commutatā veste,
permutato anulo:
13.III.1

Urbini Panapionis servus, quam admirabilis fidei! Cum cognosset milites indicio domesticorum certiores factos vēnisse in Reatinam villam ad dominum proscriptum occidendum, commutatā cum eo veste, permutato etiam anulo, illum postico clam emisit, se autem in cubiculum ac lectulum

recepit et ut Panapionem occīdī passus est. Brevis huius factī narratiō,
sed nōn parva māteria laudātiōnis: nam sī quis ante oculōs pōnere velit
subitum mīlitum accursum, convulsa iānuae claustra, minācem vōcem,
trucēs vultūs, fulgentia arma, rem vērā aestimātiōne prōsequētur; nec
tamen quam citō dīcitur aliquem prō aliō morī voluisse, tam facilier
etiam id fierī potuisse arbitrābitur. Panapiō autem quantum servō dēbēret
amplum eī faciendō monumentum ac testimōnium pietātis grātō titulō
reddendō cōnfessus est.

si: 18.I.4
quis: 7.VI.1.a

aestimatione: 3.V.3

deberet: 16.V
faciendo: 17.II
testimonium:
    3.IV.1.a
titulo: 3.V.1
reddendo: 17.II

8–10. **nec . . . arbitrabitur**: nor, however, does a person imagine, as quickly as it is said
that someone was willing to die for another, that it could even happen so easily

indicium, -i — evidence	**passus est < patior**	**aestimatio, -nis** — surmise
Reatinus, -a, -um — of Sabine	**narratio, -nis** — description	**arbitror, -ari** — think, judge
Reate	**materia, -ae** — material	**monumentum, -i** — memorial
commuto, -are — change	**laudatio, -nis** — praise	**testimonium, -i** — record
permuto, -are — exchange	**accursus, -ūs** — assault	**titulus, -i** — inscription
anulus, -i — ring	**claustrum, -i** — bolt	**confiteor, -ēri** —
posticum, -i — back door	**minax, -acis** — menacing	acknowledge
clam — secretly	**trux, -cis** — murderous	

READING FOR UNDERSTANDING

1. *Why, if Panapio memorialized him, is the slave's name not recorded here?*
2. *Why do you suppose the author only imagines the events of the slave's last moments rather than narrating them?*
3. *Of all the traits that constitute preeminence, which ones would Romans credit extraordinary slaves with and memorialize in monument and narrative?*

9.

With this passage, the author recalls an idealized past when young men paid the proper honor and respect due to their elders. The view expressed here was a commonplace: Rome's devotion to the cultural value of **mos maiorum** *contributed greatly to the nation's successes.*

READING FOR INFORMATION

1. *What did youths used to do on days when the senate was in session?*
2. *What practice did youths follow at dinner parties?*
3. *What makes the old Roman ways of acculturating the young better than other ways?*

Senectūtī iuventa ita cumulātum et circumspectum honōrem reddēbat,
tamquam maiōrēs nātū adulescentium commūnēs patrēs essent.
Quōcircā iuvenēs senātūs diē utique aliquem ex patribus cōnscrīptīs aut
propinquum aut paternum amīcum ad cūriam dēdūcēbant, adfīxīque

tamquam:
    16.XIII.1.b
natū: 3.V.10
die: 4.II.1

valvis: 3.V.7
donec: 16.XIII.3.a.i
reducendi: 17.II
officio: 3.V.13
statione: 3.V.7
sustinenda: 17.V.1
processurarum: 12.II
meditatione: 3.V.7
quinam: 7.VI.1
convivio: 3.III.7
essent interfuturi:
   17.VI; 16.V
ne: 16.III.1
discubitū: 3.V.10
sublatā mensā:
   13.III.1
cenae: 3.II.6.a
quam: 6.III
sermone: 3.V.13
his praesentibus:
   3.V.14
carmine: 3.V.1
quō: 16.III.2.c
imitanda: 17.V.1
certamine: 3.V.8
canis: 3.III.1
cursū: 3.V.13
nutrimentis: 3.V.1
disciplinae: 3.III.7
praetulerim:
   15.III.1.a
ne: 16.III.1
percurrendo: 17.II
pars: 3.VIII

valvis exspectabant, donec reducendi etiam officio fungerentur. Qua quidem voluntariā statione et corpora et animos ad publica officia impigrē sustinenda roborabant, brevique processurarum in lucem virtutum suarum verecundā laboris meditatione ipsi doctores erant. Invitati ad cenam diligenter quaerebant quinam ei convivio essent interfuturi, ne senioris adventum discubitū praecurrerent, sublatāque mensā priores consurgere et abire patiebantur. Ex quibus apparet cenae quoque tempore quam parco et quam modesto sermone his praesentibus soliti sint uti. Maiores natū in conviviis ad tibias egregia superiorum opera carmine comprehensa peragebant, quō ad ea imitanda iuventutem alacriorem redderent. Quid hōc splendidius, quid etiam utilius certamine? Pubertas canis suum decus reddebat, defuncta virili cursū aetas ingredientes actuosam vitam favoris nutrimentis prosequebatur. Quas Athenas, quam scholam, quae alienigena studia huic domesticae disciplinae praetulerim? Inde oriebantur Camilli, Scipiones, Fabricii, Marcelli, Fabii, ac ne singula imperii nostri lumina simul percurrendo sim longior, inde, inquam, caeli clarissima pars, divi fulserunt Caesares.

cumulatus, -a, -um — abundant

circumspectus, -a, -um — respectful

natus, -ūs — birth

communis, -e — joint

quocircā — and therefore

utique — especially

patres conscripti — senators

propinquus, -a, -um — related

curia, -ae — senate house

deduco, -ere — escort

adfigo, -ere — attach

valva, -ae — door

reduco, -ere — escort back

fungor, -i — perform

statio, -nis — posting

impigrē — readily

roboro, -are — grow strong

verecundus, -a, -um — modest

meditatio, -nis — consideration

doctor, -ris — instructor

adventus, -ūs — arrival

discubitus, -ūs — reclining at table

praecurro, -ere — precede, anticipate

sublata < tollo

consurgo, -ere — get up together

parcus, -a, -um — scanty

convivium, -i — party

tibia, -ae — flute

comprehendo, -ere — compile

alacer, -cris, -cre — swift

certamen, -inis — competition

pubertas, -tatis — adolescence

canus, -a, -um — gray haired

defungor, -i — spend

ingredior, -i — enter

actuosus, -a, -um — deed filled

nutrimentum, -i — support

schola, -ae — school

alienigenus, -a, -um — foreign born

singuli, -ae, -a — individual

percurro, -ere — run through

READING FOR UNDERSTANDING

1. The author here advocates educating youths through role modeling. What are the limitations of this educational method?

2. The author's critique of Greek book learning issues from what kind of prejudice?

3. The author's list of distinguished Romans at the end of this passage is impressive indeed. Can you name some other, more infamous Romans who were educated under the same system that the author here glorifies?

Verse Readings

1.

The Romans understood that a significant part of preeminence consists of maintaining a good reputation. But public opinion also has its limits. The following sententiae *from different authors examine notoriety.*

opinentur: 15.I

Male de te opinentur homines sed mali.

malis: 3.III.V
laudari: 3.I.2

Malis displicēre est laudari.

pecuniā: 3.V.8

Bona opinio hominum tutior pecuniā est.

Honesta fama melior pecuniā est.

Bonum est non laudari, sed esse laudabilem.

Bona fama in tenebris proprium splendorem tenet.

plurimum: 3.V.7
qui: 16.V
interest: 20.III.6

Plurimum qui sis, non qui habearis, interest.

Bene audire alterum patrimonium est.

Ingenuus animus non fert vocis verbera.

Si famam servare cupis, dum vivis, honestam,

(ut) fugias: 16.III.1
animo: 3.V.1

fac fugias animo, quae sunt mala, gaudia vitae.

moribus: 3.V.3
facias: 19.IV

Moribus egregiis facias tibi nomen honestum.

homini: 3.III.3

Est socia mortis homini vita ingloria.

Miser dici bonus vir, esse non potest.

probo: 3.III.3

Probo bona fama maxima est hereditas.

multis: 3.III.5
placeas: 16.V

Non quam multis placeas, sed qualibus stude.

si: 18.I.4

Nondum felix es, si non te turba deriserit.

melioribus,
   pluribus: 3.III.5

Maximum in eo vitium est, qui non melioribus vult placēre, sed pluribus.

opinio, -nis — opinion
displiceo, -ēre — displease
splendor, -ris — splendor
bene audire — to be well
   spoken of

patrimonium, -i —
   patrimony
ingenuus, -a, -um — noble
inglorius, -a, -um —
   inglorious

hereditas, -tatis —
   inheritance
nondum — not yet
derideo, -ēre — mock

READING FOR UNDERSTANDING

1. *Some celebrity publicists claim that there is no such thing as bad publicity. Which of these aphorisms contradict that claim?*
2. *Which would you rather be:* Time *magazine's Person of the Year (that is, someone who has been in the news much) or a Nobel Prize winner in the sciences (that is, someone whose name average people will probably hear only once)?*
3. *In a culture where PR image is everything, can a person achieve preeminence when opposed by scorn and ridicule? When confronted by indifference?*

2.

A militaristic culture such as ancient Rome prized the virtue of courage highly and viewed coward-ice and timidity not only as personal faults but as fundamentally unpatriotic.

Stultum est timēre quod vitari non potest.

audendo: 17.II
tardando: 3.V.1

Audendo virtus crescit, tardando timor.

Occasiones non modo accipe, adripe.

Felicitatem in dubiis virtus impetrat.

plurimi: 3.II.7

In rebus dubiis plurimi est audacia.

calamitati: 3.III.1

Non nōvit virtus calamitati cedere.

Patiens et fortis se ipsum felicem facit.

timendo: 17.II

Nemo timendo ad summum pervēnit locum.

ante . . . quam:
   16.XIII.3.a.ii.D

Pericla qui audet ante vincit, quam accipit.

multum: 3.IV.7
venturi: 12.II
ne cures: 19.IV

Multum venturi ne cures tempora fati;
non metuit mortem, qui scit contemnere vitam.

Hostili in bello dominatur dextera fortis.

Calamitas virtutis occasio est.

Etiam gerunt cum timidis bellum somnia.

tempore: 3.V.6   Ignavus omni cessat omnis tempore.

Perit voluptas, virtus immortalis est.

cum: 3.V.3   Quidquid fit cum virtute, fit cum gloriā.
cum: 3.V.3

vito, -are — avoid	**adripio, -ere** — seize	**somnium, -i** — dream
tardo, -are — delay	**hostilis, -e** — enemy-	**ignavus, -i** — coward
occasio, -nis — circumstance	**dominor, -ari** — dominate	

READING FOR UNDERSTANDING

1. *What do the Romans seem to mean by the word* **virtus**? *Is it like our expression* the right stuff?
2. *Many of these apothegms try to define courage in the contexts of disaster and crisis. Are these the only settings, or just the best settings, to observe courage?*
3. *Our society values risk taking but frowns on recklessness. Can a person be a risk taker but not courageous? Can a person be courageous but not take risks?*

3.

M. Porcius Cato (234–149 BCE) is traditionally said to have composed the following "Fifty-Eight Commandments" and passed them on to his son for instruction. Obey these, Cato claimed, and you could achieve preeminence for yourself, your family, and your state. Although they are in prose, notice how these catchphrases have a jingle quality.

1. Itaque deo supplica.
2. Parentes ama.
3. Cognatos cole.
4. Familiam cura.

patientiā: 3.V.7   5. Parentem patientiā vince.
6. Coniugem ama.
7. Liberos erudi.

ferto: 19.II.6.d   8. Libenter amorem ferto.

esto: 19.II.6.a   9. Mundus esto.

virtute: 3.V.13   10. Virtute utere.
utere: 19.I

11. Verecundiam serva.
12. Iracundiam rege.

irascere: 19.I   13. Irascere ob rem gravem.

credideris: 19.V.I	14. Nihil temerē credideris.
ne: 19.III.1	15. Maledicus ne esto.
esto: 19.II.6.a	16. Existimationem retinē.
	17. Libros lege.
quae: 3.IV.1	18. Quae lēgerīs, memento.
memento: 19.II	19. Diligentiam adhibē.
	20. Litteras disce.
liberalibus: 3.III.5	21. Liberalibus studē.
convivare: 19.I	22. Convivare rarō.
vino: 3.V.10	23. Vino tempera.
loquere: 19.I	24. Pauca in convivio loquere.
	25. Meretricem fuge.
	26. Aleam fuge.
noli: 19.III	27. Alienum noli concupiscere.
trocho: 3.V.1	28. Trocho lude.
	29. Quod satis est, dormi.

supplico, -are — pray	**maledicus, -a, -um** —	**tempero, -are** — be moderate
erudio, -ire — teach	slanderous	**meretrix, -tricis** — prostitute
mundus, -a, -um — clean	**existimatio, -nis** — good	**alea, -ae** — dice playing
verecundia, -ae —	name	**concupisco, -ere** — lust after
modesty	**convivor, -ari** — attend	**trochus, -i** — hoop game
temerē — rashly	parties	

READING FOR UNDERSTANDING

1. *Instructions 1–8 express family values. Which ones seem the most timely today? Which seem the most outdated?*
2. *Instructions 9–16 deal with personal care. Do they differ much from the Boy Scouts' code or the Girl Scouts' code?*
3. *Instructions 17–29 center on self-improvement and vice avoidance. How do these differ from the sorts of New Year's resolutions that people often make?*
4. *Which one of these first twenty-nine aphorisms should become your personal motto?*

The next precepts are social and civic and express values commonly credited for Rome's early success in the world.

maiori: 3.III.1	30. Maiori concede.
minori: 3.III.5	31. Minori parce.
	32. Saluta libenter.
esto: 19.II.6.a	33. Blandus esto.
nihil: 3.IV.7	34. Nihil mentire.
mentire: 19.I	35. Datum serva.

beneficii: 3.II.6
esto: 19.II.6.a

36. Rem tuam custodi.

37. Beneficii accepti esto memor.

38. Mutuum da.

videto: 19.II

39. Cui des, videto.

bono: 3.III.3
benefacito: 19.II
noli: 19.III

40. Bono benefacito.

41. Miserum noli irridēre.

contempserīs: 15.IV.1.a
riseris: 19.V.1

42. Minorem ne contempserīs.

43. Neminem riseris.

arbitrio: 3.V.1
feceris: 19.V.1

44. Nihil arbitrio virium feceris.

45. Patere legem, quam ipse tuleris.

46. Pugna pro patriā.

47. Magistratum metue.

stato: 19.II

48. Ad praetorium stato.

foro: 3.III.5

49. Foro parce.

50. Cum bonis ambula.

antequam: 16.XIII.3.a.ii.C
ne: 15.IV.3
accesserīs: 15.IV.1.a
adesto: 19.II.6.a

51. Antequam voceris, ne accesserīs.

52. In iudicio adesto.

53. Ius iurandum serva.

54. Consultus esto.

55. Tute consule.

56. Minimē iudica.

57. Aequum iudica.

adgredere: 19.I

58. Illud adgredere, quod iustum est.

blandus, -a, -um — easygoing

benefacio, -ere — do good turns

irrideo, -ēre — ridicule

arbitrium, -i — decision, outcome

patere = **pati**

magistratus, -ūs — magistrate

praetorium, -i — general's tent

accedo, -ere — approach

consultus, -a, -um — deliberate, thoughtful

-te — suffix conveying emphasis

READING FOR UNDERSTANDING

1. *Precepts 30–45 provide instruction in social and interpersonal matters. Which ones are most appropriate for college seniors? Which ones do you hope others will follow the year after you graduate from college?*

2. *Success in the larger community is the thrust of precepts 46–58. What differences do you notice between the larger community in Roman times and the larger community today? Would Cato's instructions be more appropriate for someone coming of age in, say, Washington DC or in Ottawa, Ontario?*

3. *Imagine that after you've lived a very long life, someone is delivering your eulogy and praising your character: which of these last twenty-nine precepts would you like your eulogist to commend you for?*

4.

The ability to lead others is a crucial aspect of greatness. The Romans were usually more worried about the tendency toward absolutism in their leaders rather than weak or ineffectual leadership skills.

Qui a multis timetur, multos timet.

(ut) timeat: 16.II   Necesse est multos timeat, quem multi timent.

agat: 15.I   Agat princeps curam non tantum salutis, sed honestae cicatricis.

rogando: 17.II   Cogit rogando, cum rogat potentior.

In sterculino plurimum gallus potest.

animo: 3.V.3   Omnes aequo animo parent, ubi digni imperant.

felicitas: 3.I.2   Potens misericors publica est felicitas.

Utrumque casum aspicere debet, qui imperat.

caveas: 19.IV
cordi: 3.III.3   Grande aliquid caveas timido committere cordi.

Qui vinci sese patitur pro tempore, vincit.

Magni magna parant, modici breviora laborant.

ne: 16.III.1
caveas: 19.IV   Ne tua paeniteat caveas victoria temet.

A duabus causis praestare princeps solet,
si aut se vindicat aut alium.

Clementia est lenitas superioris adversus inferiorem.

persuaseris,
coegeris: future
perfects   Quod persuaseris, erit diuturnum;
quod coegeris, erit in occasione.

ulciscendi: 17.II   Clementia est temperantia animi in potestate ulciscendi.

Clementia in quamcumque domum vēnerit,
felicem eam tranquillamque praestabit.

principi, medico: 3.III.2	Haud minus turpia sunt principi multa supplicia, quam medico multa funera.
virtutibus: 3.V.10	Nē virtutibus multis abundat, qui alienas amat.
	Non alia facies est quieti moderatique imperii, quam sereni caeli et nitentis.
imperio: 3.III.5	Parēre scire par imperio gloria est.
nulli: 3.III.7 **imponas:** 19.IV **possis:** 15.II	Nulli imponas, quod ipse non possis pati.
	Severitas assidua amittit auctoritatem.
	Amicos secretō admonē, palam lauda.
labor: 3.I.2	Labor imperantis militum securitas.

cicatrix, -tricis — scar

sterculinum, -i — dung heap

gallus, -i — cock, rooster

misericors, -rdis — sympathetic

aspicio, -ere — examine

grandis, -e — great

committo, -ere — entrust

modicus, -a, -um — ordinary

-met — suffix conveying emphasis

lenitas, -tatis — leniency

adversus — (with accusative) toward

diuturnus, -a, -um — enduring

occasio, -nis — moment

temperantia, -ae — self-restraint

ulciscor, -i — get revenge

supplicium, -i — death sentence

nē — indeed

abundo, -are — abound

quietus, -a, -um — calm

moderatus, -a, -um — restrained

serenus, -a, -um — mild

severitas, -tatis — severity

palam — in public

securitas, -tatis — safety

READING FOR UNDERSTANDING

1. The trait of **clementia** appears to be quite important. The mercy a winner shows to a loser is all the more praised when it's unexpected. Do Romans seem to expect **clementia** from their leaders?
2. The first two aphorisms in this section are very similar. Which do you prefer? Why?
3. The third through fifth maxims in this section are the most provocative. Explain the basic truth each of them tries to capture.

5.

The following aphorisms emphasize the importance of wisdom and prudence. The Romans, it's true, respected intelligence in all aspects of their society—nowhere more so than in the government and in the military.

Ducis in consilio posita est virtus militum.

Incertus animus dimidium est sapientiae.

Consilium in dubiis remedium prudentis est.

caveas: 16.V — Quid cautus caveas aliena exempla docebunt.

deliberandum est, statuendum est: 17.IV — Deliberandum est saepe, statuendum est semel.

(ut) legas: 16.III.1
facito: 19.II
perlectis: 3.V.18 — Multa legas facito, perlectis neglege multa;

miranda, credenda: 17.III
poetae: 3.I.1 — nam miranda canunt, sed non credenda poetae.

animo: 3.V.10 — Vir prudens animo est melior quam fortis in armis.

deliberando: 17.II — Deliberando discitur sapientia.

Gravis animus dubiam non habet sententiam.

sis: 16.V — Per quae sis tutus, illa semper cogites.

pervenias: 16.V
cogites: 19.IV — Quidquid conaris, quō pervenias cogites.

Consilii regimen virtuti corporis adde.

sequaris, fugias: 16.V
nobis: 3.III.3
magistra: 3.I.2 — Multorum disce exemplis, quae facta sequaris, quae fugias; vita est nobis aliena magistra.

monitis: 3.III.7
accommodet: 15.I — Utilibus monitis prudens accommodet aurem.

discrimine: 3.V.3
memoranda: 17.III — Magno perficitur discrimine res memoranda.

facias: 19.IV — Nil sine consilio facias: sīc facta probantur.

discute, proba: 19.I
audias, credas: 16.V — Discute quod audias omne, quod credas proba.

homini: 3.III.4 — Est homini semper diligenti aliquid super.

nesciat: 16.X — Non est beatus, ipse qui se nesciat.

felicitate: 3.V.13 — Scire uti felicitate maxima felicitas est.

Privata studia publicum evertunt bonum.

(facere) debet: 20.IV	Sapiens nihil facit, quod non debet, et nihil praetermittit, quod debet.
	Velox consilium sequitur paenitentia.
paeniteat: 16.V, 20.III.5	Specta, quod te numquam paeniteat.
priusquam: 16.XIII.3.a.ii.C **deliberes:** 19.IV **cum:** 16.I.3.a **facias:** 19.IV	Priusquam promittas, deliberes, et cum promiserīs, facias.

dimidium, -i — half

remedium, -i — cure

prudens, -ntis — prudent

cautus, -a, -um — cautious

statuo, -ere — make a decision

perlego, -ere — read thoroughly

regimen, -minis — control

addo, -ere — add

monitum, -i — advice

accommodo, -are — fit, adapt

discrimen, -minis — crisis

memoro, -are — remember

probo, -are — prove

discutio, -ere — dissect, analyze

diligens, -ntis — conscientious

everto, -ere — undermine

praetermitto, -ere — overlook

velox, -ocis — swift

paenitentia, -ae — regret

priusquam — before

READING FOR UNDERSTANDING

1. *In our culture, we talk much of the purpose-driven life or living with intentionality. Do these concepts appear synonymous with the Latin word* **consilium***?*
2. *Compare the first maxim of this section with the last in the previous section. Which do you suppose soldiers depend on more, the effort or the planning of their leaders?*
3. *Explain the sense of the second aphorism, which seems to regard the process of intelligence over the results. How well would this maxim be greeted in a corporate setting today, where leadership usually boasts itself to be results oriented? In what setting might the second aphorism make a great motto?*

6.

"Gone with the Wind": The Bald Equestrian

READING FOR INFORMATION

1. *Why did the knight come to the Campus Martius?*
2. *What caused his toupee to come off?*
3. *How did the knight react to his public embarrassment?*

religasse: 20.I.3	Calvus eques, capiti solitus religasse capillos atque alias nudo vertice ferre comas, ad Campum nitidis vēnit conspectus in armis
frenis: 3.III.2	et facilem frenis flectere coepit equum.

populo conspiciente:
13.III.1
deiecto . . . galero:
13.III.2
appositā . . . comā:
13.III.2
quod: 16.XIII.2.c
milibus: 3.III.3
calliditate: 3.V.3

mirum (est): 20.IV
capillos: 3.IV.4
deseruēre: 20.I.2

Huius ab adverso Boreae spiramina praeflant,   5
ridiculum populo conspiciente caput.
Nam mox deiecto nituit frons nuda galero,
discolor appositā quae fuit ante comā.
Ille sagax, tantis quod risus milibus esset,
distulit admotā calliditate iocum,   10
"Quid mirum," referens, "positos fūgisse capillos,
quem prius aequaevae deseruēre comae?"

calvus, -a, -um — bald

eques, -itis — knight

religo, -are — tie back

nitidus, -a, -um — shiny

conspectus, -a, -um — conspicuous

frenum, -i — rein

boreas, -ae — north wind

spiramen, -inis — gust

praeflo, -are — blow

ridiculus, -a, -um — laughable

deicio, -ere — throw down

frons, -ntis — brow

galerus, -i — helmet

sagax, -acis — clever, witty

disfero, -rre — deflect

calliditas, -tatis — wit

aequaevus, -a, -um — of the same age

READING FOR UNDERSTANDING

1. *Would you agree that an important trait of greatness is the ability to laugh at oneself? What happens to prominent people when they can't take a joke at their own expense?*
2. *Did it surprise you to learn that Roman men sometimes employed hairpieces? Did you know that Julius Caesar practiced the time-honored comb-over? What do you suppose is the connection between hair and ego?*
3. *If you belonged to the same cavalry brigade as this knight, after this incident would you feel proud to have him as your superior officer?*

7.

The Romans had an expectation—sometimes gratified, sometimes not—that personal integrity would attend preeminence. These aphorisms examine the role of honor and honesty.

viri: 3.II.5   Boni est viri, etiam in morte, nullum fallere.

hosti: 3.III.2   Etiam hosti est aequus, qui habet in consilio fidem.

Sat est disertus, e quo loquitur veritas.

Fides sīcut anima, unde abiit, numquam redit.

Honos honestum decorat, inhonestum notat.

Qui ius iurandum servat, quōvis pervenit.

eripere: 3.I.2
tollere: 12.I.3.a

Sibi primō auxilium eripere est leges tollere.

viri: 3.II.5

Viri boni est nescire facere iniuriam.

esto: 19.II.6.a
bonis: 3.III.2

Proximus esto bonis, si non potes optimus esse.

cum: 16.I.3.b

Cum accusas alium, propriam prius inspice vitam.

dicas: 19.IV
quamquam:
  16.XIII.2.c
dictū: 17.I.2
bono: 3.III.3
iustitiae: 3.III.2

Vera libens dicas, quamquam sint aspera dictū.

Bono iustitiae proxima est severitas.

Vir constans quicquid coepit complēre laborat.

aliis, sibi: 3.III.2

Bonus esse non potest aliis malus sibi.

**conscientiae,
  famae:** 3.III.7
attenderis: 19.V.1

Conscientiae potius quam famae attenderis.

Cum hominibus pacem, bella cum vitiis habē.

Cum pare contendere indecens, cum superiore furiosum,
cum inferiore sordidum.

Famam curant multi, pauci conscientiam.

quid: 7.VI

Potest quid esse honestum, quod non liberum?

Nullum laborem recusant manūs ab aratro ad arma translatae.

veris: 3.V.I
adulando: 17.II;
  3.V.1
nil: 3.IV.7

Malo veris offendere quam placēre adulando.

Nil prodest didicisse, si cessas benefacere.

aliquem: 3.IV.4
odio: 3.V.7
nocentis: 3.II.6
praestabis: 19.IV

Ridiculum est aliquem odio nocentis innocentiam suam perdere.

Praestabis parentibus pietatem, cognatis indulgentiam,
amicis fidem, omnibus aequitatem.

Non vives aliter in foro, aliter in solitudine.

ut: 16.II

Sīc vive, ut nec a superioribus contemnaris,
nec ab inferioribus timearis.

A malis hominibus tutissimum est cito effugere.

fallo, -ere — deceive

disertus, -a, -um — eloquent

veritas, -tatis — truth

decoro, -are — adorn

inhonestus, -a, -um — dishonorable

quōvis — wherever

iustitia, -ae — justice

severitas, -tatis — sternness

constans, -ntis — stable

compleo, -ēre — complete

conscientia, -ae — conscience

attendo, -ere — pay attention

indecens, -ntis — indecent

furiosus, -a, -um — crazy

recuso, -are — refuse

aratrum, -i — plow

translatae < transfero

malo, malle — prefer

adulo, -are — fawn on

cesso, -are — stop

ridiculus, -a, -um — laughable

innocentia, -ae — innocence

aequitas, -tatis — fair play

solitudo, -inis — solitude

READING FOR UNDERSTANDING

1. *According to these maxims, what are some of the things that honorable people avoid? Why?*
2. *Integrity is sometimes represented here as making the better choice between two options. What paired options are cited here? In your experience, are most ethical choices between opposites?*
3. *Of this group, what are your three favorite aphorisms? What are your three least favorite?*

8.

In this selection, the quality of self-control is given close attention. Where we often attribute success to something we call drive, the defining characteristic of preeminence for Romans was the ability to curb and hold in check one's impulses and emotions.

Bis vincit qui se vincit in victoriā.

Tacēre pro se praestat, quam contrā loqui.

Bonum ad virum cito moritur iracundia.

servis: 3.III.5

Servis imperare moderatē laus est.

effugere: 12.I.3.a
vincere: 3.I.2

Effugere cupiditatem regnum est vincere.

Medicina calamitatis est aequanimitas.

locutum (esse): 20.IV
paenitet: 20.III.5

Saepius locutum, numquam te tacuisse paenitet.

mora: 3.I.1
cogitationis: 3.IX
diligentia: 3.I.2

Mora cogitationis diligentia est.

Nocēre posse et nolle laus amplissima est.

Egregios faciet mentis constantia mores.

constantiae: 3.III.5   Nocēre casus non solet constantiae.

Patientia animi occultas divitias habet.

Quod vult habet, qui velle quod satis est potest.

virtus: 3.I.2   Quem superare potes, interdum vince ferendo;
maxima enim est hominum semper patientia virtus.

tibi: 3.III.5   Imperium habēre vis magnum? Impera tibi.

quanto, tanto: 3.V.9   Quanto maior eris, tanto moderatior esto.
esto: 19.II.6.a

dicas, cogites: 16.V   Considera quid dicas, non quid cogites.

Felicitas nutrix est iracundiae.

Iram qui vincit, hostem superat maximum.

rationi: 3.III.7   Omnia subicit, qui se subicit rationi.

Homo tacēre qui nescit, nescit loqui.

est adhibenda: Omni rei moderatio est adhibenda.
   17.IV

Severitatem abditam, clementiam in procinctū habē.

feras: 19.IV   Libenter feras, quod necesse est: dolor patientiā vincitur.

ut: 16.III.1   In hoc incumbe, ut libentius audias quam loquaris.

auribus, linguā: Auribus frequentius quam linguā utere.
   3.V.13

moderatē — moderately
cupiditas, -tatis —
   desirousness
medicina, -ae — remedy
aequanimitas, -tatis — levelheadedness
mora, -ae — postponement

cogitatio, -nis — decision
   making
constantia, -ae — constancy
divitiae, -arum — riches
nutrix, -ricis — nurturer
moderatio, -nis —
   moderation

abditus, -a, -um — hidden
procinctus, -ūs — readiness
incumbo, -ere — pay
   attention
frequenter — often

READING FOR UNDERSTANDING

1. How many of these aphorisms pertain to speech acts? What common theme do you notice in them?
2. From this selection, does it appear that the Romans had a positive or negative opinion of basic human nature?
3. How many of these maxims use language suggestive of the military? What do you suppose is the significance of that usage?

9.

The poetic fiction here is a deathbed speech by Augustus's most trusted adviser and friend, G. Cilnius Maecenas (died 8 BCE).

READING FOR INFORMATION

1. Why does the speaker wish he had died before Drusus, the prince who died prematurely?
2. What four things does the speaker seek from his wife?
3. Although he's speaking to his wife, whom does he actually address?

fato veniente: 13.III.1	Sīc est Maecenas fato veniente locutus,
cum: 16.I.4	frigidus et iam iam cum moriturus erat:
moriturus erat: 17.VI	"Me nē," inquit, "iuvenis primaevi, Iuppiter, ante
me: 3.IV.5 **cecidisse:** 12.I.3.g	angustam Drusi non cecidisse diem!
pectore: 3.V.5 **aevo:** 3.V.7 **opus:** 5.I.1	Pectore maturo fuerat puer, integer aevo, 5 et magnum magni Caesaris illud opus.
vellem: 15.II	Discidio vellemque prius—." Non omnia dixit inciditque pudor quae prope dixit amor, sed manifestus erat: moriens quaerebat amatae coniugis amplexūs, oscula, verba, manūs. 10
te . . . amico: 3.V.14	"Sed tamen hoc satis est: vixi te, Caesar, amico et morior," dixit, "dum moriorque, sat est. Mollibus ex oculis aliquis tibi procidet umor,
cum: 16.I.1	cum dicar subitā voce fuisse tibi.
contingat: 15.I **(ut) iaceam, velim:** 20.III.7.c	Hoc mihi contingat, iaceam tellure sub aequā; 15 nec tamen hoc ultrā te doluisse velim."

frigidus, -a, -um — cold

nē — indeed, truly

primaevus, -a, -um — in one's prime

angustus, -a, -um — brief, difficult

discidium, -i — civil discord

incido, -ere — fall over, fall upon

amplexus, -ūs — embrace

procido, -ere — fall forth

ultrā — further

The poem continues with Maecenas's tearful praise for Augustus and his prayers for the future of the emperor and his household.

READING FOR INFORMATION

1. What is the speaker's one hope for immortality?
2. For what selfless, impersonal reason does the speaker wish Augustus a long life?
3. How can Augustus's wife Livia be made **secura**?

velim: 15.IV vivam: 15.I si: 18.I.2.a	"Sed meminisse velim: vivam sermonibus illīc;	
	semper ero, semper si meminisse voles.	
	Et decet et certē vivam tibi semper amore,	
tibi: 3.III.8	nec tibi qui moritur desinit esse tuus.	20
	Ipse ego quicquid ero cineres interque favillas,	
tui: 3.II.6	tum quoque non potero non memor esse tui.	
te propter: 8.IV	Exemplum vixi te propter molle beati,	
	unus Maecenas teque ego propter eram.	
contigit: 20.III.7	Arbiter ipse fui: volui quod contigit esse;	25
pectus: 3.I.2	pectus eram verē pectoris ipse tui.	
	Vive diu, mi care, senex pete sidera serō:	
terris: 3.III.4 decet: 20.III.7.a tibi: 3.III.3 succrescant, tradant: 15.I Caesare: 3.V.16 sit, expleat: 15.I tibi: 3.III.8	est opus hoc terris, te quoque velle decet. Et tibi succrescant iuvenes bis Caesare digni et tradant porrō Caesaris usque genus. Sit secura tibi quam primum Livia coniunx, expleat amissi munera rupta gener.	30
cum: 16.I.3.b avitis: 3.III.7 collocet: 15.I	Cum deus intereris divis insignis avitis, te Venus in patrio collocet ipsa sinū."	

20. **nec . . . tuus**: nor does the one who dies on you cease to be yours

favilla, -ae — ash	**porrō** — onward	**intersum, -esse** — join
arbiter, -tri — adviser	**expleo, -ēre** — fulfill	**patrius, -a, -um** — ancestral
serō — late, after a long time	**amissi** = Agrippa	**colloco, -are** — place
succresco, -ere — grow together	**gener** = Tiberius	

READING FOR UNDERSTANDING

1. Do the references to civil war (line 7), the death of Claudius Nero Drusus (lines 3–6), and the death of M. Vipsanius Agrippa (line 32)—great regrets and sorrows in Augustus's life—seem tactful or awkward to you?
2. Lines 25–26 express two seemingly contradictory notions: absolute independence and complete submission. Can you explain and resolve the apparent contradiction?
3. Although Augustus officially and publicly opposed his living deification, what evidence do you see in this poem for a growing ruler cult?

10.

In this final selection of sententiae *on the topic of preeminence, we see some familiar themes and some less common ones as well.*

iudicandus est: 17.IV	Multos vitam differentes mors incerta praevenit: omnis dies velut ultimus iudicandus est.
	Nulla pusilla domus, quae amicos multos capit.
pluris: 3.II.7	Pluris docentis vita quam sententia.
sint: 16.V **ut:** 16.III.1	Intellege ecquae sint, ut et bene agas, bona.
	Gradus a magnis fit ad maiora saepius.
omnibus: 3.III.3 or 3.V.10	Bonus vir nemo est nisi qui bonus est omnibus.
	Cui omnes bene dicunt, possidet populi bona.
patriae: 3.III.3	Exsilium patitur, patriae qui se denegat.
imperando: 17.II	Male imperando summum imperium amittitur.
ignoscendo: 17.II	Multa ignoscendo fit potens potentior.
patriae: 3.III.3 **consolatio:** 3.I.2	Misericors civis patriae est consolatio.
noli: 19.III	Noli contemnere ea, quae summos sublevant.
ni: 18.I.4 **nulli:** 3.III.3	Ni gradus servetur, nulli tutus est summus locus.
neglegens: 12.II.c **teras:** 15.II	Probi delicta neglegens, leges teras.
patriae: 3.III.2	Populi est mancipium, quisquis patriae est utilis.
clementiā: 3.V.13	Perpetuō vincit, qui utitur clementiā.
ut: 16.III.1	Qui exspectat ut rogetur, officium levat.
	Satis est superare inimicum; nimium est perdere.
noli: 19.III **morte:** 3.V.6	Rebus in adversis animum submittere noli; spem retinē; spes una hominem nec morte relinquit.

pertractet: 15.I   Omnia pertractet primum mens, verba, loquelae.

Cede locum laesus Fortunae, cede potenti;
laedere qui potuit, poterit prodesse aliquandō.

malis: 19.IV   Audire malis quam loqui libentius.

differo, -rre — put on hold
incertus, -a, -um — unexpected
praevenio, -ire — overtake
pusillus, -a, -um — weak
ecqui — whether any
possideo, -ēre — possess
exsilium, -i — exile

denego, -are — deny
ignosco, -ere — forgive
misericors, -rdis — sympathetic
consolatio, -nis — consolation
sublevo, -are — elevate
delictum, -i — crime, fault

mancipium, -i — property, asset
submitto, -ere — surrender
aliquandō — sometimes
pertracto, -are — compass
loquela, -ae — speech, language
malo, malle — prefer

READING FOR UNDERSTANDING
1. *Which of the preceding seem to take a more novel view on the topic of preeminence?*
2. *Of the group, what are your three favorite aphorisms? What are your three least favorite?*
3. *All things considered, which aspects of preeminence have all the apothegms presented in this chapter not adequately addressed?*

Supplemental Readings

1.

Horatius Cocles, the famous hero of early Rome, is the subject of this anecdote. Positioned at the Sublician Bridge, he saves Rome from her dreaded enemies the Etruscans (506 BCE).

READING FOR INFORMATION
1. *What did Cocles do after he had determined that Rome was safe?*
2. *By what agency was Cocles supposedly saved?*
3. *What adversity did he overcome before rejoining his troops?*
4. *According to the author, besides Cocles, what saved Rome?*

Etruscis in urbem Ponte Sublicio irrumpentibus, Horatius Cocles extremam eius partem occupavit, totumque hostium agmen, donec post tergum suum pons abrumperetur, infatigabili pugnā sustinuit, atque, ut patriam periculo imminenti liberatam esse vīdit, armatus se in Tiberim misit. Cuius fortitudinem di immortales admirati incolumitatem sinceram ei praestiterunt: nam neque altitudine deiectūs quassatus nec pondere armorum pressus nec ullo verticis circuitū actus, ne telis quidem, quae undique congerebantur, laesus tutum natandi eventum habuit. Unus itaque tot civium, tot hostium in se oculos convertit, stupentes illos admiratione, hos inter laetitiam et metum haesitantes, unusque duos acerrimā pugnā consertos exercitūs, alterum repellendo, alterum propugnando, distraxit. Denique unus urbi nostrae tantum scuto suo quantum Tiberis alveo munimenti attulit. Quapropter discedentes Etrusci dicere potuerunt: "Romanos vicimus; ab Horatio victi sumus."

agmen, -minis — battle line	**deiectus, -ūs** — fall	**propugno, -are** — be
abrumpo, -ere — break off	**circuitus, -ūs** — swirling	aggressive
infatigabilis, -e — tireless	**stupeo, -ēre** — be amazed	**alveus, -i** — riverbank
incolumitas, -tatis — safety	**laetitia, -ae** — happiness	**munimentum, -i** — defense
sincerus, -a, -um — uninjured	**haesito, -are** — hesitate	
altitudo, -inis — height	**consero, -ere** — engage	

READING FOR UNDERSTANDING

1. *In early Rome, individualism wasn't highly prized, yet stories of individual heroism, like this one, were popular. How do you explain this apparent contradiction?*
2. *Why does the author introduce the notion that the gods helped Cocles?*
3. *Every Roman child was taught this story of Horatius Cocles, but it's interesting to note that it has no epilogue. That is, there's no account of what became of Cocles after his act of heroism. How would you explain that?*

2.

Set in 256 BCE, this story recounts the debate between the Carthaginian generals Hanno and Hamilcar over how the Romans would receive a peace party. Despite some intimidation, Hanno proved that he was right.

READING FOR INFORMATION

1. *What prompted the Carthaginians to consider suing for peace?*
2. *Why would the precedent of Cornelius Asina concern Hamilcar?*
3. *According to the author, the mere ability to put Hanno in chains would have made the Roman consuls famous, but what act made them even more famous?*

Speciosa illa quoque Romana fides. Ingenti Poenorum classe circā Siciliam devictā, duces eius fractis animis consilia petendae pacis agitabant. Quorum Hamilcar ire se ad consules negabat audēre, ne eodem modo catenae sibi inicerentur, quo ab ipsis Cornelio Asinae consuli iniectae erant. Hanno autem, certior Romani animi aestimator, nihil tale timendum esse ratus, maximā cum fiduciā ad colloquium eorum tetendit. Apud quos cum de fine belli ageret, et tribunus militum ei dixisset posse illi meritō evenire quod Cornelio accidisset, uterque consul, tribuno tacēre iusso, "Isto te," inquit, "metū, Hanno, fides civitatis nostrae liberat." Claros illos fecerat tantum hostium ducem vincire potuisse, sed multō clariores fecit noluisse.

aestimator, -ris — judge	**reor, rēri, ratus sum** — think	**colloquium, -i** — conversation

READING FOR UNDERSTANDING

1. *Why didn't the Romans avenge the humiliation of Asina by treating Hanno comparably?*
2. *Do you have any sympathy for the views of the tribune?*
3. *While Rome was a republic, it had a long tradition of treating those it defeated with considerable dignity. But after the government turned more autocratic, Rome was gradually less humane to its conquered foes. How might you explain the coincidence of these changes?*

3.

When the situation against Hannibal in the Second Punic War looked the most bleak for Rome, Q. Fabius Maximus Cunctator was named dictator (217 BCE). Because of his constant levelheadedness, Rome survived, regrouped, and finally defeated her Carthaginian enemy.

READING FOR INFORMATION

1. *What slights did Fabius suffer at the hands of the Roman government and people?*
2. *How did Fabius manage to thwart Hannibal?*
3. *According to the author, by what two means was Carthage defeated?*

Illa verō pietatis constantia admirabilis, quam Q. Fabius Maximus infatigabilem patriae praestitit. Pecuniam pro captivis Hannibali numeraverat: fraudatus eā publicē tacuit; dictatori ei magistrum equitum Minucium iure imperii aequaverant: silentium egit; compluribus praestereā iniuriis lacessitus in eodem animi habitū mansit, nec umquam sibi rei publicae permisit irasci. Tam perseverans in amore civium—quid?—in bello gerendo nonne par eius constantia? Imperium Romanum Cannensi proelio paene destructum vix sufficere ad exercitūs comparandos videbatur. Itaque frustrari et eludere Poenorum impetus quam manum cum his totā acie conserere melius ratus, plurimis comminationibus Hannibalis irritatus, saepe etiam specie bene gerendae rei oblatā, numquam a consilii salubritate ne parvi quidem certaminis discrimine recessit, quodque est difficillimum, ubique irā ac spe superior apparuit. Ergō ut Scipio pugnando, ita hic non dimicando maximē civitati nostrae succurrisse visus est: alter enim celeritate suā Carthaginem oppressit, alter cunctatione id egit, ne Roma opprimi posset.

infatigabilis, -e — tireless	**magister equitum** — second	**lacesso, -ere** — injure
fraudo, -are — cheat	in command to a dictator	**persevero, -are** — persevere

Cannensis, -e — of or at Cannae

destruo, -ere — destroy

comparo, -are — assemble

frustror, -ari — frustrate

consero, -ere — engage

comminatio, -nis — skirmish

irrito, -are — annoy

oblata < offero

salubritas, -tatis — well-being

celeritas, -tatis — speed

cunctatio, -nis — delaying

READING FOR UNDERSTANDING

1. *We commonly say "Patience is a virtue," but we more often criticize our public officials for acting too slowly. What made Fabius's slowness so commendable?*

2. *Fabius is also praised for his great patriotism, despite having been wronged several times by the state he loved so much. What do you suppose kept Fabius from simply retiring into private life in response to his public humiliations?*

3. *The judgment that Fabius saved Rome by essentially doing relatively little or nothing is historically accurate. Can you think of other great leaders in history who achieved success by doing relatively little or nothing?*

4.

After the Battle of Zama and the defeat of Carthage (203 BCE) in the Second Punic War, the elder Scipio Africanus occupied an unparalleled place in the hearts and loyalties of most Romans. The end of this passage narrates an incident that occurred in 195 BCE, when Hannibal attempted to incite the Carthaginians to war against Rome for yet another time—and how Scipio reacted to the situation.

READING FOR INFORMATION

1. *Where did Romans want to set up Scipio's statue?*

2. *What political honors did they want to give him?*

3. *On what grounds did Scipio advise the senate not to get involved in Hannibal's efforts in Carthage?*

maioribus: use of dative?
Africano: use of dative?
exsolvenda: gerund or gerundive?
ornamentis: use of ablative?
illi: use of dative?
ornatū: use of ablative?
pulvinaribus: use of dative?
plebiscito: use of ablative?
consulto: use of ablative?
patiendo: gerund or gerundive?
recusandis: what form?
emerendis: gerund or gerundive?
robore: use of ablative?
cum: type?
legatis: use of ablative?
seditiones: use of accusative?
patres: use of accusative?
rei publicae: use of dative?

Non defuit maioribus grata mens ad praemia superiori Africano exsolvenda, si quidem maxima eius merita paribus ornamentis decorare conati sunt. Voluerunt illi statuas in comitio, in rostris, in curiā, in ipsā denique Iovis Optimi Maximi cellā ponere, voluerunt imaginem eius triumphali ornatū indutam Capitolinis pulvinaribus applicare, voluerunt ei continuum per omnes vitae annos consulatum perpetuamque dictaturam tribuere: quorum nihil sibi neque plebiscito dari neque senatūs consulto decerni patiendo paene tantum se in recusandis honoribus gessit, quantum egerat in emerendis. Eodem robore mentis causam Hannibalis in senatū protexit, cum eum cives sui missis legatis tamquam seditiones apud eos moventem accusarent. Adiecit quoque non oportēre patres conscriptos se rei publicae Carthaginiensium interponere, altissimāque moderatione alterius saluti consuluit, alterius dignitati, victoriā tenus utriusque hostem egisse contentus.

moderatione: use of ablative?
saluti: use of dative?
dignitati: use of dative?
victoriā tenus: type of preposition?

8–10. **paene ... emerendis:** he conducted himself almost as greatly in refusing honors as he had done in deserving them

decoro, -are — adorn

statua, -ae — statue

comitium, -i — assembly house

cella, -ae — temple sanctuary

pulvinar, -ris — couch of the gods

dictatura, -ae — dictatorship

plebiscitum, -i — plebiscite

consultum, -i — decree

decerno, -ere — vote

emereor, -ēri — earn, deserve

protego, -ere — protect

seditio, -nis — uprising

interpono, -ere — interpose

moderatio, -nis — self-restraint

READING FOR UNDERSTANDING

1. *Why do you suppose Scipio rejected the honors offered to him?*
2. *Why do you suppose Scipio turned down the opportunity to defeat Hannibal a second (and perhaps final) time?*
3. *The principle that no sovereign nation has a right to engineer regime change in another sovereign nation has a very modern ring. Do you agree with Scipio? Does it seem odd at all to hear this principle coming from a decorated general?*

5.

This passage outlines the eventful career of the dictator Sulla (ca. 138–78 BCE), whose early years were very unpromising.

READING FOR INFORMATION

1. *Before he gained the quaestorship, what were Sulla's favorite preoccupations?*
2. *What was Marius's initial impression of Sulla when the latter first arrived in Africa?*
3. *Of all the accomplishments listed, which three happened in Italy?*

L. verō Sulla usque ad quaesturae suae comitia vitam libidine, vino, ludicrae artis amore inquinatam perduxit. Quapropter C. Marius consul molestē tulisse traditur, quod sibi asperrimum in Africā bellum gerenti tam delicatus quaestor sorte obvēnisset. Eiusdem virtus, quasi perruptis et disiectis nequitiae, qua obsidebatur, claustris, catenas Iugurthae manibus iniecit, Mitridatem compescuit, socialis belli fluctūs repressit, Cinnae dominationem fregit, eumque, qui se in Africā quaestorem fastidierat, ipsam illam provinciam proscriptum et exsulem petere coegit. Quae tam diversa tamque inter se contraria si quis apud animum suum attentiore comparatione expendere velit, duos in uno homine Sullas fuisse crediderit, turpem adulescentulum et virum, dicerem fortem, nisi ipse se felicem appellari maluisset.

quaestura, -ae — quaestorship	**delicatus, -a, -um** — effeminate	**reprimo, -ere** — repress
comitium, -i — election	**obvenio, -ire** — be allotted	**dominatio, -nis** — tyranny
ludicer, -cra, -crum — of comedy	**perrumpo, -ere** — break through	**exsul, -lis** — exile
inquinatus, -a, -um — defiled	**disicio, -ere** — discard	**comparatio, -nis** — comparison
	socialis, -e — with allies	**expendo, -ere** — dedicate

READING FOR UNDERSTANDING

1. The author portrays Sulla's great talents as all bottled up in him, just waiting for the right opportunity or conditions to break out and nullify all his bad habits. Does this seem like sound psychology to you?
2. Later, the author states that there were two Sullas, the young deadbeat and the older man of achievement. Does this seem like sound psychology to you?
3. Despite the fact that Sulla was a ruthless tyrant, the author here overlooks his many wrongdoings and seems to hold the ruler in fairly high regard. Could the case be made that Sulla's later ruthlessness and wrongdoings were consistent with his earlier misbehaviors? Why do you suppose the author didn't make this connection?
4. Without a doubt, Sulla accomplished some great things in his career, but he also committed many despicable acts. Does true preeminence require that a leader engage exclusively in good and noble acts throughout her or his career?

6.

This narrative tells how the young M. Porcius Cato Uticensis (95–46 BCE) contrived to assassinate Sulla the dictator (ca. 138–78 BCE).

READING FOR INFORMATION

1. What horror did the young Cato observe in Sulla's atrium?
2. What made Cato think he could kill Sulla?
3. What role did Cato's tutor play in all of this?
4. According to the narrator, whose deaths was Sulla responsible for?

M. Cato, cum salutandi gratiā praetextatus ad Sullam vēnisset et capita proscriptorum in atrium adlata vīdisset, atrocitate rei commotus paedagogum suum interrogavit quapropter nemo inveniretur, qui tam crudelem tyrannum occīderet: cumque is non voluntatem hominibus, sed facultatem deesse, quod salus eius magno praesidio militum custodiretur, respondisset, ut ferrum sibi daret obsecravit, adfirmando perfacile se eum interfecturum esse, quod in lecto illius considere solēret. Paedagogus et animum Catonis agnōvit et propositum exhorruit, eumque posteā ad Sullam excussum semper adduxit. Nihil hōc admirabilius: puer in officinā crudelitatis deprehensus victorem non extimuit, cum maximē consules, municipia, legiones, equestris ordinis maiorem partem trucidantem. Si ipsum Marium illo loci statuisses, celerius aliquid de suā fugā quam de Sullae nece cogitasset.

praetextatus, -a, -um — wearing the toga of manhood	**adfirmo, -are** — affirm	**adduco, -ere** — escort
atrium, -i — vestibule	**perfacilis, -e** — very easy	**crudelitas, -tatis** — cruelty
adlata < **adfero**	**agnosco, -ere** — recognize	**extimesco, -ere** — become frightened by
paedagogus, -i — attendant tutor	**propositum, -i** — prospect	**municipium, -i** — municipality
voluntas, -tatis — will	**exhorresco, -ere** — be frightened by	**equestris ordo** — equestrian class
facultas, -tatis — opportunity	**excutio, -ere** — pat down, frisk	

READING FOR UNDERSTANDING

1. *How do you feel about praise for someone who expressed a desire to commit murder?*
2. *The young Cato is commended for his utter lack of fear as though fearlessness in adolescence were a matter of principle. Can you think of other reasons why a thirteen-year-old might seem to lack fear?*
3. *Why is the unfavorable comparison with Marius (ca. 157–86 BCE) at the end of the passage rather unfair?*

7.

This anecdote recounts the judgment on the Latin town Privernum, which had unsuccessfully rebelled against Rome. The Roman senate had to determine the proper punishment for the Privernates, its erstwhile allies (329 BCE).

READING FOR INFORMATION

1. *What were the sentiments of the senators before the Privernates spoke?*
2. *What were the sentiments of the senators after the leader of the Privernates spoke?*
3. *What did the Privernate leader say that won over the senators?*

Priverno . . . interfectisque: use of ablative?
rebellandum: gerund or gerundive?
indignatione: use of ablative?
sibi: use of dative?
esset: use of subjunctive?
faciendum: gerund or gerundive?
casū: use of ablative?
victoribus et iratis: use of ablative?
cum: type?
sanguinis: use of genitive?
merērentur: use of subjunctive?

Priverno capto interfectisque qui id oppidum ad rebellandum incitaverant, senatus indignatione accensus consilium agitabat quidnam sibi de reliquis quoque Privernatibus esset faciendum. Ancipiti igitur casū salus eorum fluctuabatur, eodem tempore et victoribus et iratis subiecta. Ceterum cum auxilium unicum in precibus restare animadverterent, ingenui et Italici sanguinis oblivisci non potuerunt: princeps enim eorum in curiā interrogatus quam poenam merērentur,

libertate: use of ablative?

verbis: use of ablative?

causae: use of dative?
dicto: use of ablative?
habituri essent: use of subjunctive?
impunitate donatā: use of ablative?
vultū: use of ablative?
si: type of condition?
victis: use of dative?

daretur: use of subjunctive?

respondit, "Quam merentur qui se dignos libertate iudicant." Verbis arma sumpserat exasperatosque patrum conscriptorum animos inflammaverat. Sed Plautius consul, favens Privernatium causae, regressum animoso eius dicto obtulit, quaesivitque qualem cum eis Romani pacem habituri essent, impunitate donatā. At is constantissimo vultū, "Si bonam dederitis," inquit, "perpetuam, si malam, non diuturnam." Qua voce perfectum est ut victis non solum venia, sed etiam ius et beneficium nostrae civitatis daretur.

rebello, -are — rebel	**libertas, -tatis** — freedom	**animosus, -a, -um** — high
incito, -are — incite	**exasperatus, -a, -um** —	spirited
indignatio, -nis —	exasperated	**impunitas, -tatis** — impunity
indignation	**inflammo, -are** — inflame	**diuturnus, -a, -um** — long
anceps, -cipitis — uncertain	**regressus, -ūs** — retreat	lasting

READING FOR UNDERSTANDING

1. *How did the consul Plautius set up the Privernate leader for success?*
2. *What arguments could you make for punishing the Privernates? For not punishing the Privernates?*
3. *How do you suppose the senate communicated its decision in this case to Rome's other allies?*

8.

The bravery of certain legionary soldiers was a popular boast among Roman writers. This account commends a simple soldier from the 5th century BCE alleged to be the bravest of them all.

READING FOR INFORMATION

1. *Why, according to the author, should we believe this account of Siccius's exploits?*
2. *How many chest wounds did Siccius receive? How many back wounds?*
3. *Why was it that Siccius was conspicuous in the triumphal processions of his generals?*

Sed quod ad proeliatorum excellentem fortitudinem attinet, meritō L. Siccii Dentati commemoratio omnia Romana exempla finierit, cuius opera honoresque operum ultrā fidem veri excedere iudicari possent, nisi ea certi auctores monumentis suis testata esse voluissent. Quem centies et vicies in aciem descendisse tradunt, eo robore animi atque corporis utentem, ut maiorem semper victoriae partem traxisse vidēretur: sex et triginta spolia ex hoste retulisse, quorum in numero octo fuisse eorum, cum quibus, inspectante utroque exercitū, ex provocatione dimicasset, quattuordecim cives ex mediā morte raptos servasse, quinque et quadraginta vulnera pectore excepisse, tergo cicatricibus vacuo: novem imperatorum triumphales currūs secutum esse, totius civitatis oculos in se numerosā donorum pompā convertentem: praeferebantur enim aureae coronae octo, civicae quattuordecim, murales tres, obsidionalis una, torques octoginta tres, armillae centum sexaginta, hastae octodecim, phalerae quinque et viginti, ornamenta etiam legioni, nedum militi satis multa.

proeliator, -ris — battle soldier

excedo, -ere — excel, surpass

centies — one hundred times

vicies — twenty times

triginta — thirty

provocatio, -nis — challenge

quadraginta — forty

cicatrix, -cis — scar

numerosus, -a, -um — numerous

corona civica — awarded for saving a citizen's life

corona muralis — awarded for storming a wall

corona obsidionalis — awarded for raising a siege

torquis, -is — neck chain

octoginta — eighty

armilla, -ae — armband

sextaginta — sixty

hasta, -ae — spear

phalerae, -arum — breastplates

nedum — let alone, not to mention

READING FOR UNDERSTANDING

1. *Of all of Siccius's accomplishments, which one do you think carries the greatest honor? Why?*
2. *If you were a triumphing general, would you feel that Siccius, as a highly decorated soldier, was stealing your thunder?*
3. *Obviously, throughout his long career, Siccius was never promoted so high as to excuse him from battle duty. Does that seem unfair to you, or just smart personnel management?*

9.

The dramatic scene that this passage depicts took place in 42 BCE at the Battle of Philippi, between the forces of the Second Triumvirate and those of Cassius and Brutus, the assassins of Julius Caesar. The story illustrates how a simple mistake can affect all of history.

READING FOR INFORMATION

1. *Cassius dispatched his centurion Titinius to find out what?*
2. *What took Titinius so long on his mission?*
3. *When he finally returned to Cassius, what did Titinius discover?*
4. *What did Titinius do in response?*

Nam C. Cassium error a semet ipso poenas exigere coegit: inter illum enim pugnae quattuor exercituum apud Philippos varium ipsisque ducibus ignotum eventum missus ab eo Titinius centurio nocturno tempore, ut specularetur quonam in statū res M. Bruti essent; dum crebros excessūs viae petit, quia tenebrarum obscuritas hostesne an commilitones occurrerent dinoscere non sinebat, tardius ad Cassium rediit. Quem is exceptum esse ab hostibus omniaque in eorum potestatem recidisse existimans, finire vitam properavit, cum et castra hostium invicem capta et Bruti copiae magnā ex parte incolumes essent. Titinii verō non oblitteranda est silentio virtus, qui oculis paulisper haesit inopinato iacentis ducis spectaculo attonitus, deinde profusus in lacrimas, "Etsi imprudens," inquit, "imperator, causa tibi mortis fui, tamen, ne id ipsum impunitum sit, accipe me fati tui comitem," superque exanime corpus eius iugulo suo gladium capulo tenus demisit ac permixto utriusque sanguine duplex victima iacuit, pietatis haec, erroris illa.

nocturnus, -a, -um — night-

speculor, -ari — observe

obscuritas, -tatis — darkness

commilito, -nis — fellow soldier

dinosco, -ere — distinguish

oblittero, -are — obliterate

inopinatus, -a, -um — unexpected

impunitus, -a, -um — unpunished

iugulum, -i — throat

capulus, -i — handle

permisceo, -ēre — mix together

READING FOR UNDERSTANDING

1. *Does this passage openly praise Cassius? Criticize him? Does it seem to praise Titinius? Criticize him?*

2. *Did Titinius's final act diminish Cassius's mistake or place it in higher relief?*

3. *Cassius was a noble and principled person, and if history had turned out differently, he doubtless would have attempted to place the Roman republic back on a more steady footing. As it happens, history remembers him as just one of the assassins of Julius Caesar. What do you make of all the many, many also-rans of history?*

E. Women

Prose Readings

1.

These three anecdotes about the loyalty of wives to their husbands illustrate how women will place their own lives and dignity in jeopardy out of spousal affection.

READING FOR INFORMATION
1. *What did Tertia Aemilia do for her slave girl after her husband passed away?*
2. *How did Turia keep her husband safe after the Second Triumvirate proscribed him?*
3. *How did Sulpicia disguise herself to be reunited with her husband?*

ut: 16.III.1
comitatis et
   patientiae: 3.II.3
ut: 16.II
cum: 16.I.3.a
ancillulam: 3.IV.4
esse: 12.I.3.d
ne: 16.III.1
impatientiae: 3.II.6
ut: 16.II

a: 3.V.2

ancillulā: 3.V.16

fide: 3.V.7
ut: 16.II
cum: 16.I.2

cum: 16.I.2

ne: 16.III.1

proscribere: 12.I.3.d
ut: 16.III.1

Atque ut uxoriam fidem attingamus, Tertia Aemilia, Africani prioris uxor, mater Corneliae Gracchorum, tantae fuit comitatis et patientiae, ut, cum sciret viro suo ancillulam ex suis gratam esse, dissimulaverit, ne femina domitorem orbis Africanum magnum virum impatientiae reum ageret, tantumque a vindictā mens eius afuit, ut post mortem Africani manumissam ancillam in matrimonium liberto suo daret. Q. Lucretium, proscriptum a Triumviris, uxor Turia inter cameram et tectum cubiculi abditum, unā consciā ancillulā, ab imminente exitio non sine magno periculo suo tutum praestitit, singularique fide id egit, ut, cum ceteri proscripti in alienis et hostilibus regionibus per summos corporis et animi cruciatūs vix evaderent, ille in cubiculo et in coniugis sinū salutem retinēret. Sulpicia autem, cum a matre Iuliā diligentissimē custodiretur, ne Lentulum Cruscellionem, virum suum proscriptum a Triumviris, in Siciliam persequeretur, nihilo minus, famulari veste sumptā, cum duabus ancillis totidemque servis ad eum clandestinā fugā pervēnit, nec recusavit se ipsam proscribere, ut ei fides sua in coniuge proscripto constaret.

uxorius, -a, -um — wifely
comitas, -tatis — kindness
ancillula, -ae — slave girl
dissimulo, -are — pretend
   otherwise
domitor, -ris — conqueror
impatientia, -ae — being out
   of control
vindicta, -ae — vengeance
manumitto, -ere — set free

libertus, -i — freedman
camera, -ae — room
cubiculum, -i — bedroom
abditus, -a, -um — hidden
conscius, -a, -um — aware
immineo, -ēre — loom
exitium, -i — death
singularis, -e — unique
hostilis, -e — enemy-
cruciatus, -ūs — torment

evado, -ere — escape
persequor, -i — follow
famularis, -e — slave-
totidem — the same number
   of
clandestinus, -a, -um —
   secretive
recuso, -are — refuse
consto, -are — be established

READING FOR UNDERSTANDING

1. *The husbands in these stories had achieved degrees of public prominence. How did their wives achieve their degree of celebrity?*
2. *In what ways does the first anecdote differ from the other two? Are those differences more conspicuous to us than they would have been to the author's ancient readers?*
3. *The loyalty of the wives is presented as exemplary, but is it presented as typical or atypical?*

2.

This story celebrates a certain Sulpicia (late 3rd century BCE), who won a state-run competition to find the most chaste woman in Rome.

READING FOR INFORMATION

1. *Why was the statue of Venus Verticordia (Heart-Changer) consecrated?*
2. *How were the competitors eliminated in this contest?*
3. *What mention is made of the women who participated in this contest? What mention is made of the reaction of Sulpicia, the winner?*

commemorationi: 3.III.7	Meritō virorum commemorationi Sulpicia Servii Paterculi filia, Q. Fulvii
quae: 7.V.2	Flacci uxor, adicitur. Quae, cum senatus libris Sibyllinis per Decemviros
cum: 16.I.1	
libris ... inspectis: 13.III.1	inspectis censuisset ut Veneris Verticordiae simulacrum consecraretur,
ut: 16.IV	quō facilius virginum mulierumque mens a libidine ad pudicitiam
quō: 16.III.2.c	converteretur, et ex omnibus matronis centum, ex centum autem decem
sorte: 3.V.1	sorte ductae de sanctissimā feminā iudicium facerent, cunctis castitate
cunctis: 3.III.7	praelata est.
castitate: 3.V.10	

commemoratio, -nis — commemoration	**censeo, -ēre** — vote	**castitas, -tatis** — chastity
Decemviri — a college of priests	**simulacrum, -i** — statue	**praelata est** < **praefero**
	consecro, -are — consecrate	

READING FOR UNDERSTANDING

1. *What parties sponsored this contest?*
2. *How was this contest different from or similar to a modern beauty pageant?*
3. *Although the narrative doesn't specify how the contest was judged, do you suppose women had much of a say in its outcome?*
4. *How do you think Romans defined **castitas** (penultimate line) for a woman?*

3.

This interesting story, dating back perhaps to the 5th century BCE, impugns a mother for the will she left behind at death, while commending her daughter for making no legal challenge.

READING FOR INFORMATION

1. *Aebutia's will left money to which heirs?*
2. *Why didn't her daughter Afronia challenge the will?*
3. *What effect did her refusal to challenge have on Afronia?*

tabulae: 3.I.1
furoris: 3.II.6
cum: 16.I.2
probitatis: 3.II.3
inclinatione: 3.V.7
iniuriis aut officiis: 3.V.7
filiis: 3.III.1
Afroniae: 3.II.1
nummum: 3.II.8; 1.II.1.c
sacramento: 3.V.10
iudicio: 3.V.7
iniuriā: 3.V.16
animo: 3.V.3

Aebutiae autem, quae L. Meneni Agrippae uxor fuerat, tabulae testamenti erant plenae furoris: nam cum habēret duas simillimae probitatis filias, Pletoniam et Afroniam, animi sui potius inclinatione provecta quam ullis alteriusutrius iniuriis aut officiis commota, Pletoniam tantummodo heredem instituit: filiis etiam Afroniae ex admodum amplo patrimonio viginti milia nummum legavit. Afronia tamen cum sorore sacramento contendere noluit, testamentumque matris patientiā honorare quam iudicio convellere satius esse duxit; eō se ipsa indigniorem iniuriā ostendens quo eam aequiore animo sustinebat.

tabula, -ae — codicil
probitas, -tatis — integrity
inclinatio, -nis — inclination
proveho, -ere — carry away
alteruter — either one (of two)

commotus, -a, -um — disturbed
tantummodo — only
admodum — no less than
patrimonium, -i — inheritance

nummus, -i — sesterce
sacramentum, -i — lawsuit
honoro, -are — honor
satius — better

READING FOR UNDERSTANDING

1. *How do you suppose their mother's will affected the relationship between Afronia and her sister? Why doesn't the author explore this narrative angle?*
2. *This account seems to imply that Aebutia was insane, but what supporting evidence does it provide? Is it necessary to accept the author's word that Afronia's disinheritance was undeserved?*
3. *If Aebutia had disinherited a son and he had refused to challenge the will, would such a refusal have been portrayed as praiseworthy?*

4.

In this story, about a woman prisoner and her survival, a variety of men who control her fate change their views, if not their prejudices.

READING FOR INFORMATION

1. *By what form of execution is the woman condemned to die?*
2. *How does her daughter manage to keep her alive?*
3. *What change in the woman's punishment does the action of her daughter produce?*

Sanguinis ingenui mulierem praetor apud tribunal suum capitali crimine damnatam triumviro in carcere necandam tradidit. Quo receptam is, qui custodiae praeerat, misericordiā motus, non protinus strangulavit: aditum quoque ad eam filiae, sed diligenter excussae, ne quid cibi inferret, dedit, existimans futurum esse ut inediā consumeretur. Cum autem plures iam dies intercederent, secum ipse quaerens quidnam esset quo tam diu sustentaretur, curiosius observatā filiā animadvertit illam, exserto ubere, famem matris lactis sui subsidio lenientem. Quae tam admirabilis spectaculi novitas ab ipso ad triumvirum, a triumviro ad praetorem, a praetore ad consilium iudicum perlata, remissionem poenae mulieri impetravit. Quō non penetrat aut quid non excogitat Pietas, quae in carcere servandae genetricis novam rationem invēnit? Quid enim tam inusitatum, quid tam inauditum quam matrem uberibus natae alitam esse? Putarit aliquis hoc contrā rerum naturam factum esse, nisi diligere parentes prima naturae lex esset.

ingenuus, -a, -um — noble

praetor, -ris — judicial official

tribunal, -lis — praetor's court

capitalis, -e — capital

damno, -are — condemn

triumvir, -i — penal official

carcer, -eris — prison

custodia, -ae — guard

praesum, -esse — be in charge of

misericordia, -ae — sympathy

protinus — at once

strangulo, -are — execute

aditus, -ūs — approach

excutio, -ere — frisk, pat down

inedia, -ae — starvation

intercedo, -ere — pass

sustento, -are — sustain

curiosē — attentively

observo, -are — observe

exserto, -ere — take out

uber, -ris — breast

subsidium, -i — assistance

lenio, -ire — ease

spectaculum, -i — spectacle

novitas, -tatis — novelty

perlata < perfero

remissio, -nis — reprieve

excogito, -are — contrive

inusitatus, -a, -um — unusual

inauditus, -a, -um — unheard of

alitam esse < alo

READING FOR UNDERSTANDING

1. *Why isn't the woman executed outright?*
2. *Why should the filial piety (and ingenuity) of her daughter be grounds for the mother's legal pardon?*
3. *The author's reference to the* **lex naturae** *argues that an inversion isn't always a perversion. Do you agree with the author's praise for this story's outcome?*

5.

The daughter of one of Rome's most famous orators speaks out against a measure of the Second Triumvirate targeting only women (1st century BCE).

READING FOR INFORMATION

1. Why did Hortensia agree to speak on behalf of Roman matrons?
2. Why was her appeal successful?
3. Why was her speech in a sense a reproach of her male relations?

cum: 16.I.1
tributo: 3.V.7
virorum: 3.II.2
eis: 3.III.3

ut: 16.III.1

pecuniae: 3.II.2
his: 3.III.1
stirpe: 3.V.7
verbis: 3.III.7
si: 18.I.3

Hortensia vērō, Q. Hortensii filia, cum ordo matronarum gravi tributo a Triumviris esset oneratus nec quisquam virorum patrocinium eis accommodare audēret, causam feminarum apud Triumviros et constanter et feliciter egit: repraesentatā enim patris facundiā, impetravit ut maior pars imperatae pecuniae his remitteretur. Revixit tum muliebri stirpe Q. Hortensius verbisque filiae aspiravit; cuius si virilis sexūs posteri viam sequi voluissent, Hortensianae eloquentiae tanta hereditas unā actione feminae abscissa non esset.

tributum, -i — tax	**revivo, -ere** — live again	**hereditas, -tatis** — inheritance
onero, -are — encumber	**stirps, -pis** — offspring	
patricinium, -i — advocacy	**aspiro, -are** — favor	**actio, -nis** — declamation
accommodo, -are — provide	**virilis, -e** — masculine	**abscindo, -ere** — break off
repraesento, -are — reflect	**sexus, -ūs** — gender	
facundia, -ae — eloquence	**posteri, -orum** — posterity	

READING FOR UNDERSTANDING

1. Is there anything in this account that suggests eloquence is an inheritable trait?
2. Why would the Triumvirs, in a period of civil war, want to tax Roman matrons?
3. Why, in a period of civil war, would Roman matrons want to protect their assets?

6.

This incident from 246 BCE, during the First Punic War, involves both class conflict (the Appii Claudii were patricians) and the censorship of women's speech.

READING FOR INFORMATION

1. What was Appia doing out in public? What happened to her there?
2. How had Appia's brother recently died? Did he die alone?
3. What was the consequence of her careless speech?

vindicatum est: 20.III.4

cum: 16.I.3.a
habitam esse: 12.I.3.d
me: 3.V.10
quanto: 3.V.9
si: 18.I.3

Non in facta modo, sed in voces etiam petulantiores publicē vindicatum est; ita enim debēre esse visa est Romanae disciplinae dignitas inviolabilis. Appia namque illius Caeci filia, a ludis, quos spectaverat, exiens, turbā undique confluentis fluctuantisque populi iactata est. Atque inde egressa, cum se male habitam esse diceret: "Quid me nunc factum esset," inquit, "quantoque artius pressiusque conflictata essem, si P. Claudius,

proelio: 3.V.7
cum: 3.V.4

utinam: 15.IV

perditum: 17.I.1

factum esse:
   12.I.3.d
Fabio . . .
   consulibus: 13.VI

frater meus, navali proelio classem navium cum ingenti civium numero non perdidisset? Certē quidem maiore nunc copiā populi oppressa intercidissem. Sed utinam," inquit, "reviviscat frater aliamque classem in Siciliam ducat atque istam multitudinem perditum eat, quae me nunc male miseram convexavit!" Ob haec mulieris verba tam improba ac tam incivilia C. Fundanius et Tiberius Sempronius, aediles plebei, multam dixerunt ei aeris gravis viginti quinque milia. Id factum esse dicit Capito Ateius bello Poenico primo, Fabio Licino Otacilio Crasso consulibus.

petulans, -tis — impudent
dignitas, -tatis — dignity
inviolabilis, -e — inviolable
undique — on all sides
confluo, -ere — flow together
fluctuo, -are — swell
iacto, -are — jostle
artē — tightly

pressē — closely
conflictor, -ari — struggle
navalis, -e — naval
copia, -ae — multitude
opprimo, -ere — beleaguer
intercido, -ere — perish
revivisco, -ere — come to life
   again

classis, -is — fleet
multitudo, -dinis — mob
convexo, -are — disturb
incivilis, -e — uncivil
aedilis plebei — city
   commissioners
multa, -ae — fine
aes gravis — solid copper

READING FOR UNDERSTANDING

1. As you read them, do the words of Appia, as extensively quoted here, resemble the offhand remarks of one exiting a theater?
2. The author suggests that annoyance and discomfort motivated Appia's speech. Can you imagine her speaking out in an attempt—tactless and insensitive, to be sure—at humor?
3. In Roman naval warfare, almost all casualties were plebeians, few were patricians, and none was a woman. Does this have any bearing on the outrage against Appia?
4. Do you think Appia should have been punished for her speech act?

7.

This passage examines the practices of divorce and concubinage. The first recorded divorce in Rome—an interesting case—didn't take place until 231 BCE. On the other hand, Roman men kept concubines from an early date.

READING FOR INFORMATION

1. Why, early on, was there no need for prenups?
2. Why did Carvilius divorce his wife? Was something wrong with her? Did he want to divorce her?
3. What oath did censors require husbands to take?
4. King Numa Pompilius prescribed what penalty for a concubine who touched the temple of Juno, the temple of legitimate marriage?

memoriae: 3.V.1
annis: 4.II.2
actions neque
    cautiones: 3.IV.3
nihil: 3.IV.7
matrimoniis
    divertentibus:
    13.III.2
cum: 16.I.4
quia: 16.XIII.3.b
vitio: 3.V.7
M. . . . consulibus:
    13.VI
dilexisse, habuisse,
    praevertisse:
    12.I.3.d
gratiā: 8.III
animo atque amori:
    3.III.7
a: 3.V.2
uxorem: 3.IV.1
se: 3.IV.4
quaerundorum: 17.V
habiturum esse:
    12.I.3.d
iuncta . . . esset: 16.XI
causā: 8.III
foret: 16.XI; 10.III.7.a
ne: 19.III.1
tangito: 19.II
Iunoni: 3.III.3
crinibus demissis:
    13.III.1
caedito: 19.II

Memoriae traditum est quingentis ferē annis post Romam conditam nullas rei uxoriae neque actiones neque cautiones in urbe Romā aut in Latio fuisse, quoniam profectō nihil desiderabantur, nullis etiamtunc matrimoniis divertentibus. Servius quoque Sulpicius in libro, quem composuit *De Dotibus*, tum primum cautiones rei uxoriae necessarias esse visas scripsit, cum Spurius Carvilius, vir nobilis, divortium cum uxore fecit, quia liberi ex eā corporis vitio non gignerentur, anno urbis conditae quingentesimo vicesimo tertio M. Atilio P. Valerio consulibus. Atque is Carvilius traditur uxorem, quam dimisit, egregiē dilexisse carissimamque morum eius gratiā habuisse, sed iuris iurandi religionem animo atque amori praevertisse, quod iurare a censoribus coactus erat, uxorem se liberorum quaerundorum gratiā habiturum esse. "Paelicem" autem appellatam esse probrosamque habitam esse, quae iuncta consuetaque esset cum eo, in cuius manū mancipioque alia femina matrimonii causā foret, hac antiquissimā lege ostenditur, quam Numae regis fuisse accepimus: "Paelex aedem Iunonis ne tangito; si tangit, Iunoni crinibus demissis agnum feminam caedito."

quingenti, -ae, -a — five hundred

ferē — nearly

res uxoria — property belonging to a wife

actio, -nis — law case

cautio, -nis — bond

profectō — actually

etiamtunc — even then

diverto, -ere — go astray

divortium, -i — divorce

gigno, -ere — produce

ius, iurandum — oath

praeverto, -ere — take precedence over

censor, -ris — high magistrate

liberi, -orum — children

paelex, -icis — concubine

probosus, -a, -um — ignominious

mancipium, -i — ownership

Numa — Rome's second king

crinis, -is — hair

demitto, -ere — unbind, lower

agnus, -i — lamb

READING FOR UNDERSTANDING

1. *From a legal standpoint, infertility represented unimpeachable grounds for divorce and was attributed solely to the wife. Furthermore, the marriage oath that the censors required essentially made childbearing the only social and legal purpose of marriage. What emotional and sexual outlets were available to Roman women who didn't want to have children?*

2. *Socially and legally, it was difficult for Roman women of citizen status to become concubines. What emotional and sexual outlets were available to those who didn't want to marry?*

3. *Dowries and prenuptial contracts imposed considerable financial burdens on the fathers and husbands of Roman women. What reliable options would have been available to women who were determined either to divorce or never to marry?*

8.

This anecdote about Cornelia, the mother of the famous Gracchi brothers (2nd century BCE), serves to introduce a discussion about wealth and noble poverty.

READING FOR INFORMATION

1. *What proud possession did the Campanian hostess show Cornelia?*
2. *What problems does the author see with material possessions?*
3. *What are the advantages of poverty?*

esse: 12.I.3.d
matronis: 3.III.3
cum: 16.I.3.a

donec:
16.XIII.3.a.i.B

Maxima ornamenta esse matronis liberos sīc invēnimus: Cornelia Gracchorum mater, cum Campana matrona apud illam hospita ornamenta sua, pulcherrima illius saeculi, ostenderet, traxit eam sermone, donec e scholā redirent liberi, et "Haec," inquit, "ornamenta sunt mea." Omnia nimirum habet qui nihil concupiscit, eō quidem certius quam qui cuncta possidet, quia dominium rerum collābi solet, bonae mentis usurpatio nullum tristioris Fortunae recipit incursum. Itaque quorsum attinet aut divitias in primā felicitatis parte aut paupertatem in ultimo miseriarum

cum: 16.I.1
amaritudinibus:
3.V.7
bonis: 3.V.10
quod: 7.V.2
personis, verbis:
3.V.1

statū ponere, cum et illarum frons hilaris multis intus amaritudinibus sit referta et huius horridior aspectus solidis et certis bonis abundet? Quod melius personis quam verbis repraesentabitur.

hospitus, -a, -um — strange
saeculum, -i — age
schola, -ae — school
nimirum — surely
concupisco, -ere — desire
possideo, -ēre — possess
dominium, -i — domination
collābor, -i — pass away

usurpatio, -nis — adoption
incursus, -ūs — assault
quorsum — for what? to what end?
divitiae, -arum — riches
paupertas, -tatis — poverty
hilaris, -e — happy

intus — within
amaritudo, -dinis — bitter feeling
refertus, -a, -um — crammed
horridus, -a, -um — grim
abundo, -are — abound
repraesento, -are — reflect

READING FOR UNDERSTANDING

1. *Although Roman literature often portrays women as greedy and acquisitive, Roman history more often shows men exhibiting these traits. How would you account for this disconnect?*
2. *Why is the goddess Fortuna called* **tristior**?
3. *Is there any significance in the fact that Romans considered Fortuna, wealth, and women equally fickle and unstable?*

9.

The Oppian Law (215 BCE), a fairly severe antisumptuary law, was passed at the height of the war against Hannibal, when all of Rome's resources were needed for the war effort. About a de-

cade after Rome had defeated Hannibal and public and private wealth had been restored, Roman women (and some Roman men) pressed for the repeal of this law, which they argued was no longer necessary.

READING FOR INFORMATION

1. *According to this account, Roman women held what opinion of the Oppian Law?*
2. *Did Roman men initially grasp the strength of the women's position?*
3. *Why is the author of this narrative reluctant to pursue the issue in greater detail?*

urbi: 3.III.1

abrogationi: 3.III.7

veste: 3.V.13

auri: 3.II.2
vehiculo: 3.V.1
passūs: 3.IV.3
gratiā: 8.III
ut: 16.II

tenderet, esset: 16.V
studium, audacia: 3.I.1
si: 18.I.3
novitatis: 3.II.2
sumptuosius: 6.I.2
luxuriae: 3.III.7
loquar: 15.III
quas: 3.IV.4
studium: 3.IV.1

sui: 7.III

Urbi autem nostrae secundi Punici belli finis et Philippus, Macedoniae rex devictus, licentioris vitae fiduciam dedit. Quo tempore matronae Brutorum domum ausae sunt obsidēre, qui abrogationi Legis Oppiae intercedere parati erant; quam feminae tolli cupiebant, quia his nec veste varii coloris uti nec auri plus semunciam habēre nec iuncto vehiculo propius urbem mille passūs nisi sacrificii gratiā vehi permittebat. Et quidem obtinuerunt ut ius per continuos viginti annos servatum abolēretur: non enim provīderunt saeculi illius viri ad quem cumulum tenderet insoliti cultūs pertinax studium aut quō se usque effusura esset, legum victrix, audacia. Quod si animi apparatūs muliebres intuēri potuissent, quibus cotidiē aliquid novitatis sumptuosius adiectum est, in ipso introitū ruenti luxuriae obstitissent. Sed quid ego de feminis ulterius loquar, quas et imbecillitas mentis et graviorum operum negata adfectatio omne studium ad curiosiorem sui cultum hortatur conferre?

devinco, -ere — defeat

licens, -ntis — unrestrained

fiducia, -ae — confidence

obsideo, -ēre — besiege

abrogatio, -nis — repeal

intercedo, -ere — intervene

semuncia, -ae — half an ounce

vehiculum, -i — vehicle

mille passūs = a mile

sacrificium, -i — sacrifice

obtineo, -ēre — assert

aboleo, -ēre — abolish

provideo, -ēre — foresee

cumulus, -i — accumulation

insolitus, -a, -um — unaccustomed

victrix, -tricis — conqueror

apparatus, -ūs — accessory

intueor, -ēri — keep watch over

novitas, -tatis — novelty

sumptuosē — lavishly

introitus, -ūs — advent

luxuria, -ae — luxury

obsto, -are — block

imbecillitas, -tatis — weakness

curiosus, -a, -um — attentive

READING FOR UNDERSTANDING

1. *What made the Oppian Law divisive between men and women?*
2. *Why, on its appearance, were men slow to recognize women's objections to this law?*
3. *Although the women finally succeeded in getting the law repealed, the author fails to credit them with a political success and instead suggests that their cupidity prevailed. If the author's reaction was typical, how do you suppose the women viewed their success?*

10.

This narrative outlines the Latin practice of betrothal followed until 90 BCE. The procedures are specifically described from a technical and legal perspective.

READING FOR INFORMATION

1. What were the contents of the contract that constituted the betrothal agreement?
2. After such an agreement, what happened if the marriage didn't take place?
3. What kinds of consequences were there for an unfulfilled betrothal agreement?

solita esse: 12.I.3.d
fieri: 12.I.3.b
ducturus erat: 17.VI
ducenda erat: 17.IV
datum iri: 12.I

ducturum esse: 17.VI
si: 18.I.1

esset: 16.V

causae: 3.II.2
quanti: 3.II.7

observatum esse: 12.I.3.d
Latio: 3.III.1

Sponsalia in eā parte Italiae, quae Latium appellatur, hōc more atque iure solita esse fieri scripsit Servius Sulpicius in libro, quem inscripsit *De Dotibus*: "Qui uxorem," inquit, "ducturus erat, ab eo, unde ducenda erat, stipulabatur eam in matrimonium datum iri; qui ducturus erat, itidem spondebat. Is contractus stipulationum sponsionumque dicebatur 'sponsalia.' Tunc, quae promissa erat, 'sponsa' appellabatur; qui spoponderat se ducturum esse, 'sponsus.' Sed si post eas stipulationes uxor non dabatur aut non ducebatur, qui stipulabatur aut qui spoponderat, ex sponsū agebat. Iudices cognoscebant. Iudex quamobrem data acceptave non esset uxor quaerebat. Si nihil iustae causae videbatur, litem pecuniā aestimabat, quantique interfuerat eam uxorem accipi aut dari, eum, qui spoponderat, aut ei, qui stipulatus erat, condemnabat." Hoc ius sponsaliorum observatum esse dicit Servius ad id tempus, quo civitas universo Latio lege Iuliā data est.

sponsalia, -ium — betrothal	**stipulatio, -nis** — stipulation	**quamobrem** — why
stipulor, -ari — bargain, stipulate	**sponsio, -nis** — pledge	**aestimo, -are** — judge, assess
itidem — likewise	**sponsa, -ae** — fiancée	**condemno, -are** — convict
spondeo, -ēre — pledge	**sponsus, -i** — fiancé	**observo, -are** — observe
contractus, -ūs — contract	**sponsus, -ūs** — down payment, security deposit	

READING FOR UNDERSTANDING

1. Does the creation of such legal specifics suggest that the breach of betrothal agreements was a rare or a common occurrence? What does the preservation of the specifics here suggest?
2. Does the fact that all legal consequences for unfulfilled betrothal agreements were monetary simply make marriageable women a commodity?
3. After 90 BCE, the Latins had to comply with the Roman laws on betrothal, which stated that a breach of a betrothal agreement had to go to court only if a party felt legally aggrieved. Do you think this Roman legal dispensation made it easier for parties to enter into and renege on betrothal agreements?
4. From what you can tell, who benefited from betrothal agreements?

11.

This passage takes up, in highly moralistic tones, two topics concerning the practices of women: how they eat at the dinner table and whether they should remarry.

READING FOR INFORMATION

1. *How has the custom of men and women dining together changed up to the author's time?*
2. *In the Capitoline temple, how are Jupiter, Juno, and Minerva represented as they dine?*
3. *What is the criticism leveled here against women who have married multiple times?*

cum: 3.V.4
quae: 7.V.2

Feminae cum viris cubantibus sedentes cenabant. Quae consuetudo ex hominum convīctū ad divina penetravit: nam Iovis epulo ipse in lectulum, Iuno et Minerva in sellas ad cenam invitabantur. Quod genus severitatis

diligentius: 6.II

aetas nostra diligentius in Capitolio quam in suis domibus conservat,

disciplinam: 3.IV.4

videlicet quia magis ad rem pertinet dearum quam mulierum disciplinam continēri. Quae feminae uno contentae matrimonio fuerant coronā pudicitiae honorabantur: existimabant enim eum praecipuē matronae sincerā fide incorruptum esse animum, qui depositae virginitatis cubile

nesciret: 16.XI
experientiam: 3.IV.4
signum: 3.IV.4.a

egredi nesciret, multorum matrimoniorum experientiam quasi legitimae cuiusdam intemperantiae signum esse credentes.

ceno, -are — dine	**conservo, -are** — preserve	**virginitas, -tatis** — virginity
consuetudo, -dinis — custom	**videlicet** — evidently	**egredior, -i** — exit
convīctus, -ūs — banquet	**honoro, -are** — honor	**experientia, -ae** — experience
epulo, -nis — party friend	**incorruptus, -a, -um** — uncorrupted	**intemperantia, -ae** — lack of self-restraint
sella, -ae — chair		

READING FOR UNDERSTANDING

1. *The remark **videlicet . . . continēri** was clearly written in sarcasm, a form of humor the Romans didn't often employ. What emotion(s) would produce such a response to the subject?*
2. *Why is women's posture at the dinner table portrayed as a moral issue?*
3. *The logic concerning women who marry only once and women who have married multiple times is not applied to men in this passage. Why not?*

12.

This passage discusses women's abstinence from wine, along with their sexual fidelity and their special goddess, Viriplaca (Husband-Appeaser).

READING FOR INFORMATION

1. *Why were Roman women denied wine in the olden days?*

2. *How did Roman wives in those days try to make themselves more attractive to their husbands?*

3. *When husbands and wives quarreled, where did they go to be reconciled?*

feminis: 3.III.2
ne: 16.III.1

ut: 16.III.1

indulgentibus ...
 maritis: 13.III.2
auro, purpurā:
 3.V.13
quō: 16.III.2.c
concinniorem: 6.I
summā ...
 diligentiā: 3.V.3
cinere: 3.V.1
rutilarunt: 20.I.3
matrimoniorum:
 3.II.6.a
pudore: 3.V.3
iurgii: 3.II.2
contentione ...
 deposita: 13.III.1
placandis: 17.III
veneranda,
 colenda: 17.III
sacrificiis: 3.V.1
maiestati: 3.III.3
a: 3.V.2

Vini usus olim Romanis feminis ignotus fuit, ne scilicet in aliquod dedecus prolāberentur, quia proximus a Libero patre intemperantiae gradus ad inconcessam Venerem esse consuevit. Ceterum ut non tristis earum et horrida pudicitia, sed honesto comitatis genere temperata esset—indulgentibus namque maritis et auro abundanti et multā purpurā usae sunt—quō formam suam concinniorem efficerent, summā cum diligentiā capillos cinere rutilarunt: nulli enim tunc subsessorum alienorum matrimoniorum oculi metuebantur, sed pariter et vidēre sanctē et aspici mutuo pudore custodiebatur. Quotiens verō inter virum et uxorem aliquid iurgii intercesserat, in sacellum deae Viriplacae, quod est in Palatio, veniebant, et ibi invicem locuti quae voluerant, contentione animorum depositā, concordes revertebantur. Dea nomen hoc a placandis viris fertur adsecuta esse, veneranda quidem et nescio an praecipuis et exquisitis sacrificiis colenda utpote cotidianae ac domesticae pacis custos, in pari iugo caritatis ipsā sui appellatione virorum maiestati debitum a feminis reddens honorem.

ignotus, -a, -um — unknown
scilicet — obviously
dedecus, -coris — disgrace
prolābor, -i — fall
Liber, -eri = Bacchus
intemperantia, -ae — lack of self-restraint
inconcessus, -a, -um — unallowed
ceterum — besides
comitas, -tatis — kindness

tempero, -are — temper
abundo, -are — abound
purpura, -ae — purple
concinnus, -a, -um — pleasing
rutilo, -are — redden
subsessor, -ris — ambusher
iurgium, -i — quarrel
intercedo, -ere — come between
sacellum, -i — shrine

invicem — one after the other
contentio, -nis — contention
concors, -rdis — reconciled
placo, -are — placate
adsequor, -i — follow
exquisitus, -a, -um — expensive
utpote — as being
cotidianus, -a, -um — everyday
appellatio, -nis — name

READING FOR UNDERSTANDING

1. *The author refers to the marital* **iugum caritatis** *as* **par**. *What evidence to the contrary do you see in this passage?*

2. *If there is a direct correlation between alcohol consumption and sexual activity, why would Roman husbands deny their wives wine?*

3. *The goddess Viriplaca, praised highly here, is attested nowhere else in all of Roman literature and artifacts. If the author invented her, what was his purpose?*

13.

Here another author connects women's wine drinking and sexual infidelity. In a nasty juxtaposition, he further asserts the legal right of a husband to kill an adulterous wife.

READING FOR INFORMATION

1. Why were women expected to kiss their relatives?
2. How did women try to disguise their drinking?
3. According to M. Cato, the legal consequence of a woman's wine drinking was the same as that for what other infraction?
4. M. Cato asserts that when a man is divorcing his wife, he assumes the responsibilities of what Roman magistrate?

Romae: 4.I.3
eas: 3.IV.4
abstinuisse, institutum esse: 12.I.3.d
ut: 16.IV
cognatis: 3.III.3
ut: 16.III.1
bibissent: 16.XI
bibere: 12.I.3.b
solitas esse: 12.I.3.d
genus: 3.IV.1
pōtū: 3.V.7
libris: 3.V.1
admisissent: 18.I.3
uxores: 3.IV.1
maritis: 3.III.3
cum: 16.I.4
mulieri: 3.III.3
si: 18.I.1
quid: 7.VI.1.a
a: 3.V.2
si: 18.I.1
si: 18.I.1
probri: 3.II.2
quid: 7.VI.1.a
occidendi: 17.II
si: 18.I.2.b.i
si: 18.I.2.b
adulterere: 20.I.1
digito: 3.V.1

Qui de vīctū atque cultū populi Romani scripserunt, mulieres Romae atque in Latio aetatem abstemias egisse, hoc est, eas vino semper abstinuisse dicunt, institutumque esse ut cognatis osculum ferrent deprehendendi causā, ut odor indicium faceret, si bibissent. Bibere autem solitas esse ferunt loream, passum, murrinam et quae id genus sapiant pōtū dulcia. Atque haec quidem in his, de quibus dixi, libris pervulgata sunt; sed Marcus Cato non solum existimatas, set et multatas esse quōque a iudice mulieres refert non minus, si vinum in se, quam si probrum et adulterium admisissent. Verba Marci Catonis adscripsi ex oratione quadam, in qua id quoque scriptum est, in adulterio uxores deprehensas ius fuisse maritis necare: "Vir," inquit, "cum divortium fecit, mulieri iudex pro censore est, et imperium, quod videtur, habet, si quid perversē taetrēque factum est a muliere; multatur, si vinum bibit; si probri quid cum alieno viro fecit, condemnatur." De iure autem occidendi ita scriptum est: "In adulterio uxorem tuam si prehenderīs, sine iudicio impune neces; illa te, si adulteres sive tu adulterere, digito non audeat contingere, neque ius est."

---

vīctus, -ūs — way of life

abstemius, -a, -um — abstinent

abstineo, -ēre — abstain

cognatus, -i — relative

lorea, -ae — refined wine

passum, -i — raisin wine

murrina, -ae — spiced wine

pōtus, -ūs — drinking

pervulgo, -are — publish

set = sed

multo, -are — fine

probrum, -i — disgrace

admitto, -ere — be guilty of

divortium, -i — divorce

censor, -ris — high magistrate

perversē — wickedly

taetrē — shamefully

condemno, -are — condemn

prehendo, -ere — apprehend

impune — without punishment

adultero, -are — commit adultery

READING FOR UNDERSTANDING

1. *How do you explain the author's claims that (a) ancient Roman women didn't drink wine, (b) relatives monitored them by smelling their breath, and (c) they avoided detection by drinking other types of wine?*

2. *How do you explain the jurisprudence of a law that permits a husband to kill an adulterous wife but grants an adulterous husband complete impunity?*

3. *Though the murder of an adulterous wife may have been a justifiable homicide, do you suppose many men actually killed their wives?*

14.

This passage, excerpted from a Roman medical writer, describes "hysteria," the condition sometimes referred to as the wandering uterus. The quality of Roman gynecology is revealed here as the author explains the symptoms, treatments, and prevention of this "disease."

READING FOR INFORMATION

1. *"Wandering uterus" is compared to what other affliction?*
2. *What single abstention is recommended for this condition?*
3. *What now outdated treatments are found here?*

feminis: 3.III.3	Ex vulvā quoque feminis vehemens malum nascitur proximēque ab stomacho vel adficitur haec vel corpus adficit. Interdum etiam sīc exanimat,
ut tamquam: 16.XIII.1.b **morbo**: 3.V.7 **eo**: 3.V.19 **feminis**: 3.III.3	ut tamquam comitiali morbo prosternat. Distat tamen hic casus eo, quod neque oculi vertuntur nec spumae profluunt nec nervi distenduntur: sopor tantum est. Idque quibusdam feminis crebrō revertens perpetuum
virium: 3.II.2	est. Ubi incidit, si satis virium est, sanguis missus adiuvat; si parum est,
defigendae sunt: 17.III **ut**: 16.III.1	cucurbitulae tamen defigendae sunt in inguinibus. Ut mulierem excitet aquae frigidae perfusio efficit. Adiuvatque ruta contrita cum melle, vel ex
naturalibus: 3.III.7 **pube**: 8.IV **tenus**: 8.II.2 **ubi**: 16.XIII.2.a **circumcidendum**: 17.IV	cyprino ceratum, vel quodlibet calidum et umidum cataplasma naturalibus pube tenus impositum. Deinde ubi ad se redit, circumcidendum vinum est in totum annum, etiamsi casus īdem non revertitur. Si durities manet, mollire commodē videtur solanum in lac demissum, deinde contritum, et cera alba atque medulla cervina cum irino, aut sebum taurinum vel caprinum cum rosā mixtum.

vulva, -ae — vagina	**comitialis morbus** — epilepsy	**nervus, -i** — muscle
vehemens, -ntis — violent	**prosterno, -are** — lay low	**distendo, -ere** — tense
stomachus, -i — belly	**disto, -are** — differ	**sopor, -ris** — loss of
adficio, -ere — affect	**spuma, -ae** — frothing	consciousness
exanimo, -are — grow weak	**profluo, -ere** — come out	**incido, -ere** — occur

adiuvo, -are — benefit

cucurbitula, -ae — small cupping

defigo, -ere — attach

inguen, -inis — groin

perfusio, -nis — submersion

ruta, -ae — rue plant

contrita < contero

mel, mellis — honey

cyprinum, -i — henna oil

ceratus, -a, -um — waxed

calidus, -a, -um — warm

umidus, -a, -um — moist

cataplasma, -matis — plaster, poultice

naturalia, -ium — private parts

pubes, -is — pubic area

circumcido, -ere — cut out

durities, -ei — hardness

mollio, -ire — soften

commodē — suitably

solanum, -i — nightshade

demitto, -ere — soak

cera, -ae — wax

medulla, -ae — marrow

cervinus, -a, -um — from a deer

irinum, -i — iris ointment

sebum, -i — fat

taurinus, -a, -um — from an ox

caprinus, -a, -um — from a goat

As the passage continues, we learn how an affected uterus should be treated, how nosebleeds may be a gynecological problem, and finally what pessary (vaginal suppository) should be used to prevent hysteria.

READING FOR INFORMATION

1. *Which flower is employed most in the treatment of hysteria?*
2. *In what way is sulfur used in treatment?*
3. *Cupping is applied to what parts of an affected woman?*
4. *If a hysterical woman also experiences nosebleeds, with what frequency should cupping be administered?*

purgetur: 15.I
misceatur, apponatur: 15.I
quō: 16.III.2.c
adiecto . . . pulvere: 13.III.1
si: 18.I.1
mulieri: 3.III.5
remedio: 3.III.9
cute incisā: 13.III.1
inguinibus: 3.III.7
si: 18.I.4
eruperit: 18.I.2.b
apponenda est: 17.IV
die: 3.V.6
repetieris: 20.I.3; 19.V.1
scias: 15.II
sanasse: 20.I.3
si: 18.I.4
ei: 3.III.3
emittendus est: 17.III
curasti: 20.I.3
vitio: 3.V.7
comburendae conterendaeque sunt: 17.IV
adiciendum est: 17.IV

Si parum pura est, purgetur iunco quadrato. Si vero vulva exulcerata est, ceratum ex rosā fiet, ei recens suilla adeps et ex ōvis album misceatur, idque apponatur; vel album ex ōvo cum rosā mixtum, adiecto, quō facilius consistat, contritae rosae pulvere. Dolens vero ea sulpure suffumigari debet. At si purgatio nimia mulieri nocet, remedio sunt cucurbitulae cute incisā inguinibus vel etiam sub mammis admotae. Si vero sanguis, qui ex inferiore parte erumpere solet, is ex naribus eruperit, incisis inguinibus apponenda est cucurbita idque per tres vel quattuor menses tricesimo quōque die repetieris: tunc scias hoc vitium sanasse. Si vero non se sanguis ostenderit, scias ei dolores capitis surgere. Tunc ex bracchio ei sanguis emittendus est et statim curasti eam. Si concidere vitio locorum mulier solet, cocleae cum testis suis comburendae conterendaeque sunt, deinde his mel adiciendum est.

vulva, -ae — vagina

purgo, -are — cleanse

iuncus, -i — thin cattail

quadratus, -a, -um — quartered

exulcero, -are — ulcerate

ceratus, -a, -um — waxed

suillus, -a, -um — from a pig

adeps, -ipis — fat

consisto, -ere — stick, cohere

contritae < contero

pulvis, -veris — powder

sulpur, -ris — sulfur

suffumigo, -are — fumigate from below

purgatio, -nis — menstruation

cucurbitula, -ae — small cupping

cutis, -is — skin

incido, -ere — cut

inguen, -inis — groin

mamma, -ae — breast

naris, -is — nostril

cucurbita, -ae — cupping

tricesimus, -a, -um — thirtieth

repeto, -ere — repeat

sano, -are — cure, heal

concido, -ere — collapse

loci, -orum — private parts

coclea, -ae — snail

testa, -ae — shell

comburo, -ere — burn together

READING FOR UNDERSTANDING

1. Which strikes you as worse: the fact that the Romans had such a meager knowledge of basic female anatomy or the fact that their meager knowledge of basic bacteriology probably killed thousands and thousands of women?

2. If you were a Roman woman experiencing gynecological problems and had some knowledge of the "medical" methods of treatment, would you be inclined to consult a doctor? What alternatives might you have?

3. From diagnostic and therapeutic standpoints, hysteria shifted from a physiological to a psychological condition only relatively recently. Do you see any evidence in this passage that the Romans viewed hysteria as more than just a medical condition?

Verse Readings

1.

"Beauty and the Beast": A Brother and Sister
A father instructs his son and daughter, the former handsome and haughty, the latter unpretty and mean, how to resolve their sibling rivalry.

READING FOR INFORMATION

1. Where did the siblings find the mirror in which they discovered their differing looks?
2. Whose feelings were hurt first?
3. Did the father praise one child and rebuke the other? What did he order both children to do?

monitūs: 3.IV.1	Praecepto monitūs saepe te considera.
praecepto . . . te: 13.III.2	Habebat quidam filiam turpissimam,
pulchrā facie: 3.V.5	īdemque insignem pulchrā facie filium.
ut: 16.XIII.2.a	Hi speculum, in cathedrā matris ut positum fuit,
	pueriliter ludentes forte inspexerunt. 5
	Hic se formosum iactat; illa irascitur
	nec gloriantis sustinet fratris iocos,

accipiens—quid enim?—cuncta in contumeliam.

laesura: 12.II   Ergō ad patrem decurrit laesura invicem,

invidiā: 3.V.3   magnāque invidiā criminatur filium,   10

quod: 16.XIII   vir natus quod rem feminarum tetigerit.

Amplexus ille utrumque et carpens oscula

dulcemque in ambos caritatem partiens,

speculo: 3.V.13
uti: 12.I.3.b   "Cotidiē," inquit, "speculo vos uti volo,
ne: 16.III.1
malis: 3.V.7   tu formam ne corrumpas nequitiae malis,   15
ut: 16.III.1
moribus: 3.V.1   tu faciem ut istam moribus vincas bonis."

11. **vir natus**: though born male

praeceptus, -a, -um — advised by	**pueriliter** — childishly	**amplector, -i** — hug
monitus, -ūs — warning	**glorior, -ari** — boast	**partior, -iri** — dole out
speculum, -i — mirror	**decurro, -ere** — run off	**corrumpo, -ere** — ruin
cathedra, -ae — chair	**invicem** — in turn	**nequitia, -ae** — wickedness
	criminor, -ari — accuse	

READING FOR UNDERSTANDING

1. *Does the father's command make sense? If the children do what he orders, will the effects necessarily be as he describes?*
2. *How would the lessons of this tale have been different if the daughter were beautiful and the son ugly?*
3. *The poet instructs his readers to ponder this tale often. What lesson does it hold for readers neither beautiful nor ugly?*

2.

"Somebody's Gonna Get Hurt": The Two Rival Women
Vanity of a competitive sort has a strange (and comical) effect.

READING FOR INFORMATION

1. *The opening couplet states that the theme of this poem is what?*
2. *What is the major difference between the two women who compete for the same lover?*
3. *What does each one do to improve her situation with him?*
4. *What is the outcome?*

a: 3.V.2   A feminis utroque spoliari viros,
spoliari: 12.I.3.d
amentve amentur: amentve amentur, nempe exemplis discimus.
  16.XI
aetatis: 3.II.3   Aetatis mediae quendam mulier non rudis

tenebat, annos celans elegantiā;

animosque eiusdem pulchra iuvenis ceperat.   5

illi: 3.III.2   Ambae, vidēri dum volunt illi pares,

homini: 3.III.3
coepēre: 20.I.2
putaret: 15.II
curā: 3.V.7

capillos homini legere coepēre invicem.
Quī se putaret fingi curā mulierum,
calvus repente factus est; nam funditus
canos puella, nigros anus evellerat.   10

spolio, -are — plunder   **invicem** — each in turn   **repente** — suddenly

nempe — recently   **quī** — somehow   **funditus** — roots and all

rudis, -e — uncharming   **fingo, -ere** — groom   **canus, -a, -um** — gray

celo, -are — conceal   **calvus, -a, -um** — bald   **evellero, -are** — pluck out

READING FOR UNDERSTANDING

1. *Why doesn't this story narrate the outcome of the women's competition apart from the man's baldness?*

2. *Which parts of the story are credible? Which are not?*

3. *How does this story bear out the opening premise that men are always plundered or despoiled by women?*

3.

"No Good Can Come from Bad": A Wife and Husband at Childbirth
This clever anecdote delivers a punch line that could be used on a TV sitcom today.

Nemo libenter recolit qui laesit locum.

instante partū:
13.III.2
actis mensibus:
13.III.1
humi: 4.I.3
flebilis: 5.II.2.d
(ut) reciperet: 16.IV
melius quō:
16.III.2.c
loco: 3.V.18
malum: 3.IV.4
finiri: 12.I.3.d

Instante partū, mulier actis mensibus
humi iacebat, flebilīs gemitūs ciens.
Vir est hortatus, corpus lecto reciperet,
onus naturae melius quō deponeret.   5
"Minimē," inquit, "illo posse confido loco
malum finiri quo conceptum est initium."

recolo, -ere — revisit   **cieo, -ēre** — summon   **confido, -ere** — believe, trust

insto, -are — press   **onus, -neris** — burden   **finio, -ire** — end

flebilis, -e — tearful

READING FOR UNDERSTANDING

1. *Does the suggestion of the husband seem to you to contain any motive other than love and concern for his wife?*

2. *If the wife's reaction seems snappish, what could explain that? Would the typical adult Roman male have firsthand knowledge of childbirth?*

3. *Rewrite the last couplet in English, offering a punchy comedic one-liner appropriate for a modern audience.*

4.

"Gossip Girls": Juno, Venus, and the Hen

READING FOR INFORMATION

1. *What assertion did Juno make before the other deities?*
2. *Was Venus's interview with the chicken intended as a serious rebuttal of Juno?*
3. *According to the hen, how much grain will cause her to stop scratching and pecking?*

cum: 16.I.3.a	Cum castitatem Iuno laudaret suam,	
dis et deabus: 3.III.3	dis et deabus adserens praesentibus	
mari: 3.III.7		
melius (esse): 12.I.3.d	mari coniungi melius uni feminam,	
feminam: 3.IV.4	iocunditatis causā non renuit Venus,	
ut: 16.III.1	nullamque ut adfirmaret esse illi parem,	5
illi: 3.III.2		
interrogasse: 20.I.3	interrogasse sīc gallinam dicitur:	
possis: 16.V	"Dic, sodes, quanto possis satiari cibo?"	
	Respondit illa, "Quidquid dederis, satis erit,	
ut: 16.II	sīc ut concedas pedibus aliquid scalpere."	
ne: 16.III.1	"Ne scalpas," inquit, "satis est modius tritici?"	10
permitte: 19.I	"Plan, immō nimium est, sed permitte scalpere."	
ne: 16.III.1	"Ex toto ne quid scalpas, quid desideras?"	
quid: 7.VI.1.a	Tum denique illa fassa est naturae malum:	
pateat: 15.II	"Licet horreum mi pateat, ego scalpam tamen."	
	Risisse Iuno dicitur Veneris iocos,	15
	quia per "gallinam" denotavit "feminas."	

castitas, -tatis — chastity	**interrogo, -are** — interrogate	**triticum, -i** — wheat
adsero, -ere — assert	**gallina, -ae** — chicken	**planē** — obviously
mas, maris — male	**sodes** = si audes	**immō** — rather
iocunditas, -tatis — amusement	**satio, -are** — satisfy	**fateor, -ēri** — admit
renuo, -ere — disagree	**scalpo, -ere** — scratch and peck	**horreum, -i** — granary
adfirmo, -are — affirm	**modius, -i** — peck	**pateo, -ēre** — lie open
		denoto, -are — mean

READING FOR UNDERSTANDING

1. *In line 8, the hen says that she's satisfied with whatever food she's given. So why does she scratch and peck?*
2. *Why does Juno laugh at Venus's rebuttal? Because it was effective? Because it was funny?*
3. *Do goddesses fall within the class of **feminae**? If Juno and Venus don't mind being compared to farm animals, should we?*

5.

In this poem, the poet (doubtless a man) gives advice to a woman about the nature of beauty.

READING FOR INFORMATION

1. *According to the poet, what should a woman cultivate in order to appear beautiful?*
2. *What is wrong with pure, unadulterated beauty?*

> Non est forma satis; nec, quae vult bella vidēri,
>   debet vulgari more placēre sibi.
> Dicta, sales, lusus, sermonis gratia, risus
>   vindicant naturae candidioris opus.
> Condit enim formam, quidquid tibi sumitur artis,   5
>   et, nisi sal superest, gratia nuda perit.

more: 3.V.1
candidioris: 6.I
artis: 5.II.2
nisi: 18.I.1

bellus, -a, -um — pretty
vulgaris, -e — vulgar
sal, salis — witticism, wit

lusus, -ūs — game playing
condio, -ire — season

supersum, -esse — be abundantly present

READING FOR UNDERSTANDING

1. *What do you suppose the poet means by **mos vulgaris** (line 2)?*
2. *What do you suppose the poet means by **opus naturae candidioris** (line 4)?*
3. *When we say that someone or another is the latest It person, for all our vagueness, what do we mean?*

6.

The first of these maxims treat women quite objectively, but then the sententiae *become more tendentious.*

> Uxor legitimus debet quasi census amari:
> nec censum vellem semper amare meum.
>
> Aut amat aut odit mulier, nil est tertium.
>
> Feminae naturam regere desperare est otium.
>
> Quae vult vidēri bella nimis, nulli negat.
>
> Multis placēre quae cupit, culpam cupit.
>
> Uxoris linguam, si frugi est, ferre memento;
> namque malum est, non velle pati nec posse tacēre.

vellem: 15.II

regere: 3.I.1
desperare: 3.I.2
otium: 3.IV.1

nulli: 3.III.1

memento: 19.II
pati, tacēre: 12.I.3.d

Adulter est uxoris amator acrior.

animo, oculo: 3.V.1   Animo virum pudicae, non oculo eligunt.

parendo: 17.II   Casta ad virum matrona parendo imperat.

invenias: 15.II   Nulla tam bona uxor, de qua non invenias quid queri.

Apertē mala cum est mulier, tum demum est bona.

Muliebre est furere in irā.

ne: 16.III.1   Uxorem fuge ne ducas sub nomine dotis,
si: 18.I.2.b   nec retinēre velis, si coeperit esse molesta.

didicēre: 20.I.2   Didicēre flēre feminae in mendacium.

Malo in consilio feminae vincunt viros.

cum: 16.I.3.a   Mulier cum sola cogitat, male cogitat.

Nil temerē uxori de servis crede querenti;
semper enim mulier, quem coniunx diligit, odit.

Mulier quae multis nubit, multis non placet.

Muliebris lacrima condimentum est malitiae.

noli: 19.III   Coniugis iratae noli tu verba timēre;
cum: 16.I.3.a   nam lacrimis struit insidias, cum femina plorat.

naufragium: 3.I.1   Naufragium rerum est mulier male fida marito.
marito: 3.III.2

vīrus: 3.IV.1   Mulier intrā pectus omnis celat vīrus pestilens:
corde: 3.V.3   dulce de labris loquuntur, corde vivunt noxio.

legitimus, -a, -um —
    legitimate
census, -ūs — income
despero, -are — give up on
bellus, -a, -um — pretty
culpa, -ae — fault

frugi — good, useful
memini, -isse — remember
acer, acris, acre — keen
eligo, -ere — choose
pareo, -ēre — comply
queror, -i — complain

furo, -ere — rage
molestus, -a, -um —
    troublesome
fleo, -ēre — cry
mendacium, -i —
    deceitfulness

temerē — rashly	**struo, -ere** — contrive	**vīrus, -i** (n) — virus
queror, -i — complain	**insidiae, -arum** — plots	**pestilens, -ntis** — deadly
condimentum, -i — condiment	**ploro, -are** — weep	**labrum, -i** — lip
malitia, -ae — wickedness	**naufragium, -i** — shipwreck	**noxius, -a, -um** — noxious
	intra — within	

READING FOR UNDERSTANDING

1. *What qualities or traits seem to make the authors of these aphorisms most anxious?*
2. *If the intent of these aphorisms was to entertain, would they have differed from, for example, blond jokes in our culture?*
3. *If there had been more female Roman authors and their works had survived, do you expect that we would have a comparable selection of aphorisms about men, boyfriends, and husbands?*

7.

In these two brief poems the poet criticizes the morality of two women (Telesilla in the 3rd person and Catulla in the 2nd). The poet addresses his friend Faustinus in the first poem.

READING FOR INFORMATION

1. *The Lex Iulia, which encouraged citizen marriage, had been restored for how many days before Telesilla's marriage?*
2. *Telesilla had married how many times before?*
3. *According to the poet, Telesilla is not a bride but a what?*

Iulia lex populis ex quo, Faustine, renata est
    atque intrare domos iussa Pudicitia est,
aut minus aut certē non plus tricesima lux est,
    et nubit decimo iam Telesilla viro.
Quae nubit totiens, non nubit: adultera lege est.   5
    Offendor moechā simpliciore minus.

viro: 3.III.5
lege: 3.V.10
moechā: 3.V.7

renascor, -i — revive	**totiens** — so often	**simplex, -plicis** — straightforward
tricesimus, -a, -um — thirtieth	**moecha, -ae** — adulteress	

READING FOR INFORMATION

1. *In what two respects is Catulla a standout?*
2. *What does the poet wish for Catulla?*

fuēre: 20.I.2

Formosissima quae fuēre vel sunt,
sed vilissima quae fuēre vel sunt,

vellem: 15.II   o quam te fieri, Catulla, vellem
                     formosam minus aut magis pudicam!

vilis, -e — cheap

READING FOR UNDERSTANDING
1. *Do you suppose that the poet would be less concerned with these women's morality if they were less sexually desirable?*
2. *On what argument is a multiply married woman the same as an adulteress? Is this argument valid?*
3. *Which do you suppose is more effective in protecting public morality, the authority of law or the authority of popular literature?*

8.

*The next poem is a cute parody of funerary epitaphs dedicated throughout the Roman world to **univirae**, women who could boast that they had been married to only one man. The comedy of this parody is powered by exaggerations and, in the final line, a grossly inappropriate obscenity. Otherwise, the poem reads much like numerous surviving epitaphs.*

READING FOR INFORMATION
1. *This tomb is comparable to what two famous funerary monuments of the ancient world?*
2. *How many children did the woman produce?*
3. *What did her children do for her at her deathbed?*

cessura: 12.II   Marmora parva quidem, sed non cessura, viator,
saxis: 3.III.1   Mausoli saxis pyramidumque legis.
Tarento: 4.I.3   Bis mea Romano spectata est vita Tarento,
nihil: 3.IV.1   et nihil extremos perdidit ante rogos:
                     quinque dedit pueros, totidem mihi Iuno puellas,   5
lumina: 3.IV.1   clauserunt omnes lumina nostra manūs.
mihi: 3.III.7   Contigit et thalami mihi gloria rara fuitque
pudicitiae: 3.III.2   una pudicitiae mentula nōta meae.

marmor: -ris — marble	**pyramis, -midis** — pyramid	**totidem** — as many
viator, -ris — traveler	**Tarentum, -i** — hundred-year	**thalamus, -i** — bedchamber
Mausolus, -i — king of Caria,	festival	**mentula, -ae** — prick
occupant of the Mausoleum		

READING FOR UNDERSTANDING
1. *Why are the exaggerations of a hundred-plus-year life span and ten children who survive to adulthood successful in this poem?*

2. What is the effect of the juxtaposition of the words **pudicitia** and **mentula**? What's the effect of the word **mentula** counterbalancing the references to the Mausoleum and the Great Pyramids?

3. Who is the **viator** of this poem?

9.

This little poem is about (and to) a blue-blooded Roman matron who, in the course of lovemaking, uses Greek endearments in a manner that the poet finds whorish.

READING FOR INFORMATION

1. What neighborhood does Laelia come from?
2. To which two traditional Roman matrons does the poet refer?
3. Does the poet allow any sort of Greek learning?

cum: 16.I.2 tibi: 3.III.4	Cum tibi non Ephesos nec sit Rhodos aut Mitylene,
	sed domus in vico, Laelia, patricio,
	deque coloratis, numquam lita, mater Etruscis,
de: 3.V.18	durus Aricinā de regione pater;
	"κύριέ μου, μέλι μου, ψυχή μου," congeris usque 5
	—pro pudor!—Hersiliae civis et Egeriae.
audiat: 15.I	Lectulus has voces, nec lectulus audiat omnis,
viro: 3.III.3	sed quem lascivo stravit amica viro.
loquaris: 16.V	Scire cupis quo casta modo matrona loquaris?
cum: 16.I.3.b	Numquid, cum crisas, blandior esse potes? 10
ediscas, referas: 15.II	Tu licet ediscas totam referasque Corinthon,
	non tamen omninō, Laelia, Lais eris.

Ephesos, -i — Greek Asia Minor city

Rhodos, -i — Greek island

Mitylene, -ae — city on a Greek island

vicus, -i — neighborhood

patricius, -a, -um — patrician

coloratus, -a, -um — suntanned

lino, -ere — apply makeup

Aricinus, -a, -um — from Latin Aricia

Hersilia, -ae — wife of King Romulus

Egeria, -ae — companion of King Numa

lascivus, -a, -um — lusty

sterno, -ere — lay out

criso, -are — reach orgasm

edisco, -ere — learn about

Corinthos — Corinth (city in Greece)

omninō — entirely

READING FOR UNDERSTANDING

1. **Ephesos, Rhodos, Mitylene,** and **Corinthon** are all Greek case forms; the word **crisas** (line 10) is borrowed from Greek. Does it diminish the poet's point at all that he is pretty Greekified himself?

2. *The Greek that Laelia uses translates into "My lord, my honey, my soul." Does that seem excessive to you? What is the poet's real objection here: that Laelia's use of Greek is an affectation or that her words are unseemly for a proper Roman matron?*

3. *The wordplay in the final line with the names Laelia (a traditional and respectable Roman name) and Lais (a typical name for a Greek prostitute, made famous by two Corinthian hetaerae) is quite admirable. Can you come up with a comparable wordplay using one respectable and one disrespectable name?*

10.

The next three poems are said to have been written by the adolescent Sulpicia (second half of the 1st century BCE). They represent a great treasure, as they are some of the very few poems we have written by ancient Roman women. This first poem she wrote from her sickbed. It's addressed to her young lover Cerinthus.

tibi: 3.III.4 puellae: 3.III.3	Estne tibi, Cerinthe, tuae pia cura puellae, quod mea nunc vexat corpora fessa calor?
	A, ego non aliter tristes evincere morbos
optarim: 20.I.3 si: 18.I.2.b.i prosit: 15.II si: 18.I.4 pectore: 3.V.3	optarim, quam te si quoque velle putem. At mihi quid prosit morbos evincere, si tu 5 nostra potes lento pectore ferre mala?

vexo, -are — distress   **evinco, -ere** — overcome   **lentus, -a, -um** — sluggish

aliter — otherwise

READING FOR UNDERSTANDING

1. *How is the structure of this poem quite simple?*
2. *What is the effect of its question-statement-question arrangement?*
3. *How secure does the poet seem to be in Cerinthus's affections? Do you attribute this to her youth, to her illness, to her gendered role in society, or to an accurate appraisal of Cerinthus?*

The next poem, both naïve and sophisticated, shows the poet openly acknowledging her love—a love now requited by Cerinthus.

pudori: 3.III.9 nudasse: 20.I.3 alicui, mihi: 3.III.8	Tandem vēnit amor, qualem texisse pudori quam nudasse alicui sit mihi, Fama, magis.
Camenis: 3.V.7	Exorata meis illum Cytherea Camenis attulit in nostrum deposuitque sinum.
narret: 15.I	Exsolvit promissa Venus: mea gaudia narret, 5
si: 18.I.4 quis: 7.VI.1.a tabellis: 3.III.1	dicetur si quis non habuisse sua. Non ego signatis quicquam mandare tabellis,
ut: 16.III.1 velim: 15.II	me legat ut nemo quam meus ante, velim,

peccasse: 20.I.3
iuvat, taedet:
   20.III.5
cum: 16.I.3.b
digno: 3.V.16

sed peccasse iuvat, vultūs componere Famae

    taedet: cum digno digna fuisse ferar.   10

1–2. **qualem . . . magis:** such that, Reputation, it would be more shameful for me to hide than to expose to someone

nudo, -are — lay bare	**exsolvo, -ere** — fulfill	**pecco, -are** — do something
exoro, -are — beg, pray to	**signo, -are** — seal, sign	wrong
Cytherea = Venus	**mando, -are** — entrust	**taedet** — it's boring
Camenae = Muses	**tabella, -ae** — tablet	

READING FOR UNDERSTANDING

1. *The poem opens and closes with references to* **Fama**. *What is the best translation for this complex word in the present context?*

2. *Why does the poet credit the Muses and Venus for winning over Cerinthus, instead of just crediting herself?*

3. *Why does the poet want the joyless to recount her joys? Why is she unwilling for others to read of her love before Cerinthus does?*

4. *On the basis of this poem, what sort of intimacy does the poet appear to have shared with her lover?*

This last poem expresses a confused and bittersweet confession of Sulpicia's desire for her lover.

ne: 16.III.1
tibi: 3.III.3
lux: 3.VI
cura: 19.I

cuius: 3.II.6
fatear: 15.I
paenituisse:
   20.III.5.a
nocte: 3.V.6

Ne tibi sim, mea lux, aequē iam fervida cura

    ac videor paucos ante fuisse dies,

si quicquam totā commisi stultā iuventā,

    cuius me fatear paenituisse magis,

hesternā quam te solum quod nocte reliqui,   5

    ardorem cupiens dissimulare meum.

fervidus, -a, -um — feverish	**paenitet** — it causes shame	**dissimulo, -are** — disguise
committo, -ere — commit	**hesternus, -a, -um** —	
fateor, -ēri — confess	yesterday's	

READING FOR UNDERSTANDING

1. *How do the first couplet and the last couplet counterbalance each other?*

2. *What is the effect of the complicated syntax of this poem (a hortatory clause, a comparative clause, a relative clause, another comparative clause, a conditional clause, a causal clause, and participial and infinitive phrases, all in a single sentence)?*

3. *Judging by her poems, how old do you imagine Sulpicia to be? Would you characterize her writing as charming? Immature? Insightful? Simplistic? Heartfelt? Contrived?*

11.

The following poem was written in praise of the beautiful maiden Sulpicia.

READING FOR INFORMATION

1. *What is the occasion of this poem?*
2. *Where does Cupid/Amor get the fire to light his torches?*
3. *Is Sulpicia more attractive with her hair arranged or unarranged?*

tibi: 3.III.8 **kalendis:** 3.V.6 **spectatum:** 17.I.1 **veni:** 19.I **caveto:** 19.II	Sulpicia est tibi culta tuis, Mars magne, kalendis; spectatum e caelo, si sapis, ipse veni. Hoc Venus ignoscet; at tu, violente, caveto
ne: 16.III.1 **tibi:** 3.III.3 **cum:** 16.I.4	ne tibi miranti turpiter arma cadant. Illius ex oculis, cum vult exurere divos, 5 accendit geminas lampadas acer Amor.
	Illam, quidquid agit, quoquo vestigia movit, componit furtim subsequiturque Decor.
capillis: 3.V.14	Seu solvit crines, fusis decet esse capillis:
comis: 3.V.14	seu composit, comptis est veneranda comis. 10
	Urit, seu Tyriā voluit procedere pallā:
veste: 3.V.10	urit, seu niveā candida veste venit.

kalendae, -arum — first day of the month	**geminus, -a, -um** — twin	**como, -ere** — arrange
ignosco, -ere — forgive	**lampas, -adis** — "lamp"	**Tyrius, -a, -um** — Tyrian
violentus, -a, -um — violent	**furtim** — secretively	**palla, -ae** — cloak
exuro, -ere — inflame	**subsequor, -i** — attend	**niveus, -a, -um** — white
	crinis, -is — hair	

The praise for Sulpicia's grace and beauty continues.

READING FOR INFORMATION

1. *Vertumnus wears how many different outfits? Why?*
2. *Sulpicia deserves pearls from where? Perfume from where? Dyed wool from where?*
3. *The poet asks Phoebus and the Muses to do what on every March 1?*

	Talis in aeterno felix Vertumnus Olympo mille habet ornatūs, mille decenter habet.

cui: 3.III.1
vellera: 3.IV.1
det: 16.X
sucis: 3.V.1
Tyros: Greek
  nominative
  singular
possideat: 16.X
quidquid: 3.IV.1
arvis: 3.V.18
segetis: 3.II.6
aquis: 3.III.2
	Sola puellarum digna est cui mollia caris 15
	    vellera det sucis bis madefacta Tyros,
	possideatque metit quidquid bene olentibus arvis
	    cultor odoratae dives Arabs segetis,
	et quascumque niger rubro de litore gemmas
	    proximus Eois colligit Indus aquis. 20

Hanc vos, Pierides, festis cantate kalendis
    et testudineā, Phoebe superbe, lyrā.
Hoc sollemne sacrum multos haec sumet in annos:
    dignior est vestro nulla puella choro.

cantate: 19.I
kalendis: 3.V.6

choro: 3.V.16

Vertumnus, -i — god of changing seasons

ornatus, -ūs — ornament

decenter — appropriately

vellus, -eris — fleece

sucus, -i — juice

madefactus, -a, -um — dampened

Tyros, -i — Tyre (city of Phoenicia)

possideo, -ēre — possess

meto, -ere — harvest

olens, -tis — fragrant

cultor, -ris — farmer

odoratus, -a, -um — scented

Arabs, -bis — Arabian

seges, -getis — harvest

ruber, -bra, -brum — red

litus, -toris — shore

Eous, -a, -um — eastern

Indus, -i — Indus River

Pierides, -um — Muses

festus, -a, -um — festive

kalendae, -arum — first day of the month

testudineus, -a, -um — made of shell

lyra, -ae — lyre

sollemnis, -e — solemn

READING FOR UNDERSTANDING

1. How specific and detailed is the praise of Sulpicia's appearance? Could you draw a portrait, for example, from the description given here?
2. How many different gods does this twenty-four-line poem mention? What is the effect of such a high deity-to-line ratio?
3. On the receipt of this poem, would you be more pleased and proud if you were Sulpicia or Sulpicia's parents?

12.

The poet assumes the persona of Sulpicia for this poem and describes her love for the youth Cerinthus.

READING FOR INFORMATION

1. What is the occasion for this poem? Why are **Genius** and **Natalis deus** invoked?
2. The Fates foretold what at Cerinthus's birth?
3. What does the poet ask from Venus?
4. How are Sulpicia and Cerinthus supposedly different in their loves?

Qui mihi te, Cerinthe, dies dedit, hic mihi sanctus
    atque inter festos semper habendus erit:
te nascente, novum Parcae cecinēre puellis
    servitium, et dederunt regna superba tibi.
Uror ego ante alias: iuvat hoc, Cerinthe, quod uror,   5
    si tibi de nobis mutuus ignis adest.
Mutuus adsit amor, per te dulcissima furta
    perque tuos oculos per Geniumque rogo.

mihi: 3.III.1
mihi: 3.III.6
habendus erit: 17.IV

te nascente: 13.III.1
cecinēre: 20.I.2

si: 18.I.1
tibi: 3.III.3
adsit: 15.I

votis: 3.III.5 faveto: 19.II cum: 16.I.3.b	Magne Geni, cape tura libens votisque faveto, si modo, cum de me cogitat, ille calet. 10
	Quod si forte alios iam nunc suspirat amores,
relinque: 19.I	tunc, precor. Infidos, sancte, relinque focos.
sis: 15.IV serviat: 15.I tibi: 3.III.5 leva: 19.I teneamur: 15.I	Nec tu sis iniusta, Venus: vel serviat aequē vinctus uterque tibi, vel mea vincla leva. Sed potius validā teneamur uterque catenā, 15
queat: 15.I quam: 7.V	nulla queat posthāc quam solvisse dies.
	Optat idem iuvenis quod nos, sed tectius optat:
pudet: 20.III.5.b	nam pudet haec illum dicere verba palam.
adnue: 19.I rēfert: 20.III.6 roget: 16.V	At tu, Natalis, quoniam deus omnia sentis, adnue: quid rēfert, clamne palamne roget? 20

festus, -a, -um — holiday-	**caleo, -ēre** — be inflamed	**catena, -ae** — chain
Parcae, -arum — Fates	**suspiro, -are** — long for	**queo, -ire** — be able
cecinēre < cano	**infidus, -a, -um** — faithless	**posthāc** — hereafter
servitium, -i — servitude	**focus, -i** — fire	**palam** — openly
mutuus, -a, -um — mutual	**iniustus, -a, -um** — unfair	**adnuo, -ere** — be agreeable
furtum, -i — intrigue	**servio, -ire** — serve	**clam** — privately

READING FOR UNDERSTANDING

1. *Notice how this poem balances a tension between dominance and submission. Couched as a prayer, where does it fall within this tension?*
2. *Now notice how this poem also balances a tension between openness and concealment. Do you observe any trends or patterns of gender in this tension?*
3. *Explain the last line of the poem. Does it seem authentic or in character for a woman, or is the poet's persona slipping and exposing a male author?*

13.

The maiden Sulpicia is ill, and the poet invokes Phoebus Apollo, the god of healing, in prayer.

READING FOR INFORMATION

1. *Which feature is Phoebus said to be proud of?*
2. *What does the poet ask Phoebus to bring?*
3. *What two things does Sulpicia's boyfriend do with respect to the gods?*

ades: 10.III.3 expelle: 19.I puellae: 3.III.3 comā: 3.V.14 pigebit: 20.III.5.b	Hūc ades, et tenerae morbos expelle puellae; hūc ades, intonsā Phoebe superbe comā; crede mihi, propera: nec te iam, Phoebe, pigebit
formosae: 3.III.3	formosae medicas applicuisse manūs.
ne: 16.III.1	Effice ne macies pallentes occupet artūs, 5
neu: 16.III.1	neu notet informis languida membra color,

mali: 3.II.2	et quodcumque mali est et quidquid triste timemus,
evehat: 15.I	in pelagus rapidis evehat amnis aquis.
veni: 19.I feras: 19.IV	Sancte, veni, tecumque feras quicumque sapores
	quicumque et cantūs corpora fessa levant;
torque: 19.I puellae: 3.II.1 numeranda: 17.III	neu iuvenem torque, metuit qui fata puellae votaque pro dominā vix numeranda facit.
quod: 16.XIII.3.b.i	Interdum vovet, interdum, quod langueat illa,
	dicit in aeternos aspera verba deos.

10

hūc — here
expello, -ere — drive away
intonsus, -a, -um — unshorn
piget — it causes annoyance
applico, -are — apply
macies, -ei — thinness

palleo, -ēre — be pale
artus, -ūs — limb
informis, -e — hideous
languidus, -a, -um — weakened
pelasgus, -i — sea

rapidus, -a, -um — swift
eveho, -ere — carry away
sapor, -ris — potion
torqueo, -ēre — torment
numero, -are — count
langueo, -ēre — be sick

The poet now addresses the boyfriend, Cerinthus, before making one final appeal to Phoebus.

READING FOR INFORMATION

1. *According to the poem, why should Cerinthus have no fears?*
2. *Are there others who want to be Sulpicia's boyfriend?*
3. *Why, if Sulpicia is cured, will Phoebus be the envy of all the other gods?*

pone: 19.I	Pone metum, Cerinthe: deus non laedit amantes.
tibi: 3.III.3	Tu modo semper ama: salva puella tibi est.
fletū: 3.V.10 lacrimis: 3.V.13 aptius: 6.I si: 18.I.2.a.i quandō: 7.VI.1.a tibi: 3.III.3	Nil opus est fletū: lacrimis erit aptius uti, si quandō fuerit tristior illa tibi. At nunc tota tua est, te solum candida secum cogitat, et frustrā credula turba sedet.

fave: 19.I
tibi: 3.III.1
restituisse: 12.I.3.d
  (as if introduced
  by **laus**)
duos: 3.IV.1
cum: 16.I.3.b
focis: 3.III.1
	Phoebe, fave! Laus magna tibi tribuetur in uno
	corpore servato restituisse duos.
	Iam celeber, iam laetus eris, cum debita reddet
	certatim sanctis gratus uterque focis.

sibi: 3.III.3	Tunc te felicem dicet pia turba deorum, optabunt artes et sibi quisque tuas.

15

20

25

fletus, -ūs — weeping
aptus, -a, -um — proper
quandō = aliquandō

credulus, -a, -um — gullible
restituo, -ere — restore
celeber, -bris — celebrated

debitum, -i — debt
certatim — in rivalry
focus, -i — hearth

READING FOR UNDERSTANDING

1. *How sick is Sulpicia, according to this poem?*
2. *Whose suffering is described more, Sulpicia's or Cerinthus's?*
3. *In a culture where there were no vaccines, where childhood diseases killed many young people, and where basic infections could be fatal, juvenile and adolescent deaths were much more commonplace than today. How does that fact affect your understanding of this poem?*

Supplemental Readings

1.

The infamous tale of Tarpeia, who betrayed Rome to its Sabine enemies, is told here. This story became exemplary among Romans of the deep-seated greed (and improvidence) of women.

READING FOR INFORMATION

1. *Who was the king of Rome when this incident occurred?*
2. *What was Tarpeia supposedly doing when Tatius encountered her?*
3. *What did Tarpeia admire on the Sabines' left arms?*
4. *With what was Tarpeia rewarded from the Sabines' left arms?*

> Romulo regnante, Spurius Tarpeius arci praeerat. Cuius filiam virginem aquam sacris petitum extrā moenia egressam Tatius ut armatos Sabinos in arcem secum reciperet corrupit, mercedis nomine pactam quae in sinistris manibus gerebant: erant autem in his armillae et anuli magno ex pondere auri. Loco potitum agmen Sabinorum puellam praemium flagitantem armis obrutam necavit, perinde quasi promissum, quod ea quoque laevis gestaverant, solverit. Absit reprehensio, quia impia proditio celeri poenā vindicata est.

praesum, -esse — have command over	**armilla, -ae** — armlets	**perinde** — just
merces, -cedis — reward	**agmen, -minis** — battle line	**reprehensio, -nis** — reproach
paciscor, -i — agree, stipulate	**praemium, -i** — reward	**proditio, -nis** — treachery
sinister, -tra, -trum — left	**flagito, -are** — press for	
	obruo, -ere — bury	

READING FOR UNDERSTANDING

1. *This story suggests that what vice threatened Rome right from its very beginning?*
2. *According to the author, who was more at fault in this incident, a naïve young girl or conquest-intent warriors?*
3. *Retell this story from the viewpoint of Tarpeia. How does the message of the story change?*

2.

The notorious Servia Tullia is the subject of the next selection, which recounts how this princess ran over the corpse of her assassinated father with her carriage (traditionally 535 BCE).

READING FOR INFORMATION

1. The author justifies telling this story on what three grounds?
2. Who killed Servius Tullius? What was the relationship between the killer and Tullius's daughter?
3. What became of the street where Tullia ran her father over?

> A Tulliā ordiar, quia tempore vetustissimum, conscientiā nefarium, voce monstri simile exemplum est. Cum carpento veheretur et is, qui iumenta agebat, succussis frenis constitisset, repentinae morae causam requisivit, et ut comperit corpus patris Servii Tulli occisi ibi iacēre, suprā id duci vehiculum iussit, quō celerius in complexum interfectoris eius Tarquinii veniret. Quā tam impiā tamque probrosā festinatione non solum se aeternā infamiā, sed etiam ipsum vicum cognomine sceleris commaculavit.

ordior, -iri — begin
nefarius, -a, -um — wicked
monstrum, -i — abomination
carpentum, -i — carriage
iumentum, -i — horse
succutio, -ere — fling together

frenum, -i — rein
repentinus, -a, -um — sudden
requiesco, -ere — inquire
comperio, -ire — learn
vehiculum, -i — vehicle
complexus, -ūs — embrace

interfector, -ris — killer
probosus, -a, -um — wicked
festinatio, -nis — haste
vicus, -i — street
cognomen, -minis — name
commaculo, -are — disgrace

READING FOR UNDERSTANDING

1. Which crime does the author castigate Tullia more for, her treatment of her father's corpse or her adultery?
2. The author doesn't relate what became of Tullia and Tarquinius but does note the name change of the street where the incident occurred (**Sceleratus Vicus**). Does the latter seem like an important detail for this story?
3. What evidence can you find that this story was already well known and the author didn't have much of an interest in retelling it?

3.

This passage relates how his wife and his mother dissuaded the Roman traitor Coriolanus from attacking Rome (488 BCE). In honor of these women, Rome enacted certain measures acknowledging the value of all matrons.

READING FOR INFORMATION
1. Which neighbors of Rome did Coriolanus retain for his assault?
2. By senate decree, what were Roman men obliged to do on the street?
3. What new adornments were women permitted to wear?
4. A temple was dedicated to which goddess? Where was it erected?

Atque ut a publicis actis ordiar, Marcium Coriolanum patriae arma inferre conantem, admotoque portis urbis ingenti Volscorum exercitū funus ac tenebras Romano imperio minantem, Veturia mater et Volumnia uxor nefarium opus exsequi precibus suis non passae sunt. In quarum honorem senatus matronarum ordinem benignissimis decretis adornavit: sanxit namque ut feminis semitā viri cederent; confessus est plus salutis rei publicae in stolā quam in armis fuisse; vetustisque aurium insignibus novum vittae discrimen adiecit. Permisit quoque his purpureā veste et aureis uti segmentis. Super haec aedem et aram Fortunae Muliebri eo loco, quō Coriolanus exoratus erat, faciendam curavit, memorem beneficii esse animum suum exquisito religionis cultū testando.

10–11. **memorem . . . testando**: with this sophisticated cult of religion attesting that their intention was mindful of the favor

ordior, -iri — begin
Volsci, -orum — a tribe of Latium
minor, -ari — threaten
nefarius, -a, -um — wicked

decretum, -i — decree
adorno, -are — decorate
sancio, -ire — require
semita, -ae — path
stola, -ae — woman's dress

vitta, -ae — headband
segmentum, -i — trimming
exoro, -are — plead with

READING FOR UNDERSTANDING
1. Roman lore has several stories about women acting as peacemakers, but they invariably involve internecine conflicts. Why do you suppose women played a minimal role in the conduct of foreign war and peace?
2. What do you think of a reward system for women that features clothes and jewelry?
3. The assumption that patriotism motivated Coriolanus's mother and wife isn't really substantiated here. What other motives might they have had?

4.

The following three anecdotes narrate incidents leading to husbands divorcing their wives. As you can see, the men all acted proactively, insofar as the women weren't guilty of any serious wrongdoing.

READING FOR INFORMATION
1. Sulpicius Galus (consul in 166 BCE) divorced his wife because she did what?
2. Why did Antistius Vetus divorce his wife?

3. *Sempronius Sophus ended his marriage (circa 284 BCE) on what grounds?*

capite aperto: use of ablative?
ratione: use of ablative?
tibi: use of dative?
quibus: use of dative?
approbes: use of subjunctive?
decoris: use of genitive?
his: use of dative?
esto: what form?
notitiae: use of dative?
tui: adjective or pronoun?
irritatione: use of ablative?
haereat: use of subjunctive?
repudiando: gerund or gerundive?
libertinā: use of ablative?
dicam: use of subjunctive?
incunabulis et nutrimentis: use of ablative?
culpae: use of genitive?
culpā: use of ablative?
delicto: use of ablative?
cavēret, vindicaret: use of subjunctive?
iungendus est: use of gerundive?
notā: use of ablative?
se ignorante: use of ablative?
ludos: use of accusative?
feminis: use of dative?
occurritur: why present?

Horridum C. Sulpicii Gali maritale supercilium: nam uxorem dimisit, quod eam capite aperto forīs versatam cognōverat; abscisa est sententia, sed tamen aliquā ratione munita: "Lex enim," inquit, "tibi meos tantum praefinit oculos, quibus formam tuam approbes. His decoris instrumenta compara, his esto speciosa, horum te certiori crede notitiae. Ut ulterior tui conspectus supervacuā irritatione arcessitus in suspicione et crimine haereat necesse est." Nec aliter sensit Q. Antistius Vetus repudiando uxorem, quod illam in publico cum quādam libertinā vulgari secretō loquentem viderat: nam, ut ita dicam, incunabulis et nutrimentis culpae, non ipsā commotus culpā citeriorem delicto praebuit ultionem, ut potius cavēret iniuriam quam vindicaret. Iungendus est his P. Sempronius Sophus, qui coniugem repudii notā adfecit, nihil aliud quam se ignorante ludos ausam spectare. Ergō, dum sīc olim feminis occurritur, mens earum a delictis aberat.

supercilium, -i — pride

forīs — abroad

abscido, -ere — break off abruptly

munio, -ire — fortify

praefinio, -ire — restrict

approbo, -are — gain approval for

notitia, -ae — notice, attention

supervacuus, -a, -um — unnecessary

irritatio, -nis — provocation

arcesso, -ere — prompt

repudio, -are — divorce

libertina, -ae — freedwoman

incunabulum, -i — cradle

citerior, -ius — swifter

ultio, -nis — punishment

repudium, -i — divorce

ignoro, -are — be unknowing

occurro, -ere — oppose

READING FOR UNDERSTANDING

1. Why aren't the names of the divorced wives related in this passage?
2. Given what you read here, does it appear that men were required to provide much in the way of evidence or just cause in suing for divorce?
3. For each anecdote, supply a perfectly reasonable explanation for the woman acting as she did. Do you suppose women's innocence affected the outcome of the divorce process?

5.

This next passage relates the summary capital punishment that their kinsfolk carried out against three women. In none of these cases is any argument made that the women were entitled to legal process.

READING FOR INFORMATION

1. Publicia and Licinia were alleged to have committed what crime(s)? How were they killed?
2. On what grounds was the wife of Egnatius Mecennius killed?

3. *What arguments are adduced to justify the summary killings of these women?*

> Publicia autem, quae Postumium Albinum consulem, item Licinia, quae Claudium Asellum viros suos veneno necaverant, propinquorum decreto strangulatae sunt: non enim putaverunt severissimi viri in tam evidenti scelere longum publicae quaestionis tempus exspectandum. Itaque quarum innocentium defensores fuissent, sontium maturē vindices exstiterunt. Magno scelere severitas horum ad exigendam vindictam concitata est, Egnati autem Mecenni longē minore de causā, qui uxorem, quod vinum bibisset, fusti percussam interemit, idque factum non accusatore tantum, sed etiam reprehensore caruit, uno quōque existimante optimo illam exemplo violatae sobrietati poenas pependisse. Et sanē quaecumque femina vini usum immoderatē appetit, omnibus et virtutibus ianuam claudit et delictis aperit.

venenum, -i — poison
decretum, -i — decree
strangulo, -are — kill by strangulation
evidens, -tis — evident
quaestio, -nis — inquiry

defensor, -ris — defender
sons, -ntis — guilty
exigo, -ere — exact
vindicta, -ae — punishment
concito, -are — stir, rouse
percutio, -ere — strike, beat

interimo, -ere — kill
reprehensor, -ris — reproacher
careo, -ēre — lack
sobrietas, -tatis — sobriety
delictum, -i — crime, fault

READING FOR UNDERSTANDING

1. *Explain the logic or jurisprudence used here that if the women hadn't been guilty, their menfolk would have been the first to defend them?*
2. *Sudden, unexpected death was not an uncommon phenomenon in antiquity. Ascertaining the cause of death was usually very difficult, given the poor state of Roman forensic medicine. In what possible scenarios might accusations of poisoning plausibly be leveled against Roman women?*
3. *In several readings now, we've seen the view expressed that women and wine just don't mix. If the Romans were sincere in this view, why didn't they simply impose an absolute and universal prohibition on all alcohol use?*

6.

The following story recounts a complicated case of attempted fraud involving a man, his adulterous mistress, and a dubious IOU. This incident occurred sometime in the middle of the 1st century BCE.

READING FOR INFORMATION

1. *Why did Varro allow Oticilia to draw up a phony IOU?*
2. *What was the outcome of Varro's health crisis?*
3. *After this outcome, what did Oticilia maintain?*

4. What did Aquillius do to settle the case?

relaturus: what form?
oblitterandum est: use of
    gerundive?
silentio: use of ablative?
morbo: use of ablative?
nummum: accusative or genitive?
expensa: use of accusative?
sibi: use of dative?
consilio: use of ablative?
si: type of condition?
peteret: use of subjunctive?
nomine: use of ablative?
colorando: gerund or gerundive?
quod: with indicative or
    subjunctive?
praedae: use of dative?
morte: use of ablative?
maturasset: syncopation of?
petendo: gerund or gerundive?
fronte: use of ablative?
stipulatione: use of ablative?
auctoritatis: use of genitive?
scientiā: use of ablative?
adhibitis ... principibus: use of
    ablative?
prudentiā et religione: use of
    ablative?
si: type of condition?
formulā: use of ablative?
adversariae: use of dative?
castigaturus: what form?
fuerit: use of subjunctive?

quaestioni: use of dative?
vindicandum: gerund or
    gerundive?

Ne quod relaturus quidem sum oblitterandum est silentio. C. Visellius Varro, gravi morbo correptus, trecenta milia nummum ab Otaciliā, cum qua commercium libidinis habuerat, expensa ferri sibi passus est, eo consilio, ut, si decessisset, ab heredibus eam summam peteret, quam legati genus esse voluit, libidinosam liberalitatem debiti nomine colorando. Evasit deinde ex illā tempestate adversus vota Otaciliae. Quae offensa, quod spem praedae suae morte non maturasset, ex amicā obsequenti subitō destrictam feneratricem agere coepit, nummos petendo, quos ut fronte inverecundā, ita inani stipulatione captaverat. De qua re C. Aquillius, vir magnae auctoritatis et scientiā iuris civilis excellens, iudex adductus, adhibitis in consilium principibus civitatis, prudentiā et religione suā mulierem reppulit. Quod si eādem formulā Varro et damnari et adversariae absolvi potuisset, eius quoque non dubito quin Aquillius turpem et inconcessum errorem libenter castigaturus fuerit: nunc privatae actionis calumniam ipse compescuit, adulterii crimen publicae quaestioni vindicandum reliquit.

oblittero, -are — obliterate	**maturo, -are** — expedite	**formula, -ae** — jurisprudence
tricenti, -ae, -a — three hundred	**obsequor, -i** — yield, oblige	**adversaria, -ae** — opponent
nummus, -i — sesterce	**destringo, -ere** — expose	**inconcessus, -a, -um** — unallowable
commercium, -i — communion	**feneratrix, -tricis** — lender	**castigo, -are** — punish
debitum, -i — debt	**inverecundus, -a, -um** — shameless	**calumnia, -ae** — false prosecution
coloro, -are — color, tinge	**stipulatio, -nis** — agreement	**compesco, -ere** — curb
	adduco, -ere — bring in as	

READING FOR UNDERSTANDING

1. *What evidence is presented that Oticilia didn't loan money to Varro?*
2. *The author expresses the view that both parties in this case were culpable, but which one was more culpable? Why?*
3. *Issues concerning love and money are problematic even in marriage. How are they especially problematic when the two lovers aren't married?*

7.

This fascinating story describes a legal matter that arose in the province of Asia in 68 BCE. The case, one of homicide, was particularly hard to adjudicate, and the Roman proconsul involved refused to either convict or acquit the woman defendant.

1. *Whom did the woman murder? Why?*
2. *To what higher court and where did Dollabella refer the case?*
3. *What was the decision of the higher court? Does the author approve of their decision?*

Haesitatione P. Dolabellae, proconsulari imperio Asiam obtinentis, animus fluctuatus est. Mater familiae Zmyrnaea virum et filium interemit, cum ab his optimae indolis iuvenem, quem ex priore viro enixa fuerat, occisum esse comperisset. Quam rem Dolabella ad se delatam Athenas ad Areopagi cognitionem relegavit, quia ipse neque liberare duabus caedibus contaminatam neque punire tam iusto dolore impulsam sustinebat. Consideranter et mansuetē populi Romani magistratus, sed Areopagitae quoque non minus sapienter, qui inspectā causā et accusatorem et ream post centum annos ad se reverti iusserunt, eodem adfectū moti, quo Dolabella. Sed ille transferendo quaestionem, hi differendo inexplicabilem cunctationem damnandi atque absolvendi vitabant.

haesitatio, -nis — hesitation	**relego, -are** — bind over	**sapienter** — wisely
proconsularis, -e — proconsular	**contamino, -are** — taint	**rea, -ae** — defendant
interimo, -ere — murder	**consideranter** — deliberately	**cunctatio, -nis** — delay
enitor, -i — produce	**mansuetē** — leniently	**absolvo, -ere** — acquit
comperio, -ire — learn	**Areopagita, -ae** — member of the Areopagus	

1. *Why does the author refer to the woman's motive as **iustus dolor** (sixth line)?*
2. *Did Dollabella simply pass the buck by referring the case to the Areopagus?*
3. *Although this is a great anecdote, it's not particularly good or satisfying as a legal or historical record. What additional facts of the case would you want presented into evidence?*

8.

Claims of paternity, both true and false, were fairly common in the ancient world, before the modern advent of DNA testing. Considerably less common were claims of maternity, but this anecdote involving a famous (alleged) mother comes to a decisive outcome.

1. *Who did the claimant allege was his mother?*
2. *Why, according to the claimant, was he repudiated?*
3. *Where did he end up?*

Ne divi quidem Augusti etiamnunc terras regentis excellentissimum
numen intemptatum est ab hōc iniuriae genere. Exstitit qui clarissimae ac
sanctissimae sororis eius Octaviae utero se genitum esse fingere audēret;
propter summam autem imbecillitatem corporis iussū matris expositum
esse, sed ab eo, cui datus erat, perinde atque ipsius filium retentum esse,
subiecto in locum suum proprio filio, diceret, videlicet ut eodem tempore
sanctissimi penates et veri sanguinis memoriā spoliarentur et falsi
sordidā contagione inquinarentur. Sed dum plenis impudentiae velis ad
summum audaciae gradum fertur, imperio Augusti remo publicae triremis
adfixus est.

6. **subiecto . . . filio**: while his own son was substituted in his place

etiamnunc — even now	**penates, -ium** — household	**remus, -i** — oar
intemptatus, -a, -um —	gods	**triremis, -is** — trireme
untouched	**spolio, -are** — rob	**adfigo, -ere** — attach
imbecillitas, -tatis — weakness	**contagio, -nis** — contagion	
videlicet — obviously	**inquino, -are** — besmirch	

READING FOR UNDERSTANDING

1. *What evidence was produced that the claimant was Octavia's son? That he wasn't Octavia's son?*
2. *Why is no mention made of the claimant's alleged father?*
3. *If the claimant suffered from **summa imbecillitas corporis** (line 4), does it make sense that he was relegated to rowing on an imperial warship?*
4. *Does this anecdote belong more properly in the history books or in the grocery store tabloids?*

9.

This story, dated to the era of Augustus, tells how a certain woman remarried and altered her will out of spite for her grown sons. Later, the emperor intervened on behalf of these sons.

READING FOR INFORMATION

1. *Did Septicia and Publicius marry with the purpose of having children?*
2. *After her death, what became of Septicia's dowry?*
3. *The author suggests at the end of the passage that Augustus's ruling served what greater purpose?*

Septicia, irata filiis, in contumeliam eorum, cum iam parere non posset,
Publicio seni admodum nupsit, testamento etiam utrumque praeteriit. A
quibus aditus est divus Augustus et nuptias mulieris et suprema iudicia
improbavit: nam hereditatem maternam filios habēre iussit, dotem, quia

non creandorum liberorum causā coniugium intercesserat, virum retinēre vetuit. Si ipsa Aequitas hac de re cognosceret, potuitne iustius aut gravius pronuntiare? Spernis quos genuisti; nubis effeta; testamenti ordinem malevolo animo confundis; neque erubescis ei totum patrimonium addicere, cuius pollincto iam corpori marcidam senectutem tuam substravisti. Ergō dum sīc te geris, ad inferos usque caelesti fulmine adflata es.

admodum — altogether, fully	**effetus, -a, -um** — past reproduction	**pollingo, -ere** — prepare for burial
improbo, -are — reject	**malevolus, -a, -um** — ill willed	**marcidus, -a, -um** — withered
veto, -are — forbid	**confundo, -ere** — pervert	**substerno, -ere** — lay beneath
aequitas, -tatis — equity	**erubesco, -ere** — be ashamed	**inferi, -orum** — the dead
pronuntio, -are — render judgment	**addico, -ere** — award	**fulmen, -inis** — thunderbolt
sperno, -ere — spurn		**adflo, -are** — blast, scorch

READING FOR UNDERSTANDING

1. Why does the state care whether an older woman remarries or how she transmits her wealth and property through her will?

2. Why isn't the cause or origin of Septicia's feud with her sons related?

3. The author invokes the personified **Aequitas** to justify the actions of Augustus. Explain how the rule of law was at work in this story.

4. Governments are often put in the position of having to balance individual rights both with pro-family interests and with the interests of the state. Do you think Augustus struck a fair and effective balance in this case?

F. Love

Prose Readings

1.

The author of this passage asserts that great people experience the affection of love differently from other people. To support his assertion, he cites the marriage of Claudius Nero Drusus and Antonia Minor (second half of the 1st century BCE).

READING FOR INFORMATION

1. *According to this passage, a household or a community can maintain its health and integrity only if what conditions exist or don't exist?*
2. *Where vice is rampant, what conditions exist?*
3. *What distinguished Drusus's marital relations?*
4. *After Drusus's death, what were Antonia's sleeping arrangements?*

curā, studio: 3.V.3
referendum est: 17.IV
libidinis et avaritiae: 3.II.6
furori: 3.III.2
impetūs: 3.I.1
consilio ac ratione: 3.V.7
summoti sint: 16.V
steterit: 16.XII
virium: 3.II.2
veneris pecuniaeque: 3.II.6
sibi: 3.III.3
vindicaverit: 16.XII
penetrarunt: 20.I.3
linguis: 3.V.1
vitiis: 3.III.2
commemoremus: 15.I
Drusum: 3.IV.4
magnitudine: 3.V.7
vitrico, fratri: 3.III.5
Augustis: 3.VIII
constitit: 20.III.7.a
veneris: 3.II.6
laudibus: 3.V.10
fide: 3.V.3
formā et aetate: 3.V.10
experientiā: 3.V.7

Magnā curā praecipuoque studio referendum est quantopere libidinis et avaritiae furori similis impetūs ab illustrium virorum pectoribus consilio ac ratione summoti sint; quia ei demum penates, ea civitas, id regnum aeterno in gradū facile steterit, ubi minimum virium veneris pecuniaeque cupido sibi vindicaverit: nam quō istae generis humani certissimae pestes penetrarunt, iniuria dominatur, infamia flagrat, vis habitat, bella gignuntur. Faventibus igitur linguis contrarios his tam diris vitiis mores commemoremus. Drusum etiam Germanicum, eximiam Claudiae familiae gloriam patriaeque rarum ornamentum, et quod super omnia est, operum suorum pro habitū aetatis magnitudine vitrico pariter ac fratri, Augustis duobus mirificē respondentem, constitit usum veneris intrā coniugis caritatem clausum tenuisse. Antonia quoque, femina laudibus virilem familiae suae claritatem supergressa, amorem mariti egregiā fide pensavit; quae post eius excessum, formā et aetate florens, convīctum socrūs pro coniugio habuit, in eodemque toro alterius adulescentiae vigor exstinctus est; alterius viduitatis experientiā consenuit.

1–2. **libidinis . . . impetūs**: impulses like the madness of lust and greed
4–5. **ubi . . . vindicaverit**: where the desire for sex and money has appropriated for itself a minimum of strength

quantopere — how
avaritia, -ae — greed
illustris, -e — illustrious
summoveo, -ēre — drive away

penates, -ium — household gods
pestis, -is — pest
dominor, -ari — dominate
infamia, -ae — infamy

dirus, -a, -um — dreadful
commemoro, -are — commemorate
eximius, -a, -um — extraordinary

habitus, -ūs — state, condition
magnitudo, -dinis — greatness
vitricus, -i — stepfather
mirificē — wonderfully
clausus, -a, -um — confine
claritas, -tatis — fame
supergredior, -i — surpass
penso, -are — requite
excessus, -ūs — death
convīctus, -ūs — cohabitation
socrus, -ūs — mother-in-law
adulescentia, -ae — young adulthood
vigor, -ris — prime
viduitas, -tatis — widowhood
experentia, -ae — experience
consenesco, -ere — grow old together

READING FOR UNDERSTANDING

1. *The author claims that **libido** and **avaritia** are similar to **furor**, a view that the Stoics endorsed. Can you make arguments that either support or refute this claim? Where does the emotion of love belong in this argument?*
2. *Reading this passage of praise, do you sense that Drusus's sexual fidelity to Antonia was the norm? Was it a common exception to the norm?*
3. *Do you sense that Antonia's widowhood was the norm? Was it a common exception?*
4. *Drusus died in 9 BCE; Augustus, Livia's husband, died in 14 CE. What does this suggest about Roman sleeping arrangements?*

2.

This anecdote about the parents of the famous Gracchi brothers (2nd century BCE) is prefaced with an interesting discussion about marital love.

READING FOR INFORMATION

1. *According to the author, how is a moral example useful, even if it's hard to imitate?*
2. *What two snakes were caught in Gracchus's house?*
3. *What were the portentous implications of letting each of these snakes go?*

contemplandas: 17.III
oculis: 3.III.7
opera: 3.IV.1
imitatū: 17.I.2
excellentissima: 3.IV.1.a
animadvertenti, rubori: 3.III.10
praestare: 12.I.3.a
oportet: 20.III.7
domi: 4.I.3
anguibus . . . deprehensis: 13.III.2
mare dimisso: 13.III.4
uxori, ipsi: 3.III.3
feminā dimissā: 13.III.4
interitū: 3.V.7
occidi: 12.I
dixerim: 16.V
habuerit, amiserit: 16.XIII.3.b

Ad adfectum honestum, verum aliquantō ardentiorem et concitatiorem pergam; legitimique amoris quasi quasdam imagines non sine maximā veneratione contemplandas lectoris oculis subiciam, valenter inter coniuges stabilitae fidei opera percurrens, ardua imitatū, ceterum cognosci utilia, quia excellentissima animadvertenti ne mediocria quidem praestare rubori oportet esse. Ti. Gracchus, anguibus domi suae mare ac feminā deprehensis, certior factus est ab haruspice, mare dimisso, uxori eius, feminā dimissā, ipsi celerem obitum instare; salutarem coniugi potius quam sibi partem augurii secutus, marem necari, feminam dimitti iussit, sustinuitque in conspectū suo se ipsum interitū serpentis occidi. Itaque Corneliam nescio utrum feliciorem dixerim, quod talem virum habuerit, an esse miseriorem, quod amiserit.

adfectus, -ūs — emotion	**subicio, -ere** — submit	**haruspex, -icis** — soothsayer
aliquantō — somewhat	**valenter** — strongly	**obitus, -ūs** — death
ardens, -ntis — ardent	**stabilio, -ire** — establish	**insto, -are** — be imminent
concitatus, -a, -um — excitable	**percurro, -ere** — survey	**salutaris, -e** — salutary
	mediocris, -e — average	**augurium, -i** — augury
pergo, -ere — continue with	**rubor, -ris** — cause for shame	**interitus, -ūs** — death
contemplo, -are — ponder	**anguis, -is** — snake	
lector, -ris — reader	**mas, maris** — male	

READING FOR UNDERSTANDING

1. Gracchus's self-sacrifice was praiseworthy, to be sure, but to what extent was it also gullible?

2. The author tells this story in a context of marital love and devotion, but is it possible that Gracchus sacrificed himself for some motive other than conjugal affection?

3. In what situation(s) would you be willing to give up your life for another? Are all such situations equally honorable?

3.

Probably set in the 1st century BCE, this story recounts how a man preferred the role of loving husband to that of loyal military officer and ambitious politician.

READING FOR INFORMATION

1. What was Plautius doing in Tarentum?

2. What happened to his wife there?

3. What did he do at her funeral?

cum: 16.I.3.a
Tarentum: 4.I.2
morbo: 3.V.7
funeratā . . .
   impositā: 13.III.1
unguendi et
   osculandi: 17.II
ferro: 3.III.7
quem: 7.V.2
corpori: 3.III.3
subiectis facibus:
   13.III.1
Tarenti: 4.I.3
quin: 16.VII.2
si: 18.I.1
quis: 7.VI.1.a
exstinctis: 3.III.7
consortione: 3.V.10
tenebris: 3.III.7
ubi: 16.XIII.2.a

Nam cum M. Plautius imperio senatūs classem sociorum sexaginta navium in Asiam reduceret Tarentumque appulisset, atque ibi uxor eius Orestilla, quae illūc eum prosecuta erat, morbo oppressa decessisset, funeratā eā et in rogum impositā, inter officium unguendi et osculandi stricto ferro incubuit. Quem amici, sīcut erat, togatum et calceatum corpori coniugis iunxerunt ac deinde, subiectis facibus, utrumque unā cremaverunt. Quorum ibi factum sepulcrum est—Tarenti etiamnunc conspicitur. Nec dubito quin, si quis sensus modo exstinctis inest, Plautius et Orestilla fati consortione gestientes vultūs tenebris intulerint. Sanēque, ubi īdem et maximus et honestissimus amor est, aliquantō praestat morte iungi quam distrahi vitā.

classis, -is — fleet	**Tarentum, -i** — Sicilian city	**opprimo, -ere** — overcome
sexaginta — sixty	**appello, -ere** — put in, make landfall	**funero, -are** — give a funeral
reduco, -ere — take back		**unguo, -ere** — anoint

stringo, -ere — draw

incubo, -are — lie atop

togatus, -a, -um — wearing
   a toga

calceatus, -a, -um — wearing
   shoes

unā — together with

cremo, -are — cremate

sepulcrum, -i — tomb

etiamnunc — even now

insum, -esse — exist in

consortio, -nis — partnership

gestio, -ire — desire

sanē — obviously

aliquantō — sometimes

distraho, -ere — split

READING FOR UNDERSTANDING

1. Plautius's service to the state may well have earned him a public funeral at Rome, but he was buried instead at Tarentum. In your view, did Plautius's friends act rightly in this story?

2. What do you think of the author's assertion that where true love is concerned, a shared death is preferable to life in separation?

3. All of the anecdotes we have read here involving married love measure loyalty and devotion in terms of the death of one of the spouses. How do you explain this use of death as a yard-stick of love?

4.

The following is a letter written by a husband to his wife, who is away on family matters. It gives us an uncommon glimpse into the emotional intimacies of Roman marriage. The author portrays himself as at a real loss in the absence of his wife.

READING FOR INFORMATION

1. What reasons does the author give for missing his wife?

2. Where do his feet seem to take him in the course of his day?

3. What is his single distraction from this longing?

desiderio: 3.V.7
tui: 7.I.2
tenear: 16.V

quibus horis: 4.II.1

excluso: 3.III.2

tormentis: 3.V.10
litibus: 3.V.7
sit: 16.V

Incredibile est quanto desiderio tui tenear. In causā amor primum, deinde quod non consuevimus abesse. Inde est quod magnam noctium partem in imagine tuā vigil exigo; inde quod interdiū, quibus horis te visere solebam, ad diaetam tuam ipsi me, ut verissimē dicitur, pedes ducunt; quod denique aeger et maestus ac similis excluso a vacuo limine recedo. Unum tempus his tormentis caret, quō in foro et amicorum litibus conteror. Aestima tu, quae vita mea sit, cui es requies in labore, in miseriā curisque es solacium. Vale.

desiderium, -i — longing

vigil, -is — wakeful

exigo, -ere — spend

interdiū — sometimes

hora, -ae — hour

diaeta, -ae — dayroom

excludo, -ere — bar

vacuus, -a, -um — empty

limen, -minis — threshold

tormentum, -i — torture

careo, -ēre — be missing,
   lack

requies, -etis — relief

solacium, -i — solace

READING FOR UNDERSTANDING

1. *How is the passive **tenear** in the first sentence artful and effective? Would the active **teneo te in quanto desiderio** be as good?*
2. *The clause **similis excluso a vacuo limine recedo** is highly suggestive of a commonplace in Roman amatory poetry, of a lover rejected by his mistress. What evidence do you find in this letter that the husband is feeling a bit rejected and even begrudges his wife's absence?*
3. *Which of his wife's qualities does the author specifically miss? Is this letter more about the author or the addressee? If you were to receive such a message from a sweetheart, how would you feel?*

5.

Written by a Roman who was also an early Christian Father, this passage expresses some very negative views about love and marriage. Starting with the claim that a slave is preferable to a spouse, the author criticizes the selfishness of wives.

READING FOR INFORMATION

1. *What three motives does the author give for a man's marrying?*
2. *According to the author, how does a wife establish the fact that she is the mistress of her house?*
3. *What motive lies behind a wife's anxious tears when her husband is ill?*
4. *When a wife takes ill, what must a husband do?*

multō: 3.V.9
auctoritati,
  dispositioni:
  3.III.7

quod: 7.V
aegrotanti: 3.III.3
beneficiis: 3.V.7

coaegrotandum
  est, recedendum
  (est): 17.IV
si: 18.I.1

Si propter dispensationem domūs et languoris solacia et fugam solitudinis ducuntur uxores: multō melius servus fidelis dispensat, oboediens auctoritati domini, et dispositioni eius obtemperans, quam uxor, quae in eo se esse existimat dominam, si adversum viri faciat voluntatem, id est, quod placet, non quod iubetur. Adsidēre autem aegrotanti magis possunt amici, et vernulae beneficiis obligati, quam illa quae nobis imputat lacrimas suas (et hereditatis spe vendat illuviem) et sollicitudinem iactans, languentis animum desperatione conturbat. Quod si ipsa languerit, coaegrotandum est, et numquam ab eius lectulo recedendum. Aut si bona fuerit et suavis uxor (quae tamen rara avis est), cum parturiente gemimus, cum periclitante torquemur.

dispensatio, -nis — management	**dispenso, -are** — manage	**adsideo, -ēre** — sit by
languor, -ris — sickness	**oboedio, -ire** — be obedient	**aegroto, -are** — be sick
solacium, -i — tender loving care	**dispositio, -nis** — temperament	**vernula, -ae** — home slave
solitudo, -dinis — loneliness	**obtempero, -are** — obey	**obligo, -are** — indebted
	voluntas, -tatis — will	**imputo, -are** — impute
		hereditas, -tatis — inheritance

illuvies, -ei — dirt

sollicitudo, -inis — worry

langueo, -ēre — be sick

desperatio, -nis — despair

conturbo, -are — confound

coaegroto, -are — be sick together

suavis, -e — pleasant

periclitor, -ari — put in peril

torqueo, -ēre — torture

The author continues with the claim that excessive love (and sex) between husband and wife is disgraceful and that any relationship predicated on lust is a faulty one.

READING FOR INFORMATION

1. *How should a wise man love his wife?*
2. *In what respect should beasts be imitated?*
3. *What bitter irony does the author see in marriages whose origins began in adultery?*

iudicio, adfectū: 3.V.7 or 3.V.10
regat, feratur: 15.I

se: 3.IV.4
causā: 8.III
uxoribus: 3.III.3
imitentur: 15.I
intumuerit: future perfect
perdant: 15.II
amatores, maritos: 3.IV.1.b
exhibeant: 15.I
adulteriis: 3.V.7
rem: 3.IV.5
illis (feminis): 3.III.7

In alienā quippe uxore omnis amor turpis est, in suā nimius. Sapiens vir iudicio debet amare coniugem, non adfectū. Regat impetūs voluptatis, nec praeceps feratur in coetum. Nihil est foedius quam uxorem amare quasi adulteram. Certē qui dicunt se causā rei publicae et generis humani uxoribus iungi, et liberos tollere, imitentur saltem pecudes et, postquam uxorum venter intumuerit, non perdant filios; nec amatores uxoribus se exhibeant, sed maritos. Quorundam matrimonia adulteriis cohaeserunt: et, o rem improbam, iidem illis pudicitiam praeceperunt, qui abstulerant. Itaque cito eius modi nuptias satietas solvit. Cum primum lenocinium libidinis abscessit, quod libebat, eviluit.

adfectus, -ūs — emotion

adultera, -ae — adulteress

saltem — at least

venter, -tris — belly, womb

intumeo, -ēre — swell

cohaereo, -ēre — be brought together by

praecipio, -ere — instruct about

abstulerant < aufero

satietas, -tis — satiation

lenocinium, -i — allure

abscedo, -ere — disappear

evilesco, -ere — become vile

*The passage closes with a discussion of **pudicitia**, the feminine virtue of proper modesty. Though written at the very end of the 4th century CE, this passage would have met with the full agreement of Cato the Censor in the 2nd century BCE.*

READING FOR INFORMATION

1. *How does **pudicitia** mediate contrasts (e.g., rich/poor, unattractive/attractive) among women?*
2. *How does it mediate between generations?*
3. *What are the masculine equivalents of **pudicitia**?*

pudicitiam: 3.IV.4
esse retinendam: 17.IV
quā amissā: 13.III.1

Doctissimi viri vox est, pudicitiam in primis esse retinendam; quā amissā, omnis virtus ruit. In hac muliebrium virtutum principatus est. Haec pauperem commendat, divitem extollit, deformem redimit, exornat

subole: 3.V.7	pulchram: bene meretur de maioribus, quorum sanguinem furtivā subole
erubescendum, dubitandum est: 17.IV	non vitiat; bene de liberis, quibus nec de matre erubescendum, nec de patre dubitandum est; bene in primis de se, quam a contumeliā externi
corporis: 3.II.6	corporis pudicitia vindicat. Captivitatis nulla maior calamitas est quam ad alienam libidinem trahi. Viros consulatus illustrat; eloquentia in nomen
gentis: 3.II.3	aeternum effert; militaris gloria triumphusque novae gentis consecrat.
nobilitent: 16.X	Multa sunt quae praeclara ingenia nobilitent. Mulieris virtus propriē pudicitia est.

doctus, -a, -um — learned

principatus, -ūs — beginning point

extollo, -ere — praise

deformis, -e — ugly

redimo, -ere — redeem

exorno, -are — dress up

furtivus, -a, -um — secret

suboles, -is — offspring

vitio, -are — spoil

erubesco, -ere — blush

externus, -a, -um — external

captivitas, -tatis — captivity

illustro, -are — make illustrious

eloquentia, -ae — eloquence

effero, -rre — launch

militaris, -e — military-

triumphus, -i — triumph

consecro, -are — deify

praeclarus, -a, -um — brilliant

nobilito, -are — ennoble

READING FOR UNDERSTANDING

1. *What do you think is the main point that the author of this passage is trying to make?*
2. *Is self-control, as described in this passage, something that can be taught and learned?*
3. *The sentence* **Captivitatis nulla maior calamitas est quam ad alienam libidinem trahi** *is very provocative. What does it mean? Is it true? Does it have significance for today?*

Verse Readings

1.

"The Power of Love": The Widow and the Soldier

READING FOR INFORMATION

1. *How did the widow get a reputation for chastity?*
2. *The criminals, whose bodies the soldier was ordered to guard, had committed what crime?*
3. *The soldier asked for what from the woman's slave girl?*

	Per aliquot annos quaedam dilectum virum	
sarcophago: 3.V.1	amisit et sarcophago corpus condidit;	
a quo: 3.V.19 **nullo . . . modo:** 3.V.1 **cum:** 16.I.1	a quo revelli nullo cum posset modo et in sepulchro lugens vitam degeret, claram adsecuta est famam castae coniugis.	5
compilarant: 20.I	Intereā fanum qui compilarant Iovis,	

cruci: 3.III.7

ne: 16.III
quis: 7.VI.1.a

nocte: 3.V.6

dominae: 3.III.5

dormitum: 17.I

cruci suffixi luerunt poenas numini.
Horum reliquias ne quis posset tollere,
custodes dantur milites cadaverum,
monumentum iuxtā, mulier quō se incluserat.   10
Aliquandō sitiens unus de custodibus
aquam rogavit mediā nocte ancillulam,
quae forte dominae tunc adsistebat suae
dormitum eunti; namque lucubraverat
et usque in serum vigilias perduxerat.   15

aliquot — (indeclinable)
    some
dilectus, -a, -um — beloved
sarcophagus, -i — crypt
condo, -ere — bury
revello, -ere — tear away
lugeo, -ēre — mourn
dego, -ere — spend
adsequor, -i — attain

fanum, -i — temple
compilo, -are — plunder
crux, -cis — cross
suffigo, -ere — attach
poenas luere — pay the price
reliquiae, -arum — remains
tollo, -ere — steal
cadaver, -is — corpse
includo, -ere — enclose

aliquandō — once
sitio, -ire — thirst
ancillula, -ae — slave girl
lucubro, -are — stay up late
serum, -i — late hour
vigiliae, -arum — wakefulness
perduco, -ere — draw out

READING FOR INFORMATION
1. *How did the soldier react on first seeing the widow?*
2. *How often did the soldier visit the widow?*
3. *What happened one night during the soldier's visit?*
4. *How did the widow solve the soldier's problem?*

reclusis foribus:
    13.III.3
facie: 3.V.5

impotentis: 3.II.1

posset: 16.III
saepius: 6.II.2
consuetudine: 3.V.1

advenae: 3.III.2

artior: 6.I.2

timeas: 16.X

figendum: 17.III

subeat: 16.III

Paulum reclusis foribus miles prospicit,
videtque egregiam facie pulchrā feminam.
Correptus animus ilicō succenditur,
oriturque sensim ut impotentis cupiditas.
Sollers acumen mille causas invēnit,   20
per quas vidēre posset viduam saepius.
Cotidiānā capta consuetudine
paulatim facta est advenae submissior;
mox artior revinxit animum copula.
Hīc dum consumit noctes custos diligens,   25
desideratum est corpus ex unā cruce.
Turbatus miles factum exponit mulieri.
At sancta mulier, "Non est quod timeas," ait,
virique corpus tradit figendum cruci,
ne subeat ille poenas neglegentiae.   30
Sīc turpitudo laudis obsedit locum.

paulum — a bit

recludo, -ere — close, shut

prospicio, -ere — peer in

corripio, -ere — seize

ilicō — instantly

succendo, -ere — inflame

impotens — powerless

sollers, -tis — clever

acumen, -inis — intelligence

vidua, -ae — widow

advena, -ae — stranger

submissus, -a, -um — submissive

revincio, -ire — bind

copula, -ae — link, bond

turbatus, -a, -um — distraught

expono, -ere — explain

subeo, -ire — suffer

turpitudo, -inis — disgrace

obsideo, -ēre — take up

READING FOR UNDERSTANDING

1. *In the fable's last line, the poet expresses the view that the woman, whose conduct had been so exemplary up to that point (see, e.g.,* **sancta***, line 28), behaved disgracefully. Do you agree?*
2. *Since the widow's husband had received the proper rite of a funeral, do you think her treatment of his corpse was disrespectful?*
3. *After the death of a spouse, for how long should a person resist and be unavailable to the enticements of love?*

2.

"It's Complicated": Two Boyfriends, One Bride, and the Gods

READING FOR INFORMATION

1. *What distinguishes the two boyfriends from each other? Who wins out?*
2. *Who owns the donkey that the bride's family hired out?*
3. *How does Venus intervene?*

	Unam expetebant virginem iuvenes duo.	
	Vicit locuples genus et formam pauperis.	
ut: 16.XIII	Ut nuptiarum dictus advēnit dies,	
	amans, dolorem quia non poterat perpeti,	
	maerens propinquos contulit se in hortulos,	5
ultrā: 8.I.2	quos ultrā paulō villa splendens divitis	
erat acceptura: 17.VI	erat acceptura virginem e matris sinū,	
	parum ampla in urbe visa quod fuerat domus.	
	Pompa explicatur, turba concurrit frequens,	
	et coniugalem praefert Hymenaeus facem.	10
	Asellus autem, qui solebat pauperi	
	quaestum deferre, stabat portae in limine.	
	Illum puellae casū conducunt sui,	
laedant: 16.III	viae labores teneros ne laedant pedes.	
misericordiā: 3.V.7	Repente caelum, Veneris misericordiā,	15
	ventis movetur, intonat mundi fragor	
	noctemque densis horridam nimbis parat.	

8. **parum ... domus**: because the house in the city hadn't seemed big enough

expeto, -ere — pursue, court
perpetior, -i — endure
maereo, -ēre — grieve
conferre se — to take oneself
hortulus, -i — park, garden
ultrā — beyond
paulō — a little
parum — not at all
concurro, -ere — assemble

coniugalis, -e — conjugal
praefero, -rre — carry in front
Hymenaeus, -i — god of weddings
fax, -cis — torch
quaestus, -ūs — income
defero, -rre — earn
porta, -ae — gateway
limen, -inis — threshold

casū — by coincidence
conduco, -ere — hire
sui, suorum — loved ones
misericordia, -ae — sympathy
intono, -are — resound
fragor, -ris — crash, din
nimbus, -i — cloud

READING FOR INFORMATION
1. *Where does the donkey take the bride?*
2. *In what condition was the handsome boyfriend?*
3. *Whom did the bride finally marry?*

	Lux rapitur oculis, et simul vis grandinis	
	effusa trepidos passim comites dissipat,	
fugā: 3.V.1	sibi quemque cogens petere praesidium fugā.	20
	Asellus nōtum proximē tectum subit,	
voce: 3.V.1	et voce magnā sese vēnisse indicat.	
sese: 3.IV.4		
	Procurrunt pueri, pulchram aspiciunt virginem	
	et admirantur; deinde domino nuntiant.	
	Inter sodales ille paucos accubans	25
poculis: 3.V.1	amorem crebris avocabat poculis.	
ubi: 16.XIII	Ubi nuntiatum est, recreatus gaudiis,	
hortante ...	hortante Baccho et Venere, dulcīs perficit	
Venere: 13.III.2		
dulcīs: 5.II.2.d	aequalitatis inter plausūs nuptias.	
	Quaerunt parentes per praeconem filiam;	30
coniuge: 3.V.7	Novus maritus coniuge amissā dolet.	
esset: 16.V	Quid esset actum postquam populo innotuit,	
comprobarunt: 20.I	omnes favorem comprobarunt caelitum.	

grando, -inis — hail
trepidus, -a, -um — scared
dissipo, -are — disperse
procurro, -ere — run forth
admiror, -ari — be amazed
sodalis, -is — companion
accubo, -are — relax

avoco, -are — banish
poculum, -i — cup, drink
recreo, -are — restore, revive
aequalitas, -tatis — agemates, posse
plausus, -ūs — applause
praeco, -nis — town crier

innotesco, -ere — become known
comprobo, -are — approve
caelites, -um — gods

READING FOR UNDERSTANDING
1. *The outcome of this story is said to be commendable on the belief that the gods engineered it. Apart from the poet's assertion, is there any evidence to establish the gods' involvement in and approval of this marriage?*
2. *Which do you think is a better moral for this fable, "Love conquers all" or "When you're lucky, you're lucky"?*
3. *Try retelling the story from the perspective of the bride. Would it be the same tale?*

3.

Love, which is rarely uncomplicated in its own right, becomes a thorny psychological thicket when accompanied by other strong emotions. The following aphorisms bear this out.

quod: 7.V	Amans quod suspicatur, vigilans somniat.
	Omnis qui amicus est amat, sed non omnis qui amat amicus est.
	Amor otiosae causa est sollicitudinis.
cum: 16.I.2	Cum te detineat Veneris damnosa voluptas,
gulae: 3.III.5 **noli:** 19.III	indulgēre gulae noli, quae ventris amica est.
agitando: 17.II	Amans, sīcut fax, agitando ardescit magis.
	Non vincitur, sed vincit qui cedit suis.
concordiā: 3.V.8	Discordia fit carior concordiā.
	In venere semper certat dolor et gaudium.
	Blanditiā, non imperio, fit dulcis Venus.
est iuncta: 9.III.1.b	Cum Venere et Baccho lis est et iuncta voluptas;
quod: 7.V **animo:** 3.V.1 **complectere:** 19.I	quod lautum est animo complectere, sed fuge lites.
	Inhonesta victoria est suos vincere.
	Amor miscēri cum timore non potest.
	Amantium ira amoris integratio est.

suis: 3.III.5

Iniquē irascitur, qui suis irascitur sine dolore.

Amans iratus multa mentitur sibi.

In amore semper mendax iracundia est.

lacrimis: 3.V.1
redimas: 15.II

Ab amante lacrimis redimas iracundiam.

si: 18.I.2.b

Cogas amantem irasci, amari si velis.

suspicor, -ari — suspect
vigilo, -are — lose sleep
somnio, -are — dream
otiosus, -a, -um — idle
sollicitudo, -inis — worry
detineo, -ēre — get hold of
damnosus, -a, -um — ruinous
gula, -ae — gluttony

venter, -tris — gut, belly
ardesco, -ere — become
  inflamed
sui, suorum — loved ones
discordia, -ae — discord
blanditia, -ae — coaxing
lautus, -a, -um — fine,
  elegant

inhonestus, -a, -um —
  dishonorable
integratio, -nis — renewal
iniquē — unjustly
mendax — deceptive
redimo, -ere — undo, make
  amends for

READING FOR UNDERSTANDING

1. In what ways does love combine with other emotions? When is it positive, and when is it not?
2. Which two aphorisms seem the most true to you? Which two seem the most false?
3. In our culture, we often view the combination of love and anger as dangerous. Do the Romans seem to view it in the same way?

4.

In a poem of love lost, the poet, Lygdamus, dearly misses his Neaera (both probably pseudonyms), who has left him for another man.

READING FOR INFORMATION

1. Which two people does Lygdamus call hard hearted?
2. How well does Lygdamus claim to be holding up under his loss?
3. What common fantasy does the poet imagine in the depths of his loss?
4. What important detail do we learn about the relationship of Lygdamus and Neaera?

iuveni, puellae:
  3.III.2

Qui primus caram iuveni carumque puellae
    eripuit iuvenem, ferreus ille fuit.
Durus et ille fuit, qui tantum ferre dolorem,

erepta coniuge:
  13.III.3

    vivere et erepta coniuge qui potuit.
Non ego firmus in hōc, non haec patientia nostro

5

ingenio: 3.III.4

    ingenio. Frangit fortia corda dolor.

vitae: 3.II.6.a (after taedia)
mala: 3.IV.1.a
taedia: 3.IV.4
nata (esse): 12.I.3.d
cum: 16.I.3.a
	Nec mihi vera loqui pudor est vitaeque fatēri,
	      tot mala perpessae, taedia nata meae.
	Ergō cum tenuem fuero mutatus in umbram
	      candidaque ossa suprā nigra favilla teget, 10

veniat: 15.I capillos: 3.IV.6 fleat, veniat: 15.I	ante meum veniat longos incompta capillos. Et fleat ante meum maesta Neaera rogum;
dolore: 3.V.7 maereat: 15.I genero, viro: 3.III.3	sed veniat carae matris comitata dolore: maereat haec genero, maereat illa viro.

ferreus, -a, -um — hard hearted	**taedium, -i** — loathing	**maestus, -a, -um** — sorrowful
frango, -ere — break	**favilla, -ae** — ash	**comitatus, -a, -um** — attended
fateor, -ēri — admit	**incomptus, -a, -um** — disheveled	**maereo, -ēre** — mourn
perpetior, -i — suffer	**fleo, -ēre** — weep	**gener, -eri** — son-in-law

The poet's morbid fantasy continues with increasingly specific details, and the poem ends with Lygdamus's proposed epitaph.

READING FOR INFORMATION

1. *What details about Roman funerary practices do you learn from these lines?*
2. *Does the poet imagine an expensive burial for himself?*
3. *Besides Neaera, who is participating in Lygdamus's funeral?*

	Praefatae ante meos manes, animamque precatae, 15
liquore: 3.V.1 manūs: 3.IV.6 ossa: 3.IV.1	perfusaeque pias ante liquore manūs, pars quae sola mei superabit corporis, ossa
veste: 3.V.10	incinctae nigrā candida veste legent,
lyaeo: 3.V.1	et primum annoso spargent collecta lyaeo,

lacte: 3.V.1
parent: 15.I
tollere: 12.I.3.b
velis: 3.V.1
ponere: 12.I.3.b
	mox etiam niveo fundere lacte parent, 20
	post haec carbaseis umorem tollere velis,
	      atque in marmoreā ponere sicca domo.
	Illīc quas mittit pinguis Panchaia merces
	      Eoique Arabes, dives et Assyria,

nostri: 3.II.6
fundantur: 15.I
versūs: 3.IV.4
velim: 15.II
demonstret, notet: 15.I
huic: 3.III.3
Neaerae: 3.II.6
coniugis: 3.VIII
causa: 3.I.2
perire: 12.I.3.b
	et nostri memores lacrimae fundantur eōdem, 25
	      sīc ego componi versūs in ossa velim.
	Sed tristem mortis demonstret littera causam
	      atque haec in celebri carmina fronte notet:
	LYGDAMVS HĪC SITVS EST: DOLOR HVIC ET CVRA NEAERAE,
	      CONIVGIS EREPTAE, CAVSA PERIRE FVIT. 30

praefor, -ari — invoke	**incinctus, -a, -um** — unbelted	**niveus, -a, -um** — white
perfundo, -ere — perfume	**annosus, -a, -um** — old	**carbaseus, -a, -um** — linen-
liquor, -ris — liquid	**lyaeus, -i** — wine	

velum, -i — shroud

umor, -ris — dampness

marmoreus, -a, -um — of marble

siccus, -a, -um — dried

pinguis, -e — rich

Panchaius, -a, -um — of Panchaea (mythic Red Sea island)

merces, -edis — product

Eous, -a, -um — eastern

Arabs, -bis — Arabian

eodem — at the same place

celeber, -bis, -bre — well known

sino, -ere — lay out

READING FOR UNDERSTANDING

1. *Why do you suppose death fantasies are so common among those experiencing love, especially an obsessive or frustrated love?*

2. *Why do you suppose the poet includes his mother-in-law in his death fantasy?*

3. *Compose your own two-line epitaph. What would it say about you and/or the people you love?*

5.

In this poem, the poet exhorts his long-standing lover to persist in their love.

sit: 15.I nobis: 3.III.8 te: 3.IV.1 pectore: 3.V.10	Sit nox illa diū nobis dilecta, Nealce, quae te prima meo pectore composuit; sit torus et lecti genius secretaque lampas,
quīs: 7.V.1	quīs tenera in nostrum vēnerīs arbitrium.

duremus: 15.I
adoleverit:
  16.XIII.1.a
utamur: 15.I
	Ergō, age, duremus, quamvis adoleverit aetas, 5
	      utamurque annis, quos mora parva teret.
	Fas et iura sinunt veteres extendere amores;

fac: 19.I quod: 7.V	fac cito quod coeptum est, non cito desinere.

genius, -i — guardian spirit

lampas, -padis — lamp

arbitrium, -i — choice

duro, -are — persevere

adoleo, -ēre — burn up

extendo, -ere — extend

READING FOR UNDERSTANDING

1. *"Just 'cause there's snow on the roof don't mean there ain't fire in the furnace." This old saw reminds us that age doesn't necessarily nullify passion. Does this poem suggest that passion among older people was considered disgraceful or acceptable?*

2. *The name Nealce is Greek and suggests a prostitute or a freedwoman (or both). Does that fact change the poem for you?*

3. *The **genius lecti** is the sexual and procreative power of the head of household's bed. In what way does it seem strange that the poet should mention this mojo?*

6.

The following aphorisms examine the relationship between love, loss, and time.

Amor extorquēri non pote, elābi pote.

si: 18.I.2.a.i   Libidinis initia continebis, si exitum cogitaveris.

iuveni, seni: 3.III.3   Amare iuveni fructus est, crimen seni.

Lepores duo qui insequitur, is neutrum capit.

Amor, ut lacrima, ab oculo oritur, in pectus cadit.

Paulisper laxatus amor decedere coepit.

Amori finem tempus, non animus facit.

Homo totiens moritur, quotiens amittit suos.

In amore semper causa damni quaeritur.

nuptae: 3.II.1   Obsequium nuptae cito fit odium paelicis.
paelicis: 3.II.6

diligas: 16.XII   Quem diligas, ni rectē moneas, oderis.
ni: 18.I.4

Oculi occultē amorem incipiunt, consuetudo perficit.
Perenne coniugium animus, non corpus facit.

Quī pote transferre amorem, pote deponere.

tamquam: Amare sīc incipe, tamquam non liceat tibi desinere.
16.XIII.1.b

extorqueo, -ēre — wrestle away	**insequor, -i** — pursue	**obsequium, -i** — indulgence, allegiance
elābor, -i — slip away	**neuter, -tra, -trum** — neither	**nupta, -ae** — bride
initium, -i — beginning	**paulisper** — for a little while	**paelex, -licis** — concubine
exitus, -ūs — end	**laxo, -are** — relax	**rectē** — rightly
fructus, -ūs — pleasure	**totiens** — so often	**consuetudo, -dinis** — habit
crimen, -minis — crime	**sui, suorum** — loved ones	**perennis, -e** — lasting
lepos, -oris — pleasure	**damnum, -i** — loss	**quī** — in the way that

READING FOR UNDERSTANDING

1. *On the whole, do the Romans seem optimistic or pessimistic about the effects of time on love?*
2. *In our culture, we devote a lot of attention to lost love. If the Romans devoted less, how might you explain that difference?*
3. *Again, which two of these aphorisms seem the most true to you? Which two seem the most false?*

7.

The loss of a girlfriend named Lydia to death forms the subject of this poem. The poet starts with a complaint against the fields where his love now lies buried.

READING FOR INFORMATION

1. *In this section, which features of his beloved Lydia does the poet praise?*
2. *What secret story will Lydia furtively tell?*
3. *What will be the reactions of nature to Lydia's story?*

vobis: 3.III.5 **agri . . . prata:** 3.VI **hōc:** 3.V.10	Invideo vobis, agri formosaque prata, hōc formosa magis, mea quod formosa puella	
vobis: 3.III.4	est vobis: tacitē nostrum suspirat amorem.	
vobis: 3.III.3	Vos nunc illa videt, vobis mea Lydia ludit,	
ocellis: 3.V.1	vos nunc adloquitur, vos nunc adridet ocellis,	5
	et mea submissā meditatur carmina voce,	
	cantat et intereā, mihi quae cantabat in aurem.	
	Invideo vobis, agri: discetis amare.	
nimium multumque: 3.IV.7	O fortunati nimium multumque beati, in quibus illa pedis nivei vestigia ponet,	10
	aut roseis viridem digitis decerpserit uvam	
	(dulci namque tumet nondum viticula Baccho),	
stipendia: 3.VIII	aut inter varios, Veneris stipendia, flores	
reclinarit: 20.I.3	membra reclinarit teneramque illiserit herbam,	
	et secreta meos furtim narrabit amores.	15
	Gaudebunt silvae, gaudebunt mollia prata,	
avium: 3.II.1	et gelidi fontes, aviumque silentia fient.	
lymphae: 3.VI	Tardabunt rivi lābentes (sistite, lymphae),	
dum: 16.XIII.3.a.i.B	dum mea iucundas exponat cura querelas.	

pratum, -i — meadow	**ocellus, -i** — little eye	**roseus, -a, -um** — rosy
suspiro, -are — sigh for	**submissus, -a, -um** —	**viridis, -e** — green
adloquor, -i — speak to	lowered	**decerpo, -ere** — pluck
adrideo, -ēre — smile at	**meditor, -ari** — celebrate	**uva, -ae** — grape cluster

nondum — not yet

viticula, -ae — vine shoot

stipendium, -i — salary

reclino, -are — recline

illido, -ere — bruise

furtim — furtively

gelidus, -a, -um — chilly

tardo, -are — slow

rivus, -i — river

lympha, -ae — water

iucundus, -a, -um —
pleasant

expono, -ere — reveal

querela, -ae — complaint

The poet begins to express his sense of loss, which he situates against a backdrop of the mythological and natural worlds.

READING FOR INFORMATION

1. *What physical effects is the loss of Lydia having on the poet?*
2. *Lydia is obliquely and favorably compared to Europa and Danaë, making her worthy of which god's attention?*
3. *Why, according to the poet, are the bull and the billy goat luckier than he?*

	Invideo vobis, agri: mea gaudia habetis,	20
	et vobis nunc est mea quae fuit ante voluptas.	
mihi: 3.III.3 dolore: 3.V.7 frigore: 3.V.7	At mihi tabescunt morientia membra dolore,	
	et calor infuso decedit frigore mortis,	
mecum: 8.II.1.a	quod mea non mecum domina est: non ulla puella	
	doctior in terris fuit aut formosior, ac, si	25
tauro, auro: 3.V.16	fabula non vana est, tauro Iove digna vel auro	
avertas: 19.IV	(Iuppiter, avertas aurem; mea sola puella est).	
	Felix taure, pater magni gregis et decus, a te	
	vaccula non umquam secreta cubilia captans	
te: 3.IV.4 silvis: 3.III.3 mugire: 12.I.3.d pater: 3.VI	frustrā te patitur silvis mugire dolorem.	30
	Et pater haedorum felix semperque beatē,	
	sive petis montes praeruptos, saxa pererrans,	
silvis, campis: 3.V.18	sive tibi silvis nova pabula fastidire	
	sive libet campis: tecum tua laeta capella est.	
illi: 3.III.3	Et mas quācumque est, illi sua femina iuncta:	35
	interpellatos numquam ploravit amores.	
nobis: 3.III.2	Cur non et nobis facilis, natura, fuisti?	
	Cur ego crudelem patior tam saepe dolorem?	

tabesco, -ere — waste away

infundo, -ere — infuse

frigus, -oris — chill

doctus, -a, -um — learned

averto, -ere — avert

vaccula, -ae — calf, heifer

capto, -are — seize

mugio, -ire — bellow

haedus, -i — goat

praeruptus, -a, -um — steep

pererro, -are — wander over

pabulum, -i — food

fastidio, -ire — disdain

capella, -ae — she-goat

quācumque — wherever

interpello, -are — interrupt

ploro, -are — lament

The poet next points out that even the gods have had to deal with the loss of their loved ones, and he wonders whether the pain of humans is more acute precisely because of the pains that the gods have experienced.

READING FOR INFORMATION

1. *The mortal love of Phoebus was turned into what?*
2. *Ariadne, the daughter of King Minos, became what?*
3. *Why doesn't the poet further enumerate the gods' love affairs with mortals?*

cum: 16.I.4	Sidera per viridem redeunt cum pallida mundum,
	inque vicem Phoebi currens abit aureus orbis, 40
tuus (amor): 3.X	Luna, tuus tecum est: cur non est et mea mecum?
nōsti: 20.I.3 **sit:** 16.V **miserēre:** 19.I **dolentis:** 3.II.6.b **quae:** 3.IV.1 **deum:** 1.II.1.c **silvis:** 3.V.1	Luna, dolor nōsti quid sit: miserēre dolentis. Phoebe, recens in te laurus celebravit amorem. Et quae pompa deum, non silvis fama locuta est?
mundo: 3.III.7 **quae:** 3.IV.1 **cum:** 16.I.4	Omnia quisque deus secum sua gaudia gestat 45 aut insparsa videt mundo; quae dicere longum est. Aurea quin etiam cum saecula volvebantur,
(cum) foret: 16.I.3.a **mortalibus:** 3.III.3	condicio similisque foret mortalibus illis— haec quoque praetereo. Notum Minoidos astrum quaeque virum virgo, sīcut captiva, secuta est. 50
vos: 3.IV.1	Laedere, caelicolae, potuit vos nostra quid aetas,
quō: 16.III.2.c	condicio nobis vitae quō durior esset?

44. **quae . . . est**: what things has a gods' parade, what things has a tale of the gods not proclaimed with [kinds of] wood?

pallidus, -a, -um — pale	**celebro, -are** — celebrate	**condicio, -nis** — condition
vicis, -is — turn	**gesto, -are** — wear	**praetereo, -ire** — omit
tuus (amor) = Endymion	**insparsus, -a, -um** —	**caelicola, -ae** — deity
misereor, -ēri — pity	scattered over	
laurus, -i — laurel tree		

The poet wonders whether he was somehow responsible for Lydia's death and whether her death was a punishment for their lovemaking.

READING FOR INFORMATION

1. *Why does the poet wish that he were the first person guilty of forbidden sex?*
2. *With whom did Jupiter have sex before he was married?*

ausus (sum): 20.IV	Ausus ego primus castos violare pudores,
	sacratamque meae vittam temptare puellae,
solvere: 12.I.3.b	immatura meā cogor nece solvere fata? 55

utinam: 15.IV
facti: 3.II.6
magistra: 3.I.2
foret: 10.III.7.a
vitā: 3.V.8
esset: 15.II
moreretur: 15.II
cum: 16.I.1
furatus (esse):
  12.I.3.d
tantum: 3.IV.1
auctor: 3.I.2
ut: 16.II
sui: 7.III
mendacia: 3.IV.1
factus: 10.VIII.5
prius . . . quam:
  16.XIII.3.a.ii.D
	Istius atque utinam facti mea culpa magistra
	prima foret! Letum vitā mihi dulcius esset.
	Non mea, non ullo moreretur tempore, fama
	dulcia cum Veneris furatus gaudia primum
	dicerer, atque ex me dulcis foret orta voluptas. 60
	Nam mihi non tantum tribuerunt invida fata,
	auctor ut occulti noster foret error amoris.
	Iuppiter ante, sui semper mendacia factus,
	cum Iunone, prius coniunx quam dictus uterque est,
	gaudia libavit dulcem furatus amorem. 65

sacro, -are — sanctify	**letum, -i** — death	**error, -ris** — mistake
immaturus, -a, -um — premature	**furor, -ari** — steal **invidus, -a, -um** — jealous	**mendacium, -i** — deception

The poet continues with his description of divine sexual dalliances and ends his poem with a final lament.

READING FOR INFORMATION

1. *Adonis made an adulteress out of which deity?*
2. *Where were Mars and Vulcan when Venus was with her lover?*
3. *What natural effect was created when Aurora lost her lover Orion?*
4. *For what does the poet blame the Fates?*

moechum: 3.IV.4	Et moechum tenerā gavisa est laedere in herbā purpureos flores, quos insuper accumbebat,
Cypria: 3.I.1 collo: 3.III.7	Cypria, formoso supponens bracchia collo. (Tum, credo, fuerat Mavors distentus in armis, nam certē Vulcanus opus faciebat, et ille 70
fuligine: 3.V.7	tristi turpabat malam ac fuligine barbam.) Non Aurora novos etiam ploravit amores,
amictū: 3.V.1	atque rubens oculos roseo celavit amictū? Talia caelicolae. Numquid minus aurea proles?
deus atque heros (fecerunt): 20.VI aetas (facit): 20.VI tempore: 3.V.6 nascendi: 17.II quo: 3.V.10 fecēre: 20.I.2 ut: 16.II quod: 7.V oculis: 3.V.1 possis: 15.II	Ergō quod deus atque heros, cur non minor aetas? 75 Infelix ego, non illo qui tempore natus, quō facilis natura fuit. Sors o mea laeva nascendi, miserumque genus, quo sera libido est. Tantam Fata meae cordis fecēre rapinam, ut maneam, quod vix oculis cognoscere possis. 80

moechus, -i — adulterer	**accumbo, -ere** — lie	**Mavors, -rtis** — Mars
gaudeo, -ēre — take delight in	**Cypria, -ae** — Venus	**distendo, -ere** — distract
insuper — on top of	**suppono, -ere** — lay under	**turpo, -are** — dirty

mala, -ae — cheek	**ploro, -are** — lament	**serus, -a, -um** — slow in
fulgo, -inis — soot	**amores** = Orion	coming
barba, -ae — beard	**amictus, -ūs** — clothing	**rapina, -ae** — plundering
Aurora, -ae — goddess of	**caelicola, -ae** — deity	
dawn	**heros, -ois** — hero	

READING FOR UNDERSTANDING

1. *In our culture, we distinguish pretty clearly between premarital sex and extramarital sex (i.e., adultery). Why isn't the same distinction made clear in this poem?*
2. *Explain what the poet means in his complaint for the human race **sera libido est** (line 78).*
3. *Does this poem seem emotionally authentic to you? That is, do you think the poet's true love really died and he was left to mourn and make some sense of his loss? Alternatively, perhaps this poem is merely the result of an assignment ("Write a poem, less than a hundred lines in length, in which you lament the loss of a dead lover") given by a **grammaticus**.*

8.

In this suggestive poem, the poet expresses appreciation for his lover's "fruits" and invites her to come to him so she can bestow these favors in person.

READING FOR INFORMATION

1. *What does the poet's sweetheart send him?*
2. *What does he call these gifts?*

mihi: 3.III.3	Aurea mala mihi, dulcis mea Martia, mittis,	
	mittis et hirsutae munera castaneae.	
si: 18.I.3	Omnia grata puta; sed si magis ipsa venires,	
	ornares donum, pulchra puella, tuum.	
apportes: 15.II	Tu licet apportes stringentia mala palatum,	5
tristia: 3.IV.1.a **ore:** 3.V.18 **si:** 18.I.1 **multum:** 3.IV.7	tristia mandenti est melleus ore sapor.	
	At si dissimulas, multum mihi cara, venire,	
	oscula cum pomis mitte; vorabo libens.	

hirsutus, -a, -um — shaggy	**stringo, -ere** — pucker	**sapor, -ris** — flavor
castanea, -ae — chestnut	**palatum, -i** — mouth	**dissimulo, -are** — tell lies
orno, -are — adorn	**mando, -ere** — eat	**pomum, -i** — apple
apporto, -are — bring	**melleus, -a, -um** — honeyed	**voro, -are** — eat

READING FOR UNDERSTANDING

1. *Does the poet truly appreciate the previous gifts of "apples" and a "hairy chestnut," or does he regard them as mere come-ons?*

2. The poet says his mouth is currently "chewing on bitter things" (**tristia mandens**). What might he mean?

3. This poem is frankly oral. Many of our endearments (honey, sugar, sweetie pie, etc.) also suggest food. What do you suppose is the connection between sexual passion and orality?

9.

The poet here describes the appearance of the god Cupid in a dream, the god's words, and his own reaction.

READING FOR INFORMATION

1. At what point in the poet's sleep does the dream occur?
2. What does Cupid call the poet? Does he treat the poet accordingly?

lecto: 3.V.10	Lecto compositus vix prima silentia noctis
somno: 3.III.1	carpebam et somno lumina victa dabam,
cum: 16.I.4	cum me saevus Amor prensat, sursumque capillis
	excitat et lacerum pervigilare iubet.
cum: 16.I.2	"Tu famulus meus," inquit, "ames cum mille puellas, 5
	solus, io, solus, dure, iacēre potes?"
	Exsilio et pedibus nudis tunicāque solutā
	omne iter impedio, nullum iter expedio.
piget, paenitet: 20.III.5	Nunc propero, nunc ire piget, rursumque redire
	paenitet, et pudor est stare viā mediā. 10
	Ecce, tacent voces hominum strepitūsque viarum
volucrum, canum: 1.III.2.d	et volucrum cantūs turbaque fida canum;
	solus ego ex cunctis paveo somnumque torumque,
	et sequor imperium, magne Cupido, tuum.

silentium, -i — silence   **pervigilo, -are** — stay awake   **rursum** — again

prenso, -are — seize   **famulus, -i** — slave   **strepitus, -ūs** — sound

sursum — from behind   **io** — ha!   **paveo, -ēre** — be afraid

lacer, -era, -erum — mangled, roughed up   **exsilium, -i** — exile

expedio, -ire — make ready

READING FOR UNDERSTANDING

1. How are lines 8–13 especially dreamlike?
2. Though the poet vows to heed the god, where is the love, where is the obedience in this poem?

10.

As the following sententiae *make clear, the diagnosis is love!*

Amoris vulnus idem sanat, qui facit.

Qui propter pecuniae vel libidinis amorem moritur,
sui: 7.III   ostendit se numquam sui causā vixisse.

Amor animi arbitrio sumitur, non ponitur.

Non est hominis maior stultitia quam putare se amari ab his, quos ipse
diligat: 15.II   non diligat.

cupiat, sapiat: 16.V   Amans quid cupiat scit; quid sapiat non videt.

rationis: 3.II.2   Nil rationis est, ubi res semel in adfectum venit.

Amare et sapere vix deo conceditur.

cum: 16.I.3.a   Honestius est cum iudicaverīs amare, quam cum amaverīs iudicare.

Amantis ius iurandum poenam non habet.

cum: 16.I.1   Cum ames non sapias, aut cum sapias non ames.
sapias, ames: 15.II

In Venere semper dulcis est dementia.

Amicitia semper prodest, amor et nocet.

Nec mortem effugere quisquam nec amorem potest.

arbitrium, -i — decision   **ius iurandum** — oath
adfectus, -ūs — emotion   **dementia, -ae** — madness

READING FOR UNDERSTANDING

1. *What common view of love do all the preceding aphorisms express?*
2. *In our culture, do we share some of these views of love? Can you think of some similar song lyrics?*
3. *Some infirmities and afflictions are curable; some aren't. If viewed according to a medical model, which is love?*

11.

Duly noted: the poet describes how he publicized his love in a time-honored way.

READING FOR INFORMATION

1. *The poet claims that he was doing what when he decided to proclaim his love?*
2. *What's his purpose in proclaiming it in the manner that he does?*
3. *What is the future of this proclamation?*

quandō: 16.XIII.2.a   Quandō ponebam novellas arbores māli et piri,

cortici: 3.III.3   cortici summae notavi nomen ardoris mei.

     Nulla fit exinde finis vel quies cupidinis:

     crescit arbor, gliscit ardor: animus implet litteras.

novellus, -a, -um — young   **cortex, -icis** — bark   **glisco, -ere** — spread

mālum, -i — apple   **exinde** — thereafter   **impleo, -ēre** — fill in

pirum, -i — pear

READING FOR UNDERSTANDING

1. *What wordplay do you notice in the last line of this poem?*
2. *What ambiguity in the word **animus** does the poet exploit in the last line?*

12.

A dialogue on love: two potential lovers discuss whether to consummate their mutual attraction.

READING FOR INFORMATION

1. *According to the first speaker, what is wrong with sexual passion?*
2. *How do farm animals behave?*
3. *According to the second speaker, how should the lovers spend their time? Why?*

     "Foeda est in coetū et brevis voluptas

veneris: 3.II.6.b   et taedet veneris statim peractae.

     Non ergō, ut pecudes libidinosae,

irruamus: 15.I   caeci protinus irruamus illūc—

     nam languescit amor peritque flamma."   5

     "Sed sīc, sīc, sine fine feriati

iaceamus: 15.I   et tecum iaceamus osculantes.

     Hic nullus labor est ruborque nullus:

iuvit, iuvat, iuvabit: hoc iuvit, iuvat, et diū iuvabit;
20.III.7.a

     hoc non deficit incipitque semper."   10

taedet — it disgusts   **illūc** — there   **osculor, -ari** — kiss

libidinosus, -a, -um — lusty   **languesco, -ere** — grow weary   **rubor, -ris** — cause for shame

irruo, -ere — rush into   **feriatus, -a, -um** — at leisure

READING FOR UNDERSTANDING

1. Although the poet gives us little solid evidence either way, who speaks each side of the debate?
2. Is the first speaker really saying no?
3. Which of the two sides does it seem will win the debate?

13.

This poem purports to be by the famous poet Tibullus but is in fact just an imitative tribute to his style of writing. The poet here claims to love no one other than his girlfriend and to be exclusively devoted to her.

READING FOR INFORMATION

1. Why does the poet want others to see his girlfriend as unpretty?
2. Why doesn't the poet boast of his love?
3. In lines 9–12, what does the girlfriend supposedly provide the poet?

> Nulla tuum nobis subducet femina lectum:
>   hōc primum iuncta est foedere nostra venus.
>
> Tu mihi sola places, nec iam te praeter in urbe
>   formosa est oculis ulla puella meis.
>
> Atque utinam posses uni mihi bella vidēri!   5
>   Displiceas aliis: sīc ego tutus ero.
>
> Nil opus invidiā est; procul absit gloria vulgi:
>   qui sapit, in tacito gaudeat ille sinū.
>
> Sīc ego secretis possum bene vivere silvis,
>   quā nulla humano sit via trita pede.   10
>
> Tu mihi curarum requies, tu nocte vel atrā
>   lumen, et in solis tu mihi turba locis.

Marginal annotations:

mihi: 3.III.5
te praeter: 8.IV
oculis: 3.III.3

utinam: 15.IV

displiceas: 19.IV

invidiā: 3.V.10
absit, gaudeat: 15.I

sit: 15.II

mihi: 3.III.2

subduco, -ere — steal   **vulgus, -i** — mob   **ater, atra, atrum** — dark

foedus, -eris — bond   **tero, -ere** — wear down

bellus, -a, -um — pretty   **requies, -etis** — rest

After a bold claim and a sacred vow, the poet experiences a sudden change of thought. The poem closes with the poet acknowledging his utter subjection.

READING FOR INFORMATION

1. How, allegedly, would the poet react to a heaven-sent girlfriend?
2. What god does he make his oath to? Why?

3. *Why does he suddenly think that expressing his devotion is a mistake?*
4. *To what does he finally compare his situation?*

mittatur: 15.II	Nunc licet e caelo mittatur amica Tibullo,
	mittetur frustrā deficietque Venus.
hoc: 3.IV.1 (per) numina	Hoc tibi sancta tuae Iunonis numina iuro, 15
	quae sola ante alios est tibi magna deos.
	Quid facio demens? Heu! Heu! Mea pignora cedo.
	Iuravi stultē: proderat iste timor.
me: 3.IV.1	Nunc tu fortis eris, nunc tu me audacius ures:
(mihi) misero: 3.III.3	hoc peperit misero garrula lingua malum. 20
	Iam faciam quodcumque voles, tuus usque manebo,
dominae: 3.II.1	nec fugiam nōtae servitium dominae,
	sed Veneris sanctae considam vinctus ad aras:
supplicibus: 3.III.5	haec notat iniustos supplicibusque favet.

demens, -ntis — insane	**garrulus, -a, -um** — chatty	**iniustus, -a, -um** — unjust
pignus, -oris — promise	**servitium, -i** — slavery	
pario, -ere — produce	**consido, -ere** — be seated	

READING FOR UNDERSTANDING
1. *Why does the poet swear an oath to one goddess but sit suppliant at the altar of a different goddess?*
2. *Which motifs in this poem strike you as a little trite? Do they diminish your appreciation of the poem?*
3. *How do you reconcile the aphorism of line 8 (**qui sapit, in tacito gaudeat ille sinū**) with the confession in line 20 (**hoc peperit misero garrula lingua malum**)?*

14.

A brief, final miscellany of aphorisms on love.

    In amore forma plus valet quam auctoritas.

virtuti: 3.III.1   Virtuti amorem nemo honestē denegat.

odiis, amore: 3.V.7   Alta cadunt odiis, parva extolluntur amore.

    Iam magnum reddis modico tu munus amico,
si: 18.I.1
auro: 3.V.8   si ipsum ut amicus amas: amor est pretiosior auro.

    Si vis amari, ama.

denego, -are — refuse

extollo, -ere — praise

modicus, -a, -um — humble

pretiosus, -a, -um — expensive

READING FOR UNDERSTANDING

1. *In the first aphorism here,* **forma** *can mean "beauty" or "appearance" or even "the human body";* **auctoritas** *can mean "prestige" or "social class" or "authority" or "external influence." How should this aphorism be best understood?*

2. *For the second aphorism, does* **amor** *seem an overstatement? Would some word meaning "admiration" seem more apt?*

3. *For the third aphorism, can you provide some examples of* **alta** *and* **parva** *that bear out its truth?*

PART IV

Vocabularies

A. Acquisition Vocabulary

To achieve reading fluency in Latin, it is essential that you constantly work at building your Latin vocabulary. Mastering the following lists will virtually guarantee you a good vocabulary, suitable for future readings in both prose and poetry.

I.

1. From Morphology and Grammar Review section 6, learn all the adjectives and adverbs listed in I.4 and II.4.
2. From Morphology and Grammar Review section 8, learn all the prepositions listed in I.1 and II.1.
3. From Morphology and Grammar Review section 10, learn all the irregular compound verbs listed in I.7, II.7, and III.9.
4. From Morphology and Grammar Review section 11, learn all the deponent verbs listed in capital letters; also learn the semideponents provided in II and III.
5. From Morphology and Grammar Review section 20, learn all the impersonal verbs listed in III.1, III.5, III.6, and III.7.

II. The following words appear eight or more times throughout this text; their frequency alone justifies learning them.

1.

accipio	amica	ars
advenio	amicus	at
aeger	amitto	atque
āer	amo	aura
aes	amor	audio
aetas	ancilla	auris
ager	animus	aurum
ago	annus	aut
ales	appareo	autem
alienus	appello	avis
aliquis	aqua	avus
alius	ara	axis
alter	arbor	bellum
altus	arma	bellus

beneficium	caedo	canis
bibo	caelum	
cado	campus	

2.

cantus	coepio	cum (conjunction)
capillus	cogito	cunctus
capio	cogo	cupio
caput	colo	cura
carmen	coma	cursus
carus	compono	dea
casus	condo	debeo
cauda	coniunx	decus
causa	consilium	dein, deinde
caveo	consul	depono
cedo	contentus	deus
celer	corpus	dico
certus	cras	dies
cibus	credo	dignus
citus	creo	diligens
civis	cubiculum	diligo

3.

discedo	emo	fatum
disco	enim	faveo
diu	eo, ire	feles
divus	equus	felix
do	ergo	femina
dolor	eripio	fero, ferre
dominus	et	ferus
domus	etiam	fides
dormio	exemplum	filia
dubito	exercitus	filius
dubius	existimo	finis
duco	explico	flamen
dulcis	facilis	flamma
dum	facio	flos
duo	factum	forma
effugio	fama	
ego	fas	

4.

formosus
fors
forte
fortis
fortuna
forum
fuga
fugio
gaudium
gens
genus
gero
gradus
gratia
gratus
gravis
habeo

hīc
hic
homo
honestus
honos or honor
hostis
humanus
iaceo
iam
ibi
idem
ignis
ille
illīc
imperator
imperium
impero

impono
inde
iniuria
inquam, inquit
intellego
interficio
invenio
ipse
ira
is, ea, id
iste
ita
itaque
item
iubeo

5.

iudicium
iungo
ius
iuvenis
iuvo
labor (noun)
laboro
lacrima
laedo
laetus
laudo
lectus (adjective)
lectus (noun)
lego
leo
levis
lex

līber (adjective)
liber (noun)
līberi
lingua
locus
longus
lumen
lux
maneo
manus
mare
maritus
mater
matrimonium
matrona
maturus
medius

membrum
mens
meritus
meus
miles
mille, milia
misceo
miser
mitto
modo
mollis
mors
mos
mox
mulier

6.

mundus	nisi	olim
munus	noceo	omnis
nam	nolo	opus
natura	nomen	orbis
natus (noun)	non	ōs, oris
nauta, navita	nos	osculum
ne	nosco	ostendo
-ne	noster	par
nec	nōtus	parco
neco	novus	parens
nego	nox	pareo
negotiis	nudus	paro
nemo	nullus	pars
nemus	numen	pater
neque	numquam	patientia
nescio	nunc	
nihil, nil	oculus	

7.

patria	possum	quam
pectus	postquam	quamvis
pecunia	praesto	quando
perdo	primo, primum	quasi
peric(u)lum	procul	-que
pervenio	propero	qui
pes	proprius	quia
peto	publicus	quicumque
placeo	pudicitia	quid
plenus	pudor	quidam
plus	puella	quidem, ne quidem
poena	puer	quidquid, quicquid
poeta	pulcher	quin
pompa	puto	quis, quid
pono	quā	quisquam
pontifex	quaero	
populus	qualis	

8.

quisque
quisquis
quō
quod
quoniam
quoque
rarus
ratio
recipio
reddo
religio
relinquo
reperio
res
retineo
rex

rideo
rogo
rosa
rumpo
ruo
sacer
sacerdos
saepe
sanctus
sanguis
sapio
sat, satis
saxum
scio
scribo
se, sese

secretus
securus
sed or set
semper
senatus
senex
servio
servo
servus
seu, sive
si
sīc
sidus
signum
silva
similis

9.

sinus
sol
sōlum (adverb)
solum (noun)
sōlus
solvo
somnus
specto
spes
statim
sto
studium
stultus
subitus
sustineo
suus
taberna

taceo
talis
tam
tamen
tamquam
tango
tantum
tantus
tectum
templum
tempus
teneo
tener
terra
timeo
tollo
tot

totus
trado
traho
tres
tribuo
tristis
tu
tum
tumeo
tunc
turba
tutus
tuus
ubi
ullus

10.

umbra	verbero	vis
unde	verbum	vita
unus	verus	vitium
urbs	vestigium	vivo
usque	vestis	vivus
ut, uti, utinam	via	vix
utilis	victoria	volo, velle
utor	video, videor	volucer
uva	villa	volucris
uxor	vinco	voluptas
-ve	vinum	vos
vel	vir	votum
venio	virgo	vox
venus	virtus	
ver	vīrus	

III. The following words appear six or seven times in this text:

1.

abundo	bestia	contemno
accuso	bos	contendo
adeo (adverb)	caerimonia	contineo
adgredior	candidus	contingo
adicio	canto	converto
admoveo	castus	cornu
adversus (adjective)	cavus	cresco
aequus	cena	cruor
aeternus	civitas	cultus (noun)
aio	cognosco	cur
albus	collum	curo
amplus	color	custodio
anima	conspectus	desero
arva	conspicio	digitus
auxilium	constituo	
beatus	consumo	

2.

dimitto	fidelis	infans
discipulus	foedus	ingens
dives	fons	insignis
divinus	fortunatus	instituo
doceo	frater	iracundia
doleo	fundo	iratus
domina	funus	iter
donec	fur	iterum
dono	gloria	iudex
donum	hiems	iudico
dux	hodie	iugum
ecce	humus	iustus
egregius	iacto	levo
exspecto	impetus	libenter
felicitas	incipio	
feriatus	indignus	

3.

libido	nimium	perago
lis	nocens	pietas
littera	nodus	pingo
lucus	noto	pius
ludo	nubo	placidus
ludus	nuntio	postea
metuo	officium	potens
metus	oppidum	praecipuus
mirus	ops	precor
mons	oratio	princeps
morbus	oro	probus
moveo	os, ossis	promitto
muto	pauci	propter
narro	pauper	proscribo
navis	pax	
neu	pecus	

4.

protinus	sīcut, sīcuti	turpis
pugno	sordidus	umor
purus	sors	unda
quantus	spiritus	universus
quartus	subicio	uterque
quies	sumo	varius
quilibet	supero	veho
quondam	supplex	velut, veluti
rapio	tego	verto
repente	tempto	verum
respondeo	tendo	vetus
roseus	tenebrae	vindico
rursum, rursus	tertius	viridis
rus	timor	vitis
sentio	torus	vulnus
sermo	triumvir	

B. General Vocabulary

Aa

a (interjection) *see* **ah**

a, ab (preposition with ablative) from, away from; after; out of, of; by, at the hands of, because of; in connection with, as regards

abditus, -a, -um concealed, secret

abeo, -ire, abivi, abitus go away; die; digress; change; disappear, vanish

abicio, -ere, abieci, abiectus throw down or away; break off abruptly; get rid of, give up; dash to the ground, weaken, dishearten

aboleo, -ere, abolevi, abolitus destroy, do away with

absens, -entis absent; *see also* **absum**

absum, abesse, afui be away, be absent or missing; fail to help; be far from

abundo (1) overflow; grow in abundance; abound, be rich in

ac *see* **atque**

accedo, -ere, accessi, accessus approach, come near; enter upon, begin; be added

accendo, -ere, accendi, accensus kindle, set on fire; inflame, excite

accerso = arcesso

accido, -ere, accidi fall down; happen, fall out

accipio, -ere, accepi, acceptus take, receive, accept; hear, sense; grasp, learn; receive hospitably; treat

accommodo (1) fit, put on equipment, etc.; make suitable, adjust, adapt

accumbo, -ere, accubui, accubitus lie down, recline (especially at table)

accuso (1) accuse; blame, find fault with

acer, acris, acre sharp, cutting, keen; biting; shrill; painful; energetic
acriter (adverb) sharply, keenly

acerbus, -a, -um bitter; harsh; dark, gloomy; painful, severe; morose

acies, -ei (f) keenness, edge; insight; a piercing look or keen vision; eye; battle line; battle, battlefield

actio, -onis (f) action, doing; proposal, motion; legal formula

acumen, -inis (n) sharp point; sharpness of intellect; cunning, trickery

acutus, -a, -um sharpened, pointed, acute; shrill, piercing; painful; keen, intelligent

ad (preposition with accusative) toward, to; at or near; until or at, about; for the purpose of; concerning; compared with, in addition to; in conformity with; as far as, up to

addo, -ere, addidi, additus give, bring, place; inspire, cause; add, join

adeō (adverb) to that point, so far; so long; so much, so, to such an extent

adeo, -ire, adivi, aditus go or come to, approach, visit; undertake, undergo, incur

adfectus, -ūs (m) condition, disposition; feeling; goodwill

adfero, adferre, attuli, adlatus carry to, bring to; report; apply, bring to bear; cause, bring about; help, contribute

adficio, -ere, adfeci, adfectus influence, work on; affect; treat with; weaken

adgredior, -i, adgressus sum go to, approach; address; attack; begin, attempt

adhibeo, -ēre, adhibui, adhibitus bring up to, apply, bring to bear; invite, call in, employ for a purpose

adicio, -ere, adieci, adiectus throw to; direct, apply; add

adipiscor, -i, adeptus sum come up to, overtake; obtain

adiuvo, adiuvi, adiutus (1) help, assist, support

admirabilis, -e admirable; strange, astonishing

admiratio, -onis (f) admiration; *plural*: outbursts of admiration; wonder, astonishment

admiror, -ari, admiratus sum admire; be astonished, wonder

admoneo, -ēre, admonui, admonitus admonish, remind

admoveo, -ēre, admovi, admotus move to, bring up, apply

adnuo, -ere, adnui, adnutus nod to; indicate by nodding; nod assent to; agree

adoro (1) speak to in worship or entreaty, adore, worship

adrideo, -ēre, adrisi, adrisus laugh to, smile on; be favorable to; please

adripio, -ere, adripui, adreptus seize, snatch; grasp, comprehend quickly; arrest, bring to court, accuse; satirize

adscribo, -ere, adscripsi, adscriptus write in, add in writing; attribute, impute; enroll, include, put on a list

adsequor, -i, adsecutus sum follow after; reach, come up to, attain; grasp

adservo (1) preserve, watch

adsideo, -ēre, adsedi, adsessus sit near, sit beside; devote oneself to; besiege, blockade

adsiduus, -a, -um continuously in one place; constant, persistent

adsiduē, adsiduō (adverb) continuously, without remission

adstringo, -ere, adstrinxi, adstrictus tighten, draw together, contract, make fast; compress; bind, oblige

adulescens, -entis (adjective) young, growing; (noun) a young man or a young woman

adulo (1) fawn upon

adulter, -era, -erum (adjective) adulterous

adulter, -eri (m) an adulterer

adultera, -ae (f) an adulteress

adulterium, -i (n) adultery

adultero (1) commit adultery; defile; falsify, corrupt

advenio, -ire, advēni, adventus come to, arrive; happen, come near, break out

adversus, -a, -um turned toward, fronting, opposite; against, opposed, unfavorable

adversus, adversum (adverb) against, opposite; (preposition with accusative) toward, opposite; against, in answer to; compared with

aedes, -is (f) building, (usually) temple; *plural*: rooms, house

aeger, -gra, -grum sick, ill; unsound

aegrē (adverb) with pain, regret, or difficulty; hardly, scarcely

aequo (1) make level or equal; compare; equal, come up to

aequus, -a, -um equal, even, level; favorable, advantageous; contented, easy; impartial, fair

aequē (adverb) in like manner, equally; fairly, justly

āer, aeris (m) lower air, atmosphere

aes, aeris (n) copper; bronze; anything made of bronze, especially copper or bronze money

aestimo (1) appraise, rate, estimate the value of; judge

aestivus, -a, -um relating to summer

aetas, -atis (f) age; lifetime or time of life; epoch

aeternus, -a, -um eternal, everlasting

aether, -eris (accusative: **-era**) (m) the upper air; heaven

aevum, -i (n) eternity; time, lifetime, time of life

ager, agri (m) land, territory; field; open country

agito (1) put in motion, drive about; hunt; toss, vex, harry, trouble; argue, discuss; conduct a business; spend time; live

ago, agere, egi, actus set in motion, drive; hunt; incite to action; deal with, treat; spend time, live; act, play; take a matter up publicly

    grates or **gratias agere** express thanks

    agere causam plead a case

agrestis, -e belonging to the field or the country; wild, rustic; countrified, boorish, clownish

    agrestis, -is (noun, m) farmer

agricola, -ae (m) farmer

ah or **a** (interjection) ah!, oh!

aio (defective verb) say yes, affirm, assert, state

ala, -ae (f) wing; armpit; squadron

alacer, -cris, -cre or **alacris, -e** quick, lively, animated

albus, -a, -um white, pale, bright

ales, alitis winged; swift; *as noun (m or f)*: bird; omen, sign

alga, -ae (f) seaweed

alienus, -a, -um belonging to another; strange, foreign, unrelated; unfamiliar, unfriendly; unfavorable

alimentum, -i (n) food; maintenance

aliquandō at any time, once; sometimes, occasionally

aliquantō somewhat, considerably

aliqui, aliquae or **aliqua, aliquod** (adjective) some

aliquis, aliquid (pronoun) someone, something; anyone, anything

aliquot (indeclinable) some, several

aliter *see* **alius**

alius, alia, aliud (adjective and pronoun) another, other, different; one, another; other than (followed by **atque, quam,** etc.)

    alii . . . alii some . . . others

aliō (adverb) to another place; for another end

aliter (adverb) otherwise, in another way; else, in other conditions

alo, -ere, alui, altus or **alitus** nourish, support, rear, feed; strengthen, increase, promote, advance

alter, -tera, -terum one of two, the one, the other; second, next best; another, other, changed

altus, -a, -um high; shrill; lofty, noble; deep; secret, deep seated; ancient

alumnus, -a, -um (used as noun) nursling, foster child; pupil

amarus, -a, -um bitter, pungent; disagreeable, unpleasant; irritable; biting, acrimonious

amator, -oris (m) lover, friend, admirer

ambo, -ae, -o both, two together

ambulo (1) walk, go for a walk, travel, march

amicitia, -ae (f) friendship

amictus, -ūs (m) garment, covering

amicus, -a, -um friendly; favorable

    amica, -ae (noun, f) girlfriend; mistress

    amicē (adverb) in a friendly manner

    amicus, -i (noun, m) friend

amitto, -ere, amisi, amissus send away, let go; lose

amnis, -is (m) stream, river, current

amo (1) love (passionately), be fond of; like to, be accustomed to

amor, -oris (m) love, passion, fondness, desire; object of love, darling; Love, Cupid

amphora, -ae (f) two-handled jar; a liquid measure of about seven gallons

amplexus, -ūs (m) encircling, embrace

amplus, -a, -um large, spacious, ample; great, important, honorable; eminent, distinguished

    amplius (comparative adverb) more, further, besides

an (conjunction) or; or whether

ancilla, -ae (f) maidservant, female slave

ancillula, -ae (f) little maidservant

anima, -ae (f) breath, wind, air; breath of life, vital principle, soul; living being; sometimes = **animus** rational soul

animadverto, -ere, animadverti, animadversus turn or give the mind to; take notice of, attend to; perceive, observe; blame, censure, punish

animal, -alis (n) living being, animal

animo (1) animate, give life to; endow with a particular disposition

animus, -i (m) spiritual or rational principle of life in humankind; seat of feeling, heart; character, disposition; courage, spirit, vivacity; pride, arrogance; seat of the will, intention; seat of thought, intellect, mind, memory, consciousness

annales, -ium (m) yearly records, annals

annosus, -a, -um full of years, long lived

annus, -i (m) a circuit of the sun, year; year of office or of eligibility for office; time of year, season

ante (adverb) before; (preposition with accusative) before, sooner than, above

antequam (conjunction) before

antiquus, -a, -um coming before; previous, earlier; old, ancient, primitive; *as plural noun* **antiqui, -orum** (m): people of old time, especially ancient authors

antrum, -i (n) cave, hollow

anulus, -i (m) ring

anus, -ūs (f) old woman; *used as an adjective*: old

aperio, -ire, aperui, apertus uncover, lay bare; reveal; open up

apertus, -a, -um uncovered, clear, unconcealed, manifest; intelligible, frank; straightforward; unclosed, accessible, exposed

apertē (adverb) openly, frankly

apex, -icis (m) top; conical cap of the Roman **flamines**; any crown, tiara, helmet; highest honor, crown

apparatus, -ūs (m) preparation, preparing; provision, equipment, apparatus; splendor, pomp

appareo, -ēre, apparui, apparitus become visible, appear, be manifest

appellatio, -onis (f) addressing, speech; appeal; naming, name, title

appello (1) address, accost, speak to; approach, entreat, sue; appeal to; name, title; mention by name

appello, -ere, appuli, appulsus drive to, bring to, apply

appeto, -ere, -ivi, -itus make for, grasp at, seek; go to; attack; draw near

appono, -ere, apposui, appositus place near, put to; serve, put on table; appoint, add

appositus, -a, -um placed near, lying near; near to; fit, appropriate

apprehendo, -ere, apprehendi, apprehensus seize, lay hold of

appropinquo (1) approach, draw near

apto (1) fit, adapt, adjust; make fit

apud (preposition with accusative) at, near, by, with; at the house of

aqua, -ae (f) water

aquila, -ae (f) eagle; standard of a Roman legion

ara, -ae (f) altar; refuge, protection

aratrum, -i (n) plow

arbiter, -tri (m), **arbitra, -ae** (f) witness, spectator, arbitrator; judge, ruler, master

arbitrium, -i (n) decision, judgment, authority

arbitror, -ari, arbitratus sum witness; bear witness; arbitrate, judge, decide

arbor, -oris (f) tree; any wooden object

arcesso, -ere, arcessivi, arcessitus summon, send for, fetch

ardeo, ardēre, arsi burn, glow, be on fire; gleam; burn, smart, desire

ardor, -oris (m) flame, burning, heat; gleam; passion, desire; loved one

arduus, -a, -um steep, towering, lofty; difficult to undertake or reach

area, -ae (f) open space, site, courtyard; playground

arena, -ae (f) seashore; arena

argumentum, -i (n) argument, proof; subject, contents

arma, -orum (plural, n) defensive arms, armor, weapons; military power; protection, defense

armo (1) provide with arms, arm, equip, outfit

ars, artis (f) skill, method, technique; occupation, profession; work of art; conduct, character

artus, -a, -um narrow, tight, close; small, meager; difficult, distressing

    artē (adverb) narrowly, tightly, closely

artus, -ūs (m) joint, limb

arvum, -i (n) plowed land, field

arx, -cis (f) fortress, citadel, stronghold, height; protection

asellus, -i (m) ass, donkey

asinus, -i (m) ass, donkey

aspectus, -ūs (m) looking, sight, range or power of vision; look, aspect, appearance

asper, -era, -erum rough, uneven; pungent, sour; harsh, grating; stormy; wild, harsh, difficult, severe

aspicio, -ere, aspexi, aspectus look at, behold, survey, inspect, confront; investigate, consider; face

aspiro (1) breathe, blow, exhale; be favorable, assist; climb up, reach toward

ast *see* **at**

astrum, -i (n) star, constellation

at, ast but, yet, moreover; you may say

ater, atra, atrum dead black, dark; gloomy, sad; malicious

atque, ac and, and also, and indeed; as; than, from

atrox, -ocis terrible, cruel, horrible; harsh, fierce, severe

attero, -ere, attrivi, attritus rub against, rub away; weaken, ruin

    attritus, -a, -um (participle) rubbed away, worn out

attineo, -ēre, attinui, attentus hold, keep, detain; pertain to, concern

attingo, -ere, attigi, attactus touch, reach; border; attack, strike; handle, manage; affect a person; mention

auctoritas, -atis (f) support, backing; power, rights, command; influence, authority, prestige; influential person

audacia, -ae (f) courage, daring; audacity, impudence, temerity

audax, -acis bold

audeo, -ēre, ausus sum be daring; dare, venture

audio, -ire, audivi, auditus hear, listen; learn; listen to, obey

    bene audire be well spoken of

aufero, auferre, abstuli, ablatus carry away, remove; steal

augur, -uris (c) augur, soothsayer, seer

augurium, -i (n) the office and work of an augur, observation and interpretation of omens, augury; omen, prophecy, presentiment

augustus, -a, -um consecrated, holy; majestic, dignified

Augustus, -i (m) name assumed by all Roman emperors

aura, -ae (f) air, breath, wind; heaven; smell, glitter, echo

aureus, -a, -um golden, made of or adorned with gold; excellent, beautiful

auris, -is (f) ear; hearing

aurora, -ae (f) dawn, break of day; the east; Aurora, goddess of the morning

aurum, -i (n) gold; anything made of gold; the golden age

aut or, or else

aut . . . aut either . . . or

autem but, on the other hand, however, moreover

auxilium, -i (n) help, aid, assistance; *plural*: auxiliary troops

avarus, -a, -um covetous, greedy

aveo, -ēre long for, desire

aveo (haveo), -ēre be well

ave hail!, farewell!

avidus, -a, -um desiring, longing for; (especially) greedy for money

avidē (adverb) eagerly, greedily

avis, -is (f) bird; omen

avius, -a, -um out of the way, untrod; astray, lost

avoco (1) call away or off; withdraw, remove, divert

avus, -i (m) grandfather; ancestor

axis, -is (m) axle; wheel; chariot, wagon; the north pole; the heavens

Bb

barba, -ae (f) beard

barbarus, -a, -um foreign, strange; rough, savage; *as noun*: foreigner

beatus, -a, -um happy, blessed, prosperous; well off

beatē (adverb) happily

bellum, -i (n) war, fighting

bellus, -a, -um (colloquial) pretty, handsome

bene (adverb) well, rightly, properly; thoroughly, very; good!, excellent!

melius (comparative)

optimē (superlative)

benefacio, -ere, benefeci, benefactus benefit, do a good turn

beneficium, -i (n) a kindness, favor, service; distinction, promotion; privilege, exemption

bestia, -ae (f) animal, beast; brute

bibo, -ere, bibi, bibitus drink, drink in

bini, -ae, -a twofold; two apiece; a pair

bis twice, two times

blandior, -iri, blanditus sum (with dative) flatter, caress, coax

blandus, -a, -um flattering, caressing, alluring, tempting

blandē or **blanditer** (adverb) flatteringly

bonus, -a, -um good; useful, efficient; virtuous, honest, kind; patriotic, loyal; *as noun (n), usually plural*: goods, property

melior, melius (comparative)

optimus, -a, -um (superlative)

bos, bovis (c) ox, bullock, cow

bracchium, -i (n) forearm, arm from elbow to wrist; limb

brevis, -e short; shallow; short lived; concise

breviter or **brevi** (adverb) shortly, briefly, soon

Cc

cadaver, -eris (n) dead body, carcass

cado, -ere, cecidi, casus fall, sink, drop; set; fall in death, die; be destroyed, subside, flag, fail; be subject to; agree with, be consistent with; happen

caducus, -a, -um falling or fallen; inclined or ready to fall; destined to die; frail, perishable

caecus, -a, -um blind, not seeing; intellectually or morally blind; uncertain, objectless; unseen, hidden, obscure, dark

caedes, -is (f) cutting down, killing, bloodshed, slaughter

caedo, -ere, cecīdi, caesus cut; beat, knock about; kill, slay

caelestis, -e belonging to heaven, coming from heaven; belonging to the gods, celestial, divine, superhuman; *as plural noun (n)*: things in heaven, heavenly bodies

caelicola, -ae (c) god

caelum, -i (n) the heavens, sky, air, climate; heaven as the home of the gods; heaven as the height of joy, renown, etc.

caerimonia, -ae (f) holiness, sanctity; holy awe, reverence; religious usage, sacred ceremony

caerul(e)us, -a, -um blue, dark blue (especially of the sea or sky)

calamitas, -atis (f) loss, failure, misfortune, damage, a reverse

calamus, -i (m) reed; hence anything made of reed, e.g., a pen, a reed pipe, an arrow

calathus, -i (m) wine bowl

calco (1) tread, trample on

calculus, -i (m) little stone, pebble; voting pebble

calidus, -a, -um warm, hot; fiery, passionate

calliditas, -atis (f) expertness, cleverness

callidus, -a, -um experienced, clever, dexterous, skillful; cunning, subtle, sly
  callidē (adverb)

calor, -oris (m) warmth, heat, glow; passion, excitement

calvus, -a, -um bald, without hair

campus, -i (m) plain, field; (especially) the Campus Martius at Rome

candidatus, -i (m) candidate for office

candidus, -a, -um shining white; fair; happy; clear, lucid; honest, straightforward
  candidē (adverb) clearly, candidly

canis, -is (f) dog, hound

cano, -ere, cecini, cantus sing, play music; crow; croak; sound; sing of, celebrate in song; prophesy

canor, -oris (m) melody, song, sound

canorus, -a, -um melodious, harmonious, sweet sounding

canto (1) sing, play music; crow; play on an instrument; sound; sing of, celebrate; predict

cantus, -ūs (m) song, melody, music, poetry; prophecy; incantation

canus, -a, -um whitish gray; aged

capella, -ae (f) she-goat

capillus, -i (m) a hair, usually of the head or beard

capio, -ere, cepi, captus take, seize; reach, take possession of; take up, take in hand, adopt; choose; catch, attack, injure; charm, captivate, take in; convict; receive, suffer, undergo, take on, take in, hold, contain, keep in; grasp, comprehend

capitalis, -e deadly, mortal; first, chief, distinguished; capital

captivus, -a, -um captured; *noun (m) and (f)*: prisoner, captive

capto (1) seize, catch at; strive for, desire, seek

caput, -itis (n) head; living individual, human being, person; person's life, existence; top, summit; source; leader, chief

carcer, -eris (m) prison, cell

caritas, -atis (f) high price; (especially) high cost of living; affection, love, esteem

carmen, -inis (n) song, tune; poem, poetry, verse; prediction; incantation; religious or legal formula

caro, carnis (f) flesh, meat

carpo, -ere, carpsi, carptus pluck, pull off, select, choose; enjoy; graze; carp at, slander; weaken, annoy, harass; break up, separate, divide

carus, -a, -um high priced, expensive, costly; dear, beloved

casa, -ae (f) hut, cottage

castitas, -atis (f) chastity

castrum, -i (n) castle, fort, fortress; *plural* (**castra, -orum**): camp, encampment

castus, -a, -um clean, pure, chaste; pious, religious, holy

castē (adverb) purely, piously, religiously

casus, -ūs (m) falling, fall; accident, event, occurrence; occasion, opportunity; destruction, downfall, collapse; end

caterva, -ae (f) crowd, troop, flock

cauda, -ae (f) tail of an animal

caudex, -dicis (m) trunk of a tree; block of wood; dolt, blockhead; account book, ledger

causa, -ae (f) cause; reason, motive, pretext; interest; case at law, lawsuit, claim; situation, condition

causā (with genitive) on account of, for the sake of, with

causam dicere plead a case

cautio, -onis (f) caution, care, foresight, precaution

cautus, -a, -um cautious, wary, careful

caveo, -ēre, cavi, cautus be on one's guard (against); take care that

cavus, -a, -um hollow, concave

-ce *demonstrative particle joined to pronouns and adverbs* (*e.g.,* **hisce**)

cedo, -ere, cessi, cessus go, proceed; turn out, happen; fall to the lot of; change into something else; go away, withdraw; give ground, submit, be inferior; grant, yield

celeber, -bris, -bre filled, crowded; well attended; frequented; often repeated; famous, renowned

celebro (1) visit frequently or in large numbers; celebrate, solemnize; publish, make famous; honor

celer, -eris, -ere swift, quick, rapid; hasty, rash

celeriter (adverb)

celo (1) hide, conceal, keep secret

celsus, -a, -um upraised, lofty, elevated; proud, haughty

cena, -ae (f) dinner (the main Roman meal); dish or course at a dinner

censor, -oris (m) censor (a Roman magistrate); severe judge or rigid moralist

census, -ūs (m) the census (an enrollment of names and assessment of property); the censor's list; the amount of property necessary for enrollment in a certain rank; property, wealth

centum (indeclinable) one hundred

cera, -ae (f) wax; waxen writing tablet; wax seal; waxen image

ceratus, -a, -um smeared or covered with wax

Ceres, -eris (f) Roman goddess of agriculture; bread, grain, corn

cerno, -ere, crevi, cretus separate, sift; distinguish, discern; decide, resolve, determine

certamen, -inis (n) contest, struggle

certatim emulously, eagerly

certo (1) settle by contest; contend, struggle, dispute

certus, -a, -um settled, resolved, decided; definite, certain, fixed; sure, dependable; known, undoubted, sure

    certē or **certō** (adverb) certainly, assuredly

    certiorem facere inform

cervix, -icis (f) nape of the neck, neck

cervus, -i (m) stag, buck, deer

cesso (1) leave off, cease work, be idle, rest; be left alone, do nothing

ceterus, -a, -um the other, the rest (usually plural: **ceteri, -ae, -a**)

    ceterum (adverb) otherwise, moreover, but

ceu as, like as; as if

chors *see* **cohors**

chorus, -i (m) dance in a circle, choral dance; chorus; crowd, troop

cibus, -i (m) food, fodder, nourishment

cieo, -ēre, civi, citus move, stir, agitate; give rise to, excite, arouse; summon; call by name

cinctus, -ūs (m) girding; girdle

cingo, -ere, cinxi, cinctus equip the head or body; gird; surround; escort, accompany

cinis, -eris (m) ash, ashes

circum (adverb) roundabout, around; (preposition with accusative) round, around, about, near

circumdo, -are, circumdedi, circumdatus surround (with something); put something round

circus, -i (m) ring, circle, orbit; course for races

citus, -a, -um quick, speedy

    cito (adverb) quickly

civis, -is (c) citizen; fellow citizen; subject

civitas, -atis (f) citizenship; state, commonwealth; the inhabitants of a city, townsfolk; city, town

clades, -is (f) destruction; disaster, injury, defeat

clam (adverb) secretly, in secret; (preposition with accusative) unknown to, without the knowledge of

clamo (1) call, shout, cry aloud; call to or on, shout something; proclaim, declare

clamor, -oris (m) loud shouting, cry; echo, reverberation

clarus, -a, -um bright, clear, distinct; bringing fair weather; evident, plain; illustrious, distinguished; notorious

    clarē (adverb) clearly, brightly; illustriously

classis, -is (f) a group as summoned, division, class; social class; armed forces, (especially) fleet

claudo, -ere, clausi, clausus close, shut up, make inaccessible; blockade; shut in, confine; conclude

claustrum, -i (n) means of closing or shutting in; bolt, bar; enclosure, prison, den; barricade, dam, fortress

clementia, -ae (f) mildness, gentleness, mercy

(coepio, -ere,) coepi, coeptus (defective) begin, commence

coeptum, -i (n) thing begun or undertaken

coeptus, -ūs (m) beginning

coetus, -ūs (m) meeting, union, encounter, assembly

cogitatio, -onis (f) thinking, conception, reflection, reasoning; particular thought, idea, or intention

cogito (1) turn over in the mind, think, reflect; intend, plan

cognatus, -a, -um related, connected by blood; akin, similar; *as noun (m or f)*: relative

cognosco, -ere, cognōvi, cognitus become acquainted with, get to know, learn;

know; know again, recognize; examine, hear, decide

cogo, -ere, coegi, coactus bring, drive, or draw to a point, collect; bring close together, compress; thicken, curdle; restrict, confine; compel

cohors (chors), -tis (f) enclosure, yard; troop, company, throng; cohort (one-tenth of a legion)

collido, -ere, collisi, collisus strike or dash together, bring into collision

colligo, -ere, collegi, collectus gather or bring together, collect; contract; infer, conclude

collis, -is (m) hill, high ground

colloco (1) place, lay, set, arrange; lay out, employ, spend; settle; betroth

collum, -i (n) neck

colo, -ere, colui, cultus cultivate, till, tend; dwell in, inhabit; take care of, attend to, foster, honor, worship, court

color, -oris (m) color, tint, hue; complexion; beauty; outward show, external appearance; cast, character, tone

coma, -ae (f) hair of the head; leaves; rays of light

comedo, comesse, comedi, comesus or **comestus** eat up, consume; waste, squander

comes, -itis (c) fellow traveler; companion, comrade; attendant; *plural* (**comites**): retinue

comis, -e courteous, kind, friendly, obliging **comiter** (adverb)

comitas, -atis (f) courtesy, friendliness, civility

comitor, -ari, comitatus sum attend, accompany, follow

commemoro (1) call to mind, recollect; remind another, mention, relate, recount

commendo (1) commit to the care or protection of; recommend; set off, render agreeable

comminus hand to hand; close up, close at hand

committo, -ere, commisi, commissus unite, connect, combine; match; compare; begin, initiate; bring it about that; commit, perpetrate; incur; entrust, commit oneself

commotus, -a, -um insecure, unsteady; excited, upset

commoveo, -ēre, commovi, commotus move violently, shake, disturb, carry about or away; excite, influence, upset; start up, produce, cause

communis, -e shared, common, universal, public

commuto (1) change, alter; exchange, barter, interchange

como, -ere, compsi, comptus put together, make tidy, arrange, adorn, neaten

compello, -ere, compuli, compulsus drive together, collect; force, compel

compilo (1) bundle together; pack up and take off, plunder, rob

complector, -i, complexus sum embrace, surround, encompass; hold fast, master; attach oneself to, esteem; embrace, grasp, comprehend; unite in oneself, include

compleo, -ēre, complevi, completus fill up; bring up to strength; make up; fulfill; complete

complures, -ium several

compono, -ere, composui, compositus put together; match as opponents; compare; compose; put in place, arrange, settle; reconcile

compositus, -a, -um constructed, put together; arranged in order, settled

comprehendo, -ere, comprehendi, comprehensus grasp; take together, unite; embrace, include; take firmly, seize; capture, arrest; catch red handed; comprehend, perceive

concedo, -ere, concessi, concessus retire, withdraw; yield, submit, give way to; grant, give up; pardon, overlook; permit, allow

concido, -ere, concidi fall down; sink, perish; subside; be ruined, fail

concīdo, -ere, concīdi, concisus cut up, cut down, destroy; ruin, strike down

concilio (1) bring together, unite, reconcile, win over; bring about, cause

concipio, -ere, concepi, conceptus take together, contain, hold; express; take completely in, absorb; suck in; catch fire; draw in; take in, grasp; conceive, imagine; begin to feel; devise

concitus, -a, -um excited, violent, passionate; provoked, roused; inspired

concubitus, -ūs (m) lying or reclining together; copulation

concupisco, -ere, concupivi, concupitus desire eagerly, covet, aim at

condemno (1) condemn; urge or effect the condemnation of a person; blame, disapprove

condicio, -onis (f) arrangement, agreement; condition, stipulation, provision; state, condition, place, circumstance

condo, -ere, condidi, conditus build, found; form, establish; compose, write; put up, put away safely, store, hide, withdraw; bury; pass, dispose of

conduco, -ere, conduxi, conductus bring or lead together, collect, unite, connect; hire, contract for, farm; be of use, profit, serve

confero, conferre, contuli, collatus bring or put together, collect, concentrate; contribute; bring into contact or collision; fight foot to foot; engage; interchange, discuss; compare; bring to bear; betake oneself, devote oneself; put off, postpone; impute, attribute

conficio, -ere, confeci, confectus finish, bring about, accomplish; conclude, settle; complete; produce, cause; use up, exhaust, consume; chew, eat, and digest; waste; destroy, kill; weaken, wear out

confido, -ere, confisus sum trust completely, be assured, be confident

confirmo (1) make firm, strengthen, support; encourage; corroborate, establish, affirm, state positively

confluo, -ere, confluxi, confluxus flow, stream, or flock together

congero, -ere, congessi, congestus bring together, collect, pile up, accumulate; (especially) build up; comprise; heap on a person

congressus, -ūs (m) meeting; social intercourse; hostile encounter, combat

congrex, -regis of the same herd; intimate, close

coniugalis, -e of marriage, conjugal

coniugium, -i (n) close connection, union; (especially) marriage, wedlock; husband, wife

coniungo, -ere, coniunxi, coniunctus join together, connect, unite; marry

coniunx, -iugis (c) husband, wife; betrothed virgin, bride

conor, -ari, conatus sum undertake, try, strive

conscientia, -ae (f) knowledge shared with others, joint knowledge; consciousness, especially of right and wrong, a good or a bad conscience

conscius, -a, -um sharing knowledge with others, privy to a thing, cognizant of; conscious, especially of right and wrong; as noun (m or f): accomplice, coconspirator

conscribo, -ere, conscripsi, conscriptus enter on a list, enroll; levy; write, compose; prescribe

patres conscripti senators

consecro (1) consecrate; dedicate to the gods; curse; deify; make holy or immortal

conservo (1) keep, preserve, maintain

considero (1) look at, regard carefully, contemplate; consider, reflect on

consido, -ere, consedi, consessus sit down; take up one's position; settle, sink; be overcome or neglected; sink in; subside

consilium, -i (n) deliberation, consultation; assembly, council; judgment; resolution, plan; advice, suggestion

consimilis, -e exactly similar

consisto, -ere, constiti, constitus take one's stand, place oneself; stand still, stop; fall to, come upon, rest on; stay; stand firm; consist, be formed of

conspectus, -a, -um visible; striking, remarkable, conspicuous

conspectus, -ūs (m) seeing, looking, sight, view; mental view, survey; appearance

conspicio, -ere, conspexi, conspectus catch sight of, behold, perceive; look at with attention, watch; understand

constans, -antis steady, firm, unchanging, constant, consistent, resolute

constanter (adverb) steadily, firmly

constantia, -ae (f) steadiness, firmness

constituo, -ere, constitui, constitutus cause to stand, set up, place, establish, settle; post, station, arrange, bring to a halt; settle people; found, set up; appoint a person to an office; settle, fix upon an amount, time, etc.; decide

consto, -are, constiti, constatus stand together; be composed, consist; depend on, rest on; correspond, be consistent; cost; stand firm, stand still; remain the same, be unaltered; be established, be sure, be well known; exist

constat (impersonal) it is agreed, it is well known

construo, -ere, construxi, constructus heap up together; construct, build up; arrange

consuesco, -ere, consuevi, consuetus accustom (oneself), habituate

consuetudo, -inis (f) custom, usage, habit; intimacy, close acquaintance; romantic intrigue

consuetus, -a, -um accustomed to; usual, accustomed

consul, -sulis (m) consul (one of two chief magistrates at Rome under the Republic)

consularis, -e relating to a consul, consular; having been a consul; *as noun (m)*: ex-consul; provincial governor of consular rank

consulatus, -ūs (m) the office of consul, consulship

consulo, -ere, consului, consultus reflect, consider, consult; look to the interests of; come to a conclusion, take measures; ask the advice of, consult

consultum, -i the act of deliberation, reflection, consideration; plan, resolution, decision; decree of the senate

consultus, -a, -um well considered, deliberated upon; experienced

consultē (adverb) advisedly, after consideration

consultō (adverb) deliberately, designedly

consumo, -ere, consumpsi, consumptus spend, employ for a purpose; use up, finish; waste away, destroy

consurgo, -ere, surrexi, surrectus rise up, stand up (especially to speak or as a mark of respect); be roused to action; arise, break out

contemno, -ere, contempsi, contemptus think meanly of, despise, contemn

contemplatio, -onis (f) surveying, contemplation

contemplor, -ari, contemplatus sum mark out; look at attentively, survey, regard; consider carefully

contemptus, -a, -um despised; despicable, contemptible

contemptus, -ūs (m) contempt, disdain

contendo, -ere, contendi, contentus strain, stretch, exert; shoot, cast; strive, strain, exert oneself, hasten; assert with confidence, maintain; compare, contrast; compete

contentus, -a, -um contented, satisfied

contero, -ere, contrivi, contritus rub away, grind, pound; wear away, destroy, obliterate; consume, spend

contexo, -ere, contexui, contextus weave or twine together, connect, unite, construct, form

contineo, -ēre, continui, contentus hold together, keep together; connect, join; keep in, surround, contain, confine; include, comprise; hold back, constrain

contingo, -ere, contigi, contactus touch, reach, grasp; smear or sprinkle with; affect, infect; border; happen, befall

continuus, -a, -um joined together, successive, continuous, uninterrupted

continuō (adverb) immediately, at once

contio, -onis (f) assembly, public meeting; a speech

contrā (adverb) opposite, over against, on the opposite side; in return, back; otherwise; against; (preposition with accusative) opposite, over against; against, in opposition to

contraho, -ere, contraxi, contractus draw together, collect, unite; conclude or complete an arrangement; cause, bring on, bring about; shorten, narrow, contract, reduce; depress

contrarius, -a, -um opposite, opposed, contrary; opposed to; hostile, injurious

contumelia, -ae (f) outrage, physical violence; insult, affront

convello, -ere, convelli, convulsus pluck up, pull away, wrench off; weaken, overthrow, destroy

conveniens, -ntis agreeing, unanimous, concordant; fit, appropriate, suitable

convenio, -ire, conveni, conventus meet; come together, assemble; visit, call on; be fit, be suitable, be congenial; agree **convenit** (impersonal) it is fitting; it is agreed

converto, -ere, converti, conversus turn round, whirl round; change, alter; translate; turn in any direction, direct; devote **se convertere** turn back; flee

convīctus, -ūs (m) living together, intercourse; entertainment, feast

convinco, -ere, convici, convictus convict of a crime; prove mistaken; prove conclusively, demonstrate

convivium, -i (n) feast, party, entertainment, banquet; guests

copia, -ae (f) plenty, abundance; supplies, provisions; troops, forces (especially in the plural); means, opportunity; access

cor, cordis (n) heart; mind, judgment; person

coram (adverb) personally, openly, face to face; (preposition with ablative) in the presence of

cornix, -icis (f) crow

cornu, -ūs (n) horn; strength, courage; bow, trumpet, lantern; hoof, beak, tip of a helmet, end of a stick or spar, end of a promontory, wing of an army

corona, -ae (f) garland, chaplet, crown; constellation; circle of people, audience

corpus, -poris (n) body, substance, matter; (especially) the body of a human or an animal; flesh, trunk; corpse; person; body politic; main mass of a thing

corripio, -ere, corripui, correptus seize, snatch up; attack; overcome; blame, rebuke, accuse, bring to trial; shorten

corvus, -i (m) raven; rook

corymbus, -i (m) bunch of flowers or fruit, (especially) cluster of ivy berries

cotidianus, -a, -um daily, of every day; everyday, common, ordinary

cotidiē daily, every day

cras (adverb) tomorrow

creber, -bra, -brum thick, crowded together, close, numerous; crowded with, full of; repeated, frequent

crebrō (adverb) repeatedly, often

credo, -ere, credidi, creditus believe, trust; (with accusative and dative) entrust, commit (especially secrets and money); (with dative) trust in, rely on; believe, give credence to

cremo (1) burn, consume with fire

creo (1) make, create, produce; elect to an office; beget, bear

crepito (1) rattle, creak, crackle, rustle

cresco, -ere, crevi, cretus come into existence, spring forth, arise; grow, grow up, increase in size, height, etc.; increase in fame, power, etc.

crimen, -inis (n) accusation, charge; object of reproach; fault, guilt, crime; cause of crime

crinis, -is (m) hair (especially in the plural)

cruciatus, -ūs (m) torture, torment

crudelis, -e unfeeling, cruel

cruentus, -a, -um bloody, bloodthirsty; bloodred

cruor, -oris (m) blood, gore; murder, slaughter

crus, cruris (n) shin, shinbone, leg; pier, support

crux, crucis (f) cross; torment, trouble; gallows bird

cubiculum, -i (n) bedroom

cubile, -is (n) bed, (especially) marriage bed; lair, den, nest; seat, resting place

cubo, -are, cubui, cubitus lie down, recline (especially at table or in bed); be ill in bed

culpa, -ae (f) fault, blame; (especially) the fault of unchastity; cause of error or sin

cultor, -oris (m) cultivator, planter; inhabitant, occupier of a place; friend, supporter of a person; worshipper of gods

cultus, -ūs (m) tilling, cultivation, tending; care, careful treatment; reverence; training, education

cum (preposition with ablative) with, together with; at the same time as

cum (conjunction; older form: **quom**) when; whenever; since; although

cum . . . tum both . . . and, not only . . . but also

cumulus, -i (m) heap, pile, mass; addition, increase, finishing touch

cunctus, -a, -um all, all collectively, the whole

cupiditas, -atis (f) eager desire, passionate longing; (especially) ambition; avarice; party spirit

cupido, -inis (usually f) longing, desire (especially for power), ambition, avarice; physical desire, love

Cupido, -inis (m) Cupid (god of love); *plural* (**cupidines**): cupids

cupidus, -a, -um desirous, eager, keen, (especially) eager for power, ambitious; avaricious; physically desirous, passionate; attached, partial

cupidē (adverb) eagerly, passionately

cupio, -ere, cupivi, cupitus desire, long for, wish for

cur or **quor** why?

cura, -ae (f) care; carefulness, pains, attention, minding of things or persons; management, administration; object of care; anxiety, worry, disquiet

curia, -ae (f) meeting place of the senate, senate house

curiosus, -a, -um careful, attentive; inquisitive; worried

curo (1) care for, pay attention to, trouble about; see to something; manage, administer; minister to, cure, rest; provide or procure money

curro, -ere, cucurri, cursus run, hasten; run in a race; sail; pass

currus, -ūs (m) chariot, car; triumph; plow with wheels; ship

cursus, -ūs (m) running, rapid motion; course, direction, movement, journey

custodio, -ire, custodivi, custoditus guard, watch, keep, take care of; keep in sight, observe; keep in prison, hold captive

custos, -odis (c) guardian, keeper, watcher, attendant; jailer, guard, sentinel, spy

Dd

damno (1) cause loss or injury to; condemn, sentence, punish; condemn, disapprove of; assign, devote, make over

damnum, -i (n) loss, damage, injury; fine

de (preposition with ablative) down from, away from; coming from; taken from, made of, changed from; following from, after; in the course of, during; about, on account of; according to

dea, -ae (f) goddess

debeo, -ēre, debui, debitus owe; be indebted to; be due to, be bound to; have to; be destined to; ought

debilis, -e feeble, weak

debitum, -i a debt

decedo, -ere, decessi, decessus move away, withdraw; march away; give up; yield to, retire, depart from life, die; retire, abate, cease; go astray, deviate

decem (indeclinable) ten

decens, -entis proper, fit
  decenter (adverb)

decerpo, -ere, decerpsi, decerptus pluck off, pluck away; gather; derive; take away

decet, -ēre, decuit (impersonal) it is proper, it is fitting

decido, -ere, decidi fall down, fall dead, die; sink, fall

decīdo, -ere, decīdi, decisus cut down, cut off; cut short, settle, arrange

decipio, -ere, decepi, deceptus catch; cheat, deceive, beguile

decor, -oris (m) grace, beauty

decurro, -ere, decucurri or **decurri, decursus** run down, hasten down; move down; run through, traverse; have recourse to, take refuge in; sail downstream or to land

decus, -oris (n) distinction, honor, glory, grace; moral dignity, virtue; pride, glory; *plural* (**decora**): distinguished acts

dedecus, -oris (n) shame, dishonor, disgrace; a dishonorable action, crime, vice

deduco, -ere, deduxi, deductus lead or bring down; trace down to the present; reduce; subtract; lead or draw away; escort

defendo, -ere, defendi, defensus repel, repulse, ward off, drive away; defend, protect

defero, deferre, detuli, delatus bring down, carry down; bring or carry away;

offer, hand over, refer; communicate, report; indict

deficio, -ere, defeci, defectus do less than one might, fail; desert, rebel, revolt; run short; go out; ebb; fail, become weak; abandon, leave

deformis, -e deformed, misshapen, ugly, disgusting; foul, shameful; formless, shapeless

defungor, -i, defunctus sum perform, discharge, have done with; die

dein, deinde from that place; thereafter, thereupon, then, afterward; next, then

deleo, -ēre, delevi, deletus blot out, efface; destroy, annihilate

delibero (1) weigh carefully, consider, consult about; ask advice (especially of an oracle); resolve

delinquo, -ere, deliqui, delictus fail, be wanting; fail in duty; commit a crime

delitesco, -ere, delitui conceal oneself, lie hidden, take refuge

delphinus, -i (m) dolphin

deludo, -ere, delusi, delusus mock, cheat

dementia, -ae (f) senselessness, insanity; *plural*: mad actions

demitto, -ere, demisi, demissus send down, lower, put down; lead down; bring a vessel downstream or to land; sink, bury, plunge

demonstro (1) indicate, explain, describe

demulceo, -ēre, demulsi stroke down, caress by stroking

demum at length, at last; finally, in short

denego (1) deny, say no; refuse, reject

denique at last, finally; again, further, finally; in short, in fine

dens, dentis (m) tooth; anything biting, sharp, or destructive

depono, -ere, deposui, depositus lay down, put down; lay as a wager or prize;

put down, deposit; commit, entrust; lay aside, have done with

deprehendo, -ere, deprehendi, deprehensus seize upon, catch hold of; surprise, catch, detect a person in a crime or fault; discover, observe

derideo, -ēre, derisi, derisus laugh at, mock, deride

descendo, -ere, descendi, descensus climb down, come down, descend; march down; sink, pierce; slope down; sink; lower oneself, stoop; sink in, penetrate

desero, -ere, deserui, desertus forsake, abandon, leave; neglect, disregard

desertus, -a, -um forsaken, abandoned; *as plural noun (n)*: deserts, wildernesses

desidero (1) long for what is absent or lost, wish for; miss, find a lack of

desino, -ere, desivi, desitus cease, desist from; cease, stop, end; end in

desperatio, -nis (f) hopelessness, despair

despicio, -ere, despexi, despectus look down, regard from above; look down on, despise

desum, deesse, defui be down, fall short, fail, be missing or remiss

detraho, -ere, detraxi, detractus draw down, drag down; lower, humiliate; draw off, drag away, remove; subtract; disparage, slander

deus, -i (m) god, deity

deveho, -ere, devexi, devectus carry away or down; transport

dexter, -tera or **-tra, -terum** or **-trum** on the right hand, on the right side; dexterous, skillful; propitious, favorable, opportune; *as noun (f)*: right hand; pledge of faith

dico, -ere, dixi, dictus indicate; appoint; say, speak, tell, mention; express, put

into words; speak of, tell of, relate; name, call; mean, refer to
dicitur (impersonal) it is said
dictum, -i (n) word, saying, speech; witty saying, bon mot; order, command; prediction
dies, -ei (m or f) daytime, day; period of twenty-four hours; the business or events of the day; time; a fixed date; a historic day; day of death
in dies daily, by the day
differo, differre, distuli, dilatus carry in different directions, spread abroad, scatter; harass, disturb, discredit a person; delay, postpone business, put off persons; differ, be different
difficilis, -e difficult; hard to deal with, morose, obstinate
difficiliter or **difficulter** (adverb) with difficulty
diffundo, -ere, diffudi, diffusus pour in different directions, spread out, diffuse, extend; make relax, brighten up, gladden
digitus, -i (m) finger; inch; toe
dignus, -a, -um worthy, deserving (usually with ablative or genitive); worth having, deserved, suitable, fitting
digne (adverb)
diligens, -entis attentive, careful; (especially) careful in housekeeping, economical, saving
diligenter (adverb) attentively, carefully
diligentia, -ae (f) carefulness, attentiveness, accuracy; (especially) care in management, economy
diligo, -ere, dilexi, dilectus choose; prize, love, esteem highly
dimitto, -ere, dimisi, dimissus send forth, send in different directions; send (word) around; send away, let go, let fall; disband; break up, dismiss; give up, leave; renounce, abandon

diripio, -ere, diripui, direptus snatch apart, tear to pieces; divide; pillage, lay waste; tear away
dirus, -a, -um fearful, horrible, frightful, cruel; *as plural noun* (**dirae, -arum**, f): unlucky omens, curses
Dis, Ditis (m) a name of Pluto (god of the Underworld)
discedo, -ere, discessi, discessus go asunder, part, separate; depart, go away; march away; come off; depart, pass away; deviate, swerve, digress
disciplina, -ae (f) instruction, teaching; training, education; military training; discipline, ordered way of life; learning, body of knowledge, science; philosophical school or system
discipulus, -i (m) pupil, apprentice
disco, -ere, didici learn, get to know; receive information, find out; become acquainted with, learn to recognize
discolor, -oris of different colors; different
discordia, -ae (f) dissension, disagreement; mutiny, sedition
discutio, -ere, discussi, discussus shatter; disperse, scatter, break up
displiceo, -ere, displicui, displicitus displease
dissimilis, -e unlike, dissimilar
dissimiliter (adverb) differently
dissimulo (1) dissemble, disguise, keep secret; ignore, leave unnoticed
distendo, -ere, distendi, distentus stretch apart, expand, fill up, distend; distract, perplex
distentus, -a, -um distracted, occupied; distended, full
distinctus, -a, -um separate, distinct; set off, diversified, adorned
distinctus, -us (m) difference, distinction

distineo, -ēre, distinui, distentus hold asunder, keep apart, separate; divide in feeling; distract; keep away, prevent from happening

diū for a long time; a long time ago
diutius (comparative) longer, too long
diutissimē (superlative)

dives, -vitis rich, wealthy; (with ablative or genitive) rich in

divinus, -a, -um belonging or relating to a deity, divine; divinely inspired, prophetic; noble, admirable

divitiae, -arum (plural, f) riches, wealth; ornaments, rich offerings; richness, fertility

divortium, -i (n) separation, divorce

divum, -i (n) the open air

divus, -a, -um divine, deified; *as noun (m or f)*: god, deity

do, dare, dedi, datus offer, give, grant, bestow, lend; hand over, commit, devote; give for dispatch, tell, communicate; cause, bring about, put
datur is said

doceo, -ēre, docui, doctus teach, instruct; inform that or how; bring out, exhibit

doctus, -a, -um, taught; learned, instructed, well informed; experienced, clever, shrewd

doleo, -ēre, dolui suffer physical or mental pain, be pained, grieve; cause pain

dolor, -oris (m) physical or mental pain; (especially) grief, disappointment, resentment; cause of sorrow

dolus, -i (m) device, artifice; fraud, deceit, guile; trap

domesticus, -a, -um belonging to a house or family, domestic; native; *as noun (m), especially plural*: members of one's household

domicilium, -i (n) place of residence, dwelling

domina, -ae (f) mistress of a household; wife, mistress, lady; ruler, controller

dominor, -ari, dominatus sum rule, be supreme, domineer

dominus, -i (m) master of a house, lord; husband or lover; master, owner, possessor; employer; ruler, lord, controller

domo, -are, domui, domitus tame, break in, conquer, subdue

domus, -ūs (f) house, home; dwelling, abode; native country; household

donec up to the time when, until; so long as, while

dono (1) give as a present, present, grant, bestow, give up; remit a debt or obligation; forgive, pardon; present with

donum, -i (n) gift, present; votive offering

dormio, -ire, dormivi sleep; rest, be inactive

dorsum, -i (n) back; reef; mountain ridge

dos, dotis (f) dowry, marriage portion; gift, quality, endowment

dubito (1) doubt, waver, be uncertain; be irresolute, hesitate

dubius, -a, -um doubtful; wavering; doubting; uncertain; hesitating, irresolute; uncertain, doubted, doubtful; *as noun*: **dubium, -i** (n) doubt

duco, -ere, duxi, ductus draw; draw along or away; shape anything long, construct; spend, delay, protract; charm, influence, mislead; derive; draw in; lead; marry a wife; command; calculate, reckon; esteem, consider

dulcis, -e sweet; pleasant, delightful, agreeable; friendly, dear

dum (conjunction) while, during the time that; so long as, provided that; until; *used as adverbial enclitic*:
nedum not to say
nondum not yet
vixdum scarcely yet

dummodo provided that, so long as

duo, -ae, -o two

duodecim (indeclinable) twelve

duro (1) make hard or hardy, inure; become hard or dry; be hard or callous; endure, hold out; last, remain, continue

durus, -a, -um hard, harsh; tough, strong, enduring; rough, rude, uncouth; austere; brazen, shameless; awkward, difficult, adverse

dux, ducis (c) guide, conductor; leader, ruler, commander

Ee

e, ex (preposition with ablative) from or out of; since; immediately after; away from, out of, of; on account of, by reason of; in accordance with; for the benefit of; in regard to

ecce behold!, lo!, see!

ecqui, ecquae or **ecqua, ecquod** (interrogative adjective) is there any that?, does any?

ecquis, ecquid (interrogative pronoun) is there any that?, does anyone? at all? whether any

edo, edere or **esse, edi, esus** eat, devour, consume, waste

edo, edere, edidi, editus put forth, give out; utter; bring into the world, bring forth, give birth to; produce; make known; publish; divulge, spread; proclaim; fix, determine, nominate; bring about, cause; provide games

educo (1) bring up, raise, rear, educate

effero, efferre, extuli, elatus carry out, bring out; carry to the grave, bury; bring forth, bear; utter, express, publish words or ideas; carry off or away; raise up, lift up; praise, extol; endure to the end

efficio, -ere, effeci, effectus do, produce, effect, make; bring about, cause; make up, amount to; prove, show

effigies, -ei (f) image, likeness, effigy; shade, ghost; ideal

effugio, -ere, effūgi, effugitus flee, fly away, escape, get off; escape from, avoid, shun

effundo, -ere, effudi, effusus pour out, pour forth, shed; fling out, empty out; throw off, fling down; discharge; utter; waste, pour out freely, squander

effusus, -a, -um poured out; widespread, extensive; extravagant, wasteful; unrestrained

ego I; *plural:* **nos** we (often used for singular)

egredior, -i, egressus sum go out, pass out; march out; disembark; digress; ascend; transit, go out of, pass beyond, overstep, pass

egregius, -a, -um excellent, extraordinary, distinguished

egregiē (adverb)

elābor, -i, elapsus sum glide out, slip away, escape, disappear

eloquentia, -ae (f) eloquence

eloquor, -i, elocutus sum speak out, express; speak eloquently

emico, -are, emicui, emicatus spring out, leap forth; gleam, shine forth, be conspicuous

emitto, -ere, emisi, emissus send forth, send out, dispatch; publish; let go, let loose, free, let slip

emo, -ere, ēmi, emptus buy, purchase; bribe

emoveo, -ēre, emovi, emotus move out or away, remove

enim (conjunction) for; namely, for instance; indeed, truly, certainly

eō to there; so far, to such an extent, so long; for that reason, on that account

eo, -ire, ivi or **ii, itus** go; pass, proceed

Eos (f) dawn

epulo, -onis (m) feaster

septemviri epulones a college of priests who had charge of sacrificial feasts

equus, -i (m) horse

erga (preposition with accusative) toward; about

ergo therefore, accordingly, then

eripio, -ere, eripui, ereptus snatch away, tear out; free, rescue

error, -oris (m) wandering about; wavering, uncertainty, error, mistake; source of error, deception

erumpo, -ere, erupi, eruptus break open, cause to burst forth; vent, discharge; break out, burst forth; rush forth

esurio, -ire be hungry, desire food; long for

et (adverb) also, even; (conjunction) and; and indeed; and then; yet

et . . . et both . . . and

etiam as yet, still; also, besides, even; yes, certainly; actually?, really?

etiamsi even if, although

evado, -ere, evasi, evasus go out, go forth; climb up or out; escape, get off; go out or through, pass over

evenio, -ire, evēni, eventus come out, turn out, result; befall, happen, occur

eventum, -i (n) consequence, result; event, occurrence

everto, -ere, everti, eversus turn out, dislodge, eject; turn up, stir; overturn, throw down, demolish, destroy, ruin

evinco, -ere, evici, evictus conquer entirely, utterly subdue; prevail over, get through, get over; bring about; prove irresistibly

evoco (1) call out; summon the spirits of the dead or a deity; draw out, draw on; call forth, produce

evolo (1) fly out, fly away; come out quickly, rush forth, escape

ex *see* **e**

exanimo (1) take away the breath of, wind, stun, weaken; deprive of life, kill

excellens, -ntis high, lofty, eminent, remarkable

excelsus, -a, -um lofty, high, elevated, eminent

excipio, -ere, excepi, exceptus take out; rescue; except; take up, catch; greet, welcome a person; learn; come upon; receive, take over from, follow, succeed, come later

excito (1) arouse, rouse up; provoke, call forth, cause; console, cheer, inspire; raise, erect; kindle, inflame

exclamo (1) shout, cry aloud; exclaim; call a person by name

excutio, -ere, excussi, excussus shake out; shake out clothes to find anything hidden; search, examine a person; investigate; strike off, throw out, knock away, shake off

exemplum, -i (n) sample, example; general character, manner, fashion; example to be followed, model; precedent; warning, object lesson; copy, transcript

exeo, -ire, exivi, exitus go out, go away, go forth; pass from state to state; get out, become known; come to an end, pass away; transit, pass over

exercitus, -ūs (m) training; army; the infantry; crowd, swarm

eximius, -a, -um excepted; selected; exceptional, distinguished

existimo (1) evaluate; judge, consider, regard

exitium, -i (n) going out or away; destruction, ruin; cause of destruction

exitus, -ūs (m) going out, going forth; means of going out, exit; end, finish; issue, result

expedio, -ire, expedivi, expeditus free
from a snare, disengage, disentangle, set
free; get things ready for action; release,
clear, set straight; clear up a point,
explain

expello, -ere, expuli, expulsus drive out,
expel, thrust away

experientia, -ae (f) trial, testing, attempt;
knowledge gained by experience

experior, -iri, expertus sum try, test,
prove, put to the test; know by having
tried, know by experience; try to do

expertus, -a, -um tested, tried, approved;
with experience, experienced

expeto, -ere, expetivi, expetitus desire,
strive for, make for; demand, require;
seek to do; fall upon

explico, -are, explicavi or **explicui,
explicatus** or **explicitus** unfold, unroll,
disentangle; spread out, extend, expand;
deploy; put in order; pay off; explain,
expound, interpret; set free

explorator, -oris (m) explorer, scout, spy

expono, -ere, exposui, expositus put
outside, cast out; expose a child; land,
disembark; put on view, display, show;
set forth, explain, exhibit

exquisitus, -a, -um carefully sought or
worked out, choice, exquisite, artificial

exsanguis, -e bloodless, without blood;
deathly pale; making pale

exsaturo (1) satisfy, satiate

exsequiae, -arum (plural, f) funeral
procession

exsequor, -i, exsecutus sum follow to
the grave; follow to the end; maintain,
keep up; carry out, accomplish, execute;
avenge, punish; relate, describe, explain;
suffer, endure

exsilium, -i (n) banishment, exile; place of
exile

exspecto (1) look out for, wait for, await,
wait to see; hope for, dread

exspiro (1) breathe out, exhale, emit; blow
forth; rush forth; give up the ghost, die

exstinguo, -ere, exstinxi, exstinctus put
out, extinguish; kill; abolish, destroy,
annihilate

extendo, -ere, extendi, extensus or **exten-
tus** stretch out, expand, extend; increase,
extend; prolong; strain, exert

extollo, -ere lift up, raise up; raise, erect;
elevate, exalt; praise, exaggerate; defer,
postpone

extra (adverb) outside; except, unless;
(preposition with accusative) beyond,
outside, without; except for

exuro, -ere, exussi, exustus burn out, burn
up, consume; dry up, warm, heat

exuviae, -arum (plural, f) that which is
taken off; dress; spoils taken from the enemy (arms, etc.); animal skin, pelt, or hide

Ff

fabella, -ae (f) little story or fable

fabula, -ae (f) talk, conversation; tale,
story, fable, drama, myth

facies, -ei (f) shape, form, figure, outward
appearance; face, countenance; character, nature; seeming, pretense

facilis, -e easy to do; easy to manage,
convenient, favorable; mobile; facile,

dexterous, clever; affable, easygoing,
good natured

facile (adverb) easily, without difficulty;
indisputably, certainly

facinus, -oris (n) deed, action; bad deed,
crime, villainy; instrument of crime

facio, -ere, feci, factus make, form, do,
perform; cause, bring about; experience,

suffer; appoint, change into; regard, esteem, value; assume, make out, represent; act; behave; sacrifice; be serviceable, suit, help, be of service; *see also the passive* **fio**

certiorem facere inform

factum, -i (n) deed, act, exploit

fallax, -acis deceitful, treacherous, false
  fallaciter (adverb)

fallo, -ere, fefelli, falsus deceive, lead astray, cause to be mistaken; disappoint, fail in; beguile, wile away; escape the notice of, be concealed from

fama, -ae (f) talk, report, rumor, tradition; public opinion; standing in public opinion, repute

fames, -is (f) hunger, famine; insatiable desire

familia, -ae (f) household, establishment; family estate; family; group, sect

fas (indeclinable, n) divine command or law; fate, destiny; right, that which is allowed or lawful

fastidio, -ire, fastidivi, fastiditus loathe, feel distaste for, dislike

fateor, -ēri, fassus sum confess, admit, allow; reveal, make known

fatum, -i (n) utterance, (especially) divine utterance; destiny, fate, the will of a god; doom, fate, misfortune, ruin, calamity

faux, faucis (f) gullet, throat, jaws; chasm, gorge; isthmus, neck of land; strait

faveo, -ēre, favi, fautus favor, be favorable to, help, support; be inclined to do; speak no words of bad omen; be silent

favilla, -ae (f) glowing ashes; spark

favor, -oris (m) favor, goodwill, support, inclination; applause at the theater, acclamation

fax, facis (f) torch, (especially) torch carried at a wedding or a funeral; firebrand; instigator; stimulus; light, flame (especially of heavenly bodies); brilliance, passion

feles, -is (f) cat

felicitas, -atis (f) happiness, good fortune, success

felix, -icis fruitful, fertile; of good omen, favorable, bringing good luck; fortunate, lucky, successful
  feliciter (adverb) fruitfully; auspiciously, favorably; luckily, successfully

femina, -ae (f) female, woman

ferē almost, nearly; scarcely, hardly; just, exactly; as a rule; generally, usually

feriatus, -a, -um on holiday, idle, at leisure

ferinus, -a, -um relating to a wild beast, wild

fermē almost, nearly; hardly, scarcely; usually

fero, ferre, tuli, latus bear, bring, carry; endure, submit to; bring forth, produce; fetch, offer; cause, bring about; report to others, spread abroad, speak of; bear away, carry off; bear along, move forward, put in motion; move, impel, carry away

ferox, -ocis courageous, high spirited, warlike; wild, unbridled, arrogant

ferreus, -a, -um of iron; like iron; hard, unfeeling, cruel; immovable, firm

ferrum, -i (n) iron; plow, ax, scissors; (especially) sword

ferus, -a, -um wild, uncultivated, uncivilized, rough, cruel; *as noun (m or f)*: wild animal

ferveo, -ēre, ferbui or **fervi** be boiling hot, boil, seethe, glow; be in quick movement; be excited by passion, rage

fessus, -a, -um weary, tired, exhausted

festino (1) hasten, hurry; hasten, accelerate

festus, -a, -um of a holiday, festive; on holiday

fetus, -ūs (m) the bringing forth or hatching of young; bearing, producing; offspring, brood; fruit, produce, shoot

fidelis, -e trusty, steadfast, faithful
fideliter (adverb) faithfully; securely, without danger

fides, -ei (f) trust, confidence, reliance, belief, faith; faithfulness, conscientiousness; credibility, actuality, fulfillment; promise, assurance, word of honor, engagement; faithful protection, constant help

fides, -is (f) *usually plural*: gut string for a musical instrument; lyre, lute, harp

fidus, -a, -um trusty, true, faithful, sure

figura, -ae (f) form, shape, figure, size; ghost; kind, nature, species; figure of speech

filia, -ae (f) daughter

filius, -i (m) son

filum, -i (n) thread

fingo, fingere, finxi, fictum shape, fashion, form, mold; arrange, put in order; represent, imagine, conceive; feign, fabricate, devise

finio, -ire, finivi, finitus bound, limit, enclose, restrain; define, determine, appoint; put an end to, conclude, finish; finish speaking; die; pass, end, cease

finis, -is (usually m) boundary, limit, border; summit, end; object, aim; *plural*: enclosed area, territory

fio, fieri, factus sum (used as passive of **facio**) be made, come into existence; become, be appointed; be done; happen

firmus, -a, -um firm, strong, stout; lasting, valid

fistula, -ae (f) water pipe; reed pipe, shepherd's pipe

flagro (1) blaze, burn, glow, flame, glitter; suffer from

flamen, -inis (m) high priest of a particular god

flamma, -ae (f) flame, blazing fire; source of light, torch, star, lightning; luster, glitter; the fire or glow of passion; devouring flame, destruction

flecto, -ere, flexi, flexus bend; alter the shape of, bow, twist, curve; change, alter, influence; alter the direction of, turn, wheel

fleo, -ēre, flevi, fletus weep; drip, trickle; weep for, lament, bewail

floreo, -ēre, florui bloom, flower; be in one's prime, prosper, flourish, be in repute; abound, swarm

floridus, -a, -um flowery, blossoming; made of or rich in flowers; fresh, blooming

flos, floris (m) flower, blossom; the prime, the flower, the best, the pride; first beard, down

fluctuo (1) be wavelike, move up and down; be tossed about, waver

fluctuor, -ari, fluctatus sum toss about, waver

fluctus, -ūs (m) streaming, flowing; commotion, disturbance

fluentum, -i (n) running water, stream

flumen, -inis (n) flowing; river, stream

focus, -i (m) fireplace, hearth; house, family, home; altar fire, funeral pyre

foedus, -a, -um foul, filthy, horrible, disgusting
foedē (adverb)

foedus, -eris (n) league of states; compact, covenant, agreement; law

folium, -i (n) leaf

fons, fontis (m) spring, fountain; freshwater, springwater; origin, source

foras (adverb) outdoors, forth, out

fore, forem (etc.) *see* **sum**

forīs (adverb) situated outdoors, outside, without; abroad, outside Rome; from without, from abroad

foris, -is (f) door; opening, entrance

forma, -ae (f) form, figure, shape; beautiful shape, beauty; image, likeness; mold, stamp; manner, type

formosus, -a, -um beautifully formed, beautiful

fors, fortis (f) chance, luck

    forsitan (fors sit an) perhaps, perchance

    forte by chance, accidentally, as it happened

fortasse perhaps

forte *see* **fors**

fortis, -e strong, powerful, robust; brave, courageous, steadfast; bold, audacious

    fortiter (adverb) strongly, bravely

fortitudo, -inis (f) physical strength, moral bravery, courage; deed of bravery

fortuna, -ae (f) chance, fate, lot, luck, fortune; condition, state, mode of life; property, possessions

fortunatus, -a, -um blessed, lucky, fortunate; well off, wealthy, rich

    fortunatē (adverb) happily, fortunately

forum, -i (n) open square, marketplace; place of public commercial, political, and judicial business

fovea, -ae (f) pit, (especially) trap for game, pitfall

foveo, -ēre, fovi, fotus warm, keep warm, caress; foster, cherish, support, encourage

frango, -ere, fregi, fractus break, break in pieces, shatter; master, subdue, humble

frater, -tris (m) brother; cousin, brother-in-law; comrade, compatriot, ally

frequens, -entis crowded, numerous, full; frequented, populous; repeated, frequent, constant; often done or used

    frequenter (adverb) in large numbers; frequently, often

frigidus, -a, -um cold, cool, chilly; chilling, causing cold; dull, lifeless; flat

frigus, -oris (n) cold, coolness; the cold of winter; a cold place; the cold of death or fright; dullness, indolence; a cold reception, coolness, disfavor

frons, frondis (f) leaf, foliage; chaplet or crown of leaves

frons, frontis (f) forehead, brow; front, forepart

fructus, -ūs (m) enjoyment, enjoying; proceeds, profit, produce, income; (especially) fruits of the earth

frustrā in error; in vain, without effect; without reason

frux, frugis (f) *usually plural* (**fruges, -um**): fruits; success; *dative singular* (**frugi**) *used as an adjective*: useful, honest, discreet, moderate

fuero, fui, futurus (etc.) *see* **sum**

fuga, -ae (f) flight, running away; exile, banishment; speed; avoidance

fugio, -ere, fūgi, fugitus flee, take flight, run away; pass away, disappear; flee from, run away from, avoid; escape the notice of

fulgeo, -ēre, fulsi flash, lighten; shine, glitter, gleam; be distinguished

fulvus, -a, -um tawny, yellowish brown

fumus, -i (m) smoke, steam, vapor

fundo, -ere, fudi, fusus pour, pour out; melt, cast; shower, give abundantly; squander; utter; spread, extend, scatter; rout, defeat, put to flight

fungor, -i, functus sum (usually with ablative) occupy oneself with, perform, execute, undergo; be affected, suffer

funus, -eris (n) funeral, burial; corpse; death; destruction, ruin; cause of ruin

fur, furis (c) thief

furo, -ere rage, rave, be mad; be frantic

furor, -ari, furatus sum steal, pilfer; steal away, withdraw; counterfeit, impersonate

furor, -oris (m) madness, raving, insanity; furious anger, martial rage; passionate love; inspiration, poetic or prophetic frenzy; object of passion

furtim by stealth, stealthily

furtō secretly

furtum, -i (n) theft, robbery; stolen property; underhand methods, trick, deceit; secret or stolen love

fustis, -is (m) stick, cudgel, club

Gg

galerum, -i (n) or **galerus, -i** (m) light helmet, skullcap; wig

gallina, -ae (f) hen, chicken

garrulus, -a, -um talkative, chattering, babbling, noisy

gaudeo, -ēre, gavisus sum rejoice, be glad; (with ablative) delight in

gaudium, -i (n) joy, gladness, delight; source of delight

gelidus, -a, -um cold, frosty, icy; chilling

geminus, -a, -um twin, double; paired; similar, like

gemitus, -ūs (m) sigh, groan; groaning, roaring

gemma, -ae (f) jewel, gem, precious stone; bud or eye of a plant; literary gem

gemmeus, -a, -um made of or set with jewels; bright

gemo, -ere, gemui, gemitus sigh, groan; roar; coo; creak; sigh over, lament, bemoan

gener, -eri (m) son-in-law; granddaughter's husband; brother-in-law

genero (1) beget, produce, bring to life

genetrix, -tricis (f) one who brings forth, mother

genius, -i (m) guardian spirit of a man or place; one's taste, inclination; talent, genius

gens, gentis (f) clan, stock, people, tribe, nation; offspring, descendant; district, country

genu, -ūs (n) knee

genus, -eris (n) birth, descent, origin; race, stock, family, house; offspring, descendants; sex; class, kind, variety, sort; genus; fashion, manner, way

germen, -inis (n) embryo; bud, shoot, graft; germ, seed

gero, -ere, gessi, gestus carry, bear; wear; give birth to; carry about, display an appearance; carry on, conduct, manage business

gestio, -ire, gestivi exult, be excited, run riot; desire, long for

gesto (1) carry, bear about

gigno, -ere, genui, genitus beget, bear, bring forth; cause

gladius, -i (m) sword

gloria, -ae (f) fame, renown, glory; pride; desire of glory, ambition, boastfulness

gradus, -ūs (m) step, pace; stair; tier, gradation; degree, stage; rank, position; station, post

gramen, -inis (n) grass, turf; any plant or herb

grandis, -e full grown, big, great, large; tall; old; important; lofty, grand, sublime

granum, -i (n) grain, seed

gratia, -ae (f) charm, attraction, pleasantness; favor with others; esteem, regard, popularity; favor done, service, kindness; thankfulness, thanks

gratiā on account of

gratulatio, -onis (f) wishing joy, congratulation; thanksgiving festival

gratus, -a, -um pleasing, welcome, agreeable; thankful, grateful

gravis, -e heavy; low, deep; weighty, important; dignified, serious; elevated; burdened, laden, weighed down; pregnant; burdensome, oppressive; grievous, painful, unpleasant

graviter (adverb) heavily, weightily, reluctantly; grievously, painfully

gressus, -ūs (m) step; course

grex, gregis (m) herd, flock, drove; troop, band, sect, unit of soldiers

guberno (1) steer a ship, be at the helm; steer, direct, govern

gurges, -itis (m) whirlpool, eddy; troubled water, stream, flood, sea; abyss, depth

gutta, -ae (f) drop; spot, mark

Hh

habeo, -ēre, habui, habitus have, hold; have about one, carry, wear; contain; possess, have power over; possess property, be wealthy; own, inhabit, rule over; keep (especially in a certain state or relation); keep oneself, be in a condition

habito (1) inhabit; dwell

habitus, -ūs (m) condition, habit, bearing; style; nature, character, disposition, attitude

haedus, -i (m) kid, young goat

haereo, -ēre, haesi, haesus stick, cleave, adhere, hang on to a person or thing; come to a standstill, get stuck; be embarrassed

haud, haut not, not at all, by no means

haurio, -ire, hausi, haustus draw up, draw out, draw in; drink up, absorb, swallow; shed blood; drain, empty; derive, take in; exhaust, weaken, waste

hedera, -ae (f) ivy

herba, -ae (f) vegetation; green plant; blade, stalk (especially of corn or grass)

hereditas, -atis (f) inheritance

heres, -edis (c) heir, heiress, successor; owner

heri yesterday

hesternus, -a, -um of yesterday

heu oh!, alas!

heus hey!, ho, there!, you!

hīc here; in this place, in this matter; hereupon

hic, haec, hoc this, this one; this present; *strengthened forms*: **hice, haece, hoce**

hiems, -emis (f) winter; the cold of winter; stormy weather, storm

hilaris, -e cheerful, merry

hinc from here, hence; from this cause; henceforth, thereupon

hio (1) open, stand open; gape (especially in astonishment or longing); hang together badly

hirsutus, -a, -um hairy, shaggy, rough; unadorned

hodie today; at present, still, even now; at once

homo, -inis (c) human being, mortal; humankind; *plural*: people, the world

honestus, -a, -um honored, in good repute, respectable; honorable, proper, virtuous; fine, beautiful

honestē (adverb) respectably; honorably; properly

honoro (1) honor, show honor to, adorn, dignify

honos or **honor, -oris** (m) honor, mark of honor or respect, distinction; office of dignity, public office; offering to the gods, sacrifice; beauty, grace

hora, -ae (f) hour, twelfth part of a day or a night; time, season

horreo, -ēre, horrui bristle, be rough; stand on end; shudder, dread

horridus, -a, -um rough, shaggy, bristly; shivering with cold; wild, savage; unpolished, uncouth; frightful, horrible

hortor, -ari, hortatus sum exhort, incite, encourage; harangue troops

hospes, -pitis (m) host; guest; guest friend, friend; stranger

hospita, -ae (f) hostess; guest; guest friend, friend; stranger

hostilis, -e of, by, or for the enemy; like an enemy, unfriendly, hostile

hostis, -is (c) enemy, foe, opponent; stranger

huc hither, to this place; in addition to this; to this pitch or degree

huiusmodi or **huiuscemodi** of this kind

humanitas, -atis (f) humanity, human nature, human feeling; kindness; refinement, education, culture

humanus, -a, -um human, of human beings; humane, kind, educated, civilized, refined

humilis, -e on or near the ground, low, shallow; humble, poor, insignificant; abject, submissive; mean, plain

humus, -i (f) ground, earth, soil; land, country

humī (adverb) on the ground

Ii

iaceo, iacēre, iacui lie, be situated; lie low, lie flat; lie sick or overthrown or killed; hang loosely; be neglected or despised; be overthrown; be cast down or dejected

iacio, -ere, ieci, iactus lay; throw, cast, hurl; fling away, shed; scatter, diffuse; let fall in speaking, utter

iacto (1) throw, cast, toss, fling away or about; diffuse, spread, scatter; harass, disturb a person; broadcast words; bring up, discuss a subject; keep bringing up, boast of

iam now, by now, already; immediately, presently, soon; henceforth; further, moreover; just, indeed

  iam diu, iam dudum, iam pridem for a long time

ianua, -ae (f) door; entrance, approach

ibi there, at that place; then, thereupon; therein

icio or **ico, -ere, ici, ictus** strike, hit, smite

ictus, -ūs (m) blow, stroke; beat

īdem, eadem, idem the same; by way of addition, also; yet

idolon, -i (n) ghost, specter

igitur therefore, then; so, as I was saying

ignavus, -a, -um idle, listless, inactive, inert, sluggish; cowardly; *as noun* (m): coward

ignifer, -fera, -ferum fire bearing, fiery

ignis, -is (m) fire, conflagration; watch fire, beacon; firebrand; lightning; glow, glitter; glow of passion; beloved

ignosco, -ere, ignovi, ignotus overlook, forgive, pardon

ignotus, -a, -um passing unknown; ignoble, obscure; acting ignorant

ilico on the spot; immediately

ille, illa, illud that, that yonder, that one; (in contrast with **hic**) the former

illīc there, at that place; therein, in that matter

illic, illaec, illuc that one

illuc thither, to that place; to that matter or person

imago, -inis (f) image, copy, likeness; representation, portrait, statue; shade or ghost of the dead; mental picture, idea, conception; mere form, appearance, pretense; *plural*: waxen figures, portraits of ancestors

imber, -bris (m) shower or storm of rain, pelting rain; rain cloud; water, any fluid

imbuo, -ere, imbui, imbutus wet, steep, saturate; stain, taint; accustom

imitor, -ari, imitatus sum imitate, copy; depict; be like, act like

immanis, -e enormous, immense, monstrous; savage, horrible, inhuman

immensus, -a, -um immense, vast, boundless

immergo, -ere, immersi, immersus dip in, plunge in, immerse

immineo, -ēre, imminui project, overhang; be imminent; hang over; threaten; be on the watch or lookout for

immō no indeed, by no means; indeed

immolo (1) sacrifice; devote to death, slay

immortalis, -e deathless, immortal, imperishable

impedio, -ire, impedivi, impeditus entangle, ensnare, obstruct, surround; embarrass, hinder, prevent

imperator, -oris (m) commander, leader; emperor

imperium, -i (n) order, command; power, mastery, command; political power, authority, sovereignty; empire

impero (1) impose; requisition, order a thing; order an action to be done, give orders to a person; rule over, govern, command

impetro (1) get, accomplish, effect; obtain by asking

impetus, -ūs (m) attack, onset; any rapid motion; mental impulse, passion, force

impiger, -gra, -grum diligent, active

impigrē (adverb)

impius, -a, -um impious, undutiful, unpatriotic

impleo, -ēre, implevi, impletus fill in, fill up, complete; satisfy, content a person; fulfill, perform; contaminate

impono, -ere, imposui, impositus put, lay, place in or on; embark; lay or put on, impose; impose upon, cheat, deceive

improbus, -a, -um inferior, bad; morally bad, perverse, willful; bold, persistent, mischievous; unpatriotic

improbē (adverb) badly, wickedly; impudently, boldly

imprudens, -entis not foreseeing, not expecting; not knowing, unaware; unwise, rash, imprudent

imputo (1) lay to a charge, enter in an account; reckon, impute to

imus *see* **inferus**

in (preposition with accusative) into, on to, toward, against; until; for ever; for; (preposition with ablative) in, on, among; at, within; in relation to, in the case of

inanis, -e empty, void; empty of; empty handed, poor; vain, hollow, idle

incertus, -a, -um uncertain, doubtful, not sure as to fact; not knowing, doubting; unknown, obscure; hesitating, irresolute, undecided

incido, -ere, incidi, incasus fall in or upon; fall in with; occur, happen, crop up

incīdo, -ere, incīdi, incisus cut into, cut open; inscribe, engrave; make by cutting; cut through; cut short, bring to an end, break off

incipio, -ere, incepi, inceptus take in hand, begin, commence; begin to speak

inclino (1) bend, incline, turn; change; fall back; take a turn, verge, incline, change; waver, yield

includo, -ere, inclusi, inclusus shut in, enclose; block, obstruct, confine

incola, -ae (c) inhabitant, native; foreign resident

incolo, -ere, incolui inhabit, dwell (in)

incolumis, -e uninjured, safe and sound

incredibilis, -e not to be believed, incredible

inde thence, from there; from that cause, for that reason; from that time, thereafter; thereupon, then

indicium, -i (n) information, evidence; any mark, sign, or token

indico (1) make known, show, indicate; inform against, give evidence about; put a price on, value

indignus, -a, -um unworthy, not deserving; disgraceful, shameful

> **indignē** (adverb) unworthily, dishonorably; impatiently, indignantly

indoles, -is (f) native constitution or quality; nature, disposition, character, talents

indulgentia, -ae (f) tenderness, indulgence

indulgeo, -ēre, indulsi forbear, be patient, be indulgent; give oneself up to, indulge in; grant, allow, concede

induo, -ere, indui, indutus put on, clothe, surround, cover; assume, take up, engage in; fall into, fall on; entangle

infans, -fantis speechless, unable to speak; tongue tied, embarrassed; youthful, fresh; childish, silly; *as noun (m or f)*: little child

infelix, -icis unfruitful, barren; unhappy, unlucky; causing unhappiness

inferior, inferius *see* **inferus** and **infrā**

infero, inferre, intuli, inlatus carry in, put or place on; betake oneself, go; bring on, introduce, occasion; infer, conclude

inferus, -a, -um below, lower, southern; of the lower world; *as plural noun* (**inferi, -orum**, m): the dead, the lower world

inferior, -ius (comparative) lower, later, junior; inferior

infimus, -a, -um (superlative) lowest; meanest

> **imus, -a, -um** (superlative) lowest, deepest; last

infirmus, -a, -um weak, feeble; timorous

inflo (1) blow into; play on a wind instrument; give a blast; blow out, puff out; inspire; puff up, elate

informis, -e formless, shapeless; deformed, hideous

infrā (preposition with accusative) below, under; later than; (adverb) below, underneath; in the lower world; to the south; lower

> **inferius** (comparative) lower down

infundo, -ere, infudi, infusus pour in or on; pour out for, administer

ingemisco, -ere, ingemui sigh or groan over

ingenium, -i (n) nature, natural quality, constitution, character, mental power, ability, genius

ingens, -entis monstrous, vast, enormous

ingenuitas, -atis (f) free birth; noble mindedness, uprightness, frankness

ingenuus, -a, -um native, natural, innate; freeborn, of free birth, worthy of a free man, noble, honorable, frank

ingredior, -i, ingressus sum step in, enter, go in; walk; enter upon, begin

inguen, -guinis (n) groin

inhonestus, -a, -um degraded, dishonored; dishonorable, shameful; ugly, unsightly

> **inhonestē** (adverb) dishonorably

inicio, -ere, inieci, iniectus throw in, put in or into; cause, inspire, occasion; throw on or over; impose, lay on

inimicus, -a, -um unfriendly, adverse, hostile; hurtful, prejudicial; *as noun (m or f)*: enemy, foe

inimicē (adverb) in an unfriendly manner

iniquus, -a, -um uneven, unequal; excessive, unbalanced, adverse, disadvantageous; ill matched; unfair, unfavorable; perverse, disgruntled

    iniquē (adverb) unequally; unfairly, adversely

initium, -i (n) beginning; *plural*: elements, first principles; auspices

iniuria, -ae (f) injury, injustice, wrong; possession wrongfully obtained; revenge for an affront

iniustus, -a, -um unfair, unjust; harsh, oppressive

    iniustē (adverb)

innocens, -entis harmless, inoffensive, blameless

innocentia, -ae (f) harmlessness, innocence, integrity

innumerabilis, -e countless, innumerable

innumerus, -a, -um countless, innumerable

inquam, inquii (defective) say

inquiro, -ere, inquisivi, inquisitus search for; investigate, inquire into; search for evidence

inscribo, -ere, inscripsi, inscriptus write in or on, inscribe; mark, impress; title; ascribe

insequor, -i, insecutus sum follow after, follow on; succeed; pursue a subject; censure, reproach; attack, assail

insideo, -ēre sit in or on; dwell, remain

insignis, -e distinguished, remarkable, extraordinary; *as noun (n)*: distinguishing mark, token; badge, decoration, medal

insolitus, -a, -um unaccustomed; unusual, strange, uncommon

inspicio, -ere, inspexi, inspectus look into, see into; view, examine, inspect; consider

instituo, -ere, institui, institutus put in place, set in order; set up, make ready, build, construct; establish, introduce, arrange; settle on a course, undertake, resolve, determine; appoint; instruct, educate, train

insto, -are, insteti stand in or on; be close to, follow closely, pursue eagerly; devote oneself, persist, persevere; insist, ask pressingly; approach, impend

insulto (1) leap, prance in or on; triumph over, insult

insum, inesse, infui be in or on; be contained in, belong to

insuper above, overhead; over and above, in addition, besides

intellego, -ere, intellexi, intellectus discern, perceive; understand, grasp; judge, appreciate

intemperantia, -ae (f) lack of restraint, extravagance, excess

inter (preposition with accusative) between, among, amid; during, in the course of

intercedo, -ere, intercessi, intercessus go between, come between, intervene; interpose, stand surety; step between, withstand, protest against

interdiū in the daytime, by day

interdum sometimes, now and then

interea meanwhile; nevertheless, notwithstanding

interficio, -ere, interfeci, interfectus do away with, destroy, put an end to, kill

interim meanwhile; however

interitus, -ūs (m) destruction, ruin

interrogo (1) ask, question, interrogate; examine a witness; accuse

intersum, interesse, interfui be between; be among, be present at, take part in; intervene; differ, be different

    interest (impersonal) it makes a difference, it concerns

intestatus, -a, -um having made no will, intestate

intimus, -a, -um (superlative) innermost, inmost; most profound, most secret, intimate

intrā (adverb) inside; (preposition with accusative) inside, within, less than, short of

intro (1) go in, enter

intus within, inside; to or from the inside; inwardly

invado, -ere, invasi, invasus go in, enter, get in; undertake; attack, fall upon, assail, usurp, seize

invenio, -ire, invēni, inventus come upon, find, meet with, discover; invent, devise; procure, get, earn; show oneself

invicem in turn, alternately; mutually, reciprocally

invideo, -ēre, invīdi, invisum, envy, grudge, be envious of

invidia, -ae (f) envy, jealousy, ill will; odium, unpopularity; source of ill will

invito (1) invite, summon; receive, entertain; induce, allure; treat oneself

iocus, -i (m) joke, jest

ipse, -a, -um self; oneself; the very, actual; exactly; by oneself, of one's own accord

ira, -ae (f) wrath, anger, rage; cause of anger

iracundia, -ae (f) angry disposition, irascibility; state of anger, fury, wrath

irascor, -i grow angry

iratus, -a, -um angry

is, ea, id he, she, it; this, that

iste, ista, istud (pronoun or adjective; often contemptuous) that, that of yours, that beside you

ita so, thus; really?; certainly; and so; so very; in such a way that, only on condition that

itaque and so; therefore, for that reason

item also, likewise

iter, itineris (n) way, direction; journey, march; right of way; road; course, method

iterum again, a second time

itidem likewise, also

iubar, -aris (n) beaming light, radiance; heavenly body, (especially) the sun

iubeo, -ēre, iussi, iussus order, command, bid

iucundus, -a, -um pleasant, agreeable, delightful

iucundē (adverb)

iudex, -icis (m) judge; *plural:* panel of jurors

iudicium, -i (n) trial, legal investigation; law court; jurisdiction, judgment, considered opinion, decision; power of judging, discernment, understanding, good judgment

iudico (1) be a judge, judge, decide, declare

iugum, -i (n) yoke, collar; team of oxen or horses; pair, couple; chariot; any bond or union; bond of love, marriage tie; yoke of slavery; crossbar; yoke under which the vanquished were sent; ridge between mountains; *plural:* mountain heights

iungo, -ere, iunxi, iunctus join, unite, connect; yoke, harness; mate

Iuno, -onis (f) Juno (goddess, sister and wife of Jupiter)

Iuppiter, Iovis (m) Jupiter (the Roman supreme god)

sub Iove in the open air

iurgium, -i (n) brawl, quarrel

iurgo (1) quarrel, squabble

iuro (1) swear, take an oath

ius, iuris (n) right, law, justice, law court

iure rightly, justly

ius iurandum oath

iustus, -a, -um just, fair, lawful

iuvencus, -i (m) young bull

iuvenis, -is (m) youth, young man
iuventa, -ae (f) youth
iuventus, -tutis (f) youth, manhood

Kk

kalendae, -arum (f) first day of the month

Ll

lābor, -i, lapsus sum glide, slip, fall, sink
labor, -oris (m) work, labor, task
laboro (1) work, labor, strive
labrum, -i (n) lip, edge
lac, lactis (n) milk
lacrima, -ae (f) tear, teardrop
lacrimo (1) cry, weep, mourn
lacus, -ūs (m) lake, pool, pond
laedo, -ere, laesi, laesus strike, knock, hurt, injure, damage, offend
laetus, -a, -um glad, joyful, happy, rich, copious
  laetē (adverb)
laevus, -a, -um left, left handed; foolish; unlucky
lampas, -padis (f) torch, light
langueo, -ēre, be faint, be weak, weary; droop, flag
languesco, -ere, langui become faint, weak, or listless
languidus, -a, -um faint, weak, limp
lapsus, -ūs (m) gliding, sliding, fall; fault
lar, laris (m) *usually plural* (**lares**): Roman household deities; hearth, home
larva, -ae (f) ghost
lascivus, -a, -um playful, wanton, lewd
latebra, -ae (f) hiding place, retreat
lateo, -ēre, latui lie hidden, be concealed
latus, -a, -um broad, wide, extensive
  latē (adverb)
latus, -eris (n) side, flank
laudabilis, -e praiseworthy, laudable
laudo (1) praise, extol, commend; cite

iuvo, -are, iuvi, iutus help, please
iuxtā (adverb) nearby, just the same; (preposition with accusative) close to, next to

laurus, -i (f) laurel tree, bay tree; triumph
laus, laudis (f) praise, fame, glory
lautus, -a, -um fine, elegant, refined
lectisternium, -i (n) religious feast
lectulus, -i (m) small bed, couch
lectus, -a, -um select, choice, excellent
lectus, -i (m) bed, couch
legio, -onis (f) legion of the Roman army
legitimus, -a, -um lawful, right, proper
lēgo (1) bequeath, leave as a legacy; appoint
lego, -ere, lēgi, lectus collect, gather, pick; scan, read; choose, select
lenio, -ire, lenivi, lenitus soothe, relieve
lenis, -e smooth, mild, gentle
  leniter (adverb)
lentus, -a, -um slow, sluggish, sticky
leo, leonis (m) lion
letum, -i (n) death, ruin
levis, -e light; swift; unimportant; fickle
lēvis, -e smooth, polished; hairless
levo (1) raise, lift up; ease; impair
lex, legis (f) law, rule, agreement
libens, -entis willing, with pleasure
  libenter (adverb) willingly, with pleasure
liber, -bri (m) book, volume
līber, -era, -erum free, independent, unrestrained
Līber, -eri (m) Italic deity identified with Bacchus
liberalis, -e genteel, courteous, generous
liberi, -orum (plural, m) children
libero (1) set free, liberate, release

libertus, -i (m) freedman

libet, -ēre, libuit or **libitum est** (impersonal) it pleases, it is agreeable

libido, -inis (f) violent desire, longing; passion, lust

libo (1) taste, touch, pour

licet, -ēre, licuit or **licitum est** (impersonal) it is allowed, one can or may; although

limen, -inis (n) threshold, doorway, entrance

lingua, -ae (f) tongue; speech, language

lino, -ere, levi, litus smear, befoul, dirty; rub out

liquor, -i be fluid, flow, melt

liquor, -oris (m) liquid, fluid; sea

lis, litis (f) legal controversy, action, suit; strife, quarrel

littera, -ae (f) letter of the alphabet; letter, dispatch; *plural*: documents; literature

litus, -oris (n) shore, beach, coast

locuples, -pletis wealthy, rich

locus, -i (m) place, position, ground, situation, rank; occasion; passage in a book; *plurals*: **loci** (m) single places; **loca** (n) region

longaevus, -a, -um aged, old

longus, -a, -um long; tedious
longē (adverb) a long way off, far, at a distance

loquax, -quacis talkative, garrulous; babbling, noisy

loquor, -i, locutus sum speak, tell, say, talk of

lubricus, -a, -um slippery, smooth; uncertain, perilous

luceo, -ēre, luxi be bright, shine; be clear, evident

lucerna, -ae (f) lamp

lucesco, -ere, luxi begin to shine
lucescit (impersonal) it grows light, day is breaking

lucidus, -a, -um shining, bright, clear

luctus, -ūs (m) sorrow, lamentation, mourning

lucus, -i (m) grove, wood

ludo, -ere, lusi, lusus play, play at or with; delude

ludus, -i (m) play, game, sport, pastime; school; *plural* (**ludi**): public games

lues, -is (f) plague, pestilence, calamity

lumen, -inis (n) light; lamp; the light of day, day; life; eye; insight; glory

luna, -ae (f) moon; night; month

luo, -ere, lui, luiturus expiate, atone for, make good
luere poenam pay a penalty

lupus, -i (m) wolf

lustro (1) purify; go round, go over, traverse; review, observe, examine

luteus, -a, -um of mud or clay; dirty

lūteus, -a, -um yellow, orange

lutum, -i (n) mud, mire, dirt; clay

lux, lucis (f) light; (especially) daylight, day; life; eye, eyesight; hope

Lyaeus, -i (m) epithet of Bacchus; wine

lympha, -ae (f) water (especially of a clear spring or stream)

lyra, -ae (f) lyre, lute, stringed instrument; lyric poetry, song

Mm

macula, -ae (f) spot, mark, stain; moral blemish

maereo, -ēre, grieve, mourn, lament

maestus, -a, -um sad, dejected, gloomy

magis, mage more, to a greater extent; rather

maximē or **maxumē** (superlative) in the highest degree, most of all, especially, very much so

magister, -tri (m) master, teacher

magistra, -ae (f) directress, teacher

magistratus, -ūs (m) magistracy, office; magistrate, state official

magnitudo, -inis (f) greatness; magnanimity

magnopere greatly, very much

magnus, -a, -um great, large; loud; old; mighty, powerful, important

maior, maius (comparative); *plural noun* (**maiores**, m): ancestors

maximus, -a, -um (superlative)

maiestas, -atis (f) greatness, grandeur, majesty

maiores *see* **magnus**

male badly, ill, excessively

male audire be ill spoken of

peius (comparative)

pessimē (superlative)

maledico, -ere, maledixi, maledictus speak ill of, abuse

malo, malle, malui wish rather, prefer

malus, -a, -um bad, evil; unfavorable, unsuccessful; ugly

peior, peius (comparative)

pessimus, -a, -um (superlative)

mancipium, -i (n) legal purchasing; slave so acquired

mando (1) commit, entrust; order, command

māne (indeclinable) morning; (adverb) in the morning, early

maneo, -ēre, mansi, mansus remain, stay; endure, last; await

manes, -ium (plural, m) shades of the departed, spirits of the dead

manus, -ūs (f) hand; power; band or body of men

mare, -is (n) sea

marita, -ae (f) wife

maritus, -a, -um matrimonial, nuptial; tied or entwined together

maritus, -i (m) husband, man

marmor, -oris (n) marble; statue; stone; foamy surface of the sea

marmoreus, -a, -um of or like marble

Mars, Martis (m; old form: **Mavors, -rtis**) Mars (god of agriculture and war)

mas, maris (m) the male, masculinity

mater, matris (f) mother; source, origin

materia, -ae (f) matter, material; timber; subject matter; occasion, cause; natural disposition

matrimonium, -i (n) marriage

matrona, -ae (f) married woman, matron

maturus, -a, -um ripe, mature, grown up, developed; timely, quick, speedy

maturē (adverb) at the right time, seasonably, opportunely; early

maximus *see* **magnus**

me, mihi *see* **ego**

medicina, -ae (f) art of healing; medicine; cure

medicus, -a, -um healing, medicinal

medicus, -i (m) doctor, physician

medius, -a, -um middle, midmost, mid; central, intermediate

mel, mellis (n) honey; sweetness, pleasantness

melior, melius *see* **bonus**

membrum, -i (n) limb, member, part of the body

memini, meminisse (perfect with present meaning) remember, recollect; mention

memor, -oris mindful, remembering; grateful, thoughtful, prudent

memoria, -ae (f) memory, remembrance; tradition, history

memoro (1) mention, call to mind, relate

mendacium, -i (n) lie, falsehood

mendax, -acis lying, mendacious, false

mens, mentis (f) mind, intellect, understanding, judgment; intention, resolve; feelings, disposition; courage; opinion, thoughts

mensa, -ae (f) table; course at a meal

mensis, -is (m) month

mentior, -iri, mentitus sum lie; deceive, mislead, disappoint; say falsely, invent

mereo, -ēre, merui or **mereor, -ēri, meritus sum** deserve, earn, obtain

meretrix, -icis (f) prostitute

mergo, -ere, mersi, mersus dip, immerse, sink, overwhelm

meritum, -i (n) desert, merit; a good; grounds, reason, action, benefit, service

meritus, -a, -um deserving

meritō (adverb) deservedly, rightly

messis, -is (f) harvest, crop; harvesttime

-met *suffix added to personal and reflexive pronouns for emphasis*

metallum, -i (n) metal; mine

metuo, -ere, metui, metutus fear, be afraid

metus, -ūs (m) fear, dread; reverence, awe

meus, -a, -um my, mine

mihi *see* **ego**

miles, -itis (m) soldier; infantryman

mille (indeclinable in singular) a thousand; *plural:* **milia, -ium** thousands

minax, -acis projecting, menacing, overhanging

minimē *see* **parum**

minimus *see* **parvus**

minor *see* **parvus**

minus *see* **parum** and **parvus**

mirabilis, -e wonderful, extraordinary, unusual

miraculum, -i (n) wonderful thing, prodigy, miracle; wonder, surprise

mirificus, -a, -um causing wonder, wonderful, astonishing

mirificē (adverb)

miror, -ari, miratus sum wonder, be astonished at; admire

mirus, -a, -um wonderful, astonishing, extraordinary

mirē (adverb)

misceo, -ēre, miscui, mixtus mix, mingle; combine, unite; prepare; confuse

miser, -era, -erum wretched, unhappy, sad

miserē (adverb)

misereo, -ēre, miserui, miseritus pity, sympathize with

miseria, -ae (f) wretchedness, unhappiness, distress

misericordia, -ae (f) pity, compassion, mercy

misericors, -cordis pitiful, compassionate

mitis, -e mild, soft, ripe; gentle

mitto, -ere, misi, missus send, dispatch; fling; let go, release, give up; dismiss; pass over a subject

moderatus, -a, -um restrained, controlled

moderatē (adverb) with restraint

modicus, -a, -um moderate, within bounds, limited; average, ordinary

modo by measure; only, merely, but, just; lately; soon, directly

modus, -i (m) measure; rhythm, measure, time; limit, boundary; rule; manner, mode, way, method; *plural:* strains, numbers

eius modi in that manner, of that kind

moecha, -ae (f) adulteress

moechus, -i (m) adulterer

moenia, -ium (plural, n) walls or fortifications of a city, ramparts

molestus, -a, -um burdensome, troublesome, irksome

molestē (adverb)

molior, -iri, molitus sum stir, displace, work at; build, contrive; strive for; undermine; toil, struggle, exert oneself

mollis, -e soft, tender, pliant, supple; mild; easy; gentle, sensitive; effeminate; pleasant; moving

molliter (adverb)

moneo, -ēre, monui, monitus remind, admonish, warn, advise

monitus, -ūs (m) warning, admonition

mons, montis (m) mountain; mass

monumentum, -i (n) memorial, monument; written memorials, annals, memoirs

mora, -ae (f) delay, hindrance; any span of time

morbus, -i (m) disease, sickness

morior, -i, moriturus sum die; wither away, decay

mors, mortis (f) death; corpse; cause of death or destruction

mortalis, -e subject to death, mortal; perishable; human, earthly

mortuus, -a, -um dead; decayed, extinct; half dead

mos, moris (m) will, inclination; custom, usage, rule; *plural*: ways, conduct, character, morals

motus, -ūs (m) motion, movement; mental activity, emotion; political movement, rebellion, rising, riot

moveo, -ēre, movi, motus move, set in motion, stir; remove, dispossess, dislodge; move mentally, influence, affect, excite; cause; change, shake; arouse, disturb

mox soon, presently; then, thereupon

mugio, -ire, mugivi bellow, roar, low, groan, rumble

mugitus, -ūs (m) lowing, bellowing, rumbling, groaning

muliebris, -e of a woman, feminine; effeminate

mulier, -eris (f) woman; wife, matron

multa, -ae (f) fine, penalty

multitudo, -inis (f) large number, multitude, crowd; common people, mob

multo (1) punish

multus, -a, -um much, great; many; *plural*: many, numerous; prolix, busy

multō (adverb) by much, by far

multum (adverb) much, greatly

plus (comparative) more; *plural* (**plures, plura**): more numerous, several, many

plurimus (superlative) most, very many

mundus, -a, -um clean, neat, elegant

mundus, -i (m) adornment; the universe, world; humankind

munus, -eris (n) office, function, duty; charge, tax; service, favor, gift; public show (especially of gladiators); public building

murmur, -uris (n) murmur, humming, roaring, rumbling, crashing

musa, -ae (f) muse (a goddess of the arts)

musicus, -a, -um belonging to poetry or music, musical

mustum, -i (n) new wine, must

mutabilis, -e changeable, variable, inconstant

muto (1) move, shift; change, alter; exchange, barter

mutuus, -a, -um interchanged, mutual, reciprocal; borrowed, lent

mutuō (adverb) mutually, reciprocally

myrrha, -ae (f) myrrh tree; myrrh

myrteus, -a, -um of myrtle; adorned with myrtle

Nn

nam (conjunction) for

nanciscor, -i, nactus or **nanctus sum** light upon, obtain, meet

naris, -is (f) nostril

narratio, -onis (f) telling, relating; narrative

narro (1) make known; say, speak, tell

nascor, -i, natus or **gnatus sum** be born; come into existence, arise, be

nata, -ae (f) daughter

natalis, -e relating to birth, natal

nato (1) swim, float; stream, flow; swim with, be full of

natura, -ae (f) birth; nature, natural qualities or disposition, character; substance, essence

natus, -i (m) son

natus, -ūs (m) birth

  natū (adverb) by birth

naufragium, -i (n) shipwreck; ruin, loss; wreckage

nauta, -ae (m) sailor, seaman

navigo (1) sail, voyage, go by sea; swim; sail over, sail through, navigate

navis, -is (f) ship, vessel

navita *see* **nauta**

ne not, that not, lest

nē indeed, truly

-ne *interrogative or (more rarely) exclamatory enclitic*

nec or **neque** not; and not, nor; not even

  nec non and also

  nec . . . nec or **neque . . . neque** neither . . . nor

necessarius, -a, -um necessary, unavoidable, inevitable; pressing, urgent; closely connected

necesse or **necessum** (indeclinable adjective) necessary, unavoidable, inevitable, indispensable

neco (1) kill, slay, put to death

nectar, -aris (n) nectar, the drink of the gods; honey, milk, wine

neglegens, -entis careless

neglego, -ere, neglexi, neglectus neglect, disregard; make light of, overlook, omit

nego (1) say no; deny, say that not; deny a request, refuse

negotium, -i (n) business, task, occupation, employment; pains, trouble, difficulty; piece of business

nemo, -inis (c) no one, nobody

nemus, -oris (n) wood, grove

nepos, -otis (m) grandson; nephew; descendant

neque *see* **nec**

nequitia, -ae (f) worthlessness, badness; extravagance

nescio, -ire, nescivi, nescitus not know, be ignorant; fail to recognize; be unable to do

  nescio quis, quid (etc.) somebody, something (etc.)

neu *see* **neve**

neuter, -tra, -trum neither; of neither sex, neuter

neve, neu and not, or not, nor

nex, necis (f) death; (usually) violent death, murder

ni, nive if not, unless

nidus, -i (m) nest

niger, -gra, -grum black, dark colored; blackening; bad, unlucky

nihil (contraction: **nil**) nothing; not at all

nihilominus nevertheless

nihilum, -i (n) nothing

nil *see* **nihil**

nimbus, -i (m) cloud, mist; rain cloud; storm, shower

nimis very much; too much, excessively

nimius, -a, -um very great; too great, excessive; intemperate, immoderate

ningo, -ere, ninxi snow
  ningit (impersonal) it snows

nisi if not, unless; except

niteo, -ēre, nitui shine, glitter, be bright; glow, be sleek, flourish

nitor, -i, nisus or **nixus sum** rest, lean, or support oneself on; trust in, depend on; strive, exert oneself, make an effort; press on, climb up

nitor, -oris (m) brilliance, brightness, splendor, glow, elegance

nive *see* **ni**

niveus, -a, -um of snow, snowy, snow white

nixus, -ūs (m) pressing, straining, effort

no (1) swim; sail, flow, fly

nobilis, -e known; celebrated, renowned, infamous, notorious; of noble birth, highly bred

nocens, -entis hurtful, injurious, guilty, wicked

noceo, -ēre, nocui, nocitus (with dative) hurt, injure, harm

noctua, -ae (f) owl

nodus, -i (m) knot; girdle; any tie, bond, connection, or obligation; knotty point, difficulty

nolo, nolle, nolui be unwilling, wish not to, refuse

nomen, -inis (n) name; title; pretext; reputation

non not; no

nondum not yet

nonne *interrogative particle introducing a question to which an affirmative answer is expected*

nos *see* **ego**

nosco, -ere, nōvi, nōtus become acquainted with, get to know; be acquainted with, know; inquire into, investigate; recognize; approve, acknowledge

noster, -tra, -trum our, ours; of us, to us, for us

nota, -ae (f) mark, token, note, sign; letter, character; distinguishing mark, brand; sort, quality; mark of disgrace, stigma

noto (1) mark, mark out, denote, distinguish; observe; write; stigmatize

nōtus, -a, -um known; famous; notorious, familiar, customary

notus, -i (m) south wind

novem (indeclinable) nine

novitas, -atis (f) newness, novelty, strangeness

novus, -a, -um new, fresh, young; inexperienced; revived, refreshed; novel, unusual, extraordinary
  novē (adverb) in a new or unusual way
  novissimus, -a, -um (superlative) latest, last, extreme
  novissimē (adverb) lately, lastly, in the last place

nox, noctis (f) night; sleep, death, darkness, gloom

nubes, -is (f) cloud; gloom; veil, concealment

nubo, -ere, nupsi, nuptus cover, veil; (with dative) be married to, marry

nudo (1) make bare, strip, uncover; spoil, divest, deprive

nudus, -a, -um naked, bare, uncovered; defenseless, deprived; unadorned, plain; mere, alone, only

nullus, -a, -um no, none, not any; nonexistent, ruined

num *interrogative particle introducing a direct question to which a negative answer is expected*; whether

numen, -inis (n) nodding, nod; consent; divine will, divine command; divine majesty, divinity, deity

numero (1) count; count out money, pay; own; reckon, consider

numerus, -i (m) number, reckoning, total; mass; cipher; category, band, class; rank, position, regard, consideration; measure, part, respect; meter, time

numquam never

nunc now, at present, as things are; then, already

nuntio (1) announce, give notice

nuptiae, -arum (plural, f) marriage, wedding

nusquam nowhere, at no place; in or for nothing

nutrimentum, -i (n) nourishment; support, training

nutrix, -icis (f) nurse, foster mother

nympha, -ae (f) bride; nymph

Oo

o o! (exclamation of joy, astonishment, etc.)

ob (preposition with accusative) in front of, before; in return for; because of, on account of

obitus, -ūs (m) death, downfall, destruction

obliviscor, -i, oblitus sum forget

obruo, -ere, obrui, obrutus fall, collapse; cover, bury, swamp, drown; overwhelm, destroy, obliterate

observatio, -onis (f) observing, watching; care, accuracy, circumspection

observo (1) watch, regard, attend to; keep, regard; respect

obsideo, -ēre, obsedi, obsessus sit down near; beset, haunt, frequent; blockade, besiege; watch over, be on the lookout for

obsīdo, -ere, obsedi, obsessus blockade, besiege, invest

obsto, -are, obstiti, obstaturus stand before or in the way; (with dative) oppose, resist, obstruct

obtempero (1) (with dative) comply with, submit to

obtineo, -ēre, obtinui, obtentus hold, possess, keep, maintain; maintain an assertion; take hold of, grasp; obtain, continue

obviam in the way, on the way; (with dative) toward, against, to meet

obviam ire (with dative) go to meet, oppose

obvius, -a, -um in the way, meeting (with dative); exposed; ready at hand; affable, easy of access

occasio, -onis (f) favorable moment, opportunity

occido, -ere, occidi, occasus fall, fall down; set; die, perish, be ruined

occīdo, -ere, occīdi, occisus strike down, beat to the ground; kill, slay; plague to death, torment

occultus, -a, -um hidden, concealed, private; close, reserved

occultē (adverb) secretly, obscurely

occupatus, -a, -um busy, engaged, occupied

occupo (1) take possession of, seize, occupy, master; fall upon, attack; take up, employ; anticipate, get the start on a person, be the first to do a thing

octo (indeclinable) eight

oculus, -i (m) eye; ornament, treasure; bud or eye of a plant

odi, odisse (perfect with present meaning) hate, detest, dislike

odium, -i (n) hatred; object of hatred

odor, -oris (m) smell, odor, scent; suspicion, inkling, presentiment

odoratus, -a, -um sweet smelling

offendo, -ere, offendi, offensus strike against, knock; hit upon, fall in with;

shock, offend, displease; run aground; stumble, make a mistake

offero, offerre, obtuli, oblatus bring forward, place before, present, offer, expose; inflict, occasion trouble

officium, -i (n) dutiful or respectful action; attendance, service, duty; sense of duty, respect, courtesy; submission, allegiance

olens, -entis smelling; fragrant, stinking

olim at that time; formerly, once; hereafter, one day; for a long time now; at times, often

omen, -inis (n) omen, sign, prognostication

omitto, -ere, omisi, omissus let go, let fall; give up, lay aside; disregard; leave out, omit; cease

omninō altogether, entirely, wholly; in general, in all; certainly, admittedly

omnipotens, -entis almighty

omnis, -e all, every, whole; of all kinds; each, the whole of

onero (1) load, burden; fill, weigh down; oppress, overwhelm; make worse, aggravate

onus, -eris (n) load, burden, weight; trouble, charge; public burden, tax

opera, -ae (f) trouble, pains, exertion; time for work; work done; *plural*: laborers, workers; mobsters, gangsters

operio, -ire, opperui, oppertus cover, bury, conceal; close, shut up; overwhelm

oportet, -ēre, oportuit (impersonal) it is proper, one should, one ought

oppidum, -i (n) town

opprimo, -ere, oppressi, oppressus press upon, press down; crush, smother, stamp out; catch, take by surprise, occupy forcibly

oppugno (1) attack, assault

ops, opis (f) might, power, ability to aid; help, support; *plural* (**opes**): resources, means, wealth

optimus *see* **bonus**

opto (1) choose, select; wish for, desire

opulentus, -a, -um rich, wealthy; powerful, mighty; splendid, sumptuous; lucrative

opus, -eris (n) work, labor; work done, a finished work; a building; a literary work or work of art

opus est there is need; one needs, it is necessary

ora, -ae (f) edge, rim, boundary; coastline, coast; region, clime, country; the people of a district

oraculum, -i (n) solemn utterance, oracle, divine response, prophecy; place where an oracle is given

oratio, -onis (f) speaking, speech; language, style; eloquence; prose

orbis, -is (m) circle, ring, disk; orbit, coil; rotation, round; world

orbus, -a, -um deprived of children or parents; deprived, destitute

ordo, -inis (m) series, line, row, order; rank, file; class; arrangement

oriens, -entis (m) the rising sun; the east; morning

orior, -iri, ortus sum rise; spring up, be born, proceed from a source or cause

ornamentum, -i (n) equipment, trappings, furniture; ornament, decoration; honor, distinction

ornatus, -ūs (m) dress, attire, equipment; embellishment, ornament

orno (1) equip, furnish, fit out; adorn, decorate, embellish; honor, distinguish

oro (1) speak; treat, argue, plead; beg, pray, entreat, beseech

ortus, -ūs (m) rising; origin, birth; source

ōs, oris (n) mouth; voice, talk; opening, source; face, countenance; presence, sight; expression; boldness of expression, impudence; mask

os, ossis (n) bone

osculor, -ari, osculatus sum kiss; caress, make much of

osculum, -i (n) kiss

ostendo, -ere, ostendi, ostentus or **ostensus** hold out, show, reveal, present; make plain, declare

otium, -i (n) free time, leisure, ease; peace, repose

ovans, -antis rejoicing, exulting; celebrating

ovis, -is (f) sheep

ōvum, -i (n) egg

Pp

pabulum, -i (n) food, nourishment, fodder

paelex, -licis (f) mistress, concubine

paene nearly, almost

paenitentia, -ae (f) repentance, regret

paeniteo, -ēre, paenitui repent, regret, be sorry

    paenitet hominem (impersonal) a person feels regret, a person is sorry

palam (adverb) openly, publicly; (preposition with ablative) in the presence of

palatium, -i (n) palace

palma, -ae (f) palm of the hand; hand; oar blade; palm tree; date; victory, honor, glory

palmes, -itis (m) young branch, shoot

pando, -ere, pandi, pansus or **passus** stretch out, spread out, extend; throw open, lay open, reveal, disclose

panis, -is (m) bread; loaf

papaver, -eris (n) poppy

papilla, -ae (f) nipple, teat, breast; bud

par, paris equal, like, a match; *as noun (m or f):* companion; *as noun (n):* the like, the equivalent

paratus, -a, -um prepared, ready; provided, equipped; skilled

parco, parcere, peperci or **parci, parsus** be sparing, economize; (with dative) spare, refrain from, keep oneself from; forbear

parcus, -a, -um sparing, thrifty, economical; moderate; scanty, small, meager

parens, -entis (c) parent; ancestor; author, cause, origin

pareo, -ēre, parui, paritus appear, become evident; (with dative) obey, give way to, be subject to, serve

pario, -ere, peperi, partus bring forth, bear, produce; occasion, create, make, get

paro (1) set, put; prepare, provide, furnish, obtain; buy

pars, partis (f) part, piece, share; direction, region; side, party; actor's role; office, function, duty

parturio, -ire, parturivi desire to bring forth, have the pains of labor; teem with, be full of

partus, -ūs (m) bearing, bringing forth, birth; young, offspring

parum too little, not enough

    minus (comparative) less; (sometimes) not, not at all

    minimē (superlative) in the least degree, very little, least of all; (sometimes) not at all, by no means

parvulus, -a, -um very small; young, little

parvus, -a, -um little, small; slight, weak; short; young; poor, insignificant

    minor, minus (comparative) smaller, less; shorter; inferior

    minimus, -a, -um (superlative) smallest, least

pasco, -ere, pavi, pastus feed, lead to pasture; keep, support; nourish; give as pasture; feast, gratify; graze on; feast upon, delight in; graze, browse

passim here and there, far and wide; indiscriminately

passus, -ūs (m) step, stride, pace; (especially) measure of length equal to five Roman feet; footstep, track

pastor, -oris (m) herder, (especially) shepherd

pateo, -ēre, patui be open, stand open, be accessible or exposed; be revealed, disclosed, or clear; stretch out, extend

pater, -tris (m) father, sire; founder, head; *plural* (**patres**): forefathers; title of the senators (also **patres conscripti**)

paternus, -a, -um of a father, paternal; native

patientia, -ae (f) endurance, resignation; lack of spirit

patior, -i, passus sum suffer, undergo, experience; permit, allow

patria, -ae (f) fatherland, homeland

patrimonium, -i (n) property inherited from a father, patrimony

patulus, -a, -um open, standing open; spreading, extended

paucus, -a, -um few, little

paulatim gradually, little by little

paulisper for a little while

paulus, -a, -um little, small
  paulō or **paulum** (adverb) a little

pauper, -eris poor; scanty, meager

pavidus, -a, -um trembling, quaking, fearful; causing fear

pavo, -onis (f) peacock

pax, pacis (f) peace; calm, quiet; grace, favor

pectus, -oris (n) breast; heart, soul; mind

pecunia, -ae (f) property, wealth; money, cash

pecus, -oris (n) cattle, herd, flock

pecus, -udis (f) single head of cattle or sheep; beast, animal

peior, peius *see* **malus**

pello, -ere, pepuli, pulsus strike, knock, beat; impel, propel, move, affect; drive away, dislodge, banish

pendeo, -ēre, pependi hang; hang upon, depend on; hang loose, hover; be suspended, be discontinued; be in suspense, be uncertain, be undecided

pendo, -ere, pependi, pensus cause to hang down; weigh; pay out money; consider, judge, value, esteem

penetro (1) put into; pass through or into; make one's way in, penetrate

penso (1) weigh carefully; estimate, ponder, consider; counterbalance, requite; pay for, purchase one thing with another

per (preposition with accusative) through, along, over; before, in the presence of; throughout, during; in the course of, in a time of; by, by means of, with, by way of; because of, on account of

perago, -ere, peregi, peractus pass through; go over, mention; drive about, harass, disturb; carry through, complete, accomplish; prosecute until conviction

percurro, -ere, percucurri or **percurri, percursus** run through, hasten through, travel through; run over, mention in passing; run over in the mind or with the eye; pass through stages

perditus, -a, -um, miserable, ruined; morally lost, abandoned, profligate

perdo, -ere, perdidi, perditus destroy, do away with, ruin; lose; waste, squander

perduco, -ere, perduxi, perductus lead through, bring along; conduct; bring over to an opinion, induce; continue, prolong

pereo, -ire, perivi, peritus go to waste, be ruined or lost, pass away, perish, die

perfero, -ferre, pertuli, perlatus carry through, bear to the end; deliver, convey; bring to an end; bear, suffer, endure

perficio, -ere, perfeci, perfectus bring to an end, complete, finish, achieve; live through; make perfect

perfundo, -ere, perfudi, perfusus pour over; steep in a fluid, dye; fill with

pergo, -ere, perrexi, perrectus continue, proceed, go on with

periculosus, -a, -um dangerous, perilous

peric(u)lum, -i (n) trial, proof, test, attempt; danger, peril, hazard; action, suit

permitto, -ere, permisi, permissus let go; hurl; give up, yield, surrender, concede, sacrifice; make allowance for; allow, permit

permuto (1) change completely; exchange, interchange

perpetior, -i, perpessus sum bear to the end, endure

perpetuus, -a, -um continuous, uninterrupted; universal, general
  perpetuō (adverb) uninterruptedly

persequor, -i, persecutus sum follow constantly, pursue to the end, hunt out, overtake; strive for; imitate; proceed against an offender, punish, avenge; accomplish an action, perform, execute; treat a subject, expound, describe

persuadeo, -ēre, persuasi, persuasus persuade; convince of a fact; prevail on a person to do a thing

pertinax, -acis tenacious; tightfisted, mean; firm, persistent, stubborn, obstinate

pertineo, -ēre, pertinui reach to, extend to; tend toward, have as an object or result; relate to, belong to, apply to, attach to

pervenio, -ire, pervēni, perventus come through to, arrive at, reach, attain, be passed to

pervigilo (1) remain awake all night

pervius, -a, -um passable, accessible

pes, pedis (m) foot; foot of a table, chair, etc.; metrical foot; measure of length

pessimus *see* **malus**

peto, -ere, petivi, petitus make for, go to; attack, assail; seek, strive for; ask for, beg, request, demand; sue for; fetch, derive

pietas, -atis (f) dutifulness, dutiful conduct; piety; patriotism; devotion; kindness

piger, -gra, -grum sluggish, unwilling, slow; unfruitful
  pigrē (adverb)

piget, -ēre, piguit or **pigitum est** (impersonal) it causes annoyance, regret, or shame; it disgusts

pignus, -noris or **-neris** (n) pledge, pawn, security; wager, bet, stake; token, assurance, proof

pingo, -ere, pinxi, pictus paint, draw; embroider; stain, dye; decorate, adorn; embellish, depict

pinguis, -e fat; oily; rich, fertile; thick, dense; heavy, stupid; easy, quiet

piscis, -is (m) fish

pius, -a, -um dutiful; godly, holy; patriotic; devoted, affectionate; honest, upright, kind

placeo, -ēre, placui, placitus please, be agreeable to
  placet (impersonal) it seems good, it is agreed or resolved

placidus, -a, -um quiet, still, gentle
  placidē (adverb)

placo (1) soothe, calm; reconcile, appease

planta, -ae (f) green twig, cutting, graft; plant; sole of the foot

planus, -a, -um even, flat; plain, clear, intelligible
  planē (adverb) distinctly, intelligibly; thoroughly, wholly, quite; certainly

platanus, -i (f) sycamore tree, plane tree

plaudo, -ere, plausi, plausus strike, beat, clap together; make a clapping noise, clap, applaud

plaustrum, -i (n) wagon, cart

plebs, plebis (f) plebeians, the common people, lower classes

plenus, -a, -um full, (with genitive or ablative) full of; complete; plump, thick; pregnant; filled, satisfied; well stocked, rich; mature; strong, loud

plerusque, -raque, -rumque, *plural*: **plerique, -raeque, -raque** very many, a large part, the most part

  plerumque (adverb) for the most part, mostly, commonly

ploro (1) lament, wail; weep over, deplore

pluma, -ae (f) soft small feather; down; the first hair on the chin

plurimus *see* **multus**

plus *see* **multus**

poculum, -i (n) drinking cup, goblet; drink, draft

poena, -ae (f) money paid as atonement, fine; punishment, penalty; loss, hardship
  poenas dare be punished

poeta, -ae (m) maker, creator; poet

politus, -a, -um polished, refined, accomplished

polus, -i (m) end of an axis, pole; the sky, heaven

pompa, -ae (f) solemn procession; suite, retinue; display, parade, ostentation

pomum, -i (n) fruit; fruit tree

pomus, -i (f) fruit tree

pondus, -eris (n) weight; burden, mass; balance; authority, influence

pono, -ere, posui, positus lay, put, place, set; put in place, settle; put aside, lay down, discard; lay to rest, lay out for burial; post, station; store, deposit, invest; stake, wager; put on a table, serve; found, set up; establish, ordain; appoint; represent, picture; reckon, count, regard; assert, cite

pons, pontis (m) bridge, gangway; deck of a ship

pontifex, -ficis (m) pontiff (member of a Roman guild of priests)

pontus, -i (n) sea

pōpulus, -i (f) poplar tree

populus, -i (m) people, political community, nation; the public; crowd, host, multitude

porrigo, -ere, porrexi, porrectus stretch out, extend; offer, grant

porta, -ae (f) gate

porto (1) bear, carry, convey, bring

posco, -ere, poposci ask earnestly, request, call on; demand for punishment; challenge to fight; demand, require

possideo, -ēre, possedi, possessus possess, have, hold

possum, posse, potui be able; may, can; avail, have influence, be master

post (adverb) behind, in the rear; afterward; (preposition with accusative) behind; after; next after

postea thereafter, afterward, next

posterus, -a, -um subsequent, following, next, future; *as plural noun (m)*: posterity
  posterior, -ius (comparative) next, later; inferior, worse
  posterius (adverb) later
  postremus, -a, -um (superlative) hindmost, last; lowest, worst
  postremō (adverb) at last
  postremum for the last time
  postumus, -a, -um (superlative) the last, last born

postquam (conjunction) after, when

postremō *see* **posterus**

postremus, -a, -um *see* **posterus**

postulo (1) claim, demand, request; demand a writ, impeach, accuse a person; require

postumus, -a, -um *see* **posterus**

pote *see* **potis**

potens, -entis able, powerful, capable; influential, efficacious

potestas, -atis (f) power, ability, control; political supremacy, dominion; authority of a magistrate, office, command; officer, magistrate; opportunity, possibility, occasion

potior (adjective) *see* **potis**

potior, -iri, potitus sum (with ablative or genitive) get possession of, obtain; possess, be master of

potis or **pote** able, capable

potior, -ius (comparative) preferable, better

potius (adverb) rather, preferably

potissimus, -a, -um (superlative) best of all, chief, principal

potissimum (adverb) chiefly, above all

poto, -are, potavi, potatus or **potus** drink; drink heavily; absorb

potus, -a, -um drunk, drained; having drunk, drunken

potus, -ūs (m) drinking, draft

praebeo, -ēre, praebui, praebitus offer, hold out; provide, supply, allow; behave as

praecedo, -ere, praecessi, praecessus precede, go before, proceed; surpass, excel

praeceps, -cipitis headlong, fast falling, quick; hasty, rash, blind; steep, precipitous; dangerous

praecipio, -ere, praecepi, praeceptus take before, receive in advance; anticipate; instruct, advise, warn

praecipuus, -a, -um peculiar, special; extraordinary, distinguished, excellent

praecipuē (adverb) especially, chiefly, particularly

praeda, -ae (f) spoils of war, plunder, booty; prey; gain

praedico (1) make publicly known, publish, proclaim, declare; praise, commend; boast

praedo, -onis (m) robber, plunderer

praefero, praeferre, praetuli, praelatus carry in front; show, display; prefer; anticipate; carry by

praeruptus, -a, -um broken off; steep, precipitous; headstrong, hasty

praesens, -entis present, at hand; immediate, ready; effective, powerful, helpful, resolute, determined

praeses, -sidis sitting before, protecting

praesidium, -i (n) sitting before; protection, help, support; guard, escort; garrison; post

praestes, -stitis protecting

praesto, -are, praestiti, praestitus stand before; be outstanding, surpass, excel; become surety for, answer for, be responsible for; perform, execute, fulfill; show, manifest, exhibit; offer, present; show oneself, behave as

praestat (impersonal) it is better, it is preferable

praesum, praeesse, praefui be before; be over, preside over; take the lead

praeter (adverb) except; (preposition with accusative) beyond, past; beside, contrary to, beyond; more than; except; in addition to

praeterea besides, further; after this, hereafter

praetereo, -ire, praeterivi, praeteritus go by, pass by; escape the notice of; pass over, omit; surpass, outstrip; transgress

praetor, -oris (m) leader, chief; magistrate who helped the consuls

praetorius, -a, -um relating to the praetor, praetorian; relating to any general or commander; *as noun (n)*: official residence of the praetor or propraetor; palace; headquarters in a Roman camp

pratum, -i (n) meadow; meadow grass

pravus, -a, -um crooked, deformed; perverse; depraved

precor, -ari, precatus sum beg, entreat, pray, invoke

pre(he)ndo, -ere, pre(he)ndi, pre(he)nsus lay hold of, seize, grasp; catch, detain, arrest; take in mentally or through the senses

premo, -ere, pressi, pressus press; step on, lie on; hug, keep close to; press hard, squeeze; pursue closely, press upon; press down, strike down; disparage, slander; press together, close; check, curb

prendo, -ere, prendi, prensus *see* **prehendo, -ere**

pretium, -i (n) worth, value, price; prize, reward; ransom; bribe; punishment

prex, precis (f) request, entreaty; prayer to a god; curse

primaevus, -a, -um young, youthful

primus *see* **prior**

princeps, -cipis first, foremost; *as noun (m)*: title of the Roman emperor

principatus, -ūs (m) first place, preeminence; rule, dominion; origin, beginning

principium, -i (n) beginning, origin; groundwork, foundation; *plural*: elements, first principles; front ranks; headquarters in a camp

prior, prius (comparative) former; higher in importance

  prius (adverb) before, previously; formerly; sooner, rather

  primus, -a, -um (superlative) first, foremost; most distinguished

  primum (adverb) at first, for the first time

  primō at first

priscus, -a, -um ancient, antique; venerable; former, previous; old fashioned

prius *see* **prior**

priusquam (conjunction) before

privatus, -a, -um private, unofficial

pro (preposition with ablative) before, in front of; for, on behalf of, in favor of; in place of; like, as good as; as a reward for; in proportion to, according to, by virtue of

probitas, -atis (f) honesty, uprightness

probrum, -i (n) abuse, reproach; ground for reproach, disgrace; infamous conduct, (especially) unchastity

probus, -a, -um good, excellent, fine; morally good, upright, virtuous

procedo, -ere, processi, processus go ahead, proceed, advance, continue; come out, go out; turn out, result; prosper

procul far; at, to, or from a distance

procumbo, -ere, procubui, procubitus lean or bend forward; fall down, sink down, be laid low

prodeo, -ire, prodivi, proditus advance, go forward; project; come out, appear

prodo, -ere, prodidi, proditus put forth, bring forth; show, publish; appoint; forsake, betray; hand over, deliver, transmit

proelium, -i (n) battle, fight, strife

profectō truly, really, indeed

profero, proferre, protuli, prolatus bring forth, bring forward, offer to publish, bring to light, reveal; produce, cite, mention; advance, bring forward, impel; enlarge, extend; lengthen; put off, postpone

proficiscor, -i, profectus sum start forward, set out, depart; arise or spring from

profundo, -ere, profudi, profusus pour forth, shed, cause to flow; stretch at full length; release, discharge; utter; spend, sacrifice, give up; lavish, squander

prohibeo, -ēre, probibui, prohibitus hold back, restrain, hinder; forbid, prohibit; preserve, defend, protect

proles, -is (f) offspring, descendants, posterity; the young men of a race; fruit

promitto, -ere, promisi, promissus let go forward, send forth; let grow; promise, undertake

pronus, -a, -um inclined forward, stooping forward; rushing down or past; precipitous, steep; well disposed, favorable; easy

prope (adverb) near, nearly

propius (comparative) more nearly, more closely

proximē (superlative) just now; (preposition with accusative) near; approximating, not far from

propero (1) hasten; accelerate, complete quickly

propinquus, -a, -um near, close, neighboring; similar; nearly related, closely connected; *as noun (m or f)*: kinsperson

propior, -ius nearer; more like; more closely connected; more suitable; *see also* **prope**

proximus, -a, -um (superlative) very near, nearest; next, following, most recent; next best; most like; most nearly connected

propono, -ere, proposui, propositus put on view, expose, display; publish, relate, tell; propose, promise, offer as a reward, hold over as a threat; imagine, put before the mind; propose to oneself, purpose, intend

proprius, -a, -um one's own, special, peculiar, characteristic; lasting, permanent

propriē (adverb) exclusively, peculiarly, characteristically; in a proper sense

propter (adverb) near, close by; (preposition with accusative) near; on account of, because of

prorsus forward, straight ahead; utterly, wholly; in a word, to sum up

proscribo, -ere, proscripsi, proscriptus make publicly known, publish; offer publicly for sale or hire, advertise; confiscate; proscribe, outlaw

proscriptio, -onis (f) advertisement of sale; proscription, blacklist

prosequor, -i, prosecutus sum follow or accompany out, see off; attack, pursue; attend; go on with, continue; imitate

prosper or **prosperus, -a, -um** fortunate, favorable, lucky, prosperous

prosperē (adverb)

prosterno, -ere, prostravi, prostratus cast down; debase; overthrow, destroy, ruin

prosum, prodesse, profui (with dative) be useful, do good, benefit

protinus forward, further on; continuously; immediately

proveho, -ere, provexi, provectus carry forward; carry on; advance, promote; convey

providens, -entis provident, prudent

provideo, -ēre, providi, provisus look forward to, see at a distance; see beforehand, foresee; take precautions for or against, provide for, make preparations for

providus, -a, -um foreseeing; providing, taking measures for; cautious, prudent

proximē *see* **prope**

proximus *see* **propior**

prudens, -entis foreseeing, aware; skilled, experienced, practiced; prudent, discreet, judicious

pruina, -ae (f) frost, hoarfrost

-pte *suffix added to personal pronouns and possessive adjectives for emphasis*

pubes, -is (f) signs of puberty, growth of hair, etc.; the youth, adult male population

publicus, -a, -um belonging to the people, public; universal, general; common; ordinary

publicē (adverb) for the people, publicly, at the public expense; all together

res publica or **respublica** republic, state, commonwealth

pudeo, -ēre, pudui, puditus be ashamed; cause shame

pudet (impersonal) it causes shame

pudicitia, -ae (f) modesty, chastity, virtue

pudicus, -a, -um modest, chaste, virtuous

pudor, -oris (m) feeling of shame, bashfulness, decency, honor; chastity, purity; that which causes shame, a disgrace

puella, -ae (f) girl, maiden; young woman, young wife, sweetheart

puer, -i (m) child; boy, lad; boyhood; page, slave

pugna, -ae (f) fight, battle; battle line, array; contest

pugno (1) fight, give battle; contend, struggle; strive, exert oneself

pulcher, -chra, -chrum beautiful, lovely; excellent, fine

pullus, -i young animal; (especially) chicken, chick

pulvis, -eris (m) dust, powder; arena, scene of action

punio, -ire, punivi, punitus punish, avenge

puppis, -is (f) stern of a vessel; ship

purgo (1) clean, cleanse, purify; excuse, defend, justify; allege in defense; clear away, wash off

purpura, -ae (f) purple shellfish; purple dye, purple cloth; high rank, etc.

purpureus, -a, -um purple; dark red, dark brown; clad in purple; gleaming, bright, beautiful

purus, -a, -um clean, pure, cleared; without addition, simple, plain; upright; faultless; without conditions, absolute

puto (1) weigh up, ponder, reckon, estimate; consider, believe, think; cleanse, clear; lop; clear up, settle

pyramis, -idis (f) pyramid; cone

Qq

quā by which way, where; whereby, as far as; by what way?, how?

quaero, -ere, quaesivi, quaesitus seek, search for; obtain, get; miss, want; seek to know, ask, inquire into a matter

quaeso, -ere seek for, ask for; *1st person*: I beg, please

quaestus, -ūs (m) gaining, getting, profit; source of profit, occupation, business

qualis, -e of what kind?; of the kind that, such as

quam how, in what way; how much? how?; how!, (often with **tam**) as; (with superlative) as possible; (after comparative) than, as

quamlibet as much as you please

quamquam although, though; nevertheless, yet

quamvis (adverb) as much as you please, ever so much; (conjunction) however much, although

quandō when?; when; at any time, ever; at the time when; since, because

quantus, -a, -um how great?; how great!; (as great) as; *as noun (n)*: how much?; how much!; as much as

    quanti for how much, at what price

    quantō by how much

quapropter wherefore

quārē why, wherefore

quartus, -a, -um fourth

quasi as if, just as; as it were, a sort of; about

quater four times; again and again

quatio, -ere, quassi, quassus shake, brandish, agitate; shatter

quattuor (indeclinable) four

-que and; but

    -que . . . -que both . . . and

queo, quire, quivi, quitus be able

querel(l)a, -ae (f) complaint, complaining

queror, -i, questus sum complain, lament, bewail

quī in what manner?, how?; wherewith, wherefrom; somehow

qui, quae, quod which?, what?, what kind of?; what!; who, which, what, that

quia because, for which reason

quicumque, quaecumque, quodcumque whoever, whichever, whatever; any available

quid what?; why?; (with genitive) how much?, how many?

quidam, quaedam, quoddam (noun: **quiddam**) certain person or thing (known but not necessarily named); a kind of

quidem indeed

ne quidem not even

quies, -etis (f) rest, quiet; peace; sleep; dream; resting place

quietus, -a, -um resting; sleeping; at peace, undisturbed, neutral; quiet, calm

quietē (adverb)

quilibet, quaelibet, quodlibet (noun: **quidlibet**) any you will, anyone, anything

quin why not?; but come now; rather, but indeed; but that, without, that not, who not

quinam, quaenam, quodnam which?, what?

quindecimvir, -i (m) one of a board of fifteen priests or magistrates

quinque (indeclinable) five

quippe certainly, indeed, to be sure, of course

quis, quid who?, what?, which?

quisnam, quaenam, quidnam who?, what?

quisquam, quaequam, quidquam or **quicquam** anybody, anyone, anything

quisque, quaeque, quidque (adjective: **quodque**) each, every, everyone, everything

quisquis, quaequae, quidquid or **quicquid** (adjective: **quodquod**) whoever, whatever, whichever; anyone, anything

quō (adverb) where?, to what place?, whither?, how far?, to what extent?, to what end?; to any place; (conjunction) to the end that, in order that; because, whereby

quod (conjunction) the fact that, the point that; as to the fact that, whereas; because, on the grounds that; why, on which account; since; as far as, to the extent that; and, but, now

quom *see* **cum**

quominus so that not, by which the less

quomodo in what manner, how

quondam in the past, formerly, once; sometime; at times, sometimes

quoniam since, whereas, because

quoque also, too

quor *see* **cur**

quorsum whither?, to what place?, to what purpose?

quot (indeclinable) how many?; how many!, as many

quotiens how often?; how often!; as often as

Rr

rabidus, -a, -um raging, mad, savage

radius, -i (m) staff, rod; spoke of a wheel; radius of a circle; shuttle; ray, beam of light

ramus, -i (m) bough, branch, twig

rapidus, -a, -um rushing, swift, violent

rapidē (adverb)

rapina, -ae (f) robbery, pillage; booty, plunder

rapio, -ere, rapui, raptus seize, snatch, tear away; plunder; hurry along, rush off; pervert, lead astray

rarus, -a, -um loose, thin; scattered, scanty, far apart; rare, infrequent; extraordinary, distinguished

    rarō (adverb) seldom, rarely

ratio, -onis (f) reckoning, account, consideration, calculation; transaction, affair, business; reason, motive, ground; plan, scheme, system; reasonableness, method, order; theory, doctrine, science; the reasoning faculty

raucus, -a, -um hoarse, harsh sounding

rea, -ae (f) party in a lawsuit; (especially) defendant, accused person; *see also* **reus**

recedo, -ere, recessi, recessus go back, retreat, retire; disappear

recens, -entis new, fresh, young, recent; vigorous

    recens (adverb) lately, recently

recipio, -ere, recepi, receptus hold back, retain; take back, fetch back; regain, recover; receive, accept, take to oneself; receive hospitably; admit, allow; guarantee, promise, be responsible for

recito (1) read aloud, read out, recite

recolo, -ere, recolui, recultus work or cultivate again; resume; set up again, rehabilitate; reflect on, recall

recondo, -ere, recondidi, reconditus put away, put back, store, hide

recreo (1) restore, refresh, revive, invigorate

rectus, -a, -um straight; upright; right, correct, proper; honest; natural, plain, straightforward

    rectē (adverb) in a straight line; rightly, properly

recurro, -ere, recurri, recursus run back; revert, return

recuso (1) object to, protest against, refuse; take exception, plead in defense

reddo, -ere, reddidi, redditus give back, restore; repeat, recite; reproduce by imitation, represent, reflect; give in return; answer; translate, render, interpret; make, render, cause to be; give as due; pay up, deliver; fulfill

redeo, redire, redivi, reditus go back, come back, return; come in; fall back on, be reduced or brought to

redimo, -ere, redemi, redemptus buy back, redeem; ransom, recover; buy up, contract for, farm, hire, procure

reduco, -ere, reduxi, reductus draw backward, bring back, lead home; bring to a state or condition

refero, referre, rettuli, relatus carry back, bring back; return, go back; bring again, restore, repeat; echo; reproduce, recall; say back, answer; bring as expected, pay up, deliver; bring back a message, report; refer a matter to authority; enter in a record, etc., register, put down, enter; assign to a cause

rēfert, rēferre, rētulit (impersonal) it matters, it concerns, it makes a difference

reficio, -ere, refeci, refectus make again, restore, repair, reestablish, refresh, revive; get back, receive, get

regalis, -e of a king, royal, regal

regimen, -inis (n) control, guidance, rule, direction, government; ruler, governor

regina, -ae (f) queen; princess; lady, mistress, sovereign

regio, -onis (f) direction, line; boundary line, boundary; region, district, province; sphere, department

regno (1) be a king, rule, reign; be master, be a tyrant; prevail

regnum, -i (n) royal power, monarchy, supremacy; tyranny; realm, kingdom, estate

rego, -ere, rexi, rectus guide, direct; rule, govern, administer

religio, -onis (f) scrupulousness, conscientious exactness; religious scruple, awe, superstition, strict observance; moral scruples, conscientiousness; sanctity; object of worship, holy thing or place

religiosus, -a, -um scrupulous, conscientious; holy, strict, superstitious; required or forbidden by religion; sacred

relinquo, -ere, reliqui, relictus leave behind; bequeath; leave unchanged; omit, leave out, pass over; desert, abandon, forsake

reliquiae, -arum (plural, f) remains, relics, remnant

reliquus, -a, -um left behind, remaining, other; outstanding; future

remaneo, -ēre, remansi, remansus remain behind, stay, continue

remedium, -i (n) means of healing, cure, remedy, medicine

remitto, -ere, remisi, remissus send back, send again; throw back; echo; let go back, relax, loosen; relieve, abate; give up doing; ease off; give up, yield; abandon, sacrifice; forgive an offense, remit punishment

remotus, -a, -um, removed, withdrawn, distant, far off, remote

renascor, -i, renatus sum be born again, grow again

renovo (1) renew, restore, repair; repeat

reparo (1) restore, renew, make good; get in exchange, purchase

repello, -ere, reppuli, repulsus drive back, drive away; banish, repel

repens, -entis sudden, unexpected; fresh, recent

repente (adverb) suddenly, unexpectedly

reperio, -ire, repperi, repertus get again; find, discover, ascertain, invent

repeto, -ere, repetivi, repetitus seek again, go back for or to; ask back; return to, renew, begin again; trace back, deduce; recollect, recall

repleo, -ēre, replevi, repletus fill again, fill up; make full, fill, satisfy

repraesento (1) bring back, reproduce; perform immediately, hasten on

repulsa, -ae (f) repulse, rejection; denial, refusal

requies, -etis (f) rest, repose

res, rei (f) thing, object, matter, affair, circumstance; fact, truth, reality; possessions, property, wealth; interest, advantage, benefit; cause, ground, reason; matter of business; lawsuit, action

res publica or **respublica** republic, state, commonwealth

resideo, -ēre, resedi, resessus remain sitting, stay, rest

resīdo, -ere, resedi, resessus sit down, settle, sink, subside, abate

resolvo, -ere, resolvi, resolutus untie, loosen, open; melt; dissipate; dispel; release; reveal; weaken

resono (1) resound, echo; make resound

respicio, -ere, respexi, respectus look behind, look back (at); look back on; look to, provide for; depend on; have a regard for, care for, consider

respondeo, -ēre, respondi, responsus match, correspond to, answer to; resemble; answer to one's name, appear, be present; answer, reply

respublica *see* **res**

restituo, -ere, restitui, restitutus put back, replace, restore; reinstate, reestablish; repair, make good

resto, -are, restiti make a stand, resist, oppose; stand still, stay behind; be left over, survive; remain available or possible; await, be in store

resulto (1) spring back, rebound; echo, resound

resupinus, -a, -um bent backward, on one's back; with head thrown back

retineo, -ēre, retinui, retentus hold back, detain; restrain; keep, reserve, maintain

reus, -i (m) party in a lawsuit; (especially) defendant, accused person; *see also* **rea**

revello, -ere, revelli, revulsus tear back, pull away; remove, banish

revenio, -ire, revēni, reventus come back, return

reverto, -ere, reverti, reversus return, come back, revert

revincio, -ire, revinxi, revinctus tie back, bind fast

rex, regis (m) ruler, king, prince, chief; monarch, tyrant

rideo, -ēre, risi, risus laugh, smile, look cheerful; please; laugh at

ridiculus, -a, -um exciting laughter; droll, humorous; absurd, ridiculous

ripa, -ae (f) bank, shore

risus, -ūs (m) laughing, laughter; ridicule; object of ridicule

ritus, -ūs (m) usage, ceremony, rite

ritū after the manner of

robur, -oris (n) hardwood; oak, oak wood; hardness, strength; the pick or flower of anything

rogo (1) ask, inquire; ask for, request

rogus, -i (m) funeral pyre

ros, roris (m) dew, moisture

rosa, -ae (f) rose; garland of roses; rosebush

roseus, -a, -um of roses; rosy, rose colored

rostrum, -i (n) beak, snout; ship's prow; *plural* (**rostra, -orum**): speaker's platform in the forum

rubeo, -ēre, be red; blush

rubor, -oris (m) redness; blush; modesty; shame, disgrace

ruina, -ae (f) falling down, collapse, ruin, destruction; ruins of a building, debris

rumpo, -ere, rupi, ruptus break, shatter, burst open; cause to break forth; destroy, violate, annul; break off, interrupt

ruo, -ere, rui, rutus rush down, fall, collapse, be ruined; rush along; be precipitate; hurl down; cast up

rursus or **rursum** backward, back; on the other hand, in return; again, afresh

rus, ruris (n) country, country seat, farm, estate

rusticus, -a, -um of the country, rural, rustic; plain, simple; awkward, boorish; *as noun (m)*: farmer

Ss

sacellum, -i (n) small shrine, chapel

sacer, -cra, -crum sacred, holy, consecrated; accursed, devoted to destruction, horrible; *as singular noun*: **sacrum, -i** (n) holy thing or place; sacrifice, victim; *as plural noun*: **sacra, -orum** (n) sacred rites, worship

sacerdos, -dotis (c) priest, priestess

sacerdotium, -i (n) priesthood

sacra *see* **sacer**

sacratus, -a, -um holy, consecrated

sacrificium, -i (n) sacrifice

sacrifico (1) sacrifice

sacrum *see* **sacer**

saeculum, -i (n) generation; spirit of the age, the times; century; epoch, age

saepe often, frequently

saevio, -ire, saevii, saevitus rage, be furious, take violent action

saevus, -a, -um raging, fierce, furious, violent, savage, cruel

sagitta, -ae (f) arrow

sal, salis (m) salt; brine, seawater; wit

salio, -ire, salui, saltus spring, leap, bound

saltem at least, at all events

salto (1) dance with gesticulation; panto-
mime, sing with gestures

saltus, -ūs (m) spring, leap, bound

saltus, -ūs (m) forest or mountain pasture;
pass, dale, ravine, glade

salum, -i (n) the open sea

salus, -utis (f) health, soundness; safety,
welfare, well-being, salvation; wish for a
person's welfare, salutation, greeting

saluto (1) wish well, greet, call on, pay
respect to, revere

salvus, -a, -um safe, unhurt, well, all right

sanctus, -a, -um consecrated, holy, sacred;
pure, virtuous

sanguis, -inis (m) blood; blood relationship, race, family, progeny; lifeblood,
strength, vigor

sano (1) heal, cure, restore, repair

sanus, -a, -um sound, healthy, uninjured; of
sound mind, rational, sane
sanē (adverb) rationally, sensibly; really,
indeed, to be sure

sapiens, -entis wise, sensible, judicious;
as noun (m): sensible, judicious person;
wise man, philosopher, sage
sapienter (adverb)

sapientia, -ae (f) wisdom, good sense,
discernment; (especially) proficiency in
philosophy, science, etc.

sapio, -ere, sapivi taste; taste or smell of;
have taste, be able to taste; discern, be
sensible, be wise, think

sapor, -oris (m) taste, flavor, flavoring;
sense of taste; taste in style or conduct

satio (1) satisfy, fill; cloy, satiate

satis or **sat** enough, sufficient; sufficiently,
fairly, quite
satius (comparative) better, more
advantageous

satyrus, -i (m) satyr

saxum, -i (n) rock, stone

scalpo, -ere, scalpsi, scalptus carve,
scrape, scratch

scelestus, -a, -um guilty, wicked, accursed
scelestē (adverb)

scelus, -eris (n) crime; misfortune, calamity; scoundrel, rascal

schola, -ae (f) learned leisure; conversation, debate; lecture, dissertation;
school; sect

scientia, -ae (f) knowing, knowledge,
acquaintance, skill

scilicet evidently, certainly, of course; no
doubt; namely

scio, -ire, scivi, scitus know, understand;
know how to

scriba, -ae (m) clerk, secretary, notary

scribo, -ere, scripsi, scriptus engrave,
draw lines, write, write on, write about;
draw up laws, etc.; enroll

scriptor, -oris (m) scribe, clerk, secretary;
writer, author, composer

scriptum, -i (n) mark, line; composition,
piece of writing; law, decree

scutum, -i (n) large shield

se or **sese, sui, sibi** himself, herself, itself,
themselves

secretus, -a, -um separate, alone, special;
retired, solitary; hidden, secret
secretō (adverb) apart, secretly

secundum (adverb) after, behind; (preposition with accusative) following, after,
along beside; during; in addition to;
next after, next to; according to; in
favor of

secundus, -a, -um going after, second, following; inferior, second rate; going the
same way, attending, favoring

securus, -a, -um free from care, uncon-
cerned, fearless, tranquil; careless; safe,
secure
securē (adverb)

sed or **set** but, however; and indeed, and
what is more

sedeo, -ēre, sēdi, sessus sit; sit in council or judgment; sit about, be inactive;
remain encamped; be settled, stay fixed;
be firmly determined

sella, -ae (f) seat, chair, stool
sella curulis magistrate's seat

semel once, a single time; for the first time;
once and for all; ever, at any time

semen, -inis (n) seed; seedling, scion,
shoot; stock, race; cause, origin; author,
instigator

semper always, at all times

senator, -oris (m) member of the senate,
senator

senatus, -ūs (m) council of elders, senate

senectus, -utis (f) old age; old men

senex, senis old, aged; *as noun (m or f)*: old
person
senior (comparative)

sensim just perceptibly, gradually, by
degrees

sensus, -ūs (m) sense, sensation; feeling,
attitude; judgment, perception, understanding; sense or meaning of words,
etc.; sentence

sententia, -ae (f) way of thinking, opinion,
thought, meaning, purpose; decision,
vote; meaning or sense of words, etc.;
sentence; maxim, aphorism

sentio, -ire, sensi, sensus feel, perceive;
experience; realize a truth; hold an opinion, judge, suppose; decide, vote

sepelio, -ire, sepelivi, sepultus bury; ruin,
destroy

septem (indeclinable) seven

sepulcrum, -i (n) grave, tomb

sequor, -i, secutus sum follow, accompany,
attend; pursue, chase; ensue; follow
logically; fall to; conform to; strive for,
aim at

serenus, -a, -um clear, bright, fair; calm

sermo, -onis (m) talk, conversation; discussion; common talk, report, rumor;
subject of conversation; conversational
style; any manner of speaking, style,
expression, diction, language, dialect

sero, -ere, serui, sertus join together, put
in a row, connect

sero, -ere, sevi, satus sow, set, plant;
beget, engender, bring forth; give rise to,
produce

serpens, -entis (c) snake, serpent

sertum, -i (n) garland, wreath

serus, -a, -um late, too late; *as noun:*
serum, -i (n) late hour
serō (adverb) late, too late

servio, -ire, servivi, servitus (with dative)
be a slave, serve, help, gratify

servitium, -i (n) slavery, servitude, subjection; slaves, servants

servo (1) watch over, observe; keep, retain
a promise, etc.; keep to, stay in a place

servus, -a, -um serving, servile, subject;
as noun (m or f): slave, servant

set *see* **sed**

seu *see* **sive**

severitas, -atis (f) gravity, sternness

sex (indeclinable) six

sexus, -ūs (m) sex, gender

si if, supposing that
quod si and if, but if
si modo if only

sīc so, thus, in this way; like this, as follows;
in that case, with this limitation;
so much, to such a degree

sicco (1) make dry, dry; stanch; drain

sīcut or **sīcuti** as, just as; as for example;
as it were; just as if

sidus, -eris (n) constellation, star; lu-
minary, heavenly body; time of year,
season, weather; destiny; heaven; pride,
glory

signo (1) mark, inscribe; seal; impress, indicate; observe, notice

signum, -i (n) sign, mark, token; warning, symptom; standard, banner; order, command; watchword, password; image, statue; seal, signet; constellation

silentium, -i (n) silence, stillness, quiet; repose; obscurity

sileo, -ēre, silui be still, be silent; be silent about; rest, be inactive

silva, -ae (f) wood, forest; bush; plantation, grove; plenty, abundance

simia, -ae (f) ape, monkey

similis, -e like, resembling, similar (with genitive or dative)

   similiter (adverb) similarly

   similior, -ius (comparative)

   simillimus, -a, -um (superlative)

simul at once, at the same time, together

simulacrum, -i (n) image, likeness, portrait; effigy; shade, ghost, imitation, phantom, appearance

simulatque or **simulac** as soon as

simulo (1) make like, cause to resemble; represent, make a copy of; play the part of; pretend a thing is so, simulate, feign

sine (preposition with ablative) without

singuli, -ae, -a single, separate, one at a time; one each

sino, -ere, sivi, situs let alone, leave; let, allow, permit; place

sinus, -ūs (m) curve, fold, winding; pocket, lap; bay, gulf; heart, secret feelings

sisto, -ere, stiti, status cause to stand, set, place; cause to appear in court; stop, check; establish firmly; place oneself, stand; present oneself in court; stand still, halt; stand firm

sitio, -ire thirst, be thirsty, be dry, be parched; thirst for, thirst after, be eager for

sitis, -is (f) thirst; dryness, drought; eager desire

sive or **seu** or if

   sive or **seu** . . . **sive** or **seu** whether . . . or

smaragdus, -i (m) emerald

socius, -a, -um sharing, associated, allied; *as noun (m or f)*: partner, comrade, associate, ally

sol, solis (m) sun; day

solacium, -i (n) consolation, comfort, relief

soleo, -ēre, solitus sum be accustomed, be in the habit, usually do

solidus, -a, -um dense, solid; whole, complete, entire; firm, enduring, real

   solidē (adverb) firmly

solitudo, -inis (f) solitude, loneliness; desertion, deprivation, want

sollemnis, -e yearly, annual, recurring; solemn, festive, religious; usual, customary

sollicito (1) move violently, disturb, agitate; rouse, vex, disquiet; incite, instigate, tamper with

sollicitudo, -inis (f) uneasiness, disquiet, anxiety

solum, -i (n) bottom, floor, foundation; sole of the foot or shoe; soil, ground, earth, land, country

sōlus, -a, -um alone, only, sole; solitary, uninhabited

   sōlum (adverb) alone, only

solutus, -a, -um loosened, unbound, free, unencumbered, independent; unrestrained, unbridled; lax, lazy, negligent

solvo, -ere, solvi, solutus loosen; untie, release, free; dissolve, break up; exempt; break up, weaken, bring to an end; pay off, discharge a debt; perform duties; solve a problem, explain a difficulty

somnium, -i (n) dream; fancy, daydream; foolishness, nonsense

somnus, -i (m) sleep, slumber; drowsiness, laziness, inactivity; night

sono, -are, sonui, sonitus sound, resound, make a noise; sing of, celebrate; mean

sonus, -i (m) noise, sound; tone, character, style

sopor, -oris (m) deep sleep; laziness

sordidus, -a, -um dirty, filthy, shabby; low, base in rank; mean in conduct

soror, -oris (f) sister

sors, sortis (f) lot; casting of lots; oracular response, prophecy; share, part; fate, fortune, destiny; money, capital

sortitio, -onis (f) casting lots, deciding by lot

spargo, -ere, sparsi, sparsus scatter, sprinkle, throw about; spread, circulate, distribute; disperse, dissipate

spatium, -i (n) space, extent, room; distance, interval; dimensions, size; tract, course; open space, walk; space of time, period; leisure, opportunity; metrical time, measure, quantity

species, -ei (f) seeing, view; sight, look; shape, form, outward appearance; beauty; vision, phantom; representation, image, statue; pretext, pretense; notion, idea; kind, species

speciosus, -a, -um beautiful, handsome, imposing; plausible, specious

spectaculum, -i (n) sight, show, spectacle

spectator, -oris (m) watcher, spectator, observer; examiner, critic

specto (1) look at, contemplate, watch; test, examine; look toward, face; consider, contemplate, look for; bear in mind, have in view; tend, incline

speculum, -i (n) mirror; image, copy

specus, -ūs (m or f) cave, hole, hollow

spero (1) look for, expect; hope, hope for; anticipate, forebode

spes, -ei (f) expectation; hope; anticipation, foreboding

spina, -ae (f) thorn, prickle; thornbush; anxiety, difficulty, perplexity

spiritus, -ūs (m) breathing, breath, exhalation; sigh; life; inspiration; spirit, disposition; high spirit, pride

splendeo, -ēre shine, glitter, be bright

splendidus, -a, -um shining, bright, brilliant; distinguished, outstanding; showy, specious; clear

    splendidē (adverb) splendidly, finely, nobly

splendor, -oris (m) brilliance, brightness, luster, distinction; clarity

spondeo, -ēre, spopondi, sponsus pledge oneself to, promise solemnly, vow; be security, post bail for a person

sponsalia, -ium (plural, n) betrothal, betrothal feast

sponte willingly, of one's own accord; unaided; by itself, automatically; in itself, alone

statim firmly, steadfastly; on the spot, at once

statio, -onis (f) standing still; place of abode; post, station; anchorage

statua, -ae (f) statue, image

statuo, -ere, statui, statutus cause to stand, place, set up; establish, settle a point; give a ruling, make arrangements; decide on

status, -a, -um fixed, determined, regular

status, -ūs (m) standing posture, position, condition, state

stipulatio, -onis (f) agreement, covenant, stipulation

stipulor, -ari, stipulatus sum make demands, bargain, stipulate

stirps, stirpis (f) stock or stem of a plant; young shoot; source, origin; root, foundation

sto, -are, steti, status stand, stand still, remain standing; stand up stiffly; be stationed; lie at anchor; remain, be fixed, stand firm, persist; be resolved; stand by, support, favor; cost

stringo, -ere, strinxi, strictus draw tight together, bind, tie; strip off, pluck, prune; draw a weapon from its sheath; graze, touch lightly; affect, injure; touch on

strues, -is (f) heap, pile

struo, -ere, struxi, structus put together, arrange; pile up; build, erect, construct; devise, contrive

studeo, -ēre, studui be eager, take pains; study a subject; (usually with dative) strive for, side with, support, favor a person

studium, -i (n) zeal, eagerness, application, enthusiasm; devotion, goodwill; application to learning, study

stultitia, -ae (f) foolishness, silliness

stultus, -a, -um foolish, silly; *as noun (m)*: simpleton, fool
　stultē (adverb)

suadeo, -ēre, suasi, suasus advise, recommend

suavis, -e sweet, pleasant
　suaviter (adverb)

sub (preposition with ablative) underneath, under; close under, at the foot of; at, near; in the power of, under; under cover of; (preposition with accusative) to or along the underside of; up under, down under; along under; close to; toward, just before, immediately after; into the power of

subdo, -ere, subdidi, subditus put, place or lay under; subject, subdue; put in the place of another, substitute; counterfeit

subdolus, -a, -um with secret guile; sly, crafty

subduco, -ere, subduxi, subductus draw up from under, pull up, raise, remove; take away stealthily, steal; draw a ship up on shore; withdraw

subeo, -ire, subivi, subitus go under, pass under; support; undergo, submit to, take on oneself; come from under, approach, advance, mount, climb; come into or over the mind; come on after, follow

subicio, -ere, subieci, subiectus throw or place under; submit, subject; append, reply; throw up from below, raise, lift; put into a mind, suggest; substitute, insert by guile, counterfeit

subitus, -a, -um sudden; coming suddenly, taking by surprise; suddenly done, hastily contrived, improvised
　subitō (adverb) suddenly

sublatus, -a, -um *see* **tollo**

sublevo (1) raise, lift, support; encourage a person; alleviate troubles

sublimis, -e high, raised, lofty; elevated, sublime
　sublime (adverb) on high, aloft

submissus, -a, -um let down, lowered; mild, gentle, humble; mean, abject

submitto, -ere, submisi, submissus let down, send under, lower; subject, subordinate; send up from below, raise, rear, make grow; send as help; send secretly

suboles, -is (f) sprout, shoot, offspring, progeny

subsum, subesse, subfui be near, be close at hand; be under; be subject; be there, exist

subter (adverb and preposition with accusative) beneath, below, underneath

succedo, -ere, successi, successus go under; submit to; go from under, ascend, mount; come after; succeed, relieve, follow; turn out well, prosper, succeed

succurro, -ere, succurri, succursus run beneath, go under; undergo; come into the mind; come to aid, succor, help, assist

sucus, -i (m) juice, sap; flavor, taste; vigor, energy

sum, esse, fui, futurus be, exist, be there; be so

essem, esses (etc.) = forem, fores (etc.)
futurus esse = fore

summus, -a, -um (alternative superlative of **superus, -a, -um**) highest, uppermost, at the top; loudest; last; greatest, most distinguished; *as noun:* **summa, -ae** (f) highest place, main thing, most important point; summary, gist, sum total of an amount; **summum, -i** (n) surface, top

sumo, -ere, sumpsi, sumptus take, choose, obtain, buy; put on; exact a punishment; take on oneself, claim; take for granted, assume

super (adverb) over, above; besides, beyond, moreover; remaining, over and above; (preposition with ablative) over, above; at; concerning, about; besides, beyond; (preposition with accusative) over, above, on; during; more than

superbia, -ae (f) pride; haughtiness, arrogance

superbus, -a, -um haughty, exalted, proud; arrogant, overbearing; brilliant, splendid

superbē (adverb) haughtily, proudly

supernus, -a, -um above, upper, high

supernē (adverb) above, from above

supero (1) go above, overtop, project; prevail, conquer; abound; remain, be over; remain alive, survive; be too much, exceed; rise above, surmount, overtop, pass; surpass, excel; overcome

superstes, -stitis standing over or near; present, witnessing; surviving, living on

supersum, superesse, superfui, superfuturus be over and above; be left, remain, survive; be plentiful, abound; be superfluous, be redundant

superus, -a, -um situated above; upper, higher; *as plural noun (m):* the gods

superior, -ius (comparative) higher, upper; earlier, former, past; superior, greater

supremus, -a, -um (superlative) highest, uppermost; last, final; greatest; *see also* **summus, -a, -um**

supplex, -plicis kneeling; entreating, suppliant

supplicium, -i (n) humble entreaty, supplication, prayer; punishment; capital punishment

supplico (1) kneel, beseech, entreat; pray to the gods

suprā (adverb) over, on the top; before, previously; above; over, more, beyond; (preposition with accusative) above, over; before; more than, above, beyond

supremus, -a, -um *see* **superus**

surgo, -ere, surrexi, surrectus rise, get up; spring up, arise

sursum or **sursus** upward, on high

suscipio, -ere, suscepi, susceptus take up, catch up; support, raise; accept, receive; take on oneself, undertake, begin; maintain a point, be ready to prove

suspicio, -ere, suspexi, suspectus look from below, look upward; look up to, esteem, respect; look askance at, suspect

suspiro (1) draw a deep breath, sigh; sigh for, long for

sustineo, -ēre, sustinui, sustentus hold up, support, sustain; endure, have the heart to; maintain; put off, delay; hold back, check, restrain

suus, -a, -um (3rd person reflexive possessive adjective) his, her, its, their (own) (strengthened by **-pte** or **-met**); proper, due, suitable; favorable; independent; *as plural noun:* one's own people, property, etc.; loved ones

Tt

taberna, -ae (f) booth, hut; cottage, hovel; stall, shop; inn, tavern

tablinum, -i (n) study, den, home office

tabula, -ae (f) board, plank; painting; votive tablet; map; writing tablet; document; record, register

taceo, -ēre, tacui, tacitus be silent, say nothing; be still, be quiet; be silent about, pass over in silence

tacitus, -a, -um unmentioned; implied, tacit; secret, concealed; silent, mute, still, quiet
   tacitē (adverb)

taeda, -ae (f) pinewood; torch (especially one used at a wedding)

taedet, -ēre, taeduit or **taesum est** (impersonal) it causes weariness or boredom

talis, -e of such kind, such

tam so, so far, to such a degree

tamen however, yet, nevertheless

tametsi even if, although

tamquam as, just as, like as; just as if

tandem at length, at last; after all, may I ask?

tango, -ere, tetigi, tactus touch, strike, push, hit; border, reach; steal; defile; taste; affect the feelings; touch on a subject

tantus, -a, -um of such a size, so great
   tantum (adverb) so much, so far, only
   tanti for so much, worth so much
   tantō by so much

tardo (1) loiter, be slow; slow down, hinder, delay

tardus, -a, -um slow, tardy; dull, stupid; making slow; measured, deliberate

taurus, -i (m) bull

te, tibi *see* **tu**

-te *suffix added to pronouns for emphasis*

tectum, -i (n) roof; ceiling; shelter, dwelling

tectus, -a, -um covered, concealed; close, reserved, cautious, wary

tegmen, -inis (n) cover, covering

tego, -ere, texi, tectus cover; bury; conceal; shield, protect

tellus, -uris (f) earth, soil, land; country; the world

telum, -i (n) missile; javelin, spear; weapon; beam of light

temerē blindly, by chance, casually, heedlessly

tempero (1) be moderate, control oneself; (with dative) control, use with moderation, spare; keep from, refrain from; mix properly, temper, mitigate, regulate

tempestas, -atis (f) period of time, season; weather, (especially) bad weather, storm, tempest; attack, fury

templum, -i (n) space marked out by the augur for auspices; consecrated ground, (especially) sanctuary, asylum; place dedicated to a deity, shrine, temple; open space, quarter, region

tempto (1) prove, try, test, attempt; test by attack, assail; work on, tamper with, excite, disturb

tempus, -oris (n) division, section; temples of the head; space, period, moment; time; fit time, occasion, opportunity; state or condition of things

tendo, -ere, tetendi, tentus or **tensus** stretch, extend, spread; direct, present, give; direct one's course, tend, make toward; be inclined, aim at, strive for; try, attempt; pitch a tent, encamp

tenebrae, -arum (plural, f) darkness; night; blindness; obscurity

teneo, -ēre, tenui, tentus hold; possess, keep, preserve, maintain; understand, grasp, remember, know; contain,

comprise; occupy, garrison; master, restrain, keep back; charm, delight, amuse;
keep on, persevere, persist, endure

tener, -era, -erum tender, delicate, soft;
young
   tenerē (adverb)

tenor, -oris (m) course, continued movement; duration, career

tenuis, -e thin, slight, slender; refined,
subtle; little, trivial, feeble; mean, low

tepeo, -ēre, be warm or lukewarm

tepidus, -a, -um warm, lukewarm, tepid

ter three times, thrice

teres, -retis rounded, polished, well turned,
smooth; refined, elegant

tergum, -i (n) back; rear; hide, skin; thing
made of hide

tero, -ere, trivi, tritus rub; whet, smooth;
grind, thresh; wear out, use up, spend

terra, -ae (f) earth, land, ground, soil;
country, land, region

terreo, -ēre, terrui, territus frighten,
terrify; scare away; deter

terribilis, -e terrible, dreadful

tertius, -a, -um third
   tertium or **tertiō** (adverb) for the third
   time

testamentum, -i (n) will, testament

testimonium, -i (n) witness, evidence;
proof, indication

testis, -is (c) witness; eyewitness, spectator

testor, -ari, testatus sum bear witness to,
give evidence of; make known, pub-
lish, declare, attest; make a will; call to
witness

thalamus, -i (m) chamber, (especially)
woman's bedroom; marriage bed; abode,
dwelling

thesaurus, -i (m) treasure, trove, hoard;
treasury, storehouse

tibi *see* **tu**

tibia, -ae (f) shinbone, tibia; pipe, flute

tigillum, -i (n) small beam

timeo, -ēre, timui be afraid, fear, dread

timidus, -a, -um fearful, timid
   timidē (adverb)

timor, -oris (m) fear, dread; object of fear

tingo, -ere, tinxi, tinctus moisten, wet;
dye, color, imbue

titulus, -i (m) inscription, label, notice;
title, honor; pretense, pretext

tollo, -ere, sustuli, sublatus lift up, raise,
elevate; acknowledge as one's own, bring
up; take away, remove, carry off, steal;
destroy, abolish

torqueo, -ēre, torsi, tortus twist, wind,
curl, wrench; distort; hurl violently,
whirl; rack, torture, torment, plague, try,
test

torreo, -ēre, torrui, tostus burn, parch, dry
up; rush, seethe

torus, -i (m) muscle; bed, sofa; marriage
couch; bier; mound; ornament

tot (indeclinable) so many

totidem (indeclinable) just as many

totiens so often, so many times

totus, -a, -um whole, complete, entire;
wholehearted, absorbed

tracto (1) drag along, haul, pull about;
handle, manage, treat; behave

trado, -ere, tradidi, traditus hand over,
give up, surrender, betray; hand down to
posterity; hand down an account of an
event, report, relate, teach

tragoedia, -ae (f) tragedy; dramatic scene

traho, -ere, traxi, tractus trail, pull along;
drag, pull violently; draw in, take up;
breathe; lengthen, draw out; draw together, contract; attract; take in or on, assume, derive; prolong, spin out; ascribe,
refer, interpret

trames, -itis (m) byway, footpath

tranquillus, -a, -um quiet, calm
  tranquillē (adverb)
trans (preposition with accusative) over, across, on or to the other side of
transeo, -ire, transivi, transitus go over, cross, pass over, go past; be changed; pass time; pass beyond, transgress; ignore, touch lightly on
transfero, transferre, transtuli, translatus carry over or across; transfer, transport, convey; put off, defer; change; copy; translate into another language
tremo, -ere, tremui tremble, quake; tremble at
trepidus, -a, -um agitated, restless, disturbed, in an emergency
tres, tria three
tribunal, -alis (n) raised platform used by magistrates and generals, tribunal
tribunus, -i (m) tribune (military or civil leader)
tribuo, -ere, tribui, tributus divide out, allot, assign; grant, give, allow, yield, ascribe, attribute
tricesimus, -a, -um thirtieth
trinoctium, -i (n) span of three nights
tristis, -e sad, gloomy, dismal, forbidding, harsh; bitter
  triste (adverb) harshly
triumphalis, -e triumphal
triumphus, -i (m) triumphal procession, triumph

triumvir, -viri (m) triumvir; *usually plural* (**triumviri**): board or commission of three
trucido (1) slaughter, massacre; demolish, destroy
tu (2nd person pronoun) you, thou; *plural:* **vos** you, ye
tum then, at that time; next, thereupon, afterward
  cum . . . tum both . . . and, not only . . . but also
tumeo, -ēre swell, be swollen, be puffed up; swell with pride, anger, or excitement
tumultus, -ūs (m) confusion, uproar, bustle; political commotion, insurrection, rebellion
tunica, -ae (f) sleeved garment, tunic; jacket, coat, covering
turba, -ae (f) tumult, disturbance; mob, throng, crowd
turbo (1) disturb, throw into disorder or confusion; upset; cause political disturbance, unsettle
turpis, -e ugly, foul; disgraceful
  turpiter (adverb) foully, disgracefully
tus, turis (n) incense, frankincense
tutus, -a, -um safe, secure, out of danger; watchful, cautious
  tutō or **tutē** (adverb) safely
tuus, -a, -um (2nd person singular possessive adjective) your, of yours, thine, thy

Uu

uber, -eris (n) udder, teat, breast; richness, abundance, fertility
uber, -eris rich, fertile, fruitful, copious
  uberius (comparative adverb) more abundantly
  uberrimē (superlative adverb) most abundantly

ubi where; when, as soon as; wherein, whereby, with whom
ubique everywhere
udus, -a, -um wet, moist
ulciscor, ulcisci, ultus sum take vengeance for, avenge; take vengeance on, punish
ullus, -a, -um any; *as noun:* anyone, anything

ulmus, -i (f) elm tree

ulna, -ae (f) elbow, arm; ell

ulterior, -ius (comparative) farther, more distant, more advanced, more remote

ultimus, -a, -um (superlative) most distant, farthest, extreme; original; last, final; highest, greatest; meanest, lowest

ultrā (adverb and preposition with accusative) beyond, on the far side of, farther (than), more (than)

umbra, -ae (f) shade, shadow; shady place; protection; idleness, pleasant rest; phantom, ghost, semblance

umeo, -ēre, be moist

umerus, -i (m) upper arm, shoulder

umor, -oris (m) moisture, fluid

umquam at any time, ever

unā *see* **unus**

unda, -ae (f) water, fluid, wave; stream

unde whence, from where; how; from whom

undecim (indeclinable) eleven

undique from or on all sides, from everywhere, everywhere; altogether, in every respect

unguis, -is (m) fingernail; toenail; claw, hoof

unicus, -a, -um one, only, sole; singular, unique

universus, -a, -um combined in one, whole, entire; all together

unus, -a, -um one; only one; one and the same; any one

unā (adverb) in one, together, as one

urbs, urbis (f) walled town or city; (especially) the city of Rome

urgeo, -ēre, ursi push, press, drive, urge; beset, oppress; stress; press on with, ply hard, follow up

uro, -ere, ussi, ustus burn; dry up, parch; chafe, gall; disturb, harass

usque through and through, all the way; continuously; always

usus, -ūs (m) use, application, practice, exercise; social intercourse, familiarity; skill, experience; utility, usefulness, profit

usus est there is need of, there is occasion for

ut or **uti** (with indicative) how; as, as being; as when, while, since, when; where; (with subjunctive) how; o that; granted that; so that; namely that; in order that; that, to; that . . . not

uter, utra, utrum which of the two?; which side?, which set?; that (of two) which; either of the two

uterque, utraque, utrumque each of two; each side, each set; both

utilis, -e useful, fit, profitable

utilitas, -tatis (f) utility, usefulness

utinam would that!, o that!, if only!

utor, -i, usus sum (with ablative) use, employ; possess, enjoy; associate with

utroque to both sides, in both directions; at each point, both ways

utrum whether

utrum . . . an whether . . . or

uva, -ae (f) bunch of grapes; vine; cluster

uxor, -oris (f) wife

uxorem ducere marry a wife

uxorius, -a, -um of a wife; too devoted to one's wife, uxorious

Vv

valens, -entis strong, powerful, healthy
    valenter (adverb)
valeo, -ēre, valui, valitus be strong, be
    vigorous, be in good health, be well; have
    force, avail, prevail, be able; be worth;
    mean, signify
    vale or **valeas** farewell, good-bye
validus, -a, -um strong, powerful; healthy,
    well; mighty, influential; efficacious
    validē or **valdē** (adverb) strongly, pow-
        erfully; certainly, to be sure, really
valles or **vallis, -is** (f) vale, valley, hollow
vanus, -a, -um empty, void; vain, idle,
    worthless, meaningless; boastful, osten-
    tatious, unreliable
varius, -a, -um various, manifold, change-
    able, diverse; fickle, changeable
    variē (adverb) diversely, variously
vasto (1) empty; lay waste, ravage, devas-
    tate, prey on
vates, -is (c) prophet, seer; bard, poet
-ve or, or perhaps
vehemens, -entis violent, furious,
    impetuous
    vehementer (adverb) violently; forcibly,
        exceedingly
veho, -ere, vexi, vectus carry, convey,
    transport
vel (adverb) even, actually; for example;
    (conjunction) or
    vel . . . vel either . . . or
vellus, -eris (n) fleece; skin, hide
velox, -ocis quick, rapid, swift
velut or **veluti** as, just as; even as, as for
    instance
vena, -ae (f) blood vessel, vein, artery; wa-
    tercourse; vein of metal; vein of talent,
    disposition, natural inclination
venatus, -ūs (m) the chase, hunting
vendo, -ere, vendidi, venditus put up for
    sale, sell; betray; recommend, advertise

veneratio, -onis (f) reverence, respect
veneror, -ari, veneratus sum ask rever-
    ently; revere, respect, worship
venio, -ire, vēni, ventus come; happen,
    arrive; grow, arise
venor, -ari, venatus sum hunt
venter, -tris (m) belly, stomach; womb
ventus, -i (m) wind; rumor, favor
venus, -eris (f) charm, loveliness; sex, love;
    loved one; *capitalized*: Venus (goddess
    of love)
ver, veris (n) spring, springtime
verber, -eris (n) lash; whip, scourge, thong;
    blow, stroke; whipping
verbero (1) beat, whip, thrash; assail, lash
verbum, -i (n) word; verb; saying, expres-
    sion; mere words, talk
verecundia, -ae (f) modesty, diffidence,
    bashfulness
verecundus, -a, -um bashful, modest, shy,
    diffident
vereor, -ēri, veritus sum be afraid, fear;
    have respect for, revere
verna, -ae (c) slave born in the master's
    house; native
vernus, -a, -um of spring, vernal
verso (1) turn about, turn this way and
    that; bend, ply, twist; influence, agi-
    tate; turn over in the mind, think of;
    be engaged in
versus or **versum** turned toward; upward
versus, -ūs (m) row, line; line of writing,
    verse
vertex, -icis (m) whirl, eddy, whirlwind,
    gust; crown of the head; head, summit,
    elevation; pole of the heavens
verto, -ere, verti, versus turn, turn round,
    turn up; turn oneself; interpret, con-
    strue, understand in a certain way; im-
    pute; alter, change; translate; change for
    another, exchange; upset, overthrow

verus, -a, -um true, real, genuine; truthful, veracious; just, reasonable

    vere (adverb) truly, really, rightly

    vero (adverb) in truth, indeed, in fact; even, indeed; to be sure; but indeed, but in fact

    verum (adverb) yet, still, however

vester, -tra, -trum (2nd person plural possessive adjective) your, yours

vestigium, -i (n) footstep, track; trace, mark

vestis, -is (f) covering, garment, clothing; blanket, carpet, tapestry

veto, -are, vetui, vetitus forbid, prohibit

vetus, -eris old, ancient, of long standing; experienced; *as plural noun (m)*: the ancients

    veterrimus, -a, -um (superlative)

vexo (1) shake, toss, jostle; harass, annoy

via, -ae (f) way, passage; highway, road, street; course, march, journey; means, way, method

vicinus, -a, -um near, neighboring; *as noun (m or f)*: neighbor

vicis (genitive—nominative not found; f) change, interchange, alternation; vicissitude of fate, lot, destiny; one's place, office, or duty

    vicem, vice, in vicem, or **ad vicem** in place of, instead of, like

victima, -ae (f) animal offered in sacrifice, victim

victor, -oris (m) conqueror, victor

victoria, -ae (f) victory, conquest

victus, -us (m) living; manner of life; nourishment, food

vicus, -i (m) part of a town, street, neighborhood; village, hamlet

video, -ere, vidi, visus see; perceive, notice, observe; look into a matter, see to, provide for; *see also* **videor**

videor, -eri, visus sum be seen; seem, appear, be thought; seem good, seem right; *see also* **video**

viginti (indeclinable) twenty

vigor, -oris (m) force, energy

vilicus, -i (m) bailiff, steward, overseer of an estate

vilis, -e cheap, worth little

villa, -ae (f) country house, estate, farm

vimen, -inis (n) wicker, osier, twig; basket

vincio, -ire, vinxi, vinctus bind, tie up; surround, encompass; restrain, confine, secure

vinco, -ere, vici, victus conquer, overcome, master, surpass; prove successfully, win one's point

vinc(u)lum, -i (n) band, cord, chain, fetter, tie; imprisonment

vindico (1) claim; arrogate, assume; appropriate; claim as free; liberate, deliver, protect; avenge, punish

vinum, -i (n) wine, wine drinking

violentus, -a, -um violent, vehement, furious, impetuous

violo (1) violate, outrage, injure

vir, viri (m) man, male person; grown man; husband; soldier, infantryman; individual

virectum, -i (n) grassy meadow, turf

vireo, -ere, virui be green, be vigorous, be healthy, be fresh

vires, -ium *see* **vis**

virgineus, -a, -um maidenly, virginal

virgo, -inis (f) maiden, virgin, girl

viridis, -e green; fresh, young, vigorous

virilis, -e manly, male, virile; adult; courageous, spirited

virtus utis (f) manliness; goodness, excellence, worth, virtue; bravery, courage

virus, -i (n) slimy liquid, slime; poison, venom; any harsh taste or smell

vis, vis (f; plural: **vires, -ium**) force, power, strength; might, influence; violence; a large number or quantity; nature, meaning of a thing

visito (1) see often; visit

viso, -ere, visi, visus look at, look into, see after; go to see, visit, call on

vita, -ae (f) life

vitalis, -e of life, vital; living, surviving

viteus, -a, -um of a vine

vitis, -is (f) vine

vitium, -i (n) fault, defect, blemish; crime, vice; defect in auguries or auspices

vito (1) avoid, shun

vitulus, -i (m) bull calf

vitupero (1) blame, scold, censure

vivo, -ere, vixi, vīctus live, be alive; live well, enjoy life; survive; live on anything; dwell

vivus, -a, -um alive, living; lifelike

vix with difficulty, scarcely, only just, barely

vocalis, -e vocal; speaking, singing

voco (1) call, summon, invoke, invite; name, designate; bring or put into any state or condition

volo, velle, volui be willing, wish, want; will, ordain; suppose

volo (1) fly; move rapidly, rush

volucer, -cris, -cre flying, winged; fleet, swift, fleeting

volucris, -is (f) bird, flying insect

voluptas, -atis (f) pleasure, delight, enjoyment

volvo, -ere, volvi, volutus wind, turn, roll, twist round; unroll a book, read; make roll; turn over in the mind, consider; experience, go through

vomer, -eris (m) plowshare

vos you (plural), ye; *see also* **tu**

votum, -i (n) vow, promise to the gods; votive offering; prayer, wish, desire

voveo, -ēre, vovi, votus vow, promise to a god; pray for, wish

vox, vocis (f) voice, cry, call; accent, language; sound, tone; saying, utterance

vulgus, -i (n) the people, the public; mass, crowd, rabble, mob

vulgō (adverb) commonly, generally, in public

vulnus, -eris (n) wound, injury

vulpes, -is (f) fox

vultus, -ūs (m) facial expression, countenance, look, aspect; face

PART V

Appendix:
Latin Word Order and
Sentence Structure

I. The norm for Latin word order and sentence structure derives from literary prose. Conversational Latin, poetry, and high rhetoric, however, could deviate widely from this norm. Even literary prose, as we shall see, alters the norm for certain reasons and effects.

The word order of conversational Latin (as known to us from comedies, dialogue in satires and novels, and graffiti) was considerably looser than that of literary prose. Sentences were shorter, with more parataxis and less compound hypotaxis (see part I, section 16.VI). Similarly, there was a tendency to use an excess of conjunctions (called polysyndeton) in conversation. Also, there was less separation between modifiers and the words they modified. Finally, little value was placed on periodic sentence structure (see II.Y below).

Like English poetry, Latin poetry commonly breaks the rules of normal word order. This is, in fact, one of the three main characteristics (poetic meter and poetic diction being the other two) that make poetry poetry. So Romans would have had an easy time distinguishing a poetic text from a prose one (and easier perhaps than we might have in English today). It is important to recognize that though grammarians have always regarded prose word order as the norm, the ancient Romans viewed poetry as a loftier order of discourse, and so, in some sense, it may be more appropriate to regard poetic word order as the norm and prose word order as presenting the common deviations.

The final prefatory observation worth making on this subject is that in terms of word order and sentence structure, Roman public oratory bears more resemblance to poetry than to prose. Clearly, high rhetoric sought the same high-impact effects on its audiences that poetry did, and so it varied normal prose word order to that end. This is not so foreign to us: the homiletics of a charismatic preacher shares many of the structural qualities of skilled performances at a poetry slam.

II. We talk about norms of word order instead of rules because deviations are nearly as common as examples of the norms themselves, rendering most of the norms that follow highly porous. What enables these deviations is the inflectional nature of Latin, since the functions that word endings indicate are usually the same regardless of where the words are placed.

The following observations outline the most prominent tendencies of Latin word order and sentence structure. Each observation preceded by an asterisk is commonly subject to deviations in conversation, poetry, and high rhetoric; an example or explanation of such deviations is provided.

*A. A sentence's subject precedes its predicate, and its verb is last (or second to last).

Caesar discedebat.	Caesar was departing.
Antonius erat iratus.	Antony was angry.

1. In a different context, one might find:

discedebat Caesar.   Caesar was departing.

erat iratus Antonius.   Antony was angry.

*B. A noun is followed by any modifier or another modifying noun.

maritus fidelis   a loyal husband

maritus Agrippinae   the husband of Agrippina

1. In a different context, one might find:

fidelis maritus   a loyal husband

Agrippinae maritus   the husband of Agrippina

*C. Words dependent on a noun modifier are embedded between the noun and the modifier.

consul genere nobilis   the consul noble by birth

1. In a different context, one might find:

consul nobilis genere   the consul noble by birth

*D. If both an adjective and a genitive modify a noun, the customary order is adjective, genitive, noun:

divitissimus civium Crassus   Crassus, richest of the citizens

1. In a different context, one might find:

Crassus civium divitissimus   Crassus, richest of the citizens

or **Crassus divitissimus civium**

*E. When a noun serves as the subject of both a subordinate clause and the main clause, it precedes both; when the same noun serves as the subject of a subordinate clause and as an object of the main clause, it precedes both in the objective case.

Caesar, quod erat iratus, discedebat.

Because he was angry, Caesar left.

Caesarem, quod erat iratus, evitabamus.

We were avoiding Caesar because he was angry.

1. In other contexts, when the same noun serves in the main clause as the subject and in the dependent clause in an oblique case, it is expressed only in the dependent clause (in the oblique case) but preceding the subordinating conjunction.

Caesarem quod evitabamus, factus est iratior.

Caesar became more angry because we were avoiding him.

*F. The "antecedent" of a relative can be used as an adjective in the relative clause if the relative clause precedes the main clause.

quos equos Caesar emere volebat erant in Arabiā.

The horses that Caesar wanted to buy were in Arabia.

1. In a different context, one might find:

equi, quos Caesar emere volebat, erant in Arabiā.

The horses that Caesar wanted to buy were in Arabia.

*G. Where one noun serves as the object of two clauses, it is expressed in the first but not the second (in English, a pronoun or noun usually expresses it in the second).

Ciceronem amo sed frater odit.

I like Cicero, but my brother hates him.

I like but my brother hates Cicero.

1. In a different context, one might find:

amo sed frater Ciceronem odit.

I like Cicero, but my brother hates him.

I like but my brother hates Cicero.

*H. Predicate modifiers follow this standard order: first, adverbial nouns expressing time, place, cause, manner, means, and so forth; then the indirect object; next, the direct object; finally, the adverb(s).

magnā curā mihi librum suaviter legebat.

With great care she was sweetly reading the book for me.

1. In a different context, any permutation might be found.

I. In a list, 1st person pronouns precede 2nd and 3rd person pronouns, and 2nd person pronouns precede 3rd person pronouns.

ego atque eae   they and I

te et eos   you and them

*J. Relative, demonstrative, and determinative pronouns precede subordinating conjunctions.

eos ut legeret libros cepit.   He took the books to read them.

1. In a different context, one might find:

ut [eos] legeret libros cepit.

He took the books to read [them].

*K. Two or more personal pronouns in a sentence tend to cluster together.

magno pretio illae tibi me non libenter vendiderunt.

They sold me to you for a great price against their will.

1. In a different context, one might find:

illae non libenter me magno pretio tibi vendiderunt.

They sold me to you for a great price against their will.

*L. If a pronoun refers to an element in the preceding sentence or to the preceding sentence as a whole, it comes first or, with a preposition, second in its sentence.

. . . bella civilia. ob haec provinciae erant inquietae.

. . . the civil wars. Because of these, the provinces were restless.

> 1. In a different context, one might find:
>
> **. . . bella civilia. provinciae ob haec erant inquietae.**
>
> . . . the civil wars. Because of these, the provinces were restless.

*M. Possessive and indefinite adjectives immediately follow their nouns.

ancilla matris vestrae	your mother's slave

> 1. In a different context, one might find:
>
> | | |
> |---|---|
> | **ancilla vestrae matris** | your mother's slave |

*N. An adverb modifying an adjective precedes it; a noun dependent on an adjective follows it.

multō sapientior	far wiser
cupidus pacis	desirous of peace

> 1. In a different context, one might find:
>
> | | |
> |---|---|
> | **sapientior multō** | far wiser |
> | **pacis cupidus** | desirous of peace |

*O. An adverb immediately precedes the word that it modifies.

suaviter legebat	was reading sweetly
multō sapientior	far wiser

> 1. In a different context, one might find:
>
> | | |
> |---|---|
> | **legebat suaviter** | was reading sweetly |

*P. Interrogatives, relatives, and conjunctions come first or sometimes second in their sentence or clause.

senatus nescit *ubi* Caesar sit.

The senate doesn't know *where* Caesar is.

in Italiā *ad quam* Sulla contendebat muncipia bellum parabant.

In Italy, *to which* Sulla was hurrying, towns prepared for war.

***cum* Livia aegrotabat, Tiberius non invisit.**

Since Livia was ill, Tiberius did not go to see [her].

Tiberius, *cum* Livia aegrotabat, non invisit.

Since Livia was ill, Tiberius did not go to see [her].

> 1. In a different context, one might find:
>
> **Tiberius, Livia domi *cum* aegrotabat, non invisit.**
>
> *Since* Livia was ill at home, Tiberius did not go to see [her].

*Q. The words **autem, enim, quidem, quoque, vero**, and (usually) **igitur** come second or sometimes third in their sentence or clause.

Arabia verō est saeva.
Arabia truly is wild.
in Arabiā autem equi sunt boni.
But in Arabia the horses are good.

1. In a different context, one might find:
   Arabia est verō saeva.
   Arabia truly is wild.
   autem in Arabiā equi sunt boni.
   But in Arabia the horses are good.

R. The enclitics **-que, -ne**, and **-ve** are added to the first word in their sentence, clause, or phrase unless it is a preposition, in which case they are added to the second word.

Arabiane est saeva?	Is Arabia wild?
in Arabiāque equi sunt boni.	And in Arabia the horses are good.

*S. Prepositions follow their object if it is a relative pronoun.

montes quibus ex	the mountains from which
epistula quam ob	the letter because of which

1. In a different context, one might find:

montes ex quibus	the mountains from which
epistula ob quam	the letter because of which

T. A negative immediately precedes the word it negates; if its use is more general, it precedes the verb.

magno pretio illae tibi me non libenter vendiderunt.
They sold me to you for a great price not willingly.
magnā curā mihi librum suaviter non legebat.
She wasn't reading the book to me sweetly with great care.

*U. When used for a direct quotation, the verbs **inquam** and **inquit** appear after the second or third word.

imperator "adducite auxilia," inquit, "quam celerrimē!"
The commander said, "Bring up the auxiliaries as quickly as possible!"

1. In a different context, one might find:
   imperator inquit, "adducite auxilia quam celerrime!"
   The commander said, "Bring up the auxiliaries as quickly as possible!"

*V. Clauses are arranged in logical order (e.g., outcomes come last, while their means come first). Temporal, conditional, and concessive clauses precede the main clause; indirect questions and purpose and result clauses follow the main clause.

1. In a different context, the opposite of any of the foregoing might be found.

*W. Most dependent clauses precede main clauses, but if two comparable clauses modify the same main clause, then they flank it.

cum Nero moriturus sit, populus gaudebit, dummodo licebit.
When Nero dies, the people will rejoice, so long as it is allowed.

1. In a different context, one might find:
   populus gaudebit, dummodo licebit, cum Nero moriturus sit.
   When Nero dies, the people will rejoice, so long as it is allowed.

X. Three positions are favored for subordinate clauses: first, immediately after the subject; second, immediately before the subject; and third, especially for result and purpose clauses, immediately after the main verb.

Tiberius, cum Livia aegrotabat, non invisit.
Since Livia was ill, Tiberius did not go to see [her].
cum Livia aegrotabat, Tiberius non invisit.
Since Livia was ill, Tiberius did not go to see [her].
cum Livia aegrotabat, Tiberius non invisit ne eam vexaret.
Since Livia was ill, Tiberius did not go to see [her], so as not to bother her.

Y. In the 1st century BCE, an ideal of prose sentence structure was defined, and it dominated Latin stylistics, off and on, for centuries. The style is referred to as periodic because it relies on a type of sentence called a period. The simple definition of a *period* is a sentence that, after subordinations and modifiers, ends with the main verb. To define a periodic sentence with a little more sophistication and specificity: it is a complex sentence consisting of two or more subordinations that are inserted between the subject and the predicate of the principal clause, whose verb is its final word. From a practical standpoint, the most striking feature of a periodic sentence is its length. The best strategy for reading such a sentence is, first, to single out the main subject and the main predicate; second, to identify and demarcate each of the component parts (ablative absolutes, relative clauses, indirect statements, purpose clauses, indirect questions, etc.); and third, to translate each of those component parts in their natural or logical order within the setting of the principal clause, with its subject, verb, and modifiers. Although periodic sentences may initially appear daunting, if you're observant of punctuation and rules of grammar (the operators), they're really as simple as basic algebra.

III. There are four reasons a speaker or writer might deviate from the norms of word order, but only the first three are important: 1) for emphasis, 2) for euphony, 3) for rhetorical effect, and 4) to shoehorn words into poetic meter. Each of these requires some explanation.

A. EMPHASIS. The most emphasized words in a Latin sentence or clause would have come first and last, and when spoken, they would have been given tonal emphasis as well;

the second-most-emphasized words would have immediately followed the first word and immediately preceded the last word. The most common first word in Latin clauses and sentences is the subject; the most common last word is the verb. It may be helpful to enumerate other parts of speech and how they can be used emphatically.

1. When a genitive, dative, or ablative noun dependent on a nominative or accusative noun is emphasized, it usually precedes the nominative or accusative noun.

    ***pacis* leges sunt sacrae**   the rules *of peace* are holy

2. When a 3rd person form of the verb *to be* is the first word of its sentence, it is emphatic; this is sometimes referred to as the existential or ontological use of the verb *to be*.

    ***sunt* feminae**   there *are* women
    ***erat* sapiens**   there *was* a wise man

3. When vocatives come first in a sentence, they are emphatic.

4. A noun and its modifying adjective or genitive are emphasized by separation.
    pater, bellis civilibus gestis, *Horatii* mortuus est.
    Horace's father died while the civil wars were waged.

5. When an appositive (see part I, section 3.VIII) precedes its noun, it is emphasized.
    ***censor* Cato**   the *censor* Cato
    a. The exceptions to this concern familiar place-names:
        urbs Roma   the city Rome
        flumen Tiber   the river Tiber

6. Any verb that starts its clause or sentence is emphasized. The emphasis may be on the verb's meaning, its entire predicate, or its tense.

7. With periphrastics and passives of the perfect system, any word placed between the participle and the verb *to be* is emphasized.
    necatus *veneno* est   he was killed *by poison*

8. An object that precedes its preposition is emphatic. This reversal is called *anastrophe* (see part I, 8.IV), which is a form of *hyperbaton* (any striking variation on normal word order).
    ***Romam* propter**   because of *Rome*

When the object of a monosyllabic preposition has a modifier that is placed before the preposition, this is emphatic:
    ***summā* cum laude**   with the *highest* praise

9. All adjectives—except relative, demonstrative, determinative, and interrogative adjectives or those expressing quantity or size—that precede their nouns are emphatic.
    ***sapiens* femina**   a *wise* woman

10. A word of negation is emphatic when it opens a clause or sentence.

non rex nobis interficiendus est.   We should *not* kill the king.

11. Some words, if they come first in a sentence or clause, are emphatic: for instance, **inquam, inquit, credo, opinor, precor**. Some words typically come second in their clause or sentence, and if they do not, they are emphatic: for instance, **autem, enim, quoque, verō, igitur**. Any word that precedes **quidem** is being emphasized. If **itaque** does not occur first in its clause or sentence, it is emphatic.

12. If the apodosis precedes the protasis in a conditional sentence (see part I, 18), the apodosis is emphasized.

B. EUPHONY. To the ancient Romans, how well words sounded together was extremely important. For example, the juxtaposition of certain words was studiously avoided because it was contrary to formula (such as **Romanus populus**, which would have grated on the ears of listeners) or because it created an interruption in the flow of words (such as *hiatus*, when one word ends in a vowel or diphthong and the next begins with a vowel, a diphthong, or *h*). One important euphonious effect was prose rhythms.

The rhetorician Quintilian (2nd century CE) stated that prose sentences shouldn't begin or end in metrical or poetic forms; indeed, he called the effect "most unattractive" and "ugly" (*Inst. Orat.* 9.4.72). His views notwithstanding, the truth is that many prose authors commonly (though sparingly) employed poetic rhythms for three reasons: to delight the ears of the audience, to evoke a relevant piece of verse, and to show off a little. Certain rhythms were commonly avoided in prose, for example the meter of epic and didactic poetry. Other rhythms were more widely employed, such as meters of theater. The former was perhaps regarded as a bit too stodgy, while the latter were associated with popular entertainment.

1. A corollary may be inferred from Quintilian's remarks. The use of poetic word order by prose authors was fully acceptable, but not necessarily the use of all poetic rhythms. Poetry, on the other hand, could employ prose word order, but it had to conform to poetic prosody.

C. RHETORIC. Besides hyperbaton (see III.A.8 above), there are many rhetorical figures of word order that invite attention and admiration. It suffices here to mention three of the most common:

1. A parallelism in structure is called *anaphora*; for example:
magister optimus discipulo callido librum nōtum dat.
The excellent teacher gives the clever student a famous book.
Notice the repeated pattern of noun, adjective.

2. A crisscrossing word order is called *chiasmus*; for example:
magister non librum nōtum sed saevam poenam dat.
The teacher gives not a famous book but penalty cruel.
Notice the pattern of noun, adjective followed by adjective, noun.

3. An interlocking word order is called *synchysis*; for example:

magister librum optimus nōtum dat.

The excellent teacher gives a famous book.

Notice the alternation noun 1, noun 2, adjective 1, adjective 2.

D. METRICS. Poets sometimes altered normal Latin word order to make their writing conform to the prescribed meter in which they were working; this happened only with poets who lacked skill in metrification and was therefore not a common cause of deviations from word order norms.

IV. There is no denying the truism that Latin word order and sentence structure are much freer than what's found in English. What makes this true is Latin's reliance on inflectional endings to indicate all functions within each phrase, clause, or sentence, thus leaving no essential purpose for word order. But just the same, this doesn't mean that Latin sentences are a free-for-all regarding the order of their parts. Even poetry and conversation, whose rules were much more relaxed than those of prose, were bound by their conventions and generally followed audience expectations of order and structure.

For the intermediate Latin student, word order and sentence structure should be like the weather: if you're prepared for the possibilities, you notice the conditions, but you neither think nor worry much about them unless, of course, something truly striking presents itself.

PART VI

Indexes

A. Authors

Brackets indicate authors to whom works have been wrongly attributed. Names in all capitals are the common names used in the "Texts" section below.

Anonymous authors
> *Elegy on Maecenas* (1st century BCE/CE)
>
> *Pervigilium Veneris* (4th century CE?)
>
> Comment: The organization of the *Pervigilium Veneris* text into neat quatrains is by J. W. Mackail in his Loeb edition (1913). I concur with G. P. Goold and his Loeb revision (1988) that the original poem would certainly not have been so organized. I have preserved Mackail's organization, however, because it works better as a teaching text.
>
> *Phoenix* (4th century CE)
>
> *Prayer to Earth* (2nd century CE?)

Aphorists: Publilius Syrus (1st century BCE), [Cato the Elder], [Seneca], et al.

AVIANUS (4th–5th century CE)
> fables in the Aesopic tradition

[CATO the Elder] (3rd–2nd century BCE)
> *Dicta* (Sayings), writings of unknown date, some of which may authentically date back to M. Porcius Cato, famous for his vigorous espousal of traditional Roman values

Aulus Cornelius CELSUS (1st century CE), encyclopedist
> *On Medicine*

L. Annaeus FLORUS (2nd century CE)
> poems

Aulus GELLIUS (2nd century CE)
> *Attic Nights,* a collection of essays mostly on antiquarian topics

JEROME (Eusebius Hieronymus; 4th–5th century CE), a very important Christian Father, born in Dalmatia
> *Against Jovinian*

MARTIAL (M. Valerius Martialis; 1st century CE), unquestionably the greatest ancient epigrammatist, born in Spain
> epigrams

M. Aurelius Olympius NEMESIANUS (3rd century CE)
> eclogues

PENTADIUS (3rd century CE)
> poems

PETRONIUS Arbiter (1st century CE)
> poems attributed to him in the *Anthologia Latina* (*AL*) edited by Alexander Riese
>
> *Satyricon,* a satiric novel

Comment: For the authenticity of the various poems attributed to Petronius, see the admirable volume by Edward Courtney *The Poems of Petronius* (Atlanta: Scholars Press, 1991).

PHAEDRUS (1st century CE), slave and freedman of the emperor Augustus, somehow fell afoul of the emperor Tiberius and his minister Sejanus
fables

PLINY THE ELDER (Gaius Plinius Secundus; 1st century CE), encyclopedist
Natural History

PLINY THE YOUNGER (Gaius Plinius Caecilius Secundus; 1st–2nd century CE), active civil servant with literary interests, achieved his highest offices under the emperor Trajan
epistles

QUINTILIAN (Marcus Fabius Quintilianus; 1st century CE)
Institutio Oratoria (*Education of an Orator*), an influential and authoritative handbook on rhetoric

Sulpicius Lupercus SERVASIUS Junior (4th century CE)
poems

Gaius SUETONIUS Tranquillus (2nd century CE), most famous for his biographies of the first twelve Roman emperors, through Domitian
biographies

TIBERIANUS (4th century CE)
poems

"Lygdamus"; Sulpicia; anonymous
TIBULLAN COLLECTION, included in Tibullus, *Elegies*, book 3 (1st century BCE)

VALERIUS MAXIMUS (1st century CE), moralizing essayist who sought the approval of the emperor Tiberius for his staunchly nationalistic themes
Memorable Deeds and Sayings

[Vergil] (1st century BCE)
Lydia, a poem once wrongly thought to be the work of an immature Vergil (its authorship is debated, but it's unlikely that anyone famous wrote it)

B. Texts

Animals and Nature

Prose Reading 1. Gellius 5.2
Prose Reading 2. Pliny the Elder 10.60
Prose Reading 3. Valerius Maximus 7.3.6
Prose Reading 4. Gellius 16.19
Prose Reading 5. Pliny the Elder 8.7
Prose Reading 6. Gellius 5.14
Verse Reading 1. Petronius, *AL* 465 Riese
Verse Reading 2. Pentadius 2

Verse Reading 3. Servasius 1
Verse Reading 4. Florus 10–13
Verse Reading 5. Tiberianus 1
Verse Reading 6. Petronius *AL* 471 Riese
Verse Reading 7. Petronius *AL* 651 Riese
Verse Reading 8. Anonymous, *Pervigilium Veneris*
Supplemental Reading 1. Petronius *AL* 474 Riese
Supplemental Reading 2. Petronius *AL* 478 Riese
Supplemental Reading 3. Aphorists
Supplemental Reading 4. Petronius, *AL* 690 Riese
Supplemental Reading 5. Anonymous, *Phoenix*

Religion

Prose Reading 1. Gellius 1.19
Prose Reading 2. Valerius Maximus 1.1.12
Prose Reading 3. Valerius Maximus 1.1.10
Prose Reading 4. Valerius Maximus 1.6.11
Prose Reading 5. Valerius Maximus 2.4.5
Prose Reading 6. Valerius Maximus 1.5 init., 1.5.1
Prose Reading 7. Valerius Maximus 1.1 init., 1.1.8–9
Prose Reading 8. Gellius 10.15
Prose Reading 9. Gellius 1.12
Verse Reading 1. Avianus 32
Verse Reading 2. Phaedrus 4.1
Verse Reading 3. Phaedrus 4.11
Verse Reading 4. Phaedrus 4.10
Verse Reading 5. Phaedrus, *Per. App.* 8
Verse Reading 6. Aphorists
Verse Reading 7. Avianus 12
Verse Reading 8. Aphorists
Verse Reading 9. Anonymous, *Prayer to Earth*
Verse Reading 10. Petronius, *AL* 466 Riese
Verse Reading 11. Tiberianus 4
Verse Reading 12. Florus 4
Verse Reading 13. Nemesianus 3
Supplemental Reading 1. Valerius Maximus 7.3.1
Supplemental Reading 2. Valerius Maximus 1.6.3
Supplemental Reading 3. Valerius Maximus 7.2.5
Supplemental Reading 4. Valerius Maximus 1.8.2
Supplemental Reading 5. Valerius Maximus 4.1.10
Supplemental Reading 6. Valerius Maximus 8.15.7
Supplemental Reading 7. Valerius Maximus 8.11.2

Fables

Preeminence

Verse Reading 5. Aphorists
Verse Reading 6. Avianus 10
Verse Reading 7. Aphorists
Verse Reading 8. Aphorists
Verse Reading 9. Anonymous, *Elegy on Maecenas* 2
Verse Reading 10. Aphorists
Supplemental Reading 1. Valerius Maximus 3.2.1
Supplemental Reading 2. Valerius Maximus 6.6.2
Supplemental Reading 3. Valerius Maximus 3.8.2
Supplemental Reading 4. Valerius Maximus 4.1.6
Supplemental Reading 5. Valerius Maximus 6.9.6
Supplemental Reading 6. Valerius Maximus 3.1.2
Supplemental Reading 7. Valerius Maximus 6.2.1
Supplemental Reading 8. Valerius Maximus 3.2.24
Supplemental Reading 9. Valerius Maximus 9.9.2

Women

Prose Reading 1. Valerius Maximus 6.7.1–3
Prose Reading 2. Valerius Maximus 8.15.12
Prose Reading 3. Valerius Maximus 7.8.2
Prose Reading 4. Valerius Maximus 5.4.7
Prose Reading 5. Valerius Maximus 8.3.3
Prose Reading 6. Gellius 10.6
Prose Reading 7. Gellius 4.3
Prose Reading 8. Valerius Maximus 4.4. init.
Prose Reading 9. Valerius Maximus 9.1.3
Prose Reading 10. Gellius 4.4
Prose Reading 11. Valerius Maximus 2.1.2–3
Prose Reading 12. Valerius Maximus 2.1.5–6
Prose Reading 13. Gellius 10.23
Prose Reading 14. Celsus 4.27, 5.21B6
Verse Reading 1. Phaedrus 3.8
Verse Reading 2. Phaedrus 2.2
Verse Reading 3. Phaedrus 1.18
Verse Reading 4. Phaedrus, Per. App. 11
Verse Reading 5. Petronius, *AL* 479 Riese
Verse Reading 6. Aphorists
Verse Reading 7. Martial 6.7, 8.54
Verse Reading 8. Martial 10.63
Verse Reading 9. Martial 10.68
Verse Reading 10. Tibullan Collection 3.17, 3.13, 3.18

Love

C. Definitions

If you are unable to find a term in this index, be sure to check the table of contents for terms used in chapter headings.

Overview of Part I